Who's Buying

Groceries

THE WHO'S BUY

New Strategist Publications, Inc.
Ithaca, New York

New Strategist Publications, Inc.
P.O. Box 242, Ithaca, New York 14851
800/848-0842; 607/273-0913
www.newstrategist.com

ISBN 1-885070-63-2

Printed in the United States of America

Contents

Introduction

The spending data in *Who's Buying Groceries* are based on the Bureau of Labor Statistics' Consumer Expenditure Survey, an ongoing, nationwide survey of household spending. The Consumer Expenditure Survey is a complete accounting of household expenditures, including everything from big-ticket items such as homes and cars, to small purchases like laundry detergent and film. The survey does not include expenditures by government, business, or institutions. The lag time between data collection and dissemination is about two years. The data in this report are from the 2001 Consumer Expenditure Survey.

To produce this report, New Strategist Publications analyzed the Consumer Expenditure Survey's average household spending data in a variety of ways, calculating household spending indexes, per capita indexes, aggregate (or total) household spending, and market shares. The data are cross-tabulated by age, household income, household type, race, Hispanic origin, region, education, occupation, and homeownership status. These analyses are presented in two formats—for all product categories by demographic characteristic (tables 1 through 40) and for all demographic characteristics by product category (tables 41 through 123).

Definition of consumer units

The Consumer Expenditure Survey uses consumer units rather than households as the sampling unit. The term "household" is used interchangeably with the term "consumer unit" in this report for convenience, although they are not exactly the same. Some households contain more than one consumer unit.

Consumer units are defined by the BLS as either: 1) members of a household who are related by blood, marriage, adoption, or other legal arrangements; 2) a person living alone or sharing a household with others or living as a roomer in a private home or lodging house or in permanent living quarters in a hotel or motel, but who is financially independent; or 3) two persons or more living together who pool their income to make joint expenditure decisions. The BLS defines financial independence in terms of "the three major expenses categories: housing, food, and other living expenses. To be considered financially independent, at least two of the three major expense categories have to be provided by the respondent."

The Census Bureau uses households as its sampling unit in the decennial census and in the monthly Current Population Survey. The Census Bureau's household "consists of all persons who occupy a housing unit. A house, an apartment or other groups of rooms, or a single room is regarded as a housing unit when it is occupied or intended for occupancy as separate living quarters; that is, when the occupants do not live and eat with any other persons in the structure and there is direct access from the outside or through a common hall."

The definition goes on to specify that "a household includes the related family members and all the unrelated persons, if any, such as lodgers, foster children, wards, or employees who share the housing unit. A person living alone in a housing unit or a group of unrelated persons sharing a housing unit as partners is also counted as a household. The count of households excludes group quarters."

Because there can be more than one consumer unit in a household, consumer units outnumber households by several million. Most of the excess consumer units are headed by young adults, under age 25.

How to use the tables in this report

The starting point for all calculations in this report are the unpublished, detailed average household spending data collected by the Consumer Expenditure Survey. These numbers are shown on the report's average spending tables and on each of the product-specific tables. The other figures shown in the report were created by New Strategist based on the average figures. The indexed spending tables and the indexed spending column (Best Customers) on the product-specific tables reveal whether spending by households in a given segment is above or below the average for all households and by how much. The indexed per capita spending tables adjust average spending for household size, revealing the individual consumers who spend the most on a particular product or service. The total (or aggregate) spending tables and the total spending column on the product-specific tables show the overall size of the market. The market share tables and market share column (Biggest Customers) on the product-specific tables reveal how much spending in a market is accounted for by each household segment. These analyses are described in detail below.

Average Spending The average spending figures show the average annual spending of households on groceries in 2001. The Consumer Expenditure Survey produces average spending data for all households in a segment; i.e., all households with a householder aged 25 to 34, not just for those who purchased an item. When examining spending data, it is important to remember that by including both purchasers and nonpurchasers in the calculation, the average is less than the amount spent on the item by buyers. (See the accompanying table for the percentage of households that purchased groceries by product category during an average week of 2001 and how much those purchasers spent.)

Because average spending figures include both buyers and nonbuyers, they reveal spending patterns by demographic characteristic. By knowing who is most likely to spend on an item, marketers can target their advertising and promotions more efficiently, and businesses can determine the market potential of a product or service in a city or neighborhood. By multiplying the average amount households spend on fresh fish by the number of households in an area, for example, a store owner can estimate the potential size of the local market for fresh fish.

Indexed Spending (Best Customers) The indexed spending figures compare the spending of each household segment with that of the average household. To compute the indexes, New Strategist divides the average amount each household segment spends on an item by average household spending, multiplying the resulting figure by 100.

An index of 100 is the average for all households. An index of 125 means the spending of a household segment is 25 percent above average (100 plus 25). An index of 75 indicates spending that is 25 percent below the average for all households (100 minus 25). Indexed spending figures identify the best customers for a product or service. Households with an index of 178 for apples, for example, are a strong market for the product. Those with an index below 100 are either a weak or an underserved market.

(percent of consumer units reporting expenditure and amount spent by purchasers during an average week or quarter, 2001)

	average week	
	percent reporting expenditure	amount spent by purchasers
GROCERIES	**85.2%**	**$68.82**
Cereals and bakery products	**18.3**	**47.54**
Cereals and cereal products	49.5	6.09
Flour	7.3	2.05
Prepared flour mixes	10.9	2.30
Ready-to-eat and cooked cereals	33.6	4.91
Rice	11.0	3.45
Pasta, cornmeal, and other cereal products	23.4	2.44
Bakery products	70.4	8.08
Bread	54.0	3.04
White bread	39.1	1.79
Bread other than white	40.5	2.32
Crackers and cookies	32.7	4.13
Cookies	24.4	3.64
Crackers	15.8	2.90
Frozen and refrigerated bakery products	14.1	3.56
Other bakery products	42.9	5.10
Biscuits and rolls	28.1	2.71
Cakes and cupcakes	12.9	5.02
Bread and cracker products	3.5	2.29
Sweetrolls, coffee cakes, doughnuts	16.0	3.19
Pies, tarts, turnovers	4.9	4.12
Meats, poultry, fish, and eggs	**69.7**	**22.84**
Beef	41.1	11.62
Ground beef	29.1	5.98
Roast	9.1	9.35
Chuck roast	6.2	4.68
Round roast	4.8	4.82
Other roast	5.0	6.79
Steak	16.2	11.01
Round steak	7.0	4.99
Sirloin steak	7.4	6.59
Other steak	11.5	8.25
Pork	37.6	9.08
Bacon	14.9	1.49
Pork chops	11.5	5.43
Ham	12.4	6.68
Ham, not canned	12.0	5.95
Canned ham	0.6	4.84
Sausage	12.0	4.09
Other pork	9.5	8.21
Other meats	35.7	5.49
Frankfurters	13.5	3.11
Lunch meats (cold cuts)	28.4	4.78
Bologna, liverwurst, salami	16.2	3.03
Lamb, organ meats, and others	2.5	7.26
Poultry	34.1	8.56
Fresh and frozen chicken	29.3	7.84
Fresh and frozen whole chicken	13.8	5.00
Fresh and frozen chicken parts	25.4	6.35
Other poultry	10.8	5.74

	average week	
	percent reporting expenditure	amount spent by purchasers
Fish and seafood	24.2%	$9.03
Canned fish and seafood	9.5	3.06
Fresh fish and shellfish	11.4	10.58
Frozen fish and shellfish	8.7	7.84
Eggs	37.2	1.80
Dairy products	**71.3**	**8.95**
Fresh milk and cream	61.1	4.27
Fresh milk, all types	59.0	4.04
Cream	11.8	2.04
Other dairy products	52.7	7.16
Butter	12.9	3.19
Cheese	38.3	4.69
Ice cream and related products	23.1	4.71
Miscellaneous dairy products	15.1	3.05
Fruits and vegetables	**72.9**	**13.76**
Fresh fruits	55.0	5.60
Apples	21.6	2.73
Bananas	37.2	1.61
Oranges	13.1	2.76
Citrus fruits, excl. oranges	15.4	1.62
Other fresh fruits	31.6	4.05
Fresh vegetables	55.1	5.64
Potatoes	21.8	2.66
Lettuce	23.6	1.69
Tomatoes	23.9	2.42
Other fresh vegetables	45.1	3.44
Processed fruits	45.4	4.92
Frozen fruits and fruit juices	8.8	3.05
Frozen orange juice	5.6	2.69
Frozen fruits	1.6	3.18
Frozen fruit juices	3.3	2.14
Canned fruits	13.3	2.33
Dried fruits	4.6	2.39
Fresh fruit juice	13.6	3.53
Canned and bottled fruit juice	27.7	3.86
Processed vegetables	39.4	4.09
Frozen vegetables	17.6	3.01
Canned and dried vegetables and juices	32.8	3.29
Canned beans	13.7	1.76
Canned corn	9.4	1.49
Canned miscellaneous vegetables	16.5	2.06
Dried beans	2.3	1.76
Dried miscellaneous vegetables	5.5	2.71
Fresh and canned vegetable juices	5.5	2.75
Sugar and other sweets	**43.7**	**5.10**
Candy and chewing gum	31.6	4.47
Sugar	14.8	2.30
Artificial sweeteners	2.7	3.72
Jams, preserves, other sweets	14.0	2.71
Fats and oils	**38.2**	**4.37**
Margarine	12.7	1.74
Fats and oils	13.1	3.59
Salad dressings	17.7	3.05
Nondairy cream and imitation milk	7.9	2.40
Peanut butter	8.4	2.86

	average week	
	percent reporting expenditure	amount spent by purchasers
Miscellaneous foods	**65.3%**	**$13.39**
Frozen prepared foods	24.7	7.49
Frozen meals	8.5	6.47
Other frozen prepared foods	20.4	6.37
Canned and packaged soups	21.8	3.30
Potato chips, nuts, and other snacks	37.8	4.94
Potato chips and other snacks	34.2	4.24
Nuts	9.8	4.26
Condiments and seasonings	38.4	4.22
Salt, spices, and other seasonings	15.9	2.39
Olives, pickles, relishes	7.5	2.55
Sauces and gravies	24.7	2.88
Baking needs and miscellaneous products	12.9	2.56
Other canned/packaged prepared foods	40.8	6.59
Prepared salads	12.3	3.10
Prepared desserts	8.0	2.51
Baby food	5.1	8.86
Miscellaneous prepared foods	31.9	5.20
Nonalcoholic beverages	58.9	8.37
Cola	37.1	4.53
Other carbonated drinks	28.1	3.17
Coffee	13.4	5.51
Roasted coffee	12.1	3.97
Instant and freeze-dried coffee	8.7	3.00
Noncarbonated fruit-flavored drinks	12.8	3.06
Tea	9.8	3.46
Other nonalcoholic beverages and ice	21.1	4.17

	average quarter	
	percent reporting expenditure	amount spent by purchasers
FOOD PREPARED BY CONSUMER UNIT ON TRIPS	13.1%	$73.20

Source: Calculations by New Strategist based on the 2001 Consumer Expenditure Survey

Spending indexes can reveal hidden markets—household segments with a high propensity to buy a particular product or service but which are overshadowed by larger household segments that account for a bigger share of the total market. Householders aged 55 to 64, for example, account for a smaller share of the market for coffee than householders aged 35 to 44 (18 versus 23 percent). But a look at the indexed spending figures reveals that, in fact, older householders are the best customers, spending 35 percent more than the average household (index of 135) on coffee versus an average amount (index of 104) spent by householders aged 35 to 44. Grocery store managers can use this type of information to craft advertising and promotions to appeal to their best customers.

Note that because of sampling errors, small differences in index values may not be significant. But the broader patterns revealed by indexes can guide marketers to their best customers.

Indexed Per Capita Spending. The indexed per capita spending figures compare the spending of each household segment with the spending of the average household—after adjusting for household size. New Strategist adjusts for household size by dividing average household spending by the average number of people per household in a segment. While the indexed spending figures show which households are the biggest spenders, the indexed per capita spending figures show the individuals who spend the most.

Households with the largest number of people (such as the middle-aged and married couples with children) typically spend more on groceries simply because there are more people in the household. But after dividing average spending by the number of people in a household, larger households often turn out to spend less than average on a per capita basis. An index of 100 is the per capita average for all households. An index of 125 means that per capita spending by households in a segment is 25 percent greater than the per capita spending of the average household. An index of 75 means per capita spending by the segment is 25 percent below the per capita spending of the average household.

The spending index (not adjusted for household size) shows that householders aged 35 to 54 are the biggest spenders on fresh fruit, spending 11 to 17 percent more than the average household. But the per capita spending index (which adjusts for household size) reveals a different story. Householders aged 55 or older emerge as the biggest spenders on fresh fruit, with a per capita spending index ranging from 28 to 45 percent above average compared to a per capita index 16 percent below average for householders aged 35 to 44 and only 8 percent above average for householders aged 45 to 54. Per capita spending indexes reveal the best individual customers. By knowing who their best customers are, businesses can target those most interested in their products.

Total (Aggregate) Spending. To produce the total (aggregate) spending figures, New Strategist multiplies average spending by the number of households in a segment. The result is the dollar size of the total household market and of each market segment. All totals are shown in thousands of dollars. To convert the numbers in the total spending tables to dollars, you must append "000" to the number. For example, households headed by people aged 35 to 44 spent approximately $2.5 billion ($2,511,558,000) on ready-to-eat cereals in 2001.

When comparing the total spending figures in this report with total spending estimates from the Bureau of Economic Analysis, other government agencies, or trade associations, keep in mind that the Consumer Expenditure Survey includes only household spending, not spending by businesses or institutions. Sales data also will differ from household spending totals because sales figures for consumer products include the value of goods sold to industries, government, and foreign markets, which can be a significant proportion of sales.

Market Shares (Biggest Customers). New Strategist produces market share figures by converting total (aggregate) spending data into percentages. To calculate the percentage of total spending on an item that is controlled by each demographic segment—i.e., its market share—each segment's total spending on an item is divided by aggregate household spending on the item.

Market shares reveal the biggest customers—the demographic segments that account for the largest share of spending on a particular product or service. In 2001, for example, householders aged 35 to 54 accounted for fully half of all spending on groceries. By targeting only the middle-aged, grocery stores and food manufacturers can reach the majority of their customers. There's a danger here, however. By single-mindedly targeting the biggest customers, businesses cannot nurture potential growth markets. With competition for customers more competitive than ever, targeting potential markets is increasingly important to business survival.

Product-specific Tables. The product-specific tables reveal at a glance the demographic characteristics of spending by individual product category. These tables show average spending, indexed spending (Best Customers), total spending, and market shares (Biggest Customers) by age, income, household type, race and Hispanic origin, region, education, occupation, and homeownership status. If you want to see the spending pattern for a particular product at a glance, these are the tables for you.

History and methodology of the Consumer Expenditure Survey

The Consumer Expenditure Survey (CEX) is an ongoing study of the day-to-day spending of American households. In taking the survey, government interviewers collect spending data on products and services as well as the amount and sources of household income, changes in saving and debt, and demographic and economic characteristics of household members. Data collection for the CEX is done by the Bureau of the Census, under contract with the Bureau of Labor Statistics (BLS). The BLS is responsible for analysis and release of the survey data.

Since the late 19th century, the federal government has conducted expenditure surveys about every ten years. Although the results have been used for a variety of purposes, their primary application is to track consumer prices. Beginning in 1980, the CEX became a continuous survey with annual release of data (with a lag time of about two years between data collection and release). The survey is used to update prices for the market basket of products and services used in calculating the Consumer Price Index.

The CEX consists of two separate surveys: an interview survey and a diary survey. In the interview portion of the survey, respondents are asked each quarter for five consecutive quarters to report their expenditures for the previous three months. The purchase of big-ticket items such as houses, cars, and major appliances, or recurring expenses such as insurance premiums, utility payments, and rent are recorded by the interview survey. About 95 percent of all expenditures are covered by the interview component.

Expenditures on small, frequently purchased items are recorded during a two-week period by the diary survey. These detailed records include expenses for food and beverages purchased in grocery stores and at restaurants, as well as other items such as tobacco, housekeeping supplies, nonprescription drugs, and personal care products and services. The diary survey is intended to capture expenditures respondents are likely to forget or recall incorrectly over longer periods of time.

Two separate, nationally representative samples are used for the interview and diary surveys. For the interview survey, about 7,500 consumer units are interviewed on a rotating panel basis each quarter for five consecutive quarters. Another 7,500 consumer units keep weekly diaries of spending for two consecutive weeks. Data collection is carried out in 105 areas of the country.

The data are reviewed, audited, and cleaned by the BLS, and then weighted to reflect the number and characteristics of all U.S. consumer units. As with any sample survey, the CEX is subject to two major types of error. Nonsampling error occurs when respondents misinterpret questions or interviewers are inconsistent in the way they ask questions or record answers. Respondents may forget items, recall expenses incorrectly, or deliberately give wrong answers. A respondent may remember how much he or she spent at the grocery store but forget the items picked up at a local convenience store. Nonsampling error can also be caused by mistakes during the various stages of data processing and refinement.

Sampling error occurs when a sample does not accurately represent the population it is supposed to represent. This kind of error is present in every sample-based survey and is minimized by using a proper sampling procedure. Standard error tables documenting the extent of sampling error in the CEX are available from the BLS at http://www.bls.gov/cex/csxstnderror.htm.

Although the CEX is the best source of information about the spending behavior of American households, it should be treated with caution because of the above problems.

For more information

To find out more about the Consumer Expenditure Survey, contact the CEX specialists at the Bureau of Labor Statistics at (202) 691-6900, or visit the Consumer Expenditure Survey home page at http://www.bls.gov/cex/. The CEX web site includes news releases, technical documentation, and current and historical summary-level CEX data. The detailed average spending data shown in this report are available from the BLS only by special request.

For a comprehensive look at detailed household spending data for all products and services, see the 8th edition of *Household Spending: Who Spends How Much on What*, available from New Strategist Publications in hardcopy or online at http://www.newstrategist.com or by calling 1-800-848-0842.

Spending Overview: 1990 to 2001

Between 1990 and 2001, spending by the average household grew 6 percent to $39,518, after adjusting for inflation. The increase in spending was much less than the 13 percent income growth during those years. While the media frequently claim consumers were on a spending spree during the 1990s as the economy boomed, in fact the substantial rise in spending at the national level was the result of demographic change. Faster than predicted population growth, coupled with the aging of the baby-boom generation into its peak-earning and spending years, were the primary economic drivers. Between 2000 and 2001, spending grew about 1 percent, after adjusting for inflation.

American households have been cutting their spending on many discretionary items for years. The food-away-from-home (primarily restaurants and carry-outs) category is one the few bright spots. After declining between 1990 and 2000, spending on restaurant and carry-out meals rose 1.7 percent between 2000 and 2001, after adjusting for inflation. But spending on food-at-home (groceries) continued to decline between 2000 and 2001, as did spending on alcoholic beverages. Spending on apparel has fallen fully 18 percent since 1990. The decline in spending on women's clothes has been especially steep—a 27 percent drop. Spending on reading material plummeted 30 percent between 1990 and 2001. Spending on entertainment rose nearly 5 percent between 1990 and 2001, after adjusting for inflation, but spending on fees and admissions to entertainment events fell slightly between 2000 and 2001.

Americans cut back on many of their discretionary purchases because their nondiscretionary expenses—the spending they cannot control—were on the rise. After adjusting for inflation, the average household spent 57 percent more on property taxes in 2001 than in 1990. Mortgage interest expenses were up 20 percent. Out-of-pocket spending on health insurance increased 39 percent and drug spending was up 36 percent. Spending on vehicle insurance rose 11 percent. Spending on water and other public services increased 27 percent. Spending on education rose 22 percent.

The average American household spent cautiously during the 1990s, and the recession of 2000–01 dampened spending even more. New spending patterns are emerging as the cost of health insurance and other necessities surge and as technological change creates new priorities in the household budget. The ability to respond in a timely fashion to new spending patterns will determine business success or failure in the years ahead.

Household Spending Trends, 1990 to 2001

(average annual spending of consumer units (CU) by product and service category, 1990 to 2001; percent change 1990–2001 and 2000–01; in 2001 dollars)

	2001	2000	1990	percent change 2000–01	percent change 1990–2001
Number of consumer units (in thousands, add 000)	110,339	109,367	96,968	0.9%	13.8%
Average income before taxes	$47,507	$45,895	$41,880	3.5	13.4
Average annual spending	39,518	$39,107	37,273	1.1	6.0
FOOD	$5,321	$5,302	$5,642	0.4	−5.7
Food at home	3,086	3,105	3,264	−0.6	−5.5
Cereals and bakery products	452	466	483	−2.9	−6.4
Cereals and cereal products	156	160	169	−2.7	−7.7
Bakery products	296	305	315	−3.0	−6.0
Meats, poultry, fish, and eggs	828	817	877	1.3	−5.6
Beef	248	245	286	1.4	−13.3
Pork	177	172	173	3.1	2.3
Other meats	102	104	130	−1.8	−21.5
Poultry	152	149	142	2.0	7.0
Fish and seafood	114	113	108	0.8	5.6
Eggs	35	35	39	0.1	−10.3
Dairy products	332	334	387	−0.6	−14.2
Fresh milk and cream	136	135	184	1.0	−26.1
Other dairy products	196	198	204	−1.2	−3.9
Fruits and vegetables	522	536	536	−2.5	−2.6
Fresh fruits	160	168	167	−4.5	−4.2
Fresh vegetables	162	163	155	−0.9	4.5
Processed fruits	116	118	122	−1.9	−4.9
Processed vegetables	84	86	92	−2.7	−8.7
Other food at home	952	953	980	−0.1	−2.9
Sugar and other sweets	116	120	123	−3.5	−5.7
Fats and oils	87	85	89	2.0	−2.2
Miscellaneous foods	455	449	441	1.3	3.2
Nonalcoholic beverages	256	257	280	−0.4	−8.6
Food prepared by CU on trips	38	41	46	−7.6	−17.4
Food away from home	2,235	2,197	2,378	1.7	−6.0
ALCOHOLIC BEVERAGES	349	382	385	−8.7	−9.4
HOUSING	13,011	12,663	11,430	2.7	13.8
Shelter	7,602	7,313	6,351	4.0	19.7
Owned dwellings	4,979	4,730	3,878	5.3	28.4
Mortgage interest and charges	2,862	2,713	2,386	5.5	19.9
Property taxes	1,233	1,171	784	5.3	57.3
Maintenance, repair, insurance, other expenses	884	848	709	4.2	24.7
Rented dwellings	2,134	2,091	2,013	2.1	6.0
Other lodging	489	491	458	−0.5	6.8
Utilities, fuels, and public services	2,767	2,559	2,482	8.2	11.5
Natural gas	411	316	323	30.2	27.2
Electricity	1,009	936	995	7.8	1.4
Fuel oil and other fuels	112	100	131	12.3	−14.5
Telephone	914	902	777	1.4	17.6
Water and other public services	321	304	253	5.5	26.9
Household services	676	703	586	−3.9	15.4
Personal services	291	335	288	−13.2	1.0
Other household services	385	368	298	4.6	29.2

ROCERIES

	2001	2000	1990	percent change	
				2000–01	1990–2001
Housekeeping supplies	**$509**	**$496**	**$533**	**2.7%**	**−4.5%**
Laundry and cleaning supplies	131	135	148	−2.7	−11.5
Other household products	255	232	225	9.8	13.3
Postage and stationery	122	130	160	−5.8	−23.8
Household furnishings and equipment	**1,458**	**1,592**	**1,477**	**−8.4**	**−1.3**
Household textiles	114	109	130	4.6	−12.3
Furniture	372	402	407	−7.4	−8.6
Floor coverings	40	45	121	−11.6	−66.9
Major appliances	178	194	193	−8.4	−7.8
Small appliances, misc. housewares	87	89	98	−2.7	−11.2
Miscellaneous household equipment	667	751	528	−11.2	26.3
APPAREL AND RELATED SERVICES	**1,743**	**1,908**	**2,125**	**−8.6**	**−18.0**
Men and boys	**423**	**452**	**516**	**−6.5**	**−18.0**
Men, aged 16 or older	335	354	426	−5.3	−21.4
Boys, aged 2 to 15	88	99	92	−10.8	−4.3
Women and girls	**677**	**745**	**884**	**−9.2**	**−23.4**
Women, aged 16 or older	562	624	770	−9.9	−27.0
Girls, aged 2 to 15	115	121	114	−5.2	0.9
Children under age 2	**81**	**84**	**92**	**−3.9**	**−12.0**
Footwear	**302**	**353**	**295**	**−14.3**	**2.4**
Other apparel products and services	**259**	**273**	**339**	**−5.3**	**−23.6**
TRANSPORTATION	**7,633**	**7,624**	**6,724**	**0.1**	**13.5**
Vehicle purchases	**3,579**	**3,513**	**2,796**	**1.9**	**2.8**
Cars and trucks, new	1,685	1,650	1,522	2.1	10.7
Cars and trucks, used	1,848	1,819	1,245	1.6	48.4
Other vehicles	46	44	29	4.1	58.6
Gasoline and motor oil	**1,279**	**1,327**	**1,375**	**−3.6**	**−7.0**
Other vehicle expenses	**2,375**	**2,345**	**2,156**	**1.3**	**10.2**
Vehicle finance charges	359	337	394	6.5	−8.9
Maintenance and repairs	662	641	774	3.2	−14.5
Vehicle insurance	819	800	739	2.4	10.8
Vehicle rentals, leases, licenses, other charges	534	566	250	−5.7	113.6
Public transportation	**400**	**439**	**397**	**−8.9**	**0.8**
HEALTH CARE	**2,182**	**2,124**	**1,944**	**2.7**	**12.2**
Health insurance	1,061	1,010	763	0.5	39.1
Medical services	573	584	738	−1.9	−22.4
Drugs	449	428	331	0.5	35.6
Medical supplies	100	102	112	−1.7	−10.7
ENTERTAINMENT	**1,953**	**1,915**	**1,868**	**2.0**	**4.6**
Fees and admissions	526	529	487	−0.6	0.8
Television, radio, sound equipment	660	639	596	3.2	10.7
Pets, toys, and playground equipment	337	343	362	−1.8	−6.9
Other entertainment products and services	430	404	422	6.4	1.9
PERSONAL CARE PRODUCTS AND SERVICES	**485**	**580**	**478**	**−16.3**	**1.5**
READING	**141**	**150**	**201**	**−6.1**	**−29.9**
EDUCATION	**648**	**650**	**533**	**−0.3**	**21.6**
TOBACCO PRODUCTS AND SMOKING SUPPLIES	**308**	**328**	**360**	**−6.1**	**−14.4**
MISCELLANEOUS	**750**	**798**	**1,106**	**−6.0**	**−32.2**
CASH CONTRIBUTIONS	**1,258**	**1,225**	**1,072**	**2.7**	**17.4**
PERSONAL INSURANCE AND PENSIONS	**3,737**	**3,459**	**3,404**	**8.0**	**9.8**
Life and other personal insurance	410	410	453	−0.0	−9.5
Pensions and Social Security	3,326	3,049	2,952	9.1	12.7

	2001	2000	1990	percent change 2000–01	percent change 1990–2001
PERSONAL TAXES	**$2,920**	**$3,204**	**$3,877**	**–8.9%**	**–24.7%**
Federal income taxes	2,237	2,476	3,046	–9.7	–26.6
State and local income taxes	555	578	733	–3.9	–24.3
Other taxes	129	150	98	–14.0	31.6
GIFTS	**1,012**	**1,113**	**1,196**	**–9.1**	**–15.4**
Food	**69**	**72**	**125**	**–4.1**	**–44.8**
Alcoholic beverages	**14**	**14**	**–**	**–2.7**	**–**
Housing	**258**	**299**	**305**	**–13.7**	**–15.4**
Housekeeping supplies	41	40	46	2.3	–10.9
Household textiles	14	13	18	4.8	–22.2
Appliances and misc. housewares	25	29	35	–13.1	–28.6
Major appliances	6	8	9	–27.0	–33.3
Small appliances and misc. housewares	19	22	26	–12.0	–26.9
Miscellaneous household equipment	59	72	66	–1.8	–10.6
Other housing	119	144	141	–17.3	–15.6
Apparel and services	**237**	**251**	**310**	**–5.5**	**–23.5**
Males, aged 2 or older	61	70	80	–12.7	–23.8
Females, aged 2 or older	89	87	125	1.9	–28.8
Children under age 2	42	42	41	–0.3	2.4
Other apparel products and services	45	52	63	–14.2	–28.6
Jewelry and watches	17	21	33	–17.3	–48.5
All other apparel products and services	28	31	30	–9.2	–6.7
Transportation	**70**	**72**	**70**	**–2.7**	**0.0**
Health care	**35**	**39**	**59**	**–10.4**	**–40.7**
Entertainment	**74**	**97**	**87**	**–23.4**	**–14.9**
Toys, games, hobbies, and tricycles	30	31	33	–2.7	–9.1
Other entertainment	44	66	54	–33.1	–18.5
Personal care products and services	**21**	**20**	**–**	**7.5**	**–**
Reading	**1**	**2**	**–**	**–51.4**	**–**
EDUCATION	**160**	**155**	**126**	**3.1**	**27.0**
All other gifts	**73**	**92**	**116**	**–20.2**	**–37.1**

Note: Spending by category will not add to total spending because gift spending is also included in the preceding product and service categories and personal taxes are not included in the total. (–) means data not available.

Source: Bureau of Labor Statistics, 1990, 2000, and 2001 Consumer Expenditure Surveys, Internet site http://www.bls.gov/cex/; calculations by New Strategist

Who's Buying
GROCERIES, 2001

Between 1990 and 2001, spending on groceries by the average household fell 5 percent, after adjusting for inflation, although spending increased slightly—up 0.4 percent—between 2000 and 2001. Pork, poultry, fish, and fresh vegetables were among the handful of categories that experienced spending increases during the decade. Some categories experienced steep declines. Spending on beef fell 13 percent between 1990 and 2001, after adjusting for inflation, although the category saw a 1 percent increase between 2000 and 2001. Spending on eggs fell 10 percent and milk was down fully 26 percent since 1990. New dietary guidelines and changing food preferences are factors behind the spending declines.

The average household spent $3,086 on groceries in 2001. The Bureau of Labor Statistics reports that during an average week, 85 percent of households shopped for groceries, spending an average of $68.82 on food items.

The largest households—those headed by householders aged 35 to 44—spend 16 percent more than average on groceries. These householders are particularly big spenders on foods preferred by children, spending 20 percent more than average on colas, 26 percent more than average on cakes and cupcakes, and 28 percent more than average on potato chips and other snacks. Householders aged 45 to 54—the most affluent—spend slightly more than those aged 35 to 44 on groceries, although their households are smaller. This age group spends the most on pricey items such as sirloin steak. On a per capita basis, householders aged 65 or older are the biggest spenders on many grocery categories such as crackers, nuts, coffee, fresh fruit, and fresh vegetables.

The most affluent households spend the most in the grocery store. In 2001, households with incomes of $70,000-plus spent 40 percent more than the average household on groceries. There are only two categories of food on which households with incomes of $70,000 or more spend less than average: canned ham and dried beans. Generally, spending on groceries is above average for households with incomes of $50,000 or more, about average for those with incomes of $30,000 to $49,999, and below average for those with incomes below $30,000. Household size accounts for some of these spending differences, with the number of people in a household rising directly with income.

Spending on groceries is highest among married couples with children at home because their households are the largest. Couples with school-aged children at home spend 43 percent more than the average household on groceries, while those with adult children at home spend 55 percent more. Married couples with school-aged children spend 62 percent more than average on potato chips and other snacks, 63 percent more than average on cereal, and twice the average on noncarbonated fruit-flavored drinks.

People who live alone spend less than average on groceries, although on a per capita basis their spending is above average on most items. They are particularly big spenders on items such as frozen meals, accounting for 25 percent of the market. Single-person households account for a sizeable 21 percent share of the market for instant and freeze-dried coffee.

The food preferences of racial and ethnic minorities are critical to the grocery industry not only because of the significant share of the market they control, but also because ethnic foods are increasingly enjoyed by the general population. Households headed by Hispanics spend 15 percent more on groceries than the average household—$3,551 in 2001. Hispanics spend more because their households are large, averaging 3.4 people versus 2.5 people in the average household. Households headed by Hispanics spend 83 percent more than average on flour, 92 percent more than average on rice, and nearly three times the average on dried beans.

Households headed by blacks spend 9 percent less than the average household on groceries. But they spend more than average on pork, poultry, and fish. They are also big spenders on noncarbonated fruit-flavored drinks.

Households in the Northeast spend the most on groceries (10 percent more than average), while those in the Midwest spend the least (6 percent less than average). Northeastern households are particularly big spenders on butter, fresh fruit juice, and tea. Households in the South spend 23 percent more than average on bacon, accounting for 44 percent of the market. They also spend 20 percent more than average on baby food. Households in the West spend more than those in other regions on dried beans, in part because many Hispanics live in the region.

Spending on groceries rises with education because educated householders have higher incomes. College graduates spend 13 percent more than the average household on groceries, while those with a high school diploma spend 4 percent less than average. On some products, however, college graduates have below-average spending. They spend less than average on beef, for example, while those with a high school degree spend slightly more than average on this item. College graduates spend 26 percent more than average on fish and seafood, while those with less education spend less than average on this item. College graduates spend 23 to 30 percent more than the average household on fresh fruits and vegetables, but less than average on sugar, nondairy creamer, and colas.

By occupation, the biggest spenders on groceries are households headed by construction workers and mechanics, spending 17 percent more than the average household—an even larger amount than is spent by the most affluent households, those headed by managers and professionals. One factor behind the higher spending of construction workers and mechanics is their relatively large household size—an average of 3.0 people versus 2.6 people in households headed by managers and professionals. The pattern of spending differs significantly between these two types of households. Those headed by construction workers spend 18 percent more than average on white bread, for example, while those headed by managers and professionals spend slightly less than average on this item. Other grocery categories favored by construction workers but not managers and professionals include ground beef (with indexes of 146 versus 98), pork (135 versus 98), and eggs (122 versus 98).

Homeowners spend more than renters on groceries because their incomes are higher and their households include more people. In 2001, the before-tax income of homeowners stood at $52,966 versus $29,021 for renters. Households headed by homeowners included 2.6 people versus 2.2 people in households headed by renters. Renters spend more than homeowners on only two products—rice and dried beans. Behind this higher spending is the fact that many renters are Hispanic, and Hispanics are big spenders on these items.

Spending on Groceries by Household Type, 2001

(indexed spending on selected groceries by household type, 2001)

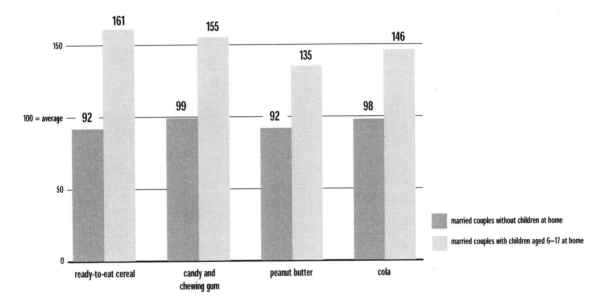

married couples without children at home

married couples with children aged 6–17 at home

1. Groceries: Average spending by age, 2001

(average annual spending of consumer units (CU) on groceries, by age of consumer unit reference person, 2001)

	total consumer units	under 25	25 to 34	35 to 44	45 to 54	55 to 64	65 to 74	75+
Number of consumer units								
(in thousands, add 000)	**110,339**	**8,598**	**18,515**	**24,422**	**22,317**	**14,549**	**11,342**	**10,596**
Average number of persons per CU	**2.5**	**1.9**	**2.9**	**3.3**	**2.7**	**2.1**	**1.9**	**1.5**
Average before-tax income of CU	**$47,507.00**	**$20,769.00**	**$49,424.00**	**$58,902.00**	**$61,093.00**	**$51,965.00**	**$32,365.00**	**$22,255.00**
Average spending of CU, total	**39,518.46**	**23,526.22**	**39,451.09**	**46,907.71**	**47,929.85**	**41,462.49**	**32,023.11**	**23,099.29**
GROCERIES	**$3,085.52**	**$1,857.28**	**$2,936.27**	**$3,588.77**	**$3,658.79**	**$3,238.19**	**$2,597.09**	**$2,261.22**
Cereals and bakery products	**452.19**	**276.43**	**418.92**	**535.15**	**522.32**	**462.61**	**385.62**	**367.26**
Cereals and cereal products	156.46	112.20	159.75	187.58	175.71	147.47	123.66	119.25
Flour	8.01	7.31	7.37	9.05	8.78	7.94	6.69	7.10
Prepared flour mixes	12.89	6.91	12.11	15.47	15.52	12.90	10.42	10.18
Ready-to-eat and cooked cereals	86.04	64.87	87.34	102.84	93.24	81.34	70.30	69.00
Rice	19.95	13.48	22.48	25.33	23.78	17.65	12.07	11.28
Pasta, cornmeal, and other cereal products	29.57	19.63	30.46	34.88	34.39	27.64	24.19	21.69
Bakery products	295.73	164.22	259.17	347.58	346.62	315.14	261.96	248.00
Bread	85.37	47.38	78.48	93.91	96.23	97.81	82.42	71.75
White bread	36.64	22.53	35.52	42.14	40.67	38.65	34.75	27.80
Crackers and cookies	70.18	38.41	61.74	80.60	83.37	70.14	65.41	64.06
Cookies	46.13	27.05	39.78	54.74	54.38	44.40	42.24	41.93
Crackers	24.05	11.36	21.96	25.86	28.99	25.74	23.17	22.13
Frozen and refrigerated bakery products	26.06	16.14	20.43	32.85	32.48	25.28	20.58	21.57
Other bakery products	114.11	62.30	98.53	140.21	134.54	121.90	93.55	90.63
Biscuits and rolls	39.34	20.21	30.57	47.30	47.46	47.96	35.04	27.49
Cakes and cupcakes	33.80	21.82	34.50	42.64	38.07	32.65	21.91	26.50
Bread and cracker products	4.05	1.51	3.84	5.05	5.30	4.18	2.90	2.52
Sweetrolls, coffee cakes, doughnuts	26.32	13.78	20.29	33.26	32.21	25.48	22.81	23.47
Pies, tarts, turnovers	10.60	4.97	9.33	11.96	11.50	11.63	10.89	10.66
Meats, poultry, fish, and eggs	**827.97**	**471.74**	**791.17**	**947.95**	**999.34**	**898.33**	**696.71**	**581.36**
Beef	248.06	147.18	240.56	273.99	308.28	265.62	215.09	166.16
Ground beef	90.48	64.07	93.21	101.54	111.08	90.38	72.42	56.62
Roast	44.44	19.31	33.89	48.41	55.61	53.07	48.14	35.29
Chuck roast	15.03	6.23	12.49	16.84	19.39	18.43	9.81	14.20
Round roast	11.88	6.09	7.90	12.58	15.83	15.93	10.01	10.25
Other roast	17.53	6.99	13.51	18.99	20.39	18.70	28.33	10.84
Steak	92.73	53.83	90.89	102.09	119.02	97.43	81.34	55.63
Round steak	18.21	10.40	19.28	19.22	23.64	16.54	18.30	11.02
Sirloin steak	25.37	16.06	27.23	28.68	32.88	26.58	15.40	14.77
Other steak	49.15	27.37	44.38	54.20	62.50	54.30	47.64	29.84
Pork	177.31	87.54	167.40	195.79	210.79	204.72	160.77	134.08
Bacon	29.30	16.12	29.01	30.19	34.58	32.25	28.89	23.79
Pork chops	42.16	24.43	47.40	46.37	49.70	44.02	33.29	28.18
Ham	39.98	15.83	32.01	45.09	49.08	46.06	39.90	34.55
Ham, not canned	38.24	15.39	31.05	43.25	47.22	43.82	36.94	32.79
Canned ham	1.74	0.44	0.96	1.83	1.86	2.24	2.96	1.76
Sausage	25.52	14.63	20.06	28.88	30.40	28.89	23.16	23.95
Other pork	40.34	16.52	38.93	45.27	47.03	53.50	35.53	23.60
Other meats	102.06	59.60	90.66	126.76	124.09	103.29	79.86	74.03
Frankfurters	22.01	14.95	23.00	25.73	25.68	21.89	16.94	15.02
Lunch meats (cold cuts)	70.88	41.65	61.07	86.80	87.48	74.19	56.70	50.02
Bologna, liverwurst, salami	25.40	12.99	22.47	30.02	30.78	29.02	20.67	18.49
Lamb, organ meats, and others	9.17	3.00	6.59	14.23	10.94	7.21	6.22	8.99

	total consumer units	under 25	25 to 34	35 to 44	45 to 54	55 to 64	65 to 74	75+
Poultry	$151.87	$92.99	$153.27	$181.00	$182.37	$154.29	$112.93	$ 101.82
Fresh and frozen chicken	119.55	78.01	125.35	145.40	142.67	115.33	83.37	76.92
Fresh and frozen whole chicken	35.75	22.50	38.69	43.05	41.44	36.35	24.53	23.00
Fresh and frozen chicken parts	83.80	55.52	86.67	102.35	101.24	78.98	58.84	53.92
Other poultry	32.32	14.97	27.92	35.60	39.70	38.96	29.56	24.90
Fish and seafood	113.67	59.11	106.59	131.25	133.52	134.03	96.66	77.44
Canned fish and seafood	15.11	8.70	15.54	16.81	16.29	16.31	13.54	13.11
Fresh fish and shellfish	63.07	32.34	57.37	73.79	74.62	75.07	50.93	45.06
Frozen fish and shellfish	35.49	18.06	33.68	40.66	42.62	42.65	32.19	19.27
Eggs	34.99	25.32	32.69	39.17	40.28	36.38	31.39	27.85
Dairy products	**331.69**	**194.01**	**317.15**	**400.05**	**388.24**	**340.43**	**273.69**	**238.09**
Fresh milk and cream	135.85	84.43	136.62	164.32	156.34	125.91	112.48	104.03
Fresh milk, all types	123.50	79.24	125.88	150.39	141.81	111.05	100.67	94.17
Cream	12.35	5.18	10.73	13.94	14.53	14.86	11.82	9.86
Other dairy products	195.84	109.58	180.53	235.73	231.90	214.52	161.21	134.05
Butter	21.55	11.24	18.61	25.61	23.64	28.73	17.47	15.68
Cheese	93.39	55.21	86.70	111.38	114.75	97.59	78.15	59.15
Ice cream and related products	56.79	30.30	51.00	68.63	66.68	62.42	44.60	45.12
Miscellaneous dairy products	24.11	12.82	24.22	30.11	26.82	25.78	20.99	14.11
Fruits and vegetables	**521.74**	**295.06**	**478.04**	**585.26**	**607.09**	**554.81**	**492.93**	**440.50**
Fresh fruits	160.41	85.21	141.93	177.97	187.32	172.63	160.62	139.91
Apples	30.83	17.76	30.11	35.88	38.64	29.81	24.43	22.51
Bananas	31.30	17.59	27.26	33.57	34.94	34.10	34.83	29.17
Oranges	18.62	11.80	16.61	21.43	23.24	17.61	16.80	14.74
Citrus fruits, excl. oranges	13.21	6.18	10.72	14.29	15.64	15.93	12.97	12.35
Other fresh fruits	66.45	31.87	57.23	72.81	74.86	75.17	71.59	61.14
Fresh vegetables	161.62	86.23	148.26	175.77	193.00	182.85	155.42	125.02
Potatoes	30.09	14.15	27.16	32.51	35.65	36.24	28.87	23.82
Lettuce	20.82	11.40	18.92	23.64	26.05	21.65	18.31	15.76
Tomatoes	30.03	18.34	29.60	33.30	35.59	30.47	28.40	22.01
Other fresh vegetables	80.68	42.34	72.58	86.32	95.72	94.49	79.85	63.43
Processed fruits	116.03	77.53	109.55	136.22	127.79	111.62	103.74	105.63
Frozen fruits and fruit juices	13.85	10.22	14.22	15.35	15.64	13.76	11.81	11.14
Frozen orange juice	7.61	6.08	8.16	8.09	8.33	8.05	5.90	6.37
Frozen fruits	2.53	1.20	1.31	2.85	3.45	3.05	2.60	2.35
Frozen fruit juices	3.72	2.94	4.76	4.41	3.85	2.66	3.31	2.41
Canned fruits	16.27	7.79	14.28	16.29	18.96	17.21	16.40	19.77
Dried fruits	5.54	2.23	4.94	5.47	5.98	5.34	7.02	7.33
Fresh fruit juice	24.86	18.26	19.64	29.24	27.03	26.57	23.67	23.59
Canned and bottled fruit juice	55.50	39.05	56.47	69.86	60.19	48.74	44.83	43.80
Processed vegetables	83.68	46.09	78.31	95.30	98.97	87.71	73.15	69.94
Frozen vegetables	27.50	14.53	24.99	32.46	32.91	28.45	24.43	21.44
Canned and dried vegetables and juices	56.18	31.56	53.32	62.84	66.07	59.26	48.72	48.50
Canned beans	12.60	7.66	13.53	13.69	14.69	12.19	9.36	12.01
Canned corn	7.13	5.12	7.83	8.61	7.54	6.45	5.77	5.49
Canned miscellaneous vegetables	17.58	7.55	14.62	19.92	19.71	20.72	18.75	15.59
Dried beans	2.28	1.24	2.16	2.17	2.80	3.05	2.26	1.41
Dried miscellaneous vegetables	7.58	4.46	6.22	7.98	9.90	8.97	6.35	6.13
Fresh and canned vegetable juices	7.65	5.22	7.54	9.37	8.85	6.84	4.94	7.17
Sugar and other sweets	**115.96**	**59.02**	**103.57**	**140.40**	**133.76**	**126.97**	**99.73**	**91.36**
Candy and chewing gum	73.49	35.84	63.58	92.25	85.54	77.01	63.92	57.48
Sugar	17.91	11.04	18.02	19.02	21.54	21.00	15.01	11.84
Artificial sweeteners	5.04	0.52	3.49	4.72	6.52	6.94	6.56	4.96
Jams, preserves, other sweets	19.52	11.62	18.48	24.42	20.16	22.02	14.24	17.07

	total consumer units	under 25	25 to 34	35 to 44	45 to 54	55 to 64	65 to 74	75+
Fats and oils	**$86.76**	**$50.23**	**$80.85**	**$96.36**	**$106.48**	**$90.70**	**$78.92**	**$65.79**
Margarine	11.43	5.37	9.34	11.82	13.80	12.78	13.03	10.66
Fats and oils	24.53	15.74	25.05	26.82	30.02	24.52	21.08	17.42
Salad dressings	28.02	15.54	25.51	31.65	35.24	30.06	24.88	19.41
Nondairy cream and imitation milk	10.09	4.98	7.29	11.38	12.15	12.24	9.81	9.27
Peanut butter	12.69	8.61	13.65	14.69	15.27	11.09	10.14	9.03
Miscellaneous foods	**454.72**	**325.39**	**474.75**	**532.69**	**537.54**	**447.52**	**326.23**	**310.13**
Frozen prepared foods	96.19	74.62	91.27	111.50	120.94	93.08	67.05	69.21
Frozen meals	28.65	16.85	22.80	28.13	35.83	35.18	23.82	31.17
Other frozen prepared foods	67.54	57.77	68.47	83.37	85.11	57.90	43.23	38.04
Canned and packaged soups	37.27	18.47	34.75	40.71	43.42	39.64	32.36	38.16
Potato chips, nuts, and other snacks	97.37	66.38	89.88	118.76	118.56	101.80	74.02	59.12
Potato chips and other snacks	75.56	57.69	74.41	97.09	93.95	73.04	47.07	35.66
Nuts	21.81	8.69	15.47	21.67	24.61	28.76	26.95	23.46
Condiments and seasonings	84.05	51.70	81.43	101.61	103.38	84.37	63.97	53.46
Salt, spices, and other seasonings	19.83	13.38	19.11	22.89	24.10	20.96	16.61	11.91
Olives, pickles, relishes	9.97	3.29	8.82	11.36	13.19	10.85	8.16	8.07
Sauces and gravies	36.84	25.58	37.15	46.51	45.03	35.27	23.52	21.49
Baking needs and miscellaneous products	17.41	9.44	16.35	20.84	21.06	17.29	15.68	11.99
Other canned/packaged prepared foods	139.85	114.23	177.42	160.12	151.24	128.63	88.83	90.18
Prepared salads	19.55	9.40	17.25	20.42	24.22	25.18	16.45	15.59
Prepared desserts	10.15	4.52	9.90	10.02	10.54	14.07	9.18	10.43
Baby food	23.62	34.65	54.69	27.47	13.24	12.32	6.07	5.30
Miscellaneous prepared foods	86.24	65.50	95.30	101.71	103.18	76.25	57.13	58.86
Nonalcoholic beverages	256.16	167.58	242.87	306.71	318.52	265.45	196.94	150.42
Cola	87.41	62.80	86.46	105.31	109.73	92.32	62.65	38.86
Other carbonated drinks	46.14	34.19	46.79	53.91	59.68	45.58	30.91	24.51
Coffee	38.35	12.84	24.26	39.91	46.74	51.77	44.48	38.37
Roasted coffee	24.98	9.65	16.36	26.65	31.27	34.14	26.59	21.57
Instant and freeze-dried coffee	13.37	3.19	7.90	13.26	15.46	17.62	17.89	16.79
Noncarbonated fruit-flavored drinks	20.36	15.65	22.79	28.70	22.88	17.29	13.42	6.14
Tea	17.57	8.41	16.28	21.23	22.13	17.43	14.28	12.78
Other nonalcoholic beverages and ice	45.67	33.69	45.84	57.15	56.34	39.74	30.63	29.34
Food prepared by CU on trips	**38.33**	**17.83**	**28.95**	**44.19**	**45.49**	**51.37**	**46.32**	**16.31**

Source: Bureau of Labor Statistics, unpublished tables from the 2001 Consumer Expenditure Survey

2. Groceries: Indexed spending by age, 2001

(indexed average annual spending of consumer units (CU) on groceries, by age of consumer unit reference person, 2001; index definition: an index of 100 is the average for all consumer units; an index of 132 means that spending by consumer units in that group is 32 percent above the average for all consumer units; an index of 68 indicates spending that is 32 percent below the average for all consumer units)

	total consumer units	under 25	25 to 34	35 to 44	45 to 54	55 to 64	65 to 74	75+
Average spending of CU, total	$39,518	$23,526	$39,451	$46,908	$47,930	$41,462	$32,023	$23,099
Average spending of CU, index	100	60	100	119	121	105	81	59
GROCERIES	100	60	95	116	119	105	84	73
Cereals and bakery products	100	61	93	118	116	102	85	81
Cereals and cereal products	100	72	102	120	112	94	79	76
Flour	100	91	92	113	110	99	84	89
Prepared flour mixes	100	54	94	120	120	100	81	79
Ready-to-eat and cooked cereals	100	75	102	120	108	95	82	80
Rice	100	68	113	127	119	89	61	57
Pasta, cornmeal, and other cereal products	100	66	103	118	116	94	82	73
Bakery products	100	56	88	118	117	107	89	84
Bread	100	56	92	110	113	115	97	84
White bread	100	62	97	115	111	106	95	76
Crackers and cookies	100	55	88	115	119	100	93	91
Cookies	100	59	86	119	118	96	92	91
Crackers	100	47	91	108	121	107	96	92
Frozen and refrigerated bakery products	100	62	78	126	125	97	79	83
Other bakery products	100	55	86	123	118	107	82	79
Biscuits and rolls	100	51	78	120	121	122	89	70
Cakes and cupcakes	100	65	102	126	113	97	65	78
Bread and cracker products	100	37	95	125	131	103	72	62
Sweetrolls, coffee cakes, doughnuts	100	52	77	126	122	97	87	89
Pies, tarts, turnovers	100	47	88	113	109	110	103	101
Meats, poultry, fish, and eggs	100	57	96	115	121	109	84	70
Beef	100	59	97	111	124	107	87	67
Ground beef	100	71	103	112	123	100	80	63
Roast	100	44	76	109	125	119	108	79
Chuck roast	100	42	83	112	129	123	65	95
Round roast	100	51	67	106	133	134	84	86
Other roast	100	40	77	108	116	107	162	62
Steak	100	58	98	110	128	105	88	60
Round steak	100	57	106	106	130	91	101	61
Sirloin steak	100	63	107	113	130	105	61	58
Other steak	100	56	90	110	127	111	97	61
Pork	100	49	94	110	119	116	91	76
Bacon	100	55	99	103	118	110	99	81
Pork chops	100	58	112	110	118	104	79	67
Ham	100	40	80	113	123	115	100	86
Ham, not canned	100	40	81	113	124	115	97	86
Canned ham	100	25	55	105	107	129	170	101
Sausage	100	57	79	113	119	113	91	94
Other pork	100	41	97	112	117	133	88	59
Other meats	100	58	89	124	122	101	78	73
Frankfurters	100	68	105	117	117	100	77	68
Lunch meats (cold cuts)	100	59	86	123	123	105	80	71
Bologna, liverwurst, salami	100	51	89	118	121	114	81	73
Lamb, organ meats, and others	100	33	72	155	119	79	68	98

	total consumer units	under 25	25 to 34	35 to 44	45 to 54	55 to 64	65 to 74	75+
Poultry	100	61	101	119	120	102	74	67
Fresh and frozen chicken	100	65	105	122	119	97	70	64
Fresh and frozen whole chicken	100	63	108	120	116	102	69	64
Fresh and frozen chicken parts	100	66	103	122	121	94	70	64
Other poultry	100	46	86	110	123	121	92	77
Fish and seafood	100	52	94	116	118	118	85	68
Canned fish and seafood	100	58	103	111	108	108	90	87
Fresh fish and shellfish	100	51	91	117	118	119	81	71
Frozen fish and shellfish	100	51	95	115	120	120	91	54
Eggs	100	72	93	112	115	104	90	80
Dairy products	**100**	**59**	**96**	**121**	**117**	**103**	**83**	**72**
Fresh milk and cream	100	62	101	121	115	93	83	77
Fresh milk, all types	100	64	102	122	115	90	82	76
Cream	100	42	87	113	118	120	96	80
Other dairy products	100	56	92	120	118	110	82	68
Butter	100	52	86	119	110	133	81	73
Cheese	100	59	93	119	123	105	84	63
Ice cream and related products	100	53	90	121	117	110	79	80
Miscellaneous dairy products	100	53	101	125	111	107	87	59
Fruits and vegetables	**100**	**57**	**92**	**112**	**116**	**106**	**95**	**84**
Fresh fruits	100	53	89	111	117	108	100	87
Apples	100	58	98	116	125	97	79	73
Bananas	100	56	87	107	112	109	111	93
Oranges	100	63	89	115	125	95	90	79
Citrus fruits, excl. oranges	100	47	81	108	118	121	98	94
Other fresh fruits	100	48	86	110	113	113	108	92
Fresh vegetables	100	53	92	109	119	113	96	77
Potatoes	100	47	90	108	119	120	96	79
Lettuce	100	55	91	114	125	104	88	76
Tomatoes	100	61	99	111	119	102	95	73
Other fresh vegetables	100	53	90	107	119	117	99	79
Processed fruits	100	67	94	117	110	96	89	91
Frozen fruits and fruit juices	100	74	103	111	113	99	85	80
Frozen orange juice	100	80	107	106	110	106	78	84
Frozen fruits	100	47	52	113	136	121	103	93
Frozen fruit juices	100	79	128	119	104	72	89	65
Canned fruits	100	48	88	100	117	106	101	122
Dried fruits	100	40	89	99	108	96	127	132
Fresh fruit juice	100	74	79	118	109	107	95	95
Canned and bottled fruit juice	100	70	102	126	109	88	81	79
Processed vegetables	100	55	94	114	118	105	87	84
Frozen vegetables	100	53	91	118	120	104	89	78
Canned and dried vegetables and juices	100	56	95	112	118	106	87	86
Canned beans	100	61	107	109	117	97	74	95
Canned corn	100	72	110	121	106	91	81	77
Canned miscellaneous vegetables	100	43	83	113	112	118	107	89
Dried beans	100	54	95	95	123	134	99	62
Dried miscellaneous vegetables	100	59	82	105	131	118	84	81
Fresh and canned vegetable juices	100	68	99	123	116	89	65	94
Sugar and other sweets	**100**	**51**	**89**	**121**	**115**	**110**	**86**	**79**
Candy and chewing gum	100	49	87	126	116	105	87	78
Sugar	100	62	101	106	120	117	84	66
Artificial sweeteners	100	10	69	94	129	138	130	98
Jams, preserves, other sweets	100	60	95	125	103	113	73	87

	total consumer units	under 25	25 to 34	35 to 44	45 to 54	55 to 64	65 to 74	75+
Fats and oils	**100**	**58**	**93**	**111**	**123**	**105**	**91**	**76**
Margarine	100	47	82	103	121	112	114	93
Fats and oils	100	64	102	109	122	100	86	71
Salad dressings	100	56	91	113	126	107	89	69
Nondairy cream and imitation milk	100	49	72	113	120	121	97	92
Peanut butter	100	68	108	116	120	87	80	71
Miscellaneous foods	**100**	**72**	**104**	**117**	**118**	**98**	**72**	**68**
Frozen prepared foods	100	78	95	116	126	97	70	72
Frozen meals	100	59	80	98	125	123	83	109
Other frozen prepared foods	100	86	101	123	126	86	64	56
Canned and packaged soups	100	50	93	109	117	106	87	102
Potato chips, nuts, and other snacks	100	68	92	122	122	105	76	61
Potato chips and other snacks	100	76	99	129	124	97	62	47
Nuts	100	40	71	99	113	132	124	108
Condiments and seasonings	100	62	97	121	123	100	76	64
Salt, spices, and other seasonings	100	68	96	115	122	106	84	60
Olives, pickles, relishes	100	33	89	114	132	109	82	81
Sauces and gravies	100	69	101	126	122	96	64	58
Baking needs and miscellaneous products	100	54	94	120	121	99	90	69
Other canned/packaged prepared foods	100	82	127	115	108	92	64	65
Prepared salads	100	48	88	105	124	129	84	80
Prepared desserts	100	45	98	99	104	139	90	103
Baby food	100	147	232	116	56	52	26	22
Miscellaneous prepared foods	100	76	111	118	120	88	66	68
Nonalcoholic beverages	100	65	95	120	124	104	77	59
Cola	100	72	99	121	126	106	72	45
Other carbonated drinks	100	74	101	117	129	99	67	53
Coffee	100	34	63	104	122	135	116	100
Roasted coffee	100	39	66	107	125	137	106	86
Instant and freeze-dried coffee	100	24	59	99	116	132	134	126
Noncarbonated fruit-flavored drinks	100	77	112	141	112	85	66	30
Tea	100	48	93	121	126	99	81	73
Other nonalcoholic beverages and ice	100	74	100	125	123	87	67	64
Food prepared by CU on trips	**100**	**47**	**76**	**115**	**119**	**134**	**121**	**43**

Source: Calculations by New Strategist based on the 2001 Consumer Expenditure Survey

3. Groceries: Indexed per capita spending by age, 2001

(indexed average annual per capita spending of consumer units (CU) on groceries, by age of consumer unit reference person, 2001; index definition: an index of 100 is the average for all consumer units; an index of 132 means that spending by consumer units in that group is 32 percent above the average for all consumer units; an index of 68 indicates spending that is 32 percent below the average for all consumer units)

	total consumer units	under 25	25 to 34	35 to 44	45 to 54	55 to 64	65 to 74	75+
Per capita spending of CU, total	**$15,807**	**$12,382**	**$13,604**	**$14,215**	**$17,752**	**$19,744**	**$16,854**	**$15,400**
Per capita spending of CU, index	**100**	**78**	**86**	**90**	**112**	**125**	**107**	**97**
GROCERIES	**100**	**79**	**82**	**88**	**110**	**125**	**111**	**122**
Cereals and bakery products	**100**	**80**	**80**	**90**	**107**	**122**	**112**	**135**
Cereals and cereal products	100	94	88	91	104	112	104	127
Flour	100	120	79	86	102	118	110	148
Prepared flour mixes	100	71	81	91	112	119	106	132
Ready-to-eat and cooked cereals	100	99	88	91	100	113	108	134
Rice	100	89	97	96	110	105	80	94
Pasta, cornmeal, and other cereal products	100	87	89	89	108	111	108	122
Bakery products	100	73	76	89	109	127	117	140
Bread	100	73	79	83	104	136	127	140
White bread	100	81	84	87	103	126	125	127
Crackers and cookies	100	72	76	87	110	119	123	152
Cookies	100	77	74	90	109	115	121	152
Crackers	100	62	79	82	112	127	127	153
Frozen and refrigerated bakery products	100	82	68	96	115	116	104	138
Other bakery products	100	72	74	93	109	127	108	132
Biscuits and rolls	100	68	67	91	112	145	117	117
Cakes and cupcakes	100	85	88	96	104	115	85	131
Bread and cracker products	100	49	82	95	121	123	94	104
Sweetrolls, coffee cakes, doughnuts	100	69	67	96	113	115	114	149
Pies, tarts, turnovers	100	62	76	86	101	131	135	168
Meats, poultry, fish, and eggs	**100**	**75**	**82**	**87**	**112**	**129**	**111**	**117**
Beef	100	78	84	84	115	128	114	112
Ground beef	100	93	89	85	114	119	105	104
Roast	100	57	66	83	116	142	143	132
Chuck roast	100	55	72	85	120	146	86	158
Round roast	100	68	57	80	123	160	111	144
Other roast	100	53	66	82	108	127	213	103
Steak	100	76	85	83	119	125	115	100
Round steak	100	75	91	80	120	108	132	101
Sirloin steak	100	83	93	86	120	125	80	97
Other steak	100	73	78	84	118	132	128	101
Pork	100	65	81	84	110	138	119	126
Bacon	100	72	85	78	109	131	130	135
Pork chops	100	76	97	83	109	124	104	111
Ham	100	52	69	85	114	137	131	144
Ham, not canned	100	53	70	86	114	136	127	143
Canned ham	100	33	48	80	99	153	224	169
Sausage	100	75	68	86	110	135	119	156
Other pork	100	54	83	85	108	158	116	98
Other meats	100	77	77	94	113	121	103	121
Frankfurters	100	89	90	89	108	118	101	114
Lunch meats (cold cuts)	100	77	74	93	114	125	105	118
Bologna, liverwurst, salami	100	67	76	90	112	136	107	121
Lamb, organ meats, and others	100	43	62	118	111	94	89	163

	total consumer units	under 25	25 to 34	35 to 44	45 to 54	55 to 64	65 to 74	75+
Poultry	100	81	87	90	111	121	98	112
Fresh and frozen chicken	100	86	90	92	111	115	92	107
Fresh and frozen whole chicken	100	83	93	91	107	121	90	107
Fresh and frozen chicken parts	100	87	89	93	112	112	92	107
Other poultry	100	61	75	83	114	144	120	128
Fish and seafood	100	68	81	88	109	140	112	114
Canned fish and seafood	100	76	89	84	100	129	118	145
Fresh fish and shellfish	100	68	78	89	110	142	106	119
Frozen fish and shellfish	100	67	82	87	111	143	119	91
Eggs	100	95	81	85	107	124	118	133
Dairy products	**100**	**77**	**82**	**91**	**108**	**122**	**109**	**120**
Fresh milk and cream	100	82	87	92	107	110	109	128
Fresh milk, all types	100	84	88	92	106	107	107	127
Cream	100	55	75	86	109	143	126	133
Other dairy products	100	74	80	91	110	130	108	114
Butter	100	69	74	90	102	159	107	121
Cheese	100	78	80	90	114	124	110	106
Ice cream and related products	100	70	77	92	109	131	103	132
Miscellaneous dairy products	100	70	87	95	103	127	115	98
Fruits and vegetables	**100**	**74**	**79**	**85**	**108**	**127**	**124**	**141**
Fresh fruits	100	70	76	84	108	128	132	145
Apples	100	76	84	88	116	115	104	122
Bananas	100	74	75	81	103	130	146	155
Oranges	100	83	77	87	116	113	119	132
Citrus fruits, excl. oranges	100	62	70	82	110	144	129	156
Other fresh fruits	100	63	74	83	104	135	142	153
Fresh vegetables	100	70	79	82	111	135	127	129
Potatoes	100	62	78	82	110	143	126	132
Lettuce	100	72	78	86	116	124	116	126
Tomatoes	100	80	85	84	110	121	124	122
Other fresh vegetables	100	69	78	81	110	139	130	131
Processed fruits	100	88	81	89	102	115	118	152
Frozen fruits and fruit juices	100	97	89	84	105	118	112	134
Frozen orange juice	100	105	92	81	101	126	102	140
Frozen fruits	100	62	45	85	126	144	135	155
Frozen fruit juices	100	104	110	90	96	85	117	108
Canned fruits	100	63	76	76	108	126	133	203
Dried fruits	100	53	77	75	100	115	167	221
Fresh fruit juice	100	97	68	89	101	127	125	158
Canned and bottled fruit juice	100	93	88	95	100	105	106	132
Processed vegetables	100	73	81	86	110	125	115	139
Frozen vegetables	100	70	78	89	111	123	117	130
Canned and dried vegetables and juices	100	74	82	85	109	126	114	144
Canned beans	100	80	93	82	108	115	98	159
Canned corn	100	95	95	92	98	108	107	128
Canned miscellaneous vegetables	100	57	72	86	104	140	140	148
Dried beans	100	72	82	72	114	159	130	103
Dried miscellaneous vegetables	100	77	71	80	121	141	110	135
Fresh and canned vegetable juices	100	90	85	93	107	106	85	156
Sugar and other sweets	**100**	**67**	**77**	**92**	**107**	**130**	**113**	**131**
Candy and chewing gum	100	64	75	95	108	125	114	130
Sugar	100	81	87	81	111	140	110	110
Artificial sweeteners	100	14	60	71	120	164	171	164
Jams, preserves, other sweets	100	78	82	95	96	134	96	146

	total consumer units	under 25	25 to 34	35 to 44	45 to 54	55 to 64	65 to 74	75+
Fats and oils	100	76	80	84	114	125	120	126
Margarine	100	62	70	78	112	133	150	155
Fats and oils	**100**	**84**	**88**	**83**	**113**	**119**	**113**	**118**
Salad dressings	100	73	79	86	117	128	117	116
Nondairy cream and imitation milk	100	65	62	85	112	144	128	153
Peanut butter	100	89	93	88	111	104	105	119
Miscellaneous foods	**100**	**94**	**90**	**89**	**110**	**117**	**94**	**114**
Frozen prepared foods	100	102	82	88	116	115	92	120
Frozen meals	100	77	69	74	116	146	109	181
Other frozen prepared foods	100	113	87	94	117	102	84	94
Canned and packaged soups	100	65	80	83	108	127	114	171
Potato chips, nuts, and other snacks	100	90	80	92	113	125	100	101
Potato chips and other snacks	100	101	85	97	115	115	82	79
Nuts	100	52	61	75	105	157	163	179
Condiments and seasonings	100	81	84	92	114	120	100	106
Salt, spices, and other seasonings	100	89	83	87	113	126	110	100
Olives, pickles, relishes	100	43	76	86	123	130	108	135
Sauces and gravies	100	91	87	96	113	114	84	97
Baking needs and miscellaneous products	100	71	81	91	112	118	119	115
Other canned/packaged prepared foods	100	108	109	87	100	110	84	108
Prepared salads	100	63	76	79	115	153	111	133
Prepared desserts	100	59	84	75	96	165	119	171
Baby food	100	193	200	88	52	62	34	37
Miscellaneous prepared foods	100	100	95	89	111	105	87	114
Nonalcoholic beverages	100	86	82	91	115	123	101	98
Cola	100	95	85	91	116	126	94	74
Other carbonated drinks	100	98	87	89	120	118	88	89
Coffee	100	44	55	79	113	161	153	167
Roasted coffee	100	51	57	81	116	163	140	144
Instant and freeze-dried coffee	100	31	51	75	107	157	176	209
Noncarbonated fruit-flavored drinks	100	101	97	107	104	101	87	50
Tea	100	63	80	92	117	118	107	121
Other nonalcoholic beverages and ice	100	97	87	95	114	104	88	107
Food prepared by CU on trips	**100**	**61**	**65**	**87**	**110**	**160**	**159**	**71**

Note: Per capita indexes account for household size and show how much each person in a particular household demographic segment spends relative to a person in the average household.
Source: Calculations by New Strategist based on the 2001 Consumer Expenditure Survey

4. Groceries: Total spending by age, 2001

(total annual spending on groceries, by consumer unit (CU) age group, 2001; numbers in thousands)

	total consumer units	under 25	25 to 34	35 to 44	45 to 54	55 to 64	65 to 74	75+
Number of consumer units	110,339	8,598	18,515	24,422	22,317	14,549	11,342	10,596
Total spending of all CUs	$4,360,427,358	$202,278,440	$730,436,931	$1,145,580,094	$1,069,650,462	$603,237,767	$363,206,114	$244,760,077
GROCERIES	$340,453,191	$15,968,893	$54,365,039	$87,644,941	$81,653,216	$47,112,426	$29,456,195	$23,959,887
Cereals and bakery products	49,894,192	2,376,745	7,756,304	13,069,433	11,656,615	6,730,513	4,373,702	3,891,487
Cereals and cereal products	17,263,640	964,696	2,957,771	4,581,079	3,921,320	2,145,541	1,402,552	1,263,573
Flour	883,815	62,851	136,456	221,019	195,943	115,519	75,878	75,232
Prepared flour mixes	1,422,270	59,412	224,217	377,808	346,360	187,682	118,184	107,867
Ready-to-eat and cooked cereals	9,493,568	557,752	1,617,100	2,511,559	2,080,837	1,183,416	797,343	731,124
Rice	2,201,263	115,901	416,217	618,609	530,698	256,790	136,898	119,523
Pasta, cornmeal, and other cereal produ	3,262,724	168,779	563,967	851,839	767,482	402,134	274,363	229,827
Bakery products	32,630,553	1,411,964	4,798,533	8,488,599	7,735,519	4,584,972	2,971,150	2,627,808
Bread	9,419,640	407,373	1,453,057	2,293,470	2,147,565	1,423,038	934,808	760,263
White bread	4,042,821	193,713	657,653	1,029,143	907,632	562,319	394,135	294,569
Crackers and cookies	7,743,591	330,249	1,143,116	1,968,413	1,860,568	1,020,467	741,880	678,780
Cookies	5,089,938	232,576	736,527	1,336,860	1,213,599	645,976	479,086	444,290
Crackers	2,653,653	97,673	406,589	631,553	646,970	374,491	262,794	234,490
Frozen and refrigerated bakery products	2,875,434	138,772	378,262	802,263	724,856	367,799	233,418	228,556
Other bakery products	12,590,783	535,655	1,824,283	3,424,209	3,002,529	1,773,523	1,061,044	960,316
Biscuits and rolls	4,340,736	173,766	566,004	1,155,161	1,059,165	697,770	397,424	291,284
Cakes and cupcakes	3,729,458	187,608	638,768	1,041,354	849,608	475,025	248,503	280,794
Bread and cracker products	446,873	12,983	71,098	123,331	118,280	60,815	32,892	26,702
Sweetrolls, coffee cakes, doughnuts	2,904,123	118,480	375,669	812,276	718,831	370,709	258,711	248,688
Pies, tarts, turnovers	1,169,593	42,732	172,745	292,087	256,646	169,205	123,514	112,953
Meats, poultry, fish, and eggs	91,357,382	4,056,021	14,648,513	23,150,835	22,302,271	13,069,803	7,902,085	6,160,091
Beef	27,370,692	1,265,454	4,453,968	6,691,384	6,879,885	3,864,505	2,439,551	1,760,631
Ground beef	9,983,473	550,874	1,725,783	2,479,810	2,478,972	1,314,939	821,388	599,946
Roast	4,903,465	166,027	627,473	1,182,269	1,241,048	772,115	546,004	373,933
Chuck roast	1,658,395	53,566	231,252	411,267	432,727	268,138	111,265	150,463
Round roast	1,310,827	52,362	146,269	307,229	353,278	231,766	113,533	108,609
Other roast	1,934,243	60,100	250,138	463,774	455,044	272,066	321,319	114,861
Steak	10,231,736	462,830	1,682,828	2,493,242	2,656,169	1,417,509	922,558	589,456
Round steak	2,009,273	89,419	356,969	469,391	527,574	240,641	207,559	116,768
Sirloin steak	2,799,300	138,084	504,164	700,423	733,783	386,712	174,667	156,503
Other steak	5,423,162	235,327	821,696	1,323,672	1,394,813	790,011	540,333	316,185
Pork	19,564,208	752,669	3,099,411	4,781,583	4,704,200	2,978,471	1,823,453	1,420,712
Bacon	3,232,933	138,600	537,120	737,300	771,722	469,205	327,670	252,079
Pork chops	4,651,892	210,049	877,611	1,132,448	1,109,155	640,447	377,575	298,595
Ham	4,411,353	136,106	592,665	1,101,188	1,095,318	670,127	452,546	366,092
Ham, not canned	4,219,363	132,323	574,891	1,056,252	1,053,809	637,537	418,974	347,443
Canned ham	191,990	3,783	17,774	44,692	41,510	32,590	33,572	18,649
Sausage	2,815,851	125,789	371,411	705,307	678,437	420,321	262,681	253,774
Other pork	4,451,075	142,039	720,789	1,105,584	1,049,569	778,372	402,981	250,066
Other meats	11,261,198	512,441	1,678,570	3,095,733	2,769,317	1,502,766	905,772	784,422
Frankfurters	2,428,561	128,540	425,845	628,378	573,101	318,478	192,134	159,152
Lunch meats (cold cuts)	7,820,828	358,107	1,130,711	2,119,830	1,952,291	1,079,390	643,091	530,012
Bologna, liverwurst, salami	2,802,611	111,688	416,032	733,148	686,917	422,212	234,439	195,920
Lamb, organ meats, and others	1,011,809	25,794	122,014	347,525	244,148	104,898	70,547	95,258

	total consumer units	under 25	25 to 34	35 to 44	45 to 54	55 to 64	65 to 74	75+
Poultry	$16,757,184	$799,528	$2,837,794	$4,420,382	$4,069,951	$2,244,765	$1,280,852	$1,078,885
Fresh and frozen chicken	13,191,027	670,730	2,320,855	3,550,959	3,183,966	1,677,936	945,583	815,044
Fresh and frozen whole chicken	3,944,619	193,455	716,345	1,051,367	924,817	528,856	278,219	243,708
Fresh and frozen chicken parts	9,246,408	477,361	1,604,695	2,499,592	2,259,373	1,149,080	667,363	571,336
Other poultry	3,566,157	128,712	516,939	869,423	885,985	566,829	335,270	263,840
Fish and seafood	12,542,234	508,228	1,973,514	3,205,388	2,979,766	1,950,003	1,096,318	820,554
Canned fish and seafood	1,667,222	74,803	287,723	410,534	363,544	237,294	153,571	138,914
Fresh fish and shellfish	6,959,081	278,059	1,062,206	1,802,099	1,665,295	1,092,193	577,648	477,456
Frozen fish and shellfish	3,915,931	155,280	623,585	992,999	951,151	620,515	365,099	204,185
Eggs	3,860,762	217,701	605,255	956,610	898,929	529,293	356,025	295,099
Dairy products	**36,598,343**	**1,668,098**	**5,872,032**	**9,770,021**	**8,664,352**	**4,952,916**	**3,104,192**	**2,522,802**
Fresh milk and cream	14,989,553	725,929	2,529,519	4,013,023	3,489,040	1,831,865	1,275,748	1,102,302
Fresh milk, all types	13,626,867	681,306	2,330,668	3,672,825	3,164,774	1,615,666	1,141,799	997,825
Cream	1,362,687	44,538	198,666	340,443	324,266	216,198	134,062	104,477
Other dairy products	21,608,790	942,169	3,342,513	5,756,998	5,175,312	3,121,052	1,828,444	1,420,394
Butter	2,377,806	96,642	344,564	625,447	527,574	417,993	198,145	166,145
Cheese	10,304,559	474,696	1,605,251	2,720,122	2,560,876	1,419,837	886,377	626,753
Ice cream and related products	6,266,152	260,519	944,265	1,676,082	1,488,098	908,149	505,853	478,092
Miscellaneous dairy products	2,660,273	110,226	448,433	735,346	598,542	375,073	238,069	149,510
Fruits and vegetables	**57,568,270**	**2,536,926**	**8,850,911**	**14,293,220**	**13,548,428**	**8,071,931**	**5,590,812**	**4,667,538**
Fresh fruits	17,699,479	732,636	2,627,834	4,346,383	4,180,420	2,511,594	1,821,752	1,482,486
Apples	3,401,751	152,701	557,487	876,261	862,329	433,706	277,085	238,516
Bananas	3,453,611	151,239	504,719	819,847	779,756	496,121	395,042	309,085
Oranges	2,054,512	101,456	307,534	523,364	518,647	256,208	190,546	156,185
Citrus fruits, excl. oranges	1,457,578	53,136	198,481	348,990	349,038	231,766	147,106	130,861
Other fresh fruits	7,332,027	274,018	1,059,613	1,778,166	1,670,651	1,093,648	811,974	647,839
Fresh vegetables	17,832,989	741,406	2,745,034	4,292,655	4,307,181	2,660,285	1,762,774	1,324,712
Potatoes	3,320,101	121,662	502,867	793,959	795,601	527,256	327,444	252,397
Lettuce	2,297,258	98,017	350,304	577,336	581,358	314,986	207,672	166,993
Tomatoes	3,313,480	157,687	548,044	813,253	794,262	443,308	322,113	233,218
Other fresh vegetables	8,902,151	364,039	1,343,819	2,108,107	2,136,183	1,374,735	905,659	672,104
Processed fruits	12,802,634	666,603	2,028,318	3,326,765	2,851,889	1,623,959	1,176,619	1,119,256
Frozen fruits and fruit juices	1,528,195	87,872	263,283	374,878	349,038	200,194	133,949	118,039
Frozen orange juice	839,680	52,276	151,082	197,574	185,901	117,119	66,918	67,497
Frozen fruits	279,158	10,318	24,255	69,603	76,994	44,374	29,489	24,901
Frozen fruit juices	410,461	25,278	88,131	107,701	85,920	38,700	37,542	25,536
Canned fruits	1,795,216	66,978	264,394	397,834	423,130	250,388	186,009	209,483
Dried fruits	611,278	19,174	91,464	133,588	133,456	77,692	79,621	77,669
Fresh fruit juice	2,743,028	157,000	363,635	714,099	603,229	386,567	268,465	249,960
Canned and bottled fruit juice	6,123,815	335,752	1,045,542	1,706,121	1,343,260	709,118	508,462	464,105
Processed vegetables	9,233,168	396,282	1,449,910	2,327,417	2,208,714	1,276,093	829,667	741,084
Frozen vegetables	3,034,323	124,929	462,690	792,738	734,453	413,919	277,085	227,178
Canned and dried vegetables and juices	6,198,845	271,353	987,220	1,534,679	1,474,484	862,174	552,582	513,906
Canned beans	1,390,271	65,861	250,508	334,337	327,837	177,352	106,161	127,258
Canned corn	786,717	44,022	144,973	210,273	168,270	93,841	65,443	58,172
Canned miscellaneous vegetables	1,939,760	64,915	270,689	486,486	439,868	301,455	212,663	165,192
Dried beans	251,573	10,662	39,992	52,996	62,488	44,374	25,633	14,940
Dried miscellaneous vegetables	836,370	38,347	115,163	194,888	220,938	130,505	72,022	64,954
Fresh and canned vegetable juices	844,093	44,882	139,603	228,834	197,506	99,515	56,030	75,973
Sugar and other sweets	**12,794,910**	**507,454**	**1,917,599**	**3,428,849**	**2,985,122**	**1,847,287**	**1,131,138**	**968,051**
Candy and chewing gum	8,108,813	308,152	1,177,184	2,252,930	1,908,996	1,120,419	724,981	609,058
Sugar	1,976,172	94,922	333,640	464,506	480,708	305,529	170,243	125,457
Artificial sweeteners	556,109	4,471	64,617	115,272	145,507	100,970	74,404	52,556
Jams, preserves, other sweets	2,153,817	99,909	342,157	596,385	449,911	320,369	161,510	180,874

	total consumer units	under 25	25 to 34	35 to 44	45 to 54	55 to 64	65 to 74	75+
Fats and oils	**$9,573,012**	**$431,878**	**$1,496,938**	**$2,353,304**	**$2,376,314**	**$1,319,594**	**$895,111**	**$697,111**
Margarine	1,261,175	46,171	172,930	288,668	307,975	185,936	147,786	112,953
Fats and oils	2,706,616	135,333	463,801	654,998	669,956	356,742	239,089	184,582
Salad dressings	3,091,699	133,613	472,318	772,956	786,451	437,343	282,189	205,668
Nondairy cream and imitation milk	1,113,321	42,818	134,974	277,922	271,152	178,080	111,265	98,225
Peanut butter	1,400,202	74,029	252,730	358,759	340,781	161,348	115,008	95,682
Miscellaneous foods	**50,173,350**	**2,797,703**	**8,789,996**	**13,009,355**	**11,996,280**	**6,510,969**	**3,700,101**	**3,286,138**
Frozen prepared foods	10,613,508	641,583	1,689,864	2,723,053	2,699,018	1,354,221	760,481	733,349
Frozen meals	3,161,212	144,876	422,142	686,991	799,618	511,834	270,166	330,277
Other frozen prepared foods	7,452,296	496,707	1,267,722	2,036,062	1,899,400	842,387	490,315	403,072
Canned and packaged soups	4,112,335	158,805	643,396	994,220	969,004	576,722	367,027	404,343
Potato chips, nuts, and other snacks	10,743,708	570,735	1,664,128	2,900,357	2,645,904	1,481,088	839,535	626,436
Potato chips and other snacks	8,337,215	496,019	1,377,701	2,371,132	2,096,682	1,062,659	533,868	377,853
Nuts	2,406,494	74,717	286,427	529,225	549,221	418,429	305,667	248,582
Condiments and seasonings	9,273,993	444,517	1,507,676	2,481,519	2,307,132	1,227,499	725,548	566,462
Salt, spices, and other seasonings	2,188,022	115,041	353,822	559,020	537,840	304,947	188,391	126,198
Olives, pickles, relishes	1,100,080	28,287	163,302	277,434	294,361	157,857	92,551	85,510
Sauces and gravies	4,064,889	219,937	687,832	1,135,867	1,004,935	513,143	266,764	227,708
Baking needs and miscellaneous products	1,921,002	81,165	302,720	508,955	469,996	251,552	177,843	127,046
Other canned/packaged prepared foods	15,430,909	982,150	3,284,931	3,910,451	3,375,223	1,871,438	1,007,510	955,547
Prepared salads	2,157,128	80,821	319,384	498,697	540,518	366,344	186,576	165,192
Prepared desserts	1,119,941	38,863	183,299	244,708	235,221	204,704	104,120	110,516
Baby food	2,606,207	297,921	1,012,585	670,872	295,477	179,244	68,846	56,159
Miscellaneous prepared foods	9,515,635	563,169	1,764,480	2,483,962	2,302,668	1,109,361	647,969	623,681
Nonalcoholic beverages	28,264,438	1,440,853	4,496,738	7,490,472	7,108,411	3,862,032	2,233,694	1,593,850
Cola	9,644,732	539,954	1,600,807	2,571,881	2,448,844	1,343,164	710,576	411,761
Other carbonated drinks	5,091,042	293,966	866,317	1,316,590	1,331,879	663,143	350,581	259,708
Coffee	4,231,501	110,398	449,174	974,682	1,043,097	753,202	504,492	406,569
Roasted coffee	2,756,268	82,971	302,905	650,846	697,853	496,703	301,584	228,556
Instant and freeze-dried coffee	1,475,232	27,428	146,269	323,836	345,021	256,353	202,908	177,907
Noncarbonated fruit-flavored drinks	2,246,502	134,559	421,957	700,911	510,613	251,552	152,210	65,059
Tea	1,938,656	72,309	301,424	518,479	493,875	253,589	161,964	135,417
Other nonalcoholic beverages and ice	5,039,182	289,667	848,728	1,395,717	1,257,340	578,177	347,406	310,887
Food prepared by CU on trips	**4,229,294**	**153,302**	**536,009**	**1,079,208**	**1,015,200**	**747,382**	**525,361**	**172,821**

Note: Numbers may not add to total because of rounding.
Source: Calculations by New Strategist based on the 2001 Consumer Expenditure Survey

5. Groceries: Market shares by age, 2001

(percentage of total annual spending on groceries accounted for by consumer unit age groups, 2001)

	total consumer units	under 25	25 to 34	35 to 44	45 to 54	55 to 64	65 to 74	75+
Share of total consumer units	100.0%	7.8%	16.8%	22.1%	20.2%	13.2%	10.3%	9.6%
Share of total before-tax income	100.0	3.4	17.5	27.4	26.0	14.4	7.0	4.5
Share of total spending	100.0	4.6	16.8	26.3	24.5	13.8	8.3	5.6
GROCERIES	**100.0**	**4.7**	**16.0**	**25.7**	**24.0**	**13.8**	**8.7**	**7.0**
Cereals and bakery products	**100.0**	**4.8**	**15.5**	**26.2**	**23.4**	**13.5**	**8.8**	**7.8**
Cereals and cereal products	100.0	5.6	17.1	26.5	22.7	12.4	8.1	7.3
Flour	100.0	7.1	15.4	2.5	22.2	13.1	8.6	8.5
Prepared flour mixes	100.0	4.2	15.8	26.6	24.4	13.2	8.3	7.6
Ready-to-eat and cooked cereals	100.0	5.9	17.0	26.5	21.9	12.5	8.4	7.7
Rice	100.0	5.3	18.9	28.1	24.1	11.7	6.2	5.4
Pasta, cornmeal, and other cereal products	100.0	5.2	17.3	26.1	23.5	12.3	8.4	7.0
Bakery products	100.0	4.3	14.7	26.0	23.7	14.1	9.1	8.1
Bread	100.0	4.3	15.4	24.3	22.8	15.1	9.9	8.1
White bread	100.0	4.8	16.3	25.5	22.5	13.9	9.7	7.3
Crackers and cookies	100.0	4.3	14.8	25.4	24.0	13.2	9.6	8.8
Cookies	100.0	4.6	14.5	26.3	23.8	12.7	9.4	8.7
Crackers	100.0	3.7	15.3	23.8	24.4	14.1	9.9	8.8
Frozen and refrigerated bakery products	100.0	4.8	13.2	27.9	25.2	12.8	8.1	7.9
Other bakery products	100.0	4.3	14.5	27.2	23.8	14.1	8.4	7.6
Biscuits and rolls	100.0	0.4	13.0	26.6	24.4	16.1	9.2	6.7
Cakes and cupcakes	100.0	5.0	17.1	27.9	22.8	12.7	6.7	7.5
Bread and cracker products	100.0	2.9	15.9	27.6	26.5	13.6	7.4	6.0
Sweetrolls, coffee cakes, doughnuts	100.0	4.1	12.9	28.0	24.8	12.8	8.9	8.6
Pies, tarts, turnovers	100.0	3.7	14.8	25.0	21.9	14.5	10.6	9.7
Meats, poultry, fish, and eggs	**100.0**	**4.4**	**16.0**	**25.3**	**24.4**	**14.3**	**8.6**	**6.7**
Beef	100.0	4.6	16.3	24.4	25.1	14.1	8.9	6.4
Ground beef	100.0	5.5	17.3	24.8	24.8	13.2	8.2	0.6
Roast	100.0	3.4	12.8	24.1	25.3	15.7	11.1	7.6
Chuck roast	100.0	3.2	13.9	24.8	26.1	16.2	6.7	9.1
Round roast	100.0	4.0	11.2	23.4	27.0	17.7	8.7	8.3
Other roast	100.0	3.1	12.9	24.0	23.5	14.1	16.6	5.9
Steak	100.0	4.5	16.4	24.4	26.0	13.9	9.0	5.8
Round steak	100.0	4.5	17.8	23.4	26.3	12.0	10.3	5.8
Sirloin steak	100.0	4.9	18.0	25.0	26.2	13.8	6.2	5.6
Other steak	100.0	4.3	15.2	24.4	25.7	14.6	10.0	5.8
Pork	100.0	3.8	15.8	24.4	24.0	15.2	9.3	7.3
Bacon	100.0	4.3	16.6	22.8	23.9	14.5	10.1	7.8
Pork chops	100.0	4.5	18.9	24.3	23.8	13.8	8.1	6.4
Ham	100.0	3.1	13.4	25.0	24.8	15.2	10.3	8.3
Ham, not canned	100.0	3.1	13.6	25.0	25.0	15.1	9.9	8.2
Canned ham	100.0	2.0	9.3	23.3	21.6	17.0	17.5	9.7
Sausage	100.0	4.5	13.2	25.1	24.1	14.9	9.3	9.0
Other pork	100.0	3.2	16.2	24.8	23.6	17.5	9.1	5.6
Other meats	100.0	4.6	14.9	27.5	24.6	13.3	8.0	7.0
Frankfurters	100.0	5.3	17.5	25.9	23.6	13.1	7.9	6.6
Lunch meats (cold cuts)	100.0	4.6	14.5	27.1	25.0	13.8	8.2	6.8
Bologna, liverwurst, salami	100.0	4.0	14.8	26.2	24.5	15.1	8.4	7.0
Lamb, organ meats, and others	100.0	2.5	12.1	34.3	24.1	10.4	7.0	9.4

	total consumer units	under 25	25 to 34	35 to 44	45 to 54	55 to 64	65 to 74	75+
Poultry	100.0%	4.8%	16.9%	26.4%	24.3%	13.4%	7.6%	6.4%
Fresh and frozen chicken	100.0	5.1	17.6	26.9	24.1	12.7	7.2	6.2
Fresh and frozen whole chicken	100.0	4.9	18.2	26.7	23.4	13.4	7.1	6.2
Fresh and frozen chicken parts	100.0	5.2	17.4	27.0	24.4	12.4	7.2	6.2
Other poultry	100.0	3.6	14.5	24.4	24.8	15.9	9.4	7.4
Fish and seafood	100.0	4.1	15.7	25.6	23.8	15.5	8.7	6.5
Canned fish and seafood	100.0	4.5	17.3	24.6	21.8	14.2	9.2	8.3
Fresh fish and shellfish	100.0	4.0	15.3	25.9	23.9	15.7	8.3	6.9
Frozen fish and shellfish	100.0	4.0	15.9	25.4	24.3	15.8	9.3	5.2
Eggs	100.0	5.6	15.7	24.8	23.3	13.7	9.2	7.6
Dairy products	**100.0**	**4.6**	**16.0**	**26.7**	**23.7**	**13.5**	**8.5**	**6.9**
Fresh milk and cream	100.0	4.8	16.9	26.8	23.3	12.2	8.5	7.4
Fresh milk, all types	100.0	5.0	17.1	27.0	23.2	11.9	8.4	7.3
Cream	100.0	3.3	14.6	25.0	23.8	15.9	9.8	7.7
Other dairy products	100.0	4.4	15.5	26.6	24.0	14.4	8.5	6.6
Butter	100.0	4.1	14.5	26.3	22.2	17.6	8.3	7.0
Cheese	100.0	4.6	15.6	26.4	24.9	13.8	8.6	6.1
Ice cream and related products	100.0	4.2	15.1	26.7	23.7	14.5	8.1	7.6
Miscellaneous dairy products	100.0	4.1	16.9	27.6	22.5	14.1	8.9	5.6
Fruits and vegetables	**100.0**	**4.4**	**15.4**	**24.8**	**23.5**	**14.0**	**9.7**	**8.1**
Fresh fruits	100.0	4.1	14.8	24.6	23.6	14.2	10.3	8.4
Apples	100.0	4.5	16.4	25.8	25.3	12.7	8.1	7.0
Bananas	100.0	4.4	14.6	23.7	22.6	14.4	11.4	8.9
Oranges	100.0	4.9	15.0	25.5	25.2	12.5	9.3	7.6
Citrus fruits, excl. oranges	100.0	3.6	13.6	23.9	23.9	15.9	10.1	9.0
Other fresh fruits	100.0	3.7	14.5	24.3	22.8	14.9	11.1	8.8
Fresh vegetables	100.0	4.2	15.4	24.1	24.2	14.9	9.9	7.4
Potatoes	100.0	3.7	15.1	23.9	24.0	15.9	9.9	7.6
Lettuce	100.0	4.3	15.2	25.1	25.3	13.7	9.0	7.3
Tomatoes	100.0	4.8	16.5	24.5	24.0	13.4	9.7	7.0
Other fresh vegetables	100.0	4.1	15.1	23.7	24.0	15.4	10.2	7.5
Processed fruits	100.0	5.2	15.8	26.0	22.3	12.7	9.2	8.7
Frozen fruits and fruit juices	100.0	5.8	17.2	24.5	22.8	13.1	8.8	7.7
Frozen orange juice	100.0	6.2	18.0	23.5	22.1	13.9	8.0	8.0
Frozen fruits	100.0	3.7	8.7	24.9	27.6	15.9	10.6	8.9
Frozen fruit juices	100.0	6.2	21.5	26.2	20.9	9.4	9.1	6.2
Canned fruits	100.0	3.7	14.7	22.2	23.6	13.9	10.4	11.7
Dried fruits	100.0	3.1	15.0	21.9	21.8	12.7	13.0	12.7
Fresh fruit juice	100.0	5.7	13.3	26.0	22.0	14.1	9.8	9.1
Canned and bottled fruit juice	100.0	5.5	17.1	27.9	21.9	11.6	8.3	7.6
Processed vegetables	100.0	4.3	15.7	25.2	23.9	13.8	9.0	8.0
Frozen vegetables	100.0	4.1	15.2	26.1	24.2	13.6	9.1	7.5
Canned and dried vegetables and juices	100.0	4.4	15.9	24.8	23.8	13.9	8.9	8.3
Canned beans	100.0	4.7	18.0	24.1	23.6	12.8	7.6	9.2
Canned corn	100.0	5.6	18.4	26.7	21.4	11.9	8.3	7.4
Canned miscellaneous vegetables	100.0	3.3	14.0	25.1	22.7	15.5	11.0	8.5
Dried beans	100.0	4.2	15.9	21.1	24.8	17.6	10.2	5.9
Dried miscellaneous vegetables	100.0	4.6	13.8	23.3	26.4	15.6	8.6	7.8
Fresh and canned vegetable juices	100.0	5.3	16.5	27.1	23.4	11.8	6.6	9.0
Sugar and other sweets	**100.0**	**4.0**	**15.0**	**26.8**	**23.3**	**14.4**	**8.8**	**7.6**
Candy and chewing gum	100.0	3.8	14.5	27.8	23.5	13.8	8.9	7.5
Sugar	100.0	4.8	16.9	23.5	24.3	15.5	8.6	6.3
Artificial sweeteners	100.0	0.8	11.6	20.7	26.2	18.2	13.4	9.5
Jams, preserves, other sweets	100.0	4.6	15.9	27.7	20.9	14.9	7.5	8.4

	total consumer units	under 25	25 to 34	35 to 44	45 to 54	55 to 64	65 to 74	75+
Fats and oils	**100.0%**	**4.5%**	**15.6%**	**24.6%**	**24.8%**	**13.8%**	**9.4%**	**7.3%**
Margarine	100.0	3.7	13.7	22.9	24.4	14.7	11.7	9.0
Fats and oils	100.0	5.0	17.1	24.2	24.8	13.2	8.8	6.8
Salad dressings	100.0	4.3	15.3	2.5	25.4	14.1	9.1	6.7
Nondairy cream and imitation milk	100.0	3.8	12.1	25.0	24.4	16.0	10.0	8.8
Peanut butter	100.0	5.3	18.1	25.6	24.3	11.5	8.2	6.8
Miscellaneous foods	**100.0**	**5.6**	**17.5**	**25.9**	**23.9**	**13.0**	**7.4**	**6.5**
Frozen prepared foods	100.0	6.0	15.9	25.7	25.4	12.8	7.2	6.9
Frozen meals	100.0	4.6	13.4	21.7	25.3	16.2	8.5	10.4
Other frozen prepared foods	100.0	6.7	17.0	27.3	25.5	11.3	6.6	5.4
Canned and packaged soups	100.0	3.9	15.6	24.2	23.6	14.0	8.9	9.8
Potato chips, nuts, and other snacks	100.0	5.3	15.5	27.0	24.6	13.8	7.8	5.8
Potato chips and other snacks	100.0	5.9	16.5	28.4	25.1	12.7	6.4	4.5
Nuts	100.0	3.1	11.9	22.0	22.8	17.4	12.7	10.3
Condiments and seasonings	100.0	4.8	16.3	26.8	24.9	13.2	7.8	6.1
Salt, spices, and other seasonings	100.0	5.3	16.2	25.5	24.6	13.9	8.6	5.8
Olives, pickles, relishes	100.0	2.6	14.8	25.2	26.8	14.3	8.4	7.8
Sauces and gravies	100.0	5.4	16.9	27.9	24.7	12.6	6.6	5.6
Baking needs and miscellaneous products	100.0	4.2	15.8	26.5	24.5	13.1	9.3	6.6
Other canned/packaged prepared foods	100.0	6.4	21.3	25.3	21.9	12.1	6.5	6.2
Prepared salads	100.0	3.7	14.8	23.1	25.1	17.0	8.6	7.7
Prepared desserts	100.0	3.5	16.4	21.9	2.1	18.3	9.3	9.9
Baby food	100.0	11.4	38.9	25.7	11.3	6.9	2.6	2.2
Miscellaneous prepared foods	100.0	5.9	18.5	26.1	24.2	11.7	6.8	6.6
Nonalcoholic beverages	100.0	5.1	15.9	26.5	25.1	13.7	7.9	5.6
Cola	100.0	5.6	16.6	26.7	25.4	13.9	7.4	4.3
Other carbonated drinks	100.0	5.8	17.0	25.9	26.2	13.0	6.9	5.1
Coffee	100.0	2.6	10.6	23.0	24.7	17.8	11.9	9.6
Roasted coffee	100.0	3.0	11.0	23.6	25.3	18.0	10.9	8.3
Instant and freeze-dried coffee	100.0	1.9	9.9	22.0	23.4	17.4	13.8	12.1
Noncarbonated fruit-flavored drinks	100.0	6.0	18.8	31.2	22.7	11.2	6.8	2.9
Tea	100.0	3.7	15.5	26.7	25.5	13.1	8.4	7.0
Other nonalcoholic beverages and ice	100.0	5.7	16.8	27.7	25.0	11.5	6.9	6.2
Food prepared by CU on trips	**100.0**	**3.6**	**12.7**	**25.5**	**2.4**	**17.7**	**12.4**	**4.1**

Note: Numbers may not add to total because of rounding.
Source: Calculations by New Strategist based on the 2001 Consumer Expenditure Survey

6. Groceries: Average spending by income, 2001

(average annual spending on groceries, by before-tax income of consumer units (CU), 2001; complete income reporters only)

	complete income reporters	Under $10,000	$10,000– $19,999	$20,000– $29,999	$30,000– $39,999	$40,000– $49,999	$50,000– $69,999	$70,000 or more
Number of consumer units								
(in thousands, add 000)	88,735	10,929	15,113	12,075	10,508	8,737	12,480	18,892
Average number of persons per CU	2.5	1.6	2.0	2.3	2.4	2.7	2.9	3.1
Average before-tax income of CU	$47,507.00	$5,420.73	$14,655.04	$24,494.00	$34,456.00	$44,418.00	$58,943.00	$113,978.00
Average spending of CU, total	41,395.25	18,085.00	22,677.53	28,622.90	35,430.40	40,899.79	50,135.75	76,123.88
GROCERIES	$3,253.03	$2,053.55	$2,356.06	$2,904.32	$3,136.21	$3,488.27	$3,741.79	$4,565.20
Cereals and bakery products	480.57	306.43	356.73	435.78	450.08	501.23	542.58	682.72
Cereals and cereal products	166.17	114.87	128.11	151.08	156.43	183.35	180.13	226.27
Flour	8.28	8.96	7.19	8.61	7.20	8.51	6.97	9.75
Prepared flour mixes	13.99	8.83	10.13	11.47	13.61	18.58	15.54	18.89
Ready-to-eat and cooked cereals	91.53	61.57	69.90	84.10	83.48	98.14	104.92	124.58
Rice	20.36	14.92	16.32	16.70	19.48	24.39	18.18	29.85
Pasta, cornmeal, and other cereal products	32.00	20.60	24.56	30.19	32.66	33.74	34.53	43.19
Bakery products	314.40	191.56	228.62	284.70	293.65	317.87	362.46	456.44
Bread	90.63	59.55	72.94	86.64	88.34	93.10	103.96	117.39
White bread	38.52	29.74	35.08	37.55	37.10	41.17	39.24	46.30
Crackers and cookies	74.28	45.90	53.53	66.67	64.77	76.94	85.57	109.96
Cookies	48.89	31.78	34.72	45.74	43.44	49.48	55.99	70.93
Crackers	25.39	14.12	18.81	20.93	21.33	27.46	29.58	39.03
Frozen and refrigerated bakery products	28.15	14.09	18.57	26.15	23.61	28.12	38.17	41.57
Other bakery products	121.33	72.01	83.59	105.23	116.92	119.70	134.76	187.52
Biscuits and rolls	42.10	23.20	27.64	31.83	36.66	41.71	51.20	69.57
Cakes and cupcakes	36.37	23.30	25.02	32.38	41.08	33.98	35.48	55.92
Bread and cracker products	4.13	3.22	2.37	2.86	3.36	4.21	5.71	6.32
Sweetrolls, coffee cakes, doughnuts	28.09	17.34	20.20	26.44	25.68	30.71	31.17	40.02
Pies, tarts, turnovers	10.64	4.97	8.35	11.72	10.14	9.11	11.20	15.69
Meats, poultry, fish, and eggs	868.91	578.51	658.93	821.09	883.44	909.90	974.36	1,145.36
Beef	264.18	169.08	191.61	267.89	277.39	267.98	294.93	346.56
Ground beef	94.96	69.67	77.03	95.12	99.00	108.58	101.53	111.17
Roast	48.12	29.29	36.33	58.54	55.80	37.33	50.53	60.50
Chuck roast	15.90	11.39	13.44	16.37	19.48	12.27	14.63	20.76
Round roast	12.99	7.30	10.40	12.79	16.70	10.27	13.99	16.94
Other roast	19.23	10.61	12.48	29.37	19.62	14.80	21.91	22.80
Steak	99.78	53.33	62.07	98.59	97.99	106.20	115.44	146.78
Round steak	19.97	11.74	11.62	27.18	18.40	23.42	22.01	24.64
Sirloin steak	28.10	15.05	20.32	22.84	29.45	29.18	34.36	40.31
Other steak	51.71	26.54	30.13	48.57	50.14	53.60	59.07	81.83
Pork	188.07	138.87	159.74	178.77	188.73	184.87	204.07	236.41
Bacon	30.25	22.01	27.07	28.27	31.60	29.69	31.58	37.39
Pork chops	44.35	34.71	36.52	39.77	39.00	47.80	48.23	58.44
Ham	43.92	31.74	35.81	50.34	40.90	34.90	48.07	56.53
Ham, not canned	42.02	29.50	34.78	48.42	39.48	30.98	45.53	55.33
Canned ham	1.90	2.24	1.03	1.92	1.43	3.92	2.55	1.20
Sausage	26.95	17.16	23.90	23.62	30.96	32.47	26.26	32.63
Other pork	42.60	33.15	36.43	36.77	46.27	40.01	49.93	51.42
Other meats	107.03	70.38	74.72	102.51	114.52	107.95	120.17	144.53
Frankfurters	23.13	18.89	17.54	20.90	24.54	23.46	26.36	28.41
Lunch meats (cold cuts)	73.98	46.77	51.49	70.81	73.91	73.51	86.78	102.43
Bologna, liverwurst, salami	26.44	19.28	21.83	27.98	25.66	24.04	29.19	33.11
Lamb, organ meats, and others	9.92	4.72	5.69	10.79	16.07	10.97	7.03	13.69

	complete income reporters	Under $10,000	$10,000–$19,999	$20,000–$29,999	$30,000–$39,999	$40,000–$49,999	$50,000–$69,999	$70,000 or more
Poultry	$159.04	$99.14	$124.00	$135.23	$149.71	$170.43	$199.85	$211.59
Fresh and frozen chicken	124.46	76.33	99.71	107.20	114.71	142.12	156.02	160.76
Fresh and frozen whole chicken	36.68	22.51	31.75	32.90	31.43	50.15	39.93	45.95
Fresh and frozen chicken parts	87.77	53.81	67.95	74.31	83.28	91.97	116.09	114.81
Other poultry	34.58	22.82	24.29	28.03	34.99	28.31	43.82	50.84
Fish and seafood	113.82	72.97	78.67	99.86	114.04	134.64	116.46	165.26
Canned fish and seafood	15.70	10.15	10.09	15.83	14.62	18.47	16.05	22.68
Fresh fish and shellfish	60.37	40.77	39.91	51.78	62.28	71.38	58.43	90.19
Frozen fish and shellfish	37.74	22.05	28.67	32.25	37.13	44.78	41.99	52.40
Eggs	36.77	28.07	30.18	36.83	39.06	44.03	38.88	41.00
Dairy products	**352.44**	**205.96**	**243.81**	**315.22**	**334.39**	**377.98**	**409.95**	**513.47**
Fresh milk and cream	145.70	97.89	113.53	136.27	145.35	162.59	161.30	188.40
Fresh milk, all types	132.96	90.99	105.72	124.38	133.70	149.74	147.64	167.67
Cream	12.74	6.90	7.81	11.89	11.65	12.85	13.66	20.73
Other dairy products	206.74	108.08	130.29	178.95	189.05	215.39	248.65	325.06
Butter	21.07	9.98	14.23	21.52	19.61	19.83	27.26	30.03
Cheese	101.17	55.56	64.89	86.10	93.60	104.65	120.21	158.35
Ice cream and related products	59.22	30.42	37.88	49.65	54.58	64.02	68.86	94.40
Miscellaneous dairy products	25.28	12.11	13.29	21.69	21.26	26.90	32.32	42.28
Fruits and vegetables	**544.55**	**347.27**	**415.69**	**501.00**	**527.44**	**572.18**	**603.26**	**754.05**
Fresh fruits	167.26	112.57	125.52	154.11	150.51	170.99	186.17	238.44
Apples	32.11	20.19	23.07	29.20	30.83	32.09	36.02	46.93
Bananas	33.08	23.81	28.44	34.17	30.78	35.07	34.94	40.74
Oranges	19.35	15.05	13.72	17.64	16.52	18.51	25.94	24.99
Citrus fruits, excl. oranges	14.07	9.18	9.75	13.78	16.32	14.43	13.11	19.94
Other fresh fruits	68.65	44.34	50.53	59.32	56.06	70.89	76.16	105.84
Fresh vegetables	168.23	101.77	128.36	151.86	173.30	178.18	183.93	233.35
Potatoes	31.36	19.46	27.52	29.39	31.01	35.34	32.00	40.66
Lettuce	20.99	12.83	16.50	17.31	20.50	19.65	23.27	31.49
Tomatoes	30.37	19.20	23.08	29.24	31.88	33.02	30.86	41.43
Other fresh vegetables	85.51	50.28	61.26	75.93	89.90	90.18	97.81	119.77
Processed fruits	120.87	78.27	93.44	112.72	117.25	122.90	133.57	166.68
Frozen fruits and fruit juices	14.69	8.53	11.27	12.11	13.32	15.91	17.06	21.70
Frozen orange juice	8.31	4.82	5.11	7.03	8.53	10.03	9.04	12.66
Frozen fruits	2.56	1.26	2.09	2.41	1.51	2.92	3.02	3.92
Frozen fruit juices	3.82	2.44	4.06	2.67	3.28	2.97	5.01	5.13
Canned fruits	17.46	11.28	12.37	15.96	19.13	18.63	19.55	23.38
Dried fruits	5.73	2.82	4.77	5.26	5.79	7.57	5.16	8.09
Fresh fruit juice	24.95	16.20	20.09	24.89	20.76	25.42	26.36	35.33
Canned and bottled fruit juice	58.04	39.45	44.95	54.51	58.23	55.37	65.44	78.18
Processed vegetables	88.19	54.66	68.37	82.31	86.38	100.11	99.60	115.58
Frozen vegetables	28.85	17.23	21.68	23.94	29.44	33.49	32.93	39.91
Canned and dried vegetables and juices	59.34	37.43	46.68	58.36	56.94	66.62	66.67	75.68
Canned beans	13.36	9.75	10.32	11.82	13.65	18.77	14.73	15.20
Canned corn	7.31	5.11	6.43	7.09	7.62	8.49	8.77	7.62
Canned miscellaneous vegetables	18.69	10.25	14.13	18.72	17.94	20.69	22.37	24.18
Dried beans	2.21	2.30	2.23	2.10	2.40	2.11	2.58	1.93
Dried miscellaneous vegetables	8.24	4.41	7.24	10.65	7.24	7.87	9.67	9.40
Fresh and canned vegetable juices	8.01	5.34	5.79	6.78	6.72	7.64	8.15	13.00
Sugar and other sweets	**122.23**	**81.73**	**84.24**	**107.60**	**104.91**	**141.09**	**140.96**	**176.08**
Candy and chewing gum	77.61	48.32	51.58	65.23	62.13	89.98	91.43	118.91
Sugar	18.88	16.50	16.41	17.82	20.73	24.13	18.95	19.46
Artificial sweeteners	4.86	4.59	2.52	6.04	2.47	4.56	5.61	7.16
Jams, preserves, other sweets	20.88	12.31	13.73	18.52	19.58	22.41	24.96	30.55

	complete income reporters	Under $10,000	$10,000– $19,999	$20,000– $29,999	$30,000– $39,999	$40,000– $49,999	$50,000– $69,999	$70,000 or more
Fats and oils	**$89.34**	**$65.47**	**$68.75**	**$78.61**	**$89.92**	**$98.09**	**$103.69**	**$113.38**
Margarine	12.11	8.54	10.04	11.09	14.04	14.60	12.79	13.74
Fats and oils	24.79	22.56	19.89	23.65	26.77	24.38	28.18	27.53
Salad dressings	29.09	17.69	20.37	23.86	27.71	33.20	34.04	42.24
Nondairy cream and imitation milk	10.75	6.98	9.40	10.21	9.51	10.03	13.37	13.63
Peanut butter	12.59	9.71	9.04	9.80	11.88	15.89	15.31	16.24
Miscellaneous foods	**481.67**	**276.54**	**312.70**	**393.14**	**453.76**	**555.59**	**583.78**	**717.44**
Frozen prepared foods	102.39	58.83	69.33	72.54	101.15	131.35	118.61	152.72
Frozen meals	29.01	19.44	22.84	21.48	30.57	43.47	29.65	36.92
Other frozen prepared foods	73.38	39.39	46.49	51.07	70.58	87.87	88.96	115.79
Canned and packaged soups	39.14	23.08	29.27	36.90	38.33	43.67	43.51	53.53
Potato chips, nuts, and other snacks	104.23	57.67	64.35	84.55	91.99	122.85	127.25	161.74
Potato chips and other snacks	81.74	44.70	51.12	64.65	71.01	98.07	104.17	124.59
Nuts	22.49	12.97	13.23	19.90	20.99	24.78	23.09	37.15
Condiments and seasonings	89.34	50.79	57.02	72.37	83.03	93.88	105.42	141.31
Salt, spices, and other seasonings	20.60	13.09	15.22	17.19	19.45	21.67	21.92	30.98
Olives, pickles, relishes	10.64	5.84	6.33	7.63	8.53	12.62	11.64	18.86
Sauces and gravies	39.60	21.86	24.47	32.58	37.53	41.57	51.04	60.01
Baking needs and miscellaneous products	18.50	10.00	10.99	14.96	17.52	18.02	20.82	31.46
Other canned/packaged prepared foods	146.57	86.16	92.72	126.77	139.26	163.84	188.98	208.14
Prepared salads	20.16	10.51	10.99	16.68	18.77	22.51	25.59	31.86
Prepared desserts	10.75	6.43	6.63	8.40	9.69	10.10	15.23	16.33
Baby food	23.72	11.87	13.84	19.78	21.50	32.08	35.59	31.21
Miscellaneous prepared foods	91.52	57.24	61.26	81.90	88.65	98.96	112.57	127.26
Nonalcoholic beverages	272.68	176.28	198.12	222.91	260.83	293.70	334.23	380.52
Cola	93.88	60.73	66.13	81.65	104.42	106.33	109.90	122.28
Other carbonated drinks	49.40	33.37	40.67	40.12	47.80	58.59	60.41	61.19
Coffee	41.26	27.09	34.91	33.63	32.66	38.02	51.02	59.59
Roasted coffee	26.66	17.09	20.23	21.82	21.01	24.59	33.52	40.43
Instant and freeze-dried coffee	14.61	10.00	14.68	11.80	11.65	13.43	17.51	19.16
Noncarbonated fruit-flavored drinks	21.37	13.94	14.63	18.30	17.90	27.81	23.86	30.61
Tea	18.79	12.37	13.42	15.49	16.28	16.44	22.13	29.77
Other nonalcoholic beverages and ice	47.39	28.77	27.75	33.31	41.31	45.70	66.67	75.81
Food prepared by CU on trips	**40.65**	**15.35**	**17.09**	**28.97**	**31.45**	**38.52**	**48.97**	**82.19**

Source: Bureau of Labor Statistics, unpublished tables from the 2001 Consumer Expenditure Survey; calculations by New Strategist

7. Groceries: Indexed spending by income, 2001

(indexed average annual spending of consumer units (CU) on groceries, by before-tax income of consumer unit, 2001; complete income reporters only; index definition: an index of 100 is the average for all consumer units; an index of 132 means that spending by consumer units in that group is 32 percent above the average for all consumer units; an index of 68 indicates spending that is 32 percent below the average for all consumer units)

	complete income reporters	Under $10,000	$10,000– $19,999	$20,000– $29,999	$30,000– $39,999	$40,000– $49,999	$50,000– $69,999	$70,000 or more
Average spending of CU, total	$41,395	$18,085	$22,678	$28,623	$35,430	$40,900	$50,136	$76,124
Average spending of CU, index	100	44	55	69	86	99	121	184
GROCERIES	**100**	**63**	**72**	**89**	**96**	**107**	**115**	**140**
Cereals and bakery products	**100**	**64**	**74**	**91**	**94**	**104**	**113**	**142**
Cereals and cereal products	100	69	77	91	94	110	108	136
Flour	100	108	87	104	87	103	84	118
Prepared flour mixes	100	63	72	82	97	133	111	135
Ready-to-eat and cooked cereals	100	67	76	92	91	107	115	136
Rice	100	73	80	82	96	120	89	147
Pasta, cornmeal, and other cereal products	100	64	77	94	102	105	108	135
Bakery products	100	61	73	91	93	101	115	145
Bread	100	66	81	96	98	103	115	130
White bread	100	77	91	98	96	107	102	120
Crackers and cookies	100	62	72	90	87	104	115	148
Cookies	100	65	71	94	89	101	115	145
Crackers	100	56	74	82	84	108	117	154
Frozen and refrigerated bakery products	100	50	66	93	84	100	136	148
Other bakery products	100	59	69	87	96	99	111	155
Biscuits and rolls	100	55	66	76	87	99	122	165
Cakes and cupcakes	100	64	69	89	113	93	98	154
Bread and cracker products	100	78	57	69	81	102	138	153
Sweetrolls, coffee cakes, doughnuts	100	62	72	94	91	109	111	143
Pies, tarts, turnovers	100	47	79	110	95	86	105	148
Meats, poultry, fish, and eggs	**100**	**67**	**76**	**95**	**102**	**105**	**112**	**132**
Beef	100	64	73	101	105	101	112	131
Ground beef	100	73	81	100	104	114	107	117
Roast	100	61	76	122	116	78	105	126
Chuck roast	100	72	85	103	123	77	92	131
Round roast	100	56	80	99	129	79	108	130
Other roast	100	55	65	153	102	77	114	119
Steak	100	53	62	99	98	106	116	147
Round steak	100	59	58	136	92	117	110	123
Sirloin steak	100	54	72	81	105	104	122	144
Other steak	100	51	58	94	97	104	114	158
Pork	100	74	85	95	100	98	109	126
Bacon	100	73	90	94	105	98	104	124
Pork chops	100	78	82	90	88	108	109	132
Ham	100	72	82	115	93	80	109	129
Ham, not canned	100	70	83	115	94	74	108	132
Canned ham	100	118	54	101	75	206	134	63
Sausage	100	64	89	88	115	121	97	121
Other pork	100	78	86	86	109	94	117	121
Other meats	100	66	70	96	107	101	112	135
Frankfurters	100	82	76	90	106	101	114	123
Lunch meats (cold cuts)	100	63	70	96	100	99	117	139
Bologna, liverwurst, salami	100	73	83	106	97	91	110	125
Lamb, organ meats, and others	100	48	57	109	162	111	71	138

	complete income reporters	Under $10,000	$10,000–$19,999	$20,000–$29,999	$30,000–$39,999	$40,000–$49,999	$50,000–$69,999	$70,000 or more
Poultry	100	62	78	85	94	107	126	133
Fresh and frozen chicken	100	61	80	86	92	114	125	129
Fresh and frozen whole chicken	100	61	87	90	86	137	109	125
Fresh and frozen chicken parts	100	61	77	85	95	105	132	131
Other poultry	100	66	70	81	101	82	127	147
Fish and seafood	100	64	69	88	100	118	102	145
Canned fish and seafood	100	65	64	101	93	118	102	145
Fresh fish and shellfish	100	68	66	86	103	118	97	149
Frozen fish and shellfish	100	58	76	86	98	119	111	139
Eggs	100	76	82	100	106	120	106	112
Dairy products	**100**	**58**	**69**	**89**	**95**	**107**	**116**	**146**
Fresh milk and cream	100	67	78	94	100	112	111	129
Fresh milk, all types	100	68	80	94	101	113	111	126
Cream	100	54	61	93	91	101	107	163
Other dairy products	100	52	63	87	91	104	120	157
Butter	100	47	68	102	93	94	129	143
Cheese	100	55	64	85	93	103	119	157
Ice cream and related products	100	51	64	84	92	108	116	159
Miscellaneous dairy products	100	48	53	86	84	106	128	167
Fruits and vegetables	**100**	**64**	**76**	**92**	**97**	**105**	**111**	**139**
Fresh fruits	100	67	75	92	90	102	111	143
Apples	100	63	72	91	96	100	112	146
Bananas	100	72	86	103	93	106	106	123
Oranges	100	78	71	91	85	96	134	129
Citrus fruits, excl. oranges	100	65	69	98	116	103	93	142
Other fresh fruits	100	65	74	86	82	103	111	154
Fresh vegetables	100	61	76	90	103	106	109	139
Potatoes	100	62	88	94	99	113	102	130
Lettuce	100	61	79	83	98	94	111	150
Tomatoes	100	63	76	96	105	109	102	136
Other fresh vegetables	100	59	72	89	105	106	114	140
Processed fruits	100	65	77	93	97	102	111	138
Frozen fruits and fruit juices	100	58	77	82	91	108	116	148
Frozen orange juice	100	58	62	85	103	121	109	152
Frozen fruits	100	49	82	94	59	114	118	153
Frozen fruit juices	100	64	106	70	86	78	131	134
Canned fruits	100	65	71	91	110	107	112	134
Dried fruits	100	49	83	92	101	132	90	141
Fresh fruit juice	100	65	81	100	83	102	106	142
Canned and bottled fruit juice	100	68	77	94	100	95	113	135
Processed vegetables	100	62	78	93	98	114	113	131
Frozen vegetables	100	60	75	83	102	116	114	138
Canned and dried vegetables and juices	100	63	79	98	96	112	112	128
Canned beans	100	73	77	89	102	141	110	114
Canned corn	100	70	88	97	104	116	120	104
Canned miscellaneous vegetables	100	55	76	100	96	111	120	129
Dried beans	100	104	101	95	109	96	117	87
Dried miscellaneous vegetables	100	54	88	129	88	96	117	114
Fresh and canned vegetable juices	100	67	72	85	84	95	102	162
Sugar and other sweets	**100**	**67**	**69**	**88**	**86**	**115**	**115**	**144**
Candy and chewing gum	100	62	67	84	80	116	118	153
Sugar	100	87	87	94	110	128	100	103
Artificial sweeteners	100	95	52	124	51	94	115	147
Jams, preserves, other sweets	100	59	66	89	94	107	120	146

	complete income reporters	Under $10,000	$10,000– $19,999	$20,000– $29,999	$30,000– $39,999	$40,000– $49,999	$50,000– $69,999	$70,000 or more
Fats and oils	**100**	**73**	**77**	**88**	**101**	**110**	**116**	**127**
Margarine	100	71	83	92	116	121	106	114
Fats and oils	100	91	80	95	108	98	114	111
Salad dressings	100	61	70	82	95	114	117	145
Nondairy cream and imitation milk	100	65	88	95	89	93	124	127
Peanut butter	100	77	72	78	94	126	122	129
Miscellaneous foods	**100**	**57**	**65**	**82**	**94**	**115**	**121**	**149**
Frozen prepared foods	100	58	68	71	99	128	116	149
Frozen meals	100	67	79	74	105	150	102	127
Other frozen prepared foods	100	54	63	70	96	120	121	158
Canned and packaged soups	100	59	75	94	98	112	111	137
Potato chips, nuts, and other snacks	100	55	62	81	88	118	122	155
Potato chips and other snacks	100	55	63	79	87	120	127	152
Nuts	100	58	59	89	93	110	103	165
Condiments and seasonings	100	57	64	81	93	105	118	158
Salt, spices, and other seasonings	100	64	74	83	94	105	106	150
Olives, pickles, relishes	100	55	60	72	80	119	109	177
Sauces and gravies	100	55	62	82	95	105	129	152
Baking needs and miscellaneous products	100	54	59	81	95	97	113	170
Other canned/packaged prepared foods	100	59	63	87	95	112	129	142
Prepared salads	100	52	55	83	93	112	127	158
Prepared desserts	100	60	62	78	90	94	142	152
Baby food	100	50	58	83	91	135	150	132
Miscellaneous prepared foods	100	63	67	90	97	108	123	139
Nonalcoholic beverages	100	65	73	82	96	108	123	140
Cola	100	65	70	87	111	113	117	130
Other carbonated drinks	100	68	82	81	97	119	122	124
Coffee	100	66	85	82	79	92	124	144
Roasted coffee	100	64	76	82	79	92	126	152
Instant and freeze-dried coffee	100	69	101	81	80	92	120	131
Noncarbonated fruit-flavored drinks	100	65	69	86	84	130	112	143
Tea	100	66	71	82	87	88	118	158
Other nonalcoholic beverages and ice	100	61	59	70	87	96	141	160
Food prepared by CU on trips	**100**	**38**	**42**	**71**	**77**	**95**	**121**	**202**

Source: Calculations by New Strategist based on the 2001 Consumer Expenditure Survey

8. Groceries: Indexed per capita spending by income, 2001

(indexed average annual per capita spending of consumer units (CU) on groceries, by before-tax income of consumer unit, 2001; complete income reporters only; index definition: an index of 100 is the average for all consumer units; an index of 132 means that spending by consumer units in that group is 32 percent above the average for all consumer units; an index of 68 indicates spending that is 32 percent below the average for all consumer units)

	complete income reporters	Under $10,000	$10,000– $19,999	$20,000– $29,999	$30,000– $39,999	$40,000– $49,999	$50,000– $69,999	$70,000 or more
Per capita spending of CU, total	$16,558	$11,044	$11,380	$12,445	$14,763	$15,148	$17,288	$24,556
Per capita spending of CU, index	100	67	69	75	89	92	104	148
GROCERIES	**100**	**96**	**91**	**97**	**100**	**99**	**99**	**113**
Cereals and bakery products	**100**	**97**	**93**	**99**	**98**	**97**	**97**	**115**
Cereals and cereal products	100	106	97	99	98	102	93	110
Flour	100	165	109	113	91	95	73	95
Prepared flour mixes	100	96	91	89	101	123	96	109
Ready-to-eat and cooked cereals	100	103	96	100	95	99	99	110
Rice	100	112	101	89	100	111	77	118
Pasta, cornmeal, and other cereal products	100	98	96	103	106	98	93	109
Bakery products	100	93	91	98	97	94	99	117
Bread	100	100	101	104	102	95	99	105
White bread	100	118	114	106	100	99	88	97
Crackers and cookies	100	94	90	98	91	96	99	119
Cookies	100	99	89	102	93	94	99	117
Crackers	100	85	93	90	88	100	100	124
Frozen and refrigerated bakery products	100	76	83	101	87	93	117	119
Other bakery products	100	91	86	94	100	91	96	125
Biscuits and rolls	100	84	82	82	91	92	105	133
Cakes and cupcakes	100	98	86	97	118	87	84	124
Bread and cracker products	100	119	72	75	85	94	119	123
Sweetrolls, coffee cakes, doughnuts	100	94	90	102	95	101	96	115
Pies, tarts, turnovers	100	71	99	120	99	79	91	119
Meats, poultry, fish, and eggs	**100**	**102**	**95**	**103**	**106**	**97**	**97**	**106**
Beef	100	98	91	110	109	94	96	106
Ground beef	100	112	102	109	109	106	92	94
Roast	100	93	95	132	121	72	91	101
Chuck roast	100	109	106	112	128	72	79	105
Round roast	100	86	101	107	134	73	93	105
Other roast	100	84	81	166	106	71	98	96
Steak	100	82	78	107	102	99	100	119
Round steak	100	90	73	148	96	109	95	100
Sirloin steak	100	82	91	88	109	96	105	116
Other steak	100	78	73	102	101	96	99	128
Pork	100	113	107	103	105	91	94	101
Bacon	100	112	112	102	109	91	90	100
Pork chops	100	120	103	98	92	100	94	106
Ham	100	110	102	125	97	74	94	104
Ham, not canned	100	107	104	125	98	68	93	106
Canned ham	100	180	68	110	78	191	116	51
Sausage	100	97	111	95	120	112	84	98
Other pork	100	119	107	94	113	87	101	97
Other meats	100	100	88	104	112	93	97	109
Frankfurters	100	125	95	98	111	94	98	99
Lunch meats (cold cuts)	100	97	87	104	104	92	101	112
Bologna, liverwurst, salami	100	111	104	115	101	84	95	101
Lamb, organ meats, and others	100	73	72	118	169	102	61	111

	complete income reporters	Under $10,000	$10,000– $19,999	$20,000– $29,999	$30,000– $39,999	$40,000– $49,999	$50,000– $69,999	$70,000 or more
Poultry	100	95	98	92	98	99	108	107
Fresh and frozen chicken	100	94	101	94	96	106	108	104
Fresh and frozen whole chicken	100	94	109	98	89	127	94	101
Fresh and frozen chicken parts	100	94	97	92	99	97	114	106
Other poultry	100	101	88	88	105	76	109	119
Fish and seafood	100	98	87	95	104	110	88	117
Canned fish and seafood	100	99	81	110	97	109	88	117
Fresh fish and shellfish	100	103	83	93	108	110	83	121
Frozen fish and shellfish	100	89	95	93	103	110	96	112
Eggs	100	117	103	109	111	111	91	90
Dairy products	**100**	**89**	**87**	**97**	**99**	**99**	**100**	**118**
Fresh milk and cream	100	103	98	102	104	103	95	104
Fresh milk, all types	100	105	100	102	105	104	96	102
Cream	100	83	77	101	95	93	92	131
Other dairy products	100	80	79	94	95	97	104	127
Butter	100	72	85	111	97	87	112	115
Cheese	100	84	81	93	96	96	102	126
Ice cream and related products	100	78	80	91	96	100	100	129
Miscellaneous dairy products	100	73	66	93	88	99	110	135
Fruits and vegetables	**100**	**97**	**96**	**100**	**101**	**97**	**96**	**112**
Fresh fruits	100	103	94	100	94	95	96	115
Apples	100	96	90	99	100	93	97	118
Bananas	100	110	108	112	97	98	91	99
Oranges	100	119	89	99	89	89	116	104
Citrus fruits, excl. oranges	100	100	87	107	121	95	80	114
Other fresh fruits	100	99	92	94	85	96	96	124
Fresh vegetables	100	92	96	98	107	98	94	112
Potatoes	100	95	110	102	103	104	88	105
Lettuce	100	93	99	90	102	87	96	121
Tomatoes	100	97	95	105	109	101	88	110
Other fresh vegetables	100	90	90	97	110	98	99	113
Processed fruits	100	99	97	101	101	94	95	111
Frozen fruits and fruit juices	100	89	96	90	95	100	100	119
Frozen orange juice	100	89	77	92	107	112	94	123
Frozen fruits	100	75	103	102	61	106	102	124
Frozen fruit juices	100	98	133	76	89	72	113	108
Canned fruits	100	99	89	99	114	99	97	108
Dried fruits	100	75	104	100	105	122	78	114
Fresh fruit juice	100	99	101	108	87	94	91	114
Canned and bottled fruit juice	100	104	97	102	105	88	97	109
Processed vegetables	100	95	97	101	102	105	97	106
Frozen vegetables	100	91	94	90	106	108	98	112
Canned and dried vegetables and juices	100	96	99	107	100	104	97	103
Canned beans	100	112	97	96	106	130	95	92
Canned corn	100	107	110	105	109	108	103	84
Canned miscellaneous vegetables	100	84	95	109	100	103	103	104
Dried beans	100	159	126	103	113	88	101	70
Dried miscellaneous vegetables	100	82	110	141	92	88	101	92
Fresh and canned vegetable juices	100	102	91	92	87	88	88	131
Sugar and other sweets	**100**	**102**	**87**	**96**	**89**	**107**	**99**	**116**
Candy and chewing gum	100	95	83	91	83	107	102	124
Sugar	100	134	109	103	114	118	87	83
Artificial sweeteners	100	144	65	135	53	87	100	119
Jams, preserves, other sweets	100	90	83	96	98	99	103	118

	complete income reporters	Under $10,000	$10,000– $19,999	$20,000– $29,999	$30,000– $39,999	$40,000– $49,999	$50,000– $69,999	$70,000 or more
Fats and oils	**100**	**112**	**97**	**96**	**105**	**102**	**100**	**102**
Margarine	100	108	104	100	121	112	91	92
Fats and oils	100	139	101	104	113	91	98	90
Salad dressings	100	93	88	89	99	106	101	117
Nondairy cream and imitation milk	100	99	110	103	92	86	107	102
Peanut butter	100	118	90	85	98	117	105	104
Miscellaneous foods	**100**	**88**	**81**	**89**	**98**	**107**	**105**	**120**
Frozen prepared foods	100	88	85	77	103	119	100	120
Frozen meals	100	102	99	81	110	139	88	103
Other frozen prepared foods	100	82	80	76	100	111	105	127
Canned and packaged soups	100	90	94	103	102	103	96	110
Potato chips, nuts, and other snacks	100	85	78	88	92	109	105	125
Potato chips and other snacks	100	84	79	86	91	111	110	123
Nuts	100	88	74	96	97	102	89	133
Condiments and seasonings	100	87	80	88	97	97	102	128
Salt, spices, and other seasonings	100	97	93	91	98	97	92	121
Olives, pickles, relishes	100	84	75	78	84	110	94	143
Sauces and gravies	100	84	78	89	99	97	111	122
Baking needs and miscellaneous products	100	83	75	88	99	90	97	137
Other canned/packaged prepared foods	100	90	79	94	99	104	111	115
Prepared salads	100	80	68	90	97	103	109	127
Prepared desserts	100	91	77	85	94	87	122	123
Baby food	100	76	73	91	94	125	129	106
Miscellaneous prepared foods	100	96	84	97	101	100	106	112
Nonalcoholic beverages	100	99	91	89	100	100	106	113
Cola	100	99	88	95	116	105	101	105
Other carbonated drinks	100	103	103	88	101	110	105	100
Coffee	100	100	106	89	83	85	107	117
Roasted coffee	100	98	95	89	82	85	108	122
Instant and freeze-dried coffee	100	105	126	88	83	85	103	106
Noncarbonated fruit-flavored drinks	100	100	86	93	87	121	96	116
Tea	100	101	90	90	90	81	102	128
Other nonalcoholic beverages and ice	100	93	74	76	91	89	121	129
Food prepared by CU on trips	**100**	**58**	**53**	**78**	**81**	**88**	**104**	**163**

Note: Per capita indexes account for household size and show how much each person in a particular household demographic segment spends relative to a person in the average household.
Source: Calculations by New Strategist based on the 2001 Consumer Expenditure Survey

(total annual spending on groceries, by before-tax income group of consumer units (CU), 2001; complete income reporters only; numbers in thousands)

	complete income reporters	Under $10,000	$10,000– $19,999	$20,000– $29,999	$30,000– $39,999	$40,000– $49,999	$50,000– $69,999	$70,000 or more
Number of consumer units	**88,735**	**10,929**	**15,113**	**12,075**	**10,508**	**8,737**	**12,480**	**18,892**
Total spending of all CUs	**$3,673,207,509**	**$197,650,992**	**$342,725,458**	**$345,621,518**	**$372,302,643**	**$357,341,465**	**$625,694,160**	**$1,438,132,341**
GROCERIES	**$288,657,617**	**$22,443,301**	**$35,607,113**	**$35,069,664**	**$32,955,295**	**$30,477,015**	**$46,697,539**	**$86,245,758**
Cereals and bakery products	**42,643,379**	**3,349,028**	**5,391,266**	**5,262,044**	**4,729,441**	**4,379,247**	**6,771,398**	**12,897,946**
Cereals and cereal products	14,745,095	1,255,453	1,936,092	1,824,291	1,643,766	1,601,929	2,248,022	4,274,693
Flour	734,726	97,940	108,634	103,966	75,658	74,352	86,986	184,197
Prepared flour mixes	1,241,403	96,460	153,154	138,500	143,014	162,334	193,939	356,870
Ready-to-eat and cooked cereals	8,121,915	672,936	1,056,437	1,015,508	877,208	857,449	1,309,402	2,353,565
Rice	1,806,645	163,024	246,708	201,653	204,696	213,095	226,886	563,926
Pasta, cornmeal, and other cereal products	2,839,520	225,163	371,240	364,544	343,191	294,786	430,934	815,946
Bakery products	27,898,284	2,093,575	3,455,174	3,437,753	3,085,674	2,777,230	4,523,501	8,623,065
Bread	8,042,053	650,838	1,102,295	1,046,178	928,277	813,415	1,297,421	2,217,732
White bread	3,418,072	325,013	530,176	453,416	389,847	359,702	489,715	874,700
Crackers and cookies	6,591,236	501,667	809,020	805,040	680,603	672,225	1,067,914	2,077,364
Cookies	4,338,254	347,356	524,704	552,311	456,468	432,307	698,755	1,340,010
Crackers	2,252,982	154,312	284,315	252,730	224,136	239,918	369,158	737,355
Frozen and refrigerated bakery products	2,497,890	153,990	280,661	315,761	248,094	245,684	476,362	785,340
Other bakery products	10,766,218	787,038	1,263,280	1,270,652	1,228,595	1,045,819	1,681,805	3,542,628
Biscuits and rolls	3,735,744	253,521	417,721	384,347	385,223	364,420	638,976	1,314,316
Cakes and cupcakes	3,227,292	254,597	378,188	390,989	431,669	296,883	442,790	1,056,441
Bread and cracker products	366,476	35,190	35,843	34,535	35,307	36,783	71,261	119,397
Sweetrolls, coffee cakes, doughnuts	2,492,566	189,510	305,317	319,263	269,845	268,313	389,002	756,058
Pies, tarts, turnovers	944,140	54,330	126,200	141,519	106,551	79,594	139,776	296,416
Meats, poultry, fish, and eggs	**77,102,729**	**6,322,523**	**9,958,343**	**9,914,662**	**9,283,188**	**7,949,796**	**12,160,013**	**21,638,141**
Beef	23,442,012	1,847,894	2,895,824	3,234,772	2,914,814	2,341,341	3,680,726	6,547,212
Ground beef	8,426,276	761,462	1,164,138	1,148,574	1,040,292	948,664	1,267,094	2,100,224
Roast	4,269,928	320,074	549,094	706,871	586,346	326,152	630,614	1,142,966
Chuck roast	1,410,887	124,439	203,190	197,668	204,696	107,203	182,582	392,198
Round roast	1,152,668	79,765	157,227	154,439	175,484	89,729	174,595	320,031
Other roast	1,706,374	115,939	188,596	354,643	206,167	129,308	273,437	430,738
Steak	8,853,978	582,838	938,059	1,190,474	1,029,679	927,869	1,440,691	2,772,968
Round steak	1,772,038	128,361	175,643	328,199	193,347	204,621	274,685	465,499
Sirloin steak	2,493,454	164,510	307,043	275,793	309,461	254,946	428,813	761,537
Other steak	4,588,487	290,009	455,373	586,483	526,871	468,303	737,194	1,545,932
Pork	16,688,391	1,517,702	2,414,093	2,158,648	1,983,175	1,615,209	2,546,794	4,466,258
Bacon	2,684,234	241,511	409,125	341,360	332,053	259,402	394,118	706,372
Pork chops	3,935,397	379,399	551,994	480,223	409,812	417,629	601,910	1,104,049
Ham	3,897,241	346,841	541,207	607,856	429,777	304,921	599,914	1,067,965
Ham, not canned	3,728,645	322,392	525,603	584,672	414,856	270,672	568,214	1,045,294
Canned ham	168,597	24,518	15,604	23,184	15,026	34,249	31,824	22,670
Sausage	2,391,408	187,514	361,194	285,212	325,328	283,690	327,725	616,446
Other pork	3,780,111	362,328	550,503	443,998	486,205	349,567	623,126	971,427
Other meats	9,497,307	769,232	1,129,260	1,237,808	1,203,376	943,159	1,499,722	2,730,461
Frankfurters	2,052,441	206,440	265,010	252,368	257,866	204,970	328,973	536,722
Lunch meats (cold cuts)	6,564,615	511,131	778,193	855,031	776,646	642,257	1,083,014	1,935,108
Bologna, liverwurst, salami	2,346,153	210,684	329,985	337,859	269,635	210,038	364,291	625,514
Lamb, organ meats, and others	880,251	51,551	86,046	130,289	168,864	95,845	87,734	258,632

	complete income reporters	Under $10,000	$10,000– $19,999	$20,000– $29,999	$30,000– $39,999	$40,000– $49,999	$50,000– $69,999	$70,000 or more
Poultry	$14,112,414	$1,083,522	$1,873,991	$1,632,902	$1,573,153	$1,489,047	$2,494,128	$3,997,358
Fresh and frozen chicken	11,043,958	834,161	1,506,869	1,294,440	1,205,373	1,241,702	1,947,130	3,037,078
Fresh and frozen whole chicken	3,254,800	246,023	479,906	397,268	330,266	438,161	498,326	868,087
Fresh and frozen chicken parts	7,788,271	588,138	1,026,963	897,293	875,106	803,542	1,448,803	2,168,991
Other poultry	3,068,456	249,429	367,122	338,462	367,675	247,345	546,874	960,469
Fish and seafood	10,099,818	797,507	1,188,931	1,205,810	1,198,332	1,176,350	1,453,421	3,122,092
Canned fish and seafood	1,393,140	110,980	152,472	191,147	153,627	161,372	200,304	428,471
Fresh fish and shellfish	5,356,932	445,564	603,230	625,244	654,438	623,647	729,206	1,703,870
Frozen fish and shellfish	3,348,859	241,004	433,300	389,419	390,162	391,243	524,035	989,941
Eggs	3,262,786	306,734	456,175	444,722	410,443	384,690	485,222	774,572
Dairy products	**31,273,763**	**2,250,956**	**3,684,756**	**3,806,282**	**3,513,770**	**3,302,411**	**5,116,176**	**9,700,475**
Fresh milk and cream	12,928,690	1,069,866	1,715,750	1,645,460	1,527,338	1,420,549	2,013,024	3,559,253
Fresh milk, all types	11,798,206	994,420	1,597,746	1,501,889	1,404,920	1,308,278	1,842,547	3,167,622
Cream	1,130,484	75,446	118,004	143,572	122,418	112,270	170,477	391,631
Other dairy products	18,345,074	1,181,159	1,969,006	2,160,821	1,986,537	1,881,862	3,103,152	6,141,034
Butter	1,869,646	109,111	215,069	259,854	206,062	173,255	340,205	567,327
Cheese	8,977,320	607,258	980,653	1,039,658	983,549	914,327	1,500,221	2,991,548
Ice cream and related products	5,254,887	332,416	572,545	599,524	573,527	559,343	859,373	1,783,405
Miscellaneous dairy products	2,243,221	132,306	200,810	261,907	223,400	235,025	403,354	798,754
Fruits and vegetables	**48,320,644**	**3,795,273**	**6,282,327**	**6,049,575**	**5,542,340**	**4,999,137**	**7,528,685**	**14,245,513**
Fresh fruits	14,841,816	1,230,293	1,896,952	1,860,878	1,581,559	1,493,940	2,323,402	4,504,609
Apples	2,849,281	220,644	348,720	352,590	323,962	280,370	449,530	886,602
Bananas	2,935,354	260,205	429,829	412,603	323,436	306,407	436,051	769,660
Oranges	1,717,022	164,520	207,325	213,003	173,592	161,722	323,731	472,111
Citrus fruits, excl. oranges	1,248,501	100,314	147,299	166,394	171,491	126,075	163,613	376,707
Other fresh fruits	6,091,658	484,570	763,709	716,289	589,079	619,366	950,477	1,999,529
Fresh vegetables	14,927,889	1,112,225	1,939,922	1,833,710	1,821,036	1,556,759	2,295,446	4,408,448
Potatoes	2,782,730	212,660	415,914	354,884	325,853	308,766	399,360	768,149
Lettuce	1,862,548	140,236	249,348	209,018	215,414	171,682	290,410	594,909
Tomatoes	2,694,882	209,868	348,778	353,073	334,995	288,496	385,133	782,696
Other fresh vegetables	7,587,730	549,502	925,883	916,855	944,669	787,903	1,220,669	2,262,695
Processed fruits	10,725,400	855,393	1,412,133	1,361,094	1,232,063	1,073,777	1,666,954	3,148,919
Frozen fruits and fruit juices	1,303,517	93,192	170,294	146,228	139,967	139,006	212,909	409,956
Frozen orange juice	737,388	52,725	77,297	84,887	89,633	87,632	112,819	239,173
Frozen fruits	227,162	13,743	31,640	29,101	15,867	25,512	37,690	74,057
Frozen fruit juices	338,968	26,656	61,358	32,240	34,466	25,949	62,525	96,916
Canned fruits	1,549,313	123,317	186,930	192,717	201,018	162,770	243,984	441,695
Dried fruits	508,452	30,836	72,042	63,515	60,841	66,139	64,397	152,836
Fresh fruit juice	2,213,938	177,073	303,551	300,547	218,146	222,095	328,973	667,454
Canned and bottled fruit juice	5,150,179	431,153	679,316	658,208	611,881	483,768	816,691	1,476,977
Processed vegetables	7,825,540	597,362	1,033,249	993,893	907,681	874,661	1,243,008	2,183,537
Frozen vegetables	2,560,005	188,357	327,712	289,076	309,356	292,602	410,966	753,980
Canned and dried vegetables and juices	5,265,535	409,046	705,537	704,697	598,326	582,059	832,042	1,429,747
Canned beans	1,185,500	106,589	155,894	142,727	143,434	163,994	183,830	287,158
Canned corn	648,653	55,869	97,167	85,612	80,071	74,177	109,450	143,957
Canned miscellaneous vegetables	1,658,457	112,054	213,571	226,044	188,514	180,769	279,178	456,809
Dried beans	196,104	25,138	33,654	25,358	25,219	18,435	32,198	36,462
Dried miscellaneous vegetables	731,176	48,239	109,412	128,599	76,078	68,760	120,682	177,585
Fresh and canned vegetable juices	710,767	58,357	87,567	81,869	70,614	66,751	101,712	245,596
Sugar and other sweets	**10,846,079**	**893,251**	**1,273,126**	**1,299,270**	**1,102,394**	**1,232,703**	**1,759,181**	**3,326,503**
Candy and chewing gum	6,886,723	528,102	779,476	787,652	652,862	786,155	1,141,046	2,246,448
Sugar	1,675,317	180,381	247,930	215,177	217,831	210,824	236,496	367,638
Artificial sweeteners	431,252	50,201	38,140	72,933	25,955	39,841	70,013	135,267
Jams, preserves, other sweets	1,852,787	134,567	207,511	223,629	205,747	195,796	311,501	577,151

	complete income reporters	Under $10,000	$10,000– $19,999	$20,000– $29,999	$30,000– $39,999	$40,000– $49,999	$50,000– $69,999	$70,000 or more
Fats and oils	**$7,927,585**	**$715,539**	**$1,038,991**	**$949,216**	**$944,879**	**$857,012**	**$1,294,051**	**$2,141,975**
Margarine	1,074,581	93,339	151,708	133,912	147,532	127,560	159,619	259,576
Fats and oils	2,199,741	246,521	300,600	285,574	281,299	213,008	351,686	520,097
Salad dressings	2,581,301	193,281	307,917	288,110	291,177	290,068	424,819	797,998
Nondairy cream and imitation milk	953,901	76,292	142,132	123,286	99,931	87,632	166,858	257,498
Peanut butter	1,117,174	106,107	136,636	118,335	124,835	138,831	191,069	306,806
Miscellaneous foods	**42,740,988**	**3,022,263**	**4,725,905**	**4,747,166**	**4,768,110**	**4,854,190**	**7,285,574**	**13,553,877**
Frozen prepared foods	9,085,577	642,983	1,047,791	875,921	1,062,884	1,147,605	1,480,253	2,885,186
Frozen meals	2,574,202	212,456	345,151	259,371	321,230	379,797	370,032	697,493
Other frozen prepared foods	6,511,374	430,527	702,651	616,670	741,655	767,720	1,110,221	2,187,505
Canned and packaged soups	3,473,088	252,270	442,417	445,568	402,772	381,545	543,005	1,011,289
Potato chips, nuts, and other snacks	9,248,849	630,270	972,526	1,020,941	966,631	1,073,340	1,588,080	3,055,592
Potato chips and other snacks	7,253,199	488,580	772,617	780,649	746,173	856,838	1,300,042	2,353,754
Nuts	1,995,650	141,759	199,909	240,293	220,563	216,503	288,163	701,838
Condiments and seasonings	7,927,585	555,064	861,806	873,868	872,479	820,230	1,315,642	2,669,629
Salt, spices, and other seasonings	1,827,941	143,095	230,015	207,569	204,381	189,331	273,562	585,274
Olives, pickles, relishes	944,140	63,812	95,699	92,132	89,633	110,261	145,267	356,303
Sauces and gravies	3,513,906	238,926	369,871	393,404	394,365	363,197	636,979	1,133,709
Baking needs and miscellaneous products	1,641,598	109,273	166,140	180,642	184,100	157,441	259,834	594,342
Other canned/packaged prepared foods	13,005,889	941,675	1,401,285	1,530,748	1,463,344	1,431,470	2,358,470	3,932,181
Prepared salads	1,788,898	114,875	166,147	201,411	197,235	196,670	319,363	601,899
Prepared desserts	953,901	70,249	100,258	101,430	101,823	88,244	190,070	308,506
Baby food	2,104,794	129,718	209,095	238,844	225,922	280,283	444,163	589,619
Miscellaneous prepared foods	8,121,027	625,535	925,784	988,943	931,534	864,614	1,404,874	2,404,196
Nonalcoholic beverages	24,196,260	1,926,586	2,994,149	2,691,638	2,740,802	2,566,057	4,171,190	7,188,784
Cola	8,330,442	663,742	999,414	985,924	1,097,245	929,005	1,371,552	2,310,114
Other carbonated drinks	4,383,509	364,739	614,607	484,449	502,282	511,901	753,917	1,156,002
Coffee	3,661,206	296,111	527,620	406,082	343,191	332,181	636,730	1,125,774
Roasted coffee	2,365,675	186,738	305,702	263,477	220,773	214,843	418,330	763,804
Instant and freeze-dried coffee	1,296,418	109,332	221,848	142,485	122,418	117,338	218,525	361,971
Noncarbonated fruit-flavored drinks	1,896,267	152,370	221,105	220,973	188,093	242,976	297,773	578,284
Tea	1,667,331	135,236	202,774	187,042	171,070	143,636	276,182	562,415
Other nonalcoholic beverages and ice	4,205,152	314,430	419,375	402,218	434,086	399,281	832,042	1,432,203
Food prepared by CU on trips	**3,607,078**	**167,785**	**258,331**	**349,813**	**330,477**	**336,549**	**611,146**	**1,552,734**

Note: Numbers may not add to total because of rounding.
Source: Calculations by New Strategist based on the 2001 Consumer Expenditure Survey

10. Groceries: Market shares by income, 2001

(percentage of total annual spending on groceries accounted for by before-tax income group of consumer units, 2001; complete income reporters only)

	complete income reporters	Under $10,000	$10,000–$19,999	$20,000–$29,999	$30,000–$39,999	$40,000–$49,999	$50,000–$69,999	$70,000 or more
Share of total consumer units	100.0%	12.3%	17.0%	13.6%	11.8%	9.8%	14.1%	21.3%
Share of total before-tax income	100.0	1.4	5.3	7.0	8.6	9.2	17.4	51.1
Share of total spending	100.0	5.4	9.3	9.4	10.1	9.7	17.0	39.2
GROCERIES	100.0	7.8	12.3	12.1	11.4	10.6	16.2	29.9
Cereals and bakery products	100.0	7.9	12.6	12.3	11.1	10.3	15.9	30.2
Cereals and cereal products	100.0	8.5	13.1	12.4	11.1	10.9	15.2	29.0
Flour	100.0	13.3	14.8	14.2	10.3	10.1	11.8	25.1
Prepared flour mixes	100.0	7.8	12.3	11.2	11.5	13.1	15.6	28.7
Ready-to-eat and cooked cereals	100.0	8.3	1.3	12.5	10.8	10.6	16.1	29.0
Rice	100.0	9.0	13.7	11.2	11.3	11.8	12.6	31.2
Pasta, cornmeal, and other cereal products	100.0	7.9	13.1	12.8	12.1	10.4	15.2	28.7
Bakery products	100.0	7.5	12.4	12.3	11.1	10.0	16.2	30.9
Bread	100.0	8.1	13.7	1.3	11.5	10.1	16.1	27.6
White bread	100.0	9.5	15.5	13.3	11.4	10.5	14.3	25.6
Crackers and cookies	100.0	7.6	12.3	12.2	10.3	10.2	16.2	31.5
Cookies	100.0	0.8	12.1	12.7	10.5	10.0	16.1	30.9
Crackers	100.0	6.8	12.6	11.2	9.9	10.6	16.4	32.7
Frozen and refrigerated bakery products	100.0	6.2	11.2	12.6	9.9	9.8	19.1	31.4
Other bakery products	100.0	7.3	11.7	11.8	11.4	9.7	15.6	32.9
Biscuits and rolls	100.0	6.8	11.2	10.3	10.3	9.8	17.1	35.2
Cakes and cupcakes	100.0	7.9	11.7	12.1	13.4	9.2	13.7	32.7
Bread and cracker products	100.0	9.6	9.8	9.4	9.6	10.0	19.4	32.6
Sweetrolls, coffee cakes, doughnuts	100.0	7.6	12.2	12.8	10.8	10.8	15.6	30.3
Pies, tarts, turnovers	100.0	5.8	13.4	15.0	11.3	8.4	14.8	31.4
Meats, poultry, fish, and eggs	100.0	8.2	12.9	12.9	12.0	10.3	15.8	28.1
Beef	100.0	7.9	12.4	13.8	12.4	10.0	15.7	27.9
Ground beef	100.0	9.0	13.8	13.6	12.3	11.3	15.0	24.9
Roast	100.0	7.5	12.9	16.6	13.7	7.6	14.8	26.8
Chuck roast	100.0	8.8	14.4	14.0	14.5	7.6	12.9	27.8
Round roast	100.0	6.9	13.6	13.4	15.2	7.8	15.1	27.8
Other roast	100.0	6.8	11.1	20.8	12.1	7.6	16.0	25.2
Steak	100.0	6.6	10.6	13.4	11.6	10.5	16.3	31.3
Round steak	100.0	7.2	9.9	18.5	10.9	11.5	15.5	26.3
Sirloin steak	100.0	6.6	12.3	11.1	12.4	10.2	17.2	30.5
Other steak	100.0	6.3	9.9	12.8	11.5	10.2	16.1	33.7
Pork	100.0	9.1	14.5	12.9	11.9	9.7	15.3	26.8
Bacon	100.0	9.0	15.2	12.7	12.4	9.7	14.7	26.3
Pork chops	100.0	9.6	14.0	12.2	10.4	10.6	15.3	28.1
Ham	100.0	8.9	13.9	15.6	11.0	7.8	15.4	27.4
Ham, not canned	100.0	8.6	14.1	15.7	11.1	7.3	15.2	28.0
Canned ham	100.0	14.5	9.3	13.8	8.9	20.3	18.9	13.4
Sausage	100.0	7.8	15.1	11.9	13.6	11.9	13.7	25.8
Other pork	100.0	9.6	14.6	11.7	12.9	9.2	16.5	25.7
Other meats	100.0	8.1	11.9	13.0	12.7	9.9	15.8	28.7
Frankfurters	100.0	10.1	12.9	12.3	12.6	10.0	16.0	26.2
Lunch meats (cold cuts)	100.0	7.8	11.9	13.0	11.8	9.8	16.5	29.5
Bologna, liverwurst, salami	100.0	9.0	14.1	14.4	11.5	9.0	15.5	26.7
Lamb, organ meats, and others	100.0	5.9	9.8	14.8	19.2	10.9	10.0	29.4

	complete income reporters	Under $10,000	$10,000–$19,999	$20,000–$29,999	$30,000–$39,999	$40,000–$49,999	$50,000–$69,999	$70,000 or more
Poultry	100.0%	7.7%	13.3%	11.6%	11.1%	10.6%	17.7%	28.3%
Fresh and frozen chicken	100.0	7.6	13.6	11.7	10.9	11.2	17.6	27.5
Fresh and frozen whole chicken	100.0	7.6	14.7	12.2	10.1	13.5	15.3	26.7
Fresh and frozen chicken parts	100.0	7.6	13.2	11.5	11.2	10.3	18.6	27.8
Other poultry	100.0	8.1	12.0	11.0	12.0	8.1	17.8	31.3
Fish and seafood	100.0	7.9	11.8	11.9	11.9	11.6	14.4	30.9
Canned fish and seafood	100.0	8.0	10.9	13.7	11.0	11.6	14.4	30.8
Fresh fish and shellfish	100.0	8.3	11.3	11.7	12.2	11.6	13.6	31.8
Frozen fish and shellfish	100.0	7.2	12.9	11.6	11.7	11.7	15.6	29.6
Eggs	100.0	9.4	14.0	13.6	12.6	11.8	14.9	23.7
Dairy products	**100.0**	**7.2**	**11.8**	**12.2**	**11.2**	**10.6**	**16.4**	**31.0**
Fresh milk and cream	100.0	8.3	13.3	12.7	11.8	11.0	15.6	27.5
Fresh milk, all types	100.0	8.4	13.5	12.7	11.9	11.1	15.6	26.8
Cream	100.0	6.7	10.4	12.7	10.8	9.9	15.1	34.6
Other dairy products	100.0	6.4	10.7	11.8	10.8	10.3	16.9	33.5
Butter	100.0	5.8	11.5	13.9	11.0	9.3	18.2	30.3
Cheese	100.0	6.8	10.9	11.6	11.0	10.2	16.7	33.3
Ice cream and related products	100.0	6.3	10.9	11.4	10.9	10.6	16.4	33.9
Miscellaneous dairy products	100.0	5.9	9.0	11.7	10.0	10.5	18.0	35.6
Fruits and vegetables	**100.0**	**7.9**	**1.3**	**12.5**	**11.5**	**10.3**	**15.6**	**29.5**
Fresh fruits	100.0	8.3	12.8	12.5	10.7	10.1	15.7	30.4
Apples	100.0	7.7	12.2	12.4	11.4	9.8	15.8	31.1
Bananas	100.0	8.9	14.6	14.1	11.0	10.4	14.9	26.2
Oranges	100.0	9.6	12.1	12.4	10.1	9.4	18.9	27.5
Citrus fruits, excl. oranges	100.0	8.0	11.8	13.3	13.7	10.1	13.1	30.2
Other fresh fruits	100.0	8.0	12.5	11.8	9.7	10.2	15.6	32.8
Fresh vegetables	100.0	7.5	13.0	12.3	12.2	10.4	15.4	29.5
Potatoes	100.0	7.6	14.9	12.8	11.7	11.1	14.4	27.6
Lettuce	100.0	7.5	13.4	11.2	11.6	9.2	15.6	31.9
Tomatoes	100.0	7.8	12.9	13.1	12.4	10.7	14.3	29.0
Other fresh vegetables	100.0	7.2	12.2	12.1	12.4	10.4	16.1	29.8
Processed fruits	100.0	8.0	13.2	12.7	11.5	10.0	15.5	29.4
Frozen fruits and fruit juices	100.0	7.1	13.1	11.2	10.7	10.7	16.3	31.5
Frozen orange juice	100.0	7.2	10.5	11.5	12.2	11.9	15.3	32.4
Frozen fruits	100.0	6.1	13.9	12.8	7.0	11.2	16.6	32.6
Frozen fruit juices	100.0	7.9	18.1	9.5	10.2	7.7	18.4	28.6
Canned fruits	100.0	8.0	12.1	12.4	13.0	10.5	15.7	28.5
Dried fruits	100.0	6.1	14.2	12.5	12.0	1.3	12.7	30.1
Fresh fruit juice	100.0	8.0	13.7	13.6	9.9	10.0	14.9	30.1
Canned and bottled fruit juice	100.0	8.4	13.2	12.8	11.9	9.4	15.9	28.7
Processed vegetables	100.0	7.6	13.2	12.7	11.6	11.2	15.9	27.9
Frozen vegetables	100.0	7.4	12.8	11.3	12.1	11.4	16.1	29.5
Canned and dried vegetables and juices	100.0	7.8	13.4	13.4	11.4	11.1	15.8	27.2
Canned beans	100.0	9.0	13.2	12.0	12.1	13.8	15.5	24.2
Canned corn	100.0	8.6	15.0	13.2	12.3	11.4	16.9	22.2
Canned miscellaneous vegetables	100.0	6.8	12.9	13.6	11.4	10.9	16.8	27.5
Dried beans	100.0	12.8	17.2	12.9	12.9	9.4	16.4	18.6
Dried miscellaneous vegetables	100.0	6.6	15.0	17.6	10.4	9.4	16.5	24.3
Fresh and canned vegetable juices	100.0	8.2	12.3	11.5	9.9	9.4	14.3	34.6
Sugar and other sweets	**100.0**	**8.2**	**11.7**	**12.0**	**10.2**	**11.4**	**16.2**	**30.7**
Candy and chewing gum	100.0	7.7	11.3	11.4	9.5	11.4	16.6	32.6
Sugar	100.0	10.8	14.8	12.8	1.3	12.6	14.1	21.9
Artificial sweeteners	100.0	11.6	8.8	16.9	6.0	9.2	16.2	31.4
Jams, preserves, other sweets	100.0	7.3	11.2	12.1	11.1	10.6	16.8	31.2

	complete income reporters	Under $10,000	$10,000–$19,999	$20,000–$29,999	$30,000–$39,999	$40,000–$49,999	$50,000–$69,999	$70,000 or more
Fats and oils	**100.0%**	**9.0%**	**13.1%**	**12.0%**	**11.9%**	**10.8%**	**16.3%**	**27.0%**
Margarine	100.0	8.7	14.1	12.5	13.7	11.9	14.9	24.2
Fats and oils	100.0	11.2	13.7	13.0	12.8	9.7	16.0	23.6
Salad dressings	100.0	7.5	11.9	11.2	11.3	11.2	16.5	30.9
Nondairy cream and imitation milk	100.0	8.0	14.9	12.9	10.5	9.2	17.5	27.0
Peanut butter	100.0	9.5	12.2	10.6	11.2	12.4	17.1	27.5
Miscellaneous foods	**100.0**	**7.1**	**11.1**	**11.1**	**11.2**	**11.4**	**17.1**	**31.7**
Frozen prepared foods	100.0	7.1	11.5	9.6	11.7	12.6	16.3	31.8
Frozen meals	100.0	8.3	13.4	10.1	12.5	14.8	14.4	27.1
Other frozen prepared foods	100.0	6.6	10.8	9.5	11.4	11.8	17.1	33.6
Canned and packaged soups	100.0	7.3	12.7	12.8	11.6	11.0	15.6	29.1
Potato chips, nuts, and other snacks	100.0	6.8	10.5	11.0	10.5	11.6	17.2	33.0
Potato chips and other snacks	100.0	6.7	10.7	10.8	10.3	11.8	17.9	32.5
Nuts	100.0	7.1	10.0	12.0	11.1	10.8	14.4	35.2
Condiments and seasonings	100.0	0.7	10.9	11.0	1.1	10.3	16.6	33.7
Salt, spices, and other seasonings	100.0	7.8	12.6	11.4	11.2	10.4	15.0	32.0
Olives, pickles, relishes	100.0	6.8	10.1	9.8	9.5	11.7	15.4	37.7
Sauces and gravies	100.0	6.8	10.5	11.2	11.2	10.3	18.1	32.3
Baking needs and miscellaneous products	100.0	6.7	10.1	1.1	11.2	9.6	15.8	36.2
Other canned/packaged prepared foods	100.0	7.2	10.8	11.8	11.3	1.1	18.1	30.2
Prepared salads	100.0	6.4	9.3	11.3	11.0	11.0	17.9	33.6
Prepared desserts	100.0	7.4	10.5	10.6	10.7	9.3	19.9	32.3
Baby food	100.0	6.2	9.9	11.3	10.7	13.3	21.1	28.0
Miscellaneous prepared foods	100.0	7.7	11.4	12.2	11.5	10.6	17.3	29.6
Nonalcoholic beverages	100.0	8.0	12.4	11.1	11.3	10.6	17.2	29.7
Cola	100.0	8.0	12.0	11.8	13.2	11.2	16.5	27.7
Other carbonated drinks	100.0	8.3	14.0	11.1	11.5	11.7	17.2	26.4
Coffee	100.0	8.1	14.4	11.1	9.4	9.1	17.4	30.7
Roasted coffee	100.0	7.9	12.9	11.1	9.3	9.1	17.7	32.3
Instant and freeze-dried coffee	100.0	8.4	17.1	11.0	9.4	9.1	16.9	27.9
Noncarbonated fruit-flavored drinks	100.0	8.0	11.7	11.7	9.9	12.8	15.7	30.5
Tea	100.0	8.1	12.2	11.2	10.3	8.6	16.6	33.7
Other nonalcoholic beverages and ice	100.0	7.5	10.0	9.6	10.3	9.5	19.8	34.1
Food prepared by CU on trips	**100.0**	**4.7**	**7.2**	**9.7**	**9.2**	**9.3**	**16.9**	**43.1**

Note: Numbers may not add to total because of rounding.
Source: Calculations by New Strategist based on the 2001 Consumer Expenditure Survey

11. Groceries: Average spending by household type, 2001

(average annual spending of consumer units (CU) on groceries, by type of consumer unit, 2001)

	total consumer units	total married couples	married couples, no children	married couples with children total	oldest child under 6	oldest child 6 to 17	oldest child 18 or older	single parent, at least one child <18	single person
Number of consumer units									
(in thousands, add 000)	**110,339**	**55,840**	**23,119**	**28,055**	**5,020**	**15,145**	**7,890**	**6,629**	**32,783**
Average number of persons per CU	**2.5**	**3.2**	**2.0**	**3.9**	**3.5**	**4.2**	**3.8**	**3.0**	**1.0**
Average before-tax income of CU	**$47,507.00**	**$64,383.00**	**$57,498.00**	**$70,157.00**	**$65,555.00**	**$69,041.00**	**$75,374.00**	**$25,908.00**	**$26,650.00**
Average spending of CU, total	**39,518.46**	**50,822.43**	**43,947.64**	**56,284.40**	**51,364.65**	**57,178.28**	**57,829.73**	**29,633.51**	**23,506.51**
GROCERIES	**$3,085.52**	**$3,927.87**	**$3,145.60**	**$4,393.42**	**$3,855.40**	**$4,399.27**	**$4,780.57**	**$3,243.05**	**$1,532.77**
Cereals and bakery products	**452.19**	**574.88**	**442.11**	**666.66**	**567.40**	**682.46**	**705.97**	**507.70**	**224.24**
Cereals and cereal products	156.46	197.23	140.87	235.36	213.96	238.15	245.18	198.53	75.11
Flour	8.01	10.16	7.19	11.21	11.24	10.18	13.41	9.25	3.40
Prepared flour mixes	12.89	16.69	12.70	19.90	16.70	21.00	19.87	15.97	5.83
Ready-to-eat and cooked cereals	86.04	109.28	78.93	132.55	121.19	138.37	128.31	110.18	43.48
Rice	19.95	25.33	15.05	30.60	27.38	28.53	37.50	24.94	7.28
Pasta, cornmeal, other cereal products	29.57	35.78	27.00	41.11	37.46	40.06	46.08	38.19	15.11
Bakery products	295.73	377.65	301.25	431.30	353.44	444.31	460.79	309.17	149.13
Bread	85.37	107.41	91.63	116.68	98.89	116.86	129.51	79.96	47.35
White bread	36.64	45.46	36.39	50.52	39.81	51.14	57.12	38.65	18.74
Crackers and cookies	70.18	88.66	70.65	103.04	86.10	107.82	105.19	73.49	37.36
Cookies	46.13	57.86	44.43	68.42	55.61	70.37	73.70	49.64	24.48
Crackers	24.05	30.80	26.22	34.61	30.49	37.45	31.50	23.85	12.88
Frozen and refrigerated bakery products	26.06	34.71	24.93	41.87	30.28	47.80	37.59	31.75	11.21
Other bakery products	114.11	146.86	114.03	169.71	138.17	171.83	188.50	123.97	53.21
Biscuits and rolls	39.34	51.98	42.71	58.04	40.87	58.65	69.45	37.34	18.81
Cakes and cupcakes	33.80	42.55	30.28	51.50	49.20	52.35	51.36	40.77	14.35
Bread and cracker products	4.05	5.26	4.23	6.30	7.35	5.54	7.19	4.25	1.71
Sweetrolls, coffee cakes, doughnuts	26.32	33.38	23.64	40.18	28.07	42.39	44.37	30.10	12.93
Pies, tarts, turnovers	10.60	13.68	13.18	13.68	12.68	12.90	16.13	11.50	5.40
Meats, poultry, fish, and eggs	**827.97**	**1,059.94**	**877.44**	**1,137.97**	**942.42**	**1,118.88**	**1,324.67**	**935.70**	**368.58**
Beef	248.06	323.35	279.31	341.56	262.24	344.52	394.00	287.68	102.53
Ground beef	90.48	113.49	88.83	128.67	99.19	131.06	145.36	109.94	39.77
Roast	44.44	61.40	54.03	62.90	35.53	62.91	83.20	45.20	13.82
Chuck roast	15.03	20.33	14.83	23.22	14.29	24.30	27.50	15.32	5.37
Round roast	11.88	16.05	14.04	17.23	9.02	16.25	25.44	9.36	3.77
Other roast	17.53	25.02	25.17	22.46	12.22	22.37	30.27	20.51	4.68
Steak	92.73	122.74	115.34	122.71	109.86	123.77	129.94	104.56	40.22
Round steak	18.21	24.45	22.80	23.88	22.99	21.98	28.66	18.27	6.72
Sirloin steak	25.37	32.49	26.42	32.89	32.20	34.38	30.15	32.23	11.55
Other steak	49.15	65.81	66.13	65.94	54.66	67.40	71.14	54.06	21.96
Pork	177.31	229.36	194.74	240.45	197.97	234.83	284.21	202.80	73.70
Bacon	29.30	37.88	32.67	39.36	37.06	38.75	42.39	37.37	14.42
Pork chops	42.16	52.74	39.31	59.59	53.82	57.14	69.21	51.89	15.86
Ham	39.98	51.85	47.99	51.85	45.50	49.88	60.86	40.31	17.18
Ham, not canned	38.24	49.57	45.57	49.62	43.42	48.00	57.75	39.03	16.53
Canned ham	1.74	2.28	2.42	2.23	2.09	1.88	3.11	1.27	0.65
Sausage	25.52	32.85	27.55	33.68	23.45	36.00	36.24	31.48	10.71
Other pork	40.34	54.04	47.22	55.97	38.14	53.07	75.50	41.74	15.53
Other meats	102.06	132.06	102.18	151.81	125.92	151.69	171.27	109.06	47.11
Frankfurters	22.01	28.16	19.83	34.01	26.95	36.46	33.92	26.74	9.81
Lunch meats (cold cuts)	70.88	90.85	74.10	102.55	89.32	99.97	117.96	76.95	33.33
Bologna, liverwurst, salami	25.40	31.67	27.11	33.92	31.43	31.79	40.41	31.99	12.51
Lamb, organ meats, and others	9.17	13.05	8.24	15.25	9.64	15.26	19.39	5.37	3.98

	total consumer units	total married couples	married couples, no children	married couples with children				single parent, at least one child <18	single person
				total	oldest child under 6	oldest child 6 to 17	oldest child 18 or older		
Poultry	$151.87	$190.82	$143.02	$217.40	$204.52	$210.80	$241.33	$176.26	$67.72
Fresh and frozen chicken	119.55	149.74	105.39	175.52	168.02	173.95	184.50	140.72	53.12
Fresh and frozen whole chicken	35.75	44.64	29.80	52.15	48.08	50.29	59.23	40.16	15.06
Fresh and frozen chicken parts	83.80	105.11	75.59	123.37	119.95	123.65	125.28	100.57	38.05
Other poultry	32.32	41.08	37.63	41.88	36.49	36.85	56.82	35.54	14.60
Fish and seafood	113.67	141.73	123.23	142.93	113.24	135.01	182.21	120.88	58.42
Canned fish and seafood	15.11	17.94	14.96	19.59	14.85	18.99	24.44	14.76	9.77
Fresh fish and shellfish	63.07	77.81	66.74	78.14	65.47	69.42	106.52	65.14	33.42
Frozen fish and shellfish	35.49	45.98	41.53	45.20	32.92	46.59	51.26	40.98	15.24
Eggs	34.99	42.61	34.95	43.83	38.53	42.04	51.65	39.03	19.09
Dairy products	**331.69**	**422.64**	**318.70**	**490.78**	**449.46**	**492.72**	**517.24**	**324.60**	**169.12**
Fresh milk and cream	135.85	172.79	120.64	205.71	196.08	206.06	212.10	134.05	68.03
Fresh milk, all types	123.50	156.82	106.90	188.76	181.86	189.98	191.24	124.72	61.98
Cream	12.35	15.97	13.74	16.95	14.22	16.09	20.86	9.33	6.04
Other dairy products	195.84	249.85	198.06	285.07	253.38	286.65	305.14	190.55	101.10
Butter	21.55	26.39	21.50	28.29	27.71	26.98	31.57	22.16	12.62
Cheese	93.39	119.06	95.44	135.14	122.02	132.78	150.01	86.38	47.09
Ice cream and related products	56.79	73.41	57.62	84.47	62.68	90.91	86.63	59.48	27.95
Miscellaneous dairy products	24.11	31.00	23.50	37.17	40.97	35.98	36.93	22.53	13.44
Fruits and vegetables	**521.74**	**658.21**	**553.99**	**712.95**	**646.96**	**696.64**	**797.42**	**498.89**	**285.01**
Fresh fruits	160.41	203.59	174.72	218.36	204.25	210.58	245.76	142.04	90.93
Apples	30.83	39.82	32.51	44.63	39.04	46.04	45.72	30.94	15.05
Bananas	31.30	38.20	33.26	40.63	38.53	38.68	46.43	28.58	18.89
Oranges	18.62	22.45	18.50	23.89	17.82	24.88	26.24	20.97	11.25
Citrus fruits, excl. oranges	13.21	17.56	14.61	18.56	17.00	17.76	21.47	9.15	7.12
Other fresh fruits	66.45	85.56	75.85	90.65	91.87	83.23	105.91	52.40	38.62
Fresh vegetables	161.62	203.90	175.58	213.41	179.13	204.95	257.28	149.39	86.18
Potatoes	30.09	37.51	32.53	38.07	31.76	37.43	44.15	28.78	15.88
Lettuce	20.82	26.81	22.55	28.58	22.86	27.70	34.75	22.49	10.55
Tomatoes	30.03	37.81	31.03	41.44	35.24	40.60	47.88	28.55	15.75
Other fresh vegetables	80.68	101.77	89.47	105.32	89.26	99.22	130.50	69.57	44.00
Processed fruits	116.03	144.31	114.46	163.72	155.97	162.93	171.19	118.82	65.15
Frozen fruits and fruit juices	13.85	17.88	13.94	21.00	16.99	21.01	23.95	12.75	7.56
Frozen orange juice	7.61	10.08	8.33	11.68	9.99	12.12	12.00	5.24	4.27
Frozen fruits	2.53	3.31	2.82	3.73	0.71	3.64	6.19	2.00	1.37
Frozen fruit juices	3.72	4.50	2.78	5.58	6.29	5.25	5.76	5.51	1.92
Canned fruits	16.27	21.73	18.04	23.48	24.21	23.16	23.62	14.23	8.47
Dried fruits	5.54	7.31	7.03	7.46	5.87	7.50	8.55	3.87	2.74
Fresh fruit juice	24.86	29.83	25.55	32.14	28.52	30.31	38.83	24.03	15.29
Canned and bottled fruit juice	55.50	67.57	49.90	79.64	80.38	80.95	76.24	63.93	31.08
Processed vegetables	83.68	106.41	89.23	117.46	107.61	118.19	123.18	88.64	42.75
Frozen vegetables	27.50	35.58	30.30	39.11	37.00	39.26	40.34	30.43	13.57
Canned and dried vegetables and juices	56.18	70.83	58.94	78.35	70.61	78.93	82.84	58.21	29.18
Canned beans	12.60	16.25	12.60	18.73	24.04	16.97	18.63	11.14	6.75
Canned corn	7.13	8.89	6.19	10.70	9.80	11.00	10.70	10.13	2.92
Canned miscellaneous vegetables	17.58	22.47	20.91	22.68	18.20	23.64	23.91	17.72	9.06
Dried beans	2.28	2.69	2.01	2.98	3.04	2.27	4.48	3.54	1.14
Dried miscellaneous vegetables	7.58	9.33	7.95	10.31	7.32	9.84	13.53	7.46	4.53
Fresh and canned vegetable juices	7.65	9.07	8.01	9.90	7.11	10.44	10.80	7.36	4.40
Sugar and other sweets	**115.96**	**148.86**	**118.39**	**168.20**	**131.49**	**171.95**	**187.29**	**118.44**	**59.28**
Candy and chewing gum	73.49	94.88	73.03	109.73	78.66	114.18	123.12	68.84	38.84
Sugar	17.91	22.87	18.36	24.57	23.35	22.30	30.41	21.34	7.92
Artificial sweeteners	5.04	6.18	6.70	5.26	4.12	4.89	6.93	4.51	3.48
Jams, preserves, other sweets	19.52	24.93	20.29	28.64	25.35	30.59	26.83	23.75	9.04

	total consumer units	total married couples	married couples, no children	married couples with children				single parent, at least one child <18	single person
				total	oldest child under 6	oldest child 6 to 17	oldest child 18 or older		
Fats and oils	**$86.76**	**$109.59**	**$91.77**	**$118.33**	**$94.11**	**$115.33**	**$142.84**	**$93.99**	**$41.80**
Margarine	11.43	14.89	13.59	15.52	11.49	14.82	20.01	12.24	5.79
Fats and oils	24.53	30.24	23.81	31.70	23.78	31.25	38.55	26.44	11.84
Salad dressings	28.02	35.85	30.83	39.12	31.75	39.50	43.74	29.80	12.77
Nondairy cream and imitation milk	10.09	12.83	11.89	13.25	8.81	12.60	17.97	8.57	5.18
Peanut butter	12.69	15.77	11.65	18.75	18.28	17.15	22.58	16.95	6.23
Miscellaneous foods	**454.72**	**579.29**	**435.94**	**685.06**	**695.81**	**689.77**	**666.81**	**487.33**	**228.74**
Frozen prepared foods	96.19	115.45	89.96	137.67	112.84	144.09	142.14	113.04	58.57
Frozen meals	28.65	29.90	29.00	30.38	20.13	30.82	37.05	32.82	24.27
Other frozen prepared foods	67.54	85.55	60.97	107.28	92.71	113.27	105.08	80.22	34.30
Canned and packaged soups	37.27	45.35	36.70	51.97	45.85	49.95	60.90	37.96	23.53
Potato chips, nuts, and other snacks	97.37	127.32	100.65	146.74	120.16	158.12	141.69	98.63	43.92
Potato chips and other snacks	75.56	98.60	70.57	119.38	99.01	132.30	106.41	81.16	31.52
Nuts	21.81	28.73	30.09	27.35	21.15	25.83	35.28	17.47	12.40
Condiments and seasonings	84.05	111.14	89.54	125.18	105.67	125.97	137.93	87.30	38.03
Salt, spices, and other seasonings	19.83	26.07	21.85	28.15	22.71	29.31	29.67	20.14	9.57
Olives, pickles, relishes	9.97	13.29	11.25	14.41	10.63	15.16	15.60	8.12	4.96
Sauces and gravies	36.84	48.48	37.35	55.93	49.80	55.56	61.27	42.73	14.94
Baking needs and miscellaneous products	17.41	23.30	19.10	26.69	22.53	25.94	31.40	16.31	8.56
Other canned/packaged prepared foods	139.85	180.02	119.09	223.51	311.29	211.64	184.15	150.41	64.69
Prepared salads	19.55	25.17	22.35	27.46	24.41	27.37	29.90	13.49	11.80
Prepared desserts	10.15	13.64	12.76	14.24	11.08	13.91	17.33	7.69	4.48
Baby food	23.62	34.59	8.88	53.20	158.14	31.96	21.51	33.40	3.60
Miscellaneous prepared foods	86.24	106.07	74.63	127.89	117.40	137.27	115.26	95.83	44.82
Nonalcoholic beverages	256.16	320.64	249.62	362.26	286.37	374.34	392.30	261.86	134.21
Cola	87.41	109.94	85.43	123.53	102.75	127.69	129.90	90.66	42.11
Other carbonated drinks	46.14	56.77	42.16	66.29	51.74	67.94	73.50	53.28	24.28
Coffee	38.35	48.14	46.17	46.03	28.64	45.53	60.01	24.14	23.81
Roasted coffee	24.98	32.33	30.96	31.19	19.39	30.23	42.05	15.59	14.32
Instant and freeze-dried coffee	13.37	15.80	15.21	14.84	9.25	15.30	17.97	8.55	9.49
Noncarbonated fruit-flavored drinks	20.36	26.37	12.78	36.14	26.15	40.63	33.78	27.68	7.28
Tea	17.57	21.47	19.95	22.00	19.19	21.10	26.02	20.48	9.19
Other nonalcoholic beverages and ice	45.67	56.89	41.95	67.57	55.59	71.28	68.38	45.61	27.29
Food prepared by CU on trips	**38.33**	**53.82**	**57.64**	**51.21**	**41.38**	**57.18**	**46.02**	**14.53**	**21.78**

Source: Bureau of Labor Statistics, unpublished tables from the 2001 Consumer Expenditure Survey

12. Groceries: Indexed spending by household type, 2001

(indexed average annual spending of consumer units (CU) on groceries, by type of consumer unit, 2001; index definition: an index of 100 is the average for all consumer units; an index of 132 means that spending by consumer units in that group is 32 percent above the average for all consumer units; an index of 68 indicates spending that is 32 percent below the average for all consumer units)

	total consumer units	total married couples	married couples, no children	married couples with children total	oldest child under 6	oldest child 6 to 17	oldest child 18 or older	single parent, at least one child <18	single person
Average spending of CU, total	$39,518	$50,822	$43,948	$56,284	$51,365	$57,178	$57,830	$29,634	$23,507
Average spending of CU, index	100	129	111	142	130	145	146	75	60
GROCERIES	100	127	102	142	125	143	155	105	50
Cereals and bakery products	100	127	98	147	126	151	156	112	50
Cereals and cereal products	100	126	90	150	137	152	157	127	48
Flour	100	127	90	140	140	127	167	116	42
Prepared flour mixes	100	130	99	154	130	163	154	124	45
Ready-to-eat and cooked cereals	100	127	92	154	141	161	149	128	51
Rice	100	127	75	153	137	143	188	125	37
Pasta, cornmeal, and other cereal products	100	121	91	139	127	136	156	129	51
Bakery products	100	128	102	146	120	150	156	105	50
Bread	100	126	107	137	116	137	152	94	56
White bread	100	124	99	138	109	140	156	106	51
Crackers and cookies	100	126	101	147	123	154	150	105	53
Cookies	100	125	96	148	121	153	160	108	53
Crackers	100	128	109	144	127	156	131	99	54
Frozen and refrigerated bakery products	100	133	96	161	116	183	144	122	43
Other bakery products	100	129	100	149	121	151	165	109	47
Biscuits and rolls	100	132	109	148	104	149	177	95	48
Cakes and cupcakes	100	126	90	152	146	155	152	121	43
Bread and cracker products	100	130	104	156	182	137	178	105	42
Sweetrolls, coffee cakes, doughnuts	100	127	90	153	107	161	169	114	49
Pies, tarts, turnovers	100	129	124	129	120	122	152	109	51
Meats, poultry, fish, and eggs	100	128	106	137	114	135	160	113	45
Beef	100	130	113	138	106	139	159	116	41
Ground beef	100	125	98	142	110	145	161	122	44
Roast	100	138	122	142	80	142	187	102	31
Chuck roast	100	135	99	155	95	162	183	102	36
Round roast	100	135	118	145	76	137	214	79	32
Other roast	100	143	144	128	70	128	173	117	27
Steak	100	132	124	132	119	134	140	113	43
Round steak	100	134	125	131	126	121	157	100	37
Sirloin steak	100	128	104	130	127	136	119	127	46
Other steak	100	134	135	134	111	137	145	110	45
Pork	100	129	110	136	112	132	160	114	42
Bacon	100	129	112	134	127	132	145	128	49
Pork chops	100	125	93	141	128	136	164	123	38
Ham	100	130	120	130	114	125	152	101	43
Ham, not canned	100	130	119	130	114	126	151	102	43
Canned ham	100	131	139	128	120	108	179	73	37
Sausage	100	129	108	132	92	141	142	123	42
Other pork	100	134	117	139	95	132	187	104	39
Other meats	100	129	100	149	123	149	168	107	46
Frankfurters	100	128	90	155	122	166	154	122	45
Lunch meats (cold cuts)	100	128	105	145	126	141	166	109	47
Bologna, liverwurst, salami	100	125	107	134	124	125	159	126	49
Lamb, organ meats, and others	100	142	90	166	105	166	212	59	43

	total consumer units	total married couples	married couples, no children	married couples with children total	oldest child under 6	oldest child 6 to 17	oldest child 18 or older	single parent, at least one child <18	single person
Poultry	100	126	94	143	135	139	159	116	45
Fresh and frozen chicken	100	125	88	147	141	146	154	118	44
Fresh and frozen whole chicken	100	125	83	146	135	141	166	112	42
Fresh and frozen chicken parts	100	125	90	147	143	148	150	120	45
Other poultry	100	127	116	130	113	114	176	110	45
Fish and seafood	100	125	108	126	100	119	160	106	51
Canned fish and seafood	100	119	99	130	98	126	162	98	65
Fresh fish and shellfish	100	123	106	124	104	110	169	103	53
Frozen fish and shellfish	100	130	117	127	93	131	144	116	43
Eggs	100	122	100	125	110	120	148	112	55
Dairy products	**100**	**127**	**96**	**148**	**136**	**149**	**156**	**98**	**51**
Fresh milk and cream	100	127	89	151	144	152	156	99	50
Fresh milk, all types	100	127	87	153	147	154	155	101	50
Cream	100	129	111	137	115	130	169	76	49
Other dairy products	100	128	101	146	129	146	156	97	52
Butter	100	123	100	131	129	125	147	103	59
Cheese	100	128	102	145	131	142	161	93	50
Ice cream and related products	100	129	102	149	110	160	153	105	49
Miscellaneous dairy products	100	129	98	154	170	149	153	93	56
Fruits and vegetables	**100**	**126**	**106**	**137**	**124**	**134**	**153**	**96**	**55**
Fresh fruits	100	127	109	136	127	131	153	89	57
Apples	100	129	105	145	127	149	148	100	49
Bananas	100	122	106	130	123	124	148	91	60
Oranges	100	121	99	128	96	134	141	113	60
Citrus fruits, excl. oranges	100	133	111	141	129	134	163	69	54
Other fresh fruits	100	129	114	136	138	125	159	79	58
Fresh vegetables	100	126	109	132	111	127	159	92	53
Potatoes	100	125	108	127	106	124	147	96	53
Lettuce	100	129	108	137	110	133	167	108	51
Tomatoes	100	126	103	138	117	135	159	95	52
Other fresh vegetables	100	126	111	131	111	123	162	86	55
Processed fruits	100	124	99	141	134	140	148	102	56
Frozen fruits and fruit juices	100	129	101	152	123	152	173	92	55
Frozen orange juice	100	133	110	154	131	159	158	69	56
Frozen fruits	100	131	112	147	28	144	245	79	54
Frozen fruit juices	100	121	75	150	169	141	155	148	52
Canned fruits	100	134	111	144	149	142	145	88	52
Dried fruits	100	132	127	135	106	135	154	70	50
Fresh fruit juice	100	120	103	129	115	122	156	97	62
Canned and bottled fruit juice	100	122	90	144	145	146	137	115	56
Processed vegetables	100	127	107	140	129	141	147	106	51
Frozen vegetables	100	129	110	142	135	143	147	111	49
Canned and dried vegetables and juices	100	126	105	140	126	141	148	104	52
Canned beans	100	129	100	149	191	135	148	88	54
Canned corn	100	125	87	150	137	154	150	142	41
Canned miscellaneous vegetables	100	128	119	129	104	135	136	101	52
Dried beans	100	118	88	131	133	100	197	155	50
Dried miscellaneous vegetables	100	123	105	136	97	130	179	98	60
Fresh and canned vegetable juices	100	119	105	129	93	137	141	96	58
Sugar and other sweets	**100**	**128**	**102**	**145**	**113**	**148**	**162**	**102**	**51**
Candy and chewing gum	100	129	99	149	107	155	168	94	53
Sugar	100	128	103	137	130	125	170	119	44
Artificial sweeteners	100	123	133	104	82	97	138	90	69
Jams, preserves, other sweets	100	128	104	147	130	157	137	122	46

	total consumer units	total married couples	married couples, no children	married couples with children total	oldest child under 6	oldest child 6 to 17	oldest child 18 or older	single parent, at least one child <18	single person
Fats and oils	**100**	**126**	**106**	**136**	**109**	**133**	**165**	**108**	**48**
Margarine	100	130	119	136	101	130	175	107	51
Fats and oils	100	123	97	129	97	127	157	108	48
Salad dressings	100	128	110	140	113	141	156	106	46
Nondairy cream and imitation milk	100	127	118	131	87	125	178	85	51
Peanut butter	100	124	92	148	144	135	178	134	49
Miscellaneous foods	**100**	**127**	**96**	**151**	**153**	**152**	**147**	**107**	**50**
Frozen prepared foods	100	120	94	143	117	150	148	118	61
Frozen meals	100	104	101	106	70	108	129	115	85
Other frozen prepared foods	100	127	90	159	137	168	156	119	51
Canned and packaged soups	100	122	99	139	123	134	163	102	63
Potato chips, nuts, and other snacks	100	131	103	151	123	162	146	101	45
Potato chips and other snacks	100	131	93	158	131	175	141	107	42
Nuts	100	132	138	125	97	118	162	80	57
Condiments and seasonings	100	132	107	149	126	150	164	104	45
Salt, spices, and other seasonings	100	132	110	142	115	148	150	102	48
Olives, pickles, relishes	100	133	113	145	107	152	157	81	50
Sauces and gravies	100	132	101	152	135	151	166	116	41
Baking needs and miscellaneous products	100	134	110	153	129	149	180	94	49
Other canned/packaged prepared foods	100	129	85	160	223	151	132	108	46
Prepared salads	100	129	114	141	125	140	153	69	60
Prepared desserts	100	134	126	140	109	137	171	76	44
Baby food	100	146	38	225	670	135	91	141	15
Miscellaneous prepared foods	100	123	87	148	136	159	134	111	52
Nonalcoholic beverages	100	125	97	141	112	146	153	102	52
Cola	100	126	98	141	118	146	149	104	48
Other carbonated drinks	100	123	91	144	112	147	159	116	53
Coffee	100	126	120	120	75	119	157	63	62
Roasted coffee	100	129	124	125	78	121	168	62	57
Instant and freeze-dried coffee	100	118	114	111	69	114	134	64	71
Noncarbonated fruit-flavored drinks	100	130	63	178	128	200	166	136	36
Tea	100	122	114	125	109	120	148	117	52
Other nonalcoholic beverages and ice	100	125	92	148	122	156	150	100	60
Food prepared by CU on trips	**100**	**140**	**150**	**134**	**108**	**149**	**120**	**38**	**57**

Source: Calculations by New Strategist based on the 2001 Consumer Expenditure Survey

13. Groceries: Indexed per capita spending by household type, 2001

(indexed average annual per capita spending of consumer units (CU) on groceries, by type of consumer unit, 2001; index definition: an index of 100 is the average for all consumer units; an index of 132 means that spending by consumer units in that group is 32 percent above the average for all consumer units; an index of 68 indicates spending that is 32 percent below the average for all consumer units)

	total consumer units	total married couples	married couples, no children	married couples with children				single parent, at least one child <18	single person
				total	oldest child under 6	oldest child 6 to 17	oldest child 18 or older		
Per capita spending of CU, total	$15,807	$15,882	$21,974	$14,432	$14,676	$13,614	$15,218	$9,878	$23,507
Per capita spending of CU, index	100	101	139	91	93	86	96	63	149
GROCERIES	**100**	**100**	**127**	**91**	**89**	**85**	**102**	**88**	**124**
Cereals and bakery products	**100**	**99**	**122**	**95**	**90**	**90**	**103**	**94**	**124**
Cereals and cereal products	100	99	113	96	98	91	103	106	120
Flour	100	99	112	90	100	76	110	96	106
Prepared flour mixes	100	101	123	99	93	97	101	103	113
Ready-to-eat and cooked cereals	100	99	115	99	101	96	98	107	126
Rice	100	99	94	98	98	85	124	104	91
Pasta, cornmeal, and other cereal products	100	95	114	89	91	81	103	108	128
Bakery products	100	100	127	94	85	89	103	87	126
Bread	100	98	134	88	83	82	100	78	139
White bread	100	97	124	88	78	83	103	88	128
Crackers and cookies	100	99	126	94	88	91	99	87	133
Cookies	100	98	120	95	86	91	105	90	133
Crackers	100	100	136	92	91	93	86	83	134
Frozen and refrigerated bakery products	100	104	120	103	83	109	95	102	108
Other bakery products	100	101	125	95	87	90	109	91	117
Biscuits and rolls	100	103	136	95	74	89	116	79	120
Cakes and cupcakes	100	98	112	98	104	92	100	101	106
Bread and cracker products	100	102	131	100	130	81	117	87	106
Sweetrolls, coffee cakes, doughnuts	100	99	112	98	76	96	111	95	123
Pies, tarts, turnovers	100	101	155	83	85	72	100	90	127
Meats, poultry, fish, and eggs	**100**	**100**	**133**	**88**	**81**	**80**	**105**	**94**	**111**
Beef	100	102	141	88	76	83	105	97	103
Ground beef	100	98	123	91	78	86	106	101	110
Roast	100	108	152	91	57	84	123	85	78
Chuck roast	100	106	123	99	68	96	120	85	89
Round roast	100	106	148	93	54	81	141	66	79
Other roast	100	112	180	82	50	76	114	98	67
Steak	100	103	156	85	85	79	92	94	108
Round steak	100	105	157	84	90	72	104	84	92
Sirloin steak	100	100	130	83	91	81	78	106	114
Other steak	100	105	168	86	79	82	95	92	112
Pork	100	101	137	87	80	79	106	95	104
Bacon	100	101	139	86	90	79	95	106	123
Pork chops	100	98	117	91	91	81	108	103	94
Ham	100	101	150	83	81	74	100	84	107
Ham, not canned	100	101	149	83	81	75	99	85	108
Canned ham	100	102	174	82	86	64	118	61	93
Sausage	100	101	135	85	66	84	93	103	105
Other pork	100	105	146	89	68	78	123	86	96
Other meats	100	101	125	95	88	89	110	89	115
Frankfurters	100	100	113	99	88	99	101	101	111
Lunch meats (cold cuts)	100	100	131	93	90	84	110	91	118
Bologna, liverwurst, salami	100	97	133	86	88	75	105	105	123
Lamb, organ meats, and others	100	111	112	107	75	99	139	49	109

	total consumer units	total married couples	married couples, no children	married couples with children				single parent, at least one child <18	single person
				total	oldest child under 6	oldest child 6 to 17	oldest child 18 or older		
Poultry	100	98	118	92	96	83	105	97	112
Fresh and frozen chicken	100	98	110	94	100	87	102	98	111
Fresh and frozen whole chicken	100	98	104	94	96	84	109	94	105
Fresh and frozen chicken parts	100	98	113	94	102	88	98	100	114
Other poultry	100	99	146	83	81	68	116	92	113
Fish and seafood	100	97	136	81	71	71	106	89	129
Canned fish and seafood	100	93	124	83	70	75	106	81	162
Fresh fish and shellfish	100	96	132	79	74	66	111	86	133
Frozen fish and shellfish	100	101	146	82	66	78	95	96	107
Eggs	100	95	125	80	79	72	97	93	136
Dairy products	**100**	**100**	**120**	**95**	**97**	**88**	**103**	**82**	**128**
Fresh milk and cream	100	99	111	97	103	90	103	82	125
Fresh milk, all types	100	99	108	98	105	92	102	84	126
Cream	100	101	139	88	82	78	111	63	122
Other dairy products	100	100	126	93	92	87	103	81	129
Butter	100	96	125	84	92	75	96	86	146
Cheese	100	100	128	93	93	85	106	77	126
Ice cream and related products	100	101	127	95	79	95	100	87	123
Miscellaneous dairy products	100	101	122	99	121	89	101	78	139
Fruits and vegetables	**100**	**99**	**133**	**88**	**89**	**80**	**101**	**80**	**137**
Fresh fruits	100	99	136	87	91	78	101	74	142
Apples	100	101	132	93	90	89	98	84	122
Bananas	100	95	133	83	88	74	98	76	151
Oranges	100	94	124	82	68	80	93	94	151
Citrus fruits, excl. oranges	100	104	138	90	92	80	107	58	135
Other fresh fruits	100	101	143	87	99	75	105	66	145
Fresh vegetables	100	99	136	85	79	76	105	77	133
Potatoes	100	97	135	81	75	74	97	80	132
Lettuce	100	101	135	88	78	79	110	90	127
Tomatoes	100	98	129	89	84	81	105	79	131
Other fresh vegetables	100	99	139	84	79	73	106	72	136
Processed fruits	100	97	123	90	96	84	97	85	140
Frozen fruits and fruit juices	100	101	126	97	88	90	114	77	137
Frozen orange juice	100	104	137	98	94	95	104	57	140
Frozen fruits	100	102	139	95	20	86	161	66	135
Frozen fruit juices	100	95	93	96	121	84	102	123	129
Canned fruits	100	104	139	93	106	85	96	73	130
Dried fruits	100	103	159	86	76	81	102	58	124
Fresh fruit juice	100	94	129	83	82	73	103	81	154
Canned and bottled fruit juice	100	95	112	92	103	87	90	96	140
Processed vegetables	100	99	133	90	92	84	97	88	128
Frozen vegetables	100	101	138	91	96	85	97	92	123
Canned and dried vegetables and juices	100	99	131	89	90	84	97	86	130
Canned beans	100	101	125	95	136	80	97	74	134
Canned corn	100	97	109	96	98	92	99	118	102
Canned miscellaneous vegetables	100	100	149	83	74	80	90	84	129
Dried beans	100	92	110	84	95	59	129	129	125
Dried miscellaneous vegetables	100	96	131	87	69	77	117	82	149
Fresh and canned vegetable juices	100	93	131	83	66	81	93	80	144
Sugar and other sweets	**100**	**100**	**128**	**93**	**81**	**88**	**106**	**85**	**128**
Candy and chewing gum	100	101	124	96	77	93	110	78	132
Sugar	100	100	128	88	93	74	112	99	111
Artificial sweeteners	100	96	166	67	58	58	91	75	173
Jams, preserves, other sweets	100	100	130	94	93	93	90	101	116

	total consumer units	total married couples	married couples, no children	married couples with children				single parent, at least one child <18	single person
				total	oldest child under 6	oldest child 6 to 17	oldest child 18 or older		
Fats and oils	**100**	**99**	**132**	**87**	**78**	**79**	**108**	**90**	**120**
Margarine	100	102	149	87	72	77	115	89	127
Fats and oils	100	96	121	83	69	76	103	90	121
Salad dressings	100	100	138	90	81	84	103	89	114
Nondairy cream and imitation milk	100	99	147	84	62	74	117	71	128
Peanut butter	100	97	115	95	103	80	117	111	123
Miscellaneous foods	**100**	**100**	**120**	**97**	**109**	**90**	**97**	**89**	**126**
Frozen prepared foods	100	94	117	92	84	89	97	98	152
Frozen meals	100	82	127	68	50	64	85	96	212
Other frozen prepared foods	100	99	113	102	98	100	102	99	127
Canned and packaged soups	100	95	123	89	88	80	108	85	158
Potato chips, nuts, and other snacks	100	102	129	97	88	97	96	84	113
Potato chips and other snacks	100	102	117	101	94	104	93	90	104
Nuts	100	103	173	80	69	71	106	67	142
Condiments and seasonings	100	103	133	96	90	89	108	87	113
Salt, spices, and other seasonings	100	103	138	91	82	88	98	85	121
Olives, pickles, relishes	100	104	141	93	76	91	103	68	124
Sauces and gravies	100	103	127	97	97	90	109	97	101
Baking needs and miscellaneous products	100	105	137	98	92	89	119	78	123
Other canned/packaged prepared foods	100	101	106	102	159	90	87	90	116
Prepared salads	100	101	143	90	89	83	101	58	151
Prepared desserts	100	105	157	90	78	82	112	63	110
Baby food	100	114	47	144	478	81	60	118	38
Miscellaneous prepared foods	100	96	108	95	97	95	88	93	130
Nonalcoholic beverages	100	98	122	91	80	87	101	85	131
Cola	100	98	122	91	84	87	98	86	120
Other carbonated drinks	100	96	114	92	80	88	105	96	132
Coffee	100	98	151	77	53	71	103	53	155
Roasted coffee	100	101	155	80	55	72	111	52	143
Instant and freeze-dried coffee	100	92	142	71	49	68	88	53	177
Noncarbonated fruit-flavored drinks	100	101	79	114	92	119	109	113	89
Tea	100	96	142	80	78	72	97	97	131
Other nonalcoholic beverages and ice	100	97	115	95	87	93	99	83	149
Food prepared by CU on trips	**100**	**110**	**188**	**86**	**77**	**89**	**79**	**32**	**142**

Note: Per capita indexes account for household size and show how much each person in a particular household demographic segment spends relative to a person in the average household.

Source: Calculations by New Strategist based on the 2001 Consumer Expenditure Survey

14. Groceries: Total spending by household type, 2001

(total annual spending on groceries, by consumer unit (CU) type, 2001; numbers in thousands)

	total consumer units	total married couples	married couples, no children	married couples with children total	oldest child under 6	oldest child 6 to 17	oldest child 18 or older	single parent, at least one child <18	single person
Number of consumer units	110,339	55,840	23,119	28,055	5,020	15,145	7,890	6,629	32,783
Total spending of all CUs	$4,360,427,358	$2,837,924,491	$1,016,025,489	$1,579,058,842	$257,850,543	$865,965,051	$456,276,570	$196,440,538	$770,613,917
GROCERIES	$340,453,191	$219,332,261	$72,723,126	$123,257,398	$19,354,108	$66,626,944	$37,718,697	$21,498,179	$50,248,799
Cereals and bakery products	49,894,192	32,101,299	10,221,141	18,703,146	2,848,348	10,335,857	5,570,103	3,365,543	7,351,260
Cereals and cereal products	17,263,640	11,013,323	3,256,774	6,603,025	1,074,079	3,606,782	1,934,470	1,316,055	2,462,331
Flour	883,815	567,334	166,226	314,497	56,425	154,176	105,805	61,318	111,462
Prepared flour mixes	1,422,270	931,970	293,611	558,295	83,834	318,045	156,774	105,865	191,125
Ready-to-eat and cooked cereals	9,493,568	6,102,195	1,824,783	3,718,690	608,374	2,095,614	1,012,366	730,383	1,425,405
Rice	2,201,263	1,414,427	347,941	858,483	137,448	432,087	295,875	165,327	238,660
Pasta, cornmeal, other cereal pdts.	3,262,724	1,997,955	624,213	1,153,341	188,049	606,709	363,571	253,162	495,351
Bakery products	32,630,553	21,087,976	6,964,599	12,100,122	1,774,269	6,729,075	3,635,633	2,049,488	4,888,929
Bread	9,419,640	5,997,774	2,118,394	3,273,457	496,428	1,769,845	1,021,834	530,055	1,552,275
White bread	4,042,821	2,538,486	841,300	1,417,339	199,846	774,515	450,677	256,211	614,353
Crackers and cookies	7,743,591	4,950,774	1,633,357	2,890,787	432,222	1,632,934	829,949	487,165	1,224,773
Cookies	5,089,938	3,230,902	1,027,177	1,919,523	279,162	1,065,754	581,493	329,064	802,528
Crackers	2,653,653	1,719,872	606,180	970,984	153,060	567,180	248,535	158,102	422,245
Frozen, refrigerated bakery products	2,875,434	1,938,206	576,357	1,174,663	152,006	723,931	296,585	210,471	367,497
Other bakery products	12,590,783	8,200,662	2,636,260	4,761,214	693,613	2,602,365	1,487,265	821,797	1,744,383
Biscuits and rolls	4,340,736	2,902,563	987,413	1,628,312	205,167	888,254	547,961	247,527	616,648
Cakes and cupcakes	3,729,458	2,375,992	700,043	1,444,833	246,984	792,841	405,230	270,264	470,436
Bread and cracker products	446,873	293,718	97,793	176,747	36,897	83,903	56,729	28,173	56,059
Sweetrolls, coffee cakes, doughnuts	2,904,123	1,863,939	546,533	1,127,250	140,911	641,997	350,079	199,533	423,884
Pies, tarts, turnovers	1,169,593	763,891	304,708	383,792	63,654	195,371	127,266	76,234	177,028
Meats, poultry, fish, and eggs	91,357,382	59,187,050	20,285,535	31,925,748	4,730,948	16,945,438	10,451,646	6,202,755	12,083,158
Beef	27,370,692	18,055,864	6,457,368	9,582,466	1,316,445	5,217,755	3,108,660	1,907,031	3,361,241
Ground beef	9,983,473	6,337,282	2,053,661	3,609,837	497,934	1,984,904	1,146,890	728,792	1,303,780
Roast	4,903,465	3,428,576	1,249,120	1,764,660	178,361	952,772	656,448	299,631	453,061
Chuck roast	1,658,395	1,135,227	342,855	651,437	71,736	368,024	216,975	101,556	176,045
Round roast	1,310,827	896,232	324,591	483,388	45,280	246,106	200,722	62,047	123,592
Other roast	1,934,243	1,397,117	581,905	630,115	61,344	338,794	238,830	135,961	153,424
Steak	10,231,736	6,853,802	2,666,546	3,442,629	551,497	1,874,497	1,025,227	693,128	1,318,532
Round steak	2,009,273	1,365,288	527,113	669,953	115,410	332,887	226,127	121,112	220,302
Sirloin steak	2,799,300	1,814,242	610,804	922,729	161,644	520,685	237,884	213,653	378,644
Other steak	5,423,162	3,674,830	1,528,860	1,849,947	274,393	1,020,773	561,295	358,364	719,915
Pork	19,564,208	12,807,462	4,502,194	6,745,825	993,809	3,556,500	2,242,417	1,344,361	2,416,107
Bacon	3,232,933	2,115,219	755,298	1,104,245	186,041	586,869	334,457	247,726	472,731
Pork chops	4,651,892	2,945,002	908,808	1,671,797	270,176	865,385	546,067	343,979	519,938
Ham	4,411,353	2,895,304	1,109,481	1,454,652	228,410	755,433	480,185	267,215	563,212
Ham, not canned	4,219,363	2,767,989	1,053,533	1,392,089	217,968	726,960	455,648	258,730	541,903
Canned ham	191,990	127,315	55,948	62,563	10,492	28,473	24,538	8,419	21,309
Sausage	2,815,851	1,834,344	636,928	944,892	117,719	545,220	285,934	208,681	351,106
Other pork	4,451,075	3,017,594	1,091,679	1,570,238	191,463	803,745	595,695	276,695	509,120
Other meats	11,261,198	7,374,230	2,362,299	4,259,030	632,118	2,297,345	1,351,320	722,959	1,544,407
Frankfurters	2,428,561	1,572,454	458,450	954,151	135,289	552,187	267,629	177,260	321,601
Lunch meats (cold cuts)	7,820,828	5,073,064	1,713,118	2,877,040	448,386	1,514,046	930,704	510,102	1,092,657
Bologna, liverwurst, salami	2,802,611	1,768,453	626,756	951,626	157,779	481,460	318,835	212,062	410,115
Lamb, organ meats, and others	1,011,809	728,712	190,501	427,839	48,393	231,113	152,987	35,598	130,476

	total consumer units	total married couples	married couples, no children	married couples with children				single parent, at least one child <18	single person
				total	oldest child under 6	oldest child 6 to 17	oldest child 18 or older		
Poultry	$16,757,184	$10,655,389	$3,306,479	$6,099,157	$1,026,690	$3,192,566	$1,904,094	$1,168,428	$2,220,065
Fresh and frozen chicken	13,191,027	8,361,482	2,436,511	4,924,214	843,460	2,634,473	1,455,705	932,833	1,741,433
Fresh and frozen whole chicken	3,944,619	2,492,698	688,946	1,463,068	241,362	761,642	467,325	266,221	493,712
Fresh and frozen chicken parts	9,246,408	5,869,342	1,747,565	3,461,145	602,149	1,872,679	988,459	666,679	1,247,393
Other poultry	3,566,157	2,293,907	869,968	1,174,943	183,180	558,093	448,310	235,595	478,632
Fish and seafood	12,542,234	7,914,203	2,848,954	4,009,901	568,465	2,044,726	1,437,637	801,314	1,915,183
Canned fish and seafood	1,667,222	1,001,770	345,860	549,597	74,547	287,604	192,832	97,844	320,290
Fresh fish and shellfish	6,959,081	4,344,910	1,542,962	2,192,218	328,659	1,051,366	840,443	431,813	1,095,608
Frozen fish and shellfish	3,915,931	2,567,523	960,132	1,268,086	165,258	705,606	404,441	271,656	499,613
Eggs	3,860,762	2,379,342	808,009	1,229,651	193,421	636,696	407,519	258,730	625,828
Dairy products	**36,598,343**	**23,600,218**	**7,368,025**	**13,768,833**	**2,256,289**	**7,462,244**	**4,081,024**	**2,151,773**	**5,544,261**
Fresh milk and cream	14,989,553	9,648,594	2,789,076	5,771,194	984,322	3,120,779	1,673,469	888,617	2,230,228
Fresh milk, all types	13,626,867	8,756,829	2,471,421	5,295,662	912,937	2,877,247	1,508,884	826,769	2,031,890
Cream	1,362,687	891,765	317,655	475,532	71,384	243,683	164,585	61,849	198,009
Other dairy products	21,608,790	13,951,624	4,578,949	7,997,639	1,271,968	4,341,314	2,407,555	1,263,156	3,314,361
Butter	2,377,806	1,473,618	497,059	793,676	139,104	408,612	249,087	146,899	413,722
Cheese	10,304,559	6,648,310	2,206,477	3,791,353	612,540	2,010,953	1,183,579	572,613	1,543,752
Ice cream and related products	6,266,152	4,099,214	1,332,117	2,369,806	314,654	1,376,832	683,511	394,293	916,285
Miscellaneous dairy products	2,660,273	1,731,040	543,297	1,042,804	205,669	544,917	291,378	149,351	440,604
Fruits and vegetables	**57,568,270**	**36,754,446**	**12,807,695**	**20,001,812**	**3,247,739**	**10,550,613**	**6,291,644**	**3,307,142**	**9,343,483**
Fresh fruits	17,699,479	11,368,466	4,039,352	6,126,090	1,025,335	3,189,234	1,939,046	941,583	2,980,958
Apples	3,401,751	2,223,549	751,599	1,252,095	195,981	697,276	360,731	205,101	493,384
Bananas	3,453,611	2,133,088	768,938	1,139,875	193,421	585,809	366,333	189,457	619,271
Oranges	2,054,512	1,253,608	427,702	670,234	89,456	376,808	207,034	139,010	368,809
Citrus fruits, excl. oranges	1,457,578	980,550	337,769	520,701	85,340	268,975	169,398	60,655	233,415
Other fresh fruits	7,332,027	4,777,670	1,753,576	2,543,186	461,187	1,260,518	835,630	347,360	1,266,080
Fresh vegetables	17,832,989	11,385,776	4,059,234	5,987,218	899,233	3,103,968	2,029,939	990,306	2,825,239
Potatoes	3,320,101	2,094,558	752,061	1,068,054	159,435	566,877	348,344	190,783	520,594
Lettuce	2,297,258	1,497,070	521,334	801,812	114,757	419,517	274,178	149,086	345,861
Tomatoes	3,313,480	2,111,310	717,383	1,162,599	176,905	614,887	377,773	189,258	516,332
Other fresh vegetables	8,902,151	5,682,837	2,068,457	2,954,753	448,085	1,502,687	1,029,645	461,180	1,442,452
Processed fruits	12,802,634	8,058,270	2,646,201	4,593,165	782,969	2,467,575	1,350,689	787,658	2,135,813
Frozen fruits and fruit juices	1,528,195	998,419	322,279	589,155	85,290	318,197	188,966	84,520	247,840
Frozen orange juice	839,680	562,867	192,581	327,682	50,150	183,557	94,680	34,736	139,983
Frozen fruits	279,158	184,830	65,196	104,645	3,564	55,128	48,839	13,258	44,913
Frozen fruit juices	410,461	251,280	64,271	156,547	31,576	79,511	45,446	36,526	62,943
Canned fruits	1,795,216	1,213,403	417,067	658,731	121,534	350,758	186,362	94,331	277,672
Dried fruits	611,278	408,190	162,527	209,290	29,467	113,588	67,460	25,654	89,825
Fresh fruit juice	2,743,028	1,665,707	590,690	901,688	143,170	459,045	306,369	159,295	501,252
Canned and bottled fruit juice	6,123,815	3,773,109	1,153,638	2,234,300	403,508	1,225,988	601,534	423,792	1,018,896
Processed vegetables	9,233,168	5,941,934	2,062,908	3,295,340	540,202	1,789,988	971,890	587,595	1,401,473
Frozen vegetables	3,034,323	1,986,787	700,506	1,097,231	185,740	594,593	318,283	201,721	444,865
Canned, dried vegetables and juices	6,198,845	3,955,147	1,362,634	2,198,109	354,462	1,195,395	653,608	385,874	956,608
Canned beans	1,390,271	907,400	291,299	525,470	120,681	257,011	146,991	73,847	221,285
Canned corn	786,717	496,418	143,107	300,189	49,196	166,595	84,423	67,152	95,726
Canned miscellaneous vegetables	1,939,760	1,254,725	483,418	636,287	91,364	358,028	188,650	117,466	297,014
Dried beans	251,573	150,210	46,469	83,604	15,261	34,379	35,347	23,467	37,373
Dried miscellaneous vegetables	836,370	520,987	183,796	289,247	36,746	149,027	106,752	49,452	148,507
Fresh and canned vegetable juices	844,093	506,469	185,183	277,745	35,692	158,114	85,212	48,789	144,245
Sugar and other sweets	**12,794,910**	**8,312,342**	**2,737,058**	**4,718,851**	**660,080**	**2,604,183**	**1,477,718**	**785,139**	**1,943,376**
Candy and chewing gum	8,108,813	5,298,099	1,688,381	3,078,475	394,873	1,729,256	971,417	456,340	1,273,292
Sugar	1,976,172	1,277,061	424,465	689,311	117,217	337,734	239,935	141,463	259,641
Artificial sweeteners	556,109	345,091	154,897	147,569	20,682	74,059	54,678	29,897	114,085
Jams, preserves, other sweets	2,153,817	1,392,091	469,085	803,495	127,257	463,286	211,689	157,439	296,358

	total consumer units	total married couples	married couples, no children	married couples with children				single parent, at least one child <18	single person
				total	oldest child under 6	oldest child 6 to 17	oldest child 18 or older		
Fats and oils	**$9,573,012**	**$6,119,506**	**$2,121,631**	**$3,319,748**	**$472,432**	**$1,746,673**	**$1,127,008**	**$623,060**	**$1,370,329**
Margarine	1,261,175	831,458	314,187	435,414	57,680	224,449	157,879	81,139	189,814
Fats and oils	2,706,616	1,688,602	550,463	889,344	119,376	473,281	304,160	175,271	388,151
Salad dressings	3,091,699	2,001,864	712,759	1,097,512	159,385	598,228	345,109	197,544	418,639
Nondairy cream and imitation milk	1,113,321	716,427	274,885	371,729	44,226	190,827	141,783	56,811	169,816
Peanut butter	1,400,202	880,597	269,336	526,031	91,766	259,737	178,156	112,362	204,238
Miscellaneous foods	**50,173,350**	**32,347,554**	**10,078,497**	**19,219,358**	**3,492,966**	**10,446,567**	**5,261,131**	**3,230,511**	**7,498,783**
Frozen prepared foods	10,613,508	6,446,728	2,079,785	3,862,332	566,457	2,182,243	1,121,485	749,342	1,920,100
Frozen meals	3,161,212	1,669,616	670,451	852,311	101,053	466,769	292,325	217,564	795,643
Other frozen prepared foods	7,452,296	4,777,112	1,409,565	3,009,740	465,404	1,715,474	829,081	531,778	1,124,457
Canned and packaged soups	4,112,335	2,532,344	848,467	1,458,018	230,167	756,493	480,501	251,637	771,384
Potato chips, nuts, and other snacks	10,743,708	7,109,549	2,326,927	4,116,791	603,203	2,394,727	1,117,934	653,818	1,439,829
Potato chips and other snacks	8,337,215	5,505,824	1,631,508	3,349,206	497,030	2,003,684	839,575	538,010	1,033,320
Nuts	2,406,494	1,604,283	695,651	767,304	106,173	391,195	278,359	115,809	406,509
Condiments and seasonings	9,273,993	6,206,058	2,070,075	3,511,925	530,463	1,907,816	1,088,268	578,712	1,246,738
Salt, spices, and other seasonings	2,188,022	1,455,749	505,150	789,748	114,004	443,900	234,096	133,508	313,733
Olives, pickles, relishes	1,100,080	742,114	260,089	404,273	53,363	229,598	123,084	53,828	162,604
Sauces and gravies	4,064,889	2,707,123	863,495	1,569,116	249,996	841,456	483,420	283,257	489,778
Baking needs and misc. products	1,921,002	1,301,072	441,573	748,788	113,101	392,861	247,746	108,119	280,623
Other canned/packaged prepared foods	15,430,909	10,052,317	2,753,242	6,270,573	1,562,676	3,205,288	1,452,944	997,068	2,120,732
Prepared salads	2,157,128	1,405,493	516,710	770,390	122,538	414,519	235,911	89,425	386,839
Prepared desserts	1,119,941	761,658	294,998	399,503	55,622	210,667	136,734	50,977	146,868
Baby food	2,606,207	1,931,506	205,297	1,492,526	793,863	484,034	169,714	221,409	118,019
Miscellaneous prepared foods	9,515,635	5,922,949	1,725,371	3,587,954	589,348	2,078,954	909,401	635,257	1,469,334
Nonalcoholic beverages	28,264,438	17,904,538	5,770,965	10,163,204	1,437,577	5,669,379	3,095,247	1,735,870	4,399,806
Cola	9,644,732	6,139,050	1,975,056	3,465,634	515,805	1,933,865	1,024,911	600,985	1,380,492
Other carbonated drinks	5,091,042	3,170,037	974,697	1,859,766	259,735	1,028,951	579,915	353,193	795,971
Coffee	4,231,501	2,688,138	1,067,404	1,291,372	143,773	689,552	473,479	160,024	780,563
Roasted coffee	2,756,268	1,805,307	715,764	875,035	97,338	457,833	331,775	103,346	469,453
Instant and freeze-dried coffee	1,475,232	882,272	351,640	416,336	46,435	231,719	141,783	56,678	311,111
Noncarbonated fruit-flavored drinks	2,246,502	1,472,501	295,461	1,013,908	131,273	615,341	266,524	183,491	238,660
Tea	1,938,656	1,198,885	461,224	617,210	96,334	319,560	205,298	135,762	301,276
Other nonalcoholic beverages and ice	5,039,182	3,176,738	969,842	1,895,676	279,062	1,079,536	539,518	302,349	894,648
Food prepared by CU on trips	**4,229,294**	**3,005,309**	**1,332,579**	**1,436,697**	**207,728**	**865,991**	**363,098**	**96,319**	**714,014**

Note: Spending by type of consumer unit will not add to total because not all types of consumer units are shown.
Source: Calculations by New Strategist based on the 2001 Consumer Expenditure Survey

15. Groceries: Market shares by household type, 2001

(percentage of total annual spending on groceries accounted for by types of consumer units, 2001)

	total consumer units	total married couples	married couples, no children	married couples with children total	oldest child under 6	oldest child 6 to 17	oldest child 18 or older	single parent, at least one child <18	single person
Share of total consumer units	100.0%	50.6%	21.0%	25.4%	4.5%	13.7%	7.2%	6.0%	29.7%
Share of total before-tax income	100.0	68.6	25.4	37.5	6.3	19.9	11.3	3.3	16.7
Share of total spending	100.0	65.1	23.3	36.2	5.9	19.9	10.5	4.5	17.7
GROCERIES	100.0	64.4	21.4	36.2	5.7	19.6	11.1	6.3	14.8
Cereals and bakery products	100.0	64.3	20.5	37.5	5.7	20.7	11.2	6.7	14.7
Cereals and cereal products	100.0	63.8	18.9	38.2	6.2	20.9	11.2	7.6	14.3
Flour	100.0	64.2	18.8	35.6	6.4	17.4	12.0	6.9	12.6
Prepared flour mixes	100.0	65.5	20.6	39.3	5.9	22.4	11.0	7.4	13.4
Ready-to-eat and cooked cereals	100.0	64.3	19.2	39.2	6.4	22.1	10.7	7.7	15.0
Rice	100.0	64.3	15.8	39.0	6.2	19.6	13.4	7.5	10.8
Pasta, cornmeal, and other cereal products	100.0	61.2	19.1	35.3	5.8	18.6	11.1	7.8	15.2
Bakery products	100.0	64.6	21.3	37.1	5.4	20.6	11.1	6.3	15.0
Bread	100.0	63.7	22.5	34.8	5.3	18.8	10.8	5.6	16.5
White bread	100.0	62.8	20.8	35.1	4.9	19.2	11.1	6.3	15.2
Crackers and cookies	100.0	63.9	21.1	37.3	5.6	21.1	10.7	6.3	15.8
Cookies	100.0	63.5	20.2	37.7	5.5	20.9	11.4	6.5	15.8
Crackers	100.0	64.8	22.8	36.6	5.8	21.4	9.4	6.0	15.9
Frozen and refrigerated bakery products	100.0	67.4	20.0	40.9	5.3	25.2	10.3	7.3	12.8
Other bakery products	100.0	65.1	20.9	37.8	5.5	20.7	11.8	6.5	13.9
Biscuits and rolls	100.0	66.9	22.7	37.5	4.7	20.5	12.6	5.7	14.2
Cakes and cupcakes	100.0	63.7	18.8	38.7	6.6	21.3	10.9	7.2	12.6
Bread and cracker products	100.0	65.7	21.9	39.6	8.3	18.8	12.7	6.3	12.5
Sweetrolls, coffee cakes, doughnuts	100.0	64.2	18.8	38.8	4.9	22.1	12.1	6.9	14.6
Pies, tarts, turnovers	100.0	65.3	26.1	32.8	5.4	16.7	10.9	6.5	15.1
Meats, poultry, fish, and eggs	100.0	64.8	22.2	34.9	5.2	18.5	11.4	6.8	13.2
Beef	100.0	66.0	23.6	35.0	4.8	19.1	11.4	7.0	12.3
Ground beef	100.0	63.5	20.6	36.2	5.0	19.9	11.5	7.3	13.1
Roast	100.0	69.9	25.5	36.0	3.6	19.4	13.4	6.1	9.2
Chuck roast	100.0	68.5	20.7	39.3	4.3	22.2	13.1	6.1	10.6
Round roast	100.0	68.4	24.8	36.9	3.5	18.8	15.3	4.7	9.4
Other roast	100.0	72.2	30.1	32.6	3.2	17.5	12.3	7.0	7.9
Steak	100.0	67.0	26.1	33.6	5.4	18.3	10.0	6.8	12.9
Round steak	100.0	67.9	26.2	33.3	5.7	16.6	11.3	6.0	11.0
Sirloin steak	100.0	64.8	21.8	33.0	5.8	18.6	8.5	7.6	13.5
Other steak	100.0	67.8	28.2	34.1	5.1	18.8	10.3	6.6	13.3
Pork	100.0	65.5	23.0	34.5	5.1	18.2	11.5	6.9	12.3
Bacon	100.0	65.4	23.4	34.2	5.8	18.2	10.3	7.7	14.6
Pork chops	100.0	63.3	19.5	35.9	5.8	18.6	11.7	7.4	11.2
Ham	100.0	65.6	25.2	33.0	5.2	17.1	10.9	6.1	12.8
Ham, not canned	100.0	65.6	25.0	33.0	5.2	17.2	10.8	6.1	12.8
Canned ham	100.0	66.3	29.1	32.6	5.5	14.8	12.8	4.4	11.1
Sausage	100.0	65.1	22.6	33.6	4.2	19.4	10.2	7.4	12.5
Other pork	100.0	67.8	24.5	35.3	4.3	18.1	13.4	6.2	11.4
Other meats	100.0	65.5	21.0	37.8	5.6	20.4	12.0	6.4	13.7
Frankfurters	100.0	64.7	18.9	39.3	5.6	22.7	11.0	7.3	13.2
Lunch meats (cold cuts)	100.0	64.9	21.9	36.8	5.7	19.4	11.9	6.5	14.0
Bologna, liverwurst, salami	100.0	63.1	22.4	34.0	5.6	17.2	11.4	7.6	14.6
Lamb, organ meats, and others	100.0	72.0	18.8	42.3	4.8	22.8	15.1	3.5	12.9

	total consumer units	total married couples	married couples, no children	married couples with children				single parent, at least one child <18	single person
				total	oldest child under 6	oldest child 6 to 17	oldest child 18 or older		
Poultry	100.0%	63.6%	19.7%	36.4%	6.1%	19.1%	11.4%	7.0%	13.2%
Fresh and frozen chicken	100.0	63.4	18.5	37.3	6.4	20.0	11.0	7.1	13.2
Fresh and frozen whole chicken	100.0	63.2	17.5	37.1	6.1	19.3	11.8	6.7	12.5
Fresh and frozen chicken parts	100.0	63.5	18.9	37.4	6.5	20.3	10.7	7.2	13.5
Other poultry	100.0	64.3	24.4	32.9	5.1	15.6	12.6	6.6	13.4
Fish and seafood	100.0	63.1	22.7	32.0	4.5	16.3	11.5	6.4	15.3
Canned fish and seafood	100.0	60.1	20.7	33.0	4.5	17.3	11.6	5.9	19.2
Fresh fish and shellfish	100.0	62.4	22.2	31.5	4.7	15.1	12.1	6.2	15.7
Frozen fish and shellfish	100.0	65.6	24.5	32.4	4.2	18.0	10.3	6.9	12.8
Eggs	100.0	61.6	20.9	31.8	5.0	16.5	10.6	6.7	16.2
Dairy products	**100.0**	**64.5**	**20.1**	**37.6**	**6.2**	**20.4**	**11.2**	**5.9**	**15.1**
Fresh milk and cream	100.0	64.4	18.6	38.5	6.6	20.8	11.2	5.9	14.9
Fresh milk, all types	100.0	64.3	18.1	38.9	6.7	21.1	11.1	6.1	14.9
Cream	100.0	65.4	23.3	34.9	5.2	17.9	12.1	4.5	14.5
Other dairy products	100.0	64.6	21.2	37.0	5.9	20.1	11.1	5.8	15.3
Butter	100.0	62.0	20.9	33.4	5.9	17.2	10.5	6.2	17.4
Cheese	100.0	64.5	21.4	36.8	5.9	19.5	11.5	5.6	15.0
Ice cream and related products	100.0	65.4	21.3	37.8	5.0	22.0	10.9	6.3	14.6
Miscellaneous dairy products	100.0	65.1	20.4	39.2	7.7	20.5	11.0	5.6	16.6
Fruits and vegetables	**100.0**	**63.8**	**22.2**	**34.7**	**5.6**	**18.3**	**10.9**	**5.7**	**16.2**
Fresh fruits	100.0	64.2	22.8	34.6	5.8	18.0	11.0	5.3	16.8
Apples	100.0	65.4	22.1	36.8	5.8	20.5	10.6	6.0	14.5
Bananas	100.0	61.8	22.3	3.3	5.6	17.0	10.6	5.5	17.9
Oranges	100.0	61.0	20.8	32.6	4.4	18.3	10.1	6.8	18.0
Citrus fruits, excl. oranges	100.0	67.3	23.2	35.7	5.9	18.5	11.6	4.2	16.0
Other fresh fruits	100.0	65.2	23.9	34.7	6.3	17.2	11.4	4.7	17.3
Fresh vegetables	100.0	63.8	22.8	33.6	5.0	17.4	11.4	5.6	15.8
Potatoes	100.0	63.1	22.7	32.2	4.8	17.1	10.5	5.7	15.7
Lettuce	100.0	65.2	22.7	34.9	5.0	18.3	11.9	6.5	15.1
Tomatoes	100.0	63.7	21.7	35.1	5.3	18.6	11.4	5.7	15.6
Other fresh vegetables	100.0	63.8	23.2	33.2	5.0	16.9	11.6	5.2	16.2
Processed fruits	100.0	62.9	20.7	35.9	6.1	19.3	10.6	6.2	16.7
Frozen fruits and fruit juices	100.0	65.3	21.1	38.6	5.6	20.8	12.4	5.5	16.2
Frozen orange juice	100.0	67.0	22.9	39.0	6.0	21.9	11.3	4.1	16.7
Frozen fruits	100.0	66.2	23.4	37.5	1.3	19.7	17.5	4.7	16.1
Frozen fruit juices	100.0	61.2	15.7	38.1	7.7	19.4	11.1	8.9	15.3
Canned fruits	100.0	67.6	23.2	36.7	6.8	19.5	10.4	5.3	15.5
Dried fruits	100.0	66.8	26.6	34.2	4.8	18.6	11.0	4.2	14.7
Fresh fruit juice	100.0	60.7	21.5	32.9	5.2	16.7	11.2	5.8	18.3
Canned and bottled fruit juice	100.0	61.6	18.8	36.5	6.6	20.0	9.8	6.9	16.6
Processed vegetables	100.0	64.4	22.3	35.7	5.9	19.4	10.5	6.4	15.2
Frozen vegetables	100.0	65.5	23.1	36.2	6.1	19.6	10.5	6.6	14.7
Canned and dried vegetables and juices	100.0	63.8	22.0	35.5	5.7	19.3	10.5	6.2	15.4
Canned beans	100.0	65.3	21.0	37.8	8.7	18.5	10.6	5.3	15.9
Canned corn	100.0	63.1	18.2	38.2	6.3	21.2	10.7	8.5	12.2
Canned miscellaneous vegetables	100.0	64.7	24.9	32.8	4.7	18.5	9.7	6.1	15.3
Dried beans	100.0	59.7	18.5	33.2	6.1	13.7	14.1	9.3	14.9
Dried miscellaneous vegetables	100.0	62.3	22.0	34.6	4.4	17.8	12.8	5.9	17.8
Fresh and canned vegetable juices	100.0	6.0	21.9	32.9	4.2	18.7	10.1	5.8	17.1
Sugar and other sweets	**100.0**	**65.0**	**21.4**	**36.9**	**5.2**	**20.4**	**11.5**	**6.1**	**15.2**
Candy and chewing gum	100.0	65.3	20.8	38.0	4.9	21.3	12.0	5.6	15.7
Sugar	100.0	64.6	21.5	34.9	5.9	17.1	12.1	7.2	13.1
Artificial sweeteners	100.0	62.1	27.9	26.5	3.7	13.3	9.8	5.4	20.5
Jams, preserves, other sweets	100.0	64.6	21.8	37.3	5.9	21.5	9.8	7.3	13.8

	total consumer units	total married couples	married couples, no children	married couples with children				single parent, at least one child <18	single person
				total	oldest child under 6	oldest child 6 to 17	oldest child 18 or older		
Fats and oils	**100.0%**	**63.9%**	**22.2%**	**34.7%**	**4.9%**	**18.2%**	**11.8%**	**6.5%**	**14.3%**
Margarine	100.0	65.9	24.9	34.5	4.6	17.8	12.5	6.4	15.1
Fats and oils	100.0	62.4	20.3	32.9	4.4	17.5	11.2	6.5	14.3
Salad dressings	100.0	64.7	23.1	35.5	5.2	19.3	11.2	6.4	13.5
Nondairy cream and imitation milk	100.0	64.4	24.7	33.4	4.0	17.1	12.7	5.1	15.3
Peanut butter	100.0	62.9	19.2	37.6	6.6	18.5	12.7	8.0	14.6
Miscellaneous foods	**100.0**	**64.5**	**20.1**	**38.3**	**7.0**	**20.8**	**10.5**	**6.4**	**14.9**
Frozen prepared foods	100.0	60.7	19.6	36.4	5.3	20.6	10.6	7.1	18.1
Frozen meals	100.0	52.8	21.2	27.0	3.2	14.8	9.2	6.9	25.2
Other frozen prepared foods	100.0	64.1	18.9	40.4	6.2	23.0	11.1	7.1	15.1
Canned and packaged soups	100.0	61.6	20.6	35.5	5.6	18.4	11.7	6.1	18.8
Potato chips, nuts, and other snacks	100.0	66.2	21.7	38.3	5.6	22.3	10.4	6.1	13.4
Potato chips and other snacks	100.0	66.0	19.6	40.2	6.0	24.0	10.1	6.5	12.4
Nuts	100.0	66.7	28.9	31.9	4.4	16.3	11.6	4.8	16.9
Condiments and seasonings	100.0	66.9	22.3	37.9	5.7	20.6	11.7	6.2	13.4
Salt, spices, and other seasonings	100.0	66.5	23.1	36.1	5.2	20.3	10.7	6.1	14.3
Olives, pickles, relishes	100.0	67.5	23.6	36.7	4.9	20.9	11.2	4.9	14.8
Sauces and gravies	100.0	66.6	21.2	38.6	6.2	20.7	11.9	7.0	12.1
Baking needs and miscellaneous products	100.0	67.7	23.0	39.0	5.9	20.5	12.9	5.6	14.6
Other canned/packaged prepared foods	100.0	65.1	17.8	40.6	10.1	20.8	9.4	6.5	13.7
Prepared salads	100.0	65.2	24.0	35.7	5.7	19.2	10.9	4.1	17.9
Prepared desserts	100.0	6.8	26.3	35.7	5.0	18.8	12.2	4.6	13.1
Baby food	100.0	74.1	7.9	57.3	30.5	18.6	6.5	8.5	4.5
Miscellaneous prepared foods	100.0	62.2	18.1	37.7	6.2	21.8	9.6	6.7	15.4
Nonalcoholic beverages	100.0	63.3	20.4	36.0	5.1	20.1	11.0	6.1	15.6
Cola	100.0	63.7	20.5	35.9	5.3	20.1	10.6	6.2	14.3
Other carbonated drinks	100.0	62.3	19.1	36.5	5.1	20.2	11.4	6.9	15.6
Coffee	100.0	63.5	25.2	30.5	3.4	16.3	11.2	3.8	18.4
Roasted coffee	100.0	65.5	26.0	31.7	3.5	16.6	12.0	3.7	17.0
Instant and freeze-dried coffee	100.0	59.8	23.8	28.2	3.1	15.7	9.6	3.8	21.1
Noncarbonated fruit-flavored drinks	100.0	65.5	13.2	45.1	5.8	27.4	11.9	8.2	10.6
Tea	100.0	61.8	23.8	31.8	5.0	16.5	10.6	0.7	15.5
Other nonalcoholic beverages and ice	100.0	63.0	19.2	37.6	5.5	21.4	10.7	6.0	17.8
Food prepared by CU on trips	**100.0**	**71.1**	**31.5**	**34.0**	**4.9**	**20.5**	**8.6**	**2.3**	**16.9**

Note: Market shares by type of consumer unit will not add to total because not all types of consumer units are shown.
Source: Calculations by New Strategist based on the 2001 Consumer Expenditure Survey

16. Groceries: Average spending by race and Hispanic origin, 2001

(average annual spending of consumer units (CU) on groceries, by race and Hispanic origin of consumer unit reference person, 2001)

	total consumer units	race black	race white and other	Hispanic origin Hispanic	Hispanic origin non-Hispanic
Number of consumer units					
(in thousands, add 000)	110,339	13,283	97,056	9,621	100,718
Average number of persons per CU	2.5	2.7	2.5	3.4	2.4
Average before-tax income of CU	$47,507.00	$33,739.00	$49,334.00	$35,886.00	$48,726.00
Average spending of CU, total	39,518.46	28,903.08	40,967.94	34,360.65	40,009.00
GROCERIES	$3,085.52	$2,803.56	$3,123.62	$3,550.97	$3,039.05
Cereals and bakery products	452.19	401.78	458.99	489.98	448.42
Cereals and cereal products	156.46	160.25	155.95	187.95	153.32
Flour	8.01	9.56	7.80	14.68	7.34
Prepared flour mixes	12.89	12.05	13.01	12.17	12.97
Ready-to-eat and cooked cereals	86.04	86.79	85.94	89.13	85.73
Rice	19.95	24.47	19.34	38.33	18.12
Pasta, cornmeal, and other cereal products	29.57	27.39	29.87	33.63	29.17
Bakery products	295.73	241.53	303.04	302.03	295.10
Bread	85.37	72.37	87.12	96.79	84.23
White bread	36.64	34.78	36.89	48.32	35.47
Crackers and cookies	70.18	60.99	71.43	62.74	70.93
Cookies	46.13	41.58	46.75	45.57	46.19
Crackers	24.05	19.40	24.68	17.16	24.74
Frozen and refrigerated bakery products	26.06	20.94	26.76	18.77	26.79
Other bakery products	114.11	87.23	117.74	123.74	113.15
Biscuits and rolls	39.34	25.27	41.24	28.63	40.41
Cakes and cupcakes	33.80	32.10	34.03	48.77	32.30
Bread and cracker products	4.05	3.00	4.19	3.10	4.14
Sweetrolls, coffee cakes, doughnuts	26.32	19.63	27.22	32.91	25.66
Pies, tarts, turnovers	10.60	7.24	11.05	10.33	10.63
Meats, poultry, fish, and eggs	827.97	941.12	812.70	1,097.76	801.06
Beef	248.06	245.25	248.44	331.38	239.75
Ground beef	90.48	97.16	89.58	110.41	88.49
Roast	44.44	45.60	44.29	55.29	43.36
Chuck roast	15.03	19.87	14.37	19.00	14.63
Round roast	11.88	11.20	11.97	13.60	11.71
Other roast	17.53	14.53	17.94	22.68	17.02
Steak	92.73	79.79	94.47	125.76	89.43
Round steak	18.21	15.66	18.56	33.23	16.71
Sirloin steak	25.37	22.92	25.70	39.42	23.96
Other steak	49.15	41.21	50.22	53.10	48.76
Pork	177.31	228.98	170.34	229.37	172.12
Bacon	29.30	40.79	27.76	29.21	29.31
Pork chops	42.16	61.69	39.52	64.58	39.92
Ham	39.98	36.50	40.45	49.33	39.05
Ham, not canned	38.24	34.47	38.75	48.26	37.24
Canned ham	1.74	2.03	1.70	1.07	1.81
Sausage	25.52	36.90	23.99	26.61	25.41
Other pork	40.34	53.10	38.62	59.63	38.42
Other meats	102.06	95.19	102.99	111.36	101.14
Frankfurters	22.01	23.74	21.78	26.95	21.52
Lunch meats (cold cuts)	70.88	61.69	72.12	71.38	70.83
Bologna, liverwurst, salami	25.40	26.41	25.26	29.95	24.94
Lamb, organ meats, and others	9.17	9.76	9.09	13.03	8.79

	total consumer units	race		Hispanic origin	
		black	white and other	Hispanic	non-Hispanic
Poultry	$151.87	$195.91	$145.93	$206.28	$146.44
Fresh and frozen chicken	119.55	154.62	114.82	176.48	113.87
Fresh and frozen whole chicken	35.75	42.93	34.78	70.10	32.32
Fresh and frozen chicken parts	83.80	111.69	80.04	106.37	81.55
Other poultry	32.32	41.29	31.11	29.80	32.57
Fish and seafood	113.67	132.38	111.15	164.07	108.64
Canned fish and seafood	15.11	14.60	15.18	17.04	14.92
Fresh fish and shellfish	63.07	77.38	61.14	102.40	59.15
Frozen fish and shellfish	35.49	40.40	34.82	44.63	34.58
Eggs	34.99	43.40	33.86	55.30	32.96
Dairy products	**331.69**	**241.27**	**343.89**	**354.51**	**329.41**
Fresh milk and cream	135.85	98.11	140.94	168.46	132.60
Fresh milk, all types	123.50	91.62	127.80	155.27	120.33
Cream	12.35	6.49	13.14	13.18	12.26
Other dairy products	195.84	143.16	202.95	186.05	196.82
Butter	21.55	16.90	22.18	16.43	22.06
Cheese	93.39	63.13	97.48	93.19	93.41
Ice cream and related products	56.79	47.07	58.10	52.42	57.22
Miscellaneous dairy products	24.11	16.06	25.20	24.01	24.12
Fruits and vegetables	**521.74**	**460.02**	**530.07**	**662.85**	**507.67**
Fresh fruits	160.41	124.35	165.28	217.95	154.67
Apples	30.83	24.69	31.66	35.70	30.34
Bananas	31.30	28.07	31.74	50.59	29.38
Oranges	18.62	17.84	18.73	24.33	18.05
Citrus fruits, excl. oranges	13.21	6.89	14.07	24.31	12.11
Other fresh fruits	66.45	46.86	69.09	83.02	64.79
Fresh vegetables	161.62	131.04	165.75	230.91	154.71
Potatoes	30.09	27.57	30.43	36.23	29.48
Lettuce	20.82	16.77	21.37	25.58	20.35
Tomatoes	30.03	24.50	30.78	55.66	27.48
Other fresh vegetables	80.68	62.20	83.17	113.43	77.41
Processed fruits	116.03	124.74	114.86	132.36	114.40
Frozen fruits and fruit juices	13.85	10.19	14.35	13.74	13.87
Frozen orange juice	7.61	5.11	7.94	8.44	7.52
Frozen fruits	2.53	1.90	2.62	2.16	2.57
Frozen fruit juices	3.72	3.18	3.79	3.14	3.77
Canned fruits	16.27	15.06	16.44	13.95	16.50
Dried fruits	5.54	4.85	5.64	4.50	5.65
Fresh fruit juice	24.86	23.46	25.05	28.11	24.53
Canned and bottled fruit juice	55.50	71.18	53.39	72.06	53.85
Processed vegetables	83.68	79.90	84.19	81.64	83.88
Frozen vegetables	27.50	29.07	27.29	18.91	28.36
Canned and dried vegetables and juices	56.18	50.82	56.90	62.73	55.52
Canned beans	12.60	12.68	12.59	14.03	12.46
Canned corn	7.13	8.95	6.88	6.77	7.16
Canned miscellaneous vegetables	17.58	14.66	17.98	13.31	18.01
Dried beans	2.28	2.28	2.28	6.67	1.84
Dried miscellaneous vegetables	7.58	5.14	7.91	8.55	7.48
Fresh and canned vegetable juices	7.65	6.47	7.81	7.54	7.66
Sugar and other sweets	**115.96**	**91.23**	**119.30**	**103.98**	**117.15**
Candy and chewing gum	73.49	45.54	77.26	59.02	74.94
Sugar	17.91	24.81	16.98	24.43	17.26
Artificial sweeteners	5.04	4.65	5.09	2.97	5.25
Jams, preserves, other sweets	19.52	16.24	19.96	17.55	19.72

	total consumer units	race		Hispanic origin	
		black	white and other	Hispanic	non-Hispanic
Fats and oils	**$86.76**	**$84.83**	**$87.02**	**$97.08**	**$85.73**
Margarine	11.43	12.59	11.27	10.36	11.53
Fats and oils	24.53	29.92	23.80	42.28	22.76
Salad dressings	28.02	25.37	28.38	27.74	28.05
Nondairy cream and imitation milk	10.09	5.11	10.76	7.20	10.38
Peanut butter	12.69	11.84	12.81	9.49	13.01
Miscellaneous foods	**454.72**	**352.88**	**468.46**	**424.78**	**457.71**
Frozen prepared foods	96.19	66.29	100.23	57.05	100.10
Frozen meals	28.65	22.13	29.53	13.07	30.20
Other frozen prepared foods	67.54	44.16	70.70	43.98	69.89
Canned and packaged soups	37.27	23.62	39.12	34.85	37.52
Potato chips, nuts, and other snacks	97.37	70.20	101.03	82.04	98.89
Potato chips and other snacks	75.56	55.12	78.31	66.00	76.51
Nuts	21.81	15.08	22.72	16.04	22.38
Condiments and seasonings	84.05	75.81	85.16	78.68	84.58
Salt, spices, and other seasonings	19.83	21.15	19.65	25.78	19.23
Olives, pickles, relishes	9.97	8.27	10.19	5.86	10.38
Sauces and gravies	36.84	34.40	37.17	33.62	37.16
Baking needs and miscellaneous products	17.41	11.98	18.14	13.41	17.81
Other canned/packaged prepared foods	139.85	116.96	142.93	172.17	136.62
Prepared salads	19.55	11.79	20.59	11.29	20.37
Prepared desserts	10.15	5.39	10.80	9.16	10.25
Baby food	23.62	30.89	22.64	28.52	23.13
Miscellaneous prepared foods	86.24	68.89	88.58	122.67	82.60
Nonalcoholic beverages	256.16	216.49	261.51	289.98	252.78
Cola	87.41	76.75	88.85	99.24	86.23
Other carbonated drinks	46.14	41.82	46.72	46.84	46.07
Coffee	38.35	20.47	40.76	38.66	38.32
Roasted coffee	24.98	11.70	26.78	23.85	25.10
Instant and freeze-dried coffee	13.37	8.77	13.99	14.81	13.22
Noncarbonated fruit-flavored drinks	20.36	28.73	19.23	27.44	19.65
Tea	17.57	14.72	17.96	21.20	17.21
Other nonalcoholic beverages and ice	45.67	34.01	47.24	56.35	44.60
Food prepared by CU on trips	**38.33**	**13.93**	**41.67**	**30.04**	**39.12**

Note: Other races include Asians, Native Americans, and Pacific Islanders.
Source: Bureau of Labor Statistics, unpublished tables from the 2001 Consumer Expenditure Survey

17. Groceries: Indexed spending by race and Hispanic origin, 2001

(indexed average annual spending of consumer units (CU) on groceries, by race and Hispanic origin of consumer unit reference person, 2001; index definition: an index of 100 is the average for all consumer units; an index of 132 means that spending by consumer units in that group is 32 percent above the average for all consumer units; an index of 68 indicates spending that is 32 percent below the average for all consumer units)

	total consumer units	race black	race white and other	Hispanic origin Hispanic	Hispanic origin non-Hispanic
Average spending of CU, total	$39,518	$28,903	$40,968	$34,361	$40,009
Average spending of CU, index	100	73	104	87	101
GROCERIES	100	91	101	115	99
Cereals and bakery products	100	89	102	108	99
Cereals and cereal products	100	102	100	120	98
Flour	100	119	97	183	92
Prepared flour mixes	100	94	101	94	101
Ready-to-eat and cooked cereals	100	101	100	104	100
Rice	100	123	97	192	91
Pasta, cornmeal, and other cereal products	100	93	101	114	99
Bakery products	100	82	103	102	100
Bread	100	85	102	113	99
White bread	100	95	101	132	97
Crackers and cookies	100	87	102	89	101
Cookies	100	90	101	99	100
Crackers	100	81	103	71	103
Frozen and refrigerated bakery products	100	80	103	72	103
Other bakery products	100	76	103	108	99
Biscuits and rolls	100	64	105	73	103
Cakes and cupcakes	100	95	101	144	96
Bread and cracker products	100	74	104	77	102
Sweetrolls, coffee cakes, doughnuts	100	75	103	125	98
Pies, tarts, turnovers	100	68	104	98	100
Meats, poultry, fish, and eggs	100	114	98	133	97
Beef	100	99	100	134	97
Ground beef	100	107	99	122	98
Roast	100	103	100	124	98
Chuck roast	100	132	96	126	97
Round roast	100	94	101	115	99
Other roast	100	83	102	129	97
Steak	100	86	102	136	96
Round steak	100	86	102	183	92
Sirloin steak	100	90	101	155	94
Other steak	100	84	102	108	99
Pork	100	129	96	129	97
Bacon	100	139	95	100	100
Pork chops	100	146	94	153	95
Ham	100	91	101	123	98
Ham, not canned	100	90	101	126	97
Canned ham	100	117	98	62	104
Sausage	100	145	94	104	100
Other pork	100	132	96	148	95
Other meats	100	93	101	109	99
Frankfurters	100	108	99	122	98
Lunch meats (cold cuts)	100	87	102	101	100
Bologna, liverwurst, salami	100	104	99	118	98
Lamb, organ meats, and others	100	106	99	142	96

	total consumer units	race		Hispanic origin	
		black	white and other	Hispanic	non-Hispanic
Poultry	100	129	96	136	96
Fresh and frozen chicken	100	129	96	148	95
Fresh and frozen whole chicken	100	120	97	196	90
Fresh and frozen chicken parts	100	133	96	127	97
Other poultry	100	128	96	92	101
Fish and seafood	100	117	98	144	96
Canned fish and seafood	100	97	101	113	99
Fresh fish and shellfish	100	123	97	162	94
Frozen fish and shellfish	100	114	98	126	97
Eggs	100	124	97	158	94
Dairy products	**100**	**73**	**104**	**107**	**99**
Fresh milk and cream	100	72	104	124	98
Fresh milk, all types	100	74	104	126	97
Cream	100	53	106	107	99
Other dairy products	100	73	104	95	101
Butter	100	78	103	76	102
Cheese	100	68	104	100	100
Ice cream and related products	100	83	102	92	101
Miscellaneous dairy products	100	67	105	100	100
Fruits and vegetables	**100**	**88**	**102**	**127**	**97**
Fresh fruits	100	78	103	136	96
Apples	100	80	103	116	98
Bananas	100	90	101	162	94
Oranges	100	96	101	131	97
Citrus fruits, excl. oranges	100	52	107	184	92
Other fresh fruits	100	71	104	125	98
Fresh vegetables	100	81	103	143	96
Potatoes	100	92	101	120	98
Lettuce	100	81	103	123	98
Tomatoes	100	82	103	185	92
Other fresh vegetables	100	77	103	141	96
Processed fruits	100	108	99	114	99
Frozen fruits and fruit juices	100	74	104	99	100
Frozen orange juice	100	67	104	111	99
Frozen fruits	100	75	104	85	102
Frozen fruit juices	100	86	102	84	101
Canned fruits	100	93	101	86	101
Dried fruits	100	88	102	81	102
Fresh fruit juice	100	94	101	113	99
Canned and bottled fruit juice	100	128	96	130	97
Processed vegetables	100	96	101	98	100
Frozen vegetables	100	106	99	69	103
Canned and dried vegetables and juices	100	91	101	112	99
Canned beans	100	101	100	111	99
Canned corn	100	126	97	95	100
Canned miscellaneous vegetables	100	83	102	76	102
Dried beans	100	100	100	293	81
Dried miscellaneous vegetables	100	68	104	113	99
Fresh and canned vegetable juices	100	85	102	99	100
Sugar and other sweets	**100**	**79**	**103**	**90**	**101**
Candy and chewing gum	100	62	105	80	102
Sugar	100	139	95	136	96
Artificial sweeteners	100	92	101	59	104
Jams, preserves, other sweets	100	83	102	90	101

	total consumer units	race		Hispanic origin	
		black	white and other	Hispanic	non-Hispanic
Fats and oils	**100**	**98**	**100**	**112**	**99**
Margarine	100	110	99	91	101
Fats and oils	100	122	97	172	93
Salad dressings	100	91	101	99	100
Nondairy cream and imitation milk	100	51	107	71	103
Peanut butter	100	93	101	75	103
Miscellaneous foods	**100**	**78**	**103**	**93**	**101**
Frozen prepared foods	100	69	104	59	104
Frozen meals	100	77	103	46	105
Other frozen prepared foods	100	65	105	65	104
Canned and packaged soups	100	63	105	94	101
Potato chips, nuts, and other snacks	100	72	104	84	102
Potato chips and other snacks	100	73	104	87	101
Nuts	100	69	104	74	103
Condiments and seasonings	100	90	101	94	101
Salt, spices, and other seasonings	100	107	99	130	97
Olives, pickles, relishes	100	83	102	59	104
Sauces and gravies	100	93	101	91	101
Baking needs and miscellaneous products	100	69	104	77	102
Other canned/packaged prepared foods	100	84	102	123	98
Prepared salads	100	60	105	58	104
Prepared desserts	100	53	106	90	101
Baby food	100	131	96	121	98
Miscellaneous prepared foods	100	80	103	142	96
Nonalcoholic beverages	100	85	102	113	99
Cola	100	88	102	114	99
Other carbonated drinks	100	91	101	102	100
Coffee	100	53	106	101	100
Roasted coffee	100	47	107	96	101
Instant and freeze-dried coffee	100	66	105	111	99
Noncarbonated fruit-flavored drinks	100	141	94	135	97
Tea	100	84	102	121	98
Other nonalcoholic beverages and ice	100	75	103	123	98
Food prepared by CU on trips	**100**	**36**	**109**	**78**	**102**

Note: Other races include Asians, Native Americans, and Pacific Islanders.
Source: Calculations by New Strategist based on the 2001 Consumer Expenditure Survey

18. Groceries: Indexed per capita spending by race and Hispanic origin, 2001

(indexed average annual per capita spending of consumer units (CU) on groceries, by race and Hispanic origin of consumer unit reference person, 2001; index definition: an index of 100 is the average for all consumer units; an index of 132 means that spending by consumer units in that group is 32 percent above the average for all consumer units; an index of 68 indicates spending that is 32 percent below the average for all consumer units)

	total consumer units	race black	race white and other	Hispanic origin Hispanic	Hispanic origin non-Hispanic
Per capita spending of CU, total	$15,807	$10,705	$16,387	$10,106	$16,670
Per capita spending of CU, index	100	68	104	64	106
GROCERIES	**100**	**84**	**101**	**85**	**103**
Cereals and bakery products	**100**	**82**	**102**	**80**	**103**
Cereals and cereal products	100	95	100	88	102
Flour	100	111	97	135	96
Prepared flour mixes	100	87	101	69	105
Ready-to-eat and cooked cereals	100	93	100	76	104
Rice	100	114	97	141	95
Pasta, cornmeal, and other cereal products	100	86	101	84	103
Bakery products	100	76	103	75	104
Bread	100	79	102	83	103
White bread	100	88	101	97	101
Crackers and cookies	100	81	102	66	105
Cookies	100	84	101	73	104
Crackers	100	75	103	53	107
Frozen and refrigerated bakery products	100	74	103	53	107
Other bakery products	100	71	103	80	103
Biscuits and rolls	100	60	105	54	107
Cakes and cupcakes	100	88	101	106	100
Bread and cracker products	100	69	104	56	107
Sweetrolls, coffee cakes, doughnuts	100	69	103	92	102
Pies, tarts, turnovers	100	63	104	72	105
Meats, poultry, fish, and eggs	**100**	**105**	**98**	**98**	**101**
Beef	100	92	100	98	101
Ground beef	100	99	99	90	102
Roast	100	95	100	92	102
Chuck roast	100	122	96	93	101
Round roast	100	87	101	84	103
Other roast	100	77	102	95	101
Steak	100	80	102	100	101
Round steak	100	80	102	134	96
Sirloin steak	100	84	101	114	98
Other steak	100	78	102	79	103
Pork	100	120	96	95	101
Bacon	100	129	95	73	104
Pork chops	100	136	94	113	99
Ham	100	85	101	91	102
Ham, not canned	100	84	101	93	101
Canned ham	100	108	98	45	108
Sausage	100	134	94	77	104
Other pork	100	122	96	109	99
Other meats	100	86	101	80	103
Frankfurters	100	100	99	90	102
Lunch meats (cold cuts)	100	81	102	74	104
Bologna, liverwurst, salami	100	96	99	87	102
Lamb, organ meats, and others	100	99	99	105	100

	total consumer units	race		Hispanic origin	
		black	white and other	Hispanic	non-Hispanic
Poultry	100	119	96	100	100
Fresh and frozen chicken	100	120	96	109	99
Fresh and frozen whole chicken	100	111	97	144	94
Fresh and frozen chicken parts	100	123	96	93	101
Other poultry	100	118	96	68	105
Fish and seafood	100	108	98	106	100
Canned fish and seafood	100	90	101	83	103
Fresh fish and shellfish	100	114	97	119	98
Frozen fish and shellfish	100	105	98	93	102
Eggs	100	115	97	116	98
Dairy products	**100**	**67**	**104**	**79**	**104**
Fresh milk and cream	100	67	104	91	102
Fresh milk, all types	100	69	104	92	102
Cream	100	49	106	79	103
Other dairy products	100	68	104	70	105
Butter	100	73	103	56	107
Cheese	100	63	104	73	104
Ice cream and related products	100	77	102	68	105
Miscellaneous dairy products	100	62	105	73	104
Fruits and vegetables	**100**	**82**	**102**	**93**	**101**
Fresh fruits	100	72	103	100	100
Apples	100	74	103	85	103
Bananas	100	83	101	119	98
Oranges	100	89	101	96	101
Citrus fruits, excl. oranges	100	48	107	135	96
Other fresh fruits	100	65	104	92	102
Fresh vegetables	100	75	103	105	100
Potatoes	100	85	101	89	102
Lettuce	100	75	103	90	102
Tomatoes	100	76	103	136	95
Other fresh vegetables	100	71	103	103	100
Processed fruits	100	100	99	84	103
Frozen fruits and fruit juices	100	68	104	73	104
Frozen orange juice	100	62	104	82	103
Frozen fruits	100	70	104	63	106
Frozen fruit juices	100	79	102	62	106
Canned fruits	100	86	101	63	106
Dried fruits	100	81	102	60	106
Fresh fruit juice	100	87	101	83	103
Canned and bottled fruit juice	100	119	96	96	101
Processed vegetables	100	88	101	72	104
Frozen vegetables	100	98	99	51	107
Canned and dried vegetables and juices	100	84	101	82	103
Canned beans	100	93	100	82	103
Canned corn	100	116	97	70	105
Canned miscellaneous vegetables	100	77	102	56	107
Dried beans	100	93	100	215	84
Dried miscellaneous vegetables	100	63	104	83	103
Fresh and canned vegetable juices	100	78	102	73	104
Sugar and other sweets	**100**	**73**	**103**	**66**	**105**
Candy and chewing gum	100	57	105	59	106
Sugar	100	128	95	100	100
Artificial sweeteners	100	85	101	43	109
Jams, preserves, other sweets	100	77	102	66	105

	total consumer units	race		Hispanic origin	
		black	white and other	Hispanic	non-Hispanic
Fats and oils	**100**	**91**	**100**	**82**	**103**
Margarine	100	102	99	67	105
Fats and oils	100	113	97	127	97
Salad dressings	100	84	101	73	104
Nondairy cream and imitation milk	100	47	107	53	107
Peanut butter	100	86	101	55	107
Miscellaneous foods	**100**	**72**	**103**	**69**	**105**
Frozen prepared foods	100	64	104	44	108
Frozen meals	100	72	103	34	110
Other frozen prepared foods	100	61	105	48	108
Canned and packaged soups	100	59	105	69	105
Potato chips, nuts, and other snacks	100	67	104	62	106
Potato chips and other snacks	100	68	104	64	106
Nuts	100	64	104	54	107
Condiments and seasonings	100	84	101	69	105
Salt, spices, and other seasonings	100	99	99	96	101
Olives, pickles, relishes	100	77	102	43	109
Sauces and gravies	100	87	101	67	105
Baking needs and miscellaneous products	100	64	104	57	107
Other canned/packaged prepared foods	100	77	102	91	102
Prepared salads	100	56	105	43	109
Prepared desserts	100	49	106	66	105
Baby food	100	121	96	89	102
Miscellaneous prepared foods	100	74	103	105	100
Nonalcoholic beverages	100	78	102	83	103
Cola	100	81	102	84	103
Other carbonated drinks	100	84	101	75	104
Coffee	100	49	106	74	104
Roasted coffee	100	43	107	70	105
Instant and freeze-dried coffee	100	61	105	81	103
Noncarbonated fruit-flavored drinks	100	131	94	99	101
Tea	100	78	102	89	102
Other nonalcoholic beverages and ice	100	69	103	91	102
Food prepared by CU on trips	**100**	**34**	**109**	**58**	**106**

Note: Per capita indexes account for household size and show how much each person in a particular household demographic segment spends relative to a person in the average household. Other races include Asians, Native Americans, and Pacific Islanders.
Source: Calculations by New Strategist based on the 2001 Consumer Expenditure Survey

19. Groceries: Total spending by race and Hispanic origin, 2001

(total annual spending on groceries, by consumer unit race and Hispanic origin groups, 2001; numbers in thousands)

	total consumer units	race black	race white and other	Hispanic origin Hispanic	Hispanic origin non-Hispanic
Number of consumer units	110,339	13,283	97,056	9,621	100,718
Total spending of all consumer units	$4,360,427,358	$383,919,612	$3,976,184,385	$330,583,814	$4,029,626,462
GROCERIES	**$340,453,191**	**$37,239,688**	**$303,166,063**	**$34,163,882**	**$306,087,038**
Cereals and bakery products	**49,894,192**	**5,336,844**	**44,547,733**	**4,714,098**	**45,163,966**
Cereals and cereal products	17,263,640	2,128,601	15,135,883	1,808,267	15,442,084
Flour	883,815	126,986	757,037	141,236	739,270
Prepared flour mixes	1,422,270	160,060	1,262,699	117,088	1,306,313
Ready-to-eat and cooked cereals	9,493,568	1,152,832	8,340,993	857,520	8,634,554
Rice	2,201,263	325,035	1,877,063	368,773	1,825,010
Pasta, cornmeal, and other cereal products	3,262,724	363,821	2,899,063	323,554	2,937,944
Bakery products	32,630,553	3,208,243	29,411,850	2,905,831	29,721,882
Bread	9,419,640	961,291	8,455,519	931,217	8,483,477
White bread	4,042,821	461,983	3,580,396	464,887	3,572,468
Crackers and cookies	7,743,591	810,130	6,932,710	603,622	7,143,928
Cookies	5,089,938	552,307	4,537,368	438,429	4,652,164
Crackers	2,653,653	257,690	2,395,342	165,096	2,491,763
Frozen and refrigerated bakery products	2,875,434	278,146	2,597,219	180,586	2,698,235
Other bakery products	12,590,783	1,158,676	11,427,373	1,190,503	11,396,242
Biscuits and rolls	4,340,736	335,661	4,002,589	275,449	4,070,014
Cakes and cupcakes	3,729,458	426,384	3,302,816	469,216	3,253,191
Bread and cracker products	446,873	39,849	406,665	29,825	416,973
Sweetrolls, coffee cakes, doughnuts	2,904,123	260,745	2,641,864	316,627	2,584,424
Pies, tarts, turnovers	1,169,593	96,169	1,072,469	99,385	1,070,632
Meats, poultry, fish, and eggs	**91,357,382**	**12,500,897**	**78,877,411**	**10,561,549**	**80,681,161**
Beef	27,370,692	3,257,656	24,112,593	3,188,207	24,147,141
Ground beef	9,983,473	1,290,576	8,694,277	1,062,255	8,912,536
Roast	4,903,465	605,705	4,298,610	531,945	4,367,133
Chuck roast	1,658,395	263,933	1,394,695	182,799	1,473,504
Round roast	1,310,827	148,770	1,161,760	130,846	1,179,408
Other roast	1,934,243	193,002	1,741,185	218,204	1,714,220
Steak	10,231,736	1,059,851	9,168,880	1,209,937	9,007,211
Round steak	2,009,273	208,012	1,801,359	319,706	1,682,998
Sirloin steak	2,799,300	304,446	2,494,339	379,260	2,413,203
Other steak	5,423,162	547,392	4,874,152	510,875	4,911,010
Pork	19,564,208	3,041,541	16,532,519	2,206,769	17,335,582
Bacon	3,232,933	541,814	2,694,275	281,029	2,952,045
Pork chops	4,651,892	819,428	3,835,653	621,324	4,020,663
Ham	4,411,353	484,830	3,925,915	474,604	3,933,038
Ham, not canned	4,219,363	457,865	3,760,920	464,310	3,750,738
Canned ham	191,990	26,965	164,995	10,295	182,300
Sausage	2,815,851	490,143	2,328,373	256,015	2,559,244
Other pork	4,451,075	705,327	3,748,303	573,700	3,869,586
Other meats	11,261,198	1,264,409	9,995,797	1,071,395	10,186,619
Frankfurters	2,428,561	315,338	2,113,880	259,286	2,167,451
Lunch meats (cold cuts)	7,820,828	819,428	6,999,679	686,747	7,133,856
Bologna, liverwurst, salami	2,802,611	350,804	2,451,635	288,149	2,511,907
Lamb, organ meats, and others	1,011,809	129,642	882,239	125,362	885,311

	total consumer units	race		Hispanic origin	
		black	white and other	Hispanic	non-Hispanic
Poultry	$16,757,184	$2,602,273	$14,163,382	$1,984,620	$14,749,144
Fresh and frozen chicken	13,191,027	2,053,818	11,143,970	1,697,914	11,468,759
Fresh and frozen whole chicken	3,944,619	570,239	3,375,608	674,432	3,255,206
Fresh and frozen chicken parts	9,246,408	1,483,578	7,768,362	1,023,386	8,213,553
Other poultry	3,566,157	548,455	3,019,412	286,706	3,280,385
Fish and seafood	12,542,234	1,758,404	10,787,774	1,578,518	10,942,004
Canned fish and seafood	1,667,222	193,932	1,473,310	163,942	1,502,713
Fresh fish and shellfish	6,959,081	1,027,839	5,934,004	985,190	5,957,470
Frozen fish and shellfish	3,915,931	536,633	3,379,490	429,385	3,482,828
Eggs	3,860,762	576,482	3,286,316	532,041	3,319,665
Dairy products	**36,598,343**	**3,204,789**	**33,376,588**	**3,410,741**	**33,177,516**
Fresh milk and cream	14,989,553	1,303,195	13,679,073	1,620,754	13,355,207
Fresh milk, all types	13,626,867	1,216,989	12,403,757	1,493,853	12,119,397
Cream	1,362,687	86,207	1,275,316	126,805	1,234,803
Other dairy products	21,608,790	1,901,594	19,697,515	1,789,987	19,823,317
Butter	2,377,806	224,483	2,152,702	158,073	2,221,839
Cheese	10,304,559	838,556	9,461,019	896,581	9,408,068
Ice cream and related products	6,266,152	625,231	5,638,954	504,333	5,763,084
Miscellaneous dairy products	2,660,273	213,325	2,445,811	231,000	2,429,318
Fruits and vegetables	**57,568,270**	**6,110,446**	**51,446,474**	**6,377,280**	**51,131,507**
Fresh fruits	17,699,479	1,651,741	16,041,416	2,096,897	15,578,053
Apples	3,401,751	327,957	3,072,793	343,470	3,055,784
Bananas	3,453,611	372,854	3,080,557	486,726	2,959,095
Oranges	2,054,512	236,969	1,817,859	234,079	1,817,960
Citrus fruits, excl. oranges	1,457,578	91,520	1,365,578	233,887	1,219,695
Other fresh fruits	7,332,027	622,441	6,705,599	798,735	6,525,519
Fresh vegetables	17,832,989	1,740,604	16,087,032	2,221,585	15,582,082
Potatoes	3,320,101	366,212	2,953,414	348,569	2,969,167
Lettuce	2,297,258	222,756	2,074,087	246,105	2,049,611
Tomatoes	3,313,480	325,434	2,987,384	535,505	2,767,731
Other fresh vegetables	8,902,151	826,203	8,072,148	1,091,310	7,796,580
Processed fruits	12,802,634	1,656,921	11,147,852	1,273,436	11,522,139
Frozen fruits and fruit juices	1,528,195	135,354	1,392,754	132,193	1,396,959
Frozen orange juice	839,680	67,876	770,625	81,201	757,399
Frozen fruits	279,158	25,238	254,287	20,781	258,845
Frozen fruit juices	410,461	42,240	367,842	30,210	379,707
Canned fruits	1,795,216	200,042	1,595,601	134,213	1,661,847
Dried fruits	611,278	64,423	547,396	43,295	569,057
Fresh fruit juice	2,743,028	311,619	2,431,253	270,446	2,470,613
Canned and bottled fruit juice	6,123,815	945,484	5,181,820	693,289	5,423,664
Processed vegetables	9,233,168	1,061,312	8,171,145	785,458	8,448,226
Frozen vegetables	3,034,323	386,137	2,648,658	181,933	2,856,363
Canned and dried vegetables and juices	6,198,845	675,042	5,522,486	603,525	5,591,863
Canned beans	1,390,271	168,428	1,221,935	134,983	1,254,946
Canned corn	786,717	118,883	667,745	65,134	721,141
Canned miscellaneous vegetables	1,939,760	194,729	1,745,067	128,056	1,813,931
Dried beans	251,573	30,285	221,288	64,172	185,321
Dried miscellaneous vegetables	836,370	68,275	767,713	82,260	753,371
Fresh and canned vegetable juices	844,093	85,941	758,007	72,542	771,500
Sugar and other sweets	**12,794,910**	**1,211,808**	**11,578,781**	**1,000,392**	**11,799,114**
Candy and chewing gum	8,108,813	604,908	7,498,547	567,831	7,547,807
Sugar	1,976,172	329,551	1,648,011	235,041	1,738,393
Artificial sweeteners	556,109	61,766	494,015	28,574	528,770
Jams, preserves, other sweets	2,153,817	215,716	1,937,238	168,849	1,986,159

	total consumer units	race		Hispanic origin	
		black	white and other	Hispanic	non-Hispanic
Fats and oils	**$9,573,012**	**$1,126,797**	**$8,445,813**	**$934,007**	**$8,634,554**
Margarine	1,261,175	167,233	1,093,821	99,674	1,161,279
Fats and oils	2,706,616	397,427	2,309,933	406,776	2,292,342
Salad dressings	3,091,699	336,990	2,754,449	266,887	2,825,140
Nondairy cream and imitation milk	1,113,321	67,876	1,044,323	69,271	1,045,453
Peanut butter	1,400,202	157,271	1,243,287	91,303	1,310,341
Miscellaneous foods	**50,173,350**	**4,687,305**	**45,466,854**	**4,086,808**	**46,099,636**
Frozen prepared foods	10,613,508	880,530	9,727,923	548,878	10,081,872
Frozen meals	3,161,212	293,953	2,866,064	125,747	3,041,684
Other frozen prepared foods	7,452,296	586,577	6,861,859	423,132	7,039,181
Canned and packaged soups	4,112,335	313,745	3,796,831	335,292	3,778,939
Potato chips, nuts, and other snacks	10,743,708	932,467	9,805,568	789,307	9,960,003
Potato chips and other snacks	8,337,215	732,159	7,600,455	634,986	7,705,934
Nuts	2,406,494	200,308	2,205,112	154,321	2,254,069
Condiments and seasonings	9,273,993	1,006,984	8,265,289	756,980	8,518,728
Salt, spices, and other seasonings	2,188,022	280,936	1,907,150	248,029	1,936,807
Olives, pickles, relishes	1,100,080	109,850	989,001	56,379	1,045,453
Sauces and gravies	4,064,889	456,935	3,607,572	323,458	3,742,681
Baking needs and miscellaneous products	1,921,002	159,130	1,760,596	129,018	1,793,788
Other canned/packaged prepared foods	15,430,909	1,553,580	13,872,214	1,656,448	13,760,093
Prepared salads	2,157,128	156,607	1,998,383	108,621	2,051,626
Prepared desserts	1,119,941	71,595	1,048,205	88,128	1,032,360
Baby food	2,606,207	410,312	2,197,348	274,391	2,329,607
Miscellaneous prepared foods	9,515,635	915,066	8,597,221	1,180,208	8,319,307
Nonalcoholic beverages	28,264,438	2,875,637	25,381,115	2,789,898	25,459,496
Cola	9,644,732	1,019,470	8,623,426	954,788	8,684,913
Other carbonated drinks	5,091,042	555,495	4,534,456	450,648	4,640,078
Coffee	4,231,501	271,903	3,956,003	371,948	3,859,514
Roasted coffee	2,756,268	155,411	2,599,160	229,461	2,528,022
Instant and freeze-dried coffee	1,475,232	116,492	1,357,813	142,487	1,331,492
Noncarbonated fruit-flavored drinks	2,246,502	381,621	1,866,387	264,000	1,979,109
Tea	1,938,656	195,526	1,743,126	203,965	1,733,357
Other nonalcoholic beverages and ice	5,039,182	451,755	4,584,925	542,143	4,492,023
Food prepared by CU on trips	**4,229,294**	**185,032**	**4,044,324**	**289,015**	**3,940,088**

Note: Other races include Asians, Native Americans, and Pacific Islanders. Numbers may not add to total because of rounding.
Source: Calculations by New Strategist based on the 2001 Consumer Expenditure Survey

20. Groceries: Market shares by race and Hispanic origin, 2001

(percentage of total annual spending on groceries accounted for by consumer unit race and Hispanic origin groups, 2001)

	total consumer units	race		Hispanic origin	
		black	white and other	Hispanic	non-Hispanic
Share of total consumer units	100.0%	12.0%	88.0%	8.7%	91.3%
Share of total before-tax income	100.0	8.5	91.3	6.6	93.6
Share of total spending	100.0	8.8	91.2	7.6	92.4
GROCERIES	100.0	10.9	89.1	10.0	89.9
Cereals and bakery products	100.0	10.7	89.3	9.4	90.5
Cereals and cereal products	100.0	12.3	87.7	10.5	89.4
Flour	100.0	14.4	85.7	16.0	83.6
Prepared flour mixes	100.0	11.3	88.8	8.2	91.8
Ready-to-eat and cooked cereals	100.0	12.1	87.9	9.0	91.0
Rice	100.0	14.8	85.3	16.8	82.9
Pasta, cornmeal, and other cereal products	100.0	11.2	88.9	9.9	90.1
Bakery products	100.0	9.8	90.1	8.9	91.1
Bread	100.0	10.2	89.8	9.9	90.1
White bread	100.0	11.4	88.6	11.5	88.4
Crackers and cookies	100.0	10.5	89.5	7.8	92.3
Cookies	100.0	10.9	89.1	8.6	91.4
Crackers	100.0	9.7	90.3	6.2	93.9
Frozen and refrigerated bakery products	100.0	9.7	90.3	6.3	93.8
Other bakery products	100.0	9.2	90.8	9.5	90.5
Biscuits and rolls	100.0	7.7	92.2	6.3	93.8
Cakes and cupcakes	100.0	11.4	88.6	12.6	87.2
Bread and cracker products	100.0	8.9	9.1	6.7	93.3
Sweetrolls, coffee cakes, doughnuts	100.0	9.0	91.0	10.9	89.0
Pies, tarts, turnovers	100.0	8.2	91.7	8.5	91.5
Meats, poultry, fish, and eggs	100.0	13.7	86.3	11.6	88.3
Beef	100.0	11.9	88.1	11.6	88.2
Ground beef	100.0	12.9	87.1	10.6	89.3
Roast	100.0	12.4	87.7	10.8	89.1
Chuck roast	100.0	15.9	84.1	11.0	88.9
Round roast	100.0	11.3	88.6	10.0	90.0
Other roast	100.0	10.0	90.0	11.3	88.6
Steak	100.0	10.4	89.6	11.8	88.0
Round steak	100.0	10.4	89.7	15.9	83.8
Sirloin steak	100.0	10.9	89.1	13.5	86.2
Other steak	100.0	10.1	89.9	9.4	90.6
Pork	100.0	15.5	84.5	11.3	88.6
Bacon	100.0	16.8	83.3	8.7	91.3
Pork chops	100.0	17.6	82.5	13.4	86.4
Ham	100.0	11.0	89.0	10.8	89.2
Ham, not canned	100.0	10.9	89.1	1.1	88.9
Canned ham	100.0	14.0	85.9	5.4	95.0
Sausage	100.0	17.4	82.7	9.1	90.9
Other pork	100.0	15.8	84.2	12.9	86.9
Other meats	100.0	11.2	88.8	9.5	90.5
Frankfurters	100.0	13.0	87.0	10.7	89.2
Lunch meats (cold cuts)	100.0	10.5	89.5	8.8	91.2
Bologna, liverwurst, salami	100.0	12.5	87.5	10.3	89.6
Lamb, organ meats, and others	100.0	12.8	87.2	12.4	87.5

	total consumer units	race		Hispanic origin	
		black	white and other	Hispanic	non-Hispanic
Poultry	100.0%	15.5%	84.5%	11.8%	88.0%
Fresh and frozen chicken	100.0	15.6	84.5	12.9	86.9
Fresh and frozen whole chicken	100.0	14.5	85.6	17.1	82.5
Fresh and frozen chicken parts	100.0	16.0	84.0	11.1	88.8
Other poultry	100.0	15.4	84.7	8.0	92.0
Fish and seafood	100.0	14.0	86.0	12.6	87.2
Canned fish and seafood	100.0	11.6	88.4	9.8	90.1
Fresh fish and shellfish	100.0	14.8	85.3	14.2	85.6
Frozen fish and shellfish	100.0	13.7	86.3	11.0	88.9
Eggs	100.0	14.9	85.1	13.8	86.0
Dairy products	**100.0**	**8.8**	**91.2**	**9.3**	**90.7**
Fresh milk and cream	100.0	8.7	91.3	10.8	89.1
Fresh milk, all types	100.0	8.9	91.0	11.0	88.9
Cream	100.0	6.3	93.6	9.3	90.6
Other dairy products	100.0	8.8	91.2	8.3	91.7
Butter	100.0	9.4	90.5	6.6	93.4
Cheese	100.0	8.1	91.8	8.7	91.3
Ice cream and related products	100.0	10.0	90.0	8.1	92.0
Miscellaneous dairy products	100.0	8.0	91.9	8.7	91.3
Fruits and vegetables	**100.0**	**10.6**	**89.4**	**11.1**	**88.8**
Fresh fruits	100.0	9.3	90.6	11.8	88.0
Apples	100.0	9.6	90.3	10.1	89.8
Bananas	100.0	10.8	89.2	14.1	85.7
Oranges	100.0	11.5	88.5	11.4	88.5
Citrus fruits, excl. oranges	100.0	6.3	93.7	16.1	83.7
Other fresh fruits	100.0	8.5	91.5	10.9	89.0
Fresh vegetables	100.0	9.8	90.2	12.5	87.4
Potatoes	100.0	11.0	89.0	10.5	89.4
Lettuce	100.0	9.7	90.3	10.7	89.2
Tomatoes	100.0	9.8	90.2	16.2	83.5
Other fresh vegetables	100.0	9.3	90.7	12.3	87.6
Processed fruits	100.0	12.9	87.1	9.9	90.0
Frozen fruits and fruit juices	100.0	8.9	91.1	8.7	91.4
Frozen orange juice	100.0	8.1	91.8	9.7	90.2
Frozen fruits	100.0	9.0	91.1	7.4	92.7
Frozen fruit juices	100.0	10.3	89.6	7.4	92.5
Canned fruits	100.0	11.1	88.9	7.5	92.6
Dried fruits	100.0	10.5	89.5	7.1	93.1
Fresh fruit juice	100.0	11.4	88.6	9.9	90.1
Canned and bottled fruit juice	100.0	15.4	84.6	11.3	88.6
Processed vegetables	100.0	11.5	88.5	8.5	91.5
Frozen vegetables	100.0	12.7	87.3	6.0	94.1
Canned and dried vegetables and juices	100.0	10.9	89.1	9.7	90.2
Canned beans	100.0	12.1	87.9	9.7	90.3
Canned corn	100.0	15.1	84.9	8.3	91.7
Canned miscellaneous vegetables	100.0	10.0	90.0	6.6	93.5
Dried beans	100.0	12.0	88.0	25.5	73.7
Dried miscellaneous vegetables	100.0	8.2	91.8	9.8	90.1
Fresh and canned vegetable juices	100.0	10.2	89.8	8.6	91.4
Sugar and other sweets	**100.0**	**9.5**	**90.5**	**7.8**	**92.2**
Candy and chewing gum	100.0	7.5	92.5	0.7	93.1
Sugar	100.0	16.7	83.4	11.9	88.0
Artificial sweeteners	100.0	11.1	88.8	5.1	95.1
Jams, preserves, other sweets	100.0	10.0	89.9	7.8	92.2

	total consumer units	race		Hispanic origin	
		black	white and other	Hispanic	non-Hispanic
Fats and oils	**100.0%**	**11.8%**	**88.2%**	**9.8%**	**90.2%**
Margarine	100.0	13.3	86.7	7.9	92.1
Fats and oils	100.0	14.7	85.3	15.0	84.7
Salad dressings	100.0	10.9	89.1	8.6	91.4
Nondairy cream and imitation milk	100.0	6.1	93.8	6.2	93.9
Peanut butter	100.0	11.2	88.8	6.5	93.6
Miscellaneous foods	**100.0**	**9.3**	**90.6**	**8.1**	**91.9**
Frozen prepared foods	100.0	8.3	91.7	5.2	95.0
Frozen meals	100.0	9.3	90.7	4.0	96.2
Other frozen prepared foods	100.0	7.9	92.1	5.7	94.5
Canned and packaged soups	100.0	7.6	92.3	8.2	91.9
Potato chips, nuts, and other snacks	100.0	8.7	91.3	7.3	92.7
Potato chips and other snacks	100.0	8.8	91.2	7.6	92.4
Nuts	100.0	8.3	91.6	6.4	93.7
Condiments and seasonings	100.0	10.9	89.1	8.2	91.9
Salt, spices, and other seasonings	100.0	12.8	87.2	11.3	88.5
Olives, pickles, relishes	100.0	10.0	89.9	5.1	95.0
Sauces and gravies	100.0	11.2	88.7	8.0	92.1
Baking needs and miscellaneous products	100.0	8.3	91.6	6.7	93.4
Other canned/packaged prepared foods	100.0	10.1	89.9	10.7	89.2
Prepared salads	100.0	7.3	92.6	5.0	95.1
Prepared desserts	100.0	6.4	93.6	7.9	92.2
Baby food	100.0	15.7	84.3	10.5	89.4
Miscellaneous prepared foods	100.0	9.6	90.3	12.4	87.4
Nonalcoholic beverages	100.0	10.2	89.8	9.9	90.1
Cola	100.0	10.6	89.4	9.9	90.1
Other carbonated drinks	100.0	10.9	89.1	8.9	91.1
Coffee	100.0	6.4	93.5	8.8	91.2
Roasted coffee	100.0	5.6	94.3	8.3	91.7
Instant and freeze-dried coffee	100.0	7.9	92.0	9.7	90.3
Noncarbonated fruit-flavored drinks	100.0	17.0	83.1	11.8	88.1
Tea	100.0	10.1	89.9	10.5	89.4
Other nonalcoholic beverages and ice	100.0	9.0	91.0	10.8	89.1
Food prepared by CU on trips	**100.0**	**4.4**	**95.6**	**6.8**	**93.2**

Note: Other races include Asians, Native Americans, and Pacific Islanders. Numbers may not add to total because of rounding.
Source: Calculations by New Strategist based on the 2001 Consumer Expenditure Survey

21. Groceries: Average spending by region, 2001

(average annual spending of consumer units (CU) on groceries, by region in which consumer unit lives, 2001)

	total consumer units	Northeast	Midwest	South	West
Number of consumer units					
(in thousands, add 000)	**110,339**	**20,940**	**25,842**	**39,177**	**24,380**
Average number of persons per CU	**2.5**	**2.5**	**2.4**	**2.5**	**2.6**
Average before-tax income of CU	**$47,507.00**	**$50,568.00**	**$47,665.00**	**$44,218.00**	**$49,960.00**
Average spending of CU, total	**39,518.46**	**41,168.71**	**39,547.66**	**36,285.41**	**43,260.53**
GROCERIES	**$3,085.52**	**$3,398.64**	**$2,892.18**	**$2,983.38**	**$3,182.91**
Cereals and bakery products	**452.19**	**510.74**	**434.66**	**431.25**	**453.70**
Cereals and cereal products	156.46	179.04	148.00	146.31	162.18
Flour	8.01	8.13	6.15	8.93	8.36
Prepared flour mixes	12.89	12.57	13.81	12.74	12.44
Ready-to-eat and cooked cereals	86.04	99.01	86.96	80.65	82.52
Rice	19.95	25.15	12.79	18.97	24.59
Pasta, cornmeal, and other cereal products	29.57	34.18	28.28	25.02	34.27
Bakery products	295.73	331.70	286.67	284.94	291.52
Bread	85.37	96.69	82.63	77.56	91.02
White bread	36.64	41.07	35.65	34.13	37.88
Crackers and cookies	70.18	77.13	68.26	70.21	66.16
Cookies	46.13	50.77	44.43	46.09	43.99
Crackers	24.05	26.36	23.83	24.12	22.17
Frozen and refrigerated bakery products	26.06	27.18	25.75	29.49	19.92
Other bakery products	114.11	130.69	110.03	107.68	114.42
Biscuits and rolls	39.34	49.16	37.87	36.21	37.44
Cakes and cupcakes	33.80	37.19	31.59	33.82	33.17
Bread and cracker products	4.05	5.30	3.72	3.73	3.83
Sweetrolls, coffee cakes, doughnuts	26.32	25.91	26.64	24.93	28.58
Pies, tarts, turnovers	10.60	13.14	10.22	8.99	11.39
Meats, poultry, fish, and eggs	**827.97**	**939.34**	**720.13**	**846.37**	**815.89**
Beef	248.06	252.18	231.63	257.15	247.24
Ground beef	90.48	83.83	90.57	99.73	81.28
Roast	44.44	43.06	48.69	45.24	39.87
Chuck roast	15.03	13.53	14.34	16.70	14.37
Round roast	11.88	13.26	12.45	10.84	11.76
Other roast	17.53	16.27	21.91	17.70	13.74
Steak	92.73	96.84	79.72	95.30	98.76
Round steak	18.21	16.82	16.79	17.86	21.47
Sirloin steak	25.37	26.81	21.72	25.95	27.02
Other steak	49.15	53.20	41.22	51.48	50.27
Pork	177.31	180.77	158.88	197.71	160.98
Bacon	29.30	24.34	26.07	36.13	26.05
Pork chops	42.16	44.58	34.94	48.78	37.05
Ham	39.98	43.30	37.10	43.63	34.27
Ham, not canned	38.24	41.34	36.17	41.15	33.06
Canned ham	1.74	1.96	0.94	2.49	1.20
Sausage	25.52	27.26	23.53	28.50	21.33
Other pork	40.34	41.29	37.24	40.67	42.28
Other meats	102.06	127.17	94.52	98.72	93.68
Frankfurters	22.01	25.95	20.47	23.47	17.90
Lunch meats (cold cuts)	70.88	88.79	68.05	67.63	63.58
Bologna, liverwurst, salami	25.40	32.83	23.33	24.65	22.34
Lamb, organ meats, and others	9.17	12.43	5.99	7.63	12.21

	total consumer units	Northeast	Midwest	South	West
Poultry	$151.87	$188.63	$124.34	$151.81	$149.22
Fresh and frozen chicken	119.55	148.18	95.64	119.01	120.89
Fresh and frozen whole chicken	35.75	48.51	25.17	33.01	40.29
Fresh and frozen chicken parts	83.80	99.68	70.47	86.00	80.60
Other poultry	32.32	40.45	28.70	32.79	28.33
Fish and seafood	113.67	153.80	82.70	106.42	123.31
Canned fish and seafood	15.11	19.15	11.62	14.92	15.61
Fresh fish and shellfish	63.07	88.89	40.15	57.72	73.53
Frozen fish and shellfish	35.49	45.75	30.93	33.77	34.17
Eggs	34.99	36.78	28.06	34.56	41.45
Dairy products	**331.69**	**375.32**	**327.59**	**300.61**	**348.22**
Fresh milk and cream	135.85	140.29	135.07	125.21	149.94
Fresh milk, all types	123.50	126.12	124.43	114.76	134.31
Cream	12.35	14.17	10.64	10.44	15.63
Other dairy products	195.84	235.03	192.53	175.40	198.28
Butter	21.55	33.51	21.49	16.89	18.76
Cheese	93.39	105.28	93.55	84.68	96.94
Ice cream and related products	56.79	64.35	55.33	54.36	55.69
Miscellaneous dairy products	24.11	31.89	22.15	19.47	26.89
Fruits and vegetables	**521.74**	**607.69**	**459.15**	**482.26**	**576.93**
Fresh fruits	160.41	191.39	146.53	140.10	180.90
Apples	30.83	35.54	29.35	27.94	32.95
Bananas	31.30	35.28	27.41	28.70	36.15
Oranges	18.62	23.96	17.30	14.54	21.96
Citrus fruits, excl. oranges	13.21	15.45	11.93	10.87	16.41
Other fresh fruits	66.45	81.16	60.53	58.06	73.44
Fresh vegetables	161.62	183.40	134.32	149.12	191.70
Potatoes	30.09	32.75	26.44	30.87	30.40
Lettuce	20.82	25.08	18.82	17.79	24.13
Tomatoes	30.03	32.36	22.40	28.62	38.35
Other fresh vegetables	80.68	93.21	66.65	71.85	98.82
Processed fruits	116.03	138.61	101.58	107.87	124.88
Frozen fruits and fruit juices	13.85	11.88	15.17	11.65	17.71
Frozen orange juice	7.61	6.44	8.31	6.54	9.58
Frozen fruits	2.53	2.34	2.59	2.26	3.08
Frozen fruit juices	3.72	3.10	4.27	2.85	5.05
Canned fruits	16.27	17.37	17.42	15.99	14.56
Dried fruits	5.54	5.58	4.59	5.59	6.43
Fresh fruit juice	24.86	36.45	21.26	20.43	25.75
Canned and bottled fruit juice	55.50	67.34	43.14	54.20	60.42
Processed vegetables	83.68	94.28	76.72	85.16	79.46
Frozen vegetables	27.50	33.73	25.46	27.92	23.61
Canned and dried vegetables and juices	56.18	60.56	51.26	57.24	55.86
Canned beans	12.60	12.44	11.21	13.48	12.79
Canned corn	7.13	7.56	6.35	7.72	6.63
Canned miscellaneous vegetables	17.58	17.40	16.84	19.08	16.13
Dried beans	2.28	2.10	1.53	2.33	3.12
Dried miscellaneous vegetables	7.58	8.64	7.86	6.53	8.05
Fresh and canned vegetable juices	7.65	8.69	6.61	7.42	8.21
Sugar and other sweets	**115.96**	**117.60**	**114.17**	**111.39**	**123.77**
Candy and chewing gum	73.49	76.31	77.76	65.64	79.17
Sugar	17.91	14.93	15.78	20.85	18.00
Artificial sweeteners	5.04	5.38	4.08	5.95	4.29
Jams, preserves, other sweets	19.52	20.98	16.55	18.95	22.31

	total consumer units	Northeast	Midwest	South	West
Fats and oils	**$86.76**	**$92.32**	**$78.14**	**$89.65**	**$86.40**
Margarine	11.43	11.29	11.92	11.76	10.48
Fats and oils	24.53	28.54	17.18	27.00	24.86
Salad dressings	28.02	29.30	26.63	27.91	28.56
Nondairy cream and imitation milk	10.09	10.07	9.74	10.19	10.31
Peanut butter	12.69	13.12	12.66	12.80	12.19
Miscellaneous foods	**454.72**	**454.80**	**459.90**	**447.77**	**460.36**
Frozen prepared foods	96.19	91.00	107.23	98.26	85.70
Frozen meals	28.65	30.60	32.28	26.39	26.74
Other frozen prepared foods	67.54	60.40	74.95	71.87	58.95
Canned and packaged soups	37.27	42.41	39.23	32.63	38.23
Potato chips, nuts, and other snacks	97.37	90.66	108.59	94.22	96.36
Potato chips and other snacks	75.56	71.17	86.87	73.38	70.92
Nuts	21.81	19.50	21.73	20.85	25.44
Condiments and seasonings	84.05	88.00	81.20	81.20	88.20
Salt, spices, and other seasonings	19.83	20.81	15.55	22.04	19.93
Olives, pickles, relishes	9.97	9.52	9.56	9.81	11.02
Sauces and gravies	36.84	40.54	38.07	33.13	38.32
Baking needs and miscellaneous products	17.41	17.13	18.03	16.21	18.93
Other canned/packaged prepared foods	139.85	142.73	123.64	141.46	151.87
Prepared salads	19.55	22.62	18.97	18.22	19.62
Prepared desserts	10.15	10.75	10.96	10.20	8.70
Baby food	23.62	27.12	16.84	28.41	20.04
Miscellaneous prepared foods	86.24	82.24	76.83	83.96	103.28
Nonalcoholic beverages	256.16	261.95	261.31	245.52	262.81
Cola	87.41	80.81	96.99	86.48	84.53
Other carbonated drinks	46.14	43.02	53.23	45.61	42.22
Coffee	38.35	45.05	36.12	33.37	42.91
Roasted coffee	24.98	30.34	25.05	20.72	27.13
Instant and freeze-dried coffee	13.37	14.71	11.07	12.65	15.78
Noncarbonated fruit-flavored drinks	20.36	22.81	16.08	21.36	21.14
Tea	17.57	24.60	14.56	17.21	15.25
Other nonalcoholic beverages and ice	45.67	44.77	43.69	41.44	55.32
Food prepared by CU on trips	**38.33**	**38.88**	**37.11**	**28.56**	**54.84**

Source: Bureau of Labor Statistics, unpublished tables from the 2001 Consumer Expenditure Survey

22. Groceries: Indexed spending by region, 2001

(indexed average annual spending of consumer units (CU) on groceries, by region in which consumer unit lives, 2001; index definition: an index of 100 is the average for all consumer units; an index of 132 means that spending by consumer units in that group is 32 percent above the average for all consumer units; an index of 68 indicates spending that is 32 percent below the average for all consumer units)

	total consumer units	Northeast	Midwest	South	West
Average spending of CU, total	**$39,518**	**$41,169**	**$39,548**	**$36,285**	**$43,261**
Average spending of CU, index	**100**	**104**	**100**	**92**	**110**
GROCERIES	**100**	**110**	**94**	**97**	**103**
Cereals and bakery products	**100**	**113**	**96**	**95**	**100**
Cereals and cereal products	100	114	95	94	104
Flour	100	102	77	112	104
Prepared flour mixes	100	98	107	99	97
Ready-to-eat and cooked cereals	100	115	101	94	96
Rice	100	126	64	95	123
Pasta, cornmeal, and other cereal products	100	116	96	85	116
Bakery products	100	112	97	96	99
Bread	100	113	97	91	107
White bread	100	112	97	93	103
Crackers and cookies	100	110	97	100	94
Cookies	100	110	96	100	95
Crackers	100	110	99	100	92
Frozen and refrigerated bakery products	100	104	99	113	76
Other bakery products	100	115	96	94	100
Biscuits and rolls	100	125	96	92	95
Cakes and cupcakes	100	110	94	100	98
Bread and cracker products	100	131	92	92	95
Sweetrolls, coffee cakes, doughnuts	100	98	101	95	109
Pies, tarts, turnovers	100	124	96	85	108
Meats, poultry, fish, and eggs	**100**	**114**	**87**	**102**	**99**
Beef	100	102	93	104	100
Ground beef	100	93	100	110	90
Roast	100	97	110	102	90
Chuck roast	100	90	95	111	96
Round roast	100	112	105	91	99
Other roast	100	93	125	101	78
Steak	100	104	86	103	107
Round steak	100	92	92	98	118
Sirloin steak	100	106	86	102	107
Other steak	100	108	84	105	102
Pork	100	102	90	112	91
Bacon	100	83	89	123	89
Pork chops	100	106	83	116	88
Ham	100	108	93	109	86
Ham, not canned	100	108	95	108	87
Canned ham	100	113	54	143	69
Sausage	100	107	92	112	84
Other pork	100	102	92	101	105
Other meats	100	125	93	97	92
Frankfurters	100	118	93	107	81
Lunch meats (cold cuts)	100	125	96	95	90
Bologna, liverwurst, salami	100	129	92	97	88
Lamb, organ meats, and others	100	136	65	83	133

	total consumer units	Northeast	Midwest	South	West
Poultry	100	124	82	100	98
Fresh and frozen chicken	100	124	80	100	101
Fresh and frozen whole chicken	100	136	70	92	113
Fresh and frozen chicken parts	100	119	84	103	96
Other poultry	100	125	89	102	88
Fish and seafood	100	135	73	94	109
Canned fish and seafood	100	127	77	99	103
Fresh fish and shellfish	100	141	64	92	117
Frozen fish and shellfish	100	129	87	95	96
Eggs	100	105	80	99	119
Dairy products	**100**	**113**	**99**	**91**	**105**
Fresh milk and cream	100	103	99	92	110
Fresh milk, all types	100	102	101	93	109
Cream	100	115	86	85	127
Other dairy products	100	120	98	90	101
Butter	100	156	100	78	87
Cheese	100	113	100	91	104
Ice cream and related products	100	113	97	96	98
Miscellaneous dairy products	100	132	92	81	112
Fruits and vegetables	**100**	**117**	**88**	**92**	**111**
Fresh fruits	100	119	91	87	113
Apples	100	115	95	91	107
Bananas	100	113	88	92	116
Oranges	100	129	93	78	118
Citrus fruits, excl. oranges	100	117	90	82	124
Other fresh fruits	100	122	91	87	111
Fresh vegetables	100	114	83	92	119
Potatoes	100	109	88	103	101
Lettuce	100	121	90	85	116
Tomatoes	100	108	75	95	128
Other fresh vegetables	100	116	83	89	123
Processed fruits	100	120	88	93	108
Frozen fruits and fruit juices	100	86	110	84	128
Frozen orange juice	100	85	109	86	126
Frozen fruits	100	93	102	89	122
Frozen fruit juices	100	83	115	77	136
Canned fruits	100	107	107	98	90
Dried fruits	100	101	83	101	116
Fresh fruit juice	100	147	86	82	104
Canned and bottled fruit juice	100	121	78	98	109
Processed vegetables	100	113	92	102	95
Frozen vegetables	100	123	93	102	86
Canned and dried vegetables and juices	100	108	91	102	99
Canned beans	100	99	89	107	102
Canned corn	100	106	89	108	93
Canned miscellaneous vegetables	100	99	96	109	92
Dried beans	100	92	67	102	137
Dried miscellaneous vegetables	100	114	104	86	106
Fresh and canned vegetable juices	100	114	86	97	107
Sugar and other sweets	**100**	**101**	**99**	**96**	**107**
Candy and chewing gum	100	104	106	89	108
Sugar	100	83	88	116	101
Artificial sweeteners	100	107	81	118	85
Jams, preserves, other sweets	100	108	85	97	114

	total consumer units	Northeast	Midwest	South	West
Fats and oils	**100**	**106**	**90**	**103**	**100**
Margarine	100	99	104	103	92
Fats and oils	100	116	70	110	101
Salad dressings	100	105	95	100	102
Nondairy cream and imitation milk	100	100	97	101	102
Peanut butter	100	103	100	101	96
Miscellaneous foods	**100**	**100**	**101**	**99**	**101**
Frozen prepared foods	100	95	112	102	89
Frozen meals	100	107	113	92	93
Other frozen prepared foods	100	89	111	106	87
Canned and packaged soups	100	114	105	88	103
Potato chips, nuts, and other snacks	100	93	112	97	99
Potato chips and other snacks	100	94	115	97	94
Nuts	100	89	100	96	117
Condiments and seasonings	100	105	97	97	105
Salt, spices, and other seasonings	100	105	78	111	101
Olives, pickles, relishes	100	96	96	98	111
Sauces and gravies	100	110	103	90	104
Baking needs and miscellaneous products	100	98	104	93	109
Other canned/packaged prepared foods	100	102	88	101	109
Prepared salads	100	116	97	93	100
Prepared desserts	100	106	108	101	86
Baby food	100	115	71	120	85
Miscellaneous prepared foods	100	95	89	97	120
Nonalcoholic beverages	100	102	102	96	103
Cola	100	92	111	99	97
Other carbonated drinks	100	93	115	99	92
Coffee	100	118	94	87	112
Roasted coffee	100	122	100	83	109
Instant and freeze-dried coffee	100	110	83	95	118
Noncarbonated fruit-flavored drinks	100	112	79	105	104
Tea	100	140	83	98	87
Other nonalcoholic beverages and ice	100	98	96	91	121
Food prepared by CU on trips	**100**	**101**	**97**	**75**	**143**

Source: Calculations by New Strategist based on the 2001 Consumer Expenditure Survey

23. Groceries: Indexed per capita spending by region, 2001

(indexed average annual per capita spending of consumer units (CU) on groceries, by region in which consumer unit lives, 2001; index definition: an index of 100 is the average for all consumer units; an index of 132 means that spending by consumer units in that group is 32 percent above the average for all consumer units; an index of 68 indicates spending that is 32 percent below the average for all consumer units)

	total consumer units	Northeast	Midwest	South	West
Per capita spending of CU, total	$15,807	$16,468	$16,478	$14,514	$16,639
Per capita spending of CU, index	100	104	104	92	105
GROCERIES	100	110	98	97	99
Cereals and bakery products	100	113	100	95	97
Cereals and cereal products	100	114	99	94	100
Flour	100	102	80	112	100
Prepared flour mixes	100	98	112	99	93
Ready-to-eat and cooked cereals	100	115	105	94	92
Rice	100	126	67	95	119
Pasta, cornmeal, and other cereal products	100	116	100	85	111
Bakery products	100	112	101	96	95
Bread	100	113	101	91	103
White bread	100	112	101	93	99
Crackers and cookies	100	110	101	100	91
Cookies	100	110	100	100	92
Crackers	100	110	103	100	89
Frozen and refrigerated bakery products	100	104	103	113	74
Other bakery products	100	115	100	94	96
Biscuits and rolls	100	125	100	92	92
Cakes and cupcakes	100	110	97	100	94
Bread and cracker products	100	131	96	92	91
Sweetrolls, coffee cakes, doughnuts	100	98	105	95	104
Pies, tarts, turnovers	100	124	100	85	103
Meats, poultry, fish, and eggs	100	114	91	102	95
Beef	100	102	97	104	96
Ground beef	100	93	104	110	86
Roast	100	97	114	102	86
Chuck roast	100	90	99	111	92
Round roast	100	112	109	91	95
Other roast	100	93	130	101	75
Steak	100	104	90	103	102
Round steak	100	92	96	98	113
Sirloin steak	100	106	89	102	102
Other steak	100	108	87	105	98
Pork	100	102	93	112	87
Bacon	100	83	93	123	86
Pork chops	100	106	86	116	85
Ham	100	108	97	109	82
Ham, not canned	100	108	99	108	83
Canned ham	100	113	56	143	66
Sausage	100	107	96	112	80
Other pork	100	102	96	101	101
Other meats	100	125	97	97	88
Frankfurters	100	118	97	107	78
Lunch meats (cold cuts)	100	125	100	95	86
Bologna, liverwurst, salami	100	129	96	97	85
Lamb, organ meats, and others	100	136	68	83	128

	total consumer units	Northeast	Midwest	South	West
Poultry	100	124	85	100	95
Fresh and frozen chicken	100	124	83	100	97
Fresh and frozen whole chicken	100	136	73	92	108
Fresh and frozen chicken parts	100	119	88	103	93
Other poultry	100	125	93	102	84
Fish and seafood	100	135	76	94	104
Canned fish and seafood	100	127	80	99	99
Fresh fish and shellfish	100	141	66	92	112
Frozen fish and shellfish	100	129	91	95	93
Eggs	100	105	84	99	114
Dairy products	**100**	**113**	**103**	**91**	**101**
Fresh milk and cream	100	103	104	92	106
Fresh milk, all types	100	102	105	93	105
Cream	100	115	90	85	122
Other dairy products	100	120	102	90	97
Butter	100	156	104	78	84
Cheese	100	113	104	91	100
Ice cream and related products	100	113	102	96	94
Miscellaneous dairy products	100	132	96	81	107
Fruits and vegetables	**100**	**117**	**92**	**92**	**106**
Fresh fruits	100	119	95	87	108
Apples	100	115	99	91	103
Bananas	100	113	91	92	111
Oranges	100	129	97	78	113
Citrus fruits, excl. oranges	100	117	94	82	119
Other fresh fruits	100	122	95	87	106
Fresh vegetables	100	114	87	92	114
Potatoes	100	109	92	103	97
Lettuce	100	121	94	85	111
Tomatoes	100	108	78	95	123
Other fresh vegetables	100	116	86	89	118
Processed fruits	100	120	91	93	104
Frozen fruits and fruit juices	100	86	114	84	123
Frozen orange juice	100	85	114	86	121
Frozen fruits	100	93	107	89	117
Frozen fruit juices	100	83	120	77	131
Canned fruits	100	107	112	98	86
Dried fruits	100	101	86	101	112
Fresh fruit juice	100	147	89	82	100
Canned and bottled fruit juice	100	121	81	98	105
Processed vegetables	100	113	96	102	91
Frozen vegetables	100	123	96	102	83
Canned and dried vegetables and juices	100	108	95	102	96
Canned beans	100	99	93	107	98
Canned corn	100	106	93	108	89
Canned miscellaneous vegetables	100	99	100	109	88
Dried beans	100	92	70	102	132
Dried miscellaneous vegetables	100	114	108	86	102
Fresh and canned vegetable juices	100	114	90	97	103
Sugar and other sweets	**100**	**101**	**103**	**96**	**103**
Candy and chewing gum	100	104	110	89	104
Sugar	100	83	92	116	97
Artificial sweeteners	100	107	84	118	82
Jams, preserves, other sweets	100	108	88	97	110

	total consumer units	Northeast	Midwest	South	West
Fats and oils	**100**	**106**	**94**	**103**	**96**
Margarine	100	99	109	103	88
Fats and oils	100	116	73	110	97
Salad dressings	100	105	99	100	98
Nondairy cream and imitation milk	100	100	101	101	98
Peanut butter	100	103	104	101	92
Miscellaneous foods	**100**	**100**	**105**	**99**	**97**
Frozen prepared foods	100	95	116	102	86
Frozen meals	100	107	117	92	90
Other frozen prepared foods	100	89	116	106	84
Canned and packaged soups	100	114	110	88	99
Potato chips, nuts, and other snacks	100	93	116	97	95
Potato chips and other snacks	100	94	120	97	90
Nuts	100	89	104	96	112
Condiments and seasonings	100	105	101	97	101
Salt, spices, and other seasonings	100	105	82	111	97
Olives, pickles, relishes	100	96	100	98	106
Sauces and gravies	100	110	108	90	100
Baking needs and miscellaneous products	100	98	108	93	105
Other canned/packaged prepared foods	100	102	92	101	104
Prepared salads	100	116	101	93	97
Prepared desserts	100	106	113	101	82
Baby food	100	115	74	120	82
Miscellaneous prepared foods	100	95	93	97	115
Nonalcoholic beverages	100	102	106	96	99
Cola	100	92	116	99	93
Other carbonated drinks	100	93	120	99	88
Coffee	100	118	98	87	108
Roasted coffee	100	122	105	83	104
Instant and freeze-dried coffee	100	110	86	95	114
Noncarbonated fruit-flavored drinks	100	112	82	105	100
Tea	100	140	86	98	84
Other nonalcoholic beverages and ice	100	98	100	91	117
Food prepared by CU on trips	**100**	**101**	**101**	**75**	**138**

Note: Per capita indexes account for household size and show how much each person in a particular household demographic segment spends relative to a person in the average household.
Source: Calculations by New Strategist based on the 2001 Consumer Expenditure Survey

24. Groceries: Total spending by region, 2001

(total annual spending on groceries, by region in which consumer units live, 2001; numbers in thousands)

	total consumer units	Northeast	Midwest	South	West
Number of consumer units	110,339	20,940	25,842	39,177	24,380
Total spending of all consumer units	$4,360,427,358	$862,072,787	$1,021,990,630	$1,421,553,508	$1,054,691,721
GROCERIES	$340,453,191	$71,167,522	$74,739,716	$116,879,878	$77,599,346
Cereals and bakery products	49,894,192	10,694,896	11,232,484	16,895,081	11,061,206
Cereals and cereal products	17,263,640	3,749,098	3,824,616	5,731,987	3,953,948
Flour	883,815	170,242	158,928	349,851	203,817
Prepared flour mixes	1,422,270	263,216	356,878	499,115	303,287
Ready-to-eat and cooked cereals	9,493,568	2,073,269	2,247,220	3,159,625	2,011,838
Rice	2,201,263	526,641	330,519	743,188	599,504
Pasta, cornmeal, and other cereal products	3,262,724	715,729	730,812	980,209	835,503
Bakery products	32,630,553	6,945,798	7,408,126	11,163,094	7,107,258
Bread	9,419,640	2,024,689	2,135,325	3,038,568	2,219,068
White bread	4,042,821	860,006	921,267	1,337,111	923,514
Crackers and cookies	7,743,591	1,615,102	1,763,975	2,750,617	1,612,981
Cookies	5,089,938	1,063,124	1,148,160	1,805,668	1,072,476
Crackers	2,653,653	551,978	615,815	944,949	540,505
Frozen and refrigerated bakery products	2,875,434	569,149	665,432	1,155,330	485,650
Other bakery products	12,590,783	2,736,649	2,843,395	4,218,579	2,789,560
Biscuits and rolls	4,340,736	1,029,410	978,637	1,418,599	912,787
Cakes and cupcakes	3,729,458	778,759	816,349	1,324,966	808,685
Bread and cracker products	446,873	110,982	96,132	146,130	93,375
Sweetrolls, coffee cakes, doughnuts	2,904,123	542,555	688,431	976,683	696,780
Pies, tarts, turnovers	1,169,593	275,152	264,105	352,201	277,688
Meats, poultry, fish, and eggs	**91,357,382**	**19,669,780**	**18,609,600**	**33,158,238**	**19,891,398**
Beef	27,370,692	5,280,649	5,985,783	10,074,366	6,027,711
Ground beef	9,983,473	1,755,400	2,340,510	3,907,122	1,981,606
Roast	4,903,465	901,676	1,258,247	1,772,368	972,031
Chuck roast	1,658,395	283,318	370,574	654,256	350,341
Round roast	1,310,827	277,664	321,733	424,679	286,709
Other roast	1,934,243	340,694	566,198	693,433	334,981
Steak	10,231,736	2,027,830	2,060,124	3,733,568	2,407,769
Round steak	2,009,273	352,211	433,887	699,701	523,439
Sirloin steak	2,799,300	561,401	561,288	1,016,643	658,748
Other steak	5,423,162	1,114,008	1,065,207	2,016,832	1,225,583
Pork	19,564,208	3,785,324	4,105,777	7,745,685	3,924,692
Bacon	3,232,933	509,680	673,701	1,415,465	635,099
Pork chops	4,651,892	933,505	902,920	1,911,054	903,279
Ham	4,411,353	906,702	958,738	1,709,293	835,503
Ham, not canned	4,219,363	865,660	934,705	1,612,134	806,003
Canned ham	191,990	41,042	24,292	97,551	29,256
Sausage	2,815,851	570,824	608,062	1,116,545	520,025
Other pork	4,451,075	864,613	962,356	1,593,329	1,030,786
Other meats	11,261,198	2,662,940	2,442,586	3,867,553	2,283,918
Frankfurters	2,428,561	543,393	528,986	919,484	436,402
Lunch meats (cold cuts)	7,820,828	1,859,263	1,758,548	2,649,541	1,550,080
Bologna, liverwurst, salami	2,802,611	687,460	602,894	965,713	544,649
Lamb, organ meats, and others	1,011,809	260,284	154,794	298,921	297,680

	total consumer units	Northeast	Midwest	South	West
Poultry	$16,757,184	$3,949,912	$3,213,194	$5,947,460	$3,637,984
Fresh and frozen chicken	13,191,027	3,102,889	2,471,529	4,662,455	2,947,298
Fresh and frozen whole chicken	3,944,619	1,015,799	650,443	1,293,233	982,270
Fresh and frozen chicken parts	9,246,408	2,087,299	1,821,086	3,369,222	1,965,028
Other poultry	3,566,157	847,023	741,665	1,284,614	690,685
Fish and seafood	12,542,234	3,220,572	2,137,133	4,169,216	3,006,298
Canned fish and seafood	1,667,222	401,001	300,284	584,521	380,572
Fresh fish and shellfish	6,959,081	1,861,357	1,037,556	2,261,296	1,792,661
Frozen fish and shellfish	3,915,931	958,005	799,293	1,323,007	833,065
Eggs	3,860,762	770,173	725,127	1,353,957	1,010,551
Dairy products	**36,598,343**	**7,859,201**	**8,465,581**	**11,776,998**	**8,489,604**
Fresh milk and cream	14,989,553	2,937,673	3,490,479	4,905,352	3,655,537
Fresh milk, all types	13,626,867	2,640,953	3,215,520	4,495,953	3,274,478
Cream	1,362,687	296,720	274,959	409,008	381,059
Other dairy products	21,608,790	4,921,528	4,975,360	6,871,646	4,834,066
Butter	2,377,806	701,699	555,345	661,700	457,369
Cheese	10,304,559	2,204,563	2,417,519	3,317,508	2,363,397
Ice cream and related products	6,266,152	1,347,489	1,429,838	2,129,662	1,357,722
Miscellaneous dairy products	2,660,273	667,777	572,400	762,776	655,578
Fruits and vegetables	**57,568,270**	**12,725,029**	**11,865,354**	**18,893,500**	**14,065,553**
Fresh fruits	17,699,479	4,007,707	3,786,628	5,488,698	4,410,342
Apples	3,401,751	744,208	758,463	1,094,605	803,321
Bananas	3,453,611	738,763	708,329	1,124,380	881,337
Oranges	2,054,512	501,722	447,067	569,634	535,385
Citrus fruits, excl. oranges	1,457,578	323,523	308,295	425,854	400,076
Other fresh fruits	7,332,027	1,699,490	1,564,216	2,274,617	1,790,467
Fresh vegetables	17,832,989	3,840,396	3,471,097	5,842,074	4,673,646
Potatoes	3,320,101	685,785	683,263	1,209,394	741,152
Lettuce	2,297,258	525,175	486,346	696,959	588,289
Tomatoes	3,313,480	677,618	578,861	1,121,246	934,973
Other fresh vegetables	8,902,151	1,951,817	1,722,369	2,814,868	2,409,232
Processed fruits	12,802,634	2,902,493	2,625,030	4,226,023	3,044,574
Frozen fruits and fruit juices	1,528,195	248,767	392,023	456,412	431,770
Frozen orange juice	839,680	134,854	214,747	256,218	233,560
Frozen fruits	279,158	49,000	66,931	88,540	75,090
Frozen fruit juices	410,461	64,914	110,345	111,654	123,119
Canned fruits	1,795,216	363,728	450,168	626,440	354,973
Dried fruits	611,278	116,845	118,615	218,999	156,763
Fresh fruit juice	2,743,028	763,263	549,401	800,386	627,785
Canned and bottled fruit juice	6,123,815	1,410,100	1,114,824	2,123,393	1,473,040
Processed vegetables	9,233,168	1,974,223	1,982,598	3,336,313	1,937,235
Frozen vegetables	3,034,323	706,306	657,937	1,093,822	575,612
Canned and dried vegetables and juices	6,198,845	1,268,126	1,324,661	2,242,492	1,361,867
Canned beans	1,390,271	260,494	289,689	528,106	311,820
Canned corn	786,717	158,306	164,097	302,446	161,639
Canned miscellaneous vegetables	1,939,760	364,356	435,179	747,497	393,249
Dried beans	251,573	43,974	39,538	91,282	76,066
Dried miscellaneous vegetables	836,370	180,922	203,118	255,826	196,259
Fresh and canned vegetable juices	844,093	181,969	170,816	290,693	200,160
Sugar and other sweets	**12,794,910**	**2,462,544**	**2,950,381**	**4,363,926**	**3,017,513**
Candy and chewing gum	8,108,813	1,597,931	2,009,474	2,571,578	1,930,165
Sugar	1,976,172	312,634	407,787	816,840	438,840
Artificial sweeteners	556,109	112,657	105,435	233,103	104,590
Jams, preserves, other sweets	2,153,817	439,321	427,685	742,404	543,918

	total consumer units	Northeast	Midwest	South	West
Fats and oils	**$9,573,012**	**$1,933,181**	**$2,019,294**	**$3,512,218**	**$2,106,432**
Margarine	1,261,175	236,413	308,037	460,722	255,502
Fats and oils	2,706,616	597,628	443,966	1,057,779	606,087
Salad dressings	3,091,699	613,542	688,173	1,093,430	696,293
Nondairy cream and imitation milk	1,113,321	210,866	251,701	399,214	251,358
Peanut butter	1,400,202	274,733	327,160	501,466	297,192
Miscellaneous foods	**50,173,350**	**9,523,512**	**11,884,736**	**17,542,285**	**11,223,577**
Frozen prepared foods	10,613,508	1,905,540	2,771,038	3,849,532	2,089,366
Frozen meals	3,161,212	640,764	834,180	1,033,881	651,921
Other frozen prepared foods	7,452,296	1,264,776	1,936,858	2,815,651	1,437,201
Canned and packaged soups	4,112,335	888,065	1,013,782	1,278,346	932,047
Potato chips, nuts, and other snacks	10,743,708	1,898,420	2,806,183	3,691,257	2,349,257
Potato chips and other snacks	8,337,215	1,490,300	2,244,895	2,874,808	1,729,030
Nuts	2,406,494	408,330	561,547	816,840	620,227
Condiments and seasonings	9,273,993	1,842,720	2,098,370	3,181,172	2,150,316
Salt, spices, and other seasonings	2,188,022	435,761	401,843	863,461	485,893
Olives, pickles, relishes	1,100,080	199,349	247,050	384,326	268,668
Sauces and gravies	4,064,889	848,908	983,805	1,297,934	934,242
Baking needs and miscellaneous products	1,921,002	358,702	465,931	635,059	461,513
Other canned/packaged prepared foods	15,430,909	2,988,766	3,195,105	5,541,978	3,702,591
Prepared salads	2,157,128	473,663	490,223	713,805	478,336
Prepared desserts	1,119,941	225,105	283,228	399,605	212,106
Baby food	2,606,207	567,893	435,179	1,113,019	488,575
Miscellaneous prepared foods	9,515,635	1,722,106	1,985,441	3,289,301	2,517,966
Nonalcoholic beverages	28,264,438	5,485,233	6,752,773	9,618,737	6,407,308
Cola	9,644,732	1,692,161	2,506,416	3,388,027	2,060,841
Other carbonated drinks	5,091,042	900,839	1,375,570	1,786,863	1,029,324
Coffee	4,231,501	943,347	933,413	1,307,337	1,046,146
Roasted coffee	2,756,268	635,320	647,342	811,747	661,429
Instant and freeze-dried coffee	1,475,232	308,027	286,071	495,589	384,716
Noncarbonated fruit-flavored drinks	2,246,502	477,641	415,539	836,821	515,393
Tea	1,938,656	515,124	376,260	674,236	371,795
Other nonalcoholic beverages and ice	5,039,182	937,484	1,129,037	1,623,495	1,348,702
Food prepared by CU on trips	**4,229,294**	**814,147**	**958,997**	**1,118,895**	**1,336,999**

Note: Numbers may not add to total because of rounding.
Source: Calculations by New Strategist based on the 2001 Consumer Expenditure Survey

25. Groceries: Market shares by region, 2001

(percentage of total annual spending on groceries accounted for by consumer units by region, 2001)

	total consumer units	Northeast	Midwest	South	West
Share of total consumer units	**100.0%**	**19.0%**	**23.4%**	**35.5%**	**22.1%**
Share of total before-tax income	**100.0**	**20.2**	**23.5**	**33.1**	**23.2**
Share of total spending	**100.0**	**19.8**	**23.4**	**32.6**	**24.2**
GROCERIES	**100.0**	**20.9**	**22.0**	**34.3**	**22.8**
Cereals and bakery products	**100.0**	**21.4**	**22.5**	**33.9**	**22.2**
Cereals and cereal products	100.0	21.7	22.2	33.2	22.9
Flour	100.0	19.3	18.0	39.6	23.1
Prepared flour mixes	100.0	18.5	25.1	35.1	21.3
Ready-to-eat and cooked cereals	100.0	21.8	23.7	33.3	21.2
Rice	100.0	23.9	15.0	33.8	27.2
Pasta, cornmeal, and other cereal products	100.0	21.9	22.4	30.0	25.6
Bakery products	100.0	21.3	22.7	34.2	21.8
Bread	100.0	21.5	22.7	32.3	23.6
White bread	100.0	21.3	22.8	33.1	22.8
Crackers and cookies	100.0	20.9	22.8	35.5	20.8
Cookies	100.0	20.9	22.6	35.5	21.1
Crackers	100.0	20.8	23.2	35.6	20.4
Frozen and refrigerated bakery products	100.0	19.8	23.1	40.2	16.9
Other bakery products	100.0	21.7	22.6	33.5	22.2
Biscuits and rolls	100.0	23.7	22.5	32.7	21.0
Cakes and cupcakes	100.0	20.9	21.9	35.5	21.7
Bread and cracker products	100.0	24.8	21.5	32.7	20.9
Sweetrolls, coffee cakes, doughnuts	100.0	18.7	23.7	33.6	24.0
Pies, tarts, turnovers	100.0	23.5	22.6	30.1	23.7
Meats, poultry, fish, and eggs	**100.0**	**21.5**	**20.4**	**36.3**	**21.8**
Beef	100.0	19.3	21.9	36.8	22.0
Ground beef	100.0	17.6	23.4	39.1	19.8
Roast	100.0	18.4	25.7	36.1	19.8
Chuck roast	100.0	17.1	22.3	39.5	21.1
Round roast	100.0	21.2	24.5	32.4	21.9
Other roast	100.0	17.6	29.3	35.9	17.3
Steak	100.0	19.8	20.1	36.5	23.5
Round steak	100.0	17.5	21.6	34.8	26.1
Sirloin steak	100.0	20.1	20.1	36.3	23.5
Other steak	100.0	20.5	19.6	37.2	22.6
Pork	100.0	19.3	21.0	39.6	20.1
Bacon	100.0	15.8	20.8	43.8	19.6
Pork chops	100.0	20.1	19.4	41.1	19.4
Ham	100.0	20.6	21.7	38.7	18.9
Ham, not canned	100.0	20.5	22.2	38.2	19.1
Canned ham	100.0	21.4	12.7	50.8	15.2
Sausage	100.0	20.3	21.6	39.7	18.5
Other pork	100.0	19.4	21.6	35.8	23.2
Other meats	100.0	23.6	21.7	34.3	20.3
Frankfurters	100.0	22.4	21.8	37.9	18.0
Lunch meats (cold cuts)	100.0	23.8	22.5	33.9	19.8
Bologna, liverwurst, salami	100.0	24.5	21.5	34.5	19.4
Lamb, organ meats, and others	100.0	25.7	15.3	29.5	29.4

	total consumer units	Northeast	Midwest	South	West
Poultry	100.0%	23.6%	19.2%	35.5%	21.7%
Fresh and frozen chicken	100.0	23.5	18.7	35.3	22.3
Fresh and frozen whole chicken	100.0	25.8	16.5	32.8	24.9
Fresh and frozen chicken parts	100.0	22.6	19.7	36.4	21.3
Other poultry	100.0	23.8	20.8	36.0	19.4
Fish and seafood	100.0	25.7	17.0	33.2	24.0
Canned fish and seafood	100.0	24.1	18.0	35.1	22.8
Fresh fish and shellfish	100.0	26.7	14.9	32.5	25.8
Frozen fish and shellfish	100.0	24.5	20.4	33.8	21.3
Eggs	100.0	19.9	18.8	35.1	26.2
Dairy products	**100.0**	**21.5**	**23.1**	**32.2**	**23.2**
Fresh milk and cream	100.0	19.6	23.3	32.7	24.4
Fresh milk, all types	100.0	19.4	23.6	33.0	24.0
Cream	100.0	21.8	20.2	30.0	28.0
Other dairy products	100.0	22.8	23.0	31.8	22.4
Butter	100.0	29.5	23.4	27.8	19.2
Cheese	100.0	21.4	23.5	32.2	22.9
Ice cream and related products	100.0	21.5	22.8	34.0	21.7
Miscellaneous dairy products	100.0	25.1	21.5	28.7	24.6
Fruits and vegetables	**100.0**	**22.1**	**20.6**	**32.8**	**24.4**
Fresh fruits	100.0	22.6	21.4	31.0	24.9
Apples	100.0	21.9	22.3	32.2	23.6
Bananas	100.0	21.4	20.5	32.6	25.5
Oranges	100.0	24.4	21.8	27.7	26.1
Citrus fruits, excl. oranges	100.0	22.2	21.2	29.2	27.4
Other fresh fruits	100.0	23.2	21.3	31.0	24.4
Fresh vegetables	100.0	21.5	19.5	32.8	26.2
Potatoes	100.0	20.7	20.6	36.4	22.3
Lettuce	100.0	22.9	21.2	30.3	25.6
Tomatoes	100.0	20.5	17.5	33.8	28.2
Other fresh vegetables	100.0	21.9	19.3	31.6	27.1
Processed fruits	100.0	22.7	20.5	3.3	23.8
Frozen fruits and fruit juices	100.0	16.3	25.7	29.9	28.3
Frozen orange juice	100.0	16.1	25.6	30.5	27.8
Frozen fruits	100.0	17.6	24.0	31.7	26.9
Frozen fruit juices	100.0	15.8	26.9	27.2	30.0
Canned fruits	100.0	20.3	25.1	34.9	19.8
Dried fruits	100.0	19.1	19.4	35.8	25.6
Fresh fruit juice	100.0	27.8	20.0	29.2	22.9
Canned and bottled fruit juice	100.0	23.0	18.2	34.7	24.1
Processed vegetables	100.0	21.4	21.5	36.1	21.0
Frozen vegetables	100.0	23.3	21.7	36.1	19.0
Canned and dried vegetables and juices	100.0	20.5	21.4	36.2	22.0
Canned beans	100.0	18.7	20.8	38.0	22.4
Canned corn	100.0	20.1	20.9	38.4	20.5
Canned miscellaneous vegetables	100.0	18.8	22.4	38.5	20.3
Dried beans	100.0	17.5	15.7	36.3	30.2
Dried miscellaneous vegetables	100.0	21.6	24.3	30.6	23.5
Fresh and canned vegetable juices	100.0	21.6	20.2	34.4	23.7
Sugar and other sweets	**100.0**	**19.2**	**23.1**	**34.1**	**23.6**
Candy and chewing gum	100.0	19.7	24.8	31.7	23.8
Sugar	100.0	15.8	20.6	41.3	22.2
Artificial sweeteners	100.0	20.3	19.0	41.9	18.8
Jams, preserves, other sweets	100.0	20.4	19.9	34.5	25.3

	total consumer units	Northeast	Midwest	South	West
Fats and oils	**100.0%**	**20.2%**	**21.1%**	**36.7%**	**2.2%**
Margarine	100.0	18.7	24.4	36.5	20.3
Fats and oils	100.0	22.1	16.4	39.1	22.4
Salad dressings	100.0	19.8	22.3	35.4	22.5
Nondairy cream and imitation milk	100.0	18.9	22.6	35.9	22.6
Peanut butter	100.0	19.6	23.4	35.8	21.2
Miscellaneous foods	**100.0**	**19.0**	**23.7**	**35.0**	**22.4**
Frozen prepared foods	100.0	18.0	26.1	36.3	19.7
Frozen meals	100.0	20.3	26.4	32.7	20.6
Other frozen prepared foods	100.0	17.0	26.0	37.8	19.3
Canned and packaged soups	100.0	21.6	24.7	31.1	22.7
Potato chips, nuts, and other snacks	100.0	17.7	26.1	34.4	21.9
Potato chips and other snacks	100.0	17.9	26.9	34.5	20.7
Nuts	100.0	17.0	23.3	33.9	25.8
Condiments and seasonings	100.0	19.9	22.6	34.3	23.2
Salt, spices, and other seasonings	100.0	19.9	18.4	39.5	22.2
Olives, pickles, relishes	100.0	18.1	22.5	34.9	24.4
Sauces and gravies	100.0	20.9	24.2	31.9	23.0
Baking needs and miscellaneous products	100.0	18.7	24.3	33.1	24.0
Other canned/packaged prepared foods	100.0	19.4	20.7	35.9	24.0
Prepared salads	100.0	22.0	22.7	33.1	22.2
Prepared desserts	100.0	20.1	25.3	35.7	18.9
Baby food	100.0	21.8	16.7	42.7	18.7
Miscellaneous prepared foods	100.0	18.1	20.9	34.6	26.5
Nonalcoholic beverages	100.0	19.4	23.9	34.0	22.7
Cola	100.0	17.5	26.0	35.1	21.4
Other carbonated drinks	100.0	17.7	27.0	35.1	20.2
Coffee	100.0	22.3	22.1	30.9	24.7
Roasted coffee	100.0	23.1	23.5	29.5	24.0
Instant and freeze-dried coffee	100.0	20.9	19.4	33.6	26.1
Noncarbonated fruit-flavored drinks	100.0	21.3	18.5	37.2	22.9
Tea	100.0	26.6	19.4	34.8	19.2
Other nonalcoholic beverages and ice	100.0	18.6	22.4	32.2	26.8
Food prepared by CU on trips	**100.0**	**19.3**	**22.7**	**26.5**	**31.6**

Note: Numbers may not add to total because of rounding.
Source: Calculations by New Strategist based on the 2001 Consumer Expenditure Survey

26. Groceries: Average spending by education, 2001

(average annual spending of consumer units (CU) on groceries, by education of consumer unit reference person, 2001)

	total consumer units	less than high school graduate	high school graduate	some college	associate's degree	college graduate total	bachelor's degree	master's, professional, doctorate
Number of consumer units								
(in thousands, add 000)	110,339	17,177	31,866	22,992	9,704	28,660	18,880	9,780
Average number of persons per CU	2.5	2.6	2.6	2.4	2.5	2.5	2.5	2.5
Average before-tax income of CU	$47,507.00	$24,390.00	$37,793.00	$41,045.00	$52,395.00	$75,833.00	$70,137.00	$86,693.00
Average spending of CU, total	39,518.46	24,080.51	33,041.32	37,070.30	43,610.31	56,461.69	53,677.88	61,757.36
GROCERIES	3,085.52	2,892.49	2,956.37	2,902.82	3,088.89	3,476.90	3,342.28	3,722.37
Cereals and bakery products	452.19	421.73	433.28	411.76	448.92	520.52	505.60	547.68
Cereals and cereal products	156.46	153.51	149.22	141.15	146.19	181.20	176.18	190.34
Flour	8.01	11.79	7.01	6.46	7.48	8.24	7.97	8.73
Prepared flour mixes	12.89	11.86	12.13	12.41	13.14	14.61	14.28	15.22
Ready-to-eat and cooked cereals	86.04	74.39	84.31	78.96	82.49	101.26	97.43	108.25
Rice	19.95	23.19	17.90	17.45	14.95	23.91	24.18	23.43
Pasta, cornmeal, and other cereal products	29.57	32.26	27.86	25.87	28.13	33.17	32.33	34.72
Bakery products	295.73	271.22	284.07	207.61	302.73	339.31	329.41	357.33
Bread	85.37	86.13	83.50	75.28	84.22	94.94	92.51	99.37
White bread	36.64	42.85	39.09	31.99	33.92	34.72	34.64	34.87
Crackers and cookies	70.18	60.38	67.35	64.71	72.43	82.36	78.02	90.25
Cookies	46.13	40.56	45.31	43.33	47.53	51.92	48.09	58.89
Crackers	24.05	19.83	22.04	21.38	24.90	30.44	29.93	31.36
Frozen and refrigerated bakery products	26.06	23.26	25.39	23.79	27.94	29.50	31.57	25.73
Other bakery products	114.11	101.44	107.83	106.83	118.14	132.51	127.31	141.99
Biscuits and rolls	39.34	30.04	36.44	38.01	41.25	48.31	46.13	52.29
Cakes and cupcakes	33.80	33.65	32.05	30.22	40.89	36.05	33.22	41.19
Bread and cracker products	4.05	3.41	3.38	3.91	3.89	5.32	5.47	5.04
Sweetrolls, coffee cakes, doughnuts	26.32	25.52	24.92	24.76	25.31	29.86	29.67	30.20
Pies, tarts, turnovers	10.60	8.81	11.03	9.92	6.80	12.98	12.83	13.27
Meats, poultry, fish, and eggs	827.97	873.61	844.07	786.91	788.16	828.07	795.44	887.45
Beef	248.06	258.88	261.22	238.36	243.19	236.17	236.10	236.29
Ground beef	90.48	104.45	98.24	83.78	87.56	79.80	82.99	74.01
Roast	44.44	45.68	48.31	41.01	46.40	41.34	43.19	37.97
Chuck roast	15.03	18.17	15.97	15.72	11.97	12.69	12.81	12.46
Round roast	11.88	12.44	12.32	9.78	12.47	12.44	12.16	12.95
Other roast	17.53	15.07	20.02	15.51	21.96	16.21	18.22	12.56
Steak	92.73	84.58	93.37	95.86	90.54	95.17	93.26	98.65
Round steak	18.21	18.90	20.48	18.84	14.89	15.97	16.69	14.66
Sirloin steak	25.37	25.35	22.73	23.33	29.68	28.33	28.36	28.26
Other steak	49.15	40.33	50.16	53.69	45.97	50.87	48.21	55.73
Pork	177.31	204.64	191.16	171.79	167.54	153.58	152.91	154.80
Bacon	29.30	31.95	31.84	27.33	30.13	26.15	27.17	24.30
Pork chops	42.16	49.72	43.49	41.77	41.72	36.73	37.57	35.19
Ham	39.98	45.31	44.83	35.03	42.10	34.48	32.61	37.90
Ham, not canned	38.24	42.74	43.03	34.04	41.48	32.35	30.62	35.51
Canned ham	1.74	2.56	1.80	0.99	0.63	2.13	1.99	2.39
Sausage	25.52	28.64	27.49	25.36	22.73	22.62	22.51	22.81
Other pork	40.34	49.02	43.51	42.29	30.86	33.60	33.05	34.59
Other meats	102.06	107.98	101.78	91.89	108.56	104.31	100.09	111.98
Frankfurters	22.01	26.31	22.42	19.75	21.84	20.82	20.36	21.65
Lunch meats (cold cuts)	70.88	71.01	71.67	64.83	80.34	71.19	69.81	73.69
Bologna, liverwurst, salami	25.40	30.58	27.73	22.48	24.13	22.41	21.58	23.93
Lamb, organ meats, and others	9.17	10.66	7.70	7.31	6.38	12.30	9.92	16.64

	total consumer units	less than high school graduate	high school graduate	some college	associate's degree	college graduate total	bachelor's degree	master's, professional, doctorate
Poultry	$151.87	$158.14	$147.02	$151.54	$139.22	$158.19	$151.43	$170.49
Fresh and frozen chicken	119.55	128.93	115.79	120.05	102.32	123.80	117.66	134.98
Fresh and frozen whole chicken	35.75	46.85	31.40	36.23	26.85	36.80	33.21	43.31
Fresh and frozen chicken parts	83.80	82.08	84.40	83.82	75.47	87.01	84.45	91.67
Other poultry	32.32	29.21	31.33	31.48	36.90	34.39	33.77	35.51
Fish and seafood	113.67	101.45	107.42	100.19	99.55	142.68	123.38	177.81
Canned fish and seafood	15.11	12.79	14.56	14.55	12.44	18.42	16.49	21.94
Fresh fish and shellfish	63.07	60.69	53.32	55.37	53.10	84.44	76.46	98.96
Frozen fish and shellfish	35.49	27.97	39.54	30.26	34.02	39.82	30.43	56.91
Eggs	34.99	42.51	35.47	33.15	30.11	33.14	31.52	36.09
Dairy products	**331.69**	**286.13**	**313.39**	**306.15**	**351.19**	**390.87**	**379.06**	**412.38**
Fresh milk and cream	135.85	131.31	131.49	128.61	136.75	148.42	145.58	153.61
Fresh milk, all types	123.50	120.21	121.21	117.38	124.97	132.03	129.71	136.24
Cream	12.35	11.09	10.28	11.23	11.78	16.40	15.86	17.37
Other dairy products	195.84	154.83	181.90	177.54	214.44	242.45	233.48	258.77
Butter	21.55	18.43	22.81	18.15	21.04	24.70	24.42	25.19
Cheese	93.39	75.32	85.49	88.01	104.76	112.78	110.06	117.72
Ice cream and related products	56.79	45.45	54.50	50.85	58.77	69.69	67.33	74.00
Miscellaneous dairy products	24.11	15.63	19.10	20.52	29.88	35.28	31.67	41.86
Fruits and vegetables	**521.74**	**490.65**	**465.18**	**478.15**	**506.74**	**640.21**	**597.05**	**718.75**
Fresh fruits	160.41	153.16	136.36	142.14	149.03	208.82	187.33	247.94
Apples	30.83	27.98	27.30	26.98	31.05	39.19	35.50	45.91
Bananas	31.30	33.49	28.60	26.59	28.50	37.50	36.35	39.59
Oranges	18.62	18.35	15.81	19.42	16.57	22.00	20.51	24.71
Citrus fruits, excl. oranges	13.21	14.59	10.42	11.59	10.92	17.51	15.39	21.36
Other fresh fruits	66.45	58.75	54.22	57.56	61.99	92.63	79.59	116.37
Fresh vegetables	161.62	157.06	140.03	147.11	163.54	198.35	186.46	219.99
Potatoes	30.09	29.64	28.40	28.29	31.12	33.22	33.02	33.58
Lettuce	20.82	18.99	17.54	18.75	23.25	26.23	23.68	30.88
Tomatoes	30.03	33.97	26.48	25.43	28.49	35.64	33.05	40.36
Other fresh vegetables	80.68	74.46	67.60	74.65	80.68	103.26	96.72	115.16
Processed fruits	116.03	99.15	108.07	110.47	113.49	139.72	132.56	152.77
Frozen fruits and fruit juices	13.85	10.02	11.18	14.49	16.30	17.72	17.98	17.25
Frozen orange juice	7.61	5.27	6.12	7.50	9.37	10.09	11.13	8.19
Frozen fruits	2.53	2.15	2.05	2.61	1.77	3.50	2.93	4.54
Frozen fruit juices	3.72	2.61	3.01	4.38	5.17	4.14	3.93	4.51
Canned fruits	16.27	14.70	17.14	14.19	14.83	18.29	16.52	21.52
Dried fruits	5.54	3.88	5.62	4.91	4.42	7.29	5.92	9.79
Fresh fruit juice	24.86	22.18	22.25	22.97	20.86	32.10	27.30	40.82
Canned and bottled fruit juice	55.50	48.37	51.87	53.92	57.08	64.32	64.83	63.39
Processed vegetables	83.68	81.27	80.72	78.43	80.68	93.31	90.71	98.05
Frozen vegetables	27.50	21.80	27.09	27.84	26.34	31.44	29.11	35.67
Canned and dried vegetables and juices	56.18	59.47	53.64	50.59	54.34	61.87	61.59	62.38
Canned beans	12.60	13.58	11.75	11.60	11.84	13.98	14.91	12.28
Canned corn	7.13	8.02	8.07	6.73	6.19	6.18	6.68	5.27
Canned miscellaneous vegetables	17.58	18.08	16.47	15.50	16.38	20.50	19.34	22.61
Dried beans	2.28	3.95	1.75	2.12	2.01	2.08	2.42	1.46
Dried miscellaneous vegetables	7.58	7.84	7.67	6.38	9.23	7.66	7.57	7.84
Fresh and canned vegetable juices	7.65	7.13	6.96	7.53	8.00	8.68	9.41	7.34
Sugar and other sweets	**115.96**	**98.73**	**112.25**	**106.46**	**120.80**	**135.55**	**132.96**	**140.27**
Candy and chewing gum	73.49	52.55	71.38	69.10	77.57	89.93	88.28	92.92
Sugar	17.91	23.10	17.72	16.20	16.08	16.99	16.98	17.02
Artificial sweeteners	5.04	5.08	4.86	4.05	6.88	5.33	4.63	6.61
Jams, preserves, other sweets	19.52	18.01	18.29	17.11	20.27	23.30	23.07	23.72

	total consumer units	less than high school graduate	high school graduate	some college	associate's degree	college graduate total	college graduate bachelor's degree	college graduate master's, professional, doctorate
Fats and oils	**$86.76**	**$90.25**	**$85.80**	**$81.40**	**$82.09**	**$91.41**	**$87.45**	**$98.63**
Margarine	11.43	11.85	12.09	11.20	8.99	11.45	11.36	11.62
Fats and oils	24.53	31.30	23.71	20.70	20.93	25.60	23.89	28.72
Salad dressings	28.02	25.56	27.72	28.01	28.18	29.74	28.71	31.63
Nondairy cream and imitation milk	10.09	10.56	9.68	10.58	10.09	9.91	9.35	10.93
Peanut butter	12.69	10.98	12.61	10.91	13.89	14.71	14.14	15.73
Miscellaneous foods	**454.72**	**367.42**	**417.79**	**450.38**	**485.26**	**539.14**	**522.77**	**568.93**
Frozen prepared foods	96.19	71.89	89.22	95.70	108.69	114.12	113.10	115.98
Frozen meals	28.65	22.97	27.07	28.32	24.66	35.32	34.72	36.40
Other frozen prepared foods	67.54	48.92	62.15	67.37	84.03	78.81	78.38	79.58
Canned and packaged soups	37.27	31.79	36.70	36.14	38.78	41.43	37.40	48.77
Potato chips, nuts, and other snacks	97.37	72.60	89.53	102.14	103.59	114.74	111.23	121.13
Potato chips and other snacks	75.56	57.13	70.61	78.24	79.52	88.39	87.72	89.62
Nuts	21.81	15.47	18.92	23.90	24.07	26.35	23.52	31.51
Condiments and seasonings	84.05	65.68	78.03	80.83	86.73	102.89	99.98	108.18
Salt, spices, and other seasonings	19.83	18.84	17.12	18.62	20.14	24.19	24.95	22.82
Olives, pickles, relishes	9.97	7.11	8.86	9.72	9.27	13.27	11.12	17.19
Sauces and gravies	36.84	27.60	36.73	35.18	38.02	43.19	43.04	43.46
Baking needs and miscellaneous products	17.41	12.13	15.31	17.32	19.30	22.23	20.87	24.72
Other canned/packaged prepared foods	139.85	125.46	124.31	135.59	147.48	165.95	161.05	174.88
Prepared salads	19.55	14.18	16.95	18.47	20.50	26.01	25.16	27.56
Prepared desserts	10.15	9.20	9.17	9.16	11.43	12.10	10.59	14.84
Baby food	23.62	18.39	24.10	25.61	18.10	26.54	27.38	24.99
Miscellaneous prepared foods	86.24	83.56	73.69	82.05	97.45	100.93	97.91	106.44
Nonalcoholic beverages	256.16	243.38	260.04	243.29	264.62	266.05	260.69	275.81
Cola	87.41	88.17	95.18	82.89	97.47	78.32	77.17	80.42
Other carbonated drinks	46.14	45.40	46.63	43.72	50.84	46.23	46.04	46.59
Coffee	38.35	36.53	39.40	32.44	35.82	43.54	41.24	47.73
Roasted coffee	24.98	21.64	25.44	21.13	22.97	30.02	28.29	33.16
Instant and freeze-dried coffee	13.37	14.89	13.97	11.32	12.85	13.52	12.95	14.57
Noncarbonated fruit-flavored drinks	20.36	21.92	19.38	19.19	17.79	22.22	23.24	20.38
Tea	17.57	14.03	17.32	16.06	17.80	20.97	19.86	22.99
Other nonalcoholic beverages and ice	45.67	36.89	41.72	48.75	42.59	53.90	52.43	56.56
Food prepared by CU on trips	**38.33**	**17.59**	**24.58**	**38.31**	**41.11**	**65.08**	**61.26**	**72.46**

Source: Bureau of Labor Statistics, unpublished tables from the 2001 Consumer Expenditure Survey

(indexed average annual spending of consumer units (CU) on groceries, by education of consumer unit reference person, 2001; index definition: an index of 100 is the average for all consumer units; an index of 132 means that spending by consumer units in that group is 32 percent above the average for all consumer units; an index of 68 indicates spending that is 32 percent below the average for all consumer units)

	total consumer units	less than high school graduate	high school graduate	some college	associate's degree	college graduate total	bachelor's degree	master's, professional, doctorate
Average spending of CU, total	$39,518	$24,081	$33,041	$37,070	$43,610	$56,462	$53,678	$61,757
Average spending of CU, index	100	61	84	94	110	143	136	156
GROCERIES	100	94	96	94	100	113	108	121
Cereals and bakery products	100	93	96	91	99	115	112	121
Cereals and cereal products	100	98	95	90	93	116	113	122
Flour	100	147	88	81	93	103	100	109
Prepared flour mixes	100	92	94	96	102	113	111	118
Ready-to-eat and cooked cereals	100	87	98	92	96	118	113	126
Rice	100	116	90	88	75	120	121	117
Pasta, cornmeal, and other cereal products	100	109	94	88	95	112	109	117
Bakery products	100	92	96	70	102	115	111	121
Bread	100	101	98	88	99	111	108	116
White bread	100	117	107	87	93	95	95	95
Crackers and cookies	100	86	96	92	103	117	111	129
Cookies	100	88	98	94	103	113	104	128
Crackers	100	83	92	89	104	127	124	130
Frozen and refrigerated bakery products	100	89	97	91	107	113	121	99
Other bakery products	100	89	95	94	104	116	112	124
Biscuits and rolls	100	76	93	97	105	123	117	133
Cakes and cupcakes	100	100	95	89	121	107	98	122
Bread and cracker products	100	84	84	97	96	131	135	124
Sweetrolls, coffee cakes, doughnuts	100	97	95	94	96	113	113	115
Pies, tarts, turnovers	100	83	104	94	64	123	121	125
Meats, poultry, fish, and eggs	100	106	102	95	95	100	96	107
Beef	100	104	105	96	98	95	95	95
Ground beef	100	115	109	93	97	88	92	82
Roast	100	103	109	92	104	93	97	85
Chuck roast	100	121	106	105	80	84	85	83
Round roast	100	105	104	82	105	105	102	109
Other roast	100	86	114	89	125	93	104	72
Steak	100	91	101	103	98	103	101	106
Round steak	100	104	113	104	82	88	92	81
Sirloin steak	100	100	90	92	117	112	112	111
Other steak	100	82	102	109	94	104	98	113
Pork	100	115	108	97	95	87	86	87
Bacon	100	109	109	93	103	89	93	83
Pork chops	100	118	103	99	99	87	89	84
Ham	100	113	112	88	105	86	82	95
Ham, not canned	100	112	113	89	109	85	80	93
Canned ham	100	147	103	57	36	122	114	137
Sausage	100	112	108	99	89	89	88	89
Other pork	100	122	108	105	77	83	82	86
Other meats	100	106	100	90	106	102	98	110
Frankfurters	100	120	102	90	99	95	93	98
Lunch meats (cold cuts)	100	100	101	92	113	100	99	104
Bologna, liverwurst, salami	100	120	109	89	95	88	85	94
Lamb, organ meats, and others	100	116	84	80	70	134	108	182

	total consumer units	less than high school graduate	high school graduate	some college	associate's degree	college graduate total	bachelor's degree	master's, professional, doctorate
Poultry	100	104	97	100	92	104	100	112
Fresh and frozen chicken	100	108	97	100	86	104	98	113
Fresh and frozen whole chicken	100	131	88	101	75	103	93	121
Fresh and frozen chicken parts	100	98	101	100	90	104	101	109
Other poultry	100	90	97	97	114	106	105	110
Fish and seafood	100	89	95	88	88	126	109	156
Canned fish and seafood	100	85	96	96	82	122	109	145
Fresh fish and shellfish	100	96	85	88	84	134	121	157
Frozen fish and shellfish	100	79	111	85	96	112	86	160
Eggs	100	122	101	95	86	95	90	103
Dairy products	**100**	**86**	**95**	**92**	**106**	**118**	**114**	**124**
Fresh milk and cream	100	97	97	95	101	109	107	113
Fresh milk, all types	100	97	98	95	101	107	105	110
Cream	100	90	83	91	95	133	128	141
Other dairy products	100	79	93	91	110	124	119	132
Butter	100	86	106	84	98	115	113	117
Cheese	100	81	92	94	112	121	118	126
Ice cream and related products	100	80	96	90	104	123	119	130
Miscellaneous dairy products	100	65	79	85	124	146	131	174
Fruits and vegetables	**100**	**94**	**89**	**92**	**97**	**123**	**114**	**138**
Fresh fruits	100	96	85	89	93	130	117	155
Apples	100	91	89	88	101	127	115	149
Bananas	100	107	91	85	91	120	116	127
Oranges	100	99	85	104	89	118	110	133
Citrus fruits, excl. oranges	100	110	79	88	83	133	117	162
Other fresh fruits	100	88	82	87	93	139	120	175
Fresh vegetables	100	97	87	91	101	123	115	136
Potatoes	100	99	94	94	103	110	110	112
Lettuce	100	91	84	90	112	126	114	148
Tomatoes	100	113	88	85	95	119	110	134
Other fresh vegetables	100	92	84	93	100	128	120	143
Processed fruits	100	86	93	95	98	120	114	132
Frozen fruits and fruit juices	100	72	81	105	118	128	130	125
Frozen orange juice	100	69	80	99	123	133	146	108
Frozen fruits	100	85	81	103	70	138	116	179
Frozen fruit juices	100	70	81	118	139	111	106	121
Canned fruits	100	90	105	87	91	112	102	132
Dried fruits	100	70	101	89	80	132	107	177
Fresh fruit juice	100	89	90	92	84	129	110	164
Canned and bottled fruit juice	100	87	94	97	103	116	117	114
Processed vegetables	100	97	97	94	96	112	108	117
Frozen vegetables	100	79	99	101	96	114	106	130
Canned and dried vegetables and juices	100	106	96	90	97	110	110	111
Canned beans	100	108	93	92	94	111	118	98
Canned corn	100	113	113	94	87	87	94	74
Canned miscellaneous vegetables	100	103	94	88	93	117	110	129
Dried beans	100	173	77	93	88	91	106	64
Dried miscellaneous vegetables	100	103	101	84	122	101	100	103
Fresh and canned vegetable juices	100	93	91	98	105	114	123	96
Sugar and other sweets	**100**	**85**	**97**	**92**	**104**	**117**	**115**	**121**
Candy and chewing gum	100	72	97	94	106	122	120	126
Sugar	100	129	99	91	90	95	95	95
Artificial sweeteners	100	101	96	80	137	106	92	131
Jams, preserves, other sweets	100	92	94	88	104	119	118	122

	total consumer units	less than high school graduate	high school graduate	some college	associate's degree	college graduate total	bachelor's degree	master's, professional, doctorate
Fats and oils	**100**	**104**	**99**	**94**	**95**	**105**	**101**	**114**
Margarine	100	104	106	98	79	100	99	102
Fats and oils	100	128	97	84	85	104	97	117
Salad dressings	100	91	99	100	101	106	103	113
Nondairy cream and imitation milk	100	105	96	105	100	98	93	108
Peanut butter	100	87	99	86	110	116	111	124
Miscellaneous foods	**100**	**81**	**92**	**99**	**107**	**119**	**115**	**125**
Frozen prepared foods	100	75	93	100	113	119	118	121
Frozen meals	100	80	95	99	86	123	121	127
Other frozen prepared foods	100	72	92	100	124	117	116	118
Canned and packaged soups	100	85	99	97	104	111	100	131
Potato chips, nuts, and other snacks	100	75	92	105	106	118	114	124
Potato chips and other snacks	100	76	93	104	105	117	116	119
Nuts	100	71	87	110	110	121	108	145
Condiments and seasonings	100	78	93	96	103	122	119	129
Salt, spices, and other seasonings	100	95	86	94	102	122	126	115
Olives, pickles, relishes	100	71	89	98	93	133	112	172
Sauces and gravies	100	75	100	96	103	117	117	118
Baking needs and miscellaneous products	100	70	88	100	111	128	120	142
Other canned/packaged prepared foods	100	90	89	97	106	119	115	125
Prepared salads	100	73	87	95	105	133	129	141
Prepared desserts	100	91	90	90	113	119	104	146
Baby food	100	78	102	108	77	112	116	106
Miscellaneous prepared foods	100	97	85	95	113	117	114	123
Nonalcoholic beverages	100	95	102	95	103	104	102	108
Cola	100	101	109	95	112	90	88	92
Other carbonated drinks	100	98	101	95	110	100	100	101
Coffee	100	95	103	85	93	114	108	125
Roasted coffee	100	87	102	85	92	120	113	133
Instant and freeze-dried coffee	100	111	105	85	96	101	97	109
Noncarbonated fruit-flavored drinks	100	108	95	94	87	109	114	100
Tea	100	80	99	91	101	119	113	131
Other nonalcoholic beverages and ice	100	81	91	107	93	118	115	124
Food prepared by CU on trips	**100**	**46**	**64**	**100**	**107**	**170**	**160**	**189**

Source: Calculations by New Strategist based on the 2001 Consumer Expenditure Survey

28. Groceries: Indexed per capita spending by education, 2001

(indexed average annual per capita spending of consumer units (CU) on groceries, by education of consumer unit reference person, 2001; index definition: an index of 100 is the average for all consumer units; an index of 132 means that spending by consumer units in that group is 32 percent above the average for all consumer units; an index of 68 indicates spending that is 32 percent below the average for all consumer units)

	total consumer units	less than high school graduate	high school graduate	some college	associate's degree	college graduate total	college graduate bachelor's degree	college graduate master's, professional, doctorate
Per capita spending of CU, total	$15,807	$9,262	$12,708	$15,446	$17,444	$22,585	$21,471	$24,703
Per capita spending of CU, index	100	59	80	98	110	143	136	156
GROCERIES	100	90	92	98	100	113	108	121
Cereals and bakery products	100	90	92	95	99	115	112	121
Cereals and cereal products	100	94	92	94	93	116	113	122
Flour	100	142	84	84	93	103	100	109
Prepared flour mixes	100	89	91	100	102	113	111	118
Ready-to-eat and cooked cereals	100	83	94	96	96	118	113	126
Rice	100	112	86	91	75	120	121	117
Pasta, cornmeal, and other cereal products	100	105	91	91	95	112	109	117
Bakery products	100	88	92	73	102	115	111	121
Bread	100	97	94	92	99	111	108	116
White bread	100	113	103	91	93	95	95	95
Crackers and cookies	100	83	92	96	103	117	111	129
Cookies	100	85	94	98	103	113	104	128
Crackers	100	79	88	93	104	127	124	130
Frozen and refrigerated bakery products	100	86	94	95	107	113	121	99
Other bakery products	100	86	91	98	104	116	112	124
Biscuits and rolls	100	73	89	101	105	123	117	133
Cakes and cupcakes	100	96	91	93	121	107	98	122
Bread and cracker products	100	81	80	101	96	131	135	124
Sweetrolls, coffee cakes, doughnuts	100	93	91	98	96	113	113	115
Pies, tarts, turnovers	100	80	100	98	64	123	121	125
Meats, poultry, fish, and eggs	100	102	98	99	95	100	96	107
Beef	100	100	101	100	98	95	95	95
Ground beef	100	111	104	97	97	88	92	82
Roast	100	99	105	96	104	93	97	85
Chuck roast	100	116	102	109	80	84	85	83
Round roast	100	101	100	86	105	105	102	109
Other roast	100	83	110	92	125	93	104	72
Steak	100	88	97	108	98	103	101	106
Round steak	100	100	108	108	82	88	92	81
Sirloin steak	100	96	86	96	117	112	112	111
Other steak	100	79	98	114	94	104	98	113
Pork	100	111	104	101	95	87	86	87
Bacon	100	105	105	97	103	89	93	83
Pork chops	100	113	99	103	99	87	89	84
Ham	100	109	108	91	105	86	82	95
Ham, not canned	100	108	108	93	109	85	80	93
Canned ham	100	142	100	59	36	122	114	137
Sausage	100	108	104	104	89	89	88	89
Other pork	100	117	104	109	77	83	82	86
Other meats	100	102	96	94	106	102	98	110
Frankfurters	100	115	98	94	99	95	93	98
Lunch meats (cold cuts)	100	96	97	95	113	100	99	104
Bologna, liverwurst, salami	100	116	105	92	95	88	85	94
Lamb, organ meats, and others	100	112	81	83	70	134	108	182

	total consumer units	less than high school graduate	high school graduate	some college	associate's degree	college graduate total	bachelor's degree	master's, professional, doctorate
Poultry	100	100	93	104	92	104	100	112
Fresh and frozen chicken	100	104	93	105	86	104	98	113
Fresh and frozen whole chicken	100	126	85	106	75	103	93	121
Fresh and frozen chicken parts	100	94	97	104	90	104	101	109
Other poultry	100	87	93	102	114	106	105	110
Fish and seafood	100	86	91	92	88	126	109	156
Canned fish and seafood	100	81	93	100	82	122	109	145
Fresh fish and shellfish	100	93	81	91	84	134	121	157
Frozen fish and shellfish	100	76	107	89	96	112	86	160
Eggs	100	117	98	99	86	95	90	103
Dairy products	**100**	**83**	**91**	**96**	**106**	**118**	**114**	**124**
Fresh milk and cream	100	93	93	99	101	109	107	113
Fresh milk, all types	100	94	94	99	101	107	105	110
Cream	100	86	80	95	95	133	128	141
Other dairy products	100	76	89	94	110	124	119	132
Butter	100	82	102	88	98	115	113	117
Cheese	100	78	88	98	112	121	118	126
Ice cream and related products	100	77	92	93	104	123	119	130
Miscellaneous dairy products	100	62	76	89	124	146	131	174
Fruits and vegetables	**100**	**90**	**86**	**96**	**97**	**123**	**114**	**138**
Fresh fruits	100	92	82	92	93	130	117	155
Apples	100	87	85	91	101	127	115	149
Bananas	100	103	88	89	91	120	116	127
Oranges	100	95	82	109	89	118	110	133
Citrus fruits, excl. oranges	100	106	76	91	83	133	117	162
Other fresh fruits	100	85	79	90	93	139	120	175
Fresh vegetables	100	93	83	95	101	123	115	136
Potatoes	100	95	91	98	103	110	110	112
Lettuce	100	88	81	94	112	126	114	148
Tomatoes	100	109	85	88	95	119	110	134
Other fresh vegetables	100	89	81	96	100	128	120	143
Processed fruits	100	82	90	99	98	120	114	132
Frozen fruits and fruit juices	100	70	78	109	118	128	130	125
Frozen orange juice	100	67	77	103	123	133	146	108
Frozen fruits	100	82	78	108	70	138	116	179
Frozen fruit juices	100	68	78	123	139	111	106	121
Canned fruits	100	87	101	91	91	112	102	132
Dried fruits	100	67	98	92	80	132	107	177
Fresh fruit juice	100	86	86	96	84	129	110	164
Canned and bottled fruit juice	100	84	90	101	103	116	117	114
Processed vegetables	100	93	93	98	96	112	108	117
Frozen vegetables	100	76	95	106	96	114	106	130
Canned and dried vegetables and juices	100	102	92	94	97	110	110	111
Canned beans	100	104	90	96	94	111	118	98
Canned corn	100	108	109	98	87	87	94	74
Canned miscellaneous vegetables	100	99	90	92	93	117	110	129
Dried beans	100	167	74	97	88	91	106	64
Dried miscellaneous vegetables	100	100	97	88	122	101	100	103
Fresh and canned vegetable juices	100	90	88	103	105	114	123	96
Sugar and other sweets	**100**	**82**	**93**	**96**	**104**	**117**	**115**	**121**
Candy and chewing gum	100	69	93	98	106	122	120	126
Sugar	100	124	95	94	90	95	95	95
Artificial sweeteners	100	97	93	84	137	106	92	131
Jams, preserves, other sweets	100	89	90	91	104	119	118	122

	total consumer units	less than high school graduate	high school graduate	some college	associate's degree	college graduate total	college graduate bachelor's degree	college graduate master's, professional, doctorate
Fats and oils	**100**	**100**	**95**	**98**	**95**	**105**	**101**	**114**
Margarine	100	100	102	102	79	100	99	102
Fats and oils	100	123	93	88	85	104	97	117
Salad dressings	100	88	95	104	101	106	103	113
Nondairy cream and imitation milk	100	101	92	109	100	98	93	108
Peanut butter	100	83	96	90	110	116	111	124
Miscellaneous foods	**100**	**78**	**88**	**103**	**107**	**119**	**115**	**125**
Frozen prepared foods	100	72	89	104	113	119	118	121
Frozen meals	100	77	91	103	86	123	121	127
Other frozen prepared foods	100	70	89	104	124	117	116	118
Canned and packaged soups	100	82	95	101	104	111	100	131
Potato chips, nuts, and other snacks	100	72	88	109	106	118	114	124
Potato chips and other snacks	100	73	90	108	105	117	116	119
Nuts	100	68	83	114	110	121	108	145
Condiments and seasonings	100	75	89	100	103	122	119	129
Salt, spices, and other seasonings	100	91	83	98	102	122	126	115
Olives, pickles, relishes	100	69	85	102	93	133	112	172
Sauces and gravies	100	72	96	100	103	117	117	118
Baking needs and miscellaneous products	100	67	85	104	111	128	120	142
Other canned/packaged prepared foods	100	86	86	101	106	119	115	125
Prepared salads	100	70	83	98	105	133	129	141
Prepared desserts	100	87	87	94	113	119	104	146
Baby food	100	75	98	113	77	112	116	106
Miscellaneous prepared foods	100	93	82	99	113	117	114	123
Nonalcoholic beverages	100	91	98	99	103	104	102	108
Cola	100	97	105	99	112	90	88	92
Other carbonated drinks	100	95	97	99	110	100	100	101
Coffee	100	92	99	88	93	114	108	125
Roasted coffee	100	83	98	88	92	120	113	133
Instant and freeze-dried coffee	100	107	101	88	96	101	97	109
Noncarbonated fruit-flavored drinks	100	104	92	98	87	109	114	100
Tea	100	77	95	95	101	119	113	131
Other nonalcoholic beverages and ice	100	78	88	111	93	118	115	124
Food prepared by CU on trips	**100**	**44**	**62**	**104**	**107**	**170**	**160**	**189**

Note: Per capita indexes account for household size and show how much each person in a particular household demographic segment spends relative to a person in the average household.
Source: Calculations by New Strategist based on the 2001 Consumer Expenditure Survey

29. Groceries: Total spending by education, 2001

(total annual spending on groceries, by consumer unit (CU) education group, 2001; numbers in thousands)

	total consumer units	less than high school graduate	high school graduate	some college	associate's degree	college graduate total	bachelor's degree	master's, professional, doctorate
Number of consumer units	110,339	17,177	31,866	22,992	9,704	28,660	18,880	9,780
Total spending of all CUs	$4,360,427,358	$413,630,920	$1,052,894,703	$852,320,338	$423,194,448	$1,618,192,035	$1,013,438,374	$603,986,981
GROCERIES	**$340,453,191**	**$49,684,301**	**$94,207,686**	**$66,741,637**	**$29,974,589**	**$99,647,954**	**$63,102,246**	**$36,404,779**
Cereals and bakery products	**49,894,192**	**7,244,056**	**13,806,901**	**9,467,186**	**4,356,320**	**14,918,103**	**9,545,728**	**5,356,310**
Cereals and cereal products	17,263,640	2,636,841	4,755,045	3,245,321	1,418,628	5,193,192	3,326,278	1,861,525
Flour	883,815	202,517	223,381	148,528	72,586	236,158	150,474	85,379
Prepared flour mixes	1,422,270	203,719	386,535	285,331	127,511	418,723	269,606	148,852
Ready-to-eat and cooked cereals	9,493,568	1,277,797	2,686,623	1,815,448	800,483	2,902,112	1,839,478	1,058,685
Rice	2,201,263	398,335	570,401	401,210	145,075	685,261	456,518	229,145
Pasta, cornmeal, and other cereal produ	3,262,724	554,130	887,787	594,803	272,974	950,652	610,390	339,562
Bakery products	32,630,553	4,658,746	9,052,175	4,773,369	2,937,692	9,724,625	6,219,261	3,494,687
Bread	9,419,640	1,479,455	2,660,811	1,730,838	817,271	2,720,980	1,746,589	971,839
White bread	4,042,821	736,034	1,245,642	735,514	329,160	995,075	654,003	341,029
Crackers and cookies	7,743,591	1,037,147	2,146,175	1,487,812	702,861	2,360,438	1,473,018	882,645
Cookies	5,089,938	696,699	1,443,849	996,243	461,231	1,488,027	907,939	575,944
Crackers	2,653,653	340,620	702,327	491,569	241,630	872,410	565,078	306,701
Frozen and refrigerated bakery products	2,875,434	399,537	809,078	546,980	271,130	845,470	596,042	251,639
Other bakery products	12,590,783	1,742,435	3,436,111	2,456,235	1,146,431	3,797,737	2,403,613	1,388,662
Biscuits and rolls	4,340,736	515,997	1,161,197	873,926	400,290	1,384,565	870,934	511,396
Cakes and cupcakes	3,729,458	578,006	1,021,305	694,818	396,797	1,033,193	627,194	402,838
Bread and cracker products	446,873	58,574	107,707	89,899	37,749	152,471	103,274	49,291
Sweetrolls, coffee cakes, doughnuts	2,904,123	438,357	794,101	569,282	245,608	855,788	560,170	295,356
Pies, tarts, turnovers	1,169,593	151,329	351,482	228,081	65,987	372,007	242,230	129,781
Meats, poultry, fish, and eggs	**91,357,382**	**15,005,999**	**26,897,135**	**18,092,635**	**7,648,305**	**23,732,486**	**15,017,964**	**8,679,261**
Beef	27,370,692	4,446,782	8,324,037	5,480,373	2,359,916	6,768,632	4,457,568	2,310,916
Ground beef	9,983,473	1,794,138	3,130,516	1,926,270	849,682	2,287,068	1,566,851	723,818
Roast	4,903,465	784,645	1,539,447	942,902	450,266	1,184,804	815,427	371,347
Chuck roast	1,658,395	312,106	508,900	361,434	116,157	363,695	241,853	121,859
Round roast	1,310,827	213,682	392,589	224,862	121,009	356,530	229,581	126,651
Other roast	1,934,243	258,857	637,957	356,606	213,100	464,579	343,994	122,837
Steak	10,231,736	1,452,831	2,975,328	2,204,013	878,600	2,727,572	1,760,749	964,797
Round steak	2,009,273	324,645	652,616	433,169	144,493	457,700	315,107	143,375
Sirloin steak	2,799,300	435,437	724,314	536,403	288,015	811,938	535,437	276,383
Other steak	5,423,162	692,748	1,598,399	1,234,441	446,093	1,457,934	910,205	545,039
Pork	19,564,208	3,515,101	6,091,505	3,949,796	1,625,808	4,401,603	2,886,941	1,513,944
Bacon	3,232,933	548,805	1,014,613	628,371	292,382	749,459	512,970	237,654
Pork chops	4,651,892	854,040	1,385,852	960,376	404,851	1,052,682	709,322	344,158
Ham	4,411,353	778,290	1,428,553	805,410	408,538	988,197	615,677	370,662
Ham, not canned	4,219,363	734,145	1,371,194	782,648	402,522	927,151	578,106	347,288
Canned ham	191,990	43,973	57,359	22,762	6,114	61,046	37,571	23,374
Sausage	2,815,851	491,949	875,996	583,077	220,572	648,289	424,989	223,082
Other pork	4,451,075	842,017	1,386,490	972,332	299,465	962,976	623,984	338,290
Other meats	11,261,198	1,854,773	3,243,322	2,112,735	1,053,466	2,989,525	1,889,699	1,095,164
Frankfurters	2,428,561	451,927	714,436	454,092	211,935	596,701	384,397	211,737
Lunch meats (cold cuts)	7,820,828	1,219,739	2,283,836	1,490,571	779,619	2,040,305	1,318,013	720,688
Bologna, liverwurst, salami	2,802,611	525,273	883,644	516,860	234,158	642,271	407,430	234,035
Lamb, organ meats, and others	1,011,809	183,107	245,368	168,072	61,912	352,518	187,290	162,739

	total consumer units	less than high school graduate	high school graduate	some college	associate's degree	college graduate total	bachelor's degree	master's, professional, doctorate
Poultry	$16,757,184	$2,716,371	$4,684,939	$3,484,208	$1,350,991	$4,533,725	$2,858,998	$1,667,392
Fresh and frozen chicken	13,191,027	2,214,631	3,689,764	2,760,190	992,913	3,548,108	2,221,421	1,320,104
Fresh and frozen whole chicken	3,944,619	804,742	1,000,592	833,000	260,552	1,054,688	627,005	423,572
Fresh and frozen chicken parts	9,246,408	1,409,888	2,689,490	1,927,189	732,361	2,493,707	1,594,416	896,533
Other poultry	3,566,157	501,740	998,362	723,788	358,078	985,617	637,578	347,288
Fish and seafood	12,542,234	1,742,607	3,423,046	2,303,569	966,033	4,089,209	2,329,414	1,738,982
Canned fish and seafood	1,667,222	219,694	463,969	334,534	120,718	527,917	311,331	214,573
Fresh fish and shellfish	6,959,081	1,042,472	1,699,095	1,273,067	515,282	2,420,050	1,443,565	967,829
Frozen fish and shellfish	3,915,931	480,441	1,259,982	695,738	330,130	1,141,241	574,518	556,580
Eggs	3,860,762	730,194	1,130,287	762,185	292,187	949,792	595,098	352,960
Dairy products	**36,598,343**	**4,914,855**	**9,986,486**	**7,039,001**	**3,407,948**	**11,202,334**	**7,156,653**	**4,033,076**
Fresh milk and cream	14,989,553	2,255,512	4,190,060	2,957,001	1,327,022	4,253,717	2,748,550	1,502,306
Fresh milk, all types	13,626,867	2,064,847	3,862,478	2,698,801	1,212,709	3,783,980	2,448,925	1,332,427
Cream	1,362,687	190,493	327,583	258,200	114,313	470,024	299,437	169,879
Other dairy products	21,608,790	2,659,515	5,796,425	4,082,000	2,080,926	6,948,617	4,408,102	2,530,771
Butter	2,377,806	316,572	726,864	417,305	204,172	707,902	461,050	246,358
Cheese	10,304,559	1,293,772	2,724,224	2,023,526	1,016,591	3,232,275	2,077,933	1,151,302
Ice cream and related products	6,266,152	780,695	1,736,697	1,169,143	570,304	1,997,315	1,271,190	723,720
Miscellaneous dairy products	2,660,273	268,477	608,641	471,796	289,956	1,011,125	597,930	409,391
Fruits and vegetables	**57,568,270**	**8,427,895**	**14,823,426**	**10,993,625**	**4,917,405**	**18,348,419**	**11,272,304**	**7,029,375**
Fresh fruits	17,699,479	2,630,829	4,345,248	3,268,083	1,446,187	5,984,781	3,536,790	2,424,853
Apples	3,401,751	480,613	869,942	620,324	301,309	1,123,185	670,240	449,000
Bananas	3,453,611	575,258	911,368	611,357	276,564	1,074,750	686,288	387,190
Oranges	2,054,512	315,198	503,802	446,505	160,795	630,520	387,229	241,664
Citrus fruits, excl. oranges	1,457,578	250,612	332,044	266,477	105,968	501,837	290,563	208,901
Other fresh fruits	7,332,027	1,009,149	1,727,775	1,323,420	601,551	2,654,776	1,502,659	1,138,099
Fresh vegetables	17,832,989	2,697,820	4,462,196	3,382,353	1,586,992	5,684,711	3,520,365	2,151,502
Potatoes	3,320,101	509,126	904,994	650,444	301,989	952,085	623,418	328,412
Lettuce	2,297,258	326,191	558,930	431,100	225,618	751,752	447,078	302,006
Tomatoes	3,313,480	583,503	843,812	584,687	276,467	1,021,442	623,984	394,721
Other fresh vegetables	8,902,151	1,278,999	2,154,142	1,716,353	782,919	2,959,432	1,826,074	1,126,265
Processed fruits	12,802,634	1,703,100	3,443,759	2,539,926	1,101,307	4,004,375	2,502,733	1,494,091
Frozen fruits and fruit juices	1,528,195	172,114	356,262	333,154	158,175	507,855	339,462	168,705
Frozen orange juice	839,680	90,523	195,020	172,440	90,927	289,179	210,134	80,098
Frozen fruits	279,158	36,931	65,325	60,009	17,176	100,310	55,318	44,401
Frozen fruit juices	410,461	44,832	95,917	100,705	50,170	118,652	74,198	44,108
Canned fruits	1,795,216	252,502	546,183	326,257	143,910	524,191	311,898	210,466
Dried fruits	611,278	66,647	179,087	112,891	42,892	208,931	111,770	95,746
Fresh fruit juice	2,743,028	380,986	709,019	528,126	202,425	919,986	515,424	399,220
Canned and bottled fruit juice	6,123,815	830,852	1,652,889	1,239,729	553,904	1,843,411	1,223,990	619,954
Processed vegetables	9,233,168	1,395,975	2,572,224	1,803,263	782,919	2,674,265	1,712,605	958,929
Frozen vegetables	3,034,323	374,459	863,250	640,097	255,603	901,070	549,597	348,853
Canned and dried vegetables and juices	6,198,845	1,021,516	1,709,292	1,163,165	527,315	1,773,194	1,162,819	610,076
Canned beans	1,390,271	233,264	374,426	266,707	114,895	400,667	281,501	120,098
Canned corn	786,717	137,760	257,159	154,736	60,068	177,119	126,118	51,541
Canned miscellaneous vegetables	1,939,760	310,560	524,833	356,376	158,952	587,530	365,139	221,126
Dried beans	251,573	67,849	55,766	48,743	19,505	59,613	45,690	14,279
Dried miscellaneous vegetables	836,370	134,668	244,412	146,689	89,568	219,536	142,922	76,675
Fresh and canned vegetable juices	844,093	122,472	221,787	173,130	77,632	248,769	177,661	71,785
Sugar and other sweets	**12,794,910**	**1,695,885**	**3,576,959**	**2,447,728**	**1,172,243**	**3,884,863**	**2,510,285**	**1,371,841**
Candy and chewing gum	8,108,813	902,651	2,274,595	1,588,747	752,739	2,577,394	1,666,726	908,758
Sugar	1,976,172	396,789	564,666	372,470	156,040	486,933	320,582	166,456
Artificial sweeteners	556,109	87,259	154,869	93,118	66,764	152,758	87,414	64,646
Jams, preserves, other sweets	2,153,817	309,358	582,829	393,393	196,700	667,778	435,562	231,982

	total consumer units	less than high school graduate	high school graduate	some college	associate's degree	college graduate total	bachelor's degree	master's, professional, doctorate
Fats and oils	**$9,573,012**	**$1,550,224**	**$2,734,103**	**$1,871,549**	**$796,601**	**$2,619,811**	**$1,651,056**	**$964,601**
Margarine	1,261,175	203,548	385,260	257,510	87,239	328,157	214,477	113,644
Fats and oils	2,706,616	537,640	755,543	475,934	203,105	733,696	451,043	280,882
Salad dressings	3,091,699	439,044	883,326	644,006	273,459	852,348	542,045	309,341
Nondairy cream and imitation milk	1,113,321	181,389	308,463	243,255	97,913	284,021	176,528	106,895
Peanut butter	1,400,202	188,604	401,830	250,843	134,789	421,589	266,963	153,839
Miscellaneous foods	**50,173,350**	**6,311,173**	**13,313,296**	**10,355,137**	**4,708,963**	**15,451,752**	**9,869,898**	**5,564,135**
Frozen prepared foods	10,613,508	1,234,855	2,843,085	2,200,334	1,054,728	3,270,679	2,135,328	1,134,284
Frozen meals	3,161,212	394,556	862,613	651,133	239,301	1,012,271	655,514	355,992
Other frozen prepared foods	7,452,296	840,299	1,980,472	1,548,971	815,427	2,258,695	1,479,814	778,292
Canned and packaged soups	4,112,335	546,057	1,169,482	830,931	376,321	1,187,384	706,112	476,971
Potato chips, nuts, and other snacks	10,743,708	1,247,050	2,852,963	2,348,403	1,005,237	3,288,448	2,100,022	1,184,651
Potato chips and other snacks	8,337,215	981,322	2,250,058	1,798,894	771,662	2,533,257	1,656,154	876,484
Nuts	2,406,494	265,728	602,905	549,509	233,575	755,191	444,058	308,168
Condiments and seasonings	9,273,993	1,128,185	2,486,504	1,858,443	841,628	2,948,827	1,887,622	1,058,000
Salt, spices, and other seasonings	2,188,022	323,615	545,546	428,111	195,439	693,285	471,056	223,180
Olives, pickles, relishes	1,100,080	122,129	282,333	223,482	89,956	380,318	209,946	168,118
Sauces and gravies	4,064,889	474,085	1,170,438	808,859	368,946	1,237,825	812,595	425,039
Baking needs and miscellaneous products	1,921,002	208,357	487,869	398,221	187,287	637,112	394,026	241,762
Other canned/packaged prepared foods	15,430,909	2,155,026	3,961,263	3,117,485	1,431,146	4,756,127	3,040,624	1,710,326
Prepared salads	2,157,128	243,570	540,129	424,662	198,932	745,447	475,021	269,537
Prepared desserts	1,119,941	158,028	292,211	210,607	110,917	346,786	199,939	145,135
Baby food	2,606,207	315,885	767,971	588,825	175,642	760,636	516,934	244,402
Miscellaneous prepared foods	9,515,635	1,435,310	2,348,206	1,886,494	945,655	2,892,654	1,848,541	1,040,983
Nonalcoholic beverages	28,264,438	4,180,538	8,286,435	5,593,724	2,567,873	7,624,993	4,921,827	2,697,422
Cola	9,644,732	1,514,496	3,033,006	1,905,807	945,849	2,244,651	1,456,970	786,508
Other carbonated drinks	5,091,042	779,836	1,485,912	1,005,210	493,351	1,324,952	869,235	455,650
Coffee	4,231,501	627,476	1,255,520	745,861	347,597	1,247,856	778,611	466,799
Roasted coffee	2,756,268	371,710	810,671	485,821	222,901	860,373	534,115	324,305
Instant and freeze-dried coffee	1,475,232	255,766	445,168	260,269	124,696	387,483	244,496	142,495
Noncarbonated fruit-flavored drinks	2,246,502	376,520	617,563	441,217	172,634	636,825	438,771	199,316
Tea	1,938,656	240,993	551,919	369,252	172,731	601,000	374,957	224,842
Other nonalcoholic beverages and ice	5,039,182	633,660	1,329,450	1,120,860	413,293	1,544,774	989,878	553,157
Food prepared by CU on trips	**4,229,294**	**302,143**	**783,266**	**880,824**	**398,931**	**1,865,193**	**1,156,589**	**708,659**

Note: Numbers may not add to total because of rounding.
Source: Calculations by New Strategist based on the 2001 Consumer Expenditure Survey

30. Groceries: Market shares by education, 2001

(percentage of total annual spending on groceries accounted for by consumer unit education groups, 2001)

	total consumer units	less than high school graduate	high school graduate	some college	associate's degree	college graduate total	bachelor's degree	master's, professional, doctorate
Share of total consumer units	100.0%	15.6%	28.9%	20.8%	8.8%	26.0%	17.1%	8.9%
Share of total before-tax income	100.0	8.0	23.0	18.0	9.7	41.5	25.3	16.2
Share of total spending	100.0	9.5	24.1	19.5	9.7	37.1	23.2	13.9
GROCERIES	**100.0**	**14.6**	**27.7**	**19.6**	**8.8**	**29.3**	**18.5**	**10.7**
Cereals and bakery products	**100.0**	**14.5**	**27.7**	**19.0**	**8.7**	**29.9**	**19.1**	**10.7**
Cereals and cereal products	100.0	15.3	27.5	18.8	8.2	30.1	19.3	10.8
Flour	100.0	22.9	25.3	16.8	8.2	26.7	17.0	9.7
Prepared flour mixes	100.0	14.3	27.2	20.1	9.0	29.4	19.0	10.5
Ready-to-eat and cooked cereals	100.0	13.5	28.3	19.1	8.4	30.6	19.4	11.2
Rice	100.0	18.1	25.9	18.2	6.6	31.1	20.7	10.4
Pasta, cornmeal, and other cereal products	100.0	17.0	27.2	18.2	8.4	29.1	18.7	10.4
Bakery products	100.0	14.3	27.7	14.6	0.9	29.8	19.1	10.7
Bread	100.0	15.7	28.2	18.4	8.7	28.9	18.5	10.3
White bread	100.0	18.2	30.8	18.2	8.1	24.6	16.2	8.4
Crackers and cookies	100.0	13.4	27.7	19.2	9.1	30.5	19.0	11.4
Cookies	100.0	13.7	28.4	19.6	9.1	29.2	17.8	11.3
Crackers	100.0	12.8	26.5	18.5	9.1	32.9	21.3	11.6
Frozen and refrigerated bakery products	100.0	13.9	28.1	19.0	9.4	29.4	20.7	8.8
Other bakery products	100.0	13.8	27.3	19.5	9.1	30.2	19.1	11.0
Biscuits and rolls	100.0	11.9	26.8	20.1	9.2	31.9	20.1	11.8
Cakes and cupcakes	100.0	15.5	27.4	18.6	10.6	27.7	16.8	10.8
Bread and cracker products	100.0	13.1	24.1	20.1	8.4	34.1	23.1	11.0
Sweetrolls, coffee cakes, doughnuts	100.0	15.1	27.3	19.6	8.5	29.5	19.3	10.2
Pies, tarts, turnovers	100.0	12.9	30.1	19.5	5.6	31.8	20.7	11.1
Meats, poultry, fish, and eggs	**100.0**	**16.4**	**29.4**	**19.8**	**8.4**	**26.0**	**16.4**	**9.5**
Beef	100.0	16.2	30.4	20.0	8.6	24.7	16.3	8.4
Ground beef	100.0	18.0	31.4	19.3	8.5	22.9	15.7	7.3
Roast	100.0	1.6	31.4	19.2	9.2	24.2	16.6	7.6
Chuck roast	100.0	18.8	30.7	21.8	0.7	21.9	14.6	7.3
Round roast	100.0	16.3	29.9	17.2	9.2	27.2	17.5	9.7
Other roast	100.0	13.4	33.0	18.4	11.0	24.0	17.8	6.4
Steak	100.0	14.2	29.1	21.5	8.6	26.7	17.2	9.4
Round steak	100.0	16.2	32.5	21.6	7.2	22.8	15.7	7.1
Sirloin steak	100.0	15.6	25.9	19.2	10.3	2.9	19.1	9.9
Other steak	100.0	12.8	29.5	22.8	8.2	26.9	16.8	10.1
Pork	100.0	18.0	31.1	20.2	8.3	22.5	14.8	7.7
Bacon	100.0	17.0	31.4	19.4	9.0	23.2	15.9	7.4
Pork chops	100.0	18.4	29.8	20.6	8.7	22.6	15.2	7.4
Ham	100.0	17.6	32.4	18.3	9.3	22.4	14.0	8.4
Ham, not canned	100.0	17.4	32.5	18.5	9.5	22.0	13.7	8.2
Canned ham	100.0	22.9	29.9	11.9	3.2	31.8	19.6	12.2
Sausage	100.0	17.5	31.1	20.7	7.8	23.0	15.1	7.9
Other pork	100.0	18.9	31.1	21.8	6.7	21.6	14.0	7.6
Other meats	100.0	16.5	28.8	18.8	9.4	26.5	16.8	9.7
Frankfurters	100.0	18.6	29.4	18.7	8.7	24.6	15.8	8.7
Lunch meats (cold cuts)	100.0	15.6	29.2	19.1	10.0	26.1	16.9	9.2
Bologna, liverwurst, salami	100.0	18.7	31.5	18.4	8.4	22.9	14.5	8.4
Lamb, organ meats, and others	100.0	18.1	24.3	16.6	6.1	34.8	18.5	16.1

	total consumer units	less than high school graduate	high school graduate	some college	associate's degree	college graduate total	bachelor's degree	master's, professional, doctorate
Poultry	100.0%	16.2%	28.0%	20.8%	8.1%	27.1%	17.1%	10.0%
Fresh and frozen chicken	100.0	16.8	28.0	20.9	7.5	26.9	16.8	1.0
Fresh and frozen whole chicken	100.0	20.4	25.4	21.1	6.6	26.7	15.9	10.7
Fresh and frozen chicken parts	100.0	15.2	29.1	20.8	7.9	27.0	17.2	9.7
Other poultry	100.0	14.1	28.0	20.3	10.0	27.6	17.9	9.7
Fish and seafood	100.0	13.9	27.3	18.4	7.7	32.6	18.6	13.9
Canned fish and seafood	100.0	13.2	27.8	20.1	7.2	31.7	18.7	12.9
Fresh fish and shellfish	100.0	15.0	24.4	18.3	7.4	34.8	20.7	13.9
Frozen fish and shellfish	100.0	12.3	32.2	17.8	8.4	29.1	14.7	14.2
Eggs	100.0	18.9	29.3	19.7	7.6	24.6	15.4	9.1
Dairy products	**100.0**	**13.4**	**27.3**	**19.2**	**9.3**	**30.6**	**19.6**	**11.0**
Fresh milk and cream	100.0	15.1	28.0	19.7	8.9	28.4	18.3	10.0
Fresh milk, all types	100.0	15.2	28.3	19.8	8.9	27.8	18.0	9.8
Cream	100.0	14.0	24.0	18.9	8.4	34.5	22.0	12.5
Other dairy products	100.0	12.3	26.8	18.9	9.6	32.2	20.4	11.7
Butter	100.0	13.3	30.6	17.5	8.6	29.8	19.4	10.4
Cheese	100.0	12.6	26.4	19.6	9.9	31.4	20.2	11.2
Ice cream and related products	100.0	12.5	27.7	18.7	9.1	31.9	20.3	11.5
Miscellaneous dairy products	100.0	10.1	22.9	17.7	10.9	3.8	22.5	15.4
Fruits and vegetables	**100.0**	**14.6**	**25.7**	**19.1**	**8.5**	**31.9**	**19.6**	**12.2**
Fresh fruits	100.0	14.9	24.6	18.5	8.2	33.8	20.0	13.7
Apples	100.0	14.1	25.6	18.2	8.9	33.0	19.7	13.2
Bananas	100.0	16.7	26.4	17.7	0.8	31.1	19.9	11.2
Oranges	100.0	15.3	24.5	21.7	7.8	30.7	18.8	11.8
Citrus fruits, excl. oranges	100.0	17.2	22.8	18.3	7.3	34.4	19.9	14.3
Other fresh fruits	100.0	13.8	23.6	18.1	8.2	36.2	20.5	15.5
Fresh vegetables	100.0	15.1	25.0	19.0	8.9	31.9	19.7	12.1
Potatoes	100.0	15.3	27.3	19.6	9.1	28.7	18.8	9.9
Lettuce	100.0	14.2	24.3	18.8	9.8	32.7	19.5	13.1
Tomatoes	100.0	17.6	25.5	17.6	8.3	30.8	18.8	11.9
Other fresh vegetables	100.0	14.4	24.2	19.3	8.8	33.2	20.5	12.7
Processed fruits	100.0	13.3	26.9	19.8	8.6	31.3	19.5	11.7
Frozen fruits and fruit juices	100.0	11.3	23.3	21.8	10.4	33.2	22.2	11.0
Frozen orange juice	100.0	10.8	23.2	20.5	10.8	34.4	25.0	9.5
Frozen fruits	100.0	13.2	23.4	21.5	6.2	35.9	19.8	15.9
Frozen fruit juices	100.0	10.9	23.4	24.5	12.2	28.9	18.1	10.7
Canned fruits	100.0	14.1	30.4	18.2	8.0	29.2	17.4	11.7
Dried fruits	100.0	10.9	29.3	18.5	7.0	34.2	18.3	15.7
Fresh fruit juice	100.0	13.9	25.8	19.3	7.4	33.5	18.8	14.6
Canned and bottled fruit juice	100.0	13.6	27.0	20.2	9.1	30.1	20.0	10.1
Processed vegetables	100.0	15.1	27.9	19.5	8.5	29.0	18.5	10.4
Frozen vegetables	100.0	12.3	28.4	21.1	8.4	29.7	18.1	11.5
Canned and dried vegetables and juices	100.0	16.5	27.6	18.8	8.5	28.6	18.8	9.8
Canned beans	100.0	16.8	26.9	19.2	8.3	28.8	20.2	8.6
Canned corn	100.0	17.5	32.7	19.7	7.6	22.5	16.0	6.6
Canned miscellaneous vegetables	100.0	16.0	27.1	18.4	8.2	30.3	18.8	11.4
Dried beans	100.0	27.0	22.2	19.4	7.8	23.7	18.2	5.7
Dried miscellaneous vegetables	100.0	16.1	29.2	17.5	10.7	26.2	17.1	9.2
Fresh and canned vegetable juices	100.0	14.5	26.3	20.5	9.2	29.5	21.1	8.5
Sugar and other sweets	**100.0**	**13.3**	**28.0**	**19.1**	**9.2**	**30.4**	**19.6**	**10.7**
Candy and chewing gum	100.0	11.1	28.1	19.6	9.3	31.8	20.6	11.2
Sugar	100.0	20.1	28.6	18.8	7.9	24.6	16.2	8.4
Artificial sweeteners	100.0	15.7	27.8	16.7	1.2	27.5	15.7	11.6
Jams, preserves, other sweets	100.0	14.4	27.1	18.3	9.1	3.1	20.2	10.8

	total consumer units	less than high school graduate	high school graduate	some college	associate's degree	college graduate total	bachelor's degree	master's, professional, doctorate
Fats and oils	**100.0%**	**16.2%**	**28.6%**	**19.6%**	**8.3%**	**27.4%**	**17.2%**	**10.1%**
Margarine	100.0	16.1	30.5	20.4	6.9	26.0	1.7	9.0
Fats and oils	100.0	19.9	27.9	17.6	7.5	27.1	16.7	10.4
Salad dressings	100.0	14.2	28.6	20.8	8.8	27.6	17.5	1.0
Nondairy cream and imitation milk	100.0	16.3	27.7	21.8	8.8	25.5	15.9	9.6
Peanut butter	100.0	13.5	28.7	17.9	9.6	30.1	19.1	11.0
Miscellaneous foods	**100.0**	**12.6**	**26.5**	**20.6**	**9.4**	**30.8**	**19.7**	**11.1**
Frozen prepared foods	100.0	11.6	26.8	20.7	9.9	30.8	20.1	10.7
Frozen meals	100.0	12.5	27.3	20.6	7.6	32.0	20.7	11.3
Other frozen prepared foods	100.0	11.3	26.6	20.8	10.9	30.3	19.9	10.4
Canned and packaged soups	100.0	13.3	28.4	20.2	9.2	28.9	17.2	11.6
Potato chips, nuts, and other snacks	100.0	11.6	26.6	21.9	9.4	30.6	19.5	11.0
Potato chips and other snacks	100.0	11.8	27.0	21.6	9.3	30.4	19.9	10.5
Nuts	100.0	11.0	25.1	22.8	9.7	31.4	18.5	12.8
Condiments and seasonings	100.0	12.2	26.8	20.0	9.1	31.8	20.4	11.4
Salt, spices, and other seasonings	100.0	14.8	24.9	19.6	8.9	31.7	21.5	10.2
Olives, pickles, relishes	100.0	11.1	25.7	20.3	8.2	34.6	19.1	15.3
Sauces and gravies	100.0	11.7	28.8	19.9	9.1	30.5	20.0	10.5
Baking needs and miscellaneous products	100.0	10.8	25.4	20.7	9.7	33.2	20.5	12.6
Other canned/packaged prepared foods	100.0	14.0	25.7	20.2	9.3	30.8	19.7	11.1
Prepared salads	100.0	11.3	25.0	19.7	9.2	34.6	22.0	12.5
Prepared desserts	100.0	14.1	26.1	18.8	9.9	31.0	17.9	13.0
Baby food	100.0	12.1	29.5	22.6	6.7	29.2	19.8	9.4
Miscellaneous prepared foods	100.0	15.1	24.7	19.8	9.9	30.4	19.4	10.9
Nonalcoholic beverages	100.0	14.8	29.3	19.8	9.1	27.0	17.4	9.5
Cola	100.0	15.7	31.4	19.8	9.8	23.3	15.1	8.2
Other carbonated drinks	100.0	15.3	29.2	19.7	9.7	26.0	17.1	9.0
Coffee	100.0	14.8	29.7	17.6	8.2	29.5	18.4	11.0
Roasted coffee	100.0	13.5	29.4	17.6	8.1	31.2	19.4	11.8
Instant and freeze-dried coffee	100.0	17.3	30.2	17.6	8.5	26.3	16.6	9.7
Noncarbonated fruit-flavored drinks	100.0	16.8	27.5	19.6	7.7	28.3	19.5	8.9
Tea	100.0	12.4	28.5	19.1	8.9	31.0	19.3	11.6
Other nonalcoholic beverages and ice	100.0	12.6	26.4	22.2	8.2	30.7	19.6	11.0
Food prepared by CU on trips	**100.0**	**7.1**	**18.5**	**20.8**	**9.4**	**44.1**	**27.3**	**16.8**

Note: Numbers may not add to total because of rounding.
Source: Calculations by New Strategist based on the 2001 Consumer Expenditure Survey

31. Groceries: Average spending by occupation, 2001

(average annual spending of consumer units (CU) on groceries, by occupation of consumer unit reference person, 2001)

	total consumer units	self-employed workers	wage and salary workers						retired
			total	managers and professionals	technical, sales and clerical workers	service workers	construction workers and mechanics	operators, fabricators, laborers	
Number of consumer units									
(in thousands, add 000)	110,339	4,874	74,016	26,766	21,137	10,227	5,045	10,841	19,331
Average number of persons per CU	2.5	2.6	2.7	2.6	2.5	2.8	3.0	2.9	1.7
Average before-tax income of CU	$47,507.00	$53,465.00	$55,254.00	$77,657.00	$46,839.00	$35,750.00	$47,580.00	$38,887.00	$24,637.00
Average spending of CU, total	39,518.46	48,317.97	43,822.07	56,058.21	39,982.24	32,515.28	40,522.76	33,671.64	26,842.53
GROCERIES	3,085.52	3,485.07	3,210.99	3,531.77	3,051.82	2,827.72	3,615.80	2,947.96	2,487.29
Cereals and bakery products	452.19	499.31	466.49	510.86	455.07	414.12	498.01	422.68	390.63
Cereals and cereal products	156.46	175.67	161.20	177.64	155.06	141.64	156.71	154.80	126.56
Flour	8.01	8.24	7.81	7.89	6.61	7.46	10.09	9.00	6.57
Prepared flour mixes	12.89	13.18	13.54	14.33	12.72	10.24	15.89	15.07	10.88
Ready-to-eat and cooked cereals	86.04	89.26	87.84	99.43	86.75	70.66	85.19	80.75	75.07
Rice	19.95	25.19	21.69	22.17	22.22	22.32	15.67	21.76	11.42
Pasta, cornmeal, and other cereal products	29.57	39.80	30.31	33.83	26.75	30.97	29.88	28.22	22.62
Bakery products	295.73	323.64	305.28	333.23	300.01	272.49	341.29	267.88	264.07
Bread	85.37	93.74	86.85	92.73	82.09	79.88	99.14	83.00	77.54
White bread	36.64	41.37	37.11	36.33	34.63	36.44	43.29	40.81	30.88
Crackers and cookies	70.18	76.95	71.88	81.86	69.51	60.99	71.92	63.83	67.19
Cookies	46.13	46.97	47.88	52.52	46.73	42.78	48.94	43.82	43.11
Crackers	24.05	29.98	24.00	29.35	22.78	18.21	22.99	20.00	24.08
Frozen and refrigerated bakery products	26.06	27.95	27.55	29.81	29.48	21.30	30.54	23.73	20.57
Other bakery products	114.11	124.99	119.01	128.82	118.92	110.31	139.69	97.32	98.78
Biscuits and rolls	39.34	46.66	40.40	46.78	39.37	39.35	38.99	29.95	33.97
Cakes and cupcakes	33.80	36.60	36.34	36.88	37.82	31.72	59.51	27.30	25.51
Bread and cracker products	4.05	4.58	4.37	4.75	4.66	3.14	3.49	4.53	3.31
Sweetrolls, coffee cakes, doughnuts	26.32	28.89	26.85	28.20	26.64	26.19	26.16	25.17	24.37
Pies, tarts, turnovers	10.60	8.26	11.05	12.20	10.43	9.92	11.54	10.37	11.62
Meats, poultry, fish, and eggs	827.97	920.69	857.86	869.29	833.02	784.55	1,073.78	848.59	657.45
Beef	248.06	268.94	255.49	260.10	251.30	216.04	345.34	249.68	202.62
Ground beef	90.48	104.70	94.08	88.43	95.93	83.93	132.09	96.31	67.62
Roast	44.44	39.87	43.93	48.42	41.03	30.66	68.34	40.52	43.60
Chuck roast	15.03	14.37	15.23	14.19	15.20	10.31	29.84	15.76	12.78
Round roast	11.88	10.23	12.25	14.05	11.21	9.20	13.56	12.19	9.43
Other roast	17.53	15.27	16.45	20.18	14.61	11.14	24.94	12.57	21.38
Steak	92.73	101.46	96.40	102.19	94.02	80.44	117.49	93.03	75.73
Round steak	18.21	20.45	18.12	16.76	19.61	15.11	22.22	19.47	16.81
Sirloin steak	25.37	26.92	27.53	29.61	23.97	23.22	39.31	27.74	16.56
Other steak	49.15	54.09	50.76	55.83	50.43	42.11	55.96	45.81	42.35
Pork	177.31	190.46	179.92	173.93	170.17	167.03	240.07	194.99	149.66
Bacon	29.30	32.13	29.71	29.79	28.47	28.34	36.75	29.86	25.09
Pork chops	42.16	46.00	44.40	41.91	39.06	43.44	75.06	46.68	30.61
Ham	39.98	45.34	40.08	38.75	36.87	37.74	47.50	47.07	37.86
Ham, not canned	38.24	42.98	38.36	37.19	35.19	36.84	47.50	43.54	35.66
Canned ham	1.74	2.35	1.72	1.55	1.68	0.90	–	3.54	2.20
Sausage	25.52	26.64	24.76	24.54	23.49	25.74	29.76	24.37	26.07
Other pork	40.34	40.37	40.98	38.94	42.27	31.77	51.00	47.01	30.02
Other meats	102.06	109.59	106.59	106.87	103.56	97.09	128.91	109.93	79.42
Frankfurters	22.01	23.89	22.84	22.76	22.75	22.98	25.12	22.08	16.56
Lunch meats (cold cuts)	70.88	77.28	74.17	74.51	71.97	66.12	93.18	76.17	55.46
Bologna, liverwurst, salami	25.40	26.46	26.08	24.56	23.65	27.07	34.11	29.14	20.25
Lamb, organ meats, and others	9.17	8.42	9.58	9.60	8.83	7.99	10.62	11.68	7.39

	total consumer units	self-employed workers	wage and salary workers						retired
			total	managers and professionals	technical, sales and clerical workers	service workers	construction workers and mechanics	operators, fabricators, laborers	
Poultry	$151.87	$159.46	$161.99	$165.50	$160.77	$154.05	$190.05	$151.86	$104.36
Fresh and frozen chicken	119.55	128.47	127.34	126.20	125.55	125.02	156.70	122.66	80.11
Fresh and frozen whole chicken	35.75	42.67	38.08	37.46	38.45	35.52	51.58	35.47	22.57
Fresh and frozen chicken parts	83.80	85.80	89.26	88.74	87.10	89.50	105.11	87.19	57.53
Other poultry	32.32	30.99	34.65	39.29	35.22	29.04	33.36	29.20	24.25
Fish and seafood	113.67	153.59	118.11	128.76	112.34	113.05	126.72	105.62	92.70
Canned fish and seafood	15.11	15.12	15.85	17.38	17.14	13.17	13.40	13.82	13.13
Fresh fish and shellfish	63.07	86.13	65.47	71.65	58.86	67.55	65.60	61.20	51.28
Frozen fish and shellfish	35.49	52.34	36.78	39.73	36.34	32.33	47.73	30.61	28.29
Eggs	34.99	38.65	35.76	34.14	34.88	37.29	42.68	36.50	28.69
Dairy products	**331.69**	**383.04**	**344.17**	**389.98**	**318.59**	**303.69**	**368.01**	**313.18**	**261.98**
Fresh milk and cream	135.85	156.62	138.99	147.49	131.16	126.35	150.21	139.84	105.50
Fresh milk, all types	123.50	141.87	126.29	131.91	119.88	115.51	139.09	128.74	95.29
Cream	12.35	14.74	12.70	15.58	11.27	10.84	11.12	11.10	10.21
Other dairy products	195.84	226.43	205.18	242.49	187.44	177.34	217.80	173.34	156.48
Butter	21.55	25.71	20.96	22.15	21.87	17.41	21.64	19.73	20.99
Cheese	93.39	108.70	98.97	113.68	92.79	85.16	116.19	82.54	69.84
Ice cream and related products	56.79	66.57	59.19	69.76	50.95	55.11	57.71	54.14	48.37
Miscellaneous dairy products	24.11	25.44	26.06	36.90	21.82	19.66	22.26	16.92	17.28
Fruits and vegetables	**521.74**	**582.42**	**531.83**	**615.47**	**492.36**	**476.43**	**568.78**	**450.39**	**460.70**
Fresh fruits	160.41	174.95	162.97	196.05	143.40	143.77	172.09	137.09	145.34
Apples	30.83	29.83	32.63	39.33	28.99	28.05	36.08	26.81	22.55
Bananas	31.30	35.84	31.08	33.61	26.70	32.78	37.62	28.68	30.49
Oranges	18.62	20.13	19.08	22.44	16.70	18.96	19.16	15.86	15.16
Citrus fruits, excl. oranges	13.21	19.30	12.99	14.98	10.93	12.03	13.25	12.82	12.17
Other fresh fruits	66.45	69.85	67.19	85.69	60.08	51.95	65.99	52.92	64.97
Fresh vegetables	161.62	187.10	164.27	187.21	153.75	146.35	188.27	138.14	141.80
Potatoes	30.09	32.96	30.31	31.63	30.36	28.81	36.43	26.25	28.36
Lettuce	20.82	23.95	21.37	25.08	18.88	20.33	23.65	17.48	16.67
Tomatoes	30.03	30.98	30.88	33.97	27.48	27.12	36.88	30.63	24.92
Other fresh vegetables	80.68	99.20	81.70	96.53	77.04	70.10	91.31	63.78	71.84
Processed fruits	116.03	127.41	117.86	134.74	114.32	109.47	114.75	96.17	103.67
Frozen fruits and fruit juices	13.85	16.53	14.53	18.15	11.13	13.64	18.36	11.56	11.43
Frozen orange juice	7.61	9.03	8.14	10.14	6.04	8.63	9.62	6.26	6.27
Frozen fruits	2.53	4.21	2.59	3.66	1.91	1.89	3.61	1.57	2.21
Frozen fruit juices	3.72	3.29	3.81	4.35	3.18	3.12	5.14	3.73	2.95
Canned fruits	16.27	23.02	15.66	17.95	15.68	12.88	16.60	12.78	17.42
Dried fruits	5.54	7.29	5.24	7.28	5.06	3.18	5.19	3.00	6.40
Fresh fruit juice	24.86	27.25	24.65	29.96	23.87	23.15	19.30	18.05	23.39
Canned and bottled fruit juice	55.50	53.32	57.78	61.40	58.58	56.62	55.29	50.78	45.03
Processed vegetables	83.68	92.96	86.73	97.46	80.89	76.84	93.66	78.99	69.90
Frozen vegetables	27.50	31.52	28.72	33.11	28.18	24.69	29.04	23.58	22.67
Canned and dried vegetables and juices	56.18	61.44	58.00	64.35	52.71	52.15	64.61	55.41	47.23
Canned beans	12.60	13.27	13.07	14.52	11.23	11.04	13.99	14.32	10.52
Canned corn	7.13	10.22	7.29	7.37	6.22	7.57	7.77	8.41	5.26
Canned miscellaneous vegetables	17.58	23.21	17.22	19.21	16.23	14.82	19.97	15.57	17.11
Dried beans	2.28	2.07	2.22	1.96	2.23	2.16	1.70	3.02	1.11
Dried miscellaneous vegetables	7.58	6.11	8.29	8.12	8.10	9.12	10.79	7.25	6.32
Fresh and canned vegetable juices	7.65	6.10	8.26	10.12	8.11	6.77	8.10	5.90	5.95
Sugar and other sweets	**115.96**	**129.29**	**120.58**	**139.92**	**114.25**	**99.77**	**122.06**	**106.97**	**95.65**
Candy and chewing gum	73.49	82.57	77.41	93.99	73.01	61.67	75.28	63.64	59.45
Sugar	17.91	21.49	18.26	17.44	17.36	17.30	18.90	22.03	12.95
Artificial sweeteners	5.04	7.01	4.66	5.27	3.33	4.29	7.84	4.54	6.49
Jams, preserves, other sweets	19.52	18.22	20.25	23.22	20.54	16.52	20.03	16.76	16.75

	total consumer units	self-employed workers	wage and salary workers total	managers and professionals	technical, sales and clerical workers	service workers	construction workers and mechanics	operators, fabricators, laborers	retired
Fats and oils	**$86.76**	**$99.65**	**$88.43**	**$93.70**	**$85.39**	**$80.92**	**$102.72**	**$82.74**	**$74.04**
Margarine	11.43	11.27	11.24	11.73	11.25	9.60	12.27	11.15	11.68
Fats and oils	24.53	27.55	25.20	24.44	22.19	26.12	30.59	28.68	19.08
Salad dressings	28.02	32.16	28.85	31.93	28.29	26.05	34.13	23.45	23.14
Nondairy cream and imitation milk	10.09	13.65	10.03	11.32	10.11	9.36	8.39	8.39	10.37
Peanut butter	12.69	15.02	13.12	14.29	13.56	9.79	17.34	11.06	9.77
Miscellaneous foods	**454.72**	**502.01**	**489.59**	**566.05**	**463.45**	**396.76**	**541.31**	**427.88**	**330.88**
Frozen prepared foods	96.19	111.25	103.68	124.31	99.70	76.26	106.21	88.74	64.44
Frozen meals	28.65	36.56	29.34	35.81	25.64	24.57	24.75	27.53	24.52
Other frozen prepared foods	67.54	74.69	74.34	88.50	74.06	51.69	81.46	61.21	39.92
Canned and packaged soups	37.27	38.73	37.43	42.10	35.03	33.45	36.27	35.25	37.44
Potato chips, nuts, and other snacks	97.37	113.88	104.63	119.55	97.59	86.69	125.52	91.17	71.51
Potato chips and other snacks	75.56	83.38	83.54	94.52	77.45	70.04	99.37	75.10	46.44
Nuts	21.81	30.49	21.09	25.02	20.14	16.65	26.15	15.99	25.07
Condiments and seasonings	84.05	103.91	88.20	100.57	85.96	67.18	96.48	80.21	63.76
Salt, spices, and other seasonings	19.83	20.31	20.63	22.47	19.69	17.01	22.79	20.44	14.60
Olives, pickles, relishes	9.97	15.14	10.42	13.55	9.23	6.04	12.63	8.56	7.74
Sauces and gravies	36.84	46.67	39.25	42.31	38.76	32.24	44.07	37.56	26.12
Baking needs and miscellaneous products	17.41	21.78	17.91	22.23	18.28	11.89	16.99	13.66	15.29
Other canned/packaged prepared foods	139.85	134.25	155.65	179.53	145.16	133.19	176.83	132.51	93.73
Prepared salads	19.55	23.78	20.89	24.03	22.10	18.36	21.21	14.29	16.58
Prepared desserts	10.15	13.06	10.39	13.29	8.87	8.47	9.03	8.89	9.42
Baby food	23.62	13.54	29.88	36.21	23.75	26.33	44.60	23.38	7.64
Miscellaneous prepared foods	86.24	83.86	94.07	105.05	90.36	80.03	100.92	85.95	60.09
Nonalcoholic beverages	256.16	308.14	270.75	287.32	254.95	244.32	306.90	269.05	184.69
Cola	87.41	109.48	93.52	92.66	88.31	82.54	115.49	104.25	55.35
Other carbonated drinks	46.14	54.94	48.77	51.49	44.40	42.71	60.45	50.47	30.42
Coffee	38.35	44.72	37.43	41.32	35.67	33.35	33.47	37.10	43.09
Roasted coffee	24.98	31.11	24.83	28.69	22.70	21.12	22.34	24.25	25.38
Instant and freeze-dried coffee	13.37	13.61	12.60	12.63	12.97	12.23	11.13	12.85	17.71
Noncarbonated fruit-flavored drinks	20.36	19.03	22.63	24.30	21.47	23.07	23.22	20.35	9.98
Tea	17.57	20.76	18.53	20.97	16.48	17.02	18.49	17.95	14.17
Other nonalcoholic beverages and ice	45.67	57.24	49.23	55.29	48.11	45.46	55.78	38.71	31.31
Food prepared by CU on trips	**38.33**	**60.52**	**41.29**	**59.18**	**34.74**	**27.15**	**34.24**	**26.49**	**31.27**

Note: (–) means sample is too small to make a reliable estimate.
Source: Bureau of Labor Statistics, unpublished tables from the 2001 Consumer Expenditure Survey

32. Groceries: Indexed spending by occupation, 2001

(indexed average annual spending of consumer units (CU) on groceries, by occupation of consumer unit reference person, 2001; index definition: an index of 100 is the average for all consumer units; an index of 132 means that spending by consumer units in that group is 32 percent above the average for all consumer units; an index of 68 indicates spending that is 32 percent below the average for all consumer units)

	total consumer units	self-employed workers	wage and salary workers						retired
			total	managers and professionals	technical, sales and clerical workers	service workers	construction workers and mechanics	operators, fabricators, laborers	
Average spending of CU, total	$39,518	$48,318	$43,822	$56,058	$39,982	$32,515	$40,523	$33,672	$26,843
Average spending of CU, index	100	122	111	142	101	82	103	85	68
GROCERIES	100	113	104	115	99	92	117	96	81
Cereals and bakery products	100	110	103	113	101	92	110	94	86
Cereals and cereal products	100	112	103	114	99	91	100	99	81
Flour	100	103	98	99	83	93	126	112	82
Prepared flour mixes	100	102	105	111	99	79	123	117	84
Ready-to-eat and cooked cereals	100	104	102	116	101	82	99	94	87
Rice	100	126	109	111	111	112	79	109	57
Pasta, cornmeal, and other cereal products	100	135	103	114	91	105	101	95	77
Bakery products	100	109	103	113	101	92	115	91	89
Bread	100	110	102	109	96	94	116	97	91
White bread	100	113	101	99	95	100	118	111	84
Crackers and cookies	100	110	102	117	99	87	103	91	96
Cookies	100	102	104	114	101	93	106	95	94
Crackers	100	125	100	122	95	76	96	83	100
Frozen and refrigerated bakery products	100	107	106	114	113	82	117	91	79
Other bakery products	100	110	104	113	104	97	122	85	87
Biscuits and rolls	100	119	103	119	100	100	99	76	86
Cakes and cupcakes	100	108	108	109	112	94	176	81	76
Bread and cracker products	100	113	108	117	115	78	86	112	82
Sweetrolls, coffee cakes, doughnuts	100	110	102	107	101	100	99	96	93
Pies, tarts, turnovers	100	78	104	115	98	94	109	98	110
Meats, poultry, fish, and eggs	100	111	104	105	101	95	130	103	79
Beef	100	108	103	105	101	87	139	101	82
Ground beef	100	116	104	98	106	93	146	106	75
Roast	100	90	99	109	92	69	154	91	98
Chuck roast	100	96	101	94	101	69	199	105	85
Round roast	100	86	103	118	94	77	114	103	79
Other roast	100	87	94	115	83	64	142	72	122
Steak	100	109	104	110	101	87	127	100	82
Round steak	100	112	100	92	108	83	122	107	92
Sirloin steak	100	106	109	117	95	92	155	109	65
Other steak	100	110	103	114	103	86	114	93	86
Pork	100	107	102	98	96	94	135	110	84
Bacon	100	110	101	102	97	97	125	102	86
Pork chops	100	109	105	99	93	103	178	111	73
Ham	100	113	100	97	92	94	119	118	95
Ham, not canned	100	112	100	97	92	96	124	114	93
Canned ham	100	135	99	89	97	52	–	203	126
Sausage	100	104	97	96	92	101	117	96	102
Other pork	100	100	102	97	105	79	126	117	74
Other meats	100	107	104	105	102	95	126	108	78
Frankfurters	100	109	104	103	103	104	114	100	75
Lunch meats (cold cuts)	100	109	105	105	102	93	132	108	78
Bologna, liverwurst, salami	100	104	103	97	93	107	134	115	80
Lamb, organ meats, and others	100	92	105	105	96	87	116	127	81

	total consumer units	self-employed workers	wage and salary workers						retired
			total	managers and professionals	technical, sales and clerical workers	service workers	construction workers and mechanics	operators, fabricators, laborers	
Poultry	100	105	107	109	106	101	125	100	69
Fresh and frozen chicken	100	108	107	106	105	105	131	103	67
Fresh and frozen whole chicken	100	119	107	105	108	99	144	99	63
Fresh and frozen chicken parts	100	102	107	106	104	107	125	104	69
Other poultry	100	96	107	122	109	90	103	90	75
Fish and seafood	100	135	104	113	99	100	112	93	82
Canned fish and seafood	100	100	105	115	113	87	89	92	87
Fresh fish and shellfish	100	137	104	114	93	107	104	97	81
Frozen fish and shellfish	100	148	104	112	102	91	135	86	80
Eggs	100	111	102	98	100	107	122	104	82
Dairy products	**100**	**116**	**104**	**118**	**96**	**92**	**111**	**94**	**79**
Fresh milk and cream	100	115	102	109	97	93	111	103	78
Fresh milk, all types	100	115	102	107	97	94	113	104	77
Cream	100	119	103	126	91	88	90	90	83
Other dairy products	100	116	105	124	96	91	111	89	80
Butter	100	119	97	103	102	81	100	92	97
Cheese	100	116	106	122	99	91	124	88	75
Ice cream and related products	100	117	104	123	90	97	102	95	85
Miscellaneous dairy products	100	106	108	153	91	82	92	70	72
Fruits and vegetables	**100**	**112**	**102**	**118**	**94**	**91**	**109**	**86**	**88**
Fresh fruits	100	109	102	122	89	90	107	86	91
Apples	100	97	106	128	94	91	117	87	73
Bananas	100	115	99	107	85	105	120	92	97
Oranges	100	108	103	121	90	102	103	85	81
Citrus fruits, excl. oranges	100	146	98	113	83	91	100	97	92
Other fresh fruits	100	105	101	129	90	78	99	80	98
Fresh vegetables	100	116	102	116	95	91	117	86	88
Potatoes	100	110	101	105	101	96	121	87	94
Lettuce	100	115	103	121	91	98	114	84	80
Tomatoes	100	103	103	113	92	90	123	102	83
Other fresh vegetables	100	123	101	120	96	87	113	79	89
Processed fruits	100	110	102	116	99	94	99	83	89
Frozen fruits and fruit juices	100	119	105	131	80	99	133	84	83
Frozen orange juice	100	119	107	133	79	113	126	82	82
Frozen fruits	100	166	102	145	76	75	143	62	87
Frozen fruit juices	100	88	102	117	86	84	138	100	79
Canned fruits	100	142	96	110	96	79	102	79	107
Dried fruits	100	132	95	131	91	57	94	54	116
Fresh fruit juice	100	110	99	121	96	93	78	73	94
Canned and bottled fruit juice	100	96	104	111	106	102	100	92	81
Processed vegetables	100	111	104	117	97	92	112	94	84
Frozen vegetables	100	115	104	120	103	90	106	86	82
Canned and dried vegetables and juices	100	109	103	115	94	93	115	99	84
Canned beans	100	105	104	115	89	88	111	114	84
Canned corn	100	143	102	103	87	106	109	118	74
Canned miscellaneous vegetables	100	132	98	109	92	84	114	89	97
Dried beans	100	91	97	86	98	95	75	133	49
Dried miscellaneous vegetables	100	81	109	107	107	120	142	96	83
Fresh and canned vegetable juices	100	80	108	132	106	89	106	77	78
Sugar and other sweets	**100**	**112**	**104**	**121**	**99**	**86**	**105**	**92**	**83**
Candy and chewing gum	100	112	105	128	99	84	102	87	81
Sugar	100	120	102	97	97	97	106	123	72
Artificial sweeteners	100	139	93	105	66	85	156	90	129
Jams, preserves, other sweets	100	93	104	119	105	85	103	86	86

	total consumer units	self-employed workers	wage and salary workers						retired
			total	managers and professionals	technical, sales and clerical workers	service workers	construction workers and mechanics	operators, fabricators, laborers	
Fats and oils	**100**	**115**	**102**	**108**	**98**	**93**	**118**	**95**	**85**
Margarine	100	99	98	103	98	84	107	98	102
Fats and oils	100	112	103	100	91	107	125	117	78
Salad dressings	100	115	103	114	101	93	122	84	83
Nondairy cream and imitation milk	100	135	99	112	100	93	83	83	103
Peanut butter	100	118	103	113	107	77	137	87	77
Miscellaneous foods	**100**	**110**	**108**	**125**	**102**	**87**	**119**	**94**	**73**
Frozen prepared foods	100	116	108	129	104	79	110	92	67
Frozen meals	100	128	102	125	90	86	86	96	86
Other frozen prepared foods	100	111	110	131	110	77	121	91	59
Canned and packaged soups	100	104	100	113	94	90	97	95	101
Potato chips, nuts, and other snacks	100	117	108	123	100	89	129	94	73
Potato chips and other snacks	100	110	111	125	103	93	132	99	62
Nuts	100	140	97	115	92	76	120	73	115
Condiments and seasonings	100	124	105	120	102	80	115	95	76
Salt, spices, and other seasonings	100	102	104	113	99	86	115	103	74
Olives, pickles, relishes	100	152	105	136	93	61	127	86	78
Sauces and gravies	100	127	107	115	105	88	120	102	71
Baking needs and miscellaneous products	100	125	103	128	105	68	98	79	88
Other canned/packaged prepared foods	100	96	111	128	104	95	126	95	67
Prepared salads	100	122	107	123	113	94	109	73	85
Prepared desserts	100	129	102	131	87	83	89	88	93
Baby food	100	57	127	153	101	112	189	99	32
Miscellaneous prepared foods	100	97	109	122	105	93	117	100	70
Nonalcoholic beverages	100	120	106	112	100	95	120	105	72
Cola	100	125	107	106	101	94	132	119	63
Other carbonated drinks	100	119	106	112	96	93	131	109	66
Coffee	100	117	98	108	93	87	87	97	112
Roasted coffee	100	125	99	115	91	85	89	97	102
Instant and freeze-dried coffee	100	102	94	95	97	92	83	96	133
Noncarbonated fruit-flavored drinks	100	94	111	119	106	113	114	100	49
Tea	100	118	106	119	94	97	105	102	81
Other nonalcoholic beverages and ice	100	125	108	121	105	100	122	85	69
Food prepared by CU on trips	**100**	**158**	**108**	**154**	**91**	**71**	**89**	**69**	**82**

Note: (–) means sample is too small to make a reliable estimate.
Source: Calculations by New Strategist based on the 2001 Consumer Expenditure Survey

33. Groceries: Indexed per capita spending by occupation, 2001

(indexed average annual per capita spending of consumer units (CU) on groceries, by occupation of consumer unit reference person, 2001; index definition: an index of 100 is the average for all consumer units; an index of 132 means that spending by consumer units in that group is 32 percent above the average for all consumer units; an index of 68 indicates spending that is 32 percent below the average for all consumer units)

	total consumer units	self-employed workers	wage and salary workers total	managers and professionals	technical, sales and clerical workers	service workers	construction workers and mechanics	operators, fabricators, laborers	retired
Per capita spending of CU, total	$15,807	$18,584	$16,230	$21,561	$15,993	$11,613	$13,508	$11,611	$15,790
Per capita spending of CU, index	100	118	103	136	101	74	86	74	100
GROCERIES	**100**	**109**	**96**	**110**	**99**	**82**	**98**	**82**	**119**
Cereals and bakery products	**100**	**106**	**96**	**109**	**101**	**82**	**92**	**81**	**127**
Cereals and cereal products	100	108	95	109	99	81	84	85	119
Flour	100	99	90	95	83	83	105	97	121
Prepared flour mixes	100	98	97	107	99	71	103	101	124
Ready-to-eat and cooked cereals	100	100	95	111	101	73	83	81	128
Rice	100	121	101	107	111	100	66	94	84
Pasta, cornmeal, and other cereal products	100	129	95	110	91	94	84	82	113
Bakery products	100	105	96	108	101	82	96	78	131
Bread	100	106	94	104	96	84	97	84	134
White bread	100	109	94	95	95	89	99	96	124
Crackers and cookies	100	105	95	112	99	78	85	78	141
Cookies	100	98	96	110	101	83	88	82	137
Crackers	100	120	92	117	95	68	80	72	147
Frozen and refrigerated bakery products	100	103	98	110	113	73	98	79	116
Other bakery products	100	105	97	109	104	86	102	74	127
Biscuits and rolls	100	114	95	114	100	89	83	66	127
Cakes and cupcakes	100	104	100	105	112	84	147	70	111
Bread and cracker products	100	109	100	113	115	69	72	96	120
Sweetrolls, coffee cakes, doughnuts	100	106	95	103	101	89	83	82	136
Pies, tarts, turnovers	100	75	97	111	98	84	91	84	161
Meats, poultry, fish, and eggs	**100**	**107**	**96**	**101**	**101**	**85**	**108**	**88**	**117**
Beef	100	104	95	101	101	78	116	87	120
Ground beef	100	111	96	94	106	83	122	92	110
Roast	100	86	92	105	92	62	128	79	144
Chuck roast	100	92	94	91	101	61	165	90	125
Round roast	100	83	96	114	94	69	95	89	117
Other roast	100	84	87	111	83	57	119	62	179
Steak	100	105	96	106	101	78	106	87	120
Round steak	100	108	92	89	108	74	102	92	136
Sirloin steak	100	102	101	112	95	82	129	94	96
Other steak	100	106	96	109	103	77	95	80	127
Pork	100	103	94	94	96	84	113	95	124
Bacon	100	105	94	98	97	86	105	88	126
Pork chops	100	105	98	96	93	92	148	95	107
Ham	100	109	93	93	92	84	99	102	139
Ham, not canned	100	108	93	94	92	86	104	98	137
Canned ham	100	130	92	86	97	46	–	175	186
Sausage	100	100	90	93	92	90	97	82	150
Other pork	100	96	94	93	105	70	105	101	109
Other meats	100	103	97	101	102	85	105	93	114
Frankfurters	100	104	96	99	103	93	95	87	111
Lunch meats (cold cuts)	100	105	97	101	102	83	110	93	115
Bologna, liverwurst, salami	100	100	95	93	93	95	112	99	117
Lamb, organ meats, and others	100	88	97	101	96	78	97	110	119

	total consumer units	self-employed workers	wage and salary workers						retired
			total	managers and professionals	technical, sales and clerical workers	service workers	construction workers and mechanics	operators, fabricators, laborers	
Poultry	100	101	99	105	106	91	104	86	101
Fresh and frozen chicken	100	103	99	102	105	93	109	88	99
Fresh and frozen whole chicken	100	115	99	101	108	89	120	86	93
Fresh and frozen chicken parts	100	98	99	102	104	95	105	90	101
Other poultry	100	92	99	117	109	80	86	78	110
Fish and seafood	100	130	96	109	99	89	93	80	120
Canned fish and seafood	100	96	97	111	113	78	74	79	128
Fresh fish and shellfish	100	131	96	109	93	96	87	84	120
Frozen fish and shellfish	100	142	96	108	102	81	112	74	117
Eggs	100	106	95	94	100	95	102	90	121
Dairy products	**100**	**111**	**96**	**113**	**96**	**82**	**93**	**81**	**116**
Fresh milk and cream	100	111	95	104	97	83	92	89	114
Fresh milk, all types	100	111	95	103	97	84	94	90	114
Cream	100	115	95	121	91	78	75	78	122
Other dairy products	100	111	97	119	96	81	93	76	118
Butter	100	115	90	99	102	72	84	79	143
Cheese	100	112	98	117	99	81	104	76	110
Ice cream and related products	100	113	97	118	90	87	85	82	125
Miscellaneous dairy products	100	102	100	147	91	73	77	61	105
Fruits and vegetables	**100**	**107**	**94**	**113**	**94**	**82**	**91**	**74**	**130**
Fresh fruits	100	105	94	118	89	80	89	74	133
Apples	100	93	98	123	94	81	98	75	108
Bananas	100	110	92	103	85	94	100	79	143
Oranges	100	104	95	116	90	91	86	73	120
Citrus fruits, excl. oranges	100	141	91	109	83	81	84	84	136
Other fresh fruits	100	101	94	124	90	70	83	69	144
Fresh vegetables	100	111	94	111	95	81	97	74	129
Potatoes	100	105	93	101	101	86	101	75	139
Lettuce	100	111	95	116	91	87	95	72	118
Tomatoes	100	99	95	109	92	81	102	88	122
Other fresh vegetables	100	118	94	115	96	78	94	68	131
Processed fruits	100	106	94	112	99	84	82	72	131
Frozen fruits and fruit juices	100	115	97	126	80	88	111	72	121
Frozen orange juice	100	114	99	128	79	101	105	71	121
Frozen fruits	100	160	95	139	76	67	119	54	129
Frozen fruit juices	100	85	95	112	86	75	115	86	117
Canned fruits	100	136	89	106	96	71	85	68	158
Dried fruits	100	127	88	126	91	51	78	47	170
Fresh fruit juice	100	105	92	116	96	83	65	63	138
Canned and bottled fruit juice	100	92	96	106	106	91	83	79	119
Processed vegetables	100	107	96	112	97	82	93	81	123
Frozen vegetables	100	110	97	116	103	80	88	74	121
Canned and dried vegetables and juices	100	105	96	110	94	83	96	85	124
Canned beans	100	101	96	111	89	78	93	98	123
Canned corn	100	138	95	99	87	95	91	102	109
Canned miscellaneous vegetables	100	127	91	105	92	75	95	76	143
Dried beans	100	87	90	83	98	85	62	114	72
Dried miscellaneous vegetables	100	78	101	103	107	107	119	83	123
Fresh and canned vegetable juices	100	77	100	127	106	79	88	67	114
Sugar and other sweets	**100**	**107**	**96**	**116**	**99**	**77**	**88**	**80**	**121**
Candy and chewing gum	100	108	98	123	99	75	85	75	119
Sugar	100	115	94	94	97	86	88	106	106
Artificial sweeteners	100	134	86	101	66	76	130	78	189
Jams, preserves, other sweets	100	90	96	114	105	76	86	74	126

	total consumer units	self-employed workers	wage and salary workers						retired
			total	managers and professionals	technical, sales and clerical workers	service workers	construction workers and mechanics	operators, fabricators, laborers	
Fats and oils	**100**	**110**	**94**	**104**	**98**	**83**	**99**	**82**	**126**
Margarine	100	95	91	99	98	75	90	84	150
Fats and oils	100	108	95	96	91	95	104	101	114
Salad dressings	100	110	95	110	101	83	102	72	121
Nondairy cream and imitation milk	100	130	92	108	100	83	69	72	151
Peanut butter	100	114	96	108	107	69	114	75	113
Miscellaneous foods	**100**	**106**	**100**	**120**	**102**	**78**	**99**	**81**	**107**
Frozen prepared foods	100	111	100	124	104	71	92	80	99
Frozen meals	100	123	95	120	90	77	72	83	126
Other frozen prepared foods	100	106	102	126	110	68	101	78	87
Canned and packaged soups	100	100	93	109	94	80	81	82	148
Potato chips, nuts, and other snacks	100	113	100	118	100	80	107	81	108
Potato chips and other snacks	100	106	102	120	103	83	110	86	90
Nuts	100	134	90	110	92	68	100	63	169
Condiments and seasonings	100	119	97	115	102	71	96	82	112
Salt, spices, and other seasonings	100	99	96	109	99	77	96	89	108
Olives, pickles, relishes	100	146	97	131	93	54	106	74	114
Sauces and gravies	100	122	99	110	105	78	100	88	104
Baking needs and miscellaneous products	100	120	95	123	105	61	81	68	129
Other canned/packaged prepared foods	100	92	103	123	104	85	105	82	99
Prepared salads	100	117	99	118	113	84	90	63	125
Prepared desserts	100	124	95	126	87	75	74	76	137
Baby food	100	55	117	147	101	100	157	85	48
Miscellaneous prepared foods	100	94	101	117	105	83	98	86	103
Nonalcoholic beverages	100	116	98	108	100	85	100	91	106
Cola	100	120	99	102	101	84	110	103	93
Other carbonated drinks	100	115	98	107	96	83	109	94	97
Coffee	100	112	90	104	93	78	73	83	165
Roasted coffee	100	120	92	110	91	76	75	84	149
Instant and freeze-dried coffee	100	98	87	91	97	82	69	83	195
Noncarbonated fruit-flavored drinks	100	90	103	115	106	101	95	86	72
Tea	100	114	98	115	94	87	88	88	119
Other nonalcoholic beverages and ice	100	121	100	116	105	89	102	73	101
Food prepared by CU on trips	**100**	**152**	**100**	**149**	**91**	**63**	**74**	**60**	**120**

Note: (–) means sample is too small to make a reliable estimate.
Note: Per capita indexes account for household size and show how much each person in a particular household demographic segment spends relative to a person in the average household.
Source: Calculations by New Strategist based on the 2001 Consumer Expenditure Survey

34. Groceries: Total spending by occupation, 2001

(total annual spending on groceries, by consumer unit (CU) occupational group, 2001; numbers in thousands)

	total consumer units	self-employed workers	wage and salary workers						retired
			total	managers and professionals	technical, sales and clerical workers	service workers	construction workers and mechanics	operators, fabricators, laborers	
Number of consumer units	110,339	4,874	74,016	26,766	21,137	10,227	5,045	10,841	19,331
Total spending of all CUs	$4,360,427,358	$235,501,786	$3,243,534,333	$1,500,454,049	$845,104,607	$332,533,769	$204,437,324	$365,034,249	$518,892,947
GROCERIES	**340,453,191**	**16,986,231**	**237,664,636**	**94,531,356**	**64,506,319**	**28,919,092**	**18,241,711**	**31,958,834**	**48,081,803**
Cereals and bakery products	**49,894,192**	**2,433,637**	**34,527,724**	**13,673,679**	**9,618,815**	**4,235,205**	**2,512,461**	**4,582,274**	**7,551,269**
Cereals and cereal products	17,263,640	856,216	11,931,379	4,754,712	3,277,503	1,448,552	790,602	1,678,187	2,446,531
Flour	883,815	40,162	578,065	211,184	139,716	76,293	50,904	97,569	127,005
Prepared flour mixes	1,422,270	64,239	1,002,177	383,557	268,863	104,725	80,165	163,374	210,321
Ready-to-eat and cooked cereals	9,493,568	435,053	6,501,565	2,661,343	1,833,635	722,640	429,784	875,411	1,451,178
Rice	2,201,263	122,776	1,605,407	593,402	469,664	228,267	79,055	235,900	220,760
Pasta, cornmeal, other cereal pdts.	3,262,724	193,985	2,243,425	905,494	565,415	316,730	150,745	305,933	437,267
Bakery products	32,630,553	1,577,421	22,595,605	8,919,234	6,341,311	2,786,755	1,721,808	2,904,087	5,104,737
Bread	9,419,640	456,889	6,428,290	2,482,011	1,735,136	816,933	500,161	899,803	1,498,926
White bread	4,042,821	201,637	2,746,734	972,409	731,974	372,672	218,398	442,421	596,941
Crackers and cookies	7,743,591	375,054	5,320,270	2,191,065	1,469,233	623,745	362,836	691,981	1,298,850
Cookies	5,089,938	228,932	3,543,886	1,405,750	987,732	437,511	246,902	475,053	833,359
Crackers	2,653,653	146,123	1,776,384	785,582	481,501	186,234	115,985	216,820	465,491
Frozen, refrigerated bakery products	2,875,434	136,228	2,039,141	797,895	623,119	217,835	154,074	257,257	397,639
Other bakery products	12,590,783	609,201	8,808,644	3,447,996	2,513,612	1,128,140	704,736	1,055,046	1,909,516
Biscuits and rolls	4,340,736	227,421	2,990,246	1,252,114	832,164	402,433	196,705	324,688	656,674
Cakes and cupcakes	3,729,458	178,388	2,689,741	987,130	799,401	324,400	300,228	295,959	493,134
Bread and cracker products	446,873	22,323	323,450	127,139	98,498	32,113	17,607	49,110	63,986
Sweetrolls, coffee cakes, doughnuts	2,904,123	140,810	1,987,330	754,801	563,090	267,845	131,977	272,868	471,097
Pies, tarts, turnovers	1,169,593	40,259	817,877	326,545	220,459	101,452	58,219	112,421	224,626
Meats, poultry, fish, and eggs	**91,357,382**	**4,487,443**	**63,495,366**	**23,267,416**	**17,607,544**	**8,023,593**	**5,417,220**	**9,199,564**	**12,709,166**
Beef	27,370,692	1,310,814	18,910,348	6,961,837	5,311,728	2,209,441	1,742,240	2,706,781	3,916,847
Ground beef	9,983,473	510,308	6,963,425	2,366,917	2,027,672	858,352	666,394	1,044,097	1,307,162
Roast	4,903,465	194,326	3,251,523	1,296,010	867,251	313,560	344,775	439,277	842,832
Chuck roast	1,658,395	70,039	1,127,264	379,810	321,282	105,440	150,543	170,854	247,050
Round roast	1,310,827	49,861	906,696	376,062	236,946	94,088	68,410	132,152	182,291
Other roast	1,934,243	74,426	1,217,563	540,138	308,812	113,929	125,822	136,271	413,297
Steak	10,231,736	494,516	7,135,142	2,735,218	1,987,301	822,660	592,737	1,008,538	1,463,937
Round steak	2,009,273	99,673	1,341,170	448,598	414,497	154,530	112,100	211,074	324,954
Sirloin steak	2,799,300	131,208	2,037,661	792,541	506,654	237,471	198,319	300,729	320,121
Other steak	5,423,162	263,635	3,757,052	1,494,346	1,065,939	430,659	282,318	496,626	818,668
Pork	19,564,208	928,302	13,316,959	4,655,410	3,596,883	1,708,216	1,211,153	2,113,887	2,893,078
Bacon	3,232,933	156,602	2,199,015	797,359	601,770	289,833	185,404	323,712	485,015
Pork chops	4,651,892	224,204	3,286,310	1,121,763	825,611	444,261	378,678	506,058	591,722
Ham	4,411,353	220,987	2,966,561	1,037,183	779,321	385,967	239,638	510,286	731,872
Ham, not canned	4,219,363	209,485	2,839,254	995,428	743,811	376,763	239,638	472,017	689,344
Canned ham	191,990	11,454	127,308	41,487	35,510	9,204	–	38,377	42,528
Sausage	2,815,851	129,843	1,832,636	656,838	496,508	263,243	150,139	264,195	503,959
Other pork	4,451,075	196,763	3,033,176	1,042,268	893,461	324,912	257,295	509,635	580,317
Other meats	11,261,198	534,142	7,889,365	2,860,482	2,188,948	992,939	650,351	1,191,751	1,535,268
Frankfurters	2,428,561	116,440	1,690,525	609,194	480,867	235,017	126,730	239,369	320,121
Lunch meats (cold cuts)	7,820,828	376,663	5,489,767	1,994,335	1,521,230	676,209	470,093	825,759	1,072,097
Bologna, liverwurst, salami	2,802,611	128,966	1,930,337	657,373	499,890	276,845	172,085	315,907	391,453
Lamb, organ meats, and others	1,011,809	41,039	709,073	256,954	186,640	81,714	53,578	126,623	142,856

	total consumer units	self-employed workers	wage and salary workers total	managers and professionals	technical, sales and clerical workers	service workers	construction workers and mechanics	operators, fabricators, laborers	retired
Poultry	$16,757,184	$777,208	$11,989,852	$4,429,773	$3,398,196	$1,575,469	$958,802	$1,646,314	$2,017,383
Fresh and frozen chicken	13,191,027	626,163	9,425,197	3,377,869	2,653,750	1,278,580	790,552	1,329,757	1,548,606
Fresh and frozen whole chicken	3,944,619	207,974	2,818,529	1,002,654	812,718	363,263	260,221	384,530	436,301
Fresh and frozen chicken parts	9,246,408	418,189	6,606,668	2,375,215	1,841,033	915,317	530,280	945,227	1,112,112
Other poultry	3,566,157	151,045	2,564,654	1,051,636	744,445	296,992	168,301	316,557	468,777
Fish and seafood	12,542,234	748,598	8,742,030	3,446,390	2,374,531	1,156,162	639,302	1,145,026	1,791,984
Canned fish and seafood	1,667,222	73,695	1,173,154	465,193	362,288	134,690	67,603	149,823	253,816
Fresh fish and shellfish	6,959,081	419,798	4,845,828	1,917,784	1,244,124	690,834	330,952	663,469	991,294
Frozen fish and shellfish	3,915,931	255,105	2,722,309	1,063,413	768,119	330,639	240,798	331,843	546,874
Eggs	3,860,762	188,380	2,646,812	913,791	737,259	381,365	215,321	395,697	554,606
Dairy products	**36,598,343**	**1,866,937**	**25,474,087**	**10,438,205**	**6,734,037**	**3,105,838**	**1,856,610**	**3,395,184**	**5,064,335**
Fresh milk and cream	14,989,553	763,366	10,287,484	3,947,717	2,772,329	1,292,181	757,809	1,516,005	2,039,421
Fresh milk, all types	13,626,867	691,474	9,347,481	3,530,703	2,533,904	1,181,321	701,709	1,395,670	1,842,051
Cream	1,362,687	71,843	940,003	417,014	238,214	110,861	56,100	120,335	197,370
Other dairy products	21,608,790	1,103,620	15,186,603	6,490,487	3,961,919	1,813,656	1,098,801	1,879,179	3,024,915
Butter	2,377,806	125,311	1,551,375	592,867	462,266	178,052	109,174	213,893	405,758
Cheese	10,304,559	529,804	7,325,364	3,042,759	1,961,302	870,931	586,179	894,816	1,350,077
Ice cream and related products	6,266,152	324,462	4,381,007	1,867,196	1,076,930	563,610	291,147	586,932	935,041
Miscellaneous dairy products	2,660,273	123,995	1,928,857	987,665	461,209	201,063	112,302	183,430	334,040
Fruits and vegetables	**57,568,270**	**2,838,715**	**39,363,929**	**16,473,670**	**10,407,013**	**4,872,450**	**2,869,495**	**4,882,678**	**8,905,792**
Fresh fruits	17,699,479	852,706	12,062,388	5,247,474	3,031,046	1,470,336	868,194	1,486,193	2,809,568
Apples	3,401,751	145,391	2,415,142	1,052,707	612,762	286,867	182,024	290,647	435,914
Bananas	3,453,611	174,684	2,300,417	899,605	564,358	335,241	189,793	310,920	589,402
Oranges	2,054,512	98,114	1,412,225	600,629	352,988	193,904	96,662	171,938	293,058
Citrus fruits, excl. oranges	1,457,578	94,068	961,468	400,955	231,027	123,031	66,846	138,982	235,258
Other fresh fruits	7,332,027	340,449	4,973,135	2,293,579	1,269,911	531,293	332,920	573,706	1,255,935
Fresh vegetables	17,832,989	911,925	12,158,608	5,010,863	3,249,814	1,496,721	949,822	1,497,576	2,741,136
Potatoes	3,320,101	160,647	2,243,425	846,609	641,719	294,640	183,789	284,576	548,227
Lettuce	2,297,258	116,732	1,581,722	671,291	399,067	207,915	119,314	189,501	322,248
Tomatoes	3,313,480	150,997	2,285,614	909,241	580,845	277,356	186,060	332,060	481,729
Other fresh vegetables	8,902,151	483,501	6,047,107	2,583,722	1,628,395	716,913	460,659	691,439	1,388,739
Processed fruits	12,802,634	620,996	8,723,526	3,606,451	2,416,382	1,119,550	578,914	1,042,579	2,004,045
Frozen fruits and fruit juices	1,528,195	80,567	1,075,453	485,803	235,255	139,496	92,626	125,322	220,953
Frozen orange juice	839,680	44,012	602,490	271,407	127,668	88,259	48,533	67,865	121,205
Frozen fruits	279,158	20,520	191,701	97,964	40,372	19,329	18,213	17,020	42,722
Frozen fruit juices	410,461	16,036	282,001	116,432	67,216	31,908	25,931	40,437	57,026
Canned fruits	1,795,216	112,200	1,159,091	480,450	331,428	131,724	83,747	138,548	336,746
Dried fruits	611,278	35,532	387,844	194,857	106,953	32,522	26,184	32,523	123,718
Fresh fruit juice	2,743,028	132,817	1,824,494	801,909	504,540	236,755	97,369	195,680	452,152
Canned and bottled fruit juice	6,123,815	259,882	4,276,645	1,643,432	1,238,206	579,053	278,938	550,506	870,475
Processed vegetables	9,233,168	453,087	6,419,408	2,608,614	1,709,772	785,843	472,515	856,331	1,351,237
Frozen vegetables	3,034,323	153,629	2,125,740	886,222	595,641	252,505	146,507	255,631	438,234
Canned, dried vegetables and juices	6,198,845	299,459	4,292,928	1,722,392	1,114,131	533,338	325,958	600,700	913,003
Canned beans	1,390,271	64,678	967,389	388,642	237,369	112,906	70,580	155,243	203,362
Canned corn	786,717	49,812	539,577	197,265	131,472	77,418	39,200	91,173	101,681
Canned miscellaneous vegetables	1,939,760	113,126	1,274,556	514,175	343,054	151,564	100,749	168,794	330,753
Dried beans	251,573	10,089	164,316	52,461	47,136	22,090	8,577	32,740	21,457
Dried miscellaneous vegetables	836,370	29,780	613,593	217,340	171,210	93,270	54,436	78,597	122,172
Fresh and canned vegetable juices	844,093	29,731	611,372	270,872	171,421	69,237	40,865	63,962	115,019
Sugar and other sweets	**12,794,910**	**630,160**	**8,924,849**	**3,745,099**	**2,414,902**	**1,020,348**	**615,793**	**1,159,662**	**1,849,010**
Candy and chewing gum	8,108,813	402,446	5,729,579	2,515,736	1,543,212	630,699	379,788	689,921	1,149,228
Sugar	1,976,172	104,742	1,351,532	466,799	366,938	176,927	95,351	238,827	250,337
Artificial sweeteners	556,109	34,167	344,915	141,057	70,386	43,874	39,553	49,218	125,458
Jams, preserves, other sweets	2,153,817	88,804	1,498,824	621,507	434,154	168,950	101,051	181,695	323,794

	total consumer units	self-employed workers	wage and salary workers						retired
			total	managers and professionals	technical, sales and clerical workers	service workers	construction workers and mechanics	operators, fabricators, laborers	
Fats and oils	**$9,573,012**	**$485,694**	**$6,545,235**	**$2,507,974**	**$1,804,888**	**$827,569**	**$518,222**	**$896,984**	**$1,431,267**
Margarine	1,261,175	54,930	831,940	313,965	237,791	98,179	61,902	120,877	225,786
Fats and oils	2,706,616	134,279	1,865,203	654,161	469,030	267,129	154,327	310,920	368,836
Salad dressings	3,091,699	156,748	2,135,362	854,638	597,966	266,413	172,186	254,222	447,319
Nondairy cream and imitation milk	1,113,321	66,530	742,381	302,991	213,695	95,725	42,328	90,956	200,463
Peanut butter	1,400,202	73,208	971,090	382,486	286,618	100,122	87,480	119,902	188,864
Miscellaneous foods	**50,173,350**	**2,446,797**	**36,237,493**	**15,150,894**	**9,795,943**	**4,057,665**	**2,730,909**	**4,638,647**	**6,396,241**
Frozen prepared foods	10,613,508	542,233	7,673,979	3,327,282	2,107,359	779,911	535,829	962,030	1,245,690
Frozen meals	3,161,212	178,193	2,171,629	958,491	541,953	251,277	124,864	298,453	473,996
Other frozen prepared foods	7,452,296	364,039	5,502,349	2,368,791	1,565,406	528,634	410,966	663,578	771,694
Canned and packaged soups	4,112,335	188,770	2,770,419	1,126,849	740,429	342,093	182,982	382,145	723,753
Potato chips, nuts, and other snacks	10,743,708	555,051	7,744,294	3,199,875	2,062,760	886,579	633,248	988,374	1,382,360
Potato chips and other snacks	8,337,215	406,394	6,183,297	2,529,922	1,637,061	716,299	501,322	814,159	897,732
Nuts	2,406,494	148,608	1,560,997	669,685	425,699	170,280	131,927	173,348	484,628
Condiments and seasonings	9,273,993	506,457	6,528,211	2,691,857	1,816,937	687,050	486,742	869,557	1,232,545
Salt, spices, and other seasonings	2,188,022	98,991	1,526,950	601,432	416,188	173,961	114,976	221,590	282,233
Olives, pickles, relishes	1,100,080	73,792	771,247	362,679	195,095	61,771	63,718	92,799	149,622
Sauces and gravies	4,064,889	227,470	2,905,128	1,132,470	819,270	329,719	222,333	407,188	504,926
Baking needs and misc. products	1,921,002	106,156	1,325,627	595,008	386,384	121,599	85,715	148,088	295,571
Other canned/packaged prepared foods	15,430,909	654,335	11,520,590	4,805,300	3,068,247	1,362,134	892,107	1,436,541	1,811,895
Prepared salads	2,157,128	115,904	1,546,194	643,187	467,128	187,768	107,004	154,918	320,508
Prepared desserts	1,119,941	63,654	769,026	355,720	187,485	86,623	45,556	96,377	182,098
Baby food	2,606,207	65,994	2,211,598	969,197	502,004	269,277	225,007	253,463	147,689
Miscellaneous prepared foods	9,515,635	408,734	6,962,685	2,811,768	1,909,939	818,467	509,141	931,784	1,161,600
Nonalcoholic beverages	28,264,438	1,501,874	20,039,832	7,690,407	5,388,878	2,498,661	1,548,311	2,916,771	3,570,242
Cola	9,644,732	533,606	6,921,976	2,480,138	1,866,609	844,137	582,647	1,130,174	1,069,971
Other carbonated drinks	5,091,042	267,778	3,609,760	1,378,181	938,483	436,795	304,970	547,145	588,049
Coffee	4,231,501	217,965	2,770,419	1,105,971	753,957	341,071	168,856	402,201	832,973
Roasted coffee	2,756,268	151,630	1,837,817	767,917	479,810	215,994	112,705	262,894	490,621
Instant and freeze-dried coffee	1,475,232	66,335	932,602	338,055	274,147	125,076	56,151	139,307	342,352
Noncarbonated fruit-flavored drinks	2,246,502	92,752	1,674,982	650,414	453,811	235,937	117,145	220,614	192,923
Tea	1,938,656	101,184	1,371,517	561,283	348,338	174,064	93,282	194,596	273,920
Other nonalcoholic beverages and ice	5,039,182	278,988	3,643,808	1,479,892	1,016,901	464,919	281,410	419,655	605,254
Food prepared by CU on trips	**4,229,294**	**294,975**	**3,056,121**	**1,584,012**	**734,299**	**277,663**	**172,741**	**287,178**	**604,480**

Note: Numbers may not add to total because of rounding; (–) means sample is too small to make a reliable estimate.
Source: Calculations by New Strategist based on the 2001 Consumer Expenditure Survey

35. Groceries: Market shares by occupation, 2001

(percentage of total annual spending on groceries accounted for by consumer unit occupation group, 2001)

	total consumer units	self-employed workers	wage and salary workers						retired
			total	managers and professionals	technical, sales and clerical workers	service workers	construction workers and mechanics	operators, fabricators, laborers	
Share of total consumer units	100.0%	4.4%	67.1%	24.3%	19.2%	9.3%	4.6%	9.8%	17.5%
Share of total before-tax income	100.0	5.0	78.0	39.7	18.9	7.0	4.6	8.0	9.1
Share of total spending	100.0	5.4	74.4	34.4	19.4	7.6	4.7	8.4	11.9
GROCERIES	100.0	5.0	69.8	27.8	18.9	8.5	5.4	9.4	14.1
Cereals and bakery products	100.0	4.9	69.2	27.4	19.3	8.5	5.0	9.2	15.1
Cereals and cereal products	100.0	5.0	69.1	27.5	19.0	8.4	4.6	9.7	14.2
Flour	100.0	4.5	65.4	23.9	15.8	8.6	5.8	11.0	14.4
Prepared flour mixes	100.0	4.5	70.5	27.0	18.9	7.4	5.6	11.5	14.8
Ready-to-eat and cooked cereals	100.0	4.6	68.5	28.0	19.3	7.6	4.5	9.2	15.3
Rice	100.0	5.6	72.9	27.0	21.3	10.4	3.6	10.7	10.0
Pasta, cornmeal, and other cereal products	100.0	5.9	68.8	27.8	17.3	9.7	4.6	9.4	13.4
Bakery products	100.0	4.8	69.2	27.3	19.4	8.5	5.3	8.9	15.6
Bread	100.0	4.9	68.2	26.3	18.4	8.7	5.3	9.6	15.9
White bread	100.0	5.0	67.9	24.1	18.1	9.2	5.4	10.9	14.8
Crackers and cookies	100.0	4.8	68.7	28.3	19.0	8.1	4.7	8.9	16.8
Cookies	100.0	4.5	69.6	27.6	19.4	8.6	4.9	9.3	16.4
Crackers	100.0	5.5	66.9	29.6	18.1	7.0	4.4	8.2	17.5
Frozen and refrigerated bakery products	100.0	4.7	70.9	27.7	21.7	7.6	5.4	8.9	13.8
Other bakery products	100.0	4.8	70.0	27.4	20.0	9.0	5.6	8.4	15.2
Biscuits and rolls	100.0	5.2	68.9	28.8	19.2	9.3	4.5	7.5	15.1
Cakes and cupcakes	100.0	4.8	72.1	26.5	21.4	8.7	8.1	7.9	13.2
Bread and cracker products	100.0	5.0	72.4	28.5	22.0	7.2	3.9	11.0	14.3
Sweetrolls, coffee cakes, doughnuts	100.0	4.8	68.4	26.0	19.4	9.2	4.5	9.4	16.2
Pies, tarts, turnovers	100.0	3.4	69.9	27.9	18.8	8.7	5.0	9.6	19.2
Meats, poultry, fish, and eggs	100.0	4.9	69.5	25.5	19.3	8.8	5.9	10.1	13.9
Beef	100.0	4.8	69.1	25.4	19.4	8.1	6.4	9.9	14.3
Ground beef	100.0	5.1	69.7	23.7	20.3	8.6	6.7	10.5	13.1
Roast	100.0	4.0	66.3	26.4	17.7	6.4	7.0	9.0	17.2
Chuck roast	100.0	4.2	68.0	22.9	19.4	6.4	9.1	10.3	14.9
Round roast	100.0	3.8	69.2	28.7	18.1	7.2	5.2	10.1	13.9
Other roast	100.0	3.8	62.9	27.9	16.0	5.9	6.5	7.1	21.4
Steak	100.0	4.8	69.7	26.7	19.4	8.0	5.8	9.9	14.3
Round steak	100.0	5.0	66.7	22.3	20.6	7.7	5.6	10.5	16.2
Sirloin steak	100.0	4.7	72.8	28.3	18.1	8.5	7.1	10.7	11.4
Other steak	100.0	4.9	69.3	27.6	19.7	7.9	5.2	9.2	15.1
Pork	100.0	4.7	68.1	23.8	18.4	8.7	6.2	10.8	14.8
Bacon	100.0	4.8	68.0	24.7	18.6	9.0	5.7	10.0	1.5
Pork chops	100.0	4.8	70.6	24.1	17.7	9.6	8.1	10.9	12.7
Ham	100.0	5.0	67.2	23.5	17.7	8.7	5.4	11.6	16.6
Ham, not canned	100.0	5.0	67.3	23.6	17.6	8.9	5.7	11.2	16.3
Canned ham	100.0	6.0	66.3	21.6	18.5	4.8	–	20.0	22.2
Sausage	100.0	4.6	65.1	23.3	17.6	9.3	5.3	9.4	17.9
Other pork	100.0	4.4	68.1	23.4	20.1	7.3	5.8	11.4	13.0
Other meats	100.0	4.7	70.1	25.4	19.4	8.8	5.8	10.6	13.6
Frankfurters	100.0	4.8	69.6	25.1	19.8	9.7	5.2	9.9	13.2
Lunch meats (cold cuts)	100.0	4.8	70.2	25.5	19.5	8.6	6.0	10.6	13.7
Bologna, liverwurst, salami	100.0	4.6	68.9	23.5	17.8	9.9	6.1	11.3	14.0
Lamb, organ meats, and others	100.0	4.1	70.1	25.4	18.4	8.1	5.3	12.5	14.1

| | total consumer units | self-employed workers | wage and salary workers | | | | | | retired |
			total	managers and professionals	technical, sales and clerical workers	service workers	construction workers and mechanics	operators, fabricators, laborers	
Poultry	100.0%	4.6%	71.6%	26.4%	20.3%	9.4%	5.7%	9.8%	12.0%
Fresh and frozen chicken	100.0	4.7	71.5	25.6	20.1	9.7	6.0	10.1	11.7
Fresh and frozen whole chicken	100.0	5.3	71.5	25.4	20.6	9.2	6.6	9.7	11.1
Fresh and frozen chicken parts	100.0	4.5	71.5	25.7	19.9	9.9	5.7	10.2	12.0
Other poultry	100.0	4.2	71.9	29.5	20.9	8.3	4.7	8.9	13.1
Fish and seafood	100.0	6.0	69.7	27.5	18.9	9.2	5.1	9.1	14.3
Canned fish and seafood	100.0	4.4	70.4	27.9	21.7	8.1	4.1	9.0	15.2
Fresh fish and shellfish	100.0	6.0	69.6	27.6	17.9	9.9	4.8	9.5	14.2
Frozen fish and shellfish	100.0	6.5	69.5	27.2	19.6	8.4	6.1	8.5	14.0
Eggs	100.0	4.9	68.6	23.7	19.1	9.9	5.6	10.2	14.4
Dairy products	**100.0**	**5.1**	**69.6**	**28.5**	**18.4**	**8.5**	**5.1**	**9.3**	**13.8**
Fresh milk and cream	100.0	5.1	68.6	26.3	18.5	8.6	5.1	10.1	13.6
Fresh milk, all types	100.0	5.1	68.6	25.9	18.6	8.7	5.1	10.2	13.5
Cream	100.0	5.3	69.0	30.6	17.5	8.1	4.1	8.8	14.5
Other dairy products	100.0	5.1	70.3	30.0	18.3	8.4	5.1	8.7	14.0
Butter	100.0	5.3	65.2	24.9	19.4	7.5	4.6	9.0	17.1
Cheese	100.0	5.1	71.1	29.5	19.0	8.5	5.7	8.7	13.1
Ice cream and related products	100.0	5.2	69.9	29.8	17.2	9.0	4.6	9.4	14.9
Miscellaneous dairy products	100.0	4.7	72.5	37.1	17.3	7.6	4.2	6.9	12.6
Fruits and vegetables	**100.0**	**4.9**	**68.4**	**28.6**	**18.1**	**8.5**	**5.0**	**8.5**	**15.5**
Fresh fruits	100.0	4.8	68.2	29.6	17.1	8.3	4.9	8.4	15.9
Apples	100.0	4.3	71.0	30.9	18.0	8.4	5.4	8.5	12.8
Bananas	100.0	5.1	66.6	26.1	16.3	9.7	5.5	0.9	17.1
Oranges	100.0	4.8	68.7	29.2	17.2	9.4	4.7	8.4	14.3
Citrus fruits, excl. oranges	100.0	6.5	66.0	27.5	15.9	8.4	4.6	9.5	16.1
Other fresh fruits	100.0	4.6	67.8	31.3	17.3	7.2	4.5	7.8	17.1
Fresh vegetables	100.0	5.1	68.2	28.1	18.2	8.4	5.3	8.4	15.4
Potatoes	100.0	4.8	67.6	25.5	19.3	8.9	5.5	8.6	16.5
Lettuce	100.0	5.1	68.9	29.2	17.4	9.1	5.2	8.2	14.0
Tomatoes	100.0	4.6	69.0	27.4	17.5	8.4	5.6	10.0	14.5
Other fresh vegetables	100.0	5.4	67.9	29.0	18.3	8.1	5.2	7.8	15.6
Processed fruits	100.0	4.9	68.1	28.2	18.9	8.7	4.5	8.1	15.7
Frozen fruits and fruit juices	100.0	5.3	70.4	31.8	15.4	9.1	6.1	8.2	14.5
Frozen orange juice	100.0	5.2	71.8	32.3	15.2	10.5	5.8	8.1	14.4
Frozen fruits	100.0	7.4	68.7	35.1	14.5	6.9	6.5	6.1	15.3
Frozen fruit juices	100.0	3.9	68.7	28.4	16.4	7.8	6.3	9.9	13.9
Canned fruits	100.0	6.2	64.6	26.8	18.5	7.3	4.7	7.7	18.8
Dried fruits	100.0	5.8	63.4	31.9	17.5	5.3	4.3	5.3	20.2
Fresh fruit juice	100.0	4.8	66.5	29.2	18.4	8.6	3.5	7.1	16.5
Canned and bottled fruit juice	100.0	4.2	69.8	26.8	20.2	9.5	4.6	9.0	14.2
Processed vegetables	100.0	4.9	69.5	28.3	18.5	8.5	5.1	9.3	14.6
Frozen vegetables	100.0	5.1	70.1	29.2	19.6	8.3	4.8	8.4	14.4
Canned and dried vegetables and juices	100.0	4.8	69.3	27.8	18.0	8.6	5.3	9.7	14.7
Canned beans	100.0	4.7	69.6	28.0	17.1	8.1	5.1	11.2	14.6
Canned corn	100.0	6.3	68.6	25.1	16.7	9.8	5.0	11.6	12.9
Canned miscellaneous vegetables	100.0	5.8	65.7	26.5	17.7	7.8	5.2	8.7	17.1
Dried beans	100.0	4.0	65.3	20.9	18.7	8.8	3.4	13.0	8.5
Dried miscellaneous vegetables	100.0	3.6	73.4	26.0	20.5	11.2	6.5	9.4	14.6
Fresh and canned vegetable juices	100.0	3.5	72.4	32.1	20.3	8.2	4.8	7.6	13.6
Sugar and other sweets	**100.0**	**4.9**	**69.8**	**29.3**	**18.9**	**8.0**	**4.8**	**9.1**	**14.5**
Candy and chewing gum	100.0	5.0	70.7	31.0	19.0	7.8	4.7	8.5	14.2
Sugar	100.0	5.3	68.4	23.6	18.6	9.0	4.8	12.1	12.7
Artificial sweeteners	100.0	6.1	62.0	25.4	12.7	7.9	7.1	8.9	22.6
Jams, preserves, other sweets	100.0	4.1	69.6	28.9	20.2	7.8	4.7	8.4	15.0

	total consumer units	self-employed workers	wage and salary workers						retired
			total	managers and professionals	technical, sales and clerical workers	service workers	construction workers and mechanics	operators, fabricators, laborers	
Fats and oils	**100.0%**	**5.1%**	**68.4%**	**26.2%**	**18.9%**	**8.6%**	**5.4%**	**9.4%**	**15.0%**
Margarine	100.0	4.4	66.0	24.9	18.9	7.8	4.9	9.6	17.9
Fats and oils	100.0	5.0	68.9	24.2	17.3	9.9	5.7	11.5	13.6
Salad dressings	100.0	5.1	69.1	27.6	19.3	8.6	5.6	8.2	14.5
Nondairy cream and imitation milk	100.0	6.0	66.7	27.2	19.2	8.6	3.8	8.2	1.8
Peanut butter	100.0	5.2	69.4	27.3	20.5	7.2	6.2	8.6	13.5
Miscellaneous foods	**100.0**	**4.9**	**72.2**	**30.2**	**19.5**	**8.1**	**5.4**	**9.2**	**12.7**
Frozen prepared foods	100.0	5.1	72.3	31.3	19.9	7.3	5.1	9.1	11.7
Frozen meals	100.0	5.6	68.7	30.3	17.1	7.9	3.9	9.4	15.0
Other frozen prepared foods	100.0	4.9	73.8	31.8	2.1	7.1	5.5	8.9	10.4
Canned and packaged soups	100.0	4.6	67.4	27.4	1.8	8.3	4.4	9.3	17.6
Potato chips, nuts, and other snacks	100.0	5.2	72.1	29.8	19.2	8.3	5.9	9.2	12.9
Potato chips and other snacks	100.0	4.9	74.2	30.3	19.6	8.6	6.0	9.8	10.8
Nuts	100.0	6.2	64.9	27.8	17.7	7.1	5.5	7.2	20.1
Condiments and seasonings	100.0	5.5	70.4	29.0	19.6	7.4	5.2	9.4	13.3
Salt, spices, and other seasonings	100.0	4.5	69.8	27.5	19.0	8.0	5.3	10.1	12.9
Olives, pickles, relishes	100.0	6.7	70.1	33.0	17.7	5.6	5.8	8.4	13.6
Sauces and gravies	100.0	5.6	71.5	27.9	20.2	8.1	5.5	10.0	12.4
Baking needs and miscellaneous products	100.0	5.5	6.9	31.0	20.1	6.3	4.5	7.7	15.4
Other canned/packaged prepared foods	100.0	4.2	74.7	31.1	19.9	8.8	5.8	9.3	11.7
Prepared salads	100.0	5.4	71.7	29.8	21.7	8.7	5.0	7.2	14.9
Prepared desserts	100.0	5.7	68.7	31.8	16.7	7.7	4.1	8.6	16.3
Baby food	100.0	2.5	84.9	37.2	19.3	10.3	8.6	9.7	5.7
Miscellaneous prepared foods	100.0	4.3	73.2	29.5	20.1	8.6	5.4	9.8	12.2
Nonalcoholic beverages	100.0	5.3	70.9	27.2	19.1	8.8	5.5	10.3	12.6
Cola	100.0	5.5	71.8	25.7	19.4	8.8	6.0	11.7	11.1
Other carbonated drinks	100.0	5.3	70.9	27.1	18.4	8.6	6.0	10.7	11.6
Coffee	100.0	5.2	65.5	26.1	17.8	8.1	4.0	9.5	19.7
Roasted coffee	100.0	5.5	66.7	27.9	17.4	7.8	4.1	9.5	17.8
Instant and freeze-dried coffee	100.0	4.5	63.2	22.9	18.6	8.5	3.8	9.4	23.2
Noncarbonated fruit-flavored drinks	100.0	4.1	74.6	29.0	20.2	10.5	5.2	9.8	8.6
Tea	100.0	5.2	70.7	29.0	18.0	9.0	4.8	10.0	14.1
Other nonalcoholic beverages and ice	100.0	5.5	72.3	29.4	20.2	9.2	5.6	8.3	12.0
Food prepared by CU on trips	**100.0**	**7.0**	**72.3**	**37.5**	**17.4**	**6.6**	**4.1**	**6.8**	**14.3**

Note: Numbers may not add to total because of rounding; (–) means sample is too small to make a reliable estimate.
Source: Calculations by New Strategist based on the 2001 Consumer Expenditure Survey

36. Groceries: Average spending by homeownership status, 2001

(average annual spending of consumer units (CU) on groceries, by homeownership status, 2001)

	total consumer units	homeowners	renters
Number of consumer units (in thousands, add 000)	**110,339**	**73,010**	**37,329**
Average number of persons per CU	**2.5**	**2.6**	**2.2**
Average before-tax income of CU	**$47,507.00**	**$52,966.00**	**$29,021.00**
Average spending of CU, total	**39,518.46**	**45,398.53**	**28,016.06**
GROCERIES	**3,085.52**	**3,380.16**	**2,508.66**
Cereals and bakery products	**452.19**	**494.78**	**368.82**
Cereals and cereal products	156.46	165.29	139.17
Flour	8.01	8.41	7.21
Prepared flour mixes	12.89	14.45	9.85
Ready-to-eat and cooked cereals	86.04	92.51	73.36
Rice	19.95	18.69	22.41
Pasta, cornmeal, and other cereal products	29.57	31.23	26.34
Bakery products	295.73	329.48	229.65
Bread	85.37	93.04	70.34
White bread	36.64	39.04	31.92
Crackers and cookies	70.18	77.96	54.96
Cookies	46.13	50.77	37.06
Crackers	24.05	27.19	17.90
Frozen and refrigerated bakery products	26.06	30.10	18.16
Other bakery products	114.11	128.38	86.19
Biscuits and rolls	39.34	45.77	26.76
Cakes and cupcakes	33.80	37.56	26.44
Bread and cracker products	4.05	4.47	3.22
Sweetrolls, coffee cakes, doughnuts	26.32	29.21	20.67
Pies, tarts, turnovers	10.60	11.37	9.10
Meats, poultry, fish, and eggs	**827.97**	**899.92**	**687.09**
Beef	248.06	273.88	197.51
Ground beef	90.48	97.90	75.96
Roast	44.44	51.24	31.13
Chuck roast	15.03	16.83	11.50
Round roast	11.88	13.68	8.36
Other roast	17.53	20.73	11.28
Steak	92.73	102.29	73.99
Round steak	18.21	19.62	15.45
Sirloin steak	25.37	26.90	22.36
Other steak	49.15	55.77	36.19
Pork	177.31	195.65	141.40
Bacon	29.30	32.21	23.62
Pork chops	42.16	45.46	35.70
Ham	39.98	44.62	30.90
Ham, not canned	38.24	42.75	29.41
Canned ham	1.74	1.86	1.50
Sausage	25.52	28.31	20.07
Other pork	40.34	45.07	31.10
Other meats	102.06	112.00	82.62
Frankfurters	22.01	24.05	18.03
Lunch meats (cold cuts)	70.88	78.23	56.47
Bologna, liverwurst, salami	25.40	27.19	21.88
Lamb, organ meats, and others	9.17	9.71	8.12

	total consumer units	homeowners	renters
Poultry	$151.87	$161.82	$132.39
Fresh and frozen chicken	119.55	125.20	108.50
Fresh and frozen whole chicken	35.75	36.38	34.51
Fresh and frozen chicken parts	83.80	88.81	73.99
Other poultry	32.32	36.62	23.89
Fish and seafood	113.67	120.01	101.25
Canned fish and seafood	15.11	16.46	12.48
Fresh fish and shellfish	63.07	35.32	58.67
Frozen fish and shellfish	35.49	38.23	30.11
Eggs	34.99	36.56	31.93
Dairy products	**331.69**	**366.81**	**262.92**
Fresh milk and cream	135.85	147.55	112.94
Fresh milk, all types	123.50	133.46	104.01
Cream	12.35	14.09	8.93
Other dairy products	195.84	219.26	149.98
Butter	21.55	23.85	17.04
Cheese	93.39	104.27	72.09
Ice cream and related products	56.79	63.59	43.48
Miscellaneous dairy products	24.11	27.55	17.37
Fruits and vegetables	**521.74**	**568.50**	**430.20**
Fresh fruits	160.41	176.76	128.39
Apples	30.83	33.71	25.19
Bananas	31.30	33.53	26.93
Oranges	18.62	19.92	16.09
Citrus fruits, excl. oranges	13.21	14.76	10.20
Other fresh fruits	66.45	74.85	49.98
Fresh vegetables	161.62	174.50	136.40
Potatoes	30.09	32.36	25.64
Lettuce	20.82	22.87	16.82
Tomatoes	30.03	31.44	27.28
Other fresh vegetables	80.68	87.83	66.66
Processed fruits	116.03	125.62	97.26
Frozen fruits and fruit juices	13.85	15.91	9.84
Frozen orange juice	7.61	8.68	5.51
Frozen fruits	2.53	3.06	1.50
Frozen fruit juices	3.72	4.17	2.83
Canned fruits	16.27	18.83	11.27
Dried fruits	5.54	6.39	3.88
Fresh fruit juice	24.86	26.52	21.60
Canned and bottled fruit juice	55.50	57.98	50.67
Processed vegetables	83.68	91.61	68.15
Frozen vegetables	27.50	30.29	22.04
Canned and dried vegetables and juices	56.18	61.32	46.11
Canned beans	12.60	13.74	10.37
Canned corn	7.13	7.41	6.58
Canned miscellaneous vegetables	17.58	20.21	12.45
Dried beans	2.28	2.12	2.58
Dried miscellaneous vegetables	7.58	8.41	5.95
Fresh and canned vegetable juices	7.65	7.73	7.48
Sugar and other sweets	**115.96**	**131.16**	**86.19**
Candy and chewing gum	73.49	84.50	51.94
Sugar	17.91	19.27	15.25
Artificial sweeteners	5.04	5.78	3.59
Jams, preserves, other sweets	19.52	21.62	15.41

	total consumer units	homeowners	renters
Fats and oils	**$86.76**	**$94.22**	**$72.15**
Margarine	11.43	12.81	8.72
Fats and oils	24.53	24.58	24.43
Salad dressings	28.02	31.39	21.42
Nondairy cream and imitation milk	10.09	11.69	6.96
Peanut butter	12.69	13.75	10.62
Miscellaneous foods	**454.72**	**500.18**	**365.71**
Frozen prepared foods	96.19	105.40	78.16
Frozen meals	28.65	30.65	24.73
Other frozen prepared foods	67.54	74.75	53.43
Canned and packaged soups	37.27	41.36	29.27
Potato chips, nuts, and other snacks	97.37	108.65	75.28
Potato chips and other snacks	75.56	83.15	60.70
Nuts	21.81	25.50	14.58
Condiments and seasonings	84.05	93.76	65.02
Salt, spices, and other seasonings	19.83	21.67	16.21
Olives, pickles, relishes	9.97	11.70	6.56
Sauces and gravies	36.84	40.44	29.79
Baking needs and miscellaneous products	17.41	19.95	12.45
Other canned/packaged prepared foods	139.85	151.01	117.98
Prepared salads	19.55	22.67	13.43
Prepared desserts	10.15	11.89	6.75
Baby food	23.62	25.27	20.39
Miscellaneous prepared foods	86.24	90.83	77.25
Nonalcoholic beverages	256.16	278.72	211.98
Cola	87.41	96.06	70.50
Other carbonated drinks	46.14	49.26	40.04
Coffee	38.35	44.01	27.26
Roasted coffee	24.98	29.05	17.03
Instant and freeze-dried coffee	13.37	14.97	10.23
Noncarbonated fruit-flavored drinks	20.36	21.57	17.98
Tea	17.57	18.50	15.76
Other nonalcoholic beverages and ice	45.67	48.53	40.06
Food prepared by CU on trips	**38.33**	**45.86**	**23.60**

Source: Bureau of Labor Statistics, unpublished tables from the 2001 Consumer Expenditure Survey

37. Groceries: Indexed spending by homeownership status, 2001

(indexed average annual spending of consumer units (CU) on groceries, by homeownership status, 2001; index definition: an index of 100 is the average for all consumer units; an index of 132 means that spending by consumer units in that group is 32 percent above the average for all consumer units; an index of 68 indicates spending that is 32 percent below the average for all consumer units)

	total consumer units	homeowners	renters
Average spending of CU, total	$39,518	$45,399	$28,016
Average spending of CU, index	100	60	100
GROCERIES	**100**	**110**	**81**
Cereals and bakery products	**100**	**109**	**82**
Cereals and cereal products	100	106	89
Flour	100	105	90
Prepared flour mixes	100	112	76
Ready-to-eat and cooked cereals	100	108	85
Rice	100	94	112
Pasta, cornmeal, and other cereal products	100	106	89
Bakery products	100	111	78
Bread	100	109	82
White bread	100	107	87
Crackers and cookies	100	111	78
Cookies	100	110	80
Crackers	100	113	74
Frozen and refrigerated bakery products	100	116	70
Other bakery products	100	113	76
Biscuits and rolls	100	116	68
Cakes and cupcakes	100	111	78
Bread and cracker products	100	110	80
Sweetrolls, coffee cakes, doughnuts	100	111	79
Pies, tarts, turnovers	100	107	86
Meats, poultry, fish, and eggs	**100**	**109**	**83**
Beef	100	110	80
Ground beef	100	108	84
Roast	100	115	70
Chuck roast	100	112	77
Round roast	100	115	70
Other roast	100	118	64
Steak	100	110	80
Round steak	100	108	85
Sirloin steak	100	106	88
Other steak	100	114	74
Pork	100	110	80
Bacon	100	110	81
Pork chops	100	108	85
Ham	100	112	77
Ham, not canned	100	112	77
Canned ham	100	107	86
Sausage	100	111	79
Other pork	100	112	77
Other meats	100	110	81
Frankfurters	100	109	82
Lunch meats (cold cuts)	100	110	80
Bologna, liverwurst, salami	100	107	86
Lamb, organ meats, and others	100	106	89

	total consumer units	homeowners	renters
Poultry	100	107	87
Fresh and frozen chicken	100	105	91
Fresh and frozen whole chicken	100	102	97
Fresh and frozen chicken parts	100	106	88
Other poultry	100	113	74
Fish and seafood	100	106	89
Canned fish and seafood	100	109	83
Fresh fish and shellfish	100	56	93
Frozen fish and shellfish	100	108	85
Eggs	100	105	91
Dairy products	**100**	**111**	**79**
Fresh milk and cream	100	109	83
Fresh milk, all types	100	108	84
Cream	100	114	72
Other dairy products	100	112	77
Butter	100	111	79
Cheese	100	112	77
Ice cream and related products	100	112	77
Miscellaneous dairy products	100	114	72
Fruits and vegetables	**100**	**109**	**83**
Fresh fruits	100	110	80
Apples	100	109	82
Bananas	100	107	86
Oranges	100	107	86
Citrus fruits, excl. oranges	100	112	77
Other fresh fruits	100	113	75
Fresh vegetables	100	108	84
Potatoes	100	108	85
Lettuce	100	110	81
Tomatoes	100	105	91
Other fresh vegetables	100	109	83
Processed fruits	100	108	84
Frozen fruits and fruit juices	100	115	71
Frozen orange juice	100	114	72
Frozen fruits	100	121	59
Frozen fruit juices	100	112	76
Canned fruits	100	116	69
Dried fruits	100	115	70
Fresh fruit juice	100	107	87
Canned and bottled fruit juice	100	105	91
Processed vegetables	100	110	81
Frozen vegetables	100	110	80
Canned and dried vegetables and juices	100	109	82
Canned beans	100	109	82
Canned corn	100	104	92
Canned miscellaneous vegetables	100	115	71
Dried beans	100	93	113
Dried miscellaneous vegetables	100	111	79
Fresh and canned vegetable juices	100	101	98
Sugar and other sweets	**100**	**113**	**74**
Candy and chewing gum	100	115	71
Sugar	100	108	85
Artificial sweeteners	100	115	71
Jams, preserves, other sweets	100	111	79

	total consumer units	homeowners	renters
Fats and oils	**100**	**109**	**83**
Margarine	100	112	76
Fats and oils	100	100	100
Salad dressings	100	112	76
Nondairy cream and imitation milk	100	116	69
Peanut butter	100	108	84
Miscellaneous foods	**100**	**110**	**80**
Frozen prepared foods	100	110	81
Frozen meals	100	107	86
Other frozen prepared foods	100	111	79
Canned and packaged soups	100	111	79
Potato chips, nuts, and other snacks	100	112	77
Potato chips and other snacks	100	110	80
Nuts	100	117	67
Condiments and seasonings	100	112	77
Salt, spices, and other seasonings	100	109	82
Olives, pickles, relishes	100	117	66
Sauces and gravies	100	110	81
Baking needs and miscellaneous products	100	115	72
Other canned/packaged prepared foods	100	108	84
Prepared salads	100	116	69
Prepared desserts	100	117	67
Baby food	100	107	86
Miscellaneous prepared foods	100	105	90
Nonalcoholic beverages	100	109	83
Cola	100	110	81
Other carbonated drinks	100	107	87
Coffee	100	115	71
Roasted coffee	100	116	68
Instant and freeze-dried coffee	100	112	77
Noncarbonated fruit-flavored drinks	100	106	88
Tea	100	105	90
Other nonalcoholic beverages and ice	100	106	88
Food prepared by CU on trips	**100**	**120**	**62**

Source: Calculations by New Strategist based on the 2001 Consumer Expenditure Survey

38. Groceries: Indexed per capita spending by homeownership status, 2001

(indexed average annual per capita spending of consumer units (CU) on groceries, by homeownership status, 2001; index definition: an index of 100 is the average for all consumer units; an index of 132 means that spending by consumer units in that group is 32 percent above the average for all consumer units; an index of 68 indicates spending that is 32 percent below the average for all consumer units)

	total consumer units	homeowners	renters
Per capita spending of CU, total	$15,807	$17,461	$12,735
Per capita spending of CU, index	100	111	81
GROCERIES	100	105	92
Cereals and bakery products	100	105	93
Cereals and cereal products	100	102	101
Flour	100	101	102
Prepared flour mixes	100	108	87
Ready-to-eat and cooked cereals	100	103	97
Rice	100	90	128
Pasta, cornmeal, and other cereal products	100	102	101
Bakery products	100	107	88
Bread	100	105	94
White bread	100	103	99
Crackers and cookies	100	107	89
Cookies	100	106	91
Crackers	100	109	85
Frozen and refrigerated bakery products	100	111	79
Other bakery products	100	108	86
Biscuits and rolls	100	112	77
Cakes and cupcakes	100	107	89
Bread and cracker products	100	106	90
Sweetrolls, coffee cakes, doughnuts	100	107	89
Pies, tarts, turnovers	100	103	98
Meats, poultry, fish, and eggs	100	105	94
Beef	100	106	91
Ground beef	100	104	95
Roast	100	111	80
Chuck roast	100	108	87
Round roast	100	111	80
Other roast	100	114	73
Steak	100	106	91
Round steak	100	104	96
Sirloin steak	100	102	100
Other steak	100	109	84
Pork	100	106	91
Bacon	100	106	92
Pork chops	100	104	96
Ham	100	107	88
Ham, not canned	100	108	87
Canned ham	100	103	98
Sausage	100	107	89
Other pork	100	107	88
Other meats	100	106	92
Frankfurters	100	105	93
Lunch meats (cold cuts)	100	106	91
Bologna, liverwurst, salami	100	103	98
Lamb, organ meats, and others	100	102	101

	total consumer units	homeowners	renters
Poultry	100	103	99
Fresh and frozen chicken	100	101	103
Fresh and frozen whole chicken	100	98	110
Fresh and frozen chicken parts	100	102	100
Other poultry	100	109	84
Fish and seafood	100	102	101
Canned fish and seafood	100	105	94
Fresh fish and shellfish	100	54	106
Frozen fish and shellfish	100	104	96
Eggs	100	101	104
Dairy products	**100**	**106**	**90**
Fresh milk and cream	100	104	95
Fresh milk, all types	100	104	96
Cream	100	110	82
Other dairy products	100	108	87
Butter	100	106	90
Cheese	100	107	88
Ice cream and related products	100	108	87
Miscellaneous dairy products	100	110	82
Fruits and vegetables	**100**	**105**	**94**
Fresh fruits	100	106	91
Apples	100	105	93
Bananas	100	103	98
Oranges	100	103	98
Citrus fruits, excl. oranges	100	107	88
Other fresh fruits	100	108	86
Fresh vegetables	100	104	96
Potatoes	100	103	97
Lettuce	100	106	92
Tomatoes	100	101	103
Other fresh vegetables	100	105	94
Processed fruits	100	104	95
Frozen fruits and fruit juices	100	111	81
Frozen orange juice	100	110	82
Frozen fruits	100	116	67
Frozen fruit juices	100	108	86
Canned fruits	100	111	79
Dried fruits	100	111	80
Fresh fruit juice	100	103	99
Canned and bottled fruit juice	100	101	104
Processed vegetables	100	105	93
Frozen vegetables	100	106	91
Canned and dried vegetables and juices	100	105	93
Canned beans	100	105	94
Canned corn	100	100	105
Canned miscellaneous vegetables	100	111	81
Dried beans	100	89	129
Dried miscellaneous vegetables	100	107	89
Fresh and canned vegetable juices	100	97	111
Sugar and other sweets	**100**	**109**	**85**
Candy and chewing gum	100	111	80
Sugar	100	104	97
Artificial sweeteners	100	110	81
Jams, preserves, other sweets	100	107	90

	total consumer units	homeowners	renters
Fats and oils	**100**	**104**	**95**
Margarine	100	108	87
Fats and oils	100	96	113
Salad dressings	100	108	87
Nondairy cream and imitation milk	100	111	78
Peanut butter	100	104	95
Miscellaneous foods	**100**	**106**	**91**
Frozen prepared foods	100	105	92
Frozen meals	100	103	98
Other frozen prepared foods	100	106	90
Canned and packaged soups	100	107	89
Potato chips, nuts, and other snacks	100	107	88
Potato chips and other snacks	100	106	91
Nuts	100	112	76
Condiments and seasonings	100	107	88
Salt, spices, and other seasonings	100	105	93
Olives, pickles, relishes	100	113	75
Sauces and gravies	100	106	92
Baking needs and miscellaneous products	100	110	81
Other canned/packaged prepared foods	100	104	96
Prepared salads	100	112	78
Prepared desserts	100	113	76
Baby food	100	103	98
Miscellaneous prepared foods	100	101	102
Nonalcoholic beverages	100	105	94
Cola	100	106	92
Other carbonated drinks	100	103	99
Coffee	100	110	81
Roasted coffee	100	112	78
Instant and freeze-dried coffee	100	108	87
Noncarbonated fruit-flavored drinks	100	102	100
Tea	100	101	102
Other nonalcoholic beverages and ice	100	102	100
Food prepared by CU on trips	**100**	**115**	**70**

Note: Per capita indexes account for household size and show how much each person in a particular household demographic segment spends relative to a person in the average household.
Source: Calculations by New Strategist based on the 2001 Consumer Expenditure Survey

39. Groceries: Total spending by homeownership status, 2001

(total annual spending on groceries, by homeownership status, 2001; numbers in thousands)

	total consumer units	homeowners	renters
Number of consumer units	110,339	73,010	37,329
Total spending of all CUs	$4,360,427,358	$3,314,546,675	$1,045,811,504
GROCERIES	34,045,319,128	24,678,548,160	9,364,576,914
Cereals and bakery products	4,989,419,241	3,612,388,780	1,376,768,178
Cereals and cereal products	1,726,363,994	1,206,782,290	519,507,693
Flour	88,381,539	61,401,410	26,914,209
Prepared flour mixes	142,226,971	105,499,450	36,769,065
Ready-to-eat and cooked cereals	949,356,756	675,415,510	273,845,544
Rice	220,126,305	136,455,690	83,654,289
Pasta, cornmeal, and other cereal products	326,272,423	228,010,230	98,324,586
Bakery products	3,263,055,247	2,405,533,480	857,260,485
Bread	941,964,043	679,285,040	262,572,186
White bread	404,282,096	285,031,040	119,154,168
Crackers and cookies	774,359,102	569,185,960	205,160,184
Cookies	508,993,807	370,671,770	138,341,274
Crackers	265,365,295	198,514,190	66,818,910
Frozen and refrigerated bakery products	287,543,434	219,760,100	67,789,464
Other bakery products	1,259,078,329	937,302,380	321,738,651
Biscuits and rolls	434,073,626	334,166,770	99,892,404
Cakes and cupcakes	372,945,820	274,225,560	98,697,876
Bread and cracker products	44,687,295	32,635,470	12,019,938
Sweetrolls, coffee cakes, doughnuts	290,412,248	213,262,210	77,159,043
Pies, tarts, turnovers	116,959,340	83,012,370	33,969,390
Meats, poultry, fish, and eggs	**9,135,738,183**	**6,570,315,920**	**2,564,838,261**
Beef	2,737,069,234	1,999,597,880	737,285,079
Ground beef	998,347,272	714,767,900	283,551,084
Roast	490,346,516	374,103,240	116,205,177
Chuck roast	165,839,517	122,875,830	42,928,350
Round roast	131,082,732	99,877,680	31,207,044
Other roast	193,424,267	151,349,730	42,107,112
Steak	1,023,173,547	746,819,290	276,197,271
Round steak	200,927,319	143,245,620	57,673,305
Sirloin steak	279,930,043	196,396,900	83,467,644
Other steak	542,316,185	407,176,770	135,093,651
Pork	1,956,420,809	1,428,440,650	527,832,060
Bacon	323,293,270	235,165,210	88,171,098
Pork chops	465,189,224	331,903,460	133,264,530
Ham	441,135,322	325,770,620	115,346,610
Ham, not canned	421,936,336	312,117,750	109,784,589
Canned ham	19,198,986	13,579,860	5,599,350
Sausage	281,585,128	206,691,310	74,919,303
Other pork	445,107,526	329,056,070	116,093,190
Other meats	1,126,119,834	817,712,000	308,412,198
Frankfurters	242,856,139	175,589,050	67,304,187
Lunch meats (cold cuts)	782,082,832	571,157,230	210,796,863
Bologna, liverwurst, salami	280,261,060	198,514,190	81,675,852
Lamb, organ meats, and others	101,180,863	70,892,710	30,311,148

	total consumer units	homeowners	renters
Poultry	$1,675,718,393	$1,181,447,820	$494,198,631
Fresh and frozen chicken	1,319,102,745	914,085,200	405,019,650
Fresh and frozen whole chicken	394,461,925	265,610,380	128,822,379
Fresh and frozen chicken parts	924,640,820	648,401,810	276,197,271
Other poultry	356,615,648	267,362,620	89,178,981
Fish and seafood	1,254,223,413	876,193,010	377,956,125
Canned fish and seafood	166,722,229	120,174,460	46,586,592
Fresh fish and shellfish	695,908,073	257,871,320	219,009,243
Frozen fish and shellfish	391,593,111	279,117,230	112,397,619
Eggs	386,076,161	266,924,560	119,191,497
Dairy products	**3,659,834,291**	**2,678,079,810**	**981,454,068**
Fresh milk and cream	1,498,955,315	1,077,262,550	421,593,726
Fresh milk, all types	1,362,686,650	974,391,460	388,258,929
Cream	136,268,665	102,871,090	33,334,797
Other dairy products	2,160,878,976	1,600,817,260	559,860,342
Butter	237,780,545	174,128,850	63,608,616
Cheese	1,030,455,921	761,275,270	269,104,761
Ice cream and related products	626,615,181	464,270,590	162,306,492
Miscellaneous dairy products	266,027,329	201,142,550	64,840,473
Fruits and vegetables	**5,756,826,986**	**4,150,618,500**	**1,605,893,580**
Fresh fruits	1,769,947,899	1,290,524,760	479,267,031
Apples	340,175,137	246,116,710	94,031,751
Bananas	345,361,070	244,802,530	100,526,997
Oranges	205,451,218	145,435,920	60,062,361
Citrus fruits, excl. oranges	145,757,819	107,762,760	38,075,580
Other fresh fruits	733,202,655	546,479,850	186,570,342
Fresh vegetables	1,783,298,918	1,274,024,500	509,167,560
Potatoes	332,010,051	236,260,360	95,711,556
Lettuce	229,725,798	166,973,870	62,787,378
Tomatoes	331,348,017	229,543,440	101,833,512
Other fresh vegetables	890,215,052	641,246,830	248,835,114
Processed fruits	1,280,263,417	917,151,620	363,061,854
Frozen fruits and fruit juices	152,819,515	116,158,910	36,731,736
Frozen orange juice	83,967,979	63,372,680	20,568,279
Frozen fruits	27,915,767	22,341,060	5,599,350
Frozen fruit juices	41,046,108	30,445,170	10,564,107
Canned fruits	179,521,553	137,477,830	42,069,783
Dried fruits	61,127,806	46,653,390	14,483,652
Fresh fruit juice	274,302,754	193,622,520	80,630,640
Canned and bottled fruit juice	612,381,450	423,311,980	189,146,043
Processed vegetables	923,316,752	668,844,610	254,397,135
Frozen vegetables	303,432,250	221,147,290	82,273,116
Canned and dried vegetables and juices	619,884,502	447,697,320	172,124,019
Canned beans	139,027,140	100,315,740	38,710,173
Canned corn	78,671,707	54,100,410	24,562,482
Canned miscellaneous vegetables	193,975,962	147,553,210	46,474,605
Dried beans	25,157,292	15,478,120	9,630,882
Dried miscellaneous vegetables	83,636,962	61,401,410	22,210,755
Fresh and canned vegetable juices	84,409,335	56,436,730	27,922,092
Sugar and other sweets	**1,279,491,044**	**957,599,160**	**321,738,651**
Candy and chewing gum	810,881,311	616,934,500	193,886,826
Sugar	197,617,149	140,690,270	56,926,725
Artificial sweeteners	55,610,856	42,199,780	13,401,111
Jams, preserves, other sweets	215,381,728	157,847,620	57,523,989

	total consumer units	homeowners	renters
Fats and oils	**$957,301,164**	**$687,900,220**	**$269,328,735**
Margarine	126,117,477	93,525,810	32,550,888
Fats and oils	270,661,567	179,458,580	91,194,747
Salad dressings	309,169,878	229,178,390	79,958,718
Nondairy cream and imitation milk	111,332,051	85,348,690	25,980,984
Peanut butter	140,020,191	100,388,750	39,643,398
Miscellaneous foods	**5,017,335,008**	**3,651,814,180**	**1,365,158,859**
Frozen prepared foods	1,061,350,841	769,525,400	291,763,464
Frozen meals	316,121,235	223,775,650	92,314,617
Other frozen prepared foods	745,229,606	545,749,750	199,448,847
Canned and packaged soups	411,233,453	301,969,360	109,261,983
Potato chips, nuts, and other snacks	1,074,370,843	793,253,650	281,012,712
Potato chips and other snacks	833,721,484	607,078,150	226,587,030
Nuts	240,649,359	186,175,500	54,425,682
Condiments and seasonings	927,399,295	684,541,760	242,713,158
Salt, spices, and other seasonings	218,802,237	158,212,670	60,510,309
Olives, pickles, relishes	110,007,983	85,421,700	24,487,824
Sauces and gravies	406,488,876	295,252,440	111,203,091
Baking needs and miscellaneous products	192,100,199	145,654,950	46,474,605
Other canned/packaged prepared foods	1,543,090,915	1,102,524,010	440,407,542
Prepared salads	215,712,745	165,513,670	50,132,847
Prepared desserts	111,994,085	86,808,890	25,197,075
Baby food	260,620,718	184,496,270	76,113,831
Miscellaneous prepared foods	951,563,536	663,149,830	288,366,525
Nonalcoholic beverages	2,826,443,824	2,034,934,720	791,300,142
Cola	964,473,199	701,334,060	263,169,450
Other carbonated drinks	509,104,146	359,647,260	149,465,316
Coffee	423,150,065	321,317,010	101,758,854
Roasted coffee	275,626,822	212,094,050	63,571,287
Instant and freeze-dried coffee	147,523,243	109,295,970	38,187,567
Noncarbonated fruit-flavored drinks	224,650,204	157,482,570	67,117,542
Tea	193,865,623	135,068,500	58,830,504
Other nonalcoholic beverages and ice	503,918,213	354,317,530	149,539,974
Food prepared by CU on trips	**422,929,387**	**334,823,860**	**88,096,440**

Note: Numbers may not add to total because of rounding.
Source: Calculations by New Strategist based on the 2001 Consumer Expenditure Survey

40. Groceries: Market shares by homeownership status, 2001

(percentage of total annual spending on groceries accounted for by homeowners and renters, 2001)

	total consumer units	homeowners	renters
Share of total consumer units	**100.0%**	**66.2%**	**33.8%**
Share of total before-tax income	**100.0**	**73.8**	**20.7**
Share of total spending	**100.0**	**76.0**	**24.0**
GROCERIES	**100.0**	**72.5**	**27.5**
Cereals and bakery products	**100.0**	**72.4**	**27.6**
Cereals and cereal products	100.0	69.9	30.1
Flour	100.0	69.5	30.5
Prepared flour mixes	100.0	74.2	25.9
Ready-to-eat and cooked cereals	100.0	71.1	28.8
Rice	100.0	62.0	3.8
Pasta, cornmeal, and other cereal products	100.0	69.9	30.1
Bakery products	100.0	73.7	26.3
Bread	100.0	72.1	27.9
White bread	100.0	70.5	29.5
Crackers and cookies	100.0	73.5	26.5
Cookies	100.0	72.8	27.2
Crackers	100.0	74.8	25.2
Frozen and refrigerated bakery products	100.0	76.4	23.6
Other bakery products	100.0	74.4	25.6
Biscuits and rolls	100.0	77.0	23.0
Cakes and cupcakes	100.0	73.5	26.5
Bread and cracker products	100.0	73.0	26.9
Sweetrolls, coffee cakes, doughnuts	100.0	73.4	26.6
Pies, tarts, turnovers	100.0	71.0	29.0
Meats, poultry, fish, and eggs	**100.0**	**71.9**	**28.1**
Beef	100.0	73.1	26.9
Ground beef	100.0	71.6	28.4
Roast	100.0	76.3	23.7
Chuck roast	100.0	74.1	25.9
Round roast	100.0	76.2	23.8
Other roast	100.0	78.2	21.8
Steak	100.0	73.0	27.0
Round steak	100.0	71.3	28.7
Sirloin steak	100.0	70.2	29.8
Other steak	100.0	75.1	24.9
Pork	100.0	73.0	27.0
Bacon	100.0	72.7	27.3
Pork chops	100.0	71.3	28.6
Ham	100.0	73.8	26.1
Ham, not canned	100.0	74.0	26.0
Canned ham	100.0	70.7	29.2
Sausage	100.0	73.4	26.6
Other pork	100.0	73.9	26.1
Other meats	100.0	72.6	27.4
Frankfurters	100.0	72.3	27.7
Lunch meats (cold cuts)	100.0	73.0	27.0
Bologna, liverwurst, salami	100.0	70.8	29.1
Lamb, organ meats, and others	100.0	70.1	30.0

	total consumer units	homeowners	renters
Poultry	100.0%	70.5%	29.5%
Fresh and frozen chicken	100.0	69.3	30.7
Fresh and frozen whole chicken	100.0	67.3	32.7
Fresh and frozen chicken parts	100.0	70.1	29.9
Other poultry	100.0	75.0	2.5
Fish and seafood	100.0	69.9	30.1
Canned fish and seafood	100.0	72.1	27.9
Fresh fish and shellfish	100.0	37.1	31.5
Frozen fish and shellfish	100.0	71.3	28.7
Eggs	100.0	69.1	30.9
Dairy products	**100.0**	**73.2**	**26.8**
Fresh milk and cream	100.0	71.9	28.1
Fresh milk, all types	100.0	71.5	28.5
Cream	100.0	75.5	24.5
Other dairy products	100.0	74.1	25.9
Butter	100.0	73.2	26.8
Cheese	100.0	73.9	26.1
Ice cream and related products	100.0	74.1	25.9
Miscellaneous dairy products	100.0	75.6	24.4
Fruits and vegetables	**100.0**	**72.1**	**27.9**
Fresh fruits	100.0	72.9	27.1
Apples	100.0	72.3	27.6
Bananas	100.0	70.9	29.1
Oranges	100.0	70.8	29.2
Citrus fruits, excl. oranges	100.0	73.9	26.1
Other fresh fruits	100.0	74.5	25.4
Fresh vegetables	100.0	71.4	28.6
Potatoes	100.0	71.2	28.8
Lettuce	100.0	72.7	27.3
Tomatoes	100.0	69.3	30.7
Other fresh vegetables	100.0	72.0	28.0
Processed fruits	100.0	71.6	28.4
Frozen fruits and fruit juices	100.0	76.0	24.0
Frozen orange juice	100.0	75.5	24.5
Frozen fruits	100.0	80.0	20.1
Frozen fruit juices	100.0	74.2	25.7
Canned fruits	100.0	76.6	23.4
Dried fruits	100.0	76.3	23.7
Fresh fruit juice	100.0	70.6	29.4
Canned and bottled fruit juice	100.0	69.1	30.9
Processed vegetables	100.0	72.4	27.6
Frozen vegetables	100.0	72.9	27.1
Canned and dried vegetables and juices	100.0	72.2	27.8
Canned beans	100.0	72.2	27.8
Canned corn	100.0	68.8	31.2
Canned miscellaneous vegetables	100.0	76.1	24.0
Dried beans	100.0	61.5	38.3
Dried miscellaneous vegetables	100.0	73.4	26.6
Fresh and canned vegetable juices	100.0	66.9	33.1
Sugar and other sweets	**100.0**	**74.8**	**25.1**
Candy and chewing gum	100.0	76.1	23.9
Sugar	100.0	71.2	28.8
Artificial sweeteners	100.0	75.9	24.1
Jams, preserves, other sweets	100.0	73.3	26.7

	total consumer units	homeowners	renters
Fats and oils	**100.0%**	**71.9%**	**28.1%**
Margarine	100.0	74.2	25.8
Fats and oils	100.0	66.3	33.7
Salad dressings	100.0	74.1	25.9
Nondairy cream and imitation milk	100.0	76.7	23.3
Peanut butter	100.0	71.7	28.3
Miscellaneous foods	**100.0**	**72.8**	**27.2**
Frozen prepared foods	100.0	72.5	27.5
Frozen meals	100.0	70.8	29.2
Other frozen prepared foods	100.0	73.2	26.8
Canned and packaged soups	100.0	73.4	26.6
Potato chips, nuts, and other snacks	100.0	73.8	26.2
Potato chips and other snacks	100.0	72.8	27.2
Nuts	100.0	77.4	22.6
Condiments and seasonings	100.0	73.8	26.2
Salt, spices, and other seasonings	100.0	72.3	27.7
Olives, pickles, relishes	100.0	77.7	22.3
Sauces and gravies	100.0	72.6	27.4
Baking needs and miscellaneous products	100.0	75.8	24.2
Other canned/packaged prepared foods	100.0	71.4	28.5
Prepared salads	100.0	76.7	23.2
Prepared desserts	100.0	77.5	22.5
Baby food	100.0	70.8	29.2
Miscellaneous prepared foods	100.0	69.7	30.3
Nonalcoholic beverages	100.0	72.0	28.0
Cola	100.0	72.7	27.3
Other carbonated drinks	100.0	70.6	29.4
Coffee	100.0	75.9	24.1
Roasted coffee	100.0	76.9	23.1
Instant and freeze-dried coffee	100.0	74.1	25.9
Noncarbonated fruit-flavored drinks	100.0	70.1	29.9
Tea	100.0	69.7	30.3
Other nonalcoholic beverages and ice	100.0	70.3	29.7
Food prepared by CU on trips	**100.0**	**79.2**	**20.8**

Note: Numbers may not add to total because of rounding.
Source: Calculations by New Strategist based on the 2001 Consumer Expenditure Survey

41. SPENDING ON BABY FOOD, 2001

Total (aggregate) household spending in 2001	$4,360,427,357,940
Total (aggregate) household spending on baby food	$2,606,207,180
Average household spending on baby food	$23.62

	AVERAGE ANNUAL SPENDING PER HOUSEHOLD (in dollars)	BEST CUSTOMERS (index)	BIGGEST CUSTOMERS (percent market share)	TOTAL (AGGREGATE) HH SPENDING (in thousands of dollars)
AGE OF HOUSEHOLDER				
Average household	**$23.62**	**100**	**100.0%**	**$2,606,207**
Under age 25	34.65	147	11.4	297,921
Aged 25 to 34	54.69	232	38.9	1,012,585
Aged 35 to 44	27.47	116	25.7	670,872
Aged 45 to 54	13.24	56	11.3	295,477
Aged 55 to 64	12.32	52	6.9	179,244
Aged 65 to 74	6.07	26	2.6	68,846
Aged 75 or older	5.30	22	2.2	56,159
HOUSEHOLD INCOME				
Average household reporting income	**23.72**	**100**	**100.0**	**2,104,794**
Under $10,000	11.87	50	6.2	129,718
$10,000 to $19,999	13.84	58	9.9	209,095
$20,000 to $29,999	19.78	83	11.3	238,844
$30,000 to $39,999	21.50	91	10.7	225,922
$40,000 to $49,999	32.08	135	13.3	280,283
$50,000 to $69,999	35.59	150	21.1	444,163
$70,000 or more	31.21	132	28.0	589,619
HOUSEHOLD TYPE				
Average household	**23.62**	**100**	**100.0**	**2,606,207**
Married couples	34.59	146	74.1	1,931,506
Married couples, no children	8.88	38	7.9	205,297
Married couples, with children	53.20	225	57.3	1,492,526
Oldest child under 6	158.14	670	30.5	793,863
Oldest child 6 to 17	31.96	135	18.6	484,034
Oldest child 18 or older	21.51	91	6.5	169,714
Single parent with child under 18	33.40	141	8.5	221,409
Single person	3.60	15	4.5	118,019
RACE				
Average household	**23.62**	**100**	**100.0**	**2,606,207**
Black	30.89	131	15.7	410,312
White and other	22.64	96	84.3	2,197,348
HISPANIC ORIGIN				
Average household	**23.62**	**100**	**100.0**	**2,606,207**
Hispanic	28.52	121	10.5	274,391
Non-Hispanic	23.13	98	89.4	2,329,607
REGION				
Average household	**23.62**	**100**	**100.0**	**2,606,207**
Northeast	27.12	115	21.8	567,893
Midwest	16.84	71	16.7	435,179
South	28.41	120	42.7	1,113,019
West	20.04	85	18.7	488,575

	AVERAGE ANNUAL SPENDING PER HOUSEHOLD (in dollars)	BEST CUSTOMERS (index)	BIGGEST CUSTOMERS (percent market share)	TOTAL (AGGREGATE) HH SPENDING (in thousands of dollars)
EDUCATION				
Average household	**$23.62**	**100**	**100.0%**	**$2,606,207**
Less than high school graduate	18.39	78	12.1	315,885
High school graduate	24.10	102	29.5	767,971
Some college	25.61	108	22.6	588,825
Associate's degree	18.10	77	6.7	175,642
College graduate	26.54	112	29.2	760,636
Bachelor's degree	27.38	116	19.8	516,934
Master's, professional, doctoral degree	24.99	106	9.4	244,402
OCCUPATION				
Average household	**23.62**	**100**	**100.0**	**2,606,207**
Self-employed	13.54	57	2.5	65,994
Wage-and-salary workers, total	29.88	127	84.9	2,211,598
Managers and professionals	36.21	153	37.2	969,197
Technical, sales, and clerical	23.75	101	19.3	502,004
Service workers	26.33	112	10.3	269,277
Construction workers and mechanics	44.60	189	8.6	225,007
Operators, fabricators, laborers	23.38	99	9.7	253,463
Retired	7.64	32	5.7	147,689
HOMEOWNERSHIP STATUS				
Average household	**23.62**	**100**	**100.0**	**2,606,207**
Homeowners	25.27	107	70.8	1,844,963
Renters	20.39	86	29.2	761,138

Note: Households by type will not sum to the total because not all household types are shown. Hispanics may be of any race and most are white. Total household spending and market shares may not sum to total due to rounding. For an explanation of terms, see the introduction to this report.
Source: Calculations by New Strategist based on the Bureau of Labor Statistics' 2001 Consumer Expenditure Survey

42. SPENDING ON BACON, 2001

Total (aggregate) household spending in 2001	$4,360,427,357,940
Total (aggregate) household spending on bacon	$3,232,932,700
Average annual household spending on bacon	$29.30

	AVERAGE ANNUAL SPENDING PER HOUSEHOLD (in dollars)	BEST CUSTOMERS (index)	BIGGEST CUSTOMERS (percent market share)	TOTAL (AGGREGATE) HH SPENDING (in thousands of dollars)
AGE OF HOUSEHOLDER				
Average household	**$29.30**	**100**	**100.0%**	**$3,232,933**
Under age 25	16.12	55	4.3	138,600
Aged 25 to 34	29.01	99	16.6	537,120
Aged 35 to 44	30.19	103	22.8	737,300
Aged 45 to 54	34.58	118	23.9	771,722
Aged 55 to 64	32.25	110	14.5	469,205
Aged 65 to 74	28.89	99	10.1	327,670
Aged 75 or older	23.79	81	7.8	252,079
HOUSEHOLD INCOME				
Average household reporting income	**30.25**	**100**	**100.0**	**2,684,234**
Under $10,000	22.01	73	9.0	241,511
$10,000 to $19,999	27.07	90	15.2	409,125
$20,000 to $29,999	28.27	94	12.7	341,360
$30,000 to $39,999	31.60	105	12.4	332,053
$40,000 to $49,999	29.69	98	9.7	259,402
$50,000 to $69,999	31.58	104	14.7	394,118
$70,000 or more	37.39	124	26.3	706,372
HOUSEHOLD TYPE				
Average household	**29.30**	**100**	**100.0**	**3,232,933**
Married couples	37.88	129	65.4	2,115,219
Married couples, no children	32.67	112	23.4	755,298
Married couples, with children	39.36	134	34.2	1,104,245
Oldest child under 6	37.06	127	5.8	186,041
Oldest child 6 to 17	38.75	132	18.2	586,869
Oldest child 18 or older	42.39	145	10.3	334,457
Single parent with child under 18	37.37	128	7.7	247,726
Single person	14.42	49	14.6	472,731
RACE				
Average household	**29.30**	**100**	**100.0**	**3,232,933**
Black	40.79	139	16.8	541,814
White and other	27.76	95	83.3	2,694,275
HISPANIC ORIGIN				
Average household	**29.30**	**100**	**100.0**	**3,232,933**
Hispanic	29.21	100	8.7	281,029
Non-Hispanic	29.31	100	91.3	2,952,045
REGION				
Average household	**29.30**	**100**	**100.0**	**3,232,933**
Northeast	24.34	83	15.8	509,680
Midwest	26.07	89	20.8	673,701
South	36.13	123	43.8	1,415,465
West	26.05	89	19.6	635,099

	AVERAGE ANNUAL SPENDING PER HOUSEHOLD (in dollars)	BEST CUSTOMERS (index)	BIGGEST CUSTOMERS (percent market share)	TOTAL (AGGREGATE) HH SPENDING (in thousands of dollars)
EDUCATION				
Average household	**$29.30**	**100**	**100.0%**	**$3,232,933**
Less than high school graduate	31.95	109	17.0	548,805
High school graduate	31.84	109	31.4	1,014,613
Some college	27.33	93	19.4	628,371
Associate's degree	30.13	103	9.0	292,382
College graduate	26.15	89	23.2	749,459
Bachelor's degree	27.17	93	15.9	512,970
Master's, professional, doctoral degree	24.30	83	7.4	237,654
OCCUPATION				
Average household	**29.30**	**100**	**100.0**	**3,232,933**
Self-employed	32.13	110	4.8	156,602
Wage-and-salary workers, total	29.71	101	68.0	2,199,015
Managers and professionals	29.79	102	24.7	797,359
Technical, sales, and clerical	28.47	97	18.6	601,770
Service workers	28.34	97	9.0	289,833
Construction workers and mechanics	36.75	125	5.7	185,404
Operators, fabricators, laborers	29.86	102	10.0	323,712
Retired	25.09	86	1.5	485,015
HOMEOWNERSHIP STATUS				
Average household	**29.30**	**100**	**100.0**	**3,232,933**
Homeowners	32.21	110	72.7	2,351,652
Renters	23.62	81	27.3	881,711

Note: Households by type will not sum to the total because not all household types are shown. Hispanics may be of any race and most are white. Total household spending and market shares may not sum to total due to rounding. For an explanation of terms, see the introduction to this report.
Source: Calculations by New Strategist based on the Bureau of Labor Statistics' 2001 Consumer Expenditure Survey

43. SPENDING ON BAKERY PRODUCTS, FROZEN AND REFRIGERATED, 2001

Total (aggregate) household spending in 2001 $4,360,427,357,940
Total (aggregate) household spending on bakery products, frozen and refrigerated $2,875,434,340
Average annual household spending on bakery products, frozen and refrigerated $26.06

	AVERAGE ANNUAL SPENDING PER HOUSEHOLD (in dollars)	BEST CUSTOMERS (index)	BIGGEST CUSTOMERS (percent market share)	TOTAL (AGGREGATE) HH SPENDING (in thousands of dollars)
AGE OF HOUSEHOLDER				
Average household	**$26.06**	**100**	**100.0%**	**$2,875,434**
Under age 25	16.14	62	4.8	138,772
Aged 25 to 34	20.43	78	13.2	378,262
Aged 35 to 44	32.85	126	27.9	802,263
Aged 45 to 54	32.48	125	25.2	724,856
Aged 55 to 64	25.28	97	12.8	367,799
Aged 65 to 74	20.58	79	8.1	233,418
Aged 75 or older	21.57	83	7.9	228,556
HOUSEHOLD INCOME				
Average household reporting income	**28.15**	**100**	**100.0**	**2,497,890**
Under $10,000	14.09	50	6.2	153,990
$10,000 to $19,999	18.57	66	11.2	280,661
$20,000 to $29,999	26.15	93	12.6	315,761
$30,000 to $39,999	23.61	84	9.9	248,094
$40,000 to $49,999	28.12	100	9.8	245,684
$50,000 to $69,999	38.17	136	19.1	476,362
$70,000 or more	41.57	148	31.4	785,340
HOUSEHOLD TYPE				
Average household	**26.06**	**100**	**100.0**	**2,875,434**
Married couples	34.71	133	67.4	1,938,206
Married couples, no children	24.93	96	20.0	576,357
Married couples, with children	41.87	161	40.9	1,174,663
Oldest child under 6	30.28	116	5.3	152,006
Oldest child 6 to 17	47.80	183	25.2	723,931
Oldest child 18 or older	37.59	144	10.3	296,585
Single parent with child under 18	31.75	122	7.3	210,471
Single person	11.21	43	12.8	367,497
RACE				
Average household	**26.06**	**100**	**100.0**	**2,875,434**
Black	20.94	80	9.7	278,146
White and other	26.76	103	90.3	2,597,219
HISPANIC ORIGIN				
Average household	**26.06**	**100**	**100.0**	**2,875,434**
Hispanic	18.77	72	6.3	180,586
Non-Hispanic	26.79	103	93.8	2,698,235
REGION				
Average household	**26.06**	**100**	**100.0**	**2,875,434**
Northeast	27.18	104	19.8	569,149
Midwest	25.75	99	23.1	665,432
South	29.49	113	40.2	1,155,330
West	19.92	76	16.9	485,650

	AVERAGE ANNUAL SPENDING PER HOUSEHOLD (in dollars)	BEST CUSTOMERS (index)	BIGGEST CUSTOMERS (percent market share)	TOTAL (AGGREGATE) HH SPENDING (in thousands of dollars)
EDUCATION				
Average household	**$26.06**	**100**	**100.0%**	**$2,875,434**
Less than high school graduate	23.26	89	13.9	399,537
High school graduate	25.39	97	28.1	809,078
Some college	23.79	91	19.0	546,980
Associate's degree	27.94	107	9.4	271,130
College graduate	29.50	113	29.4	845,470
Bachelor's degree	31.57	121	20.7	596,042
Master's, professional, doctoral degree	25.73	99	8.8	251,639
OCCUPATION				
Average household	**26.06**	**100**	**100.0**	**2,875,434**
Self-employed	27.95	107	4.7	136,228
Wage-and-salary workers, total	27.55	106	70.9	2,039,141
Managers and professionals	29.81	114	27.7	797,895
Technical, sales, and clerical	29.48	113	21.7	623,119
Service workers	21.30	82	7.6	217,835
Construction workers and mechanics	30.54	117	5.4	154,074
Operators, fabricators, laborers	23.73	91	8.9	257,257
Retired	20.57	79	13.8	397,639
HOMEOWNERSHIP STATUS				
Average household	**26.06**	**100**	**100.0**	**2,875,434**
Homeowners	30.10	116	76.4	2,197,601
Renters	18.16	70	23.6	677,895

Note: Households by type will not sum to the total because not all household types are shown. Hispanics may be of any race and most are white. Total household spending and market shares may not sum to total due to rounding. For an explanation of terms, see the introduction to this report.
Source: Calculations by New Strategist based on the Bureau of Labor Statistics' 2001 Consumer Expenditure Survey

44. SPENDING ON BAKING NEEDS AND MISCELLANEOUS PRODUCTS, 2001

Total (aggregate) household spending in 2001	$4,360,427,357,940
Total (aggregate) household spending on baking needs and miscellaneous products	$1,921,001,990
Average annual household spending on baking needs and miscellaneous products	$17.41

	AVERAGE ANNUAL SPENDING PER HOUSEHOLD (in dollars)	BEST CUSTOMERS (index)	BIGGEST CUSTOMERS (percent market share)	TOTAL (AGGREGATE) HH SPENDING (in thousands of dollars)
AGE OF HOUSEHOLDER				
Average household	**$17.41**	**100**	**100.0%**	**$1,921,002**
Under age 25	9.44	54	4.2	81,165
Aged 25 to 34	16.35	94	15.8	302,720
Aged 35 to 44	20.84	120	26.5	508,955
Aged 45 to 54	21.06	121	24.5	469,996
Aged 55 to 64	17.29	99	13.1	251,552
Aged 65 to 74	15.68	90	9.3	177,843
Aged 75 or older	11.99	69	6.6	127,046
HOUSEHOLD INCOME				
Average household reporting income	**18.50**	**100**	**100.0**	**1,641,598**
Under $10,000	10.00	54	6.7	109,273
$10,000 to $19,999	10.99	59	10.1	166,140
$20,000 to $29,999	14.96	81	1.1	180,642
$30,000 to $39,999	17.52	95	11.2	184,100
$40,000 to $49,999	18.02	97	9.6	157,441
$50,000 to $69,999	20.82	113	15.8	259,834
$70,000 or more	31.46	170	36.2	594,342
HOUSEHOLD TYPE				
Average household	**17.41**	**100**	**100.0**	**1,921,002**
Married couples	23.30	134	67.7	1,301,072
Married couples, no children	19.10	110	23.0	441,573
Married couples, with children	26.69	153	39.0	748,788
Oldest child under 6	22.53	129	5.9	113,101
Oldest child 6 to 17	25.94	149	20.5	392,861
Oldest child 18 or older	31.40	180	12.9	247,746
Single parent with child under 18	16.31	94	5.6	108,119
Single person	8.56	49	14.6	280,623
RACE				
Average household	**17.41**	**100**	**100.0**	**1,921,002**
Black	11.98	69	8.3	159,130
White and other	18.14	104	91.6	1,760,596
HISPANIC ORIGIN				
Average household	**17.41**	**100**	**100.0**	**1,921,002**
Hispanic	13.41	77	6.7	129,018
Non-Hispanic	17.81	102	93.4	1,793,788
REGION				
Average household	**17.41**	**100**	**100.0**	**1,921,002**
Northeast	17.13	98	18.7	358,702
Midwest	18.03	104	24.3	465,931
South	16.21	93	33.1	635,059
West	18.93	109	24.0	461,513

	AVERAGE ANNUAL SPENDING PER HOUSEHOLD (in dollars)	BEST CUSTOMERS (index)	BIGGEST CUSTOMERS (percent market share)	TOTAL (AGGREGATE) HH SPENDING (in thousands of dollars)
EDUCATION				
Average household	**$17.41**	**100**	**100.0%**	**$1,921,002**
Less than high school graduate	12.13	70	10.8	208,357
High school graduate	15.31	88	25.4	487,869
Some college	17.32	100	20.7	398,221
Associate's degree	19.30	111	9.7	187,287
College graduate	22.23	128	33.2	637,112
Bachelor's degree	20.87	120	20.5	394,026
Master's, professional, doctoral degree	24.72	142	12.6	241,762
OCCUPATION				
Average household	**17.41**	**100**	**100.0**	**1,921,002**
Self-employed	21.78	125	5.5	106,156
Wage-and-salary workers, total	17.91	103	6.9	1,325,627
Managers and professionals	22.23	128	31.0	595,008
Technical, sales, and clerical	18.28	105	20.1	386,384
Service workers	11.89	68	6.3	121,599
Construction workers and mechanics	16.99	98	4.5	85,715
Operators, fabricators, laborers	13.66	79	7.7	148,088
Retired	15.29	88	15.4	295,571
HOMEOWNERSHIP STATUS				
Average household	**17.41**	**100**	**100.0**	**1,921,002**
Homeowners	19.95	115	75.8	1,456,550
Renters	12.45	72	24.2	464,746

Note: Households by type will not sum to the total because not all household types are shown. Hispanics may be of any race and most are white. Total household spending and market shares may not sum to total due to rounding. For an explanation of terms, see the introduction to this report.
Source: Calculations by New Strategist based on the Bureau of Labor Statistics' 2001 Consumer Expenditure Survey

45. SPENDING ON BISCUITS AND ROLLS, 2001

Total (aggregate) household spending in 2001	$4,360,427,357,940
Total (aggregate) household spending on biscuits and rolls	$4,340,736,260
Average annual household spending on biscuits and rolls	$39.34

	AVERAGE ANNUAL SPENDING PER HOUSEHOLD (in dollars)	BEST CUSTOMERS (index)	BIGGEST CUSTOMERS (percent market share)	TOTAL (AGGREGATE) HH SPENDING (in thousands of dollars)
AGE OF HOUSEHOLDER				
Average household	**$39.34**	**100**	**100.0%**	**$4,340,736**
Under age 25	20.21	51	0.4	173,766
Aged 25 to 34	30.57	78	13.0	566,004
Aged 35 to 44	47.30	120	26.6	1,155,161
Aged 45 to 54	47.46	121	24.4	1,059,165
Aged 55 to 64	47.96	122	16.1	697,770
Aged 65 to 74	35.04	89	9.2	397,424
Aged 75 or older	27.49	70	6.7	291,284
HOUSEHOLD INCOME				
Average household reporting income	**42.10**	**100**	**100.0**	**3,735,744**
Under $10,000	23.20	55	6.8	253,521
$10,000 to $19,999	27.64	66	11.2	417,721
$20,000 to $29,999	31.83	76	10.3	384,347
$30,000 to $39,999	36.66	87	10.3	385,223
$40,000 to $49,999	41.71	99	9.8	364,420
$50,000 to $69,999	51.20	122	17.1	638,976
$70,000 or more	69.57	165	35.2	1,314,316
HOUSEHOLD TYPE				
Average household	**39.34**	**100**	**100.0**	**4,340,736**
Married couples	51.98	132	66.9	2,902,563
Married couples, no children	42.71	109	22.7	987,413
Married couples, with children	58.04	148	37.5	1,628,312
Oldest child under 6	40.87	104	4.7	205,167
Oldest child 6 to 17	58.65	149	20.5	888,254
Oldest child 18 or older	69.45	177	12.6	547,961
Single parent with child under 18	37.34	95	5.7	247,527
Single person	18.81	48	14.2	616,648
RACE				
Average household	**39.34**	**100**	**100.0**	**4,340,736**
Black	25.27	64	7.7	335,661
White and other	41.24	105	92.2	4,002,589
HISPANIC ORIGIN				
Average household	**39.34**	**100**	**100.0**	**4,340,736**
Hispanic	28.63	73	6.3	275,449
Non-Hispanic	40.41	103	93.8	4,070,014
REGION				
Average household	**39.34**	**100**	**100.0**	**4,340,736**
Northeast	49.16	125	23.7	1,029,410
Midwest	37.87	96	22.5	978,637
South	36.21	92	32.7	1,418,599
West	37.44	95	21.0	912,787

	AVERAGE ANNUAL SPENDING PER HOUSEHOLD (in dollars)	BEST CUSTOMERS (index)	BIGGEST CUSTOMERS (percent market share)	TOTAL (AGGREGATE) HH SPENDING (in thousands of dollars)
EDUCATION				
Average household	**$39.34**	**100**	**100.0%**	**$4,340,736**
Less than high school graduate	30.04	76	11.9	515,997
High school graduate	36.44	93	26.8	1,161,197
Some college	38.01	97	20.1	873,926
Associate's degree	41.25	105	9.2	400,290
College graduate	48.31	123	31.9	1,384,565
Bachelor's degree	46.13	117	20.1	870,934
Master's, professional, doctoral degree	52.29	133	11.8	511,396
OCCUPATION				
Average household	**39.34**	**100**	**100.0**	**4,340,736**
Self-employed	46.66	119	5.2	227,421
Wage-and-salary workers, total	40.4	103	68.9	2,990,246
Managers and professionals	46.78	119	28.8	1,252,114
Technical, sales, and clerical	39.37	100	19.2	832,164
Service workers	39.35	100	9.3	402,433
Construction workers and mechanics	38.99	99	4.5	196,705
Operators, fabricators, laborers	29.95	76	7.5	324,688
Retired	33.97	86	15.1	656,674
HOMEOWNERSHIP STATUS				
Average household	**39.34**	**100**	**100.0**	**4,340,736**
Homeowners	45.77	116	77.0	3,341,668
Renters	26.76	68	23.0	998,924

Note: Households by type will not sum to the total because not all household types are shown. Hispanics may be of any race and most are white. Total household spending and market shares may not sum to total due to rounding. For an explanation of terms, see the introduction to this report.
Source: Calculations by New Strategist based on the Bureau of Labor Statistics' 2001 Consumer Expenditure Survey

46. SPENDING ON BREAD, 2001

Total (aggregate) household spending in 2001	$4,360,427,357,940
Total (aggregate) household spending on bread	$9,419,640,430
Average annual household spending on bread	$85.37

	AVERAGE ANNUAL SPENDING PER HOUSEHOLD (in dollars)	BEST CUSTOMERS (index)	BIGGEST CUSTOMERS (percent market share)	TOTAL (AGGREGATE) HH SPENDING (in thousands of dollars)
AGE OF HOUSEHOLDER				
Average household	**$85.37**	**100**	**100.0%**	**$9,419,640**
Under age 25	47.38	56	4.3	407,373
Aged 25 to 34	78.48	92	15.4	1,453,057
Aged 35 to 44	93.91	110	24.3	2,293,470
Aged 45 to 54	96.23	113	22.8	2,147,565
Aged 55 to 64	97.81	115	15.1	1,423,038
Aged 65 to 74	82.42	97	9.9	934,808
Aged 75 or older	71.75	84	8.1	760,263
HOUSEHOLD INCOME				
Average household reporting income	**90.63**	**100**	**100.0**	**8,042,053**
Under $10,000	59.55	66	8.1	650,838
$10,000 to $19,999	72.94	81	13.7	1,102,295
$20,000 to $29,999	86.64	96	1.3	1,046,178
$30,000 to $39,999	88.34	98	11.5	928,277
$40,000 to $49,999	93.10	103	10.1	813,415
$50,000 to $69,999	103.96	115	16.1	1,297,421
$70,000 or more	117.39	130	27.6	2,217,732
HOUSEHOLD TYPE				
Average household	**85.37**	**100**	**100.0**	**9,419,640**
Married couples	107.41	126	63.7	5,997,774
Married couples, no children	91.63	107	22.5	2,118,394
Married couples, with children	116.68	137	34.8	3,273,457
Oldest child under 6	98.89	116	5.3	496,428
Oldest child 6 to 17	116.86	137	18.8	1,769,845
Oldest child 18 or older	129.51	152	10.8	1,021,834
Single parent with child under 18	79.96	94	5.6	530,055
Single person	47.35	56	16.5	1,552,275
RACE				
Average household	**85.37**	**100**	**100.0**	**9,419,640**
Black	72.37	85	10.2	961,291
White and other	87.12	102	89.8	8,455,519
HISPANIC ORIGIN				
Average household	**85.37**	**100**	**100.0**	**9,419,640**
Hispanic	96.79	113	9.9	931,217
Non-Hispanic	84.23	99	90.1	8,483,477
REGION				
Average household	**85.37**	**100**	**100.0**	**9,419,640**
Northeast	96.69	113	21.5	2,024,689
Midwest	82.63	97	22.7	2,135,325
South	77.56	91	32.3	3,038,568
West	91.02	107	23.6	2,219,068

	AVERAGE ANNUAL SPENDING PER HOUSEHOLD (in dollars)	BEST CUSTOMERS (index)	BIGGEST CUSTOMERS (percent market share)	TOTAL (AGGREGATE) HH SPENDING (in thousands of dollars)
EDUCATION				
Average household	**$85.37**	**100**	**100.0%**	**$9,419,640**
Less than high school graduate	86.13	101	15.7	1,479,455
High school graduate	83.50	98	28.2	2,660,811
Some college	75.28	88	18.4	1,730,838
Associate's degree	84.22	99	8.7	817,271
College graduate	94.94	111	28.9	2,720,980
Bachelor's degree	92.51	108	18.5	1,746,589
Master's, professional, doctoral degree	99.37	116	10.3	971,839
OCCUPATION				
Average household	**85.37**	**100**	**100.0**	**9,419,640**
Self-employed	93.74	110	4.9	456,889
Wage-and-salary workers, total	86.85	102	68.2	6,428,290
Managers and professionals	92.73	109	26.3	2,482,011
Technical, sales, and clerical	82.09	96	18.4	1,735,136
Service workers	79.88	94	8.7	816,933
Construction workers and mechanics	99.14	116	5.3	500,161
Operators, fabricators, laborers	83.00	97	9.6	899,803
Retired	77.54	91	15.9	1,498,926
HOMEOWNERSHIP STATUS				
Average household	**85.37**	**100**	**100.0**	**9,419,640**
Homeowners	93.04	109	72.1	6,792,850
Renters	70.34	82	27.9	2,625,722

Note: Households by type will not sum to the total because not all household types are shown. Hispanics may be of any race and most are white. Total household spending and market shares may not sum to total due to rounding. For an explanation of terms, see the introduction to this report.
Source: Calculations by New Strategist based on the Bureau of Labor Statistics' 2001 Consumer Expenditure Survey

47. SPENDING ON BUTTER, 2001

Total (aggregate) household spending in 2001	$4,360,427,357,940
Total (aggregate) household spending on butter	$2,377,805,450
Average annual household spending on butter	$21.55

	AVERAGE ANNUAL SPENDING PER HOUSEHOLD (in dollars)	BEST CUSTOMERS (index)	BIGGEST CUSTOMERS (percent market share)	TOTAL (AGGREGATE) HH SPENDING (in thousands of dollars)
AGE OF HOUSEHOLDER				
Average household	**$21.55**	**100**	**100.0%**	**$2,377,806**
Under age 25	11.24	52	4.1	96,642
Aged 25 to 34	18.61	86	14.5	344,564
Aged 35 to 44	25.61	119	26.3	625,447
Aged 45 to 54	23.64	110	22.2	527,574
Aged 55 to 64	28.73	133	17.6	417,993
Aged 65 to 74	17.47	81	8.3	198,145
Aged 75 or older	15.68	73	7.0	166,145
HOUSEHOLD INCOME				
Average household reporting income	**21.07**	**100**	**100.0**	**1,869,646**
Under $10,000	9.98	47	5.8	109,111
$10,000 to $19,999	14.23	68	11.5	215,069
$20,000 to $29,999	21.52	102	13.9	259,854
$30,000 to $39,999	19.61	93	11.0	206,062
$40,000 to $49,999	19.83	94	9.3	173,255
$50,000 to $69,999	27.26	129	18.2	340,205
$70,000 or more	30.03	143	30.3	567,327
HOUSEHOLD TYPE				
Average household	**21.55**	**100**	**100.0**	**2,377,806**
Married couples	26.39	123	62.0	1,473,618
Married couples, no children	21.50	100	20.9	497,059
Married couples, with children	28.29	131	33.4	793,676
Oldest child under 6	27.71	129	5.9	139,104
Oldest child 6 to 17	26.98	125	17.2	408,612
Oldest child 18 or older	31.57	147	10.5	249,087
Single parent with child under 18	22.16	103	6.2	146,899
Single person	12.62	59	17.4	413,722
RACE				
Average household	**21.55**	**100**	**100.0**	**2,377,806**
Black	16.90	78	9.4	224,483
White and other	22.18	103	90.5	2,152,702
HISPANIC ORIGIN				
Average household	**21.55**	**100**	**100.0**	**2,377,806**
Hispanic	16.43	76	6.6	158,073
Non-Hispanic	22.06	102	93.4	2,221,839
REGION				
Average household	**21.55**	**100**	**100.0**	**2,377,806**
Northeast	33.51	156	29.5	701,699
Midwest	21.49	100	23.4	555,345
South	16.89	78	27.8	661,700
West	18.76	87	19.2	457,369

	AVERAGE ANNUAL SPENDING PER HOUSEHOLD (in dollars)	BEST CUSTOMERS (index)	BIGGEST CUSTOMERS (percent market share)	TOTAL (AGGREGATE) HH SPENDING (in thousands of dollars)
EDUCATION				
Average household	**$21.55**	**100**	**100.0%**	**$2,377,806**
Less than high school graduate	18.43	86	13.3	316,572
High school graduate	22.81	106	30.6	726,864
Some college	18.15	84	17.5	417,305
Associate's degree	21.04	98	8.6	204,172
College graduate	24.70	115	29.8	707,902
Bachelor's degree	24.42	113	19.4	461,050
Master's, professional, doctoral degree	25.19	117	10.4	246,358
OCCUPATION				
Average household	**21.55**	**100**	**100.0**	**2,377,806**
Self-employed	25.71	119	5.3	125,311
Wage-and-salary workers, total	20.96	97	65.2	1,551,375
Managers and professionals	22.15	103	24.9	592,867
Technical, sales, and clerical	21.87	102	19.4	462,266
Service workers	17.41	81	7.5	178,052
Construction workers and mechanics	21.64	100	4.6	109,174
Operators, fabricators, laborers	19.73	92	9.0	213,893
Retired	20.99	97	17.1	405,758
HOMEOWNERSHIP STATUS				
Average household	**21.55**	**100**	**100.0**	**2,377,806**
Homeowners	23.85	111	73.2	1,741,289
Renters	17.04	79	26.8	636,086

Note: Households by type will not sum to the total because not all household types are shown. Hispanics may be of any race and most are white. Total household spending and market shares may not sum to total due to rounding. For an explanation of terms, see the introduction to this report.
Source: Calculations by New Strategist based on the Bureau of Labor Statistics' 2001 Consumer Expenditure Survey

48. SPENDING ON CAKES AND CUPCAKES, 2001

Total (aggregate) household spending in 2001	$4,360,427,357,940
Total (aggregate) household spending on cakes and cupcakes	$3,729,458,200
Average annual household spending on cakes and cupcakes	$33.80

	AVERAGE ANNUAL SPENDING PER HOUSEHOLD (in dollars)	BEST CUSTOMERS (index)	BIGGEST CUSTOMERS (percent market share)	TOTAL (AGGREGATE) HH SPENDING (in thousands of dollars)
AGE OF HOUSEHOLDER				
Average household	**$33.80**	**100**	**100.0%**	**$3,729,458**
Under age 25	21.82	65	5.0	187,608
Aged 25 to 34	34.50	102	17.1	638,768
Aged 35 to 44	42.64	126	27.9	1,041,354
Aged 45 to 54	38.07	113	22.8	849,608
Aged 55 to 64	32.65	97	12.7	475,025
Aged 65 to 74	21.91	65	6.7	248,503
Aged 75 or older	26.50	78	7.5	280,794
HOUSEHOLD INCOME				
Average household reporting income	**36.37**	**100**	**100.0**	**3,227,292**
Under $10,000	23.30	64	7.9	254,597
$10,000 to $19,999	25.02	69	11.7	378,188
$20,000 to $29,999	32.38	89	12.1	390,989
$30,000 to $39,999	41.08	113	13.4	431,669
$40,000 to $49,999	33.98	93	9.2	296,883
$50,000 to $69,999	35.48	98	13.7	442,790
$70,000 or more	55.92	154	32.7	1,056,441
HOUSEHOLD TYPE				
Average household	**33.80**	**100**	**100.0**	**3,729,458**
Married couples	42.55	126	63.7	2,375,992
Married couples, no children	30.28	90	18.8	700,043
Married couples, with children	51.50	152	38.7	1,444,833
Oldest child under 6	49.20	146	6.6	246,984
Oldest child 6 to 17	52.35	155	21.3	792,841
Oldest child 18 or older	51.36	152	10.9	405,230
Single parent with child under 18	40.77	121	7.2	270,264
Single person	14.35	43	12.6	470,436
RACE				
Average household	**33.80**	**100**	**100.0**	**3,729,458**
Black	32.10	95	11.4	426,384
White and other	34.03	101	88.6	3,302,816
HISPANIC ORIGIN				
Average household	**33.80**	**100**	**100.0**	**3,729,458**
Hispanic	48.77	144	12.6	469,216
Non-Hispanic	32.30	96	87.2	3,253,191
REGION				
Average household	**33.80**	**100**	**100.0**	**3,729,458**
Northeast	37.19	110	20.9	778,759
Midwest	31.59	94	21.9	816,349
South	33.82	100	35.5	1,324,966
West	33.17	98	21.7	808,685

	AVERAGE ANNUAL SPENDING PER HOUSEHOLD (in dollars)	BEST CUSTOMERS (index)	BIGGEST CUSTOMERS (percent market share)	TOTAL (AGGREGATE) HH SPENDING (in thousands of dollars)
EDUCATION				
Average household	**$33.80**	**100**	**100.0%**	**$3,729,458**
Less than high school graduate	33.65	100	15.5	578,006
High school graduate	32.05	95	27.4	1,021,305
Some college	30.22	89	18.6	694,818
Associate's degree	40.89	121	10.6	396,797
College graduate	36.05	107	27.7	1,033,193
Bachelor's degree	33.22	98	16.8	627,194
Master's, professional, doctoral degree	41.19	122	10.8	402,838
OCCUPATION				
Average household	**33.80**	**100**	**100.0**	**3,729,458**
Self-employed	36.60	108	4.8	178,388
Wage-and-salary workers, total	36.34	108	72.1	2,689,741
Managers and professionals	36.88	109	26.5	987,130
Technical, sales, and clerical	37.82	112	21.4	799,401
Service workers	31.72	94	8.7	324,400
Construction workers and mechanics	59.51	176	8.1	300,228
Operators, fabricators, laborers	27.30	81	7.9	295,959
Retired	25.51	76	13.2	493,134
HOMEOWNERSHIP STATUS				
Average household	**33.80**	**100**	**100.0**	**3,729,458**
Homeowners	37.56	111	73.5	2,742,256
Renters	26.44	78	26.5	986,979

Note: Households by type will not sum to the total because not all household types are shown. Hispanics may be of any race and most are white. Total household spending and market shares may not sum to total due to rounding. For an explanation of terms, see the introduction to this report.
Source: Calculations by New Strategist based on the Bureau of Labor Statistics' 2001 Consumer Expenditure Survey

49. SPENDING ON CANDY AND CHEWING GUM, 2001

Total (aggregate) household spending in 2001	$4,360,427,357,940
Total (aggregate) household spending on candy and chewing gum	$8,108,813,110
Average annual household spending on candy and chewing gum	$73.49

	AVERAGE ANNUAL SPENDING PER HOUSEHOLD (in dollars)	BEST CUSTOMERS (index)	BIGGEST CUSTOMERS (percent market share)	TOTAL (AGGREGATE) HH SPENDING (in thousands of dollars)
AGE OF HOUSEHOLDER				
Average household	**$73.49**	**100**	**100.0%**	**$8,108,813**
Under age 25	35.84	49	3.8	308,152
Aged 25 to 34	63.58	87	14.5	1,177,184
Aged 35 to 44	92.25	126	27.8	2,252,930
Aged 45 to 54	85.54	116	23.5	1,908,996
Aged 55 to 64	77.01	105	13.8	1,120,419
Aged 65 to 74	63.92	87	8.9	724,981
Aged 75 or older	57.48	78	7.5	609,058
HOUSEHOLD INCOME				
Average household reporting income	**77.61**	**100**	**100.0**	**6,886,723**
Under $10,000	48.32	62	7.7	528,102
$10,000 to $19,999	51.58	67	11.3	779,476
$20,000 to $29,999	65.23	84	11.4	787,652
$30,000 to $39,999	62.13	80	9.5	652,862
$40,000 to $49,999	89.98	116	11.4	786,155
$50,000 to $69,999	91.43	118	16.6	1,141,046
$70,000 or more	118.91	153	32.6	2,246,448
HOUSEHOLD TYPE				
Average household	**73.49**	**100**	**100.0**	**8,108,813**
Married couples	94.88	129	65.3	5,298,099
Married couples, no children	73.03	99	20.8	1,688,381
Married couples, with children	109.73	149	38.0	3,078,475
Oldest child under 6	78.66	107	4.9	394,873
Oldest child 6 to 17	114.18	155	21.3	1,729,256
Oldest child 18 or older	123.12	168	12.0	971,417
Single parent with child under 18	68.84	94	5.6	456,340
Single person	38.84	53	15.7	1,273,292
RACE				
Average household	**73.49**	**100**	**100.0**	**8,108,813**
Black	45.54	62	7.5	604,908
White and other	77.26	105	92.5	7,498,547
HISPANIC ORIGIN				
Average household	**73.49**	**100**	**100.0**	**8,108,813**
Hispanic	59.02	80	0.7	567,831
Non-Hispanic	74.94	102	93.1	7,547,807
REGION				
Average household	**73.49**	**100**	**100.0**	**8,108,813**
Northeast	76.31	104	19.7	1,597,931
Midwest	77.76	106	24.8	2,009,474
South	65.64	89	31.7	2,571,578
West	79.17	108	23.8	1,930,165

	AVERAGE ANNUAL SPENDING PER HOUSEHOLD (in dollars)	BEST CUSTOMERS (index)	BIGGEST CUSTOMERS (percent market share)	TOTAL (AGGREGATE) HH SPENDING (in thousands of dollars)
EDUCATION				
Average household	**$73.49**	**100**	**100.0%**	**$8,108,813**
Less than high school graduate	52.55	72	11.1	902,651
High school graduate	71.38	97	28.1	2,274,595
Some college	69.10	94	19.6	1,588,747
Associate's degree	77.57	106	9.3	752,739
College graduate	89.93	122	31.8	2,577,394
Bachelor's degree	88.28	120	20.6	1,666,726
Master's, professional, doctoral degree	92.92	126	11.2	908,758
OCCUPATION				
Average household	**73.49**	**100**	**100.0**	**8,108,813**
Self-employed	82.57	112	5.0	402,446
Wage-and-salary workers, total	77.41	105	70.7	5,729,579
Managers and professionals	93.99	128	31.0	2,515,736
Technical, sales, and clerical	73.01	99	19.0	1,543,212
Service workers	61.67	84	7.8	630,699
Construction workers and mechanics	75.28	102	4.7	379,788
Operators, fabricators, laborers	63.64	87	8.5	689,921
Retired	59.45	81	14.2	1,149,228
HOMEOWNERSHIP STATUS				
Average household	**73.49**	**100**	**100.0**	**8,108,813**
Homeowners	84.50	115	76.1	6,169,345
Renters	51.94	71	23.9	1,938,868

Note: Households by type will not sum to the total because not all household types are shown. Hispanics may be of any race and most are white. Total household spending and market shares may not sum to total due to rounding. For an explanation of terms, see the introduction to this report.
Source: Calculations by New Strategist based on the Bureau of Labor Statistics' 2001 Consumer Expenditure Survey

50. SPENDING ON CANNED BEANS, 2001

Total (aggregate) household spending in 2001	$4,360,427,357,940
Total (aggregate) household spending on vegetables, canned beans	$1,390,271,400
Average annual household spending on vegetables, canned beans	$12.60

	AVERAGE ANNUAL SPENDING PER HOUSEHOLD (in dollars)	BEST CUSTOMERS (index)	BIGGEST CUSTOMERS (percent market share)	TOTAL (AGGREGATE) HH SPENDING (in thousands of dollars)
AGE OF HOUSEHOLDER				
Average household	**$12.60**	**100**	**100.0%**	**$1,390,271**
Under age 25	7.66	61	4.7	65,861
Aged 25 to 34	13.53	107	18.0	250,508
Aged 35 to 44	13.69	109	24.1	334,337
Aged 45 to 54	14.69	117	23.6	327,837
Aged 55 to 64	12.19	97	12.8	177,352
Aged 65 to 74	9.36	74	7.6	106,161
Aged 75 or older	12.01	95	9.2	127,258
HOUSEHOLD INCOME				
Average household reporting income	**13.36**	**100**	**100.0**	**1,185,500**
Under $10,000	9.75	73	9.0	106,589
$10,000 to $19,999	10.32	77	13.2	155,894
$20,000 to $29,999	11.82	89	12.0	142,727
$30,000 to $39,999	13.65	102	12.1	143,434
$40,000 to $49,999	18.77	141	13.8	163,994
$50,000 to $69,999	14.73	110	15.5	183,830
$70,000 or more	15.20	114	24.2	287,158
HOUSEHOLD TYPE				
Average household	**12.60**	**100**	**100.0**	**1,390,271**
Married couples	16.25	129	65.3	907,400
Married couples, no children	12.60	100	21.0	291,299
Married couples, with children	18.73	149	37.8	525,470
Oldest child under 6	24.04	191	8.7	120,681
Oldest child 6 to 17	16.97	135	18.5	257,011
Oldest child 18 or older	18.63	148	10.6	146,991
Single parent with child under 18	11.14	88	5.3	73,847
Single person	6.75	54	15.9	221,285
RACE				
Average household	**12.60**	**100**	**100.0**	**1,390,271**
Black	12.68	101	12.1	168,428
White and other	12.59	100	87.9	1,221,935
HISPANIC ORIGIN				
Average household	**12.60**	**100**	**100.0**	**1,390,271**
Hispanic	14.03	111	9.7	134,983
Non-Hispanic	12.46	99	90.3	1,254,946
REGION				
Average household	**12.60**	**100**	**100.0**	**1,390,271**
Northeast	12.44	99	18.7	260,494
Midwest	11.21	89	20.8	289,689
South	13.48	107	38.0	528,106
West	12.79	102	22.4	311,820

	AVERAGE ANNUAL SPENDING PER HOUSEHOLD (in dollars)	BEST CUSTOMERS (index)	BIGGEST CUSTOMERS (percent market share)	TOTAL (AGGREGATE) HH SPENDING (in thousands of dollars)
EDUCATION				
Average household	**12.60**	**100**	**100.0%**	**$1,390,271**
Less than high school graduate	13.58	108	16.8	233,264
High school graduate	11.75	93	26.9	374,426
Some college	11.60	92	19.2	266,707
Associate's degree	11.84	94	8.3	114,895
College graduate	13.98	111	28.8	400,667
Bachelor's degree	14.91	118	20.2	281,501
Master's, professional, doctoral degree	12.28	98	8.6	120,098
OCCUPATION				
Average household	**12.60**	**100**	**100.0**	**1,390,271**
Self-employed	13.27	105	4.7	64,678
Wage-and-salary workers, total	13.07	104	69.6	967,389
Managers and professionals	14.52	115	28.0	388,642
Technical, sales, and clerical	11.23	89	17.1	237,369
Service workers	11.04	88	8.1	112,906
Construction workers and mechanics	13.99	111	5.1	70,580
Operators, fabricators, laborers	14.32	114	11.2	155,243
Retired	10.52	84	14.6	203,362
HOMEOWNERSHIP STATUS				
Average household	**12.60**	**100**	**100.0**	**1,390,271**
Homeowners	13.74	109	72.2	1,003,157
Renters	10.37	82	27.8	387,102

Note: Households by type will not sum to the total because not all household types are shown. Hispanics may be of any race and most are white. Total household spending and market shares may not sum to total due to rounding. For an explanation of terms, see the introduction to this report.
Source: Calculations by New Strategist based on the Bureau of Labor Statistics' 2001 Consumer Expenditure Survey

51. SPENDING ON CANNED CORN, 2001

Total (aggregate) household spending in 2001	$4,360,427,357,940
Total (aggregate) household spending on vegetables, canned corn	$786,717,070
Average annual household spending on vegetables, canned corn	$7.13

	AVERAGE ANNUAL SPENDING PER HOUSEHOLD (in dollars)	BEST CUSTOMERS (index)	BIGGEST CUSTOMERS (percent market share)	TOTAL (AGGREGATE) HH SPENDING (in thousands of dollars)
AGE OF HOUSEHOLDER				
Average household	**$7.13**	**100**	**100.0%**	**$786,717**
Under age 25	5.12	72	5.6	44,022
Aged 25 to 34	7.83	110	18.4	144,973
Aged 35 to 44	8.61	121	26.7	210,273
Aged 45 to 54	7.54	106	21.4	168,270
Aged 55 to 64	6.45	91	11.9	93,841
Aged 65 to 74	5.77	81	8.3	65,443
Aged 75 or older	5.49	77	7.4	58,172
HOUSEHOLD INCOME				
Average household reporting income	**7.31**	**100**	**100.0**	**648,653**
Under $10,000	5.11	70	8.6	55,869
$10,000 to $19,999	6.43	88	15.0	97,167
$20,000 to $29,999	7.09	97	13.2	85,612
$30,000 to $39,999	7.62	104	12.3	80,071
$40,000 to $49,999	8.49	116	11.4	74,177
$50,000 to $69,999	8.77	120	16.9	109,450
$70,000 or more	7.62	104	22.2	143,957
HOUSEHOLD TYPE				
Average household	**7.13**	**100**	**100.0**	**786,717**
Married couples	8.89	125	63.1	496,418
Married couples, no children	6.19	87	18.2	143,107
Married couples, with children	10.70	150	38.2	300,189
Oldest child under 6	9.80	137	6.3	49,196
Oldest child 6 to 17	11.00	154	21.2	166,595
Oldest child 18 or older	10.70	150	10.7	84,423
Single parent with child under 18	10.13	142	8.5	67,152
Single person	2.92	41	12.2	95,726
RACE				
Average household	**7.13**	**100**	**100.0**	**786,717**
Black	8.95	126	15.1	118,883
White and other	6.88	97	84.9	667,745
HISPANIC ORIGIN				
Average household	**7.13**	**100**	**100.0**	**786,717**
Hispanic	6.77	95	8.3	65,134
Non-Hispanic	7.16	100	91.7	721,141
REGION				
Average household	**7.13**	**100**	**100.0**	**786,717**
Northeast	7.56	106	20.1	158,306
Midwest	6.35	89	20.9	164,097
South	7.72	108	38.4	302,446
West	6.63	93	20.5	161,639

	AVERAGE ANNUAL SPENDING PER HOUSEHOLD (in dollars)	BEST CUSTOMERS (index)	BIGGEST CUSTOMERS (percent market share)	TOTAL (AGGREGATE) HH SPENDING (in thousands of dollars)
EDUCATION				
Average household	**$7.13**	**100**	**100.0%**	**$786,717**
Less than high school graduate	8.02	113	17.5	137,760
High school graduate	8.07	113	32.7	257,159
Some college	6.73	94	19.7	154,736
Associate's degree	6.19	87	7.6	60,068
College graduate	6.18	87	22.5	177,119
Bachelor's degree	6.68	94	16.0	126,118
Master's, professional, doctoral degree	5.27	74	6.6	51,541
OCCUPATION				
Average household	**7.13**	**100**	**100.0**	**786,717**
Self-employed	10.22	143	6.3	49,812
Wage-and-salary workers, total	7.29	102	68.6	539,577
Managers and professionals	7.37	103	25.1	197,265
Technical, sales, and clerical	6.22	87	16.7	131,472
Service workers	7.57	106	9.8	77,418
Construction workers and mechanics	7.77	109	5.0	39,200
Operators, fabricators, laborers	8.41	118	11.6	91,173
Retired	5.26	74	12.9	101,681
HOMEOWNERSHIP STATUS				
Average household	**7.13**	**100**	**100.0**	**786,717**
Homeowners	7.41	104	68.8	541,004
Renters	6.58	92	31.2	245,625

Note: Households by type will not sum to the total because not all household types are shown. Hispanics may be of any race and most are white. Total household spending and market shares may not sum to total due to rounding. For an explanation of terms, see the introduction to this report.
Source: Calculations by New Strategist based on the Bureau of Labor Statistics' 2001 Consumer Expenditure Survey

52. SPENDING ON CANNED FRUIT, 2001

Total (aggregate) household spending in 2001	$4,360,427,357,940
Total (aggregate) household spending on fruit, canned	$1,795,215,530
Average annual household spending on fruit, canned	$16.27

	AVERAGE ANNUAL SPENDING PER HOUSEHOLD (in dollars)	BEST CUSTOMERS (index)	BIGGEST CUSTOMERS (percent market share)	TOTAL (AGGREGATE) HH SPENDING (in thousands of dollars)
AGE OF HOUSEHOLDER				
Average household	**$16.27**	**100**	**100.0%**	**$1,795,216**
Under age 25	7.79	48	3.7	66,978
Aged 25 to 34	14.28	88	14.7	264,394
Aged 35 to 44	16.29	100	22.2	397,834
Aged 45 to 54	18.96	117	23.6	423,130
Aged 55 to 64	17.21	106	13.9	250,388
Aged 65 to 74	16.40	101	10.4	186,009
Aged 75 or older	19.77	122	11.7	209,483
HOUSEHOLD INCOME				
Average household reporting income	**17.46**	**100**	**100.0**	**1,549,313**
Under $10,000	11.28	65	8.0	123,317
$10,000 to $19,999	12.37	71	12.1	186,930
$20,000 to $29,999	15.96	91	12.4	192,717
$30,000 to $39,999	19.13	110	13.0	201,018
$40,000 to $49,999	18.63	107	10.5	162,770
$50,000 to $69,999	19.55	112	15.7	243,984
$70,000 or more	23.38	134	28.5	441,695
HOUSEHOLD TYPE				
Average household	**16.27**	**100**	**100.0**	**1,795,216**
Married couples	21.73	134	67.6	1,213,403
Married couples, no children	18.04	111	23.2	417,067
Married couples, with children	23.48	144	36.7	658,731
Oldest child under 6	24.21	149	6.8	121,534
Oldest child 6 to 17	23.16	142	19.5	350,758
Oldest child 18 or older	23.62	145	10.4	186,362
Single parent with child under 18	14.23	88	5.3	94,331
Single person	8.47	52	15.5	277,672
RACE				
Average household	**16.27**	**100**	**100.0**	**1,795,216**
Black	15.06	93	11.1	200,042
White and other	16.44	101	88.9	1,595,601
HISPANIC ORIGIN				
Average household	**16.27**	**100**	**100.0**	**1,795,216**
Hispanic	13.95	86	7.5	134,213
Non-Hispanic	16.50	101	92.6	1,661,847
REGION				
Average household	**16.27**	**100**	**100.0**	**1,795,216**
Northeast	17.37	107	20.3	363,728
Midwest	17.42	107	25.1	450,168
South	15.99	98	34.9	626,440
West	14.56	90	19.8	354,973

	AVERAGE ANNUAL SPENDING PER HOUSEHOLD (in dollars)	BEST CUSTOMERS (index)	BIGGEST CUSTOMERS (percent market share)	TOTAL (AGGREGATE) HH SPENDING (in thousands of dollars)
EDUCATION				
Average household	**$16.27**	**100**	**100.0%**	**$1,795,216**
Less than high school graduate	14.70	90	14.1	252,502
High school graduate	17.14	105	30.4	546,183
Some college	14.19	87	18.2	326,257
Associate's degree	14.83	91	8.0	143,910
College graduate	18.29	112	29.2	524,191
Bachelor's degree	16.52	102	17.4	311,898
Master's, professional, doctoral degree	21.52	132	11.7	210,466
OCCUPATION				
Average household	**16.27**	**100**	**100.0**	**1,795,216**
Self-employed	23.02	142	6.2	112,200
Wage-and-salary workers, total	15.66	96	64.6	1,159,091
Managers and professionals	17.95	110	26.8	480,450
Technical, sales, and clerical	15.68	96	18.5	331,428
Service workers	12.88	79	7.3	131,724
Construction workers and mechanics	16.60	102	4.7	83,747
Operators, fabricators, laborers	12.78	79	7.7	138,548
Retired	17.42	107	18.8	336,746
HOMEOWNERSHIP STATUS				
Average household	**16.27**	**100**	**100.0**	**1,795,216**
Homeowners	18.83	116	76.6	1,374,778
Renters	11.27	69	23.4	420,698

Note: Households by type will not sum to the total because not all household types are shown. Hispanics may be of any race and most are white. Total household spending and market shares may not sum to total due to rounding. For an explanation of terms, see the introduction to this report.
Source: Calculations by New Strategist based on the Bureau of Labor Statistics' 2001 Consumer Expenditure Survey

53. SPENDING ON CANNED VEGETABLES (OTHER THAN BEANS OR CORN), 2001

Total (aggregate) household spending in 2001	$4,360,427,357,940
Total (aggregate) household spending on canned vegetables (other than beans or corn)	$1,939,759,620
Average annual household spending on canned vegetables (other than beans or corn)	$17.58

	AVERAGE ANNUAL SPENDING PER HOUSEHOLD (in dollars)	BEST CUSTOMERS (index)	BIGGEST CUSTOMERS (percent market share)	TOTAL (AGGREGATE) HH SPENDING (in thousands of dollars)
AGE OF HOUSEHOLDER				
Average household	**$17.58**	**100**	**100.0%**	**$1,939,760**
Under age 25	7.55	43	3.3	64,915
Aged 25 to 34	14.62	83	14.0	270,689
Aged 35 to 44	19.92	113	25.1	486,486
Aged 45 to 54	19.71	112	22.7	439,868
Aged 55 to 64	20.72	118	15.5	301,455
Aged 65 to 74	18.75	107	11.0	212,663
Aged 75 or older	15.59	89	8.5	165,192
HOUSEHOLD INCOME				
Average household reporting income	**18.69**	**100**	**100.0**	**1,658,457**
Under $10,000	10.25	55	6.8	112,054
$10,000 to $19,999	14.13	76	12.9	213,571
$20,000 to $29,999	18.72	100	13.6	226,044
$30,000 to $39,999	17.94	96	11.4	188,514
$40,000 to $49,999	20.69	111	10.9	180,769
$50,000 to $69,999	22.37	120	16.8	279,178
$70,000 or more	24.18	129	27.5	456,809
HOUSEHOLD TYPE				
Average household	**17.58**	**100**	**100.0**	**1,939,760**
Married couples	22.47	128	64.7	1,254,725
Married couples, no children	20.91	119	24.9	483,418
Married couples, with children	22.68	129	32.8	636,287
Oldest child under 6	18.20	104	4.7	91,364
Oldest child 6 to 17	23.64	135	18.5	358,028
Oldest child 18 or older	23.91	136	9.7	188,650
Single parent with child under 18	17.72	101	6.1	117,466
Single person	9.06	52	15.3	297,014
RACE				
Average household	**17.58**	**100**	**100.0**	**1,939,760**
Black	14.66	83	10.0	194,729
White and other	17.98	102	90.0	1,745,067
HISPANIC ORIGIN				
Average household	**17.58**	**100**	**100.0**	**1,939,760**
Hispanic	13.31	76	6.6	128,056
Non-Hispanic	18.01	102	93.5	1,813,931
REGION				
Average household	**17.58**	**100**	**100.0**	**1,939,760**
Northeast	17.40	99	18.8	364,356
Midwest	16.84	96	22.4	435,179
South	19.08	109	38.5	747,497
West	16.13	92	20.3	393,249

	AVERAGE ANNUAL SPENDING PER HOUSEHOLD (in dollars)	BEST CUSTOMERS (index)	BIGGEST CUSTOMERS (percent market share)	TOTAL (AGGREGATE) HH SPENDING (in thousands of dollars)
EDUCATION				
Average household	**$17.58**	**100**	**100.0%**	**$1,939,760**
Less than high school graduate	18.08	103	16.0	310,560
High school graduate	16.47	94	27.1	524,833
Some college	15.50	88	18.4	356,376
Associate's degree	16.38	93	8.2	158,952
College graduate	20.50	117	30.3	587,530
Bachelor's degree	19.34	110	18.8	365,139
Master's, professional, doctoral degree	22.61	129	11.4	221,126
OCCUPATION				
Average household	**17.58**	**100**	**100.0**	**1,939,760**
Self-employed	23.21	132	5.8	113,126
Wage-and-salary workers, total	17.22	98	65.7	1,274,556
Managers and professionals	19.21	109	26.5	514,175
Technical, sales, and clerical	16.23	92	17.7	343,054
Service workers	14.82	84	7.8	151,564
Construction workers and mechanics	19.97	114	5.2	100,749
Operators, fabricators, laborers	15.57	89	8.7	168,794
Retired	17.11	97	17.1	330,753
HOMEOWNERSHIP STATUS				
Average household	**17.58**	**100**	**100.0**	**1,939,760**
Homeowners	20.21	115	76.1	1,475,532
Renters	12.45	71	24.0	464,746

Note: Households by type will not sum to the total because not all household types are shown. Hispanics may be of any race and most are white. Total household spending and market shares may not sum to total due to rounding. For an explanation of terms, see the introduction to this report.
Source: Calculations by New Strategist based on the Bureau of Labor Statistics' 2001 Consumer Expenditure Survey

54. SPENDING ON COLA CARBONATED DRINKS, 2001

Total (aggregate) household spending in 2001	$4,360,427,357,940
Total (aggregate) household spending on cola carbonated drinks	$9,644,731,990
Average annual household spending on cola carbonated drinks	$87.41

	AVERAGE ANNUAL SPENDING PER HOUSEHOLD (in dollars)	BEST CUSTOMERS (index)	BIGGEST CUSTOMERS (percent market share)	TOTAL (AGGREGATE) HH SPENDING (in thousands of dollars)
AGE OF HOUSEHOLDER				
Average household	**$87.41**	**100**	**100.0%**	**$9,644,732**
Under age 25	62.80	72	5.6	539,954
Aged 25 to 34	86.46	99	16.6	1,600,807
Aged 35 to 44	105.31	121	26.7	2,571,881
Aged 45 to 54	109.73	126	25.4	2,448,844
Aged 55 to 64	92.32	106	13.9	1,343,164
Aged 65 to 74	62.65	72	7.4	710,576
Aged 75 or older	38.86	45	4.3	411,761
HOUSEHOLD INCOME				
Average household reporting income	**93.88**	**100**	**100.0**	**8,330,442**
Under $10,000	60.73	65	8.0	663,742
$10,000 to $19,999	66.13	70	12.0	999,414
$20,000 to $29,999	81.65	87	11.8	985,924
$30,000 to $39,999	104.42	111	13.2	1,097,245
$40,000 to $49,999	106.33	113	11.2	929,005
$50,000 to $69,999	109.90	117	16.5	1,371,552
$70,000 or more	122.28	130	27.7	2,310,114
HOUSEHOLD TYPE				
Average household	**87.41**	**100**	**100.0**	**9,644,732**
Married couples	109.94	126	63.7	6,139,050
Married couples, no children	85.43	98	20.5	1,975,056
Married couples, with children	123.53	141	35.9	3,465,634
Oldest child under 6	102.75	118	5.3	515,805
Oldest child 6 to 17	127.69	146	20.1	1,933,865
Oldest child 18 or older	129.90	149	10.6	1,024,911
Single parent with child under 18	90.66	104	6.2	600,985
Single person	42.11	48	14.3	1,380,492
RACE				
Average household	**87.41**	**100**	**100.0**	**9,644,732**
Black	76.75	88	10.6	1,019,470
White and other	88.85	102	89.4	8,623,426
HISPANIC ORIGIN				
Average household	**87.41**	**100**	**100.0**	**9,644,732**
Hispanic	99.24	114	9.9	954,788
Non-Hispanic	86.23	99	90.1	8,684,913
REGION				
Average household	**87.41**	**100**	**100.0**	**9,644,732**
Northeast	80.81	92	17.5	1,692,161
Midwest	96.99	111	26.0	2,506,416
South	86.48	99	35.1	3,388,027
West	84.53	97	21.4	2,060,841

	AVERAGE ANNUAL SPENDING PER HOUSEHOLD (in dollars)	BEST CUSTOMERS (index)	BIGGEST CUSTOMERS (percent market share)	TOTAL (AGGREGATE) HH SPENDING (in thousands of dollars)
EDUCATION				
Average household	**$87.41**	**100**	**100.0%**	**$9,644,732**
Less than high school graduate	88.17	101	15.7	1,514,496
High school graduate	95.18	109	31.4	3,033,006
Some college	82.89	95	19.8	1,905,807
Associate's degree	97.47	112	9.8	945,849
College graduate	78.32	90	23.3	2,244,651
Bachelor's degree	77.17	88	15.1	1,456,970
Master's, professional, doctoral degree	80.42	92	8.2	786,508
OCCUPATION				
Average household	**87.41**	**100**	**100.0**	**9,644,732**
Self-employed	109.48	125	5.5	533,606
Wage-and-salary workers, total	93.52	107	71.8	6,921,976
Managers and professionals	92.66	106	25.7	2,480,138
Technical, sales, and clerical	88.31	101	19.4	1,866,609
Service workers	82.54	94	8.8	844,137
Construction workers and mechanics	115.49	132	6.0	582,647
Operators, fabricators, laborers	104.25	119	11.7	1,130,174
Retired	55.35	63	11.1	1,069,971
HOMEOWNERSHIP STATUS				
Average household	**87.41**	**100**	**100.0**	**9,644,732**
Homeowners	96.06	110	72.7	7,013,341
Renters	70.50	81	27.3	2,631,695

Note: Households by type will not sum to the total because not all household types are shown. Hispanics may be of any race and most are white. Total household spending and market shares may not sum to total due to rounding. For an explanation of terms, see the introduction to this report.
Source: Calculations by New Strategist based on the Bureau of Labor Statistics' 2001 Consumer Expenditure Survey

55. SPENDING ON NONCOLA CARBONATED DRINKS, 2001

Total (aggregate) household spending in 2001		$4,360,427,357,940
Total (aggregate) household spending on noncola carbonated drinks		$5,091,041,460
Average annual household spending on noncola carbonated drinks		$46.14

	AVERAGE ANNUAL SPENDING PER HOUSEHOLD (in dollars)	BEST CUSTOMERS (index)	BIGGEST CUSTOMERS (percent market share)	TOTAL (AGGREGATE) HH SPENDING (in thousands of dollars)
AGE OF HOUSEHOLDER				
Average household	**$46.14**	**100**	**100.0%**	**$5,091,042**
Under age 25	34.19	74	5.8	293,966
Aged 25 to 34	46.79	101	17.0	866,317
Aged 35 to 44	53.91	117	25.9	1,316,590
Aged 45 to 54	59.68	129	26.2	1,331,879
Aged 55 to 64	45.58	99	13.0	663,143
Aged 65 to 74	30.91	67	6.9	350,581
Aged 75 or older	24.51	53	5.1	259,708
HOUSEHOLD INCOME				
Average household reporting income	**49.40**	**100**	**100.0**	**4,383,509**
Under $10,000	33.37	68	8.3	364,739
$10,000 to $19,999	40.67	82	14.0	614,607
$20,000 to $29,999	40.12	81	11.1	484,449
$30,000 to $39,999	47.80	97	11.5	502,282
$40,000 to $49,999	58.59	119	11.7	511,901
$50,000 to $69,999	60.41	122	17.2	753,917
$70,000 or more	61.19	124	26.4	1,156,002
HOUSEHOLD TYPE				
Average household	**46.14**	**100**	**100.0**	**5,091,042**
Married couples	56.77	123	62.3	3,170,037
Married couples, no children	42.16	91	19.1	974,697
Married couples, with children	66.29	144	36.5	1,859,766
Oldest child under 6	51.74	112	5.1	259,735
Oldest child 6 to 17	67.94	147	20.2	1,028,951
Oldest child 18 or older	73.50	159	11.4	579,915
Single parent with child under 18	53.28	116	6.9	353,193
Single person	24.28	53	15.6	795,971
RACE				
Average household	**46.14**	**100**	**100.0**	**5,091,042**
Black	41.82	91	10.9	555,495
White and other	46.72	101	89.1	4,534,456
HISPANIC ORIGIN				
Average household	**46.14**	**100**	**100.0**	**5,091,042**
Hispanic	46.84	102	8.9	450,648
Non-Hispanic	46.07	100	91.1	4,640,078
REGION				
Average household	**46.14**	**100**	**100.0**	**5,091,042**
Northeast	43.02	93	17.7	900,839
Midwest	53.23	115	27.0	1,375,570
South	45.61	99	35.1	1,786,863
West	42.22	92	20.2	1,029,324

	AVERAGE ANNUAL SPENDING PER HOUSEHOLD (in dollars)	BEST CUSTOMERS (index)	BIGGEST CUSTOMERS (percent market share)	TOTAL (AGGREGATE) HH SPENDING (in thousands of dollars)
EDUCATION				
Average household	**$46.14**	**100**	**100.0%**	**$5,091,042**
Less than high school graduate	45.40	98	15.3	779,836
High school graduate	46.63	101	29.2	1,485,912
Some college	43.72	95	19.7	1,005,210
Associate's degree	50.84	110	9.7	493,351
College graduate	46.23	100	26.0	1,324,952
Bachelor's degree	46.04	100	17.1	869,235
Master's, professional, doctoral degree	46.59	101	9.0	455,650
OCCUPATION				
Average household	**46.14**	**100**	**100.0**	**5,091,042**
Self-employed	54.94	119	5.3	267,778
Wage-and-salary workers, total	48.77	106	70.9	3,609,760
Managers and professionals	51.49	112	27.1	1,378,181
Technical, sales, and clerical	44.40	96	18.4	938,483
Service workers	42.71	93	8.6	436,795
Construction workers and mechanics	60.45	131	6.0	304,970
Operators, fabricators, laborers	50.47	109	10.7	547,145
Retired	30.42	66	11.6	588,049
HOMEOWNERSHIP STATUS				
Average household	**46.14**	**100**	**100.0**	**5,091,042**
Homeowners	49.26	107	70.6	3,596,473
Renters	40.04	87	29.4	1,494,653

Note: Households by type will not sum to the total because not all household types are shown. Hispanics may be of any race and most are white. Total household spending and market shares may not sum to total due to rounding. For an explanation of terms, see the introduction to this report.
Source: Calculations by New Strategist based on the Bureau of Labor Statistics' 2001 Consumer Expenditure Survey

56. SPENDING ON CEREAL, READY-TO-EAT AND COOKED, 2001

Total (aggregate) household spending in 2001	$4,360,427,357,940
Total (aggregate) household spending on cereal, ready-to-eat and cooked	$9,493,567,560
Average annual household spending on cereal, ready-to-eat and cooked	$86.04

	AVERAGE ANNUAL SPENDING PER HOUSEHOLD (in dollars)	BEST CUSTOMERS (index)	BIGGEST CUSTOMERS (percent market share)	TOTAL (AGGREGATE) HH SPENDING (in thousands of dollars)
AGE OF HOUSEHOLDER				
Average household	**$86.04**	**100**	**100.0%**	**$9,493,568**
Under age 25	64.87	75	5.9	557,752
Aged 25 to 34	87.34	102	17.0	1,617,100
Aged 35 to 44	102.84	120	26.5	2,511,559
Aged 45 to 54	93.24	108	21.9	2,080,837
Aged 55 to 64	81.34	95	12.5	1,183,416
Aged 65 to 74	70.30	82	8.4	797,343
Aged 75 or older	69.00	80	7.7	731,124
HOUSEHOLD INCOME				
Average household reporting income	**91.53**	**100**	**100.0**	**8,121,915**
Under $10,000	61.57	67	8.3	672,936
$10,000 to $19,999	69.90	76	1.3	1,056,437
$20,000 to $29,999	84.10	92	12.5	1,015,508
$30,000 to $39,999	83.48	91	10.8	877,208
$40,000 to $49,999	98.14	107	10.6	857,449
$50,000 to $69,999	104.92	115	16.1	1,309,402
$70,000 or more	124.58	136	29.0	2,353,565
HOUSEHOLD TYPE				
Average household	**86.04**	**100**	**100.0**	**9,493,568**
Married couples	109.28	127	64.3	6,102,195
Married couples, no children	78.93	92	19.2	1,824,783
Married couples, with children	132.55	154	39.2	3,718,690
Oldest child under 6	121.19	141	6.4	608,374
Oldest child 6 to 17	138.37	161	22.1	2,095,614
Oldest child 18 or older	128.31	149	10.7	1,012,366
Single parent with child under 18	110.18	128	7.7	730,383
Single person	43.48	51	15.0	1,425,405
RACE				
Average household	**86.04**	**100**	**100.0**	**9,493,568**
Black	86.79	101	12.1	1,152,832
White and other	85.94	100	87.9	8,340,993
HISPANIC ORIGIN				
Average household	**86.04**	**100**	**100.0**	**9,493,568**
Hispanic	89.13	104	9.0	857,520
Non-Hispanic	85.73	100	91.0	8,634,554
REGION				
Average household	**86.04**	**100**	**100.0**	**9,493,568**
Northeast	99.01	115	21.8	2,073,269
Midwest	86.96	101	23.7	2,247,220
South	80.65	94	33.3	3,159,625
West	82.52	96	21.2	2,011,838

	AVERAGE ANNUAL SPENDING PER HOUSEHOLD (in dollars)	BEST CUSTOMERS (index)	BIGGEST CUSTOMERS (percent market share)	TOTAL (AGGREGATE) HH SPENDING (in thousands of dollars)
EDUCATION				
Average household	**$86.04**	**100**	**100.0%**	**$9,493,568**
Less than high school graduate	74.39	87	13.5	1,277,797
High school graduate	84.31	98	28.3	2,686,623
Some college	78.96	92	19.1	1,815,448
Associate's degree	82.49	96	8.4	800,483
College graduate	101.26	118	30.6	2,902,112
Bachelor's degree	97.43	113	19.4	1,839,478
Master's, professional, doctoral degree	108.25	126	11.2	1,058,685
OCCUPATION				
Average household	**86.04**	**100**	**100.0**	**9,493,568**
Self-employed	89.26	104	4.6	435,053
Wage-and-salary workers, total	87.84	102	68.5	6,501,565
Managers and professionals	99.43	116	28.0	2,661,343
Technical, sales, and clerical	86.75	101	19.3	1,833,635
Service workers	70.66	82	7.6	722,640
Construction workers and mechanics	85.19	99	4.5	429,784
Operators, fabricators, laborers	80.75	94	9.2	875,411
Retired	75.07	87	15.3	1,451,178
HOMEOWNERSHIP STATUS				
Average household	**86.04**	**100**	**100.0**	**9,493,568**
Homeowners	92.51	108	71.1	6,754,155
Renters	73.36	85	28.8	2,738,455

Note: Households by type will not sum to the total because not all household types are shown. Hispanics may be of any race and most are white. Total household spending and market shares may not sum to total due to rounding. For an explanation of terms, see the introduction to this report.
Source: Calculations by New Strategist based on the Bureau of Labor Statistics' 2001 Consumer Expenditure Survey

57. SPENDING ON CHEESE, 2001

Total (aggregate) household spending in 2001	$4,360,427,357,940
Total (aggregate) household spending on cheese	$10,304,559,210
Average annual household spending on cheese	$93.39

	AVERAGE ANNUAL SPENDING PER HOUSEHOLD (in dollars)	BEST CUSTOMERS (index)	BIGGEST CUSTOMERS (percent market share)	TOTAL (AGGREGATE) HH SPENDING (in thousands of dollars)
AGE OF HOUSEHOLDER				
Average household	**$93.39**	**100**	**100.0%**	**$10,304,559**
Under age 25	55.21	59	4.6	474,696
Aged 25 to 34	86.70	93	15.6	1,605,251
Aged 35 to 44	111.38	119	26.4	2,720,122
Aged 45 to 54	114.75	123	24.9	2,560,876
Aged 55 to 64	97.59	105	13.8	1,419,837
Aged 65 to 74	78.15	84	8.6	886,377
Aged 75 or older	59.15	63	6.1	626,753
HOUSEHOLD INCOME				
Average household reporting income	**101.17**	**100**	**100.0**	**8,977,320**
Under $10,000	55.56	55	6.8	607,258
$10,000 to $19,999	64.89	64	10.9	980,653
$20,000 to $29,999	86.10	85	11.6	1,039,658
$30,000 to $39,999	93.60	93	11.0	983,549
$40,000 to $49,999	104.65	103	10.2	914,327
$50,000 to $69,999	120.21	119	16.7	1,500,221
$70,000 or more	158.35	157	33.3	2,991,548
HOUSEHOLD TYPE				
Average household	**93.39**	**100**	**100.0**	**10,304,559**
Married couples	119.06	128	64.5	6,648,310
Married couples, no children	95.44	102	21.4	2,206,477
Married couples, with children	135.14	145	36.8	3,791,353
Oldest child under 6	122.02	131	5.9	612,540
Oldest child 6 to 17	132.78	142	19.5	2,010,953
Oldest child 18 or older	150.01	161	11.5	1,183,579
Single parent with child under 18	86.38	93	5.6	572,613
Single person	47.09	50	15.0	1,543,752
RACE				
Average household	**93.39**	**100**	**100.0**	**10,304,559**
Black	63.13	68	8.1	838,556
White and other	97.48	104	91.8	9,461,019
HISPANIC ORIGIN				
Average household	**93.39**	**100**	**100.0**	**10,304,559**
Hispanic	93.19	100	8.7	896,581
Non-Hispanic	93.41	100	91.3	9,408,068
REGION				
Average household	**93.39**	**100**	**100.0**	**10,304,559**
Northeast	105.28	113	21.4	2,204,563
Midwest	93.55	100	23.5	2,417,519
South	84.68	91	32.2	3,317,508
West	96.94	104	22.9	2,363,397

	AVERAGE ANNUAL SPENDING PER HOUSEHOLD (in dollars)	BEST CUSTOMERS (index)	BIGGEST CUSTOMERS (percent market share)	TOTAL (AGGREGATE) HH SPENDING (in thousands of dollars)
EDUCATION				
Average household	**$93.39**	**100**	**100.0%**	**$10,304,559**
Less than high school graduate	75.32	81	12.6	1,293,772
High school graduate	85.49	92	26.4	2,724,224
Some college	88.01	94	19.6	2,023,526
Associate's degree	104.76	112	9.9	1,016,591
College graduate	112.78	121	31.4	3,232,275
Bachelor's degree	110.06	118	20.2	2,077,933
Master's, professional, doctoral degree	117.72	126	11.2	1,151,302
OCCUPATION				
Average household	**93.39**	**100**	**100.0**	**10,304,559**
Self-employed	108.70	116	5.1	529,804
Wage-and-salary workers, total	98.97	106	71.1	7,325,364
Managers and professionals	113.68	122	29.5	3,042,759
Technical, sales, and clerical	92.79	99	19.0	1,961,302
Service workers	85.16	91	8.5	870,931
Construction workers and mechanics	116.19	124	5.7	586,179
Operators, fabricators, laborers	82.54	88	8.7	894,816
Retired	69.84	75	13.1	1,350,077
HOMEOWNERSHIP STATUS				
Average household	**93.39**	**100**	**100.0**	**10,304,559**
Homeowners	104.27	112	73.9	7,612,753
Renters	72.09	77	26.1	2,691,048

Note: Households by type will not sum to the total because not all household types are shown. Hispanics may be of any race and most are white. Total household spending and market shares may not sum to total due to rounding. For an explanation of terms, see the introduction to this report.
Source: Calculations by New Strategist based on the Bureau of Labor Statistics' 2001 Consumer Expenditure Survey

58. SPENDING ON COFFEE, INSTANT AND FREEZE-DRIED, 2001

Total (aggregate) household spending in 2001	$4,360,427,357,940
Total (aggregate) household spending on coffee, instant and freeze-dried	$1,475,232,430
Average annual household spending on coffee, instant and freeze-dried	$13.37

	AVERAGE ANNUAL SPENDING PER HOUSEHOLD (in dollars)	BEST CUSTOMERS (index)	BIGGEST CUSTOMERS (percent market share)	TOTAL (AGGREGATE) HH SPENDING (in thousands of dollars)
AGE OF HOUSEHOLDER				
Average household	**$13.37**	**100**	**100.0%**	**$1,475,232**
Under age 25	3.19	24	1.9	27,428
Aged 25 to 34	7.90	59	9.9	146,269
Aged 35 to 44	13.26	99	22.0	323,836
Aged 45 to 54	15.46	116	23.4	345,021
Aged 55 to 64	17.62	132	17.4	256,353
Aged 65 to 74	17.89	134	13.8	202,908
Aged 75 or older	16.79	126	12.1	177,907
HOUSEHOLD INCOME				
Average household reporting income	**14.61**	**100**	**100.0**	**1,296,418**
Under $10,000	10.00	69	8.4	109,332
$10,000 to $19,999	14.68	101	17.1	221,848
$20,000 to $29,999	11.80	81	11.0	142,485
$30,000 to $39,999	11.65	80	9.4	122,418
$40,000 to $49,999	13.43	92	9.1	117,338
$50,000 to $69,999	17.51	120	16.9	218,525
$70,000 or more	19.16	131	27.9	361,971
HOUSEHOLD TYPE				
Average household	**13.37**	**100**	**100.0**	**1,475,232**
Married couples	15.80	118	59.8	882,272
Married couples, no children	15.21	114	23.8	351,640
Married couples, with children	14.84	111	28.2	416,336
Oldest child under 6	9.25	69	3.1	46,435
Oldest child 6 to 17	15.30	114	15.7	231,719
Oldest child 18 or older	17.97	134	9.6	141,783
Single parent with child under 18	8.55	64	3.8	56,678
Single person	9.49	71	21.1	311,111
RACE				
Average household	**13.37**	**100**	**100.0**	**1,475,232**
Black	8.77	66	7.9	116,492
White and other	13.99	105	92.0	1,357,813
HISPANIC ORIGIN				
Average household	**13.37**	**100**	**100.0**	**1,475,232**
Hispanic	14.81	111	9.7	142,487
Non-Hispanic	13.22	99	90.3	1,331,492
REGION				
Average household	**13.37**	**100**	**100.0**	**1,475,232**
Northeast	14.71	110	20.9	308,027
Midwest	11.07	83	19.4	286,071
South	12.65	95	33.6	495,589
West	15.78	118	26.1	384,716

	AVERAGE ANNUAL SPENDING PER HOUSEHOLD (in dollars)	BEST CUSTOMERS (index)	BIGGEST CUSTOMERS (percent market share)	TOTAL (AGGREGATE) HH SPENDING (in thousands of dollars)
EDUCATION				
Average household	**$13.37**	**100**	**100.0%**	**$1,475,232**
Less than high school graduate	14.89	111	17.3	255,766
High school graduate	13.97	105	30.2	445,168
Some college	11.32	85	17.6	260,269
Associate's degree	12.85	96	8.5	124,696
College graduate	13.52	101	26.3	387,483
Bachelor's degree	12.95	97	16.6	244,496
Master's, professional, doctoral degree	14.57	109	9.7	142,495
OCCUPATION				
Average household	**13.37**	**100**	**100.0**	**1,475,232**
Self-employed	13.61	102	4.5	66,335
Wage-and-salary workers, total	12.60	94	63.2	932,602
Managers and professionals	12.63	95	22.9	338,055
Technical, sales, and clerical	12.97	97	18.6	274,147
Service workers	12.23	92	8.5	125,076
Construction workers and mechanics	11.13	83	3.8	56,151
Operators, fabricators, laborers	12.85	96	9.4	139,307
Retired	17.71	133	23.2	342,352
HOMEOWNERSHIP STATUS				
Average household	**13.37**	**100**	**100.0**	**1,475,232**
Homeowners	14.97	112	74.1	1,092,960
Renters	10.23	77	25.9	381,876

Note: Households by type will not sum to the total because not all household types are shown. Hispanics may be of any race and most are white. Total household spending and market shares may not sum to total due to rounding. For an explanation of terms, see the introduction to this report.
Source: Calculations by New Strategist based on the Bureau of Labor Statistics' 2001 Consumer Expenditure Survey

59. SPENDING ON COFFEE, ROASTED, 2001

Total (aggregate) household spending in 2001 $4,360,427,357,940
Total (aggregate) household spending on coffee, roasted $2,756,268,220
Average annual household spending on coffee, roasted $24.98

	AVERAGE ANNUAL SPENDING PER HOUSEHOLD (in dollars)	BEST CUSTOMERS (index)	BIGGEST CUSTOMERS (percent market share)	TOTAL (AGGREGATE) HH SPENDING (in thousands of dollars)
AGE OF HOUSEHOLDER				
Average household	**$24.98**	**100**	**100.0%**	**$2,756,268**
Under age 25	9.65	39	3.0	82,971
Aged 25 to 34	16.36	66	11.0	302,905
Aged 35 to 44	26.65	107	23.6	650,846
Aged 45 to 54	31.27	125	25.3	697,853
Aged 55 to 64	34.14	137	18.0	496,703
Aged 65 to 74	26.59	106	10.9	301,584
Aged 75 or older	21.57	86	8.3	228,556
HOUSEHOLD INCOME				
Average household reporting income	**26.66**	**100**	**100.0**	**2,365,675**
Under $10,000	17.09	64	7.9	186,738
$10,000 to $19,999	20.23	76	12.9	305,702
$20,000 to $29,999	21.82	82	11.1	263,477
$30,000 to $39,999	21.01	79	9.3	220,773
$40,000 to $49,999	24.59	92	9.1	214,843
$50,000 to $69,999	33.52	126	17.7	418,330
$70,000 or more	40.43	152	32.3	763,804
HOUSEHOLD TYPE				
Average household	**24.98**	**100**	**100.0**	**2,756,268**
Married couples	32.33	129	65.5	1,805,307
Married couples, no children	30.96	124	26.0	715,764
Married couples, with children	31.19	125	31.7	875,035
Oldest child under 6	19.39	78	3.5	97,338
Oldest child 6 to 17	30.23	121	16.6	457,833
Oldest child 18 or older	42.05	168	12.0	331,775
Single parent with child under 18	15.59	62	3.7	103,346
Single person	14.32	57	17.0	469,453
RACE				
Average household	**24.98**	**100**	**100.0**	**2,756,268**
Black	11.70	47	5.6	155,411
White and other	26.78	107	94.3	2,599,160
HISPANIC ORIGIN				
Average household	**24.98**	**100**	**100.0**	**2,756,268**
Hispanic	23.85	96	8.3	229,461
Non-Hispanic	25.10	101	91.7	2,528,022
REGION				
Average household	**24.98**	**100**	**100.0**	**2,756,268**
Northeast	30.34	122	23.1	635,320
Midwest	25.05	100	23.5	647,342
South	20.72	83	29.5	811,747
West	27.13	109	24.0	661,429

	AVERAGE ANNUAL SPENDING PER HOUSEHOLD (in dollars)	BEST CUSTOMERS (index)	BIGGEST CUSTOMERS (percent market share)	TOTAL (AGGREGATE) HH SPENDING (in thousands of dollars)
EDUCATION				
Average household	**$24.98**	**100**	**100.0%**	**$2,756,268**
Less than high school graduate	21.64	87	13.5	371,710
High school graduate	25.44	102	29.4	810,671
Some college	21.13	85	17.6	485,821
Associate's degree	22.97	92	8.1	222,901
College graduate	30.02	120	31.2	860,373
Bachelor's degree	28.29	113	19.4	534,115
Master's, professional, doctoral degree	33.16	133	11.8	324,305
OCCUPATION				
Average household	**24.98**	**100**	**100.0**	**2,756,268**
Self-employed	31.11	125	5.5	151,630
Wage-and-salary workers, total	24.83	99	66.7	1,837,817
Managers and professionals	28.69	115	27.9	767,917
Technical, sales, and clerical	22.70	91	17.4	479,810
Service workers	21.12	85	7.8	215,994
Construction workers and mechanics	22.34	89	4.1	112,705
Operators, fabricators, laborers	24.25	97	9.5	262,894
Retired	25.38	102	17.8	490,621
HOMEOWNERSHIP STATUS				
Average household	**24.98**	**100**	**100.0**	**2,756,268**
Homeowners	29.05	116	76.9	2,120,941
Renters	17.03	68	23.1	635,713

Note: Households by type will not sum to the total because not all household types are shown. Hispanics may be of any race and most are white. Total household spending and market shares may not sum to total due to rounding. For an explanation of terms, see the introduction to this report.
Source: Calculations by New Strategist based on the Bureau of Labor Statistics' 2001 Consumer Expenditure Survey

60. SPENDING ON COOKIES, 2001

Total (aggregate) household spending in 2001	$4,360,427,357,940
Total (aggregate) household spending on cookies	$5,089,938,070
Average annual household spending on cookies	$46.13

	AVERAGE ANNUAL SPENDING PER HOUSEHOLD (in dollars)	BEST CUSTOMERS (index)	BIGGEST CUSTOMERS (percent market share)	TOTAL (AGGREGATE) HH SPENDING (in thousands of dollars)
AGE OF HOUSEHOLDER				
Average household	**$46.13**	**100**	**100.0%**	**$5,089,938**
Under age 25	27.05	59	4.6	232,576
Aged 25 to 34	39.78	86	14.5	736,527
Aged 35 to 44	54.74	119	26.3	1,336,860
Aged 45 to 54	54.38	118	23.8	1,213,599
Aged 55 to 64	44.40	96	12.7	645,976
Aged 65 to 74	42.24	92	9.4	479,086
Aged 75 or older	41.93	91	8.7	444,290
HOUSEHOLD INCOME				
Average household reporting income	**48.89**	**100**	**100.0**	**4,338,254**
Under $10,000	31.78	65	0.8	347,356
$10,000 to $19,999	34.72	71	12.1	524,704
$20,000 to $29,999	45.74	94	12.7	552,311
$30,000 to $39,999	43.44	89	10.5	456,468
$40,000 to $49,999	49.48	101	10.0	432,307
$50,000 to $69,999	55.99	115	16.1	698,755
$70,000 or more	70.93	145	30.9	1,340,010
HOUSEHOLD TYPE				
Average household	**46.13**	**100**	**100.0**	**5,089,938**
Married couples	57.86	125	63.5	3,230,902
Married couples, no children	44.43	96	20.2	1,027,177
Married couples, with children	68.42	148	37.7	1,919,523
Oldest child under 6	55.61	121	5.5	279,162
Oldest child 6 to 17	70.37	153	20.9	1,065,754
Oldest child 18 or older	73.70	160	11.4	581,493
Single parent with child under 18	49.64	108	6.5	329,064
Single person	24.48	53	15.8	802,528
RACE				
Average household	**46.13**	**100**	**100.0**	**5,089,938**
Black	41.58	90	10.9	552,307
White and other	46.75	101	89.1	4,537,368
HISPANIC ORIGIN				
Average household	**46.13**	**100**	**100.0**	**5,089,938**
Hispanic	45.57	99	8.6	438,429
Non-Hispanic	46.19	100	91.4	4,652,164
REGION				
Average household	**46.13**	**100**	**100.0**	**5,089,938**
Northeast	50.77	110	20.9	1,063,124
Midwest	44.43	96	22.6	1,148,160
South	46.09	100	35.5	1,805,668
West	43.99	95	21.1	1,072,476

	AVERAGE ANNUAL SPENDING PER HOUSEHOLD (in dollars)	BEST CUSTOMERS (index)	BIGGEST CUSTOMERS (percent market share)	TOTAL (AGGREGATE) HH SPENDING (in thousands of dollars)
EDUCATION				
Average household	**$46.13**	**100**	**100.0%**	**$5,089,938**
Less than high school graduate	40.56	88	13.7	696,699
High school graduate	45.31	98	28.4	1,443,849
Some college	43.33	94	19.6	996,243
Associate's degree	47.53	103	9.1	461,231
College graduate	51.92	113	29.2	1,488,027
Bachelor's degree	48.09	104	17.8	907,939
Master's, professional, doctoral degree	58.89	128	11.3	575,944
OCCUPATION				
Average household	**46.13**	**100**	**100.0**	**5,089,938**
Self-employed	46.97	102	4.5	228,932
Wage-and-salary workers, total	47.88	104	69.6	3,543,886
Managers and professionals	52.52	114	27.6	1,405,750
Technical, sales, and clerical	46.73	101	19.4	987,732
Service workers	42.78	93	8.6	437,511
Construction workers and mechanics	48.94	106	4.9	246,902
Operators, fabricators, laborers	43.82	95	9.3	475,053
Retired	43.11	94	16.4	833,359
HOMEOWNERSHIP STATUS				
Average household	**46.13**	**100**	**100.0**	**5,089,938**
Homeowners	50.77	110	72.8	3,706,718
Renters	37.06	80	27.2	1,383,413

Note: Households by type will not sum to the total because not all household types are shown. Hispanics may be of any race and most are white. Total household spending and market shares may not sum to total due to rounding. For an explanation of terms, see the introduction to this report.
Source: Calculations by New Strategist based on the Bureau of Labor Statistics' 2001 Consumer Expenditure Survey

61. SPENDING ON CRACKERS, 2001

Total (aggregate) household spending in 2001	$4,360,427,357,940
Total (aggregate) household spending on crackers	$2,653,652,950
Average annual household spending on crackers	$24.05

	AVERAGE ANNUAL SPENDING PER HOUSEHOLD (in dollars)	BEST CUSTOMERS (index)	BIGGEST CUSTOMERS (percent market share)	TOTAL (AGGREGATE) HH SPENDING (in thousands of dollars)
AGE OF HOUSEHOLDER				
Average household	**$24.05**	**100**	**100.0%**	**$2,653,653**
Under age 25	11.36	47	3.7	97,673
Aged 25 to 34	21.96	91	15.3	406,589
Aged 35 to 44	25.86	108	23.8	631,553
Aged 45 to 54	28.99	121	24.4	646,970
Aged 55 to 64	25.74	107	14.1	374,491
Aged 65 to 74	23.17	96	9.9	262,794
Aged 75 or older	22.13	92	8.8	234,490
HOUSEHOLD INCOME				
Average household reporting income	**25.39**	**100**	**100.0**	**2,252,982**
Under $10,000	14.12	56	6.8	154,312
$10,000 to $19,999	18.81	74	12.6	284,315
$20,000 to $29,999	20.93	82	11.2	252,730
$30,000 to $39,999	21.33	84	9.9	224,136
$40,000 to $49,999	27.46	108	10.6	239,918
$50,000 to $69,999	29.58	117	16.4	369,158
$70,000 or more	39.03	154	32.7	737,355
HOUSEHOLD TYPE				
Average household	**24.05**	**100**	**100.0**	**2,653,653**
Married couples	30.80	128	64.8	1,719,872
Married couples, no children	26.22	109	22.8	606,180
Married couples, with children	34.61	144	36.6	970,984
Oldest child under 6	30.49	127	5.8	153,060
Oldest child 6 to 17	37.45	156	21.4	567,180
Oldest child 18 or older	31.50	131	9.4	248,535
Single parent with child under 18	23.85	99	6.0	158,102
Single person	12.88	54	15.9	422,245
RACE				
Average household	**24.05**	**100**	**100.0**	**2,653,653**
Black	19.40	81	9.7	257,690
White and other	24.68	103	90.3	2,395,342
HISPANIC ORIGIN				
Average household	**24.05**	**100**	**100.0**	**2,653,653**
Hispanic	17.16	71	6.2	165,096
Non-Hispanic	24.74	103	93.9	2,491,763
REGION				
Average household	**24.05**	**100**	**100.0**	**2,653,653**
Northeast	26.36	110	20.8	551,978
Midwest	23.83	99	23.2	615,815
South	24.12	100	35.6	944,949
West	22.17	92	20.4	540,505

	AVERAGE ANNUAL SPENDING PER HOUSEHOLD (in dollars)	BEST CUSTOMERS (index)	BIGGEST CUSTOMERS (percent market share)	TOTAL (AGGREGATE) HH SPENDING (in thousands of dollars)
EDUCATION				
Average household	**$24.05**	**100**	**100.0%**	**$2,653,653**
Less than high school graduate	19.83	83	12.8	340,620
High school graduate	22.04	92	26.5	702,327
Some college	21.38	89	18.5	491,569
Associate's degree	24.90	104	9.1	241,630
College graduate	30.44	127	32.9	872,410
Bachelor's degree	29.93	124	21.3	565,078
Master's, professional, doctoral degree	31.36	130	11.6	306,701
OCCUPATION				
Average household	**24.05**	**100**	**100.0**	**2,653,653**
Self-employed	29.98	125	5.5	146,123
Wage-and-salary workers, total	24.00	100	66.9	1,776,384
Managers and professionals	29.35	122	29.6	785,582
Technical, sales, and clerical	22.78	95	18.1	481,501
Service workers	18.21	76	7.0	186,234
Construction workers and mechanics	22.99	96	4.4	115,985
Operators, fabricators, laborers	20.00	83	8.2	216,820
Retired	24.08	100	17.5	465,491
HOMEOWNERSHIP STATUS				
Average household	**24.05**	**100**	**100.0**	**2,653,653**
Homeowners	27.19	113	74.8	1,985,142
Renters	17.90	74	25.2	668,189

Note: Households by type will not sum to the total because not all household types are shown. Hispanics may be of any race and most are white. Total household spending and market shares may not sum to total due to rounding. For an explanation of terms, see the introduction to this report.
Source: Calculations by New Strategist based on the Bureau of Labor Statistics' 2001 Consumer Expenditure Survey

62. SPENDING ON CREAM, 2001

Total (aggregate) household spending in 2001	$4,360,427,357,940
Total (aggregate) household spending on cream	$1,362,686,650
Average annual household spending on cream	$12.35

	AVERAGE ANNUAL SPENDING PER HOUSEHOLD (in dollars)	BEST CUSTOMERS (index)	BIGGEST CUSTOMERS (percent market share)	TOTAL (AGGREGATE) HH SPENDING (in thousands of dollars)
AGE OF HOUSEHOLDER				
Average household	**$12.35**	**100**	**100.0%**	**$1,362,687**
Under age 25	5.18	42	3.3	44,538
Aged 25 to 34	10.73	87	14.6	198,666
Aged 35 to 44	13.94	113	25.0	340,443
Aged 45 to 54	14.53	118	23.8	324,266
Aged 55 to 64	14.86	120	15.9	216,198
Aged 65 to 74	11.82	96	9.8	134,062
Aged 75 or older	9.86	80	7.7	104,477
HOUSEHOLD INCOME				
Average household reporting income	**12.74**	**100**	**100.0**	**1,130,484**
Under $10,000	6.90	54	6.7	75,446
$10,000 to $19,999	7.81	61	10.4	118,004
$20,000 to $29,999	11.89	93	12.7	143,572
$30,000 to $39,999	11.65	91	10.8	122,418
$40,000 to $49,999	12.85	101	9.9	112,270
$50,000 to $69,999	13.66	107	15.1	170,477
$70,000 or more	20.73	163	34.6	391,631
HOUSEHOLD TYPE				
Average household	**12.35**	**100**	**100.0**	**1,362,687**
Married couples	15.97	129	65.4	891,765
Married couples, no children	13.74	111	23.3	317,655
Married couples, with children	16.95	137	34.9	475,532
Oldest child under 6	14.22	115	5.2	71,384
Oldest child 6 to 17	16.09	130	17.9	243,683
Oldest child 18 or older	20.86	169	12.1	164,585
Single parent with child under 18	9.33	76	4.5	61,849
Single person	6.04	49	14.5	198,009
RACE				
Average household	**12.35**	**100**	**100.0**	**1,362,687**
Black	6.49	53	6.3	86,207
White and other	13.14	106	93.6	1,275,316
HISPANIC ORIGIN				
Average household	**12.35**	**100**	**100.0**	**1,362,687**
Hispanic	13.18	107	9.3	126,805
Non-Hispanic	12.26	99	90.6	1,234,803
REGION				
Average household	**12.35**	**100**	**100.0**	**1,362,687**
Northeast	14.17	115	21.8	296,720
Midwest	10.64	86	20.2	274,959
South	10.44	85	30.0	409,008
West	15.63	127	28.0	381,059

	AVERAGE ANNUAL SPENDING PER HOUSEHOLD (in dollars)	BEST CUSTOMERS (index)	BIGGEST CUSTOMERS (percent market share)	TOTAL (AGGREGATE) HH SPENDING (in thousands of dollars)
EDUCATION				
Average household	**$12.35**	**100**	**100.0%**	**$1,362,687**
Less than high school graduate	11.09	90	14.0	190,493
High school graduate	10.28	83	24.0	327,583
Some college	11.23	91	18.9	258,200
Associate's degree	11.78	95	8.4	114,313
College graduate	16.40	133	34.5	470,024
Bachelor's degree	15.86	128	22.0	299,437
Master's, professional, doctoral degree	17.37	141	12.5	169,879
OCCUPATION				
Average household	**12.35**	**100**	**100.0**	**1,362,687**
Self-employed	14.74	119	5.3	71,843
Wage-and-salary workers, total	12.70	103	69.0	940,003
Managers and professionals	15.58	126	30.6	417,014
Technical, sales, and clerical	11.27	91	17.5	238,214
Service workers	10.84	88	8.1	110,861
Construction workers and mechanics	11.12	90	4.1	56,100
Operators, fabricators, laborers	11.10	90	8.8	120,335
Retired	10.21	83	14.5	197,370
HOMEOWNERSHIP STATUS				
Average household	**12.35**	**100**	**100.0**	**1,362,687**
Homeowners	14.09	114	75.5	1,028,711
Renters	8.93	72	24.5	333,348

Note: Households by type will not sum to the total because not all household types are shown. Hispanics may be of any race and most are white. Total household spending and market shares may not sum to total due to rounding. For an explanation of terms, see the introduction to this report.
Source: Calculations by New Strategist based on the Bureau of Labor Statistics' 2001 Consumer Expenditure Survey

63. SPENDING ON DESSERTS, PREPARED

Total (aggregate) household spending in 2001	$4,360,427,357,940
Total (aggregate) household spending on prepared desserts	$1,119,940,850
Average annual household spending on prepared desserts	$10.15

	AVERAGE ANNUAL SPENDING PER HOUSEHOLD (in dollars)	BEST CUSTOMERS (index)	BIGGEST CUSTOMERS (percent market share)	TOTAL (AGGREGATE) HH SPENDING (in thousands of dollars)
AGE OF HOUSEHOLDER				
Average household	**$10.15**	**100**	**100.0%**	**$1,119,941**
Under age 25	4.52	45	3.5	38,863
Aged 25 to 34	9.90	98	16.4	183,299
Aged 35 to 44	10.02	99	21.9	244,708
Aged 45 to 54	10.54	104	2.1	235,221
Aged 55 to 64	14.07	139	18.3	204,704
Aged 65 to 74	9.18	90	9.3	104,120
Aged 75 or older	10.43	103	9.9	110,516
HOUSEHOLD INCOME				
Average household reporting income	**10.75**	**100**	**100.0**	**953,901**
Under $10,000	6.43	60	7.4	70,249
$10,000 to $19,999	6.63	62	10.5	100,258
$20,000 to $29,999	8.40	78	10.6	101,430
$30,000 to $39,999	9.69	90	10.7	101,823
$40,000 to $49,999	10.10	94	9.3	88,244
$50,000 to $69,999	15.23	142	19.9	190,070
$70,000 or more	16.33	152	32.3	308,506
HOUSEHOLD TYPE				
Average household	**10.15**	**100**	**100.0**	**1,119,941**
Married couples	13.64	134	6.8	761,658
Married couples, no children	12.76	126	26.3	294,998
Married couples, with children	14.24	140	35.7	399,503
Oldest child under 6	11.08	109	5.0	55,622
Oldest child 6 to 17	13.91	137	18.8	210,667
Oldest child 18 or older	17.33	171	12.2	136,734
Single parent with child under 18	7.69	76	4.6	50,977
Single person	4.48	44	13.1	146,868
RACE				
Average household	**10.15**	**100**	**100.0**	**1,119,941**
Black	5.39	53	6.4	71,595
White and other	10.80	106	93.6	1,048,205
HISPANIC ORIGIN				
Average household	**10.15**	**100**	**100.0**	**1,119,941**
Hispanic	9.16	90	7.9	88,128
Non-Hispanic	10.25	101	92.2	1,032,360
REGION				
Average household	**10.15**	**100**	**100.0**	**1,119,941**
Northeast	10.75	106	20.1	225,105
Midwest	10.96	108	25.3	283,228
South	10.20	101	35.7	399,605
West	8.70	86	18.9	212,106

	AVERAGE ANNUAL SPENDING PER HOUSEHOLD (in dollars)	BEST CUSTOMERS (index)	BIGGEST CUSTOMERS (percent market share)	TOTAL (AGGREGATE) HH SPENDING (in thousands of dollars)
EDUCATION				
Average household	**$10.15**	**100**	**100.0%**	**$1,119,941**
Less than high school graduate	9.20	91	14.1	158,028
High school graduate	9.17	90	26.1	292,211
Some college	9.16	90	18.8	210,607
Associate's degree	11.43	113	9.9	110,917
College graduate	12.10	119	31.0	346,786
Bachelor's degree	10.59	104	17.9	199,939
Master's, professional, doctoral degree	14.84	146	13.0	145,135
OCCUPATION				
Average household	**10.15**	**100**	**100.0**	**1,119,941**
Self-employed	13.06	129	5.7	63,654
Wage-and-salary workers, total	10.39	102	68.7	769,026
Managers and professionals	13.29	131	31.8	355,720
Technical, sales, and clerical	8.87	87	16.7	187,485
Service workers	8.47	83	7.7	86,623
Construction workers and mechanics	9.03	89	4.1	45,556
Operators, fabricators, laborers	8.89	88	8.6	96,377
Retired	9.42	93	16.3	182,098
HOMEOWNERSHIP STATUS				
Average household	**10.15**	**100**	**100.0**	**1,119,941**
Homeowners	11.89	117	77.5	868,089
Renters	6.75	67	22.5	251,971

Note: Households by type will not sum to the total because not all household types are shown. Hispanics may be of any race and most are white. Total household spending and market shares may not sum to total due to rounding. For an explanation of terms, see the introduction to this report.
Source: Calculations by New Strategist based on the Bureau of Labor Statistics' 2001 Consumer Expenditure Survey

64. SPENDING ON DRIED BEANS, 2001

Total (aggregate) household spending in 2001	$4,360,427,357,940
Total (aggregate) household spending on dried beans	$251,572,920
Average annual household spending on dried beans	$2.28

	AVERAGE ANNUAL SPENDING PER HOUSEHOLD (in dollars)	BEST CUSTOMERS (index)	BIGGEST CUSTOMERS (percent market share)	TOTAL (AGGREGATE) HH SPENDING (in thousands of dollars)
AGE OF HOUSEHOLDER				
Average household	**$2.28**	**100**	**100.0%**	**$251,573**
Under age 25	1.24	54	4.2	10,662
Aged 25 to 34	2.16	95	15.9	39,992
Aged 35 to 44	2.17	95	21.1	52,996
Aged 45 to 54	2.80	123	24.8	62,488
Aged 55 to 64	3.05	134	17.6	44,374
Aged 65 to 74	2.26	99	10.2	25,633
Aged 75 or older	1.41	62	5.9	14,940
HOUSEHOLD INCOME				
Average household reporting income	**2.21**	**100**	**100.0**	**196,104**
Under $10,000	2.30	104	12.8	25,138
$10,000 to $19,999	2.23	101	17.2	33,654
$20,000 to $29,999	2.10	95	12.9	25,358
$30,000 to $39,999	2.40	109	12.9	25,219
$40,000 to $49,999	2.11	96	9.4	18,435
$50,000 to $69,999	2.58	117	16.4	32,198
$70,000 or more	1.93	87	18.6	36,462
HOUSEHOLD TYPE				
Average household	**2.28**	**100**	**100.0**	**251,573**
Married couples	2.69	118	59.7	150,210
Married couples, no children	2.01	88	18.5	46,469
Married couples, with children	2.98	131	33.2	83,604
Oldest child under 6	3.04	133	6.1	15,261
Oldest child 6 to 17	2.27	100	13.7	34,379
Oldest child 18 or older	4.48	197	14.1	35,347
Single parent with child under 18	3.54	155	9.3	23,467
Single person	1.14	50	14.9	37,373
RACE				
Average household	**2.28**	**100**	**100.0**	**251,573**
Black	2.28	100	12.0	30,285
White and other	2.28	100	88.0	221,288
HISPANIC ORIGIN				
Average household	**2.28**	**100**	**100.0**	**251,573**
Hispanic	6.67	293	25.5	64,172
Non-Hispanic	1.84	81	73.7	185,321
REGION				
Average household	**2.28**	**100**	**100.0**	**251,573**
Northeast	2.10	92	17.5	43,974
Midwest	1.53	67	15.7	39,538
South	2.33	102	36.3	91,282
West	3.12	137	30.2	76,066

	AVERAGE ANNUAL SPENDING PER HOUSEHOLD (in dollars)	BEST CUSTOMERS (index)	BIGGEST CUSTOMERS (percent market share)	TOTAL (AGGREGATE) HH SPENDING (in thousands of dollars)
EDUCATION				
Average household	**$2.28**	**100**	**100.0%**	**$251,573**
Less than high school graduate	3.95	173	27.0	67,849
High school graduate	1.75	77	22.2	55,766
Some college	2.12	93	19.4	48,743
Associate's degree	2.01	88	7.8	19,505
College graduate	2.08	91	23.7	59,613
Bachelor's degree	2.42	106	18.2	45,690
Master's, professional, doctoral degree	1.46	64	5.7	14,279
OCCUPATION				
Average household	**2.28**	**100**	**100.0**	**251,573**
Self-employed	2.07	91	4.0	10,089
Wage-and-salary workers, total	2.22	97	65.3	164,316
Managers and professionals	1.96	86	20.9	52,461
Technical, sales, and clerical	2.23	98	18.7	47,136
Service workers	2.16	95	8.8	22,090
Construction workers and mechanics	1.70	75	3.4	8,577
Operators, fabricators, laborers	3.02	133	13.0	32,740
Retired	1.11	49	8.5	21,457
HOMEOWNERSHIP STATUS				
Average household	**2.28**	**100**	**100.0**	**251,573**
Homeowners	2.12	93	61.5	154,781
Renters	2.58	113	38.3	96,309

Note: Households by type will not sum to the total because not all household types are shown. Hispanics may be of any race and most are white. Total household spending and market shares may not sum to total due to rounding. For an explanation of terms, see the introduction to this report.
Source: Calculations by New Strategist based on the Bureau of Labor Statistics' 2001 Consumer Expenditure Survey

65. SPENDING ON DRIED VEGETABLES OTHER THAN BEANS, 2001

Total (aggregate) household spending in 2001	$4,360,427,357,940
Total (aggregate) household spending on dried vegetables other than beans	$836,369,620
Average annual household spending on dried vegetables other than beans	$7.58

	AVERAGE ANNUAL SPENDING PER HOUSEHOLD (in dollars)	BEST CUSTOMERS (index)	BIGGEST CUSTOMERS (percent market share)	TOTAL (AGGREGATE) HH SPENDING (in thousands of dollars)
AGE OF HOUSEHOLDER				
Average household	**$7.58**	**100**	**100.0%**	**$836,370**
Under age 25	4.46	59	4.6	38,347
Aged 25 to 34	6.22	82	13.8	115,163
Aged 35 to 44	7.98	105	23.3	194,888
Aged 45 to 54	9.90	131	26.4	220,938
Aged 55 to 64	8.97	118	15.6	130,505
Aged 65 to 74	6.35	84	8.6	72,022
Aged 75 or older	6.13	81	7.8	64,954
HOUSEHOLD INCOME				
Average household reporting income	**8.24**	**100**	**100.0**	**731,176**
Under $10,000	4.41	54	6.6	48,239
$10,000 to $19,999	7.24	88	15.0	109,412
$20,000 to $29,999	10.65	129	17.6	128,599
$30,000 to $39,999	7.24	88	10.4	76,078
$40,000 to $49,999	7.87	96	9.4	68,760
$50,000 to $69,999	9.67	117	16.5	120,682
$70,000 or more	9.40	114	24.3	177,585
HOUSEHOLD TYPE				
Average household	**7.58**	**100**	**100.0**	**836,370**
Married couples	9.33	123	62.3	520,987
Married couples, no children	7.95	105	22.0	183,796
Married couples, with children	10.31	136	34.6	289,247
Oldest child under 6	7.32	97	4.4	36,746
Oldest child 6 to 17	9.84	130	17.8	149,027
Oldest child 18 or older	13.53	179	12.8	106,752
Single parent with child under 18	7.46	98	5.9	49,452
Single person	4.53	60	17.8	148,507
RACE				
Average household	**7.58**	**100**	**100.0**	**836,370**
Black	5.14	68	8.2	68,275
White and other	7.91	104	91.8	767,713
HISPANIC ORIGIN				
Average household	**7.58**	**100**	**100.0**	**836,370**
Hispanic	8.55	113	9.8	82,260
Non-Hispanic	7.48	99	90.1	753,371
REGION				
Average household	**7.58**	**100**	**100.0**	**836,370**
Northeast	8.64	114	21.6	180,922
Midwest	7.86	104	24.3	203,118
South	6.53	86	30.6	255,826
West	8.05	106	23.5	196,259

	AVERAGE ANNUAL SPENDING PER HOUSEHOLD (in dollars)	BEST CUSTOMERS (index)	BIGGEST CUSTOMERS (percent market share)	TOTAL (AGGREGATE) HH SPENDING (in thousands of dollars)
EDUCATION				
Average household	**$7.58**	**100**	**100.0%**	**$836,370**
Less than high school graduate	7.84	103	16.1	134,668
High school graduate	7.67	101	29.2	244,412
Some college	6.38	84	17.5	146,689
Associate's degree	9.23	122	10.7	89,568
College graduate	7.66	101	26.2	219,536
Bachelor's degree	7.57	100	17.1	142,922
Master's, professional, doctoral degree	7.84	103	9.2	76,675
OCCUPATION				
Average household	**7.58**	**100**	**100.0**	**836,370**
Self-employed	6.11	81	3.6	29,780
Wage-and-salary workers, total	8.29	109	73.4	613,593
Managers and professionals	8.12	107	26.0	217,340
Technical, sales, and clerical	8.10	107	20.5	171,210
Service workers	9.12	120	11.2	93,270
Construction workers and mechanics	10.79	142	6.5	54,436
Operators, fabricators, laborers	7.25	96	9.4	78,597
Retired	6.32	83	14.6	122,172
HOMEOWNERSHIP STATUS				
Average household	**7.58**	**100**	**100.0**	**836,370**
Homeowners	8.41	111	73.4	614,014
Renters	5.95	79	26.6	222,108

Note: Households by type will not sum to the total because not all household types are shown. Hispanics may be of any race and most are white. Total household spending and market shares may not sum to total due to rounding. For an explanation of terms, see the introduction to this report.
Source: Calculations by New Strategist based on the Bureau of Labor Statistics' 2001 Consumer Expenditure Survey

66. SPENDING ON EGGS, 2001

Total (aggregate) household spending in 2001	$4,360,427,357,940		
Total (aggregate) household spending on eggs	$3,860,761,610		
Average annual household spending on eggs	$34.99		

	AVERAGE ANNUAL SPENDING PER HOUSEHOLD (in dollars)	BEST CUSTOMERS (index)	BIGGEST CUSTOMERS (percent market share)	TOTAL (AGGREGATE) HH SPENDING (in thousands of dollars)
AGE OF HOUSEHOLDER				
Average household	**$34.99**	**100**	**100.0%**	**$3,860,762**
Under age 25	25.32	72	5.6	217,701
Aged 25 to 34	32.69	93	15.7	605,255
Aged 35 to 44	39.17	112	24.8	956,610
Aged 45 to 54	40.28	115	23.3	898,929
Aged 55 to 64	36.38	104	13.7	529,293
Aged 65 to 74	31.39	90	9.2	356,025
Aged 75 or older	27.85	80	7.6	295,099
HOUSEHOLD INCOME				
Average household reporting income	**36.77**	**100**	**100.0**	**3,262,786**
Under $10,000	28.07	76	9.4	306,734
$10,000 to $19,999	30.18	82	14.0	456,175
$20,000 to $29,999	36.83	100	13.6	444,722
$30,000 to $39,999	39.06	106	12.6	410,443
$40,000 to $49,999	44.03	120	11.8	384,690
$50,000 to $69,999	38.88	106	14.9	485,222
$70,000 or more	41.00	112	23.7	774,572
HOUSEHOLD TYPE				
Average household	**34.99**	**100**	**100.0**	**3,860,762**
Married couples	42.61	122	61.6	2,379,342
Married couples, no children	34.95	100	20.9	808,009
Married couples, with children	43.83	125	31.8	1,229,651
Oldest child under 6	38.53	110	5.0	193,421
Oldest child 6 to 17	42.04	120	16.5	636,696
Oldest child 18 or older	51.65	148	10.6	407,519
Single parent with child under 18	39.03	112	6.7	258,730
Single person	19.09	55	16.2	625,828
RACE				
Average household	**34.99**	**100**	**100.0**	**3,860,762**
Black	43.40	124	14.9	576,482
White and other	33.86	97	85.1	3,286,316
HISPANIC ORIGIN				
Average household	**34.99**	**100**	**100.0**	**3,860,762**
Hispanic	55.30	158	13.8	532,041
Non-Hispanic	32.96	94	86.0	3,319,665
REGION				
Average household	**34.99**	**100**	**100.0**	**3,860,762**
Northeast	36.78	105	19.9	770,173
Midwest	28.06	80	18.8	725,127
South	34.56	99	35.1	1,353,957
West	41.45	119	26.2	1,010,551

	AVERAGE ANNUAL SPENDING PER HOUSEHOLD (in dollars)	BEST CUSTOMERS (index)	BIGGEST CUSTOMERS (percent market share)	TOTAL (AGGREGATE) HH SPENDING (in thousands of dollars)
EDUCATION				
Average household	**$34.99**	**100**	**100.0%**	**$3,860,762**
Less than high school graduate	42.51	122	18.9	730,194
High school graduate	35.47	101	29.3	1,130,287
Some college	33.15	95	19.7	762,185
Associate's degree	30.11	86	7.6	292,187
College graduate	33.14	95	24.6	949,792
Bachelor's degree	31.52	90	15.4	595,098
Master's, professional, doctoral degree	36.09	103	9.1	352,960
OCCUPATION				
Average household	**34.99**	**100**	**100.0**	**3,860,762**
Self-employed	38.65	111	4.9	188,380
Wage-and-salary workers, total	35.76	102	68.6	2,646,812
Managers and professionals	34.14	98	23.7	913,791
Technical, sales, and clerical	34.88	100	19.1	737,259
Service workers	37.29	107	9.9	381,365
Construction workers and mechanics	42.68	122	5.6	215,321
Operators, fabricators, laborers	36.50	104	10.2	395,697
Retired	28.69	82	14.4	554,606
HOMEOWNERSHIP STATUS				
Average household	**34.99**	**100**	**100.0**	**3,860,762**
Homeowners	36.56	105	69.1	2,669,246
Renters	31.93	91	30.9	1,191,915

Note: Households by type will not sum to the total because not all household types are shown. Hispanics may be of any race and most are white. Total household spending and market shares may not sum to total due to rounding. For an explanation of terms, see the introduction to this report.
Source: Calculations by New Strategist based on the Bureau of Labor Statistics' 2001 Consumer Expenditure Survey

67. SPENDING ON FATS AND OILS, 2001

Total (aggregate) household spending in 2001	$4,360,427,357,940	
Total (aggregate) household spending on fats and oils	$2,706,615,670	
Average annual household spending on fats and oils	$24.53	

	AVERAGE ANNUAL SPENDING PER HOUSEHOLD (in dollars)	BEST CUSTOMERS (index)	BIGGEST CUSTOMERS (percent market share)	TOTAL (AGGREGATE) HH SPENDING (in thousands of dollars)
AGE OF HOUSEHOLDER				
Average household	**$24.53**	**100**	**100.0%**	**$2,706,616**
Under age 25	15.74	64	5.0	135,333
Aged 25 to 34	25.05	102	17.1	463,801
Aged 35 to 44	26.82	109	24.2	654,998
Aged 45 to 54	30.02	122	24.8	669,956
Aged 55 to 64	24.52	100	13.2	356,742
Aged 65 to 74	21.08	86	8.8	239,089
Aged 75 or older	17.42	71	6.8	184,582
HOUSEHOLD INCOME				
Average household reporting income	**24.79**	**100**	**100.0**	**2,199,741**
Under $10,000	22.56	91	11.2	246,521
$10,000 to $19,999	19.89	80	13.7	300,600
$20,000 to $29,999	23.65	95	13.0	285,574
$30,000 to $39,999	26.77	108	12.8	281,299
$40,000 to $49,999	24.38	98	9.7	213,008
$50,000 to $69,999	28.18	114	16.0	351,686
$70,000 or more	27.53	111	23.6	520,097
HOUSEHOLD TYPE				
Average household	**24.53**	**100**	**100.0**	**2,706,616**
Married couples	30.24	123	62.4	1,688,602
Married couples, no children	23.81	97	20.3	550,463
Married couples, with children	31.70	129	32.9	889,344
Oldest child under 6	23.78	97	4.4	119,376
Oldest child 6 to 17	31.25	127	17.5	473,281
Oldest child 18 or older	38.55	157	11.2	304,160
Single parent with child under 18	26.44	108	6.5	175,271
Single person	11.84	48	14.3	388,151
RACE				
Average household	**24.53**	**100**	**100.0**	**2,706,616**
Black	29.92	122	14.7	397,427
White and other	23.80	97	85.3	2,309,933
HISPANIC ORIGIN				
Average household	**24.53**	**100**	**100.0**	**2,706,616**
Hispanic	42.28	172	15.0	406,776
Non-Hispanic	22.76	93	84.7	2,292,342
REGION				
Average household	**24.53**	**100**	**100.0**	**2,706,616**
Northeast	28.54	116	22.1	597,628
Midwest	17.18	70	16.4	443,966
South	27.00	110	39.1	1,057,779
West	24.86	101	22.4	606,087

	AVERAGE ANNUAL SPENDING PER HOUSEHOLD (in dollars)	BEST CUSTOMERS (index)	BIGGEST CUSTOMERS (percent market share)	TOTAL (AGGREGATE) HH SPENDING (in thousands of dollars)
EDUCATION				
Average household	**$24.53**	**100**	**100.0%**	**$2,706,616**
Less than high school graduate	31.30	128	19.9	537,640
High school graduate	23.71	97	27.9	755,543
Some college	20.70	84	17.6	475,934
Associate's degree	20.93	85	7.5	203,105
College graduate	25.60	104	27.1	733,696
Bachelor's degree	23.89	97	16.7	451,043
Master's, professional, doctoral degree	28.72	117	10.4	280,882
OCCUPATION				
Average household	**24.53**	**100**	**100.0**	**2,706,616**
Self-employed	27.55	112	5.0	134,279
Wage-and-salary workers, total	25.20	103	68.9	1,865,203
Managers and professionals	24.44	100	24.2	654,161
Technical, sales, and clerical	22.19	91	17.3	469,030
Service workers	26.12	107	9.9	267,129
Construction workers and mechanics	30.59	125	5.7	154,327
Operators, fabricators, laborers	28.68	117	11.5	310,920
Retired	19.08	78	13.6	368,836
HOMEOWNERSHIP STATUS				
Average household	**24.53**	**100**	**100.0**	**2,706,616**
Homeowners	24.58	100	66.3	1,794,586
Renters	24.43	100	33.7	911,948

Note: Households by type will not sum to the total because not all household types are shown. Hispanics may be of any race and most are white. Total household spending and market shares may not sum to total due to rounding. For an explanation of terms, see the introduction to this report.
Source: Calculations by New Strategist based on the Bureau of Labor Statistics' 2001 Consumer Expenditure Survey

68. SPENDING ON FISH AND SEAFOOD, CANNED, 2001

Total (aggregate) household spending in 2001	$4,360,427,357,940
Total (aggregate) household spending on fish and seafood, canned	$1,667,222,290
Average annual household spending on fish and seafood, canned	$15.11

	AVERAGE ANNUAL SPENDING PER HOUSEHOLD (in dollars)	BEST CUSTOMERS (index)	BIGGEST CUSTOMERS (percent market share)	TOTAL (AGGREGATE) HH SPENDING (in thousands of dollars)
AGE OF HOUSEHOLDER				
Average household	**$15.11**	**100**	**100.0%**	**$1,667,222**
Under age 25	8.70	58	4.5	74,803
Aged 25 to 34	15.54	103	17.3	287,723
Aged 35 to 44	16.81	111	24.6	410,534
Aged 45 to 54	16.29	108	21.8	363,544
Aged 55 to 64	16.31	108	14.2	237,294
Aged 65 to 74	13.54	90	9.2	153,571
Aged 75 or older	13.11	87	8.3	138,914
HOUSEHOLD INCOME				
Average household reporting income	**15.70**	**100**	**100.0**	**1,393,140**
Under $10,000	10.15	65	8.0	110,980
$10,000 to $19,999	10.09	64	10.9	152,472
$20,000 to $29,999	15.83	101	13.7	191,147
$30,000 to $39,999	14.62	93	11.0	153,627
$40,000 to $49,999	18.47	118	11.6	161,372
$50,000 to $69,999	16.05	102	14.4	200,304
$70,000 or more	22.68	145	30.8	428,471
HOUSEHOLD TYPE				
Average household	**15.11**	**100**	**100.0**	**1,667,222**
Married couples	17.94	119	60.1	1,001,770
Married couples, no children	14.96	99	20.7	345,860
Married couples, with children	19.59	130	33.0	549,597
Oldest child under 6	14.85	98	4.5	74,547
Oldest child 6 to 17	18.99	126	17.3	287,604
Oldest child 18 or older	24.44	162	11.6	192,832
Single parent with child under 18	14.76	98	5.9	97,844
Single person	9.77	65	19.2	320,290
RACE				
Average household	**15.11**	**100**	**100.0**	**1,667,222**
Black	14.60	97	11.6	193,932
White and other	15.18	101	88.4	1,473,310
HISPANIC ORIGIN				
Average household	**15.11**	**100**	**100.0**	**1,667,222**
Hispanic	17.04	113	9.8	163,942
Non-Hispanic	14.92	99	90.1	1,502,713
REGION				
Average household	**15.11**	**100**	**100.0**	**1,667,222**
Northeast	19.15	127	24.1	401,001
Midwest	11.62	77	18.0	300,284
South	14.92	99	35.1	584,521
West	15.61	103	22.8	380,572

	AVERAGE ANNUAL SPENDING PER HOUSEHOLD (in dollars)	BEST CUSTOMERS (index)	BIGGEST CUSTOMERS (percent market share)	TOTAL (AGGREGATE) HH SPENDING (in thousands of dollars)
EDUCATION				
Average household	**$15.11**	**100**	**100.0%**	**$1,667,222**
Less than high school graduate	12.79	85	13.2	219,694
High school graduate	14.56	96	27.8	463,969
Some college	14.55	96	20.1	334,534
Associate's degree	12.44	82	7.2	120,718
College graduate	18.42	122	31.7	527,917
Bachelor's degree	16.49	109	18.7	311,331
Master's, professional, doctoral degree	21.94	145	12.9	214,573
OCCUPATION				
Average household	**15.11**	**100**	**100.0**	**1,667,222**
Self-employed	15.12	100	4.4	73,695
Wage-and-salary workers, total	15.85	105	70.4	1,173,154
Managers and professionals	17.38	115	27.9	465,193
Technical, sales, and clerical	17.14	113	21.7	362,288
Service workers	13.17	87	8.1	134,690
Construction workers and mechanics	13.40	89	4.1	67,603
Operators, fabricators, laborers	13.82	92	9.0	149,823
Retired	13.13	87	15.2	253,816
HOMEOWNERSHIP STATUS				
Average household	**15.11**	**100**	**100.0**	**1,667,222**
Homeowners	16.46	109	72.1	1,201,745
Renters	12.48	83	27.9	465,866

Note: Households by type will not sum to the total because not all household types are shown. Hispanics may be of any race and most are white. Total household spending and market shares may not sum to total due to rounding. For an explanation of terms, see the introduction to this report.
Source: Calculations by New Strategist based on the Bureau of Labor Statistics' 2001 Consumer Expenditure Survey

69. SPENDING ON FISH AND SHELLFISH, FRESH, 2001

Total (aggregate) household spending in 2001	$4,360,427,357,940
Total (aggregate) household spending on fish and shellfish, fresh	$6,959,080,730
Average annual household spending on fish and shellfish, fresh	$63.07

	AVERAGE ANNUAL SPENDING PER HOUSEHOLD (in dollars)	BEST CUSTOMERS (index)	BIGGEST CUSTOMERS (percent market share)	TOTAL (AGGREGATE) HH SPENDING (in thousands of dollars)
AGE OF HOUSEHOLDER				
Average household	**$63.07**	**100**	**100.0%**	**$6,959,081**
Under age 25	32.34	51	4.0	278,059
Aged 25 to 34	57.37	91	15.3	1,062,206
Aged 35 to 44	73.79	117	25.9	1,802,099
Aged 45 to 54	74.62	118	23.9	1,665,295
Aged 55 to 64	75.07	119	15.7	1,092,193
Aged 65 to 74	50.93	81	8.3	577,648
Aged 75 or older	45.06	71	6.9	477,456
HOUSEHOLD INCOME				
Average household reporting income	**60.37**	**100**	**100.0**	**5,356,932**
Under $10,000	40.77	68	8.3	445,564
$10,000 to $19,999	39.91	66	11.3	603,230
$20,000 to $29,999	51.78	86	11.7	625,244
$30,000 to $39,999	62.28	103	12.2	654,438
$40,000 to $49,999	71.38	118	11.6	623,647
$50,000 to $69,999	58.43	97	13.6	729,206
$70,000 or more	90.19	149	31.8	1,703,870
HOUSEHOLD TYPE				
Average household	**63.07**	**100**	**100.0**	**6,959,081**
Married couples	77.81	123	62.4	4,344,910
Married couples, no children	66.74	106	22.2	1,542,962
Married couples, with children	78.14	124	31.5	2,192,218
Oldest child under 6	65.47	104	4.7	328,659
Oldest child 6 to 17	69.42	110	15.1	1,051,366
Oldest child 18 or older	106.52	169	12.1	840,443
Single parent with child under 18	65.14	103	6.2	431,813
Single person	33.42	53	15.7	1,095,608
RACE				
Average household	**63.07**	**100**	**100.0**	**6,959,081**
Black	77.38	123	14.8	1,027,839
White and other	61.14	97	85.3	5,934,004
HISPANIC ORIGIN				
Average household	**63.07**	**100**	**100.0**	**6,959,081**
Hispanic	102.40	162	14.2	985,190
Non-Hispanic	59.15	94	85.6	5,957,470
REGION				
Average household	**63.07**	**100**	**100.0**	**6,959,081**
Northeast	88.89	141	26.7	1,861,357
Midwest	40.15	64	14.9	1,037,556
South	57.72	92	32.5	2,261,296
West	73.53	117	25.8	1,792,661

	AVERAGE ANNUAL SPENDING PER HOUSEHOLD (in dollars)	BEST CUSTOMERS (index)	BIGGEST CUSTOMERS (percent market share)	TOTAL (AGGREGATE) HH SPENDING (in thousands of dollars)
EDUCATION				
Average household	**$63.07**	**100**	**100.0%**	**$6,959,081**
Less than high school graduate	60.69	96	15.0	1,042,472
High school graduate	53.32	85	24.4	1,699,095
Some college	55.37	88	18.3	1,273,067
Associate's degree	53.10	84	7.4	515,282
College graduate	84.44	134	34.8	2,420,050
Bachelor's degree	76.46	121	20.7	1,443,565
Master's, professional, doctoral degree	98.96	157	13.9	967,829
OCCUPATION				
Average household	**63.07**	**100**	**100.0**	**6,959,081**
Self-employed	86.13	137	6.0	419,798
Wage-and-salary workers, total	65.47	104	69.6	4,845,828
Managers and professionals	71.65	114	27.6	1,917,784
Technical, sales, and clerical	58.86	93	17.9	1,244,124
Service workers	67.55	107	9.9	690,834
Construction workers and mechanics	65.60	104	4.8	330,952
Operators, fabricators, laborers	61.20	97	9.5	663,469
Retired	51.28	81	14.2	991,294
HOMEOWNERSHIP STATUS				
Average household	**63.07**	**100**	**100.0**	**6,959,081**
Homeowners	35.32	56	37.1	2,578,713
Renters	58.67	93	31.5	2,190,092

Note: Households by type will not sum to the total because not all household types are shown. Hispanics may be of any race and most are white. Total household spending and market shares may not sum to total due to rounding. For an explanation of terms, see the introduction to this report.
Source: Calculations by New Strategist based on the Bureau of Labor Statistics' 2001 Consumer Expenditure Survey

70. SPENDING ON FISH AND SHELLFISH, FROZEN, 2001

Total (aggregate) household spending in 2001		$4,360,427,357,940
Total (aggregate) household spending on fish and shellfish, frozen		$3,915,931,110
Average annual household spending on fish and shellfish, frozen		$35.49

	AVERAGE ANNUAL SPENDING PER HOUSEHOLD (in dollars)	BEST CUSTOMERS (index)	BIGGEST CUSTOMERS (percent market share)	TOTAL (AGGREGATE) HH SPENDING (in thousands of dollars)
AGE OF HOUSEHOLDER				
Average household	**$35.49**	**100**	**100.0%**	**$3,915,931**
Under age 25	18.06	51	4.0	155,280
Aged 25 to 34	33.68	95	15.9	623,585
Aged 35 to 44	40.66	115	25.4	992,999
Aged 45 to 54	42.62	120	24.3	951,151
Aged 55 to 64	42.65	120	15.8	620,515
Aged 65 to 74	32.19	91	9.3	365,099
Aged 75 or older	19.27	54	5.2	204,185
HOUSEHOLD INCOME				
Average household reporting income	**37.74**	**100**	**100.0**	**3,348,859**
Under $10,000	22.05	58	7.2	241,004
$10,000 to $19,999	28.67	76	12.9	433,300
$20,000 to $29,999	32.25	86	11.6	389,419
$30,000 to $39,999	37.13	98	11.7	390,162
$40,000 to $49,999	44.78	119	11.7	391,243
$50,000 to $69,999	41.99	111	15.6	524,035
$70,000 or more	52.40	139	29.6	989,941
HOUSEHOLD TYPE				
Average household	**35.49**	**100**	**100.0**	**3,915,931**
Married couples	45.98	130	65.6	2,567,523
Married couples, no children	41.53	117	24.5	960,132
Married couples, with children	45.20	127	32.4	1,268,086
Oldest child under 6	32.92	93	4.2	165,258
Oldest child 6 to 17	46.59	131	18.0	705,606
Oldest child 18 or older	51.26	144	10.3	404,441
Single parent with child under 18	40.98	116	6.9	271,656
Single person	15.24	43	12.8	499,613
RACE				
Average household	**35.49**	**100**	**100.0**	**3,915,931**
Black	40.40	114	13.7	536,633
White and other	34.82	98	86.3	3,379,490
HISPANIC ORIGIN				
Average household	**35.49**	**100**	**100.0**	**3,915,931**
Hispanic	44.63	126	11.0	429,385
Non-Hispanic	34.58	97	88.9	3,482,828
REGION				
Average household	**35.49**	**100**	**100.0**	**3,915,931**
Northeast	45.75	129	24.5	958,005
Midwest	30.93	87	20.4	799,293
South	33.77	95	33.8	1,323,007
West	34.17	96	21.3	833,065

	AVERAGE ANNUAL SPENDING PER HOUSEHOLD (in dollars)	BEST CUSTOMERS (index)	BIGGEST CUSTOMERS (percent market share)	TOTAL (AGGREGATE) HH SPENDING (in thousands of dollars)
EDUCATION				
Average household	**$35.49**	**100**	**100.0%**	**$3,915,931**
Less than high school graduate	27.97	79	12.3	480,441
High school graduate	39.54	111	32.2	1,259,982
Some college	30.26	85	17.8	695,738
Associate's degree	34.02	96	8.4	330,130
College graduate	39.82	112	29.1	1,141,241
Bachelor's degree	30.43	86	14.7	574,518
Master's, professional, doctoral degree	56.91	160	14.2	556,580
OCCUPATION				
Average household	**35.49**	**100**	**100.0**	**3,915,931**
Self-employed	52.34	148	6.5	255,105
Wage-and-salary workers, total	36.78	104	69.5	2,722,309
Managers and professionals	39.73	112	27.2	1,063,413
Technical, sales, and clerical	36.34	102	19.6	768,119
Service workers	32.33	91	8.4	330,639
Construction workers and mechanics	47.73	135	6.1	240,798
Operators, fabricators, laborers	30.61	86	8.5	331,843
Retired	28.29	80	14.0	546,874
HOMEOWNERSHIP STATUS				
Average household	**35.49**	**100**	**100.0**	**3,915,931**
Homeowners	38.23	108	71.3	2,791,172
Renters	30.11	85	28.7	1,123,976

Note: Households by type will not sum to the total because not all household types are shown. Hispanics may be of any race and most are white. Total household spending and market shares may not sum to total due to rounding. For an explanation of terms, see the introduction to this report.
Source: Calculations by New Strategist based on the Bureau of Labor Statistics' 2001 Consumer Expenditure Survey

71. SPENDING ON FLOUR, 2001

Total (aggregate) household spending in 2001	$4,360,427,357,940
Total (aggregate) household spending on flour	$883,815,390
Average annual household spending on flour	$8.01

	AVERAGE ANNUAL SPENDING PER HOUSEHOLD (in dollars)	BEST CUSTOMERS (index)	BIGGEST CUSTOMERS (percent market share)	TOTAL (AGGREGATE) HH SPENDING (in thousands of dollars)
AGE OF HOUSEHOLDER				
Average household	**$8.01**	**100**	**100.0%**	**$883,815**
Under age 25	7.31	91	7.1	62,851
Aged 25 to 34	7.37	92	15.4	136,456
Aged 35 to 44	9.05	113	2.5	221,019
Aged 45 to 54	8.78	110	22.2	195,943
Aged 55 to 64	7.94	99	13.1	115,519
Aged 65 to 74	6.69	84	8.6	75,878
Aged 75 or older	7.10	89	8.5	75,232
HOUSEHOLD INCOME				
Average household reporting income	**8.28**	**100**	**100.0**	**734,726**
Under $10,000	8.96	108	13.3	97,940
$10,000 to $19,999	7.19	87	14.8	108,634
$20,000 to $29,999	8.61	104	14.2	103,966
$30,000 to $39,999	7.20	87	10.3	75,658
$40,000 to $49,999	8.51	103	10.1	74,352
$50,000 to $69,999	6.97	84	11.8	86,986
$70,000 or more	9.75	118	25.1	184,197
HOUSEHOLD TYPE				
Average household	**8.01**	**100**	**100.0**	**883,815**
Married couples	10.16	127	64.2	567,334
Married couples, no children	7.19	90	18.8	166,226
Married couples, with children	11.21	140	35.6	314,497
Oldest child under 6	11.24	140	6.4	56,425
Oldest child 6 to 17	10.18	127	17.4	154,176
Oldest child 18 or older	13.41	167	12.0	105,805
Single parent with child under 18	9.25	116	6.9	61,318
Single person	3.40	42	12.6	111,462
RACE				
Average household	**8.01**	**100**	**100.0**	**883,815**
Black	9.56	119	14.4	126,986
White and other	7.80	97	85.7	757,037
HISPANIC ORIGIN				
Average household	**8.01**	**100**	**100.0**	**883,815**
Hispanic	14.68	183	16.0	141,236
Non-Hispanic	7.34	92	83.6	739,270
REGION				
Average household	**8.01**	**100**	**100.0**	**883,815**
Northeast	8.13	102	19.3	170,242
Midwest	6.15	77	18.0	158,928
South	8.93	112	39.6	349,851
West	8.36	104	23.1	203,817

	AVERAGE ANNUAL SPENDING PER HOUSEHOLD (in dollars)	BEST CUSTOMERS (index)	BIGGEST CUSTOMERS (percent market share)	TOTAL (AGGREGATE) HH SPENDING (in thousands of dollars)
EDUCATION				
Average household	**$8.01**	**100**	**100.0%**	**$883,815**
Less than high school graduate	11.79	147	22.9	202,517
High school graduate	7.01	88	25.3	223,381
Some college	6.46	81	16.8	148,528
Associate's degree	7.48	93	8.2	72,586
College graduate	8.24	103	26.7	236,158
Bachelor's degree	7.97	100	17.0	150,474
Master's, professional, doctoral degree	8.73	109	9.7	85,379
OCCUPATION				
Average household	**8.01**	**100**	**100.0**	**883,815**
Self-employed	8.24	103	4.5	40,162
Wage-and-salary workers, total	7.81	98	65.4	578,065
Managers and professionals	7.89	99	23.9	211,184
Technical, sales, and clerical	6.61	83	15.8	139,716
Service workers	7.46	93	8.6	76,293
Construction workers and mechanics	10.09	126	5.8	50,904
Operators, fabricators, laborers	9.00	112	11.0	97,569
Retired	6.57	82	14.4	127,005
HOMEOWNERSHIP STATUS				
Average household	**8.01**	**100**	**100.0**	**883,815**
Homeowners	8.41	105	69.5	614,014
Renters	7.21	90	30.5	269,142

Note: Households by type will not sum to the total because not all household types are shown. Hispanics may be of any race and most are white. Total household spending and market shares may not sum to total due to rounding. For an explanation of terms, see the introduction to this report.
Source: Calculations by New Strategist based on the Bureau of Labor Statistics' 2001 Consumer Expenditure Survey

72. SPENDING ON PREPARED FLOUR MIXES, 2001

Total (aggregate) household spending in 2001	$4,360,427,357,940
Total (aggregate) household spending on prepared flour mixes	$1,422,269,710
Average annual household spending on prepared flour mixes	$12.89

	AVERAGE ANNUAL SPENDING PER HOUSEHOLD (in dollars)	BEST CUSTOMERS (index)	BIGGEST CUSTOMERS (percent market share)	TOTAL (AGGREGATE) HH SPENDING (in thousands of dollars)
AGE OF HOUSEHOLDER				
Average household	**$12.89**	**100**	**100.0%**	**$1,422,270**
Under age 25	6.91	54	4.2	59,412
Aged 25 to 34	12.11	94	15.8	224,217
Aged 35 to 44	15.47	120	26.6	377,808
Aged 45 to 54	15.52	120	24.4	346,360
Aged 55 to 64	12.90	100	13.2	187,682
Aged 65 to 74	10.42	81	8.3	118,184
Aged 75 or older	10.18	79	7.6	107,867
HOUSEHOLD INCOME				
Average household reporting income	**13.99**	**100**	**100.0**	**1,241,403**
Under $10,000	8.83	63	7.8	96,460
$10,000 to $19,999	10.13	72	12.3	153,154
$20,000 to $29,999	11.47	82	11.2	138,500
$30,000 to $39,999	13.61	97	11.5	143,014
$40,000 to $49,999	18.58	133	13.1	162,334
$50,000 to $69,999	15.54	111	15.6	193,939
$70,000 or more	18.89	135	28.7	356,870
HOUSEHOLD TYPE				
Average household	**12.89**	**100**	**100.0**	**1,422,270**
Married couples	16.69	130	65.5	931,970
Married couples, no children	12.70	99	20.6	293,611
Married couples, with children	19.90	154	39.3	558,295
Oldest child under 6	16.70	130	5.9	83,834
Oldest child 6 to 17	21.00	163	22.4	318,045
Oldest child 18 or older	19.87	154	11.0	156,774
Single parent with child under 18	15.97	124	7.4	105,865
Single person	5.83	45	13.4	191,125
RACE				
Average household	**12.89**	**100**	**100.0**	**1,422,270**
Black	12.05	94	11.3	160,060
White and other	13.01	101	88.8	1,262,699
HISPANIC ORIGIN				
Average household	**12.89**	**100**	**100.0**	**1,422,270**
Hispanic	12.17	94	8.2	117,088
Non-Hispanic	12.97	101	91.8	1,306,313
REGION				
Average household	**12.89**	**100**	**100.0**	**1,422,270**
Northeast	12.57	98	18.5	263,216
Midwest	13.81	107	25.1	356,878
South	12.74	99	35.1	499,115
West	12.44	97	21.3	303,287

	AVERAGE ANNUAL SPENDING PER HOUSEHOLD (in dollars)	BEST CUSTOMERS (index)	BIGGEST CUSTOMERS (percent market share)	TOTAL (AGGREGATE) HH SPENDING (in thousands of dollars)
EDUCATION				
Average household	**$12.89**	**100**	**100.0%**	**$1,422,270**
Less than high school graduate	11.86	92	14.3	203,719
High school graduate	12.13	94	27.2	386,535
Some college	12.41	96	20.1	285,331
Associate's degree	13.14	102	9.0	127,511
College graduate	14.61	113	29.4	418,723
Bachelor's degree	14.28	111	19.0	269,606
Master's, professional, doctoral degree	15.22	118	10.5	148,852
OCCUPATION				
Average household	**12.89**	**100**	**100.0**	**1,422,270**
Self-employed	13.18	102	4.5	64,239
Wage-and-salary workers, total	13.54	105	70.5	1,002,177
Managers and professionals	14.33	111	27.0	383,557
Technical, sales, and clerical	12.72	99	18.9	268,863
Service workers	10.24	79	7.4	104,725
Construction workers and mechanics	15.89	123	5.6	80,165
Operators, fabricators, laborers	15.07	117	11.5	163,374
Retired	10.88	84	14.8	210,321
HOMEOWNERSHIP STATUS				
Average household	**12.89**	**100**	**100.0**	**1,422,270**
Homeowners	14.45	112	74.2	1,054,995
Renters	9.85	76	25.9	367,691

Note: Households by type will not sum to the total because not all household types are shown. Hispanics may be of any race and most are white. Total household spending and market shares may not sum to total due to rounding. For an explanation of terms, see the introduction to this report.
Source: Calculations by New Strategist based on the Bureau of Labor Statistics' 2001 Consumer Expenditure Survey

73. SPENDING ON FRESH APPLES, 2001

Total (aggregate) household spending in 2001	$4,360,427,357,940	
Total (aggregate) household spending on fresh apples	$3,401,751,370	
Average annual household spending on fresh apples	$30.83	

	AVERAGE ANNUAL SPENDING PER HOUSEHOLD (in dollars)	BEST CUSTOMERS (index)	BIGGEST CUSTOMERS (percent market share)	TOTAL (AGGREGATE) HH SPENDING (in thousands of dollars)
AGE OF HOUSEHOLDER				
Average household	**$30.83**	**100**	**100.0%**	**$3,401,751**
Under age 25	17.76	58	4.5	152,701
Aged 25 to 34	30.11	98	16.4	557,487
Aged 35 to 44	35.88	116	25.8	876,261
Aged 45 to 54	38.64	125	25.3	862,329
Aged 55 to 64	29.81	97	12.7	433,706
Aged 65 to 74	24.43	79	8.1	277,085
Aged 75 or older	22.51	73	7.0	238,516
HOUSEHOLD INCOME				
Average household reporting income	**32.11**	**100**	**100.0**	**2,849,281**
Under $10,000	20.19	63	7.7	220,644
$10,000 to $19,999	23.07	72	12.2	348,720
$20,000 to $29,999	29.20	91	12.4	352,590
$30,000 to $39,999	30.83	96	11.4	323,962
$40,000 to $49,999	32.09	100	9.8	280,370
$50,000 to $69,999	36.02	112	15.8	449,530
$70,000 or more	46.93	146	31.1	886,602
HOUSEHOLD TYPE				
Average household	**30.83**	**100**	**100.0**	**3,401,751**
Married couples	39.82	129	65.4	2,223,549
Married couples, no children	32.51	105	22.1	751,599
Married couples, with children	44.63	145	36.8	1,252,095
Oldest child under 6	39.04	127	5.8	195,981
Oldest child 6 to 17	46.04	149	20.5	697,276
Oldest child 18 or older	45.72	148	10.6	360,731
Single parent with child under 18	30.94	100	6.0	205,101
Single person	15.05	49	14.5	493,384
RACE				
Average household	**30.83**	**100**	**100.0**	**3,401,751**
Black	24.69	80	9.6	327,957
White and other	31.66	103	90.3	3,072,793
HISPANIC ORIGIN				
Average household	**30.83**	**100**	**100.0**	**3,401,751**
Hispanic	35.70	116	10.1	343,470
Non-Hispanic	30.34	98	89.8	3,055,784
REGION				
Average household	**30.83**	**100**	**100.0**	**3,401,751**
Northeast	35.54	115	21.9	744,208
Midwest	29.35	95	22.3	758,463
South	27.94	91	32.2	1,094,605
West	32.95	107	23.6	803,321

	AVERAGE ANNUAL SPENDING PER HOUSEHOLD (in dollars)	BEST CUSTOMERS (index)	BIGGEST CUSTOMERS (percent market share)	TOTAL (AGGREGATE) HH SPENDING (in thousands of dollars)
EDUCATION				
Average household	**$30.83**	**100**	**100.0%**	**$3,401,751**
Less than high school graduate	27.98	91	14.1	480,613
High school graduate	27.30	89	25.6	869,942
Some college	26.98	88	18.2	620,324
Associate's degree	31.05	101	8.9	301,309
College graduate	39.19	127	33.0	1,123,185
Bachelor's degree	35.50	115	19.7	670,240
Master's, professional, doctoral degree	45.91	149	13.2	449,000
OCCUPATION				
Average household	**30.83**	**100**	**100.0**	**3,401,751**
Self-employed	29.83	97	4.3	145,391
Wage-and-salary workers, total	32.63	106	71.0	2,415,142
Managers and professionals	39.33	128	30.9	1,052,707
Technical, sales, and clerical	28.99	94	18.0	612,762
Service workers	28.05	91	8.4	286,867
Construction workers and mechanics	36.08	117	5.4	182,024
Operators, fabricators, laborers	26.81	87	8.5	290,647
Retired	22.55	73	12.8	435,914
HOMEOWNERSHIP STATUS				
Average household	**30.83**	**100**	**100.0**	**3,401,751**
Homeowners	33.71	109	72.3	2,461,167
Renters	25.19	82	27.6	940,318

Note: Households by type will not sum to the total because not all household types are shown. Hispanics may be of any race and most are white. Total household spending and market shares may not sum to total due to rounding. For an explanation of terms, see the introduction to this report.
Source: Calculations by New Strategist based on the Bureau of Labor Statistics' 2001 Consumer Expenditure Survey

74. SPENDING ON FRESH BANANAS, 2001

Total (aggregate) household spending in 2001	$4,360,427,357,940
Total (aggregate) household spending on fresh bananas	$3,453,610,700
Average annual household spending on fresh bananas	$31.30

	AVERAGE ANNUAL SPENDING PER HOUSEHOLD (in dollars)	BEST CUSTOMERS (index)	BIGGEST CUSTOMERS (percent market share)	TOTAL (AGGREGATE) HH SPENDING (in thousands of dollars)
AGE OF HOUSEHOLDER				
Average household	**$31.30**	**100**	**100.0%**	**$3,453,611**
Under age 25	17.59	56	4.4	151,239
Aged 25 to 34	27.26	87	14.6	504,719
Aged 35 to 44	33.57	107	23.7	819,847
Aged 45 to 54	34.94	112	22.6	779,756
Aged 55 to 64	34.10	109	14.4	496,121
Aged 65 to 74	34.83	111	11.4	395,042
Aged 75 or older	29.17	93	8.9	309,085
HOUSEHOLD INCOME				
Average household reporting income	**33.08**	**100**	**100.0**	**2,935,354**
Under $10,000	23.81	72	8.9	260,205
$10,000 to $19,999	28.44	86	14.6	429,829
$20,000 to $29,999	34.17	103	14.1	412,603
$30,000 to $39,999	30.78	93	11.0	323,436
$40,000 to $49,999	35.07	106	10.4	306,407
$50,000 to $69,999	34.94	106	14.9	436,051
$70,000 or more	40.74	123	26.2	769,660
HOUSEHOLD TYPE				
Average household	**31.30**	**100**	**100.0**	**3,453,611**
Married couples	38.20	122	61.8	2,133,088
Married couples, no children	33.26	106	22.3	768,938
Married couples, with children	40.63	130	3.3	1,139,875
Oldest child under 6	38.53	123	5.6	193,421
Oldest child 6 to 17	38.68	124	17.0	585,809
Oldest child 18 or older	46.43	148	10.6	366,333
Single parent with child under 18	28.58	91	5.5	189,457
Single person	18.89	60	17.9	619,271
RACE				
Average household	**31.30**	**100**	**100.0**	**3,453,611**
Black	28.07	90	10.8	372,854
White and other	31.74	101	89.2	3,080,557
HISPANIC ORIGIN				
Average household	**31.30**	**100**	**100.0**	**3,453,611**
Hispanic	50.59	162	14.1	486,726
Non-Hispanic	29.38	94	85.7	2,959,095
REGION				
Average household	**31.30**	**100**	**100.0**	**3,453,611**
Northeast	35.28	113	21.4	738,763
Midwest	27.41	88	20.5	708,329
South	28.70	92	32.6	1,124,380
West	36.15	116	25.5	881,337

	AVERAGE ANNUAL SPENDING PER HOUSEHOLD (in dollars)	BEST CUSTOMERS (index)	BIGGEST CUSTOMERS (percent market share)	TOTAL (AGGREGATE) HH SPENDING (in thousands of dollars)
EDUCATION				
Average household	**$31.30**	**100**	**100.0%**	**$3,453,611**
Less than high school graduate	33.49	107	16.7	575,258
High school graduate	28.60	91	26.4	911,368
Some college	26.59	85	17.7	611,357
Associate's degree	28.50	91	0.8	276,564
College graduate	37.50	120	31.1	1,074,750
Bachelor's degree	36.35	116	19.9	686,288
Master's, professional, doctoral degree	39.59	127	11.2	387,190
OCCUPATION				
Average household	**31.30**	**100**	**100.0**	**3,453,611**
Self-employed	35.84	115	5.1	174,684
Wage-and-salary workers, total	31.08	99	66.6	2,300,417
Managers and professionals	33.61	107	26.1	899,605
Technical, sales, and clerical	26.70	85	16.3	564,358
Service workers	32.78	105	9.7	335,241
Construction workers and mechanics	37.62	120	5.5	189,793
Operators, fabricators, laborers	28.68	92	0.9	310,920
Retired	30.49	97	17.1	589,402
HOMEOWNERSHIP STATUS				
Average household	**31.30**	**100**	**100.0**	**3,453,611**
Homeowners	33.53	107	70.9	2,448,025
Renters	26.93	86	29.1	1,005,270

Note: Households by type will not sum to the total because not all household types are shown. Hispanics may be of any race and most are white. Total household spending and market shares may not sum to total due to rounding. For an explanation of terms, see the introduction to this report.
Source: Calculations by New Strategist based on the Bureau of Labor Statistics' 2001 Consumer Expenditure Survey

75. SPENDING ON FRESH CITRUS FRUIT OTHER THAN ORANGES, 2001

Total (aggregate) household spending in 2001		$4,360,427,357,940	
Total (aggregate) household spending on fresh citrus fruit other than oranges		$1,457,578,190	
Average annual household spending on fresh citrus fruit other than oranges		$13.21	

	AVERAGE ANNUAL SPENDING PER HOUSEHOLD (in dollars)	BEST CUSTOMERS (index)	BIGGEST CUSTOMERS (percent market share)	TOTAL (AGGREGATE) HH SPENDING (in thousands of dollars)
AGE OF HOUSEHOLDER				
Average household	**$13.21**	**100**	**100.0%**	**$1,457,578**
Under age 25	6.18	47	3.6	53,136
Aged 25 to 34	10.72	81	13.6	198,481
Aged 35 to 44	14.29	108	23.9	348,990
Aged 45 to 54	15.64	118	23.9	349,038
Aged 55 to 64	15.93	121	15.9	231,766
Aged 65 to 74	12.97	98	10.1	147,106
Aged 75 or older	12.35	94	9.0	130,861
HOUSEHOLD INCOME				
Average household reporting income	**14.07**	**100**	**100.0**	**1,248,501**
Under $10,000	9.18	65	8.0	100,314
$10,000 to $19,999	9.75	69	11.8	147,299
$20,000 to $29,999	13.78	98	13.3	166,394
$30,000 to $39,999	16.32	116	13.7	171,491
$40,000 to $49,999	14.43	103	10.1	126,075
$50,000 to $69,999	13.11	93	13.1	163,613
$70,000 or more	19.94	142	30.2	376,707
HOUSEHOLD TYPE				
Average household	**13.21**	**100**	**100.0**	**1,457,578**
Married couples	17.56	133	67.3	980,550
Married couples, no children	14.61	111	23.2	337,769
Married couples, with children	18.56	141	35.7	520,701
Oldest child under 6	17.00	129	5.9	85,340
Oldest child 6 to 17	17.76	134	18.5	268,975
Oldest child 18 or older	21.47	163	11.6	169,398
Single parent with child under 18	9.15	69	4.2	60,655
Single person	7.12	54	16.0	233,415
RACE				
Average household	**13.21**	**100**	**100.0**	**1,457,578**
Black	6.89	52	6.3	91,520
White and other	14.07	107	93.7	1,365,578
HISPANIC ORIGIN				
Average household	**13.21**	**100**	**100.0**	**1,457,578**
Hispanic	24.31	184	16.1	233,887
Non-Hispanic	12.11	92	83.7	1,219,695
REGION				
Average household	**13.21**	**100**	**100.0**	**1,457,578**
Northeast	15.45	117	22.2	323,523
Midwest	11.93	90	21.2	308,295
South	10.87	82	29.2	425,854
West	16.41	124	27.4	400,076

	AVERAGE ANNUAL SPENDING PER HOUSEHOLD (in dollars)	BEST CUSTOMERS (index)	BIGGEST CUSTOMERS (percent market share)	TOTAL (AGGREGATE) HH SPENDING (in thousands of dollars)
EDUCATION				
Average household	**$13.21**	**100**	**100.0%**	**$1,457,578**
Less than high school graduate	14.59	110	17.2	250.612
High school graduate	10.42	79	22.8	332,044
Some college	11.59	88	18.3	266,477
Associate's degree	10.92	83	7.3	105,968
College graduate	17.51	133	34.4	501,837
Bachelor's degree	15.39	117	19.9	290,563
Master's, professional, doctoral degree	21.36	162	14.3	208,901
OCCUPATION				
Average household	**13.21**	**100**	**100.0**	**1,457,578**
Self-employed	19.30	146	6.5	94,068
Wage-and-salary workers, total	12.99	98	66.0	961,468
Managers and professionals	14.98	113	27.5	400,955
Technical, sales, and clerical	10.93	83	15.9	231,027
Service workers	12.03	91	8.4	123,031
Construction workers and mechanics	13.25	100	4.6	66,846
Operators, fabricators, laborers	12.82	97	9.5	138,982
Retired	12.17	92	16.1	235,258
HOMEOWNERSHIP STATUS				
Average household	**13.21**	**100**	**100.0**	**1,457,578**
Homeowners	14.76	112	73.9	1,077,628
Renters	10.20	77	26.1	380,756

Note: Households by type will not sum to the total because not all household types are shown. Hispanics may be of any race and most are white. Total household spending and market shares may not sum to total due to rounding. For an explanation of terms, see the introduction to this report.
Source: Calculations by New Strategist based on the Bureau of Labor Statistics' 2001 Consumer Expenditure Survey

76. SPENDING ON LETTUCE, 2001

Total (aggregate) household spending in 2001	$4,360,427,357,940
Total (aggregate) household spending on lettuce	$2,297,257,980
Average annual household spending on lettuce	$20.82

	AVERAGE ANNUAL SPENDING PER HOUSEHOLD (in dollars)	BEST CUSTOMERS (index)	BIGGEST CUSTOMERS (percent market share)	TOTAL (AGGREGATE) HH SPENDING (in thousands of dollars)
AGE OF HOUSEHOLDER				
Average household	**$20.82**	**100**	**100.0%**	**$2,297,258**
Under age 25	11.40	55	4.3	98,017
Aged 25 to 34	18.92	91	15.2	350,304
Aged 35 to 44	23.64	114	25.1	577,336
Aged 45 to 54	26.05	125	25.3	581,358
Aged 55 to 64	21.65	104	13.7	314,986
Aged 65 to 74	18.31	88	9.0	207,672
Aged 75 or older	15.76	76	7.3	166,993
HOUSEHOLD INCOME				
Average household reporting income	**20.99**	**100**	**100.0**	**1,862,548**
Under $10,000	12.83	61	7.5	140,236
$10,000 to $19,999	16.50	79	13.4	249,348
$20,000 to $29,999	17.31	83	11.2	209,018
$30,000 to $39,999	20.50	98	11.6	215,414
$40,000 to $49,999	19.65	94	9.2	171,682
$50,000 to $69,999	23.27	111	15.6	290,410
$70,000 or more	31.49	150	31.9	594,909
HOUSEHOLD TYPE				
Average household	**20.82**	**100**	**100.0**	**2,297,258**
Married couples	26.81	129	65.2	1,497,070
Married couples, no children	22.55	108	22.7	521,334
Married couples, with children	28.58	137	34.9	801,812
Oldest child under 6	22.86	110	5.0	114,757
Oldest child 6 to 17	27.70	133	18.3	419,517
Oldest child 18 or older	34.75	167	11.9	274,178
Single parent with child under 18	22.49	108	6.5	149,086
Single person	10.55	51	15.1	345,861
RACE				
Average household	**20.82**	**100**	**100.0**	**2,297,258**
Black	16.77	81	9.7	222,756
White and other	21.37	103	90.3	2,074,087
HISPANIC ORIGIN				
Average household	**20.82**	**100**	**100.0**	**2,297,258**
Hispanic	25.58	123	10.7	246,105
Non-Hispanic	20.35	98	89.2	2,049,611
REGION				
Average household	**20.82**	**100**	**100.0**	**2,297,258**
Northeast	25.08	121	22.9	525,175
Midwest	18.82	90	21.2	486,346
South	17.79	85	30.3	696,959
West	24.13	116	25.6	588,289

	AVERAGE ANNUAL SPENDING PER HOUSEHOLD (in dollars)	BEST CUSTOMERS (index)	BIGGEST CUSTOMERS (percent market share)	TOTAL (AGGREGATE) HH SPENDING (in thousands of dollars)
EDUCATION				
Average household	**$20.82**	**100**	**100.0%**	**$2,297,258**
Less than high school graduate	18.99	91	14.2	326,191
High school graduate	17.54	84	24.3	558,930
Some college	18.75	90	18.8	431,100
Associate's degree	23.25	112	9.8	225,618
College graduate	26.23	126	32.7	751,752
Bachelor's degree	23.68	114	19.5	447,078
Master's, professional, doctoral degree	30.88	148	13.1	302,006
OCCUPATION				
Average household	**20.82**	**100**	**100.0**	**2,297,258**
Self-employed	23.95	115	5.1	116,732
Wage-and-salary workers, total	21.37	103	68.9	1,581,722
Managers and professionals	25.08	121	29.2	671,291
Technical, sales, and clerical	18.88	91	17.4	399,067
Service workers	20.33	98	9.1	207,915
Construction workers and mechanics	23.65	114	5.2	119,314
Operators, fabricators, laborers	17.48	84	8.2	189,501
Retired	16.67	80	14.0	322,248
HOMEOWNERSHIP STATUS				
Average household	**20.82**	**100**	**100.0**	**2,297,258**
Homeowners	22.87	110	72.7	1,669,739
Renters	16.82	81	27.3	627,874

Note: Households by type will not sum to the total because not all household types are shown. Hispanics may be of any race and most are white. Total household spending and market shares may not sum to total due to rounding. For an explanation of terms, see the introduction to this report.
Source: Calculations by New Strategist based on the Bureau of Labor Statistics' 2001 Consumer Expenditure Survey

77. SPENDING ON FRESH ORANGES, 2001

Total (aggregate) household spending in 2001	$4,360,427,357,940
Total (aggregate) household spending on fresh oranges	$2,054,512,180
Average annual household spending on fresh oranges	$18.62

	AVERAGE ANNUAL SPENDING PER HOUSEHOLD (in dollars)	BEST CUSTOMERS (index)	BIGGEST CUSTOMERS (percent market share)	TOTAL (AGGREGATE) HH SPENDING (in thousands of dollars)
AGE OF HOUSEHOLDER				
Average household	**$18.62**	**100**	**100.0%**	**$2,054,512**
Under age 25	11.80	63	4.9	101,456
Aged 25 to 34	16.61	89	15.0	307,534
Aged 35 to 44	21.43	115	25.5	523,364
Aged 45 to 54	23.24	125	25.2	518,647
Aged 55 to 64	17.61	95	12.5	256,208
Aged 65 to 74	16.80	90	9.3	190,546
Aged 75 or older	14.74	79	7.6	156,185
HOUSEHOLD INCOME				
Average household reporting income	**19.35**	**100**	**100.0**	**1,717,022**
Under $10,000	15.05	78	9.6	164,520
$10,000 to $19,999	13.72	71	12.1	207,325
$20,000 to $29,999	17.64	91	12.4	213,003
$30,000 to $39,999	16.52	85	10.1	173,592
$40,000 to $49,999	18.51	96	9.4	161,722
$50,000 to $69,999	25.94	134	18.9	323,731
$70,000 or more	24.99	129	27.5	472,111
HOUSEHOLD TYPE				
Average household	**18.62**	**100**	**100.0**	**2,054,512**
Married couples	22.45	121	61.0	1,253,608
Married couples, no children	18.50	99	20.8	427,702
Married couples, with children	23.89	128	32.6	670,234
Oldest child under 6	17.82	96	4.4	89,456
Oldest child 6 to 17	24.88	134	18.3	376,808
Oldest child 18 or older	26.24	141	10.1	207,034
Single parent with child under 18	20.97	113	6.8	139,010
Single person	11.25	60	18.0	368,809
RACE				
Average household	**18.62**	**100**	**100.0**	**2,054,512**
Black	17.84	96	11.5	236,969
White and other	18.73	101	88.5	1,817,859
HISPANIC ORIGIN				
Average household	**18.62**	**100**	**100.0**	**2,054,512**
Hispanic	24.33	131	11.4	234,079
Non-Hispanic	18.05	97	88.5	1,817,960
REGION				
Average household	**18.62**	**100**	**100.0**	**2,054,512**
Northeast	23.96	129	24.4	501,722
Midwest	17.30	93	21.8	447,067
South	14.54	78	27.7	569,634
West	21.96	118	26.1	535,385

	AVERAGE ANNUAL SPENDING PER HOUSEHOLD (in dollars)	BEST CUSTOMERS (index)	BIGGEST CUSTOMERS (percent market share)	TOTAL (AGGREGATE) HH SPENDING (in thousands of dollars)
EDUCATION				
Average household	**$18.62**	**100**	**100.0%**	**$2,054,512**
Less than high school graduate	18.35	99	15.3	315,198
High school graduate	15.81	85	24.5	503,802
Some college	19.42	104	21.7	446,505
Associate's degree	16.57	89	7.8	160,795
College graduate	22.00	118	30.7	630,520
Bachelor's degree	20.51	110	18.8	387,229
Master's, professional, doctoral degree	24.71	133	11.8	241,664
OCCUPATION				
Average household	**18.62**	**100**	**100.0**	**2,054,512**
Self-employed	20.13	108	4.8	98,114
Wage-and-salary workers, total	19.08	103	68.7	1,412,225
Managers and professionals	22.44	121	29.2	600,629
Technical, sales, and clerical	16.70	90	17.2	352,988
Service workers	18.96	102	9.4	193,904
Construction workers and mechanics	19.16	103	4.7	96,662
Operators, fabricators, laborers	15.86	85	8.4	171,938
Retired	15.16	81	14.3	293,058
HOMEOWNERSHIP STATUS				
Average household	**18.62**	**100**	**100.0**	**2,054,512**
Homeowners	19.92	107	70.8	1,454,359
Renters	16.09	86	29.2	600,624

Note: Households by type will not sum to the total because not all household types are shown. Hispanics may be of any race and most are white. Total household spending and market shares may not sum to total due to rounding. For an explanation of terms, see the introduction to this report.
Source: Calculations by New Strategist based on the Bureau of Labor Statistics' 2001 Consumer Expenditure Survey

78. SPENDING ON FRESH FRUIT OTHER THAN APPLES, BANANAS, AND CITRUS, 2001

Total (aggregate) household spending in 2001	$4,360,427,357,940
Total (aggregate) household spending on fresh fruit other than apples, bananas, and citrus	$7,332,026,550
Average annual household spending on fresh fruit other than apples, bananas, and citrus	$66.45

	AVERAGE ANNUAL SPENDING PER HOUSEHOLD (in dollars)	BEST CUSTOMERS (index)	BIGGEST CUSTOMERS (percent market share)	TOTAL (AGGREGATE) HH SPENDING (in thousands of dollars)
AGE OF HOUSEHOLDER				
Average household	**$66.45**	**100**	**100.0%**	**$7,332,027**
Under age 25	31.87	48	3.7	274,018
Aged 25 to 34	57.23	86	14.5	1,059,613
Aged 35 to 44	72.81	110	24.3	1,778,166
Aged 45 to 54	74.86	113	22.8	1,670,651
Aged 55 to 64	75.17	113	14.9	1,093,648
Aged 65 to 74	71.59	108	11.1	811,974
Aged 75 or older	61.14	92	8.8	647,839
HOUSEHOLD INCOME				
Average household reporting income	**68.65**	**100**	**100.0**	**6,091,658**
Under $10,000	44.34	65	8.0	484,570
$10,000 to $19,999	50.53	74	12.5	763,709
$20,000 to $29,999	59.32	86	11.8	716,289
$30,000 to $39,999	56.06	82	9.7	589,079
$40,000 to $49,999	70.89	103	10.2	619,366
$50,000 to $69,999	76.16	111	15.6	950,477
$70,000 or more	105.84	154	32.8	1,999,529
HOUSEHOLD TYPE				
Average household	**66.45**	**100**	**100.0**	**7,332,027**
Married couples	85.56	129	65.2	4,777,670
Married couples, no children	75.85	114	23.9	1,753,576
Married couples, with children	90.65	136	34.7	2,543,186
Oldest child under 6	91.87	138	6.3	461,187
Oldest child 6 to 17	83.23	125	17.2	1,260,518
Oldest child 18 or older	105.91	159	11.4	835,630
Single parent with child under 18	52.40	79	4.7	347,360
Single person	38.62	58	17.3	1,266,080
RACE				
Average household	**66.45**	**100**	**100.0**	**7,332,027**
Black	46.86	71	8.5	622,441
White and other	69.09	104	91.5	6,705,599
HISPANIC ORIGIN				
Average household	**66.45**	**100**	**100.0**	**7,332,027**
Hispanic	83.02	125	10.9	798,735
Non-Hispanic	64.79	98	89.0	6,525,519
REGION				
Average household	**66.45**	**100**	**100.0**	**7,332,027**
Northeast	81.16	122	23.2	1,699,490
Midwest	60.53	91	21.3	1,564,216
South	58.06	87	31.0	2,274,617
West	73.44	111	24.4	1,790,467

	AVERAGE ANNUAL SPENDING PER HOUSEHOLD (in dollars)	BEST CUSTOMERS (index)	BIGGEST CUSTOMERS (percent market share)	TOTAL (AGGREGATE) HH SPENDING (in thousands of dollars)
EDUCATION				
Average household	**$66.45**	**100**	**100.0%**	**$7,332,027**
Less than high school graduate	58.75	88	13.8	1,009,149
High school graduate	54.22	82	23.6	1,727,775
Some college	57.56	87	18.1	1,323,420
Associate's degree	61.99	93	8.2	601,551
College graduate	92.63	139	36.2	2,654,776
Bachelor's degree	79.59	120	20.5	1,502,659
Master's, professional, doctoral degree	116.37	175	15.5	1,138,099
OCCUPATION				
Average household	**66.45**	**100**	**100.0**	**7,332,027**
Self-employed	69.85	105	4.6	340,449
Wage-and-salary workers, total	67.19	101	67.8	4,973,135
Managers and professionals	85.69	129	31.3	2,293,579
Technical, sales, and clerical	60.08	90	17.3	1,269,911
Service workers	51.95	78	7.2	531,293
Construction workers and mechanics	65.99	99	4.5	332,920
Operators, fabricators, laborers	52.92	80	7.8	573,706
Retired	64.97	98	17.1	1,255,935
HOMEOWNERSHIP STATUS				
Average household	**66.45**	**100**	**100.0**	**7,332,027**
Homeowners	74.85	113	74.5	5,464,799
Renters	49.98	75	25.4	1,865,703

Note: Households by type will not sum to the total because not all household types are shown. Hispanics may be of any race and most are white. Total household spending and market shares may not sum to total due to rounding. For an explanation of terms, see the introduction to this report.
Source: Calculations by New Strategist based on the Bureau of Labor Statistics' 2001 Consumer Expenditure Survey

79. SPENDING ON FRESH POTATOES, 2001

Total (aggregate) household spending in 2001	$4,360,427,357,940
Total (aggregate) household spending on fresh potatoes	$3,320,100,510
Average annual household spending on fresh potatoes	$30.09

	AVERAGE ANNUAL SPENDING PER HOUSEHOLD (in dollars)	BEST CUSTOMERS (index)	BIGGEST CUSTOMERS (percent market share)	TOTAL (AGGREGATE) HH SPENDING (in thousands of dollars)
AGE OF HOUSEHOLDER				
Average household	**$30.09**	**100**	**100.0%**	**$3,320,101**
Under age 25	14.15	47	3.7	121,662
Aged 25 to 34	27.16	90	15.1	502,867
Aged 35 to 44	32.51	108	23.9	793,959
Aged 45 to 54	35.65	119	24.0	795,601
Aged 55 to 64	36.24	120	15.9	527,256
Aged 65 to 74	28.87	96	9.9	327,444
Aged 75 or older	23.82	79	7.6	252,397
HOUSEHOLD INCOME				
Average household reporting income	**31.36**	**100**	**100.0**	**2,782,730**
Under $10,000	19.46	62	7.6	212,660
$10,000 to $19,999	27.52	88	14.9	415,914
$20,000 to $29,999	29.39	94	12.8	354,884
$30,000 to $39,999	31.01	99	11.7	325,853
$40,000 to $49,999	35.34	113	11.1	308,766
$50,000 to $69,999	32.00	102	14.4	399,360
$70,000 or more	40.66	130	27.6	768,149
HOUSEHOLD TYPE				
Average household	**30.09**	**100**	**100.0**	**3,320,101**
Married couples	37.51	125	63.1	2,094,558
Married couples, no children	32.53	108	22.7	752,061
Married couples, with children	38.07	127	32.2	1,068,054
Oldest child under 6	31.76	106	4.8	159,435
Oldest child 6 to 17	37.43	124	17.1	566,877
Oldest child 18 or older	44.15	147	10.5	348,344
Single parent with child under 18	28.78	96	5.7	190,783
Single person	15.88	53	15.7	520,594
RACE				
Average household	**30.09**	**100**	**100.0**	**3,320,101**
Black	27.57	92	11.0	366,212
White and other	30.43	101	89.0	2,953,414
HISPANIC ORIGIN				
Average household	**30.09**	**100**	**100.0**	**3,320,101**
Hispanic	36.23	120	10.5	348,569
Non-Hispanic	29.48	98	89.4	2,969,167
REGION				
Average household	**30.09**	**100**	**100.0**	**3,320,101**
Northeast	32.75	109	20.7	685,785
Midwest	26.44	88	20.6	683,263
South	30.87	103	36.4	1,209,394
West	30.40	101	22.3	741,152

	AVERAGE ANNUAL SPENDING PER HOUSEHOLD (in dollars)	BEST CUSTOMERS (index)	BIGGEST CUSTOMERS (percent market share)	TOTAL (AGGREGATE) HH SPENDING (in thousands of dollars)
EDUCATION				
Average household	**$30.09**	**100**	**100.0%**	**$3,320,101**
Less than high school graduate	29.64	99	15.3	509,126
High school graduate	28.40	94	27.3	904,994
Some college	28.29	94	19.6	650,444
Associate's degree	31.12	103	9.1	301,989
College graduate	33.22	110	28.7	952,085
Bachelor's degree	33.02	110	18.8	623,418
Master's, professional, doctoral degree	33.58	112	9.9	328,412
OCCUPATION				
Average household	**30.09**	**100**	**100.0**	**3,320,101**
Self-employed	32.96	110	4.8	160,647
Wage-and-salary workers, total	30.31	101	67.6	2,243,425
Managers and professionals	31.63	105	25.5	846,609
Technical, sales, and clerical	30.36	101	19.3	641,719
Service workers	28.81	96	8.9	294,640
Construction workers and mechanics	36.43	121	5.5	183,789
Operators, fabricators, laborers	26.25	87	8.6	284,576
Retired	28.36	94	16.5	548,227
HOMEOWNERSHIP STATUS				
Average household	**30.09**	**100**	**100.0**	**3,320,101**
Homeowners	32.36	108	71.2	2,362,604
Renters	25.64	85	28.8	957,116

Note: Households by type will not sum to the total because not all household types are shown. Hispanics may be of any race and most are white. Total household spending and market shares may not sum to total due to rounding. For an explanation of terms, see the introduction to this report.
Source: Calculations by New Strategist based on the Bureau of Labor Statistics' 2001 Consumer Expenditure Survey

80. SPENDING ON FRESH TOMATOES, 2001

Total (aggregate) household spending in 2001 $4,360,427,357,940
Total (aggregate) household spending on fresh tomatoes $3,313,480,170
Average annual household spending on fresh tomatoes $30.03

	AVERAGE ANNUAL SPENDING PER HOUSEHOLD (in dollars)	BEST CUSTOMERS (index)	BIGGEST CUSTOMERS (percent market share)	TOTAL (AGGREGATE) HH SPENDING (in thousands of dollars)
AGE OF HOUSEHOLDER				
Average household	**$30.03**	**100**	**100.0%**	**$3,313,480**
Under age 25	18.34	61	4.8	157,687
Aged 25 to 34	29.60	99	16.5	548,044
Aged 35 to 44	33.30	111	24.5	813,253
Aged 45 to 54	35.59	119	24.0	794,262
Aged 55 to 64	30.47	102	13.4	443,308
Aged 65 to 74	28.40	95	9.7	322,113
Aged 75 or older	22.01	73	7.0	233,218
HOUSEHOLD INCOME				
Average household reporting income	**30.37**	**100**	**100.0**	**2,694,882**
Under $10,000	19.20	63	7.8	209,868
$10,000 to $19,999	23.08	76	12.9	348,778
$20,000 to $29,999	29.24	96	13.1	353,073
$30,000 to $39,999	31.88	105	12.4	334,995
$40,000 to $49,999	33.02	109	10.7	288,496
$50,000 to $69,999	30.86	102	14.3	385,133
$70,000 or more	41.43	136	29.0	782,696
HOUSEHOLD TYPE				
Average household	**30.03**	**100**	**100.0**	**3,313,480**
Married couples	37.81	126	63.7	2,111,310
Married couples, no children	31.03	103	21.7	717,383
Married couples, with children	41.44	138	35.1	1,162,599
Oldest child under 6	35.24	117	5.3	176,905
Oldest child 6 to 17	40.60	135	18.6	614,887
Oldest child 18 or older	47.88	159	11.4	377,773
Single parent with child under 18	28.55	95	5.7	189,258
Single person	15.75	52	15.6	516,332
RACE				
Average household	**30.03**	**100**	**100.0**	**3,313,480**
Black	24.50	82	9.8	325,434
White and other	30.78	103	90.2	2,987,384
HISPANIC ORIGIN				
Average household	**30.03**	**100**	**100.0**	**3,313,480**
Hispanic	55.66	185	16.2	535,505
Non-Hispanic	27.48	92	83.5	2,767,731
REGION				
Average household	**30.03**	**100**	**100.0**	**3,313,480**
Northeast	32.36	108	20.5	677,618
Midwest	22.40	75	17.5	578,861
South	28.62	95	33.8	1,121,246
West	38.35	128	28.2	934,973

	AVERAGE ANNUAL SPENDING PER HOUSEHOLD (in dollars)	BEST CUSTOMERS (index)	BIGGEST CUSTOMERS (percent market share)	TOTAL (AGGREGATE) HH SPENDING (in thousands of dollars)
EDUCATION				
Average household	**$30.03**	**100**	**100.0%**	**$3,313,480**
Less than high school graduate	33.97	113	17.6	583,503
High school graduate	26.48	88	25.5	843,812
Some college	25.43	85	17.6	584,687
Associate's degree	28.49	95	8.3	276,467
College graduate	35.64	119	30.8	1,021,442
Bachelor's degree	33.05	110	18.8	623,984
Master's, professional, doctoral degree	40.36	134	11.9	394,721
OCCUPATION				
Average household	**30.03**	**100**	**100.0**	**3,313,480**
Self-employed	30.98	103	4.6	150,997
Wage-and-salary workers, total	30.88	103	69.0	2,285,614
Managers and professionals	33.97	113	27.4	909,241
Technical, sales, and clerical	27.48	92	17.5	580,845
Service workers	27.12	90	8.4	277,356
Construction workers and mechanics	36.88	123	5.6	186,060
Operators, fabricators, laborers	30.63	102	10.0	332,060
Retired	24.92	83	14.5	481,729
HOMEOWNERSHIP STATUS				
Average household	**30.03**	**100**	**100.0**	**3,313,480**
Homeowners	31.44	105	69.3	2,295,434
Renters	27.28	91	30.7	1,018,335

Note: Households by type will not sum to the total because not all household types are shown. Hispanics may be of any race and most are white. Total household spending and market shares may not sum to total due to rounding. For an explanation of terms, see the introduction to this report.
Source: Calculations by New Strategist based on the Bureau of Labor Statistics' 2001 Consumer Expenditure Survey

81. SPENDING ON FRESH VEGETABLES OTHER THAN POTATOES, LETTUCE, AND TOMATOES, 2001

Total (aggregate) household spending in 2001	$4,360,427,357,940
Total (aggregate) household spending on fresh vegetables other than potatoes, lettuce, and tomatoes	$8,902,150,520
Average annual household spending on fresh vegetables other than potatoes, lettuce, and tomatoes	$80.68

	AVERAGE ANNUAL SPENDING PER HOUSEHOLD (in dollars)	BEST CUSTOMERS (index)	BIGGEST CUSTOMERS (percent market share)	TOTAL (AGGREGATE) HH SPENDING (in thousands of dollars)
AGE OF HOUSEHOLDER				
Average household	**$80.68**	**100**	**100.0%**	**$8,902,151**
Under age 25	42.34	53	4.1	364,039
Aged 25 to 34	72.58	90	15.1	1,343,819
Aged 35 to 44	86.32	107	23.7	2,108,107
Aged 45 to 54	95.72	119	24.0	2,136,183
Aged 55 to 64	94.49	117	15.4	1,374,735
Aged 65 to 74	79.85	99	10.2	905,659
Aged 75 or older	63.43	79	7.5	672,104
HOUSEHOLD INCOME				
Average household reporting income	**85.51**	**100**	**100.0**	**7,587,730**
Under $10,000	50.28	59	7.2	549,502
$10,000 to $19,999	61.26	72	12.2	925,883
$20,000 to $29,999	75.93	89	12.1	916,855
$30,000 to $39,999	89.90	105	12.4	944,669
$40,000 to $49,999	90.18	106	10.4	787,903
$50,000 to $69,999	97.81	114	16.1	1,220,669
$70,000 or more	119.77	140	29.8	2,262,695
HOUSEHOLD TYPE				
Average household	**80.68**	**100**	**100.0**	**8,902,151**
Married couples	101.77	126	63.8	5,682,837
Married couples, no children	89.47	111	23.2	2,068,457
Married couples, with children	105.32	131	33.2	2,954,753
Oldest child under 6	89.26	111	5.0	448,085
Oldest child 6 to 17	99.22	123	16.9	1,502,687
Oldest child 18 or older	130.50	162	11.6	1,029,645
Single parent with child under 18	69.57	86	5.2	461,180
Single person	44.00	55	16.2	1,442,452
RACE				
Average household	**80.68**	**100**	**100.0**	**8,902,151**
Black	62.20	77	9.3	826,203
White and other	83.17	103	90.7	8,072,148
HISPANIC ORIGIN				
Average household	**80.68**	**100**	**100.0**	**8,902,151**
Hispanic	113.43	141	12.3	1,091,310
Non-Hispanic	77.41	96	87.6	7,796,580
REGION				
Average household	**80.68**	**100**	**100.0**	**8,902,151**
Northeast	93.21	116	21.9	1,951,817
Midwest	66.65	83	19.3	1,722,369
South	71.85	89	31.6	2,814,868
West	98.82	123	27.1	2,409,232

	AVERAGE ANNUAL SPENDING PER HOUSEHOLD (in dollars)	BEST CUSTOMERS (index)	BIGGEST CUSTOMERS (percent market share)	TOTAL (AGGREGATE) HH SPENDING (in thousands of dollars)
EDUCATION				
Average household	**$80.68**	**100**	**100.0%**	**$8,902,151**
Less than high school graduate	74.46	92	14.4	1,278,999
High school graduate	67.60	84	24.2	2,154,142
Some college	74.65	93	19.3	1,716,353
Associate's degree	80.68	100	8.8	782,919
College graduate	103.26	128	33.2	2,959,432
Bachelor's degree	96.72	120	20.5	1,826,074
Master's, professional, doctoral degree	115.16	143	12.7	1,126,265
OCCUPATION				
Average household	**80.68**	**100**	**100.0**	**8,902,151**
Self-employed	99.20	123	5.4	483,501
Wage-and-salary workers, total	81.70	101	67.9	6,047,107
Managers and professionals	96.53	120	29.0	2,583,722
Technical, sales, and clerical	77.04	96	18.3	1,628,395
Service workers	70.10	87	8.1	716,913
Construction workers and mechanics	91.31	113	5.2	460,659
Operators, fabricators, laborers	63.78	79	7.8	691,439
Retired	71.84	89	15.6	1,388,739
HOMEOWNERSHIP STATUS				
Average household	**80.68**	**100**	**100.0**	**8,902,151**
Homeowners	87.83	109	72.0	6,412,468
Renters	66.66	83	28.0	2,488,351

Note: Households by type will not sum to the total because not all household types are shown. Hispanics may be of any race and most are white. Total household spending and market shares may not sum to total due to rounding. For an explanation of terms, see the introduction to this report.
Source: Calculations by New Strategist based on the Bureau of Labor Statistics' 2001 Consumer Expenditure Survey

82. SPENDING ON FROZEN FRUIT, 2001

Total (aggregate) household spending in 2001	$4,360,427,357,940
Total (aggregate) household spending on frozen fruit	$279,157,670
Average annual household spending on frozen fruit	$2.53

	AVERAGE ANNUAL SPENDING PER HOUSEHOLD (in dollars)	BEST CUSTOMERS (index)	BIGGEST CUSTOMERS (percent market share)	TOTAL (AGGREGATE) HH SPENDING (in thousands of dollars)
AGE OF HOUSEHOLDER				
Average household	**$2.53**	**100**	**100.0%**	**$279,158**
Under age 25	1.20	47	3.7	10,318
Aged 25 to 34	1.31	52	8.7	24,255
Aged 35 to 44	2.85	113	24.9	69,603
Aged 45 to 54	3.45	136	27.6	76,994
Aged 55 to 64	3.05	121	15.9	44,374
Aged 65 to 74	2.60	103	10.6	29,489
Aged 75 or older	2.35	93	8.9	24,901
HOUSEHOLD INCOME				
Average household reporting income	**2.56**	**100**	**100.0**	**227,162**
Under $10,000	1.26	49	6.1	13,743
$10,000 to $19,999	2.09	82	13.9	31,640
$20,000 to $29,999	2.41	94	12.8	29,101
$30,000 to $39,999	1.51	59	7.0	15,867
$40,000 to $49,999	2.92	114	11.2	25,512
$50,000 to $69,999	3.02	118	16.6	37,690
$70,000 or more	3.92	153	32.6	74,057
HOUSEHOLD TYPE				
Average household	**2.53**	**100**	**100.0**	**279,158**
Married couples	3.31	131	66.2	184,830
Married couples, no children	2.82	112	23.4	65,196
Married couples, with children	3.73	147	37.5	104,645
Oldest child under 6	0.71	28	1.3	3,564
Oldest child 6 to 17	3.64	144	19.7	55,128
Oldest child 18 or older	6.19	245	17.5	48,839
Single parent with child under 18	2.00	79	4.7	13,258
Single person	1.37	54	16.1	44,913
RACE				
Average household	**2.53**	**100**	**100.0**	**279,158**
Black	1.90	75	9.0	25,238
White and other	2.62	104	91.1	254,287
HISPANIC ORIGIN				
Average household	**2.53**	**100**	**100.0**	**279,158**
Hispanic	2.16	85	7.4	20,781
Non-Hispanic	2.57	102	92.7	258,845
REGION				
Average household	**2.53**	**100**	**100.0**	**279,158**
Northeast	2.34	93	17.6	49,000
Midwest	2.59	102	24.0	66,931
South	2.26	89	31.7	88,540
West	3.08	122	26.9	75,090

	AVERAGE ANNUAL SPENDING PER HOUSEHOLD (in dollars)	BEST CUSTOMERS (index)	BIGGEST CUSTOMERS (percent market share)	TOTAL (AGGREGATE) HH SPENDING (in thousands of dollars)
EDUCATION				
Average household	**$2.53**	**100**	**100.0%**	**$279,158**
Less than high school graduate	2.15	85	13.2	36,931
High school graduate	2.05	81	23.4	65,325
Some college	2.61	103	21.5	60,009
Associate's degree	1.77	70	6.2	17,176
College graduate	3.50	138	35.9	100,310
Bachelor's degree	2.93	116	19.8	55,318
Master's, professional, doctoral degree	4.54	179	15.9	44,401
OCCUPATION				
Average household	**2.53**	**100**	**100.0**	**279,158**
Self-employed	4.21	166	7.4	20,520
Wage-and-salary workers, total	2.59	102	68.7	191,701
Managers and professionals	3.66	145	35.1	97,964
Technical, sales, and clerical	1.91	76	14.5	40,372
Service workers	1.89	75	6.9	19,329
Construction workers and mechanics	3.61	143	6.5	18,213
Operators, fabricators, laborers	1.57	62	6.1	17,020
Retired	2.21	87	15.3	42,722
HOMEOWNERSHIP STATUS				
Average household	**2.53**	**100**	**100.0**	**279,158**
Homeowners	3.06	121	80.0	223,411
Renters	1.50	59	20.1	55,994

Note: Households by type will not sum to the total because not all household types are shown. Hispanics may be of any race and most are white. Total household spending and market shares may not sum to total due to rounding. For an explanation of terms, see the introduction to this report.
Source: Calculations by New Strategist based on the Bureau of Labor Statistics' 2001 Consumer Expenditure Survey

83. SPENDING ON FROZEN MEALS, 2001

Total (aggregate) household spending in 2001	$4,360,427,357,940
Total (aggregate) household spending on frozen meals	$3,161,212,350
Average annual household spending on frozen meals	$28.65

	AVERAGE ANNUAL SPENDING PER HOUSEHOLD (in dollars)	BEST CUSTOMERS (index)	BIGGEST CUSTOMERS (percent market share)	TOTAL (AGGREGATE) HH SPENDING (in thousands of dollars)
AGE OF HOUSEHOLDER				
Average household	**$28.65**	**100**	**100.0%**	**$3,161,212**
Under age 25	16.85	59	4.6	144,876
Aged 25 to 34	22.80	80	13.4	422,142
Aged 35 to 44	28.13	98	21.7	686,991
Aged 45 to 54	35.83	125	25.3	799,618
Aged 55 to 64	35.18	123	16.2	511,834
Aged 65 to 74	23.82	83	8.5	270,166
Aged 75 or older	31.17	109	10.4	330,277
HOUSEHOLD INCOME				
Average household reporting income	**29.01**	**100**	**100.0**	**2,574,202**
Under $10,000	19.44	67	8.3	212,456
$10,000 to $19,999	22.84	79	13.4	345,151
$20,000 to $29,999	21.48	74	10.1	259,371
$30,000 to $39,999	30.57	105	12.5	321,230
$40,000 to $49,999	43.47	150	14.8	379,797
$50,000 to $69,999	29.65	102	14.4	370,032
$70,000 or more	36.92	127	27.1	697,493
HOUSEHOLD TYPE				
Average household	**28.65**	**100**	**100.0**	**3,161,212**
Married couples	29.90	104	52.8	1,669,616
Married couples, no children	29.00	101	21.2	670,451
Married couples, with children	30.38	106	27.0	852,311
Oldest child under 6	20.13	70	3.2	101,053
Oldest child 6 to 17	30.82	108	14.8	466,769
Oldest child 18 or older	37.05	129	9.2	292,325
Single parent with child under 18	32.82	115	6.9	217,564
Single person	24.27	85	25.2	795,643
RACE				
Average household	**28.65**	**100**	**100.0**	**3,161,212**
Black	22.13	77	9.3	293,953
White and other	29.53	103	90.7	2,866,064
HISPANIC ORIGIN				
Average household	**28.65**	**100**	**100.0**	**3,161,212**
Hispanic	13.07	46	4.0	125,747
Non-Hispanic	30.20	105	96.2	3,041,684
REGION				
Average household	**28.65**	**100**	**100.0**	**3,161,212**
Northeast	30.60	107	20.3	640,764
Midwest	32.28	113	26.4	834,180
South	26.39	92	32.7	1,033,881
West	26.74	93	20.6	651,921

	AVERAGE ANNUAL SPENDING PER HOUSEHOLD (in dollars)	BEST CUSTOMERS (index)	BIGGEST CUSTOMERS (percent market share)	TOTAL (AGGREGATE) HH SPENDING (in thousands of dollars)
EDUCATION				
Average household	**$28.65**	**100**	**100.0%**	**$3,161,212**
Less than high school graduate	22.97	80	12.5	394,556
High school graduate	27.07	95	27.3	862,613
Some college	28.32	99	20.6	651,133
Associate's degree	24.66	86	7.6	239,301
College graduate	35.32	123	32.0	1,012,271
Bachelor's degree	34.72	121	20.7	655,514
Master's, professional, doctoral degree	36.40	127	11.3	355,992
OCCUPATION				
Average household	**28.65**	**100**	**100.0**	**3,161,212**
Self-employed	36.56	128	5.6	178,193
Wage-and-salary workers, total	29.34	102	68.7	2,171,629
Managers and professionals	35.81	125	30.3	958,491
Technical, sales, and clerical	25.64	90	17.1	541,953
Service workers	24.57	86	7.9	251,277
Construction workers and mechanics	24.75	86	3.9	124,864
Operators, fabricators, laborers	27.53	96	9.4	298,453
Retired	24.52	86	15.0	473,996
HOMEOWNERSHIP STATUS				
Average household	**28.65**	**100**	**100.0**	**3,161,212**
Homeowners	30.65	107	70.8	2,237,757
Renters	24.73	86	29.2	923,146

Note: Households by type will not sum to the total because not all household types are shown. Hispanics may be of any race and most are white. Total household spending and market shares may not sum to total due to rounding. For an explanation of terms, see the introduction to this report.
Source: Calculations by New Strategist based on the Bureau of Labor Statistics' 2001 Consumer Expenditure Survey

84. SPENDING ON FROZEN PREPARED FOODS OTHER THAN MEALS, 2001

Total (aggregate) household spending in 2001	$4,360,427,357,940
Total (aggregate) household spending on frozen prepared foods other than meals	$7,452,296,060
Average annual household spending on frozen prepared foods other than meals	$67.54

	AVERAGE ANNUAL SPENDING PER HOUSEHOLD (in dollars)	BEST CUSTOMERS (index)	BIGGEST CUSTOMERS (percent market share)	TOTAL (AGGREGATE) HH SPENDING (in thousands of dollars)
AGE OF HOUSEHOLDER				
Average household	**$67.54**	**100**	**100.0%**	**$7,452,296**
Under age 25	57.77	86	6.7	496,707
Aged 25 to 34	68.47	101	17.0	1,267,722
Aged 35 to 44	83.37	123	27.3	2,036,062
Aged 45 to 54	85.11	126	25.5	1,899,400
Aged 55 to 64	57.90	86	11.3	842,387
Aged 65 to 74	43.23	64	6.6	490,315
Aged 75 or older	38.04	56	5.4	403,072
HOUSEHOLD INCOME				
Average household reporting income	**73.38**	**100**	**100.0**	**6,511,374**
Under $10,000	39.39	54	6.6	430,527
$10,000 to $19,999	46.49	63	10.8	702,651
$20,000 to $29,999	51.07	70	9.5	616,670
$30,000 to $39,999	70.58	96	11.4	741,655
$40,000 to $49,999	87.87	120	11.8	767,720
$50,000 to $69,999	88.96	121	17.1	1,110,221
$70,000 or more	115.79	158	33.6	2,187,505
HOUSEHOLD TYPE				
Average household	**67.54**	**100**	**100.0**	**7,452,296**
Married couples	85.55	127	64.1	4,777,112
Married couples, no children	60.97	90	18.9	1,409,565
Married couples, with children	107.28	159	40.4	3,009,740
Oldest child under 6	92.71	137	6.2	465,404
Oldest child 6 to 17	113.27	168	23.0	1,715,474
Oldest child 18 or older	105.08	156	11.1	829,081
Single parent with child under 18	80.22	119	7.1	531,778
Single person	34.30	51	15.1	1,124,457
RACE				
Average household	**67.54**	**100**	**100.0**	**7,452,296**
Black	44.16	65	7.9	586,577
White and other	70.70	105	92.1	6,861,859
HISPANIC ORIGIN				
Average household	**67.54**	**100**	**100.0**	**7,452,296**
Hispanic	43.98	65	5.7	423,132
Non-Hispanic	69.89	104	94.5	7,039,181
REGION				
Average household	**67.54**	**100**	**100.0**	**7,452,296**
Northeast	60.40	89	17.0	1,264,776
Midwest	74.95	111	26.0	1,936,858
South	71.87	106	37.8	2,815,651
West	58.95	87	19.3	1,437,201

	AVERAGE ANNUAL SPENDING PER HOUSEHOLD (in dollars)	BEST CUSTOMERS (index)	BIGGEST CUSTOMERS (percent market share)	TOTAL (AGGREGATE) HH SPENDING (in thousands of dollars)
EDUCATION				
Average household	**$67.54**	**100**	**100.0%**	**$7,452,296**
Less than high school graduate	48.92	72	11.3	840,299
High school graduate	62.15	92	26.6	1,980,472
Some college	67.37	100	20.8	1,548,971
Associate's degree	84.03	124	10.9	815,427
College graduate	78.81	117	30.3	2,258,695
Bachelor's degree	78.38	116	19.9	1,479,814
Master's, professional, doctoral degree	79.58	118	10.4	778,292
OCCUPATION				
Average household	**67.54**	**100**	**100.0**	**7,452,296**
Self-employed	74.69	111	4.9	364,039
Wage-and-salary workers, total	74.34	110	73.8	5,502,349
Managers and professionals	88.50	131	31.8	2,368,791
Technical, sales, and clerical	74.06	110	2.1	1,565,406
Service workers	51.69	77	7.1	528,634
Construction workers and mechanics	81.46	121	5.5	410,966
Operators, fabricators, laborers	61.21	91	8.9	663,578
Retired	39.92	59	10.4	771,694
HOMEOWNERSHIP STATUS				
Average household	**67.54**	**100**	**100.0**	**7,452,296**
Homeowners	74.75	111	73.2	5,457,498
Renters	53.43	79	26.8	1,994,489

Note: Households by type will not sum to the total because not all household types are shown. Hispanics may be of any race and most are white. Total household spending and market shares may not sum to total due to rounding. For an explanation of terms, see the introduction to this report.
Source: Calculations by New Strategist based on the Bureau of Labor Statistics' 2001 Consumer Expenditure Survey

85. SPENDING ON FROZEN VEGETABLES, 2001

Total (aggregate) household spending in 2001	$4,360,427,357,940
Total (aggregate) household spending on frozen vegetables	$3,034,322,500
Average annual household spending on frozen vegetables	$27.50

	AVERAGE ANNUAL SPENDING PER HOUSEHOLD (in dollars)	BEST CUSTOMERS (index)	BIGGEST CUSTOMERS (percent market share)	TOTAL (AGGREGATE) HH SPENDING (in thousands of dollars)
AGE OF HOUSEHOLDER				
Average household	**$27.50**	**100**	**100.0%**	**$3,034,323**
Under age 25	14.53	53	4.1	124,929
Aged 25 to 34	24.99	91	15.2	462,690
Aged 35 to 44	32.46	118	26.1	792,738
Aged 45 to 54	32.91	120	24.2	734,453
Aged 55 to 64	28.45	104	13.6	413,919
Aged 65 to 74	24.43	89	9.1	277,085
Aged 75 or older	21.44	78	7.5	227,178
HOUSEHOLD INCOME				
Average household reporting income	**28.85**	**100**	**100.0**	**2,560,005**
Under $10,000	17.23	60	7.4	188,357
$10,000 to $19,999	21.68	75	12.8	327,712
$20,000 to $29,999	23.94	83	11.3	289,076
$30,000 to $39,999	29.44	102	12.1	309,356
$40,000 to $49,999	33.49	116	11.4	292,602
$50,000 to $69,999	32.93	114	16.1	410,966
$70,000 or more	39.91	138	29.5	753,980
HOUSEHOLD TYPE				
Average household	**27.50**	**100**	**100.0**	**3,034,323**
Married couples	35.58	129	65.5	1,986,787
Married couples, no children	30.30	110	23.1	700,506
Married couples, with children	39.11	142	36.2	1,097,231
Oldest child under 6	37.00	135	6.1	185,740
Oldest child 6 to 17	39.26	143	19.6	594,593
Oldest child 18 or older	40.34	147	10.5	318,283
Single parent with child under 18	30.43	111	6.6	201,721
Single person	13.57	49	14.7	444,865
RACE				
Average household	**27.50**	**100**	**100.0**	**3,034,323**
Black	29.07	106	12.7	386,137
White and other	27.29	99	87.3	2,648,658
HISPANIC ORIGIN				
Average household	**27.50**	**100**	**100.0**	**3,034,323**
Hispanic	18.91	69	6.0	181,933
Non-Hispanic	28.36	103	94.1	2,856,363
REGION				
Average household	**27.50**	**100**	**100.0**	**3,034,323**
Northeast	33.73	123	23.3	706,306
Midwest	25.46	93	21.7	657,937
South	27.92	102	36.1	1,093,822
West	23.61	86	19.0	575,612

	AVERAGE ANNUAL SPENDING PER HOUSEHOLD (in dollars)	BEST CUSTOMERS (index)	BIGGEST CUSTOMERS (percent market share)	TOTAL (AGGREGATE) HH SPENDING (in thousands of dollars)
EDUCATION				
Average household	**$27.50**	**100**	**100.0%**	**$3,034,323**
Less than high school graduate	21.80	79	12.3	374,459
High school graduate	27.09	99	28.4	863,250
Some college	27.84	101	21.1	640,097
Associate's degree	26.34	96	8.4	255,603
College graduate	31.44	114	29.7	901,070
Bachelor's degree	29.11	106	18.1	549,597
Master's, professional, doctoral degree	35.67	130	11.5	348,853
OCCUPATION				
Average household	**27.50**	**100**	**100.0**	**3,034,323**
Self-employed	31.52	115	5.1	153,629
Wage-and-salary workers, total	28.72	104	70.1	2,125,740
Managers and professionals	33.11	120	29.2	886,222
Technical, sales, and clerical	28.18	103	19.6	595,641
Service workers	24.69	90	8.3	252,505
Construction workers and mechanics	29.04	106	4.8	146,507
Operators, fabricators, laborers	23.58	86	8.4	255,631
Retired	22.67	82	14.4	438,234
HOMEOWNERSHIP STATUS				
Average household	**27.50**	**100**	**100.0**	**3,034,323**
Homeowners	30.29	110	72.9	2,211,473
Renters	22.04	80	27.1	822,731

Note: Households by type will not sum to the total because not all household types are shown. Hispanics may be of any race and most are white. Total household spending and market shares may not sum to total due to rounding. For an explanation of terms, see the introduction to this report.
Source: Calculations by New Strategist based on the Bureau of Labor Statistics' 2001 Consumer Expenditure Survey

86. SPENDING ON FRUIT JUICE, CANNED AND BOTTLED, 2001

Total (aggregate) household spending in 2001	$4,360,427,357,940
Total (aggregate) household spending on fruit juice, canned and bottled	$6,123,814,500
Average annual household spending on fruit juice, canned and bottled	$55.50

	AVERAGE ANNUAL SPENDING PER HOUSEHOLD (in dollars)	BEST CUSTOMERS (index)	BIGGEST CUSTOMERS (percent market share)	TOTAL (AGGREGATE) HH SPENDING (in thousands of dollars)
AGE OF HOUSEHOLDER				
Average household	**$55.50**	**100**	**100.0%**	**$6,123,815**
Under age 25	39.05	70	5.5	335,752
Aged 25 to 34	56.47	102	17.1	1,045,542
Aged 35 to 44	69.86	126	27.9	1,706,121
Aged 45 to 54	60.19	109	21.9	1,343,260
Aged 55 to 64	48.74	88	11.6	709,118
Aged 65 to 74	44.83	81	8.3	508,462
Aged 75 or older	43.80	79	7.6	464,105
HOUSEHOLD INCOME				
Average household reporting income	**58.04**	**100**	**100.0**	**5,150,179**
Under $10,000	39.45	68	8.4	431,153
$10,000 to $19,999	44.95	77	13.2	679,316
$20,000 to $29,999	54.51	94	12.8	658,208
$30,000 to $39,999	58.23	100	11.9	611,881
$40,000 to $49,999	55.37	95	9.4	483,768
$50,000 to $69,999	65.44	113	15.9	816,691
$70,000 or more	78.18	135	28.7	1,476,977
HOUSEHOLD TYPE				
Average household	**55.50**	**100**	**100.0**	**6,123,815**
Married couples	67.57	122	61.6	3,773,109
Married couples, no children	49.90	90	18.8	1,153,638
Married couples, with children	79.64	144	36.5	2,234,300
Oldest child under 6	80.38	145	6.6	403,508
Oldest child 6 to 17	80.95	146	20.0	1,225,988
Oldest child 18 or older	76.24	137	9.8	601,534
Single parent with child under 18	63.93	115	6.9	423,792
Single person	31.08	56	16.6	1,018,896
RACE				
Average household	**55.50**	**100**	**100.0**	**6,123,815**
Black	71.18	128	15.4	945,484
White and other	53.39	96	84.6	5,181,820
HISPANIC ORIGIN				
Average household	**55.50**	**100**	**100.0**	**6,123,815**
Hispanic	72.06	130	11.3	693,289
Non-Hispanic	53.85	97	88.6	5,423,664
REGION				
Average household	**55.50**	**100**	**100.0**	**6,123,815**
Northeast	67.34	121	23.0	1,410,100
Midwest	43.14	78	18.2	1,114,824
South	54.20	98	34.7	2,123,393
West	60.42	109	24.1	1,473,040

	AVERAGE ANNUAL SPENDING PER HOUSEHOLD (in dollars)	BEST CUSTOMERS (index)	BIGGEST CUSTOMERS (percent market share)	TOTAL (AGGREGATE) HH SPENDING (in thousands of dollars)
EDUCATION				
Average household	**$55.50**	**100**	**100.0%**	**$6,123,815**
Less than high school graduate	48.37	87	13.6	830,852
High school graduate	51.87	94	27.0	1,652,889
Some college	53.92	97	20.2	1,239,729
Associate's degree	57.08	103	9.1	553,904
College graduate	64.32	116	30.1	1,843,411
Bachelor's degree	64.83	117	20.0	1,223,990
Master's, professional, doctoral degree	63.39	114	10.1	619,954
OCCUPATION				
Average household	**55.50**	**100**	**100.0**	**6,123,815**
Self-employed	53.32	96	4.2	259,882
Wage-and-salary workers, total	57.78	104	69.8	4,276,645
Managers and professionals	61.40	111	26.8	1,643,432
Technical, sales, and clerical	58.58	106	20.2	1,238,206
Service workers	56.62	102	9.5	579,053
Construction workers and mechanics	55.29	100	4.6	278,938
Operators, fabricators, laborers	50.78	92	9.0	550,506
Retired	45.03	81	14.2	870,475
HOMEOWNERSHIP STATUS				
Average household	**55.50**	**100**	**100.0**	**6,123,815**
Homeowners	57.98	105	69.1	4,233,120
Renters	50.67	91	30.9	1,891,460

Note: Households by type will not sum to the total because not all household types are shown. Hispanics may be of any race and most are white. Total household spending and market shares may not sum to total due to rounding. For an explanation of terms, see the introduction to this report.
Source: Calculations by New Strategist based on the Bureau of Labor Statistics' 2001 Consumer Expenditure Survey

87. SPENDING ON FRUIT JUICE, FRESH, 2001

Total (aggregate) household spending in 2001 $4,360,427,357,940
Total (aggregate) household spending on fruit juice, fresh $2,743,027,540
Average annual household spending on fruit juice, fresh $24.86

	AVERAGE ANNUAL SPENDING PER HOUSEHOLD (in dollars)	BEST CUSTOMERS (index)	BIGGEST CUSTOMERS (percent market share)	TOTAL (AGGREGATE) HH SPENDING (in thousands of dollars)
AGE OF HOUSEHOLDER				
Average household	**$24.86**	**100**	**100.0%**	**$2,743,028**
Under age 25	18.26	74	5.7	157,000
Aged 25 to 34	19.64	79	13.3	363,635
Aged 35 to 44	29.24	118	26.0	714,099
Aged 45 to 54	27.03	109	22.0	603,229
Aged 55 to 64	26.57	107	14.1	386,567
Aged 65 to 74	23.67	95	9.8	268,465
Aged 75 or older	23.59	95	9.1	249,960
HOUSEHOLD INCOME				
Average household reporting income	**24.95**	**100**	**100.0**	**2,213,938**
Under $10,000	16.20	65	8.0	177,073
$10,000 to $19,999	20.09	81	13.7	303,551
$20,000 to $29,999	24.89	100	13.6	300,547
$30,000 to $39,999	20.76	83	9.9	218,146
$40,000 to $49,999	25.42	102	10.0	222,095
$50,000 to $69,999	26.36	106	14.9	328,973
$70,000 or more	35.33	142	30.1	667,454
HOUSEHOLD TYPE				
Average household	**24.86**	**100**	**100.0**	**2,743,028**
Married couples	29.83	120	60.7	1,665,707
Married couples, no children	25.55	103	21.5	590,690
Married couples, with children	32.14	129	32.9	901,688
Oldest child under 6	28.52	115	5.2	143,170
Oldest child 6 to 17	30.31	122	16.7	459,045
Oldest child 18 or older	38.83	156	11.2	306,369
Single parent with child under 18	24.03	97	5.8	159,295
Single person	15.29	62	18.3	501,252
RACE				
Average household	**24.86**	**100**	**100.0**	**2,743,028**
Black	23.46	94	11.4	311,619
White and other	25.05	101	88.6	2,431,253
HISPANIC ORIGIN				
Average household	**24.86**	**100**	**100.0**	**2,743,028**
Hispanic	28.11	113	9.9	270,446
Non-Hispanic	24.53	99	90.1	2,470,613
REGION				
Average household	**24.86**	**100**	**100.0**	**2,743,028**
Northeast	36.45	147	27.8	763,263
Midwest	21.26	86	20.0	549,401
South	20.43	82	29.2	800,386
West	25.75	104	22.9	627,785

	AVERAGE ANNUAL SPENDING PER HOUSEHOLD (in dollars)	BEST CUSTOMERS (index)	BIGGEST CUSTOMERS (percent market share)	TOTAL (AGGREGATE) HH SPENDING (in thousands of dollars)
EDUCATION				
Average household	**$24.86**	**100**	**100.0%**	**$2,743,028**
Less than high school graduate	22.18	89	13.9	380,986
High school graduate	22.25	90	25.8	709,019
Some college	22.97	92	19.3	528,126
Associate's degree	20.86	84	7.4	202,425
College graduate	32.10	129	33.5	919,986
Bachelor's degree	27.30	110	18.8	515,424
Master's, professional, doctoral degree	40.82	164	14.6	399,220
OCCUPATION				
Average household	**24.86**	**100**	**100.0**	**2,743,028**
Self-employed	27.25	110	4.8	132,817
Wage-and-salary workers, total	24.65	99	66.5	1,824,494
Managers and professionals	29.96	121	29.2	801,909
Technical, sales, and clerical	23.87	96	18.4	504,540
Service workers	23.15	93	8.6	236,755
Construction workers and mechanics	19.30	78	3.5	97,369
Operators, fabricators, laborers	18.05	73	7.1	195,680
Retired	23.39	94	16.5	452,152
HOMEOWNERSHIP STATUS				
Average household	**24.86**	**100**	**100.0**	**2,743,028**
Homeowners	26.52	107	70.6	1,936,225
Renters	21.60	87	29.4	806,306

Note: Households by type will not sum to the total because not all household types are shown. Hispanics may be of any race and most are white. Total household spending and market shares may not sum to total due to rounding. For an explanation of terms, see the introduction to this report.
Source: Calculations by New Strategist based on the Bureau of Labor Statistics' 2001 Consumer Expenditure Survey

88. SPENDING ON FRUIT JUICE OTHER THAN ORANGE, FROZEN, 2001

Total (aggregate) household spending in 2001	$4,360,427,357,940
Total (aggregate) household spending on fruit juice other than orange, frozen	$410,461,080
Average annual household spending on fruit juice other than orange, frozen	$3.72

	AVERAGE ANNUAL SPENDING PER HOUSEHOLD (in dollars)	BEST CUSTOMERS (index)	BIGGEST CUSTOMERS (percent market share)	TOTAL (AGGREGATE) HH SPENDING (in thousands of dollars)
AGE OF HOUSEHOLDER				
Average household	**$3.72**	**100**	**100.0%**	**$410,461**
Under age 25	2.94	79	6.2	25,278
Aged 25 to 34	4.76	128	21.5	88,131
Aged 35 to 44	4.41	119	26.2	107,701
Aged 45 to 54	3.85	104	20.9	85,920
Aged 55 to 64	2.66	72	9.4	38,700
Aged 65 to 74	3.31	89	9.1	37,542
Aged 75 or older	2.41	65	6.2	25,536
HOUSEHOLD INCOME				
Average household reporting income	**3.82**	**100**	**100.0**	**338,968**
Under $10,000	2.44	64	7.9	26,656
$10,000 to $19,999	4.06	106	18.1	61,358
$20,000 to $29,999	2.67	70	9.5	32,240
$30,000 to $39,999	3.28	86	10.2	34,466
$40,000 to $49,999	2.97	78	7.7	25,949
$50,000 to $69,999	5.01	131	18.4	62,525
$70,000 or more	5.13	134	28.6	96,916
HOUSEHOLD TYPE				
Average household	**3.72**	**100**	**100.0**	**410,461**
Married couples	4.50	121	61.2	251,280
Married couples, no children	2.78	75	15.7	64,271
Married couples, with children	5.58	150	38.1	156,547
Oldest child under 6	6.29	169	7.7	31,576
Oldest child 6 to 17	5.25	141	19.4	79,511
Oldest child 18 or older	5.76	155	11.1	45,446
Single parent with child under 18	5.51	148	8.9	36,526
Single person	1.92	52	15.3	62,943
RACE				
Average household	**3.72**	**100**	**100.0**	**410,461**
Black	3.18	86	10.3	42,240
White and other	3.79	102	89.6	367,842
HISPANIC ORIGIN				
Average household	**3.72**	**100**	**100.0**	**410,461**
Hispanic	3.14	84	7.4	30,210
Non-Hispanic	3.77	101	92.5	379,707
REGION				
Average household	**3.72**	**100**	**100.0**	**410,461**
Northeast	3.10	83	15.8	64,914
Midwest	4.27	115	26.9	110,345
South	2.85	77	27.2	111,654
West	5.05	136	30.0	123,119

	AVERAGE ANNUAL SPENDING PER HOUSEHOLD (in dollars)	BEST CUSTOMERS (index)	BIGGEST CUSTOMERS (percent market share)	TOTAL (AGGREGATE) HH SPENDING (in thousands of dollars)
EDUCATION				
Average household	**$3.72**	**100**	**100.0%**	**$410,461**
Less than high school graduate	2.61	70	10.9	44,832
High school graduate	3.01	81	23.4	95,917
Some college	4.38	118	24.5	100,705
Associate's degree	5.17	139	12.2	50,170
College graduate	4.14	111	28.9	118,652
Bachelor's degree	3.93	106	18.1	74,198
Master's, professional, doctoral degree	4.51	121	10.7	44,108
OCCUPATION				
Average household	**3.72**	**100**	**100.0**	**410,461**
Self-employed	3.29	88	3.9	16,036
Wage-and-salary workers, total	3.81	102	68.7	282,001
Managers and professionals	4.35	117	28.4	116,432
Technical, sales, and clerical	3.18	86	16.4	67,216
Service workers	3.12	84	7.8	31,908
Construction workers and mechanics	5.14	138	6.3	25,931
Operators, fabricators, laborers	3.73	100	9.9	40,437
Retired	2.95	79	13.9	57,026
HOMEOWNERSHIP STATUS				
Average household	**3.72**	**100**	**100.0**	**410,461**
Homeowners	4.17	112	74.2	304,452
Renters	2.83	76	25.7	105,641

Note: Households by type will not sum to the total because not all household types are shown. Hispanics may be of any race and most are white. Total household spending and market shares may not sum to total due to rounding. For an explanation of terms, see the introduction to this report.
Source: Calculations by New Strategist based on the Bureau of Labor Statistics' 2001 Consumer Expenditure Survey

89. SPENDING ON ORANGE JUICE, FROZEN, 2001

Total (aggregate) household spending in 2001 $4,360,427,357,940
Total (aggregate) household spending on orange juice, frozen $839,679,790
Average annual household spending on orange juice, frozen $7.61

	AVERAGE ANNUAL SPENDING PER HOUSEHOLD (in dollars)	BEST CUSTOMERS (index)	BIGGEST CUSTOMERS (percent market share)	TOTAL (AGGREGATE) HH SPENDING (in thousands of dollars)
AGE OF HOUSEHOLDER				
Average household	**$7.61**	**100**	**100.0%**	**$839,680**
Under age 25	6.08	80	6.2	52,276
Aged 25 to 34	8.16	107	18.0	151,082
Aged 35 to 44	8.09	106	23.5	197,574
Aged 45 to 54	8.33	110	22.1	185,901
Aged 55 to 64	8.05	106	13.9	117,119
Aged 65 to 74	5.90	78	8.0	66,918
Aged 75 or older	6.37	84	8.0	67,497
HOUSEHOLD INCOME				
Average household reporting income	**8.31**	**100**	**100.0**	**737,388**
Under $10,000	4.82	58	7.2	52,725
$10,000 to $19,999	5.11	62	10.5	77,297
$20,000 to $29,999	7.03	85	11.5	84,887
$30,000 to $39,999	8.53	103	12.2	89,633
$40,000 to $49,999	10.03	121	11.9	87,632
$50,000 to $69,999	9.04	109	15.3	112,819
$70,000 or more	12.66	152	32.4	239,173
HOUSEHOLD TYPE				
Average household	**7.61**	**100**	**100.0**	**839,680**
Married couples	10.08	133	67.0	562,867
Married couples, no children	8.33	110	22.9	192,581
Married couples, with children	11.68	154	39.0	327,682
Oldest child under 6	9.99	131	6.0	50,150
Oldest child 6 to 17	12.12	159	21.9	183,557
Oldest child 18 or older	12.00	158	11.3	94,680
Single parent with child under 18	5.24	69	4.1	34,736
Single person	4.27	56	16.7	139,983
RACE				
Average household	**7.61**	**100**	**100.0**	**839,680**
Black	5.11	67	8.1	67,876
White and other	7.94	104	91.8	770,625
HISPANIC ORIGIN				
Average household	**7.61**	**100**	**100.0**	**839,680**
Hispanic	8.44	111	9.7	81,201
Non-Hispanic	7.52	99	90.2	757,399
REGION				
Average household	**7.61**	**100**	**100.0**	**839,680**
Northeast	6.44	85	16.1	134,854
Midwest	8.31	109	25.6	214,747
South	6.54	86	30.5	256,218
West	9.58	126	27.8	233,560

	AVERAGE ANNUAL SPENDING PER HOUSEHOLD (in dollars)	BEST CUSTOMERS (index)	BIGGEST CUSTOMERS (percent market share)	TOTAL (AGGREGATE) HH SPENDING (in thousands of dollars)
EDUCATION				
Average household	**$7.61**	**100**	**100.0%**	**$839,680**
Less than high school graduate	5.27	69	10.8	90,523
High school graduate	6.12	80	23.2	195,020
Some college	7.50	99	20.5	172,440
Associate's degree	9.37	123	10.8	90,927
College graduate	10.09	133	34.4	289,179
Bachelor's degree	11.13	146	25.0	210,134
Master's, professional, doctoral degree	8.19	108	9.5	80,098
OCCUPATION				
Average household	**7.61**	**100**	**100.0**	**839,680**
Self-employed	9.03	119	5.2	44,012
Wage-and-salary workers, total	8.14	107	71.8	602,490
Managers and professionals	10.14	133	32.3	271,407
Technical, sales, and clerical	6.04	79	15.2	127,668
Service workers	8.63	113	10.5	88,259
Construction workers and mechanics	9.62	126	5.8	48,533
Operators, fabricators, laborers	6.26	82	8.1	67,865
Retired	6.27	82	14.4	121,205
HOMEOWNERSHIP STATUS				
Average household	**7.61**	**100**	**100.0**	**839,680**
Homeowners	8.68	114	75.5	633,727
Renters	5.51	`72	24.5	205,683

Note: Households by type will not sum to the total because not all household types are shown. Hispanics may be of any race and most are white. Total household spending and market shares may not sum to total due to rounding. For an explanation of terms, see the introduction to this report.
Source: Calculations by New Strategist based on the Bureau of Labor Statistics' 2001 Consumer Expenditure Survey

90. SPENDING ON FRUIT-FLAVORED DRINKS, NONCARBONATED, 2001

Total (aggregate) household spending in 2001	$4,360,427,357,940
Total (aggregate) household spending on fruit-flavored drinks, noncarbonated	$2,246,502,040
Average annual household spending on fruit-flavored drinks, noncarbonated	$20.36

	AVERAGE ANNUAL SPENDING PER HOUSEHOLD (in dollars)	BEST CUSTOMERS (index)	BIGGEST CUSTOMERS (percent market share)	TOTAL (AGGREGATE) HH SPENDING (in thousands of dollars)
AGE OF HOUSEHOLDER				
Average household	**$20.36**	**100**	**100.0%**	**$2,246,502**
Under age 25	15.65	77	6.0	134,559
Aged 25 to 34	22.79	112	18.8	421,957
Aged 35 to 44	28.70	141	31.2	700,911
Aged 45 to 54	22.88	112	22.7	510,613
Aged 55 to 64	17.29	85	11.2	251,552
Aged 65 to 74	13.42	66	6.8	152,210
Aged 75 or older	6.14	30	2.9	65,059
HOUSEHOLD INCOME				
Average household reporting income	**21.37**	**100**	**100.0**	**1,896,267**
Under $10,000	13.94	65	8.0	152,370
$10,000 to $19,999	14.63	69	11.7	221,105
$20,000 to $29,999	18.30	86	11.7	220,973
$30,000 to $39,999	17.90	84	9.9	188,093
$40,000 to $49,999	27.81	130	12.8	242,976
$50,000 to $69,999	23.86	112	15.7	297,773
$70,000 or more	30.61	143	30.5	578,284
HOUSEHOLD TYPE				
Average household	**20.36**	**100**	**100.0**	**2,246,502**
Married couples	26.37	130	65.5	1,472,501
Married couples, no children	12.78	63	13.2	295,461
Married couples, with children	36.14	178	45.1	1,013,908
Oldest child under 6	26.15	128	5.8	131,273
Oldest child 6 to 17	40.63	200	27.4	615,341
Oldest child 18 or older	33.78	166	11.9	266,524
Single parent with child under 18	27.68	136	8.2	183,491
Single person	7.28	36	10.6	238,660
RACE				
Average household	**20.36**	**100**	**100.0**	**2,246,502**
Black	28.73	141	17.0	381,621
White and other	19.23	94	83.1	1,866,387
HISPANIC ORIGIN				
Average household	**20.36**	**100**	**100.0**	**2,246,502**
Hispanic	27.44	135	11.8	264,000
Non-Hispanic	19.65	97	88.1	1,979,109
REGION				
Average household	**20.36**	**100**	**100.0**	**2,246,502**
Northeast	22.81	112	21.3	477,641
Midwest	16.08	79	18.5	415,539
South	21.36	105	37.2	836,821
West	21.14	104	22.9	515,393

	AVERAGE ANNUAL SPENDING PER HOUSEHOLD (in dollars)	BEST CUSTOMERS (index)	BIGGEST CUSTOMERS (percent market share)	TOTAL (AGGREGATE) HH SPENDING (in thousands of dollars)
EDUCATION				
Average household	**$20.36**	**100**	**100.0%**	**$2,246,502**
Less than high school graduate	21.92	108	16.8	376,520
High school graduate	19.38	95	27.5	617,563
Some college	19.19	94	19.6	441,217
Associate's degree	17.79	87	7.7	172,634
College graduate	22.22	109	28.3	636,825
Bachelor's degree	23.24	114	19.5	438,771
Master's, professional, doctoral degree	20.38	100	8.9	199,316
OCCUPATION				
Average household	**20.36**	**100**	**100.0**	**2,246,502**
Self-employed	19.03	94	4.1	92,752
Wage-and-salary workers, total	22.63	111	74.6	1,674,982
Managers and professionals	24.30	119	29.0	650,414
Technical, sales, and clerical	21.47	106	20.2	453,811
Service workers	23.07	113	10.5	235,937
Construction workers and mechanics	23.22	114	5.2	117,145
Operators, fabricators, laborers	20.35	100	9.8	220,614
Retired	9.98	49	8.6	192,923
HOMEOWNERSHIP STATUS				
Average household	**20.36**	**100**	**100.0**	**2,246,502**
Homeowners	21.57	106	70.1	1,574,826
Renters	17.98	88	29.9	671,175

Note: Households by type will not sum to the total because not all household types are shown. Hispanics may be of any race and most are white. Total household spending and market shares may not sum to total due to rounding. For an explanation of terms, see the introduction to this report.
Source: Calculations by New Strategist based on the Bureau of Labor Statistics' 2001 Consumer Expenditure Survey

91. SPENDING ON GROCERIES ON TRIPS, 2001

Total (aggregate) household spending in 2001	$4,360,427,357,940
Total (aggregate) household spending on groceries on trips	$4,229,293,870
Average annual household spending on groceries on trips	$38.33

	AVERAGE ANNUAL SPENDING PER HOUSEHOLD (in dollars)	BEST CUSTOMERS (index)	BIGGEST CUSTOMERS (percent market share)	TOTAL (AGGREGATE) HH SPENDING (in thousands of dollars)
AGE OF HOUSEHOLDER				
Average household	**$38.33**	**100**	**100.0%**	**$4,229,294**
Under age 25	17.83	47	3.6	153,302
Aged 25 to 34	28.95	76	12.7	536,009
Aged 35 to 44	44.19	115	25.5	1,079,208
Aged 45 to 54	45.49	119	2.4	1,015,200
Aged 55 to 64	51.37	134	17.7	747,382
Aged 65 to 74	46.32	121	12.4	525,361
Aged 75 or older	16.31	43	4.1	172,821
HOUSEHOLD INCOME				
Average household reporting income	**40.65**	**100**	**100.0**	**3,607,078**
Under $10,000	15.35	38	4.7	167,785
$10,000 to $19,999	17.09	42	7.2	258,331
$20,000 to $29,999	28.97	71	9.7	349,813
$30,000 to $39,999	31.45	77	9.2	330,477
$40,000 to $49,999	38.52	95	9.3	336,549
$50,000 to $69,999	48.97	121	16.9	611,146
$70,000 or more	82.19	202	43.1	1,552,734
HOUSEHOLD TYPE				
Average household	**38.33**	**100**	**100.0**	**4,229,294**
Married couples	53.82	140	71.1	3,005,309
Married couples, no children	57.64	150	31.5	1,332,579
Married couples, with children	51.21	134	34.0	1,436,697
Oldest child under 6	41.38	108	4.9	207,728
Oldest child 6 to 17	57.18	149	20.5	865,991
Oldest child 18 or older	46.02	120	8.6	363,098
Single parent with child under 18	14.53	38	2.3	96,319
Single person	21.78	57	16.9	714,014
RACE				
Average household	**38.33**	**100**	**100.0**	**4,229,294**
Black	13.93	36	4.4	185,032
White and other	41.67	109	95.6	4,044,324
HISPANIC ORIGIN				
Average household	**38.33**	**100**	**100.0**	**4,229,294**
Hispanic	30.04	78	6.8	289,015
Non-Hispanic	39.12	102	93.2	3,940,088
REGION				
Average household	**38.33**	**100**	**100.0**	**4,229,294**
Northeast	38.88	101	19.3	814,147
Midwest	37.11	97	22.7	958,997
South	28.56	75	26.5	1,118,895
West	54.84	143	31.6	1,336,999

	AVERAGE ANNUAL SPENDING PER HOUSEHOLD (in dollars)	BEST CUSTOMERS (index)	BIGGEST CUSTOMERS (percent market share)	TOTAL (AGGREGATE) HH SPENDING (in thousands of dollars)
EDUCATION				
Average household	**$38.33**	**100**	**100.0%**	**$4,229,294**
Less than high school graduate	17.59	46	7.1	302,143
High school graduate	24.58	64	18.5	783,266
Some college	38.31	100	20.8	880,824
Associate's degree	41.11	107	9.4	398,931
College graduate	65.08	170	44.1	1,865,193
Bachelor's degree	61.26	160	27.3	1,156,589
Master's, professional, doctoral degree	72.46	189	16.8	708,659
OCCUPATION				
Average household	**38.33**	**100**	**100.0**	**4,229,294**
Self-employed	60.52	158	7.0	294,975
Wage-and-salary workers, total	41.29	108	72.3	3,056,121
Managers and professionals	59.18	154	37.5	1,584,012
Technical, sales, and clerical	34.74	91	17.4	734,299
Service workers	27.15	71	6.6	277,663
Construction workers and mechanics	34.24	89	4.1	172,741
Operators, fabricators, laborers	26.49	69	6.8	287,178
Retired	31.27	82	14.3	604,480
HOMEOWNERSHIP STATUS				
Average household	**38.33**	**100**	**100.0**	**4,229,294**
Homeowners	45.86	120	79.2	3,348,239
Renters	23.60	62	20.8	880,964

Note: Households by type will not sum to the total because not all household types are shown. Hispanics may be of any race and most are white. Total household spending and market shares may not sum to total due to rounding. For an explanation of terms, see the introduction to this report.
Source: Calculations by New Strategist based on the Bureau of Labor Statistics' 2001 Consumer Expenditure Survey

92. SPENDING ON GROUND BEEF, 2001

Total (aggregate) household spending in 2001	$4,360,427,357,940
Total (aggregate) household spending on ground beef	$9,983,472,720
Average annual household spending on ground beef	$90.48

	AVERAGE ANNUAL SPENDING PER HOUSEHOLD (in dollars)	BEST CUSTOMERS (index)	BIGGEST CUSTOMERS (percent market share)	TOTAL (AGGREGATE) HH SPENDING (in thousands of dollars)
AGE OF HOUSEHOLDER				
Average household	**$90.48**	**100**	**100.0%**	**$9,983,473**
Under age 25	64.07	71	5.5	550,874
Aged 25 to 34	93.21	103	17.3	1,725,783
Aged 35 to 44	101.54	112	24.8	2,479,810
Aged 45 to 54	111.08	123	24.8	2,478,972
Aged 55 to 64	90.38	100	13.2	1,314,939
Aged 65 to 74	72.42	80	8.2	821,388
Aged 75 or older	56.62	63	0.6	599,946
HOUSEHOLD INCOME				
Average household reporting income	**94.96**	**100**	**100.0**	**8,426,276**
Under $10,000	69.67	73	9.0	761,462
$10,000 to $19,999	77.03	81	13.8	1,164,138
$20,000 to $29,999	95.12	100	13.6	1,148,574
$30,000 to $39,999	99.00	104	12.3	1,040,292
$40,000 to $49,999	108.58	114	11.3	948,664
$50,000 to $69,999	101.53	107	15.0	1,267,094
$70,000 or more	111.17	117	24.9	2,100,224
HOUSEHOLD TYPE				
Average household	**90.48**	**100**	**100.0**	**9,983,473**
Married couples	113.49	125	63.5	6,337,282
Married couples, no children	88.83	98	20.6	2,053,661
Married couples, with children	128.67	142	36.2	3,609,837
Oldest child under 6	99.19	110	5.0	497,934
Oldest child 6 to 17	131.06	145	19.9	1,984,904
Oldest child 18 or older	145.36	161	11.5	1,146,890
Single parent with child under 18	109.94	122	7.3	728,792
Single person	39.77	44	13.1	1,303,780
RACE				
Average household	**90.48**	**100**	**100.0**	**9,983,473**
Black	97.16	107	12.9	1,290,576
White and other	89.58	99	87.1	8,694,277
HISPANIC ORIGIN				
Average household	**90.48**	**100**	**100.0**	**9,983,473**
Hispanic	110.41	122	10.6	1,062,255
Non-Hispanic	88.49	98	89.3	8,912,536
REGION				
Average household	**90.48**	**100**	**100.0**	**9,983,473**
Northeast	83.83	93	17.6	1,755,400
Midwest	90.57	100	23.4	2,340,510
South	99.73	110	39.1	3,907,122
West	81.28	90	19.8	1,981,606

	AVERAGE ANNUAL SPENDING PER HOUSEHOLD (in dollars)	BEST CUSTOMERS (index)	BIGGEST CUSTOMERS (percent market share)	TOTAL (AGGREGATE) HH SPENDING (in thousands of dollars)
EDUCATION				
Average household	**$90.48**	**100**	**100.0%**	**$9,983,473**
Less than high school graduate	104.45	115	18.0	1,794,138
High school graduate	98.24	109	31.4	3,130,516
Some college	83.78	93	19.3	1,926,270
Associate's degree	87.56	97	8.5	849,682
College graduate	79.80	88	22.9	2,287,068
Bachelor's degree	82.99	92	15.7	1,566,851
Master's, professional, doctoral degree	74.01	82	7.3	723,818
OCCUPATION				
Average household	**90.48**	**100**	**100.0**	**9,983,473**
Self-employed	104.70	116	5.1	510,308
Wage-and-salary workers, total	94.08	104	69.7	6,963,425
Managers and professionals	88.43	98	23.7	2,366,917
Technical, sales, and clerical	95.93	106	20.3	2,027,672
Service workers	83.93	93	8.6	858,352
Construction workers and mechanics	132.09	146	6.7	666,394
Operators, fabricators, laborers	96.31	106	10.5	1,044,097
Retired	67.62	75	13.1	1,307,162
HOMEOWNERSHIP STATUS				
Average household	**90.48**	**100**	**100.0**	**9,983,473**
Homeowners	97.90	108	71.6	7,147,679
Renters	75.96	84	28.4	2,835,511

Note: Households by type will not sum to the total because not all household types are shown. Hispanics may be of any race and most are white. Total household spending and market shares may not sum to total due to rounding. For an explanation of terms, see the introduction to this report.
Source: Calculations by New Strategist based on the Bureau of Labor Statistics' 2001 Consumer Expenditure Survey

93. SPENDING ON HAM, 2001

Total (aggregate) household spending in 2001	$4,360,427,357,940
Total (aggregate) household spending on ham	$4,411,353,220
Average annual household spending on ham	$39.98

	AVERAGE ANNUAL SPENDING PER HOUSEHOLD (in dollars)	BEST CUSTOMERS (index)	BIGGEST CUSTOMERS (percent market share)	TOTAL (AGGREGATE) HH SPENDING (in thousands of dollars)
AGE OF HOUSEHOLDER				
Average household	**$39.98**	**100**	**100.0%**	**$4,411,353**
Under age 25	15.83	40	3.1	136,106
Aged 25 to 34	32.01	80	13.4	592,665
Aged 35 to 44	45.09	113	25.0	1,101,188
Aged 45 to 54	49.08	123	24.8	1,095,318
Aged 55 to 64	46.06	115	15.2	670,127
Aged 65 to 74	39.90	100	10.3	452,546
Aged 75 or older	34.55	86	8.3	366,092
HOUSEHOLD INCOME				
Average household reporting income	**43.92**	**100**	**100.0**	**3,897,241**
Under $10,000	31.74	72	8.9	346,841
$10,000 to $19,999	35.81	82	13.9	541,207
$20,000 to $29,999	50.34	115	15.6	607,856
$30,000 to $39,999	40.90	93	11.0	429,777
$40,000 to $49,999	34.90	80	7.8	304,921
$50,000 to $69,999	48.07	109	15.4	599,914
$70,000 or more	56.53	129	27.4	1,067,965
HOUSEHOLD TYPE				
Average household	**39.98**	**100**	**100.0**	**4,411,353**
Married couples	51.85	130	65.6	2,895,304
Married couples, no children	47.99	120	25.2	1,109,481
Married couples, with children	51.85	130	33.0	1,454,652
Oldest child under 6	45.50	114	5.2	228,410
Oldest child 6 to 17	49.88	125	17.1	755,433
Oldest child 18 or older	60.86	152	10.9	480,185
Single parent with child under 18	40.31	101	6.1	267,215
Single person	17.18	43	12.8	563,212
RACE				
Average household	**39.98**	**100**	**100.0**	**4,411,353**
Black	36.50	91	11.0	484,830
White and other	40.45	101	89.0	3,925,915
HISPANIC ORIGIN				
Average household	**39.98**	**100**	**100.0**	**4,411,353**
Hispanic	49.33	123	10.8	474,604
Non-Hispanic	39.05	98	89.2	3,933,038
REGION				
Average household	**39.98**	**100**	**100.0**	**4,411,353**
Northeast	43.30	108	20.6	906,702
Midwest	37.10	93	21.7	958,738
South	43.63	109	38.7	1,709,293
West	34.27	86	18.9	835,503

	AVERAGE ANNUAL SPENDING PER HOUSEHOLD (in dollars)	BEST CUSTOMERS (index)	BIGGEST CUSTOMERS (percent market share)	TOTAL (AGGREGATE) HH SPENDING (in thousands of dollars)
EDUCATION				
Average household	**$39.98**	**100**	**100.0%**	**$4,411,353**
Less than high school graduate	45.31	113	17.6	778,290
High school graduate	44.83	112	32.4	1,428,553
Some college	35.03	88	18.3	805,410
Associate's degree	42.10	105	9.3	408,538
College graduate	34.48	86	22.4	988,197
Bachelor's degree	32.61	82	14.0	615,677
Master's, professional, doctoral degree	37.90	95	8.4	370,662
OCCUPATION				
Average household	**39.98**	**100**	**100.0**	**4,411,353**
Self-employed	45.34	113	5.0	220,987
Wage-and-salary workers, total	40.08	100	67.2	2,966,561
Managers and professionals	38.75	97	23.5	1,037,183
Technical, sales, and clerical	36.87	92	17.7	779,321
Service workers	37.74	94	8.7	385,967
Construction workers and mechanics	47.50	119	5.4	239,638
Operators, fabricators, laborers	47.07	118	11.6	510,286
Retired	37.86	95	16.6	731,872
HOMEOWNERSHIP STATUS				
Average household	**39.98**	**100**	**100.0**	**4,411,353**
Homeowners	44.62	112	73.8	3,257,706
Renters	30.90	77	26.1	1,153,466

Note: Households by type will not sum to the total because not all household types are shown. Hispanics may be of any race and most are white. Total household spending and market shares may not sum to total due to rounding. For an explanation of terms, see the introduction to this report.
Source: Calculations by New Strategist based on the Bureau of Labor Statistics' 2001 Consumer Expenditure Survey

94. SPENDING ON HOT DOGS, 2001

Total (aggregate) household spending in 2001	$4,360,427,357,940
Total (aggregate) household spending on hot dogs	$2,428,561,390
Average annual household spending on hot dogs	$22.01

	AVERAGE ANNUAL SPENDING PER HOUSEHOLD (in dollars)	BEST CUSTOMERS (index)	BIGGEST CUSTOMERS (percent market share)	TOTAL (AGGREGATE) HH SPENDING (in thousands of dollars)
AGE OF HOUSEHOLDER				
Average household	**$22.01**	**100**	**100.0%**	**$2,428,561**
Under age 25	14.95	68	5.3	128,540
Aged 25 to 34	23.00	105	17.5	425,845
Aged 35 to 44	25.73	117	25.9	628,378
Aged 45 to 54	25.68	117	23.6	573,101
Aged 55 to 64	21.89	100	13.1	318,478
Aged 65 to 74	16.94	77	7.9	192,134
Aged 75 or older	15.02	68	6.6	159,152
HOUSEHOLD INCOME				
Average household reporting income	**23.13**	**100**	**100.0**	**2,052,441**
Under $10,000	18.89	82	10.1	206,440
$10,000 to $19,999	17.54	76	12.9	265,010
$20,000 to $29,999	20.90	90	12.3	252,368
$30,000 to $39,999	24.54	106	12.6	257,866
$40,000 to $49,999	23.46	101	10.0	204,970
$50,000 to $69,999	26.36	114	16.0	328,973
$70,000 or more	28.41	123	26.2	536,722
HOUSEHOLD TYPE				
Average household	**22.01**	**100**	**100.0**	**2,428,561**
Married couples	28.16	128	64.7	1,572,454
Married couples, no children	19.83	90	18.9	458,450
Married couples, with children	34.01	155	39.3	954,151
Oldest child under 6	26.95	122	5.6	135,289
Oldest child 6 to 17	36.46	166	22.7	552,187
Oldest child 18 or older	33.92	154	11.0	267,629
Single parent with child under 18	26.74	122	7.3	177,260
Single person	9.81	45	13.2	321,601
RACE				
Average household	**22.01**	**100**	**100.0**	**2,428,561**
Black	23.74	108	13.0	315,338
White and other	21.78	99	87.0	2,113,880
HISPANIC ORIGIN				
Average household	**22.01**	**100**	**100.0**	**2,428,561**
Hispanic	26.95	122	10.7	259,286
Non-Hispanic	21.52	98	89.2	2,167,451
REGION				
Average household	**22.01**	**100**	**100.0**	**2,428,561**
Northeast	25.95	118	22.4	543,393
Midwest	20.47	93	21.8	528,986
South	23.47	107	37.9	919,484
West	17.90	81	18.0	436,402

	AVERAGE ANNUAL SPENDING PER HOUSEHOLD (in dollars)	BEST CUSTOMERS (index)	BIGGEST CUSTOMERS (percent market share)	TOTAL (AGGREGATE) HH SPENDING (in thousands of dollars)
EDUCATION				
Average household	**$22.01**	**100**	**100.0%**	**$2,428,561**
Less than high school graduate	26.31	120	18.6	451,927
High school graduate	22.42	102	29.4	714,436
Some college	19.75	90	18.7	454,092
Associate's degree	21.84	99	8.7	211,935
College graduate	20.82	95	24.6	596,701
Bachelor's degree	20.36	93	15.8	384,397
Master's, professional, doctoral degree	21.65	98	8.7	211,737
OCCUPATION				
Average household	**22.01**	**100**	**100.0**	**2,428,561**
Self-employed	23.89	109	4.8	116,440
Wage-and-salary workers, total	22.84	104	69.6	1,690,525
Managers and professionals	22.76	103	25.1	609,194
Technical, sales, and clerical	22.75	103	19.8	480,867
Service workers	22.98	104	9.7	235,017
Construction workers and mechanics	25.12	114	5.2	126,730
Operators, fabricators, laborers	22.08	100	9.9	239,369
Retired	16.56	75	13.2	320,121
HOMEOWNERSHIP STATUS				
Average household	**22.01**	**100**	**100.0**	**2,428,561**
Homeowners	24.05	109	72.3	1,755,891
Renters	18.03	82	27.7	673,042

Note: Households by type will not sum to the total because not all household types are shown. Hispanics may be of any race and most are white. Total household spending and market shares may not sum to total due to rounding. For an explanation of terms, see the introduction to this report.
Source: Calculations by New Strategist based on the Bureau of Labor Statistics' 2001 Consumer Expenditure Survey

95. SPENDING ON ICE CREAM AND RELATED PRODUCTS, 2001

Total (aggregate) household spending in 2001	$4,360,427,357,940
Total (aggregate) household spending on ice cream and related products	$6,266,151,810
Average annual household spending on ice cream and related products	$56.79

	AVERAGE ANNUAL SPENDING PER HOUSEHOLD (in dollars)	BEST CUSTOMERS (index)	BIGGEST CUSTOMERS (percent market share)	TOTAL (AGGREGATE) HH SPENDING (in thousands of dollars)
AGE OF HOUSEHOLDER				
Average household	**$56.79**	**100**	**100.0%**	**$6,266,152**
Under age 25	30.30	53	4.2	260,519
Aged 25 to 34	51.00	90	15.1	944,265
Aged 35 to 44	68.63	121	26.7	1,676,082
Aged 45 to 54	66.68	117	23.7	1,488,098
Aged 55 to 64	62.42	110	14.5	908,149
Aged 65 to 74	44.60	79	8.1	505,853
Aged 75 or older	45.12	80	7.6	478,092
HOUSEHOLD INCOME				
Average household reporting income	**59.22**	**100**	**100.0**	**5,254,887**
Under $10,000	30.42	51	6.3	332,416
$10,000 to $19,999	37.88	64	10.9	572,545
$20,000 to $29,999	49.65	84	11.4	599,524
$30,000 to $39,999	54.58	92	10.9	573,527
$40,000 to $49,999	64.02	108	10.6	559,343
$50,000 to $69,999	68.86	116	16.4	859,373
$70,000 or more	94.40	159	33.9	1,783,405
HOUSEHOLD TYPE				
Average household	**56.79**	**100**	**100.0**	**6,266,152**
Married couples	73.41	129	65.4	4,099,214
Married couples, no children	57.62	102	21.3	1,332,117
Married couples, with children	84.47	149	37.8	2,369,806
Oldest child under 6	62.68	110	5.0	314,654
Oldest child 6 to 17	90.91	160	22.0	1,376,832
Oldest child 18 or older	86.63	153	10.9	683,511
Single parent with child under 18	59.48	105	6.3	394,293
Single person	27.95	49	14.6	916,285
RACE				
Average household	**56.79**	**100**	**100.0**	**6,266,152**
Black	47.07	83	10.0	625,231
White and other	58.10	102	90.0	5,638,954
HISPANIC ORIGIN				
Average household	**56.79**	**100**	**100.0**	**6,266,152**
Hispanic	52.42	92	8.1	504,333
Non-Hispanic	57.22	101	92.0	5,763,084
REGION				
Average household	**56.79**	**100**	**100.0**	**6,266,152**
Northeast	64.35	113	21.5	1,347,489
Midwest	55.33	97	22.8	1,429,838
South	54.36	96	34.0	2,129,662
West	55.69	98	21.7	1,357,722

	AVERAGE ANNUAL SPENDING PER HOUSEHOLD (in dollars)	BEST CUSTOMERS (index)	BIGGEST CUSTOMERS (percent market share)	TOTAL (AGGREGATE) HH SPENDING (in thousands of dollars)
EDUCATION				
Average household	**$56.79**	**100**	**100.0%**	**$6,266,152**
Less than high school graduate	45.45	80	12.5	780,695
High school graduate	54.50	96	27.7	1,736,697
Some college	50.85	90	18.7	1,169,143
Associate's degree	58.77	104	9.1	570,304
College graduate	69.69	123	31.9	1,997,315
Bachelor's degree	67.33	119	20.3	1,271,190
Master's, professional, doctoral degree	74.00	130	11.5	723,720
OCCUPATION				
Average household	**56.79**	**100**	**100.0**	**6,266,152**
Self-employed	66.57	117	5.2	324,462
Wage-and-salary workers, total	59.19	104	69.9	4,381,007
Managers and professionals	69.76	123	29.8	1,867,196
Technical, sales, and clerical	50.95	90	17.2	1,076,930
Service workers	55.11	97	9.0	563,610
Construction workers and mechanics	57.71	102	4.6	291,147
Operators, fabricators, laborers	54.14	95	9.4	586,932
Retired	48.37	85	14.9	935,041
HOMEOWNERSHIP STATUS				
Average household	**56.79**	**100**	**100.0**	**6,266,152**
Homeowners	63.59	112	74.1	4,642,706
Renters	43.48	77	25.9	1,623,065

Note: Households by type will not sum to the total because not all household types are shown. Hispanics may be of any race and most are white. Total household spending and market shares may not sum to total due to rounding. For an explanation of terms, see the introduction to this report.
Source: Calculations by New Strategist based on the Bureau of Labor Statistics' 2001 Consumer Expenditure Survey

96. SPENDING ON JAMS, PRESERVES, AND OTHER SWEETS EXCEPT CANDY, 2001

Total (aggregate) household spending in 2001	$4,360,427,357,940
Total (aggregate) household spending on jams, preserves, and other sweets except candy	$2,153,817,280
Average annual household spending on jams, preserves, and other sweets except candy	$19.52

	AVERAGE ANNUAL SPENDING PER HOUSEHOLD (in dollars)	BEST CUSTOMERS (index)	BIGGEST CUSTOMERS (percent market share)	TOTAL (AGGREGATE) HH SPENDING (in thousands of dollars)
AGE OF HOUSEHOLDER				
Average household	**$19.52**	**100**	**100.0%**	**$2,153,817**
Under age 25	11.62	60	4.6	99,909
Aged 25 to 34	18.48	95	15.9	342,157
Aged 35 to 44	24.42	125	27.7	596,385
Aged 45 to 54	20.16	103	20.9	449,911
Aged 55 to 64	22.02	113	14.9	320,369
Aged 65 to 74	14.24	73	7.5	161,510
Aged 75 or older	17.07	87	8.4	180,874
HOUSEHOLD INCOME				
Average household reporting income	**20.88**	**100**	**100.0**	**1,852,787**
Under $10,000	12.31	59	7.3	134,567
$10,000 to $19,999	13.73	66	11.2	207,511
$20,000 to $29,999	18.52	89	12.1	223,629
$30,000 to $39,999	19.58	94	11.1	205,747
$40,000 to $49,999	22.41	107	10.6	195,796
$50,000 to $69,999	24.96	120	16.8	311,501
$70,000 or more	30.55	146	31.2	577,151
HOUSEHOLD TYPE				
Average household	**19.52**	**100**	**100.0**	**2,153,817**
Married couples	24.93	128	64.6	1,392,091
Married couples, no children	20.29	104	21.8	469,085
Married couples, with children	28.64	147	37.3	803,495
Oldest child under 6	25.35	130	5.9	127,257
Oldest child 6 to 17	30.59	157	21.5	463,286
Oldest child 18 or older	26.83	137	9.8	211,689
Single parent with child under 18	23.75	122	7.3	157,439
Single person	9.04	46	13.8	296,358
RACE				
Average household	**19.52**	**100**	**100.0**	**2,153,817**
Black	16.24	83	10.0	215,716
White and other	19.96	102	89.9	1,937,238
HISPANIC ORIGIN				
Average household	**19.52**	**100**	**100.0**	**2,153,817**
Hispanic	17.55	90	7.8	168,849
Non-Hispanic	19.72	101	92.2	1,986,159
REGION				
Average household	**19.52**	**100**	**100.0**	**2,153,817**
Northeast	20.98	108	20.4	439,321
Midwest	16.55	85	19.9	427,685
South	18.95	97	34.5	742,404
West	22.31	114	25.3	543,918

	AVERAGE ANNUAL SPENDING PER HOUSEHOLD (in dollars)	BEST CUSTOMERS (index)	BIGGEST CUSTOMERS (percent market share)	TOTAL (AGGREGATE) HH SPENDING (in thousands of dollars)
EDUCATION				
Average household	**$19.52**	**100**	**100.0%**	**$2,153,817**
Less than high school graduate	18.01	92	14.4	309,358
High school graduate	18.29	94	27.1	582,829
Some college	17.11	88	18.3	393,393
Associate's degree	20.27	104	9.1	196,700
College graduate	23.30	119	3.1	667,778
Bachelor's degree	23.07	118	20.2	435,562
Master's, professional, doctoral degree	23.72	122	10.8	231,982
OCCUPATION				
Average household	**19.52**	**100**	**100.0**	**2,153,817**
Self-employed	18.22	93	4.1	88,804
Wage-and-salary workers, total	20.25	104	69.6	1,498,824
Managers and professionals	23.22	119	28.9	621,507
Technical, sales, and clerical	20.54	105	20.2	434,154
Service workers	16.52	85	7.8	168,950
Construction workers and mechanics	20.03	103	4.7	101,051
Operators, fabricators, laborers	16.76	86	8.4	181,695
Retired	16.75	86	15.0	323,794
HOMEOWNERSHIP STATUS				
Average household	**19.52**	**100**	**100.0**	**2,153,817**
Homeowners	21.62	111	73.3	1,578,476
Renters	15.41	79	26.7	575,240

Note: Households by type will not sum to the total because not all household types are shown. Hispanics may be of any race and most are white. Total household spending and market shares may not sum to total due to rounding. For an explanation of terms, see the introduction to this report.
Source: Calculations by New Strategist based on the Bureau of Labor Statistics' 2001 Consumer Expenditure Survey

97. SPENDING ON LUNCH MEATS (COLD CUTS), 2001

Total (aggregate) household spending in 2001		$4,360,427,357,940
Total (aggregate) household spending on lunch meats (cold cuts)		$7,820,828,320
Average annual household spending on lunch meats (cold cuts)		$70.88

	AVERAGE ANNUAL SPENDING PER HOUSEHOLD (in dollars)	BEST CUSTOMERS (index)	BIGGEST CUSTOMERS (percent market share)	TOTAL (AGGREGATE) HH SPENDING (in thousands of dollars)
AGE OF HOUSEHOLDER				
Average household	**$70.88**	**100**	**100.0%**	**$7,820,828**
Under age 25	41.65	59	4.6	358,107
Aged 25 to 34	61.07	86	14.5	1,130,711
Aged 35 to 44	86.80	123	27.1	2,119,830
Aged 45 to 54	87.48	123	25.0	1,952,291
Aged 55 to 64	74.19	105	13.8	1,079,390
Aged 65 to 74	56.70	80	8.2	643,091
Aged 75 or older	50.02	71	6.8	530,012
HOUSEHOLD INCOME				
Average household reporting income	**73.98**	**100**	**100.0**	**6,564,615**
Under $10,000	46.77	63	7.8	511,131
$10,000 to $19,999	51.49	70	11.9	778,193
$20,000 to $29,999	70.81	96	13.0	855,031
$30,000 to $39,999	73.91	100	11.8	776,646
$40,000 to $49,999	73.51	99	9.8	642,257
$50,000 to $69,999	86.78	117	16.5	1,083,014
$70,000 or more	102.43	139	29.5	1,935,108
HOUSEHOLD TYPE				
Average household	**70.88**	**100**	**100.0**	**7,820,828**
Married couples	90.85	128	64.9	5,073,064
Married couples, no children	74.10	105	21.9	1,713,118
Married couples, with children	102.55	145	36.8	2,877,040
Oldest child under 6	89.32	126	5.7	448,386
Oldest child 6 to 17	99.97	141	19.4	1,514,046
Oldest child 18 or older	117.96	166	11.9	930,704
Single parent with child under 18	76.95	109	6.5	510,102
Single person	33.33	47	14.0	1,092,657
RACE				
Average household	**70.88**	**100**	**100.0**	**7,820,828**
Black	61.69	87	10.5	819,428
White and other	72.12	102	89.5	6,999,679
HISPANIC ORIGIN				
Average household	**70.88**	**100**	**100.0**	**7,820,828**
Hispanic	71.38	101	8.8	686,747
Non-Hispanic	70.83	100	91.2	7,133,856
REGION				
Average household	**70.88**	**100**	**100.0**	**7,820,828**
Northeast	88.79	125	23.8	1,859,263
Midwest	68.05	96	22.5	1,758,548
South	67.63	95	33.9	2,649,541
West	63.58	90	19.8	1,550,080

	AVERAGE ANNUAL SPENDING PER HOUSEHOLD (in dollars)	BEST CUSTOMERS (index)	BIGGEST CUSTOMERS (percent market share)	TOTAL (AGGREGATE) HH SPENDING (in thousands of dollars)
EDUCATION				
Average household	**$70.88**	**100**	**100.0%**	**$7,820,828**
Less than high school graduate	71.01	100	15.6	1,219,739
High school graduate	71.67	101	29.2	2,283,836
Some college	64.83	92	19.1	1,490,571
Associate's degree	80.34	113	10.0	779,619
College graduate	71.19	100	26.1	2,040,305
Bachelor's degree	69.81	99	16.9	1,318,013
Master's, professional, doctoral degree	73.69	104	9.2	720,688
OCCUPATION				
Average household	**70.88**	**100**	**100.0**	**7,820,828**
Self-employed	77.28	109	4.8	376,663
Wage-and-salary workers, total	74.17	105	70.2	5,489,767
Managers and professionals	74.51	105	25.5	1,994,335
Technical, sales, and clerical	71.97	102	19.5	1,521,230
Service workers	66.12	93	8.6	676,209
Construction workers and mechanics	93.18	132	6.0	470,093
Operators, fabricators, laborers	76.17	108	10.6	825,759
Retired	55.46	78	13.7	1,072,097
HOMEOWNERSHIP STATUS				
Average household	**70.88**	**100**	**100.0**	**7,820,828**
Homeowners	78.23	110	73.0	5,711,572
Renters	56.47	80	27.0	2,107,969

Note: Households by type will not sum to the total because not all household types are shown. Hispanics may be of any race and most are white. Total household spending and market shares may not sum to total due to rounding. For an explanation of terms, see the introduction to this report.
Source: Calculations by New Strategist based on the Bureau of Labor Statistics' 2001 Consumer Expenditure Survey

98. SPENDING ON MARGARINE 2001

Total (aggregate) household spending in 2001	$4,360,427,357,940
Total (aggregate) household spending on margarine	$1,261,174,770
Average annual household spending on margarine	$11.43

	AVERAGE ANNUAL SPENDING PER HOUSEHOLD (in dollars)	BEST CUSTOMERS (index)	BIGGEST CUSTOMERS (percent market share)	TOTAL (AGGREGATE) HH SPENDING (in thousands of dollars)
AGE OF HOUSEHOLDER				
Average household	**$11.43**	**100**	**100.0%**	**$1,261,175**
Under age 25	5.37	47	3.7	46,171
Aged 25 to 34	9.34	82	13.7	172,930
Aged 35 to 44	11.82	103	22.9	288,668
Aged 45 to 54	13.80	121	24.4	307,975
Aged 55 to 64	12.78	112	14.7	185,936
Aged 65 to 74	13.03	114	11.7	147,786
Aged 75 or older	10.66	93	9.0	112,953
HOUSEHOLD INCOME				
Average household reporting income	**12.11**	**100**	**100.0**	**1,074,581**
Under $10,000	8.54	71	8.7	93,339
$10,000 to $19,999	10.04	83	14.1	151,708
$20,000 to $29,999	11.09	92	12.5	133,912
$30,000 to $39,999	14.04	116	13.7	147,532
$40,000 to $49,999	14.60	121	11.9	127,560
$50,000 to $69,999	12.79	106	14.9	159,619
$70,000 or more	13.74	114	24.2	259,576
HOUSEHOLD TYPE				
Average household	**11.43**	**100**	**100.0**	**1,261,175**
Married couples	14.89	130	65.9	831,458
Married couples, no children	13.59	119	24.9	314,187
Married couples, with children	15.52	136	34.5	435,414
Oldest child under 6	11.49	101	4.6	57,680
Oldest child 6 to 17	14.82	130	17.8	224,449
Oldest child 18 or older	20.01	175	12.5	157,879
Single parent with child under 18	12.24	107	6.4	81,139
Single person	5.79	51	15.1	189,814
RACE				
Average household	**11.43**	**100**	**100.0**	**1,261,175**
Black	12.59	110	13.3	167,233
White and other	11.27	99	86.7	1,093,821
HISPANIC ORIGIN				
Average household	**11.43**	**100**	**100.0**	**1,261,175**
Hispanic	10.36	91	7.9	99,674
Non-Hispanic	11.53	101	92.1	1,161,279
REGION				
Average household	**11.43**	**100**	**100.0**	**1,261,175**
Northeast	11.29	99	18.7	236,413
Midwest	11.92	104	24.4	308,037
South	11.76	103	36.5	460,722
West	10.48	92	20.3	255,502

	AVERAGE ANNUAL SPENDING PER HOUSEHOLD (in dollars)	BEST CUSTOMERS (index)	BIGGEST CUSTOMERS (percent market share)	TOTAL (AGGREGATE) HH SPENDING (in thousands of dollars)
EDUCATION				
Average household	**$11.43**	**100**	**100.0%**	**$1,261,175**
Less than high school graduate	11.85	104	16.1	203,548
High school graduate	12.09	106	30.5	385,260
Some college	11.20	98	20.4	257,510
Associate's degree	8.99	79	6.9	87,239
College graduate	11.45	100	26.0	328,157
Bachelor's degree	11.36	99	1.7	214,477
Master's, professional, doctoral degree	11.62	102	9.0	113,644
OCCUPATION				
Average household	**11.43**	**100**	**100.0**	**1,261,175**
Self-employed	11.27	99	4.4	54,930
Wage-and-salary workers, total	11.24	98	66.0	831,940
Managers and professionals	11.73	103	24.9	313,965
Technical, sales, and clerical	11.25	98	18.9	237,791
Service workers	9.60	84	7.8	98,179
Construction workers and mechanics	12.27	107	4.9	61,902
Operators, fabricators, laborers	11.15	98	9.6	120,877
Retired	11.68	102	17.9	225,786
HOMEOWNERSHIP STATUS				
Average household	**11.43**	**100**	**100.0**	**1,261,175**
Homeowners	12.81	112	74.2	935,258
Renters	8.72	76	25.8	325,509

Note: Households by type will not sum to the total because not all household types are shown. Hispanics may be of any race and most are white. Total household spending and market shares may not sum to total due to rounding. For an explanation of terms, see the introduction to this report.
Source: Calculations by New Strategist based on the Bureau of Labor Statistics' 2001 Consumer Expenditure Survey

99. SPENDING ON MILK, FRESH, 2001

Total (aggregate) household spending in 2001	$4,360,427,357,940
Total (aggregate) household spending on milk, fresh	$13,626,866,500
Average annual household spending on milk, fresh	$123.50

	AVERAGE ANNUAL SPENDING PER HOUSEHOLD (in dollars)	BEST CUSTOMERS (index)	BIGGEST CUSTOMERS (percent market share)	TOTAL (AGGREGATE) HH SPENDING (in thousands of dollars)
AGE OF HOUSEHOLDER				
Average household	**$123.50**	**100**	**100.0%**	**$13,626,867**
Under age 25	79.24	64	5.0	681,306
Aged 25 to 34	125.88	102	17.1	2,330,668
Aged 35 to 44	150.39	122	27.0	3,672,825
Aged 45 to 54	141.81	115	23.2	3,164,774
Aged 55 to 64	111.05	90	11.9	1,615,666
Aged 65 to 74	100.67	82	8.4	1,141,799
Aged 75 or older	94.17	76	7.3	997,825
HOUSEHOLD INCOME				
Average household reporting income	**132.96**	**100**	**100.0**	**11,798,206**
Under $10,000	90.99	68	8.4	994,420
$10,000 to $19,999	105.72	80	13.5	1,597,746
$20,000 to $29,999	124.38	94	12.7	1,501,889
$30,000 to $39,999	133.70	101	11.9	1,404,920
$40,000 to $49,999	149.74	113	11.1	1,308,278
$50,000 to $69,999	147.64	111	15.6	1,842,547
$70,000 or more	167.67	126	26.8	3,167,622
HOUSEHOLD TYPE				
Average household	**123.50**	**100**	**100.0**	**13,626,867**
Married couples	156.82	127	64.3	8,756,829
Married couples, no children	106.90	87	18.1	2,471,421
Married couples, with children	188.76	153	38.9	5,295,662
Oldest child under 6	181.86	147	6.7	912,937
Oldest child 6 to 17	189.98	154	21.1	2,877,247
Oldest child 18 or older	191.24	155	11.1	1,508,884
Single parent with child under 18	124.72	101	6.1	826,769
Single person	61.98	50	14.9	2,031,890
RACE				
Average household	**123.50**	**100**	**100.0**	**13,626,867**
Black	91.62	74	8.9	1,216,989
White and other	127.80	104	91.0	12,403,757
HISPANIC ORIGIN				
Average household	**123.50**	**100**	**100.0**	**13,626,867**
Hispanic	155.27	126	11.0	1,493,853
Non-Hispanic	120.33	97	88.9	12,119,397
REGION				
Average household	**123.50**	**100**	**100.0**	**13,626,867**
Northeast	126.12	102	19.4	2,640,953
Midwest	124.43	101	23.6	3,215,520
South	114.76	93	33.0	4,495,953
West	134.31	109	24.0	3,274,478

	AVERAGE ANNUAL SPENDING PER HOUSEHOLD (in dollars)	BEST CUSTOMERS (index)	BIGGEST CUSTOMERS (percent market share)	TOTAL (AGGREGATE) HH SPENDING (in thousands of dollars)
EDUCATION				
Average household	**$123.50**	**100**	**100.0%**	**$13,626,867**
Less than high school graduate	120.21	97	15.2	2,064,847
High school graduate	121.21	98	28.3	3,862,478
Some college	117.38	95	19.8	2,698,801
Associate's degree	124.97	101	8.9	1,212,709
College graduate	132.03	107	27.8	3,783,980
Bachelor's degree	129.71	105	18.0	2,448,925
Master's, professional, doctoral degree	136.24	110	9.8	1,332,427
OCCUPATION				
Average household	**123.50**	**100**	**100.0**	**13,626,867**
Self-employed	141.87	115	5.1	691,474
Wage-and-salary workers, total	126.29	102	68.6	9,347,481
Managers and professionals	131.91	107	25.9	3,530,703
Technical, sales, and clerical	119.88	97	18.6	2,533,904
Service workers	115.51	94	8.7	1,181,321
Construction workers and mechanics	139.09	113	5.1	701,709
Operators, fabricators, laborers	128.74	104	10.2	1,395,670
Retired	95.29	77	13.5	1,842,051
HOMEOWNERSHIP STATUS				
Average household	**123.50**	**100**	**100.0**	**13,626,867**
Homeowners	133.46	108	71.5	9,743,915
Renters	104.01	84	28.5	3,882,589

Note: Households by type will not sum to the total because not all household types are shown. Hispanics may be of any race and most are white. Total household spending and market shares may not sum to total due to rounding. For an explanation of terms, see the introduction to this report.
Source: Calculations by New Strategist based on the Bureau of Labor Statistics' 2001 Consumer Expenditure Survey

100. SPENDING ON NONDAIRY CREAM AND IMITATION MILK, 2001

Total (aggregate) household spending in 2001	$4,360,427,357,940
Total (aggregate) household spending on nondairy cream and imitation milk	$1,113,320,510
Average annual household spending on nondairy cream and imitation milk	$10.09

	AVERAGE ANNUAL SPENDING PER HOUSEHOLD (in dollars)	BEST CUSTOMERS (index)	BIGGEST CUSTOMERS (percent market share)	TOTAL (AGGREGATE) HH SPENDING (in thousands of dollars)
AGE OF HOUSEHOLDER				
Average household	**$10.09**	**100**	**100.0%**	**$1,113,321**
Under age 25	4.98	49	3.8	42,818
Aged 25 to 34	7.29	72	12.1	134,974
Aged 35 to 44	11.38	113	25.0	277,922
Aged 45 to 54	12.15	120	24.4	271,152
Aged 55 to 64	12.24	121	16.0	178,080
Aged 65 to 74	9.81	97	10.0	111,265
Aged 75 or older	9.27	92	8.8	98,225
HOUSEHOLD INCOME				
Average household reporting income	**10.75**	**100**	**100.0**	**953,901**
Under $10,000	6.98	65	8.0	76,292
$10,000 to $19,999	9.40	88	14.9	142,132
$20,000 to $29,999	10.21	95	12.9	123,286
$30,000 to $39,999	9.51	89	10.5	99,931
$40,000 to $49,999	10.03	93	9.2	87,632
$50,000 to $69,999	13.37	124	17.5	166,858
$70,000 or more	13.63	127	27.0	257,498
HOUSEHOLD TYPE				
Average household	**10.09**	**100**	**100.0**	**1,113,321**
Married couples	12.83	127	64.4	716,427
Married couples, no children	11.89	118	24.7	274,885
Married couples, with children	13.25	131	33.4	371,729
Oldest child under 6	8.81	87	4.0	44,226
Oldest child 6 to 17	12.60	125	17.1	190,827
Oldest child 18 or older	17.97	178	12.7	141,783
Single parent with child under 18	8.57	85	5.1	56,811
Single person	5.18	51	15.3	169,816
RACE				
Average household	**10.09**	**100**	**100.0**	**1,113,321**
Black	5.11	51	6.1	67,876
White and other	10.76	107	93.8	1,044,323
HISPANIC ORIGIN				
Average household	**10.09**	**100**	**100.0**	**1,113,321**
Hispanic	7.20	71	6.2	69,271
Non-Hispanic	10.38	103	93.9	1,045,453
REGION				
Average household	**10.09**	**100**	**100.0**	**1,113,321**
Northeast	10.07	100	18.9	210,866
Midwest	9.74	97	22.6	251,701
South	10.19	101	35.9	399,214
West	10.31	102	22.6	251,358

	AVERAGE ANNUAL SPENDING PER HOUSEHOLD (in dollars)	BEST CUSTOMERS (index)	BIGGEST CUSTOMERS (percent market share)	TOTAL (AGGREGATE) HH SPENDING (in thousands of dollars)
EDUCATION				
Average household	**$10.09**	**100**	**100.0%**	**$1,113,321**
Less than high school graduate	10.56	105	16.3	181,389
High school graduate	9.68	96	27.7	308,463
Some college	10.58	105	21.8	243,255
Associate's degree	10.09	100	8.8	97,913
College graduate	9.91	98	25.5	284,021
Bachelor's degree	9.35	93	15.9	176,528
Master's, professional, doctoral degree	10.93	108	9.6	106,895
OCCUPATION				
Average household	**10.09**	**100**	**100.0**	**1,113,321**
Self-employed	13.65	135	6.0	66,530
Wage-and-salary workers, total	10.03	99	66.7	742,381
Managers and professionals	11.32	112	27.2	302,991
Technical, sales, and clerical	10.11	100	19.2	213,695
Service workers	9.36	93	8.6	95,725
Construction workers and mechanics	8.39	83	3.8	42,328
Operators, fabricators, laborers	8.39	83	8.2	90,956
Retired	10.37	103	1.8	200,463
HOMEOWNERSHIP STATUS				
Average household	**10.09**	**100**	**100.0**	**1,113,321**
Homeowners	11.69	116	76.7	853,487
Renters	6.96	69	23.3	259,810

Note: Households by type will not sum to the total because not all household types are shown. Hispanics may be of any race and most are white. Total household spending and market shares may not sum to total due to rounding. For an explanation of terms, see the introduction to this report.
Source: Calculations by New Strategist based on the Bureau of Labor Statistics' 2001 Consumer Expenditure Survey

101. SPENDING ON NUTS, 2001

Total (aggregate) household spending in 2001	$4,360,427,357,940
Total (aggregate) household spending on nuts	$2,406,493,590
Average annual household spending on nuts	$21.81

	AVERAGE ANNUAL SPENDING PER HOUSEHOLD (in dollars)	BEST CUSTOMERS (index)	BIGGEST CUSTOMERS (percent market share)	TOTAL (AGGREGATE) HH SPENDING (in thousands of dollars)
AGE OF HOUSEHOLDER				
Average household	**$21.81**	**100**	**100.0%**	**$2,406,494**
Under age 25	8.69	40	3.1	74,717
Aged 25 to 34	15.47	71	11.9	286,427
Aged 35 to 44	21.67	99	22.0	529,225
Aged 45 to 54	24.61	113	22.8	549,221
Aged 55 to 64	28.76	132	17.4	418,429
Aged 65 to 74	26.95	124	12.7	305,667
Aged 75 or older	23.46	108	10.3	248,582
HOUSEHOLD INCOME				
Average household reporting income	**22.49**	**100**	**100.0**	**1,995,650**
Under $10,000	12.97	58	7.1	141,759
$10,000 to $19,999	13.23	59	10.0	199,909
$20,000 to $29,999	19.90	89	12.0	240,293
$30,000 to $39,999	20.99	93	11.1	220,563
$40,000 to $49,999	24.78	110	10.8	216,503
$50,000 to $69,999	23.09	103	14.4	288,163
$70,000 or more	37.15	165	35.2	701,838
HOUSEHOLD TYPE				
Average household	**21.81**	**100**	**100.0**	**2,406,494**
Married couples	28.73	132	66.7	1,604,283
Married couples, no children	30.09	138	28.9	695,651
Married couples, with children	27.35	125	31.9	767,304
Oldest child under 6	21.15	97	4.4	106,173
Oldest child 6 to 17	25.83	118	16.3	391,195
Oldest child 18 or older	35.28	162	11.6	278,359
Single parent with child under 18	17.47	80	4.8	115,809
Single person	12.40	57	16.9	406,509
RACE				
Average household	**21.81**	**100**	**100.0**	**2,406,494**
Black	15.08	69	8.3	200,308
White and other	22.72	104	91.6	2,205,112
HISPANIC ORIGIN				
Average household	**21.81**	**100**	**100.0**	**2,406,494**
Hispanic	16.04	74	6.4	154,321
Non-Hispanic	22.38	103	93.7	2,254,069
REGION				
Average household	**21.81**	**100**	**100.0**	**2,406,494**
Northeast	19.50	89	17.0	408,330
Midwest	21.73	100	23.3	561,547
South	20.85	96	33.9	816,840
West	25.44	117	25.8	620,227

	AVERAGE ANNUAL SPENDING PER HOUSEHOLD (in dollars)	BEST CUSTOMERS (index)	BIGGEST CUSTOMERS (percent market share)	TOTAL (AGGREGATE) HH SPENDING (in thousands of dollars)
EDUCATION				
Average household	**$21.81**	**100**	**100.0%**	**$2,406,494**
Less than high school graduate	15.47	71	11.0	265,728
High school graduate	18.92	87	25.1	602,905
Some college	23.90	110	22.8	549,509
Associate's degree	24.07	110	9.7	233,575
College graduate	26.35	121	31.4	755,191
Bachelor's degree	23.52	108	18.5	444,058
Master's, professional, doctoral degree	31.51	145	12.8	308,168
OCCUPATION				
Average household	**21.81**	**100**	**100.0**	**2,406,494**
Self-employed	30.49	140	6.2	148,608
Wage-and-salary workers, total	21.09	97	64.9	1,560,997
Managers and professionals	25.02	115	27.8	669,685
Technical, sales, and clerical	20.14	92	17.7	425,699
Service workers	16.65	76	7.1	170,280
Construction workers and mechanics	26.15	120	5.5	131,927
Operators, fabricators, laborers	15.99	73	7.2	173,348
Retired	25.07	115	20.1	484,628
HOMEOWNERSHIP STATUS				
Average household	**21.81**	**100**	**100.0**	**2,406,494**
Homeowners	25.50	117	77.4	1,861,755
Renters	14.58	67	22.6	544,257

Note: Households by type will not sum to the total because not all household types are shown. Hispanics may be of any race and most are white. Total household spending and market shares may not sum to total due to rounding. For an explanation of terms, see the introduction to this report.
Source: Calculations by New Strategist based on the Bureau of Labor Statistics' 2001 Consumer Expenditure Survey

102. SPENDING ON OLIVES, PICKLES, RELISHES, 2001

Total (aggregate) household spending in 2001	$4,360,427,357,940	
Total (aggregate) household spending on olives, pickles, and relishes	$1,100,079,830	
Average annual household spending on olives, pickles, and relishes	$9.97	

	AVERAGE ANNUAL SPENDING PER HOUSEHOLD (in dollars)	BEST CUSTOMERS (index)	BIGGEST CUSTOMERS (percent market share)	TOTAL (AGGREGATE) HH SPENDING (in thousands of dollars)
AGE OF HOUSEHOLDER				
Average household	**$9.97**	**100**	**100.0%**	**$1,100,080**
Under age 25	3.29	33	2.6	28,287
Aged 25 to 34	8.82	89	14.8	163,302
Aged 35 to 44	11.36	114	25.2	277,434
Aged 45 to 54	13.19	132	26.8	294,361
Aged 55 to 64	10.85	109	14.3	157,857
Aged 65 to 74	8.16	82	8.4	92,551
Aged 75 or older	8.07	81	7.8	85,510
HOUSEHOLD INCOME				
Average household reporting income	**10.64**	**100**	**100.0**	**944,140**
Under $10,000	5.84	55	6.8	63,812
$10,000 to $19,999	6.33	60	10.1	95,699
$20,000 to $29,999	7.63	72	9.8	92,132
$30,000 to $39,999	8.53	80	9.5	89,633
$40,000 to $49,999	12.62	119	11.7	110,261
$50,000 to $69,999	11.64	109	15.4	145,267
$70,000 or more	18.86	177	37.7	356,303
HOUSEHOLD TYPE				
Average household	**9.97**	**100**	**100.0**	**1,100,080**
Married couples	13.29	133	67.5	742,114
Married couples, no children	11.25	113	23.6	260,089
Married couples, with children	14.41	145	36.7	404,273
Oldest child under 6	10.63	107	4.9	53,363
Oldest child 6 to 17	15.16	152	20.9	229,598
Oldest child 18 or older	15.60	157	11.2	123,084
Single parent with child under 18	8.12	81	4.9	53,828
Single person	4.96	50	14.8	162,604
RACE				
Average household	**9.97**	**100**	**100.0**	**1,100,080**
Black	8.27	83	10.0	109,850
White and other	10.19	102	89.9	989,001
HISPANIC ORIGIN				
Average household	**9.97**	**100**	**100.0**	**1,100,080**
Hispanic	5.86	59	5.1	56,379
Non-Hispanic	10.38	104	95.0	1,045,453
REGION				
Average household	**9.97**	**100**	**100.0**	**1,100,080**
Northeast	9.52	96	18.1	199,349
Midwest	9.56	96	22.5	247,050
South	9.81	98	34.9	384,326
West	11.02	111	24.4	268,668

	AVERAGE ANNUAL SPENDING PER HOUSEHOLD (in dollars)	BEST CUSTOMERS (index)	BIGGEST CUSTOMERS (percent market share)	TOTAL (AGGREGATE) HH SPENDING (in thousands of dollars)
EDUCATION				
Average household	**$9.97**	**100**	**100.0%**	**$1,100,080**
Less than high school graduate	7.11	71	11.1	122,129
High school graduate	8.86	89	25.7	282,333
Some college	9.72	98	20.3	223,482
Associate's degree	9.27	93	8.2	89,956
College graduate	13.27	133	34.6	380,318
Bachelor's degree	11.12	112	19.1	209,946
Master's, professional, doctoral degree	17.19	172	15.3	168,118
OCCUPATION				
Average household	**9.97**	**100**	**100.0**	**1,100,080**
Self-employed	15.14	152	6.7	73,792
Wage-and-salary workers, total	10.42	105	70.1	771,247
Managers and professionals	13.55	136	33.0	362,679
Technical, sales, and clerical	9.23	93	17.7	195,095
Service workers	6.04	61	5.6	61,771
Construction workers and mechanics	12.63	127	5.8	63,718
Operators, fabricators, laborers	8.56	86	8.4	92,799
Retired	7.74	78	13.6	149,622
HOMEOWNERSHIP STATUS				
Average household	**9.97**	**100**	**100.0**	**1,100,080**
Homeowners	11.70	117	77.7	854,217
Renters	6.56	66	22.3	244,878

Note: Households by type will not sum to the total because not all household types are shown. Hispanics may be of any race and most are white. Total household spending and market shares may not sum to total due to rounding. For an explanation of terms, see the introduction to this report.
Source: Calculations by New Strategist based on the Bureau of Labor Statistics' 2001 Consumer Expenditure Survey

103. SPENDING ON OTHER BEVERAGES AND ICE, 2001

(excludes alcoholic beverages, carbonated beverages, coffee, fruit-flavored beverages, nonalcoholic beer, and tea)

Total (aggregate) household spending in 2001	$4,360,427,357,940
Total (aggregate) household spending on other beverages and ice	$5,039,182,130
Average annual household spending on other beverages and ice	$45.67

	AVERAGE ANNUAL SPENDING PER HOUSEHOLD (in dollars)	BEST CUSTOMERS (index)	BIGGEST CUSTOMERS (percent market share)	TOTAL (AGGREGATE) HH SPENDING (in thousands of dollars)
AGE OF HOUSEHOLDER				
Average household	**$45.67**	**100**	**100.0%**	**$5,039,182**
Under age 25	33.69	74	5.7	289,667
Aged 25 to 34	45.84	100	16.8	848,728
Aged 35 to 44	57.15	125	27.7	1,395,717
Aged 45 to 54	56.34	123	25.0	1,257,340
Aged 55 to 64	39.74	87	11.5	578,177
Aged 65 to 74	30.63	67	6.9	347,406
Aged 75 or older	29.34	64	6.2	310,887
HOUSEHOLD INCOME				
Average household reporting income	**47.39**	**100**	**100.0**	**4,205,152**
Under $10,000	28.77	61	7.5	314,430
$10,000 to $19,999	27.75	59	10.0	419,375
$20,000 to $29,999	33.31	70	9.6	402,218
$30,000 to $39,999	41.31	87	10.3	434,086
$40,000 to $49,999	45.70	96	9.5	399,281
$50,000 to $69,999	66.67	141	19.8	832,042
$70,000 or more	75.81	160	34.1	1,432,203
HOUSEHOLD TYPE				
Average household	**45.67**	**100**	**100.0**	**5,039,182**
Married couples	56.89	125	63.0	3,176,738
Married couples, no children	41.95	92	19.2	969,842
Married couples, with children	67.57	148	37.6	1,895,676
Oldest child under 6	55.59	122	5.5	279,062
Oldest child 6 to 17	71.28	156	21.4	1,079,536
Oldest child 18 or older	68.38	150	10.7	539,518
Single parent with child under 18	45.61	100	6.0	302,349
Single person	27.29	60	17.8	894,648
RACE				
Average household	**45.67**	**100**	**100.0**	**5,039,182**
Black	34.01	75	9.0	451,755
White and other	47.24	103	91.0	4,584,925
HISPANIC ORIGIN				
Average household	**45.67**	**100**	**100.0**	**5,039,182**
Hispanic	56.35	123	10.8	542,143
Non-Hispanic	44.60	98	89.1	4,492,023
REGION				
Average household	**45.67**	**100**	**100.0**	**5,039,182**
Northeast	44.77	98	18.6	937,484
Midwest	43.69	96	22.4	1,129,037
South	41.44	91	32.2	1,623,495
West	55.32	121	26.8	1,348,702

	AVERAGE ANNUAL SPENDING PER HOUSEHOLD (in dollars)	BEST CUSTOMERS (index)	BIGGEST CUSTOMERS (percent market share)	TOTAL (AGGREGATE) HH SPENDING (in thousands of dollars)
EDUCATION				
Average household	**$45.67**	**100**	**100.0%**	**$5,039,182**
Less than high school graduate	36.89	81	12.6	633,660
High school graduate	41.72	91	26.4	1,329,450
Some college	48.75	107	22.2	1,120,860
Associate's degree	42.59	93	8.2	413,293
College graduate	53.90	118	30.7	1,544,774
Bachelor's degree	52.43	115	19.6	989,878
Master's, professional, doctoral degree	56.56	124	11.0	553,157
OCCUPATION				
Average household	**45.67**	**100**	**100.0**	**5,039,182**
Self-employed	57.24	125	5.5	278,988
Wage-and-salary workers, total	49.23	108	72.3	3,643,808
Managers and professionals	55.29	121	29.4	1,479,892
Technical, sales, and clerical	48.11	105	20.2	1,016,901
Service workers	45.46	100	9.2	464,919
Construction workers and mechanics	55.78	122	5.6	281,410
Operators, fabricators, laborers	38.71	85	8.3	419,655
Retired	31.31	69	12.0	605,254
HOMEOWNERSHIP STATUS				
Average household	**45.67**	**100**	**100.0**	**5,039,182**
Homeowners	48.53	106	70.3	3,543,175
Renters	40.06	88	29.7	1,495,400

Note: Households by type will not sum to the total because not all household types are shown. Hispanics may be of any race and most are white. Total household spending and market shares may not sum to total due to rounding. For an explanation of terms, see the introduction to this report.
Source: Calculations by New Strategist based on the Bureau of Labor Statistics' 2001 Consumer Expenditure Survey

104. SPENDING ON PASTA, CORNMEAL, OTHER CEREAL PRODUCTS, 2001

(except flour and rice)

Total (aggregate) household spending in 2001	$4,360,427,357,940
Total (aggregate) household spending on pasta, cornmeal, and other cereal products	$3,262,724,230
Average annual household spending on pasta, cornmeal, and other cereal products	$29.57

	AVERAGE ANNUAL SPENDING PER HOUSEHOLD (in dollars)	BEST CUSTOMERS (index)	BIGGEST CUSTOMERS (percent market share)	TOTAL (AGGREGATE) HH SPENDING (in thousands of dollars)
AGE OF HOUSEHOLDER				
Average household	**$29.57**	**100**	**100.0%**	**$3,262,724**
Under age 25	19.63	66	5.2	168,779
Aged 25 to 34	30.46	103	17.3	563,967
Aged 35 to 44	34.88	118	26.1	851,839
Aged 45 to 54	34.39	116	23.5	767,482
Aged 55 to 64	27.64	94	12.3	402,134
Aged 65 to 74	24.19	82	8.4	274,363
Aged 75 or older	21.69	73	7.0	229,827
HOUSEHOLD INCOME				
Average household reporting income	**32.00**	**100**	**100.0**	**2,839,520**
Under $10,000	20.60	64	7.9	225,163
$10,000 to $19,999	24.56	77	13.1	371,240
$20,000 to $29,999	30.19	94	12.8	364,544
$30,000 to $39,999	32.66	102	12.1	343,191
$40,000 to $49,999	33.74	105	10.4	294,786
$50,000 to $69,999	34.53	108	15.2	430,934
$70,000 or more	43.19	135	28.7	815,946
HOUSEHOLD TYPE				
Average household	**29.57**	**100**	**100.0**	**3,262,724**
Married couples	35.78	121	61.2	1,997,955
Married couples, no children	27.00	91	19.1	624,213
Married couples, with children	41.11	139	35.3	1,153,341
Oldest child under 6	37.46	127	5.8	188,049
Oldest child 6 to 17	40.06	136	18.6	606,709
Oldest child 18 or older	46.08	156	11.1	363,571
Single parent with child under 18	38.19	129	7.8	253,162
Single person	15.11	51	15.2	495,351
RACE				
Average household	**29.57**	**100**	**100.0**	**3,262,724**
Black	27.39	93	11.2	363,821
White and other	29.87	101	88.9	2,899,063
HISPANIC ORIGIN				
Average household	**29.57**	**100**	**100.0**	**3,262,724**
Hispanic	33.63	114	9.9	323,554
Non-Hispanic	29.17	99	90.1	2,937,944
REGION				
Average household	**29.57**	**100**	**100.0**	**3,262,724**
Northeast	34.18	116	21.9	715,729
Midwest	28.28	96	22.4	730,812
South	25.02	85	30.0	980,209
West	34.27	116	25.6	835,503

	AVERAGE ANNUAL SPENDING PER HOUSEHOLD (in dollars)	BEST CUSTOMERS (index)	BIGGEST CUSTOMERS (percent market share)	TOTAL (AGGREGATE) HH SPENDING (in thousands of dollars)
EDUCATION				
Average household	**$29.57**	**100**	**100.0%**	**$3,262,724**
Less than high school graduate	32.26	109	17.0	554,130
High school graduate	27.86	94	27.2	887,787
Some college	25.87	88	18.2	594,803
Associate's degree	28.13	95	8.4	272,974
College graduate	33.17	112	29.1	950,652
Bachelor's degree	32.33	109	18.7	610,390
Master's, professional, doctoral degree	34.72	117	10.4	339,562
OCCUPATION				
Average household	**29.57**	**100**	**100.0**	**3,262,724**
Self-employed	39.80	135	5.9	193,985
Wage-and-salary workers, total	30.31	103	68.8	2,243,425
Managers and professionals	33.83	114	27.8	905,494
Technical, sales, and clerical	26.75	91	17.3	565,415
Service workers	30.97	105	9.7	316,730
Construction workers and mechanics	29.88	101	4.6	150,745
Operators, fabricators, laborers	28.22	95	9.4	305,933
Retired	22.62	77	13.4	437,267
HOMEOWNERSHIP STATUS				
Average household	**29.57**	**100**	**100.0**	**3,262,724**
Homeowners	31.23	106	69.9	2,280,102
Renters	26.34	89	30.1	983,246

Note: Households by type will not sum to the total because not all household types are shown. Hispanics may be of any race and most are white. Total household spending and market shares may not sum to total due to rounding. For an explanation of terms, see the introduction to this report.
Source: Calculations by New Strategist based on the Bureau of Labor Statistics' 2001 Consumer Expenditure Survey

105. SPENDING ON PEANUT BUTTER, 2001

Total (aggregate) household spending in 2001	$4,360,427,357,940
Total (aggregate) household spending on peanut butter	$1,400,201,910
Average annual household spending on peanut butter	$12.69

	AVERAGE ANNUAL SPENDING PER HOUSEHOLD (in dollars)	BEST CUSTOMERS (index)	BIGGEST CUSTOMERS (percent market share)	TOTAL (AGGREGATE) HH SPENDING (in thousands of dollars)
AGE OF HOUSEHOLDER				
Average household	**$12.69**	**100**	**100.0%**	**$1,400,202**
Under age 25	8.61	68	5.3	74,029
Aged 25 to 34	13.65	108	18.1	252,730
Aged 35 to 44	14.69	116	25.6	358,759
Aged 45 to 54	15.27	120	24.3	340,781
Aged 55 to 64	11.09	87	11.5	161,348
Aged 65 to 74	10.14	80	8.2	115,008
Aged 75 or older	9.03	71	6.8	95,682
HOUSEHOLD INCOME				
Average household reporting income	**12.59**	**100**	**100.0**	**1,117,174**
Under $10,000	9.71	77	9.5	106,107
$10,000 to $19,999	9.04	72	12.2	136,636
$20,000 to $29,999	9.80	78	10.6	118,335
$30,000 to $39,999	11.88	94	11.2	124,835
$40,000 to $49,999	15.89	126	12.4	138,831
$50,000 to $69,999	15.31	122	17.1	191,069
$70,000 or more	16.24	129	27.5	306,806
HOUSEHOLD TYPE				
Average household	**12.69**	**100**	**100.0**	**1,400,202**
Married couples	15.77	124	62.9	880,597
Married couples, no children	11.65	92	19.2	269,336
Married couples, with children	18.75	148	37.6	526,031
Oldest child under 6	18.28	144	6.6	91,766
Oldest child 6 to 17	17.15	135	18.5	259,737
Oldest child 18 or older	22.58	178	12.7	178,156
Single parent with child under 18	16.95	134	8.0	112,362
Single person	6.23	49	14.6	204,238
RACE				
Average household	**12.69**	**100**	**100.0**	**1,400,202**
Black	11.84	93	11.2	157,271
White and other	12.81	101	88.8	1,243,287
HISPANIC ORIGIN				
Average household	**12.69**	**100**	**100.0**	**1,400,202**
Hispanic	9.49	75	6.5	91,303
Non-Hispanic	13.01	103	93.6	1,310,341
REGION				
Average household	**12.69**	**100**	**100.0**	**1,400,202**
Northeast	13.12	103	19.6	274,733
Midwest	12.66	100	23.4	327,160
South	12.80	101	35.8	501,466
West	12.19	96	21.2	297,192

	AVERAGE ANNUAL SPENDING PER HOUSEHOLD (in dollars)	BEST CUSTOMERS (index)	BIGGEST CUSTOMERS (percent market share)	TOTAL (AGGREGATE) HH SPENDING (in thousands of dollars)
EDUCATION				
Average household	**$12.69**	**100**	**100.0%**	**$1,400,202**
Less than high school graduate	10.98	87	13.5	188,604
High school graduate	12.61	99	28.7	401,830
Some college	10.91	86	17.9	250,843
Associate's degree	13.89	110	9.6	134,789
College graduate	14.71	116	30.1	421,589
Bachelor's degree	14.14	111	19.1	266,963
Master's, professional, doctoral degree	15.73	124	11.0	153,839
OCCUPATION				
Average household	**12.69**	**100**	**100.0**	**1,400,202**
Self-employed	15.02	118	5.2	73,208
Wage-and-salary workers, total	13.12	103	69.4	971,090
Managers and professionals	14.29	113	27.3	382,486
Technical, sales, and clerical	13.56	107	20.5	286,618
Service workers	9.79	77	7.2	100,122
Construction workers and mechanics	17.34	137	6.2	87,480
Operators, fabricators, laborers	11.06	87	8.6	119,902
Retired	9.77	77	13.5	188,864
HOMEOWNERSHIP STATUS				
Average household	**12.69**	**100**	**100.0**	**1,400,202**
Homeowners	13.75	108	71.7	1,003,888
Renters	10.62	84	28.3	396,434

Note: Households by type will not sum to the total because not all household types are shown. Hispanics may be of any race and most are white. Total household spending and market shares may not sum to total due to rounding. For an explanation of terms, see the introduction to this report.
Source: Calculations by New Strategist based on the Bureau of Labor Statistics' 2001 Consumer Expenditure Survey

106. SPENDING ON PIES, TARTS, AND TURNOVERS, 2001

Total (aggregate) household spending in 2001	$4,360,427,357,940
Total (aggregate) household spending on pies, tarts, and turnovers	$1,169,593,400
Average annual household spending on pies, tarts, and turnovers	$10.60

	AVERAGE ANNUAL SPENDING PER HOUSEHOLD (in dollars)	BEST CUSTOMERS (index)	BIGGEST CUSTOMERS (percent market share)	TOTAL (AGGREGATE) HH SPENDING (in thousands of dollars)
AGE OF HOUSEHOLDER				
Average household	**$10.60**	**100**	**100.0%**	**$1,169,593**
Under age 25	4.97	47	3.7	42,732
Aged 25 to 34	9.33	88	14.8	172,745
Aged 35 to 44	11.96	113	25.0	292,087
Aged 45 to 54	11.50	109	21.9	256,646
Aged 55 to 64	11.63	110	14.5	169,205
Aged 65 to 74	10.89	103	10.6	123,514
Aged 75 or older	10.66	101	9.7	112,953
HOUSEHOLD INCOME				
Average household reporting income	**10.64**	**100**	**100.0**	**944,140**
Under $10,000	4.97	47	5.8	54,330
$10,000 to $19,999	8.35	79	13.4	126,200
$20,000 to $29,999	11.72	110	15.0	141,519
$30,000 to $39,999	10.14	95	11.3	106,551
$40,000 to $49,999	9.11	86	8.4	79,594
$50,000 to $69,999	11.20	105	14.8	139,776
$70,000 or more	15.69	148	31.4	296,416
HOUSEHOLD TYPE				
Average household	**10.60**	**100**	**100.0**	**1,169,593**
Married couples	13.68	129	65.3	763,891
Married couples, no children	13.18	124	26.1	304,708
Married couples, with children	13.68	129	32.8	383,792
Oldest child under 6	12.68	120	5.4	63,654
Oldest child 6 to 17	12.90	122	16.7	195,371
Oldest child 18 or older	16.13	152	10.9	127,266
Single parent with child under 18	11.50	109	6.5	76,234
Single person	5.40	51	15.1	177,028
RACE				
Average household	**10.60**	**100**	**100.0**	**1,169,593**
Black	7.24	68	8.2	96,169
White and other	11.05	104	91.7	1,072,469
HISPANIC ORIGIN				
Average household	**10.60**	**100**	**100.0**	**1,169,593**
Hispanic	10.33	98	8.5	99,385
Non-Hispanic	10.63	100	91.5	1,070,632
REGION				
Average household	**10.60**	**100**	**100.0**	**1,169,593**
Northeast	13.14	124	23.5	275,152
Midwest	10.22	96	22.6	264,105
South	8.99	85	30.1	352,201
West	11.39	108	23.7	277,688

	AVERAGE ANNUAL SPENDING PER HOUSEHOLD (in dollars)	BEST CUSTOMERS (index)	BIGGEST CUSTOMERS (percent market share)	TOTAL (AGGREGATE) HH SPENDING (in thousands of dollars)
EDUCATION				
Average household	**$10.60**	**100**	**100.0%**	**$1,169,593**
Less than high school graduate	8.81	83	12.9	151,329
High school graduate	11.03	104	30.1	351,482
Some college	9.92	94	19.5	228,081
Associate's degree	6.80	64	5.6	65,987
College graduate	12.98	123	31.8	372,007
Bachelor's degree	12.83	121	20.7	242,230
Master's, professional, doctoral degree	13.27	125	11.1	129,781
OCCUPATION				
Average household	**10.60**	**100**	**100.0**	**1,169,593**
Self-employed	8.26	78	3.4	40,259
Wage-and-salary workers, total	11.05	104	69.9	817,877
Managers and professionals	12.20	115	27.9	326,545
Technical, sales, and clerical	10.43	98	18.8	220,459
Service workers	9.92	94	8.7	101,452
Construction workers and mechanics	11.54	109	5.0	58,219
Operators, fabricators, laborers	10.37	98	9.6	112,421
Retired	11.62	110	19.2	224,626
HOMEOWNERSHIP STATUS				
Average household	**10.60**	**100**	**100.0**	**1,169,593**
Homeowners	11.37	107	71.0	830,124
Renters	9.10	86	29.0	339,694

Note: Households by type will not sum to the total because not all household types are shown. Hispanics may be of any race and most are white. Total household spending and market shares may not sum to total due to rounding. For an explanation of terms, see the introduction to this report.
Source: Calculations by New Strategist based on the Bureau of Labor Statistics' 2001 Consumer Expenditure Survey

107. SPENDING ON PORK CHOPS, 2001

Total (aggregate) household spending in 2001	$4,360,427,357,940
Total (aggregate) household spending on pork chops	$4,651,892,240
Average annual household spending on pork chops	$42.16

	AVERAGE ANNUAL SPENDING PER HOUSEHOLD (in dollars)	BEST CUSTOMERS (index)	BIGGEST CUSTOMERS (percent market share)	TOTAL (AGGREGATE) HH SPENDING (in thousands of dollars)
AGE OF HOUSEHOLDER				
Average household	**$42.16**	**100**	**100.0%**	**$4,651,892**
Under age 25	24.43	58	4.5	210,049
Aged 25 to 34	47.40	112	18.9	877,611
Aged 35 to 44	46.37	110	24.3	1,132,448
Aged 45 to 54	49.70	118	23.8	1,109,155
Aged 55 to 64	44.02	104	13.8	640,447
Aged 65 to 74	33.29	79	8.1	377,575
Aged 75 or older	28.18	67	6.4	298,595
HOUSEHOLD INCOME				
Average household reporting income	**44.35**	**100**	**100.0**	**3,935,397**
Under $10,000	34.71	78	9.6	379,399
$10,000 to $19,999	36.52	82	14.0	551,994
$20,000 to $29,999	39.77	90	12.2	480,223
$30,000 to $39,999	39.00	88	10.4	409,812
$40,000 to $49,999	47.80	108	10.6	417,629
$50,000 to $69,999	48.23	109	15.3	601,910
$70,000 or more	58.44	132	28.1	1,104,049
HOUSEHOLD TYPE				
Average household	**42.16**	**100**	**100.0**	**4,651,892**
Married couples	52.74	125	63.3	2,945,002
Married couples, no children	39.31	93	19.5	908,808
Married couples, with children	59.59	141	35.9	1,671,797
Oldest child under 6	53.82	128	5.8	270,176
Oldest child 6 to 17	57.14	136	18.6	865,385
Oldest child 18 or older	69.21	164	11.7	546,067
Single parent with child under 18	51.89	123	7.4	343,979
Single person	15.86	38	11.2	519,938
RACE				
Average household	**42.16**	**100**	**100.0**	**4,651,892**
Black	61.69	146	17.6	819,428
White and other	39.52	94	82.5	3,835,653
HISPANIC ORIGIN				
Average household	**42.16**	**100**	**100.0**	**4,651,892**
Hispanic	64.58	153	13.4	621,324
Non-Hispanic	39.92	95	86.4	4,020,663
REGION				
Average household	**42.16**	**100**	**100.0**	**4,651,892**
Northeast	44.58	106	20.1	933,505
Midwest	34.94	83	19.4	902,920
South	48.78	116	41.1	1,911,054
West	37.05	88	19.4	903,279

	AVERAGE ANNUAL SPENDING PER HOUSEHOLD (in dollars)	BEST CUSTOMERS (index)	BIGGEST CUSTOMERS (percent market share)	TOTAL (AGGREGATE) HH SPENDING (in thousands of dollars)
EDUCATION				
Average household	**$42.16**	**100**	**100.0%**	**$4,651,892**
Less than high school graduate	49.72	118	18.4	854,040
High school graduate	43.49	103	29.8	1,385,852
Some college	41.77	99	20.6	960,376
Associate's degree	41.72	99	8.7	404,851
College graduate	36.73	87	22.6	1,052,682
Bachelor's degree	37.57	89	15.2	709,322
Master's, professional, doctoral degree	35.19	84	7.4	344,158
OCCUPATION				
Average household	**42.16**	**100**	**100.0**	**4,651,892**
Self-employed	46.00	109	4.8	224,204
Wage-and-salary workers, total	44.40	105	70.6	3,286,310
Managers and professionals	41.91	99	24.1	1,121,763
Technical, sales, and clerical	39.06	93	17.7	825,611
Service workers	43.44	103	9.6	444,261
Construction workers and mechanics	75.06	178	8.1	378,678
Operators, fabricators, laborers	46.68	111	10.9	506,058
Retired	30.61	73	12.7	591,722
HOMEOWNERSHIP STATUS				
Average household	**42.16**	**100**	**100.0**	**4,651,892**
Homeowners	45.46	108	71.3	3,319,035
Renters	35.70	85	28.6	1,332,645

Note: Households by type will not sum to the total because not all household types are shown. Hispanics may be of any race and most are white. Total household spending and market shares may not sum to total due to rounding. For an explanation of terms, see the introduction to this report.
Source: Calculations by New Strategist based on the Bureau of Labor Statistics' 2001 Consumer Expenditure Survey

108. SPENDING ON PORK OTHER THAN BACON, HOT DOGS, HAM, PORK CHOPS, SAUSAGE, 2001

(includes pork ribs, roast, ground, etc.)

Total (aggregate) household spending in 2001	$4,360,427,357,940
Total (aggregate) household spending on pork other than bacon, hot dogs, ham, pork chops, sausage	$4,451,075,260
Average annual household spending on pork other than bacon, hot dogs, ham, pork chops, sausage	$40.34

	AVERAGE ANNUAL SPENDING PER HOUSEHOLD (in dollars)	TOTAL BEST CUSTOMERS (index)	BIGGEST CUSTOMERS (percent market share)	(AGGREGATE) HH SPENDING (in thousands of dollars)
AGE OF HOUSEHOLDER				
Average household	**$40.34**	**100**	**100.0%**	**$4,451,075**
Under age 25	16.52	41	3.2	142,039
Aged 25 to 34	38.93	97	16.2	720,789
Aged 35 to 44	45.27	112	24.8	1,105,584
Aged 45 to 54	47.03	117	23.6	1,049,569
Aged 55 to 64	53.50	133	17.5	778,372
Aged 65 to 74	35.53	88	9.1	402,981
Aged 75 or older	23.60	59	5.6	250,066
HOUSEHOLD INCOME				
Average household reporting income	**42.60**	**100**	**100.0**	**3,780,111**
Under $10,000	33.15	78	9.6	362,328
$10,000 to $19,999	36.43	86	14.6	550,503
$20,000 to $29,999	36.77	86	11.7	443,998
$30,000 to $39,999	46.27	109	12.9	486,205
$40,000 to $49,999	40.01	94	9.2	349,567
$50,000 to $69,999	49.93	117	16.5	623,126
$70,000 or more	51.42	121	25.7	971,427
HOUSEHOLD TYPE				
Average household	**40.34**	**100**	**100.0**	**4,451,075**
Married couples	54.04	134	67.8	3,017,594
Married couples, no children	47.22	117	24.5	1,091,679
Married couples, with children	55.97	139	35.3	1,570,238
Oldest child under 6	38.14	95	4.3	191,463
Oldest child 6 to 17	53.07	132	18.1	803,745
Oldest child 18 or older	75.50	187	13.4	595,695
Single parent with child under 18	41.74	104	6.2	276,695
Single person	15.53	39	11.4	509,120
RACE				
Average household	**40.34**	**100**	**100.0**	**4,451,075**
Black	53.10	132	15.8	705,327
White and other	38.62	96	84.2	3,748,303
HISPANIC ORIGIN				
Average household	**40.34**	**100**	**100.0**	**4,451,075**
Hispanic	59.63	148	12.9	573,700
Non-Hispanic	38.42	95	86.9	3,869,586
REGION				
Average household	**40.34**	**100**	**100.0**	**4,451,075**
Northeast	41.29	102	19.4	864,613
Midwest	37.24	92	21.6	962,356
South	40.67	101	35.8	1,593,329

	AVERAGE ANNUAL SPENDING PER HOUSEHOLD (in dollars)	BEST CUSTOMERS (index)	BIGGEST CUSTOMERS (percent market share)	TOTAL (AGGREGATE) HH SPENDING (in thousands of dollars)
West	42.28	105	23.2	1,030,786
EDUCATION				
Average household	**$40.34**	**100**	**100.0%**	**$4,451,075**
Less than high school graduate	49.02	122	18.9	842,017
High school graduate	43.51	108	31.1	1,386,490
Some college	42.29	105	21.8	972,332
Associate's degree	30.86	77	6.7	299,465
College graduate	33.60	83	21.6	962,976
Bachelor's degree	33.05	82	14.0	623,984
Master's, professional, doctoral degree	34.59	86	7.6	338,290
OCCUPATION				
Average household	**40.34**	**100**	**100.0**	**4,451,075**
Self-employed	40.37	100	4.4	196,763
Wage-and-salary workers, total	40.98	102	68.1	3,033,176
Managers and professionals	38.94	97	23.4	1,042,268
Technical, sales, and clerical	42.27	105	20.1	893,461
Service workers	31.77	79	7.3	324,912
Construction workers and mechanics	51.00	126	5.8	257,295
Operators, fabricators, laborers	47.01	117	11.4	509,635
Retired	30.02	74	13.0	580,317
HOMEOWNERSHIP STATUS				
Average household	**40.34**	**100**	**100.0**	**4,451,075**
Homeowners	45.07	112	73.9	3,290,561
Renters	31.10	77	26.1	1,160,932

Note: Households by type will not sum to the total because not all household types are shown. Hispanics may be of any race and most are white. Total household spending and market shares may not sum to total due to rounding. For an explanation of terms, see the introduction to this report.
Source: Calculations by New Strategist based on the Bureau of Labor Statistics' 2001 Consumer Expenditure Survey

109. SPENDING ON POTATO CHIPS AND OTHER SNACKS, 2001

Total (aggregate) household spending in 2001	$4,360,427,357,940
Total (aggregate) household spending on potato chips and other snacks	$8,337,214,840
Average annual household spending on potato chips and other snacks	$75.56

	AVERAGE ANNUAL SPENDING PER HOUSEHOLD (in dollars)	BEST CUSTOMERS (index)	BIGGEST CUSTOMERS (percent market share)	TOTAL (AGGREGATE) HH SPENDING (in thousands of dollars)
AGE OF HOUSEHOLDER				
Average household	**$75.56**	**100**	**100.0%**	**$8,337,215**
Under age 25	57.69	76	5.9	496,019
Aged 25 to 34	74.41	99	16.5	1,377,701
Aged 35 to 44	97.09	129	28.4	2,371,132
Aged 45 to 54	93.95	124	25.1	2,096,682
Aged 55 to 64	73.04	97	12.7	1,062,659
Aged 65 to 74	47.07	62	6.4	533,868
Aged 75 or older	35.66	47	4.5	377,853
HOUSEHOLD INCOME				
Average household reporting income	**81.74**	**100**	**100.0**	**7,253,199**
Under $10,000	44.70	55	6.7	488,580
$10,000 to $19,999	51.12	63	10.7	772,617
$20,000 to $29,999	64.65	79	10.8	780,649
$30,000 to $39,999	71.01	87	10.3	746,173
$40,000 to $49,999	98.07	120	11.8	856,838
$50,000 to $69,999	104.17	127	17.9	1,300,042
$70,000 or more	124.59	152	32.5	2,353,754
HOUSEHOLD TYPE				
Average household	**75.56**	**100**	**100.0**	**8,337,215**
Married couples	98.60	131	66.0	5,505,824
Married couples, no children	70.57	93	19.6	1,631,508
Married couples, with children	119.38	158	40.2	3,349,206
Oldest child under 6	99.01	131	6.0	497,030
Oldest child 6 to 17	132.30	175	24.0	2,003,684
Oldest child 18 or older	106.41	141	10.1	839,575
Single parent with child under 18	81.16	107	6.5	538,010
Single person	31.52	42	12.4	1,033,320
RACE				
Average household	**75.56**	**100**	**100.0**	**8,337,215**
Black	55.12	73	8.8	732,159
White and other	78.31	104	91.2	7,600,455
HISPANIC ORIGIN				
Average household	**75.56**	**100**	**100.0**	**8,337,215**
Hispanic	66.00	87	7.6	634,986
Non-Hispanic	76.51	101	92.4	7,705,934
REGION				
Average household	**75.56**	**100**	**100.0**	**8,337,215**
Northeast	71.17	94	17.9	1,490,300
Midwest	86.87	115	26.9	2,244,895
South	73.38	97	34.5	2,874,808
West	70.92	94	20.7	1,729,030

	AVERAGE ANNUAL SPENDING PER HOUSEHOLD (in dollars)	BEST CUSTOMERS (index)	BIGGEST CUSTOMERS (percent market share)	TOTAL (AGGREGATE) HH SPENDING (in thousands of dollars)
EDUCATION				
Average household	**$75.56**	**100**	**100.0%**	**$8,337,215**
Less than high school graduate	57.13	76	11.8	981,322
High school graduate	70.61	93	27.0	2,250,058
Some college	78.24	104	21.6	1,798,894
Associate's degree	79.52	105	9.3	771,662
College graduate	88.39	117	30.4	2,533,257
Bachelor's degree	87.72	116	19.9	1,656,154
Master's, professional, doctoral degree	89.62	119	10.5	876,484
OCCUPATION				
Average household	**75.56**	**100**	**100.0**	**8,337,215**
Self-employed	83.38	110	4.9	406,394
Wage-and-salary workers, total	83.54	111	74.2	6,183,297
Managers and professionals	94.52	125	30.3	2,529,922
Technical, sales, and clerical	77.45	103	19.6	1,637,061
Service workers	70.04	93	8.6	716,299
Construction workers and mechanics	99.37	132	6.0	501,322
Operators, fabricators, laborers	75.10	99	9.8	814,159
Retired	46.44	62	10.8	897,732
HOMEOWNERSHIP STATUS				
Average household	**75.56**	**100**	**100.0**	**8,337,215**
Homeowners	83.15	110	72.8	6,070,782
Renters	60.70	80	27.2	2,265,870

Note: Households by type will not sum to the total because not all household types are shown. Hispanics may be of any race and most are white. Total household spending and market shares may not sum to total due to rounding. For an explanation of terms, see the introduction to this report.
Source: Calculations by New Strategist based on the Bureau of Labor Statistics' 2001 Consumer Expenditure Survey

110. SPENDING ON POULTRY, 2001

Total (aggregate) household spending in 2001	$4,360,427,357,940
Total (aggregate) household spending on poultry	$16,757,183,930
Average annual household spending on poultry	$151.87

	AVERAGE ANNUAL SPENDING PER HOUSEHOLD (in dollars)	BEST CUSTOMERS (index)	BIGGEST CUSTOMERS (percent market share)	TOTAL (AGGREGATE) HH SPENDING (in thousands of dollars)
AGE OF HOUSEHOLDER				
Average household	**$151.87**	**100**	**100.0%**	**$16,757,184**
Under age 25	92.99	61	4.8	799,528
Aged 25 to 34	153.27	101	16.9	2,837,794
Aged 35 to 44	181.00	119	26.4	4,420,382
Aged 45 to 54	182.37	120	24.3	4,069,951
Aged 55 to 64	154.29	102	13.4	2,244,765
Aged 65 to 74	112.93	74	7.6	1,280,852
Aged 75 or older	101.82	67	6.4	1,078,885
HOUSEHOLD INCOME				
Average household reporting income	**159.04**	**100**	**100.0**	**14,112,414**
Under $10,000	99.14	62	7.7	1,083,522
$10,000 to $19,999	124.00	78	13.3	1,873,991
$20,000 to $29,999	135.23	85	11.6	1,632,902
$30,000 to $39,999	149.71	94	11.1	1,573,153
$40,000 to $49,999	170.43	107	10.6	1,489,047
$50,000 to $69,999	199.85	126	17.7	2,494,128
$70,000 or more	211.59	133	28.3	3,997,358
HOUSEHOLD TYPE				
Average household	**151.87**	**100**	**100.0**	**16,757,184**
Married couples	190.82	126	63.6	10,655,389
Married couples, no children	143.02	94	19.7	3,306,479
Married couples, with children	217.40	143	36.4	6,099,157
Oldest child under 6	204.52	135	6.1	1,026,690
Oldest child 6 to 17	210.80	139	19.1	3,192,566
Oldest child 18 or older	241.33	159	11.4	1,904,094
Single parent with child under 18	176.26	116	7.0	1,168,428
Single person	67.72	45	13.2	2,220,065
RACE				
Average household	**151.87**	**100**	**100.0**	**16,757,184**
Black	195.91	129	15.5	2,602,273
White and other	145.93	96	84.5	14,163,382
HISPANIC ORIGIN				
Average household	**151.87**	**100**	**100.0**	**16,757,184**
Hispanic	206.28	136	11.8	1,984,620
Non-Hispanic	146.44	96	88.0	14,749,144
REGION				
Average household	**151.87**	**100**	**100.0**	**16,757,184**
Northeast	188.63	124	23.6	3,949,912
Midwest	124.34	82	19.2	3,213,194
South	151.81	100	35.5	5,947,460
West	149.22	98	21.7	3,637,984

	AVERAGE ANNUAL SPENDING PER HOUSEHOLD (in dollars)	BEST CUSTOMERS (index)	BIGGEST CUSTOMERS (percent market share)	TOTAL (AGGREGATE) HH SPENDING (in thousands of dollars)
EDUCATION				
Average household	**$151.87**	**100**	**100.0%**	**$16,757,184**
Less than high school graduate	158.14	104	16.2	2,716,371
High school graduate	147.02	97	28.0	4,684,939
Some college	151.54	100	20.8	3,484,208
Associate's degree	139.22	92	8.1	1,350,991
College graduate	158.19	104	27.1	4,533,725
Bachelor's degree	151.43	100	17.1	2,858,998
Master's, professional, doctoral degree	170.49	112	10.0	1,667,392
OCCUPATION				
Average household	**151.87**	**100**	**100.0**	**16,757,184**
Self-employed	159.46	105	4.6	777,208
Wage-and-salary workers, total	161.99	107	71.6	11,989,852
Managers and professionals	165.50	109	26.4	4,429,773
Technical, sales, and clerical	160.77	106	20.3	3,398,196
Service workers	154.05	101	9.4	1,575,469
Construction workers and mechanics	190.05	125	5.7	958,802
Operators, fabricators, laborers	151.86	100	9.8	1,646,314
Retired	104.36	69	12.0	2,017,383
HOMEOWNERSHIP STATUS				
Average household	**151.87**	**100**	**100.0**	**16,757,184**
Homeowners	161.82	107	70.5	11,814,478
Renters	132.39	87	29.5	4,941,986

Note: Households by type will not sum to the total because not all household types are shown. Hispanics may be of any race and most are white. Total household spending and market shares may not sum to total due to rounding. For an explanation of terms, see the introduction to this report.
Source: Calculations by New Strategist based on the Bureau of Labor Statistics' 2001 Consumer Expenditure Survey

111. SPENDING ON RICE, 2001

Total (aggregate) household spending in 2001	$4,360,427,357,940
Total (aggregate) household spending on rice	$2,201,263,050
Average annual household spending on rice	$19.95

	AVERAGE ANNUAL SPENDING PER HOUSEHOLD (in dollars)	BEST CUSTOMERS (index)	BIGGEST CUSTOMERS (percent market share)	TOTAL (AGGREGATE) HH SPENDING (in thousands of dollars)
AGE OF HOUSEHOLDER				
Average household	**$19.95**	**100**	**100.0%**	**$2,201,263**
Under age 25	13.48	68	5.3	115,901
Aged 25 to 34	22.48	113	18.9	416,217
Aged 35 to 44	25.33	127	28.1	618,609
Aged 45 to 54	23.78	119	24.1	530,698
Aged 55 to 64	17.65	89	11.7	256,790
Aged 65 to 74	12.07	61	6.2	136,898
Aged 75 or older	11.28	57	5.4	119,523
HOUSEHOLD INCOME				
Average household reporting income	**20.36**	**100**	**100.0**	**1,806,645**
Under $10,000	14.92	73	9.0	163,024
$10,000 to $19,999	16.32	80	13.7	246,708
$20,000 to $29,999	16.70	82	11.2	201,653
$30,000 to $39,999	19.48	96	11.3	204,696
$40,000 to $49,999	24.39	120	11.8	213,095
$50,000 to $69,999	18.18	89	12.6	226,886
$70,000 or more	29.85	147	31.2	563,926
HOUSEHOLD TYPE				
Average household	**19.95**	**100**	**100.0**	**2,201,263**
Married couples	25.33	127	64.3	1,414,427
Married couples, no children	15.05	75	15.8	347,941
Married couples, with children	30.60	153	39.0	858,483
Oldest child under 6	27.38	137	6.2	137,448
Oldest child 6 to 17	28.53	143	19.6	432,087
Oldest child 18 or older	37.50	188	13.4	295,875
Single parent with child under 18	24.94	125	7.5	165,327
Single person	7.28	37	10.8	238,660
RACE				
Average household	**19.95**	**100**	**100.0**	**2,201,263**
Black	24.47	123	14.8	325,035
White and other	19.34	97	85.3	1,877,063
HISPANIC ORIGIN				
Average household	**19.95**	**100**	**100.0**	**2,201,263**
Hispanic	38.33	192	16.8	368,773
Non-Hispanic	18.12	91	82.9	1,825,010
REGION				
Average household	**19.95**	**100**	**100.0**	**2,201,263**
Northeast	25.15	126	23.9	526,641
Midwest	12.79	64	15.0	330,519
South	18.97	95	33.8	743,188
West	24.59	123	27.2	599,504

	AVERAGE ANNUAL SPENDING PER HOUSEHOLD (in dollars)	BEST CUSTOMERS (index)	BIGGEST CUSTOMERS (percent market share)	TOTAL (AGGREGATE) HH SPENDING (in thousands of dollars)
EDUCATION				
Average household	**$19.95**	**100**	**100.0%**	**$2,201,263**
Less than high school graduate	23.19	116	18.1	398,335
High school graduate	17.90	90	25.9	570,401
Some college	17.45	88	18.2	401,210
Associate's degree	14.95	75	6.6	145,075
College graduate	23.91	120	31.1	685,261
Bachelor's degree	24.18	121	20.7	456,518
Master's, professional, doctoral degree	23.43	117	10.4	229,145
OCCUPATION				
Average household	**19.95**	**100**	**100.0**	**2,201,263**
Self-employed	25.19	126	5.6	122,776
Wage-and-salary workers, total	21.69	109	72.9	1,605,407
Managers and professionals	22.17	111	27.0	593,402
Technical, sales, and clerical	22.22	111	21.3	469,664
Service workers	22.32	112	10.4	228,267
Construction workers and mechanics	15.67	79	3.6	79,055
Operators, fabricators, laborers	21.76	109	10.7	235,900
Retired	11.42	57	10.0	220,760
HOMEOWNERSHIP STATUS				
Average household	**19.95**	**100**	**100.0**	**2,201,263**
Homeowners	18.69	94	62.0	1,364,557
Renters	22.41	112	3.8	836,543

Note: Households by type will not sum to the total because not all household types are shown. Hispanics may be of any race and most are white. Total household spending and market shares may not sum to total due to rounding. For an explanation of terms, see the introduction to this report.
Source: Calculations by New Strategist based on the Bureau of Labor Statistics' 2001 Consumer Expenditure Survey

112. SPENDING ON ROAST BEEF, 2001

Total (aggregate) household spending in 2001	$4,360,427,357,940
Total (aggregate) household spending on roast beef	$4,903,465,160
Average annual household spending on roast beef	$44.44

	AVERAGE ANNUAL SPENDING PER HOUSEHOLD (in dollars)	BEST CUSTOMERS (index)	BIGGEST CUSTOMERS (percent market share)	TOTAL (AGGREGATE) HH SPENDING (in thousands of dollars)
AGE OF HOUSEHOLDER				
Average household	**$44.44**	**100**	**100.0%**	**$4,903,465**
Under age 25	19.31	44	3.4	166,027
Aged 25 to 34	33.89	76	12.8	627,473
Aged 35 to 44	48.41	109	24.1	1,182,269
Aged 45 to 54	55.61	125	25.3	1,241,048
Aged 55 to 64	53.07	119	15.7	772,115
Aged 65 to 74	48.14	108	11.1	546,004
Aged 75 or older	35.29	79	7.6	373,933
HOUSEHOLD INCOME				
Average household reporting income	**48.12**	**100**	**100.0**	**4,269,928**
Under $10,000	29.29	61	7.5	320,074
$10,000 to $19,999	36.33	76	12.9	549,094
$20,000 to $29,999	58.54	122	16.6	706,871
$30,000 to $39,999	55.80	116	13.7	586,346
$40,000 to $49,999	37.33	78	7.6	326,152
$50,000 to $69,999	50.53	105	14.8	630,614
$70,000 or more	60.50	126	26.8	1,142,966
HOUSEHOLD TYPE				
Average household	**44.44**	**100**	**100.0**	**4,903,465**
Married couples	61.40	138	69.9	3,428,576
Married couples, no children	54.03	122	25.5	1,249,120
Married couples, with children	62.90	142	36.0	1,764,660
Oldest child under 6	35.53	80	3.6	178,361
Oldest child 6 to 17	62.91	142	19.4	952,772
Oldest child 18 or older	83.20	187	13.4	656,448
Single parent with child under 18	45.20	102	6.1	299,631
Single person	13.82	31	9.2	453,061
RACE				
Average household	**44.44**	**100**	**100.0**	**4,903,465**
Black	45.60	103	12.4	605,705
White and other	44.29	100	87.7	4,298,610
HISPANIC ORIGIN				
Average household	**44.44**	**100**	**100.0**	**4,903,465**
Hispanic	55.29	124	10.8	531,945
Non-Hispanic	43.36	98	89.1	4,367,133
REGION				
Average household	**44.44**	**100**	**100.0**	**4,903,465**
Northeast	43.06	97	18.4	901,676
Midwest	48.69	110	25.7	1,258,247
South	45.24	102	36.1	1,772,368
West	39.87	90	19.8	972,031

	AVERAGE ANNUAL SPENDING PER HOUSEHOLD (in dollars)	BEST CUSTOMERS (index)	BIGGEST CUSTOMERS (percent market share)	TOTAL (AGGREGATE) HH SPENDING (in thousands of dollars)
EDUCATION				
Average household	**$44.44**	**100**	**100.0%**	**$4,903,465**
Less than high school graduate	45.68	103	1.6	784,645
High school graduate	48.31	109	31.4	1,539,447
Some college	41.01	92	19.2	942,902
Associate's degree	46.40	104	9.2	450,266
College graduate	41.34	93	24.2	1,184,804
Bachelor's degree	43.19	97	16.6	815,427
Master's, professional, doctoral degree	37.97	85	7.6	371,347
OCCUPATION				
Average household	**44.44**	**100**	**100.0**	**4,903,465**
Self-employed	39.87	90	4.0	194,326
Wage-and-salary workers, total	43.93	99	66.3	3,251,523
Managers and professionals	48.42	109	26.4	1,296,010
Technical, sales, and clerical	41.03	92	17.7	867,251
Service workers	30.66	69	6.4	313,560
Construction workers and mechanics	68.34	154	7.0	344,775
Operators, fabricators, laborers	40.52	91	9.0	439,277
Retired	43.60	98	17.2	842,832
HOMEOWNERSHIP STATUS				
Average household	**44.44**	**100**	**100.0**	**4,903,465**
Homeowners	51.24	115	76.3	3,741,032
Renters	31.13	70	23.7	1,162,052

Note: Households by type will not sum to the total because not all household types are shown. Hispanics may be of any race and most are white. Total household spending and market shares may not sum to total due to rounding. For an explanation of terms, see the introduction to this report.
Source: Calculations by New Strategist based on the Bureau of Labor Statistics' 2001 Consumer Expenditure Survey

113. SPENDING ON SALAD DRESSINGS, 2001

Total (aggregate) household spending in 2001	$4,360,427,357,940
Total (aggregate) household spending on salad dressings	$3,091,698,780
Average annual household spending on salad dressings	$28.02

	AVERAGE ANNUAL SPENDING PER HOUSEHOLD (in dollars)	BEST CUSTOMERS (index)	BIGGEST CUSTOMERS (percent market share)	TOTAL (AGGREGATE) HH SPENDING (in thousands of dollars)
AGE OF HOUSEHOLDER				
Average household	**$28.02**	**100**	**100.0%**	**$3,091,699**
Under age 25	15.54	56	4.3	133,613
Aged 25 to 34	25.51	91	15.3	472,318
Aged 35 to 44	31.65	113	2.5	772,956
Aged 45 to 54	35.24	126	25.4	786,451
Aged 55 to 64	30.06	107	14.1	437,343
Aged 65 to 74	24.88	89	9.1	282,189
Aged 75 or older	19.41	69	6.7	205,668
HOUSEHOLD INCOME				
Average household reporting income	**29.09**	**100**	**100.0**	**2,581,301**
Under $10,000	17.69	61	7.5	193,281
$10,000 to $19,999	20.37	70	11.9	307,917
$20,000 to $29,999	23.86	82	11.2	288,110
$30,000 to $39,999	27.71	95	11.3	291,177
$40,000 to $49,999	33.20	114	11.2	290,068
$50,000 to $69,999	34.04	117	16.5	424,819
$70,000 or more	42.24	145	30.9	797,998
HOUSEHOLD TYPE				
Average household	**28.02**	**100**	**100.0**	**3,091,699**
Married couples	35.85	128	64.7	2,001,864
Married couples, no children	30.83	110	23.1	712,759
Married couples, with children	39.12	140	35.5	1,097,512
Oldest child under 6	31.75	113	5.2	159,385
Oldest child 6 to 17	39.50	141	19.3	598,228
Oldest child 18 or older	43.74	156	11.2	345,109
Single parent with child under 18	29.80	106	6.4	197,544
Single person	12.77	46	13.5	418,639
RACE				
Average household	**28.02**	**100**	**100.0**	**3,091,699**
Black	25.37	91	10.9	336,990
White and other	28.38	101	89.1	2,754,449
HISPANIC ORIGIN				
Average household	**28.02**	**100**	**100.0**	**3,091,699**
Hispanic	27.74	99	8.6	266,887
Non-Hispanic	28.05	100	91.4	2,825,140
REGION				
Average household	**28.02**	**100**	**100.0**	**3,091,699**
Northeast	29.30	105	19.8	613,542
Midwest	26.63	95	22.3	688,173
South	27.91	100	35.4	1,093,430
West	28.56	102	22.5	696,293

	AVERAGE ANNUAL SPENDING PER HOUSEHOLD (in dollars)	BEST CUSTOMERS (index)	BIGGEST CUSTOMERS (percent market share)	TOTAL (AGGREGATE) HH SPENDING (in thousands of dollars)
EDUCATION				
Average household	**$28.02**	**100**	**100.0%**	**$3,091,699**
Less than high school graduate	25.56	91	14.2	439,044
High school graduate	27.72	99	28.6	883,326
Some college	28.01	100	20.8	644,006
Associate's degree	28.18	101	8.8	273,459
College graduate	29.74	106	27.6	852,348
Bachelor's degree	28.71	103	17.5	542,045
Master's, professional, doctoral degree	31.63	113	1.0	309,341
OCCUPATION				
Average household	**28.02**	**100**	**100.0**	**3,091,699**
Self-employed	32.16	115	5.1	156,748
Wage-and-salary workers, total	28.85	103	69.1	2,135,362
Managers and professionals	31.93	114	27.6	854,638
Technical, sales, and clerical	28.29	101	19.3	597,966
Service workers	26.05	93	8.6	266,413
Construction workers and mechanics	34.13	122	5.6	172,186
Operators, fabricators, laborers	23.45	84	8.2	254,222
Retired	23.14	83	14.5	447,319
HOMEOWNERSHIP STATUS				
Average household	**28.02**	**100**	**100.0**	**3,091,699**
Homeowners	31.39	112	74.1	2,291,784
Renters	21.42	76	25.9	799,587

Note: Households by type will not sum to the total because not all household types are shown. Hispanics may be of any race and most are white. Total household spending and market shares may not sum to total due to rounding. For an explanation of terms, see the introduction to this report.
Source: Calculations by New Strategist based on the Bureau of Labor Statistics' 2001 Consumer Expenditure Survey

114. SPENDING ON SALADS, PREPARED, 2001

Total (aggregate) household spending in 2001	$4,360,427,357,940
Total (aggregate) household spending on prepared salads	$2,157,127,450
Average annual household spending on prepared salads	$19.55

	AVERAGE ANNUAL SPENDING PER HOUSEHOLD (in dollars)	BEST CUSTOMERS (index)	BIGGEST CUSTOMERS (percent market share)	TOTAL (AGGREGATE) HH SPENDING (in thousands of dollars)
AGE OF HOUSEHOLDER				
Average household	**$19.55**	**100**	**100.0%**	**$2,157,128**
Under age 25	9.40	48	3.7	80,821
Aged 25 to 34	17.25	88	14.8	319,384
Aged 35 to 44	20.42	105	23.1	498,697
Aged 45 to 54	24.22	124	25.1	540,518
Aged 55 to 64	25.18	129	17.0	366,344
Aged 65 to 74	16.45	84	8.6	186,576
Aged 75 or older	15.59	80	7.7	165,192
HOUSEHOLD INCOME				
Average household reporting income	**20.16**	**100**	**100.0**	**1,788,898**
Under $10,000	10.51	52	6.4	114,875
$10,000 to $19,999	10.99	55	9.3	166,147
$20,000 to $29,999	16.68	83	11.3	201,411
$30,000 to $39,999	18.77	93	11.0	197,235
$40,000 to $49,999	22.51	112	11.0	196,670
$50,000 to $69,999	25.59	127	17.9	319,363
$70,000 or more	31.86	158	33.6	601,899
HOUSEHOLD TYPE				
Average household	**19.55**	**100**	**100.0**	**2,157,128**
Married couples	25.17	129	65.2	1,405,493
Married couples, no children	22.35	114	24.0	516,710
Married couples, with children	27.46	141	35.7	770,390
Oldest child under 6	24.41	125	5.7	122,538
Oldest child 6 to 17	27.37	140	19.2	414,519
Oldest child 18 or older	29.90	153	10.9	235,911
Single parent with child under 18	13.49	69	4.1	89,425
Single person	11.80	60	17.9	386,839
RACE				
Average household	**19.55**	**100**	**100.0**	**2,157,128**
Black	11.79	60	7.3	156,607
White and other	20.59	105	92.6	1,998,383
HISPANIC ORIGIN				
Average household	**19.55**	**100**	**100.0**	**2,157,128**
Hispanic	11.29	58	5.0	108,621
Non-Hispanic	20.37	104	95.1	2,051,626
REGION				
Average household	**19.55**	**100**	**100.0**	**2,157,128**
Northeast	22.62	116	22.0	473,663
Midwest	18.97	97	22.7	490,223
South	18.22	93	33.1	713,805
West	19.62	100	22.2	478,336

	AVERAGE ANNUAL SPENDING PER HOUSEHOLD (in dollars)	BEST CUSTOMERS (index)	BIGGEST CUSTOMERS (percent market share)	TOTAL (AGGREGATE) HH SPENDING (in thousands of dollars)
EDUCATION				
Average household	**$19.55**	**100**	**100.0%**	**$2,157,128**
Less than high school graduate	14.18	73	11.3	243,570
High school graduate	16.95	87	25.0	540,129
Some college	18.47	95	19.7	424,662
Associate's degree	20.50	105	9.2	198,932
College graduate	26.01	133	34.6	745,447
Bachelor's degree	25.16	129	22.0	475,021
Master's, professional, doctoral degree	27.56	141	12.5	269,537
OCCUPATION				
Average household	**19.55**	**100**	**100.0**	**2,157,128**
Self-employed	23.78	122	5.4	115,904
Wage-and-salary workers, total	20.89	107	71.7	1,546,194
Managers and professionals	24.03	123	29.8	643,187
Technical, sales, and clerical	22.10	113	21.7	467,128
Service workers	18.36	94	8.7	187,768
Construction workers and mechanics	21.21	109	5.0	107,004
Operators, fabricators, laborers	14.29	73	7.2	154,918
Retired	16.58	85	14.9	320,508
HOMEOWNERSHIP STATUS				
Average household	**19.55**	**100**	**100.0**	**2,157,128**
Homeowners	22.67	116	76.7	1,655,137
Renters	13.43	69	23.2	501,329

Note: Households by type will not sum to the total because not all household types are shown. Hispanics may be of any race and most are white. Total household spending and market shares may not sum to total due to rounding. For an explanation of terms, see the introduction to this report.
Source: Calculations by New Strategist based on the Bureau of Labor Statistics' 2001 Consumer Expenditure Survey

115. SPENDING ON SALT, SPICES, AND OTHER SEASONINGS, 2001

Total (aggregate) household spending in 2001	$4,360,427,357,940
Total (aggregate) household spending on salt, spices, and other seasonings	$2,188,022,370
Average annual household spending on salt, spices, and other seasonings	$19.83

	AVERAGE ANNUAL SPENDING PER HOUSEHOLD (in dollars)	BEST CUSTOMERS (index)	BIGGEST CUSTOMERS (percent market share)	TOTAL (AGGREGATE) HH SPENDING (in thousands of dollars)
AGE OF HOUSEHOLDER				
Average household	**$19.83**	**100**	**100.0%**	**$2,188,022**
Under age 25	13.38	68	5.3	115,041
Aged 25 to 34	19.11	96	16.2	353,822
Aged 35 to 44	22.89	115	25.5	559,020
Aged 45 to 54	24.10	122	24.6	537,840
Aged 55 to 64	20.96	106	13.9	304,947
Aged 65 to 74	16.61	84	8.6	188,391
Aged 75 or older	11.91	60	5.8	126,198
HOUSEHOLD INCOME				
Average household reporting income	**20.60**	**100**	**100.0**	**1,827,941**
Under $10,000	13.09	64	7.8	143,095
$10,000 to $19,999	15.22	74	12.6	230,015
$20,000 to $29,999	17.19	83	11.4	207,569
$30,000 to $39,999	19.45	94	11.2	204,381
$40,000 to $49,999	21.67	105	10.4	189,331
$50,000 to $69,999	21.92	106	15.0	273,562
$70,000 or more	30.98	150	32.0	585,274
HOUSEHOLD TYPE				
Average household	**19.83**	**100**	**100.0**	**2,188,022**
Married couples	26.07	132	66.5	1,455,749
Married couples, no children	21.85	110	23.1	505,150
Married couples, with children	28.15	142	36.1	789,748
Oldest child under 6	22.71	115	5.2	114,004
Oldest child 6 to 17	29.31	148	20.3	443,900
Oldest child 18 or older	29.67	150	10.7	234,096
Single parent with child under 18	20.14	102	6.1	133,508
Single person	9.57	48	14.3	313,733
RACE				
Average household	**19.83**	**100**	**100.0**	**2,188,022**
Black	21.15	107	12.8	280,936
White and other	19.65	99	87.2	1,907,150
HISPANIC ORIGIN				
Average household	**19.83**	**100**	**100.0**	**2,188,022**
Hispanic	25.78	130	11.3	248,029
Non-Hispanic	19.23	97	88.5	1,936,807
REGION				
Average household	**19.83**	**100**	**100.0**	**2,188,022**
Northeast	20.81	105	19.9	435,761
Midwest	15.55	78	18.4	401,843
South	22.04	111	39.5	863,461
West	19.93	101	22.2	485,893

	AVERAGE ANNUAL SPENDING PER HOUSEHOLD (in dollars)	BEST CUSTOMERS (index)	BIGGEST CUSTOMERS (percent market share)	TOTAL (AGGREGATE) HH SPENDING (in thousands of dollars)
EDUCATION				
Average household	**$19.83**	**100**	**100.0%**	**$2,188,022**
Less than high school graduate	18.84	95	14.8	323,615
High school graduate	17.12	86	24.9	545,546
Some college	18.62	94	19.6	428,111
Associate's degree	20.14	102	8.9	195,439
College graduate	24.19	122	31.7	693,285
Bachelor's degree	24.95	126	21.5	471,056
Master's, professional, doctoral degree	22.82	115	10.2	223,180
OCCUPATION				
Average household	**19.83**	**100**	**100.0**	**2,188,022**
Self-employed	20.31	102	4.5	98,991
Wage-and-salary workers, total	20.63	104	69.8	1,526,950
Managers and professionals	22.47	113	27.5	601,432
Technical, sales, and clerical	19.69	99	19.0	416,188
Service workers	17.01	86	8.0	173,961
Construction workers and mechanics	22.79	115	5.3	114,976
Operators, fabricators, laborers	20.44	103	10.1	221,590
Retired	14.60	74	12.9	282,233
HOMEOWNERSHIP STATUS				
Average household	**19.83**	**100**	**100.0**	**2,188,022**
Homeowners	21.67	109	72.3	1,582,127
Renters	16.21	82	27.7	605,103

Note: Households by type will not sum to the total because not all household types are shown. Hispanics may be of any race and most are white. Total household spending and market shares may not sum to total due to rounding. For an explanation of terms, see the introduction to this report.
Source: Calculations by New Strategist based on the Bureau of Labor Statistics' 2001 Consumer Expenditure Survey

116. SPENDING ON SAUCES AND GRAVIES, 2001

Total (aggregate) household spending in 2001	$4,360,427,357,940
Total (aggregate) household spending on sauces and gravies	$4,064,888,760
Average annual household spending on sauces and gravies	$36.84

	AVERAGE ANNUAL SPENDING PER HOUSEHOLD (in dollars)	BEST CUSTOMERS (index)	BIGGEST CUSTOMERS (percent market share)	TOTAL (AGGREGATE) HH SPENDING (in thousands of dollars)
AGE OF HOUSEHOLDER				
Average household	**$36.84**	**100**	**100.0%**	**$4,064,889**
Under age 25	25.58	69	5.4	219,937
Aged 25 to 34	37.15	101	16.9	687,832
Aged 35 to 44	46.51	126	27.9	1,135,867
Aged 45 to 54	45.03	122	24.7	1,004,935
Aged 55 to 64	35.27	96	12.6	513,143
Aged 65 to 74	23.52	64	6.6	266,764
Aged 75 or older	21.49	58	5.6	227,708
HOUSEHOLD INCOME				
Average household reporting income	**39.60**	**100**	**100.0**	**3,513,906**
Under $10,000	21.86	55	6.8	238,926
$10,000 to $19,999	24.47	62	10.5	369,871
$20,000 to $29,999	32.58	82	11.2	393,404
$30,000 to $39,999	37.53	95	11.2	394,365
$40,000 to $49,999	41.57	105	10.3	363,197
$50,000 to $69,999	51.04	129	18.1	636,979
$70,000 or more	60.01	152	32.3	1,133,709
HOUSEHOLD TYPE				
Average household	**36.84**	**100**	**100.0**	**4,064,889**
Married couples	48.48	132	66.6	2,707,123
Married couples, no children	37.35	101	21.2	863,495
Married couples, with children	55.93	152	38.6	1,569,116
Oldest child under 6	49.80	135	6.2	249,996
Oldest child 6 to 17	55.56	151	20.7	841,456
Oldest child 18 or older	61.27	166	11.9	483,420
Single parent with child under 18	42.73	116	7.0	283,257
Single person	14.94	41	12.1	489,778
RACE				
Average household	**36.84**	**100**	**100.0**	**4,064,889**
Black	34.40	93	11.2	456,935
White and other	37.17	101	88.7	3,607,572
HISPANIC ORIGIN				
Average household	**36.84**	**100**	**100.0**	**4,064,889**
Hispanic	33.62	91	8.0	323,458
Non-Hispanic	37.16	101	92.1	3,742,681
REGION				
Average household	**36.84**	**100**	**100.0**	**4,064,889**
Northeast	40.54	110	20.9	848,908
Midwest	38.07	103	24.2	983,805
South	33.13	90	31.9	1,297,934
West	38.32	104	23.0	934,242

	AVERAGE ANNUAL SPENDING PER HOUSEHOLD (in dollars)	BEST CUSTOMERS (index)	BIGGEST CUSTOMERS (percent market share)	TOTAL (AGGREGATE) HH SPENDING (in thousands of dollars)
EDUCATION				
Average household	**$36.84**	**100**	**100.0%**	**$4,064,889**
Less than high school graduate	27.60	75	11.7	474,085
High school graduate	36.73	100	28.8	1,170,438
Some college	35.18	96	19.9	808,859
Associate's degree	38.02	103	9.1	368,946
College graduate	43.19	117	30.5	1,237,825
Bachelor's degree	43.04	117	20.0	812,595
Master's, professional, doctoral degree	43.46	118	10.5	425,039
OCCUPATION				
Average household	**36.84**	**100**	**100.0**	**4,064,889**
Self-employed	46.67	127	5.6	227,470
Wage-and-salary workers, total	39.25	107	71.5	2,905,128
Managers and professionals	42.31	115	27.9	1,132,470
Technical, sales, and clerical	38.76	105	20.2	819,270
Service workers	32.24	88	8.1	329,719
Construction workers and mechanics	44.07	120	5.5	222,333
Operators, fabricators, laborers	37.56	102	10.0	407,188
Retired	26.12	71	12.4	504,926
HOMEOWNERSHIP STATUS				
Average household	**36.84**	**100**	**100.0**	**4,064,889**
Homeowners	40.44	110	72.6	2,952,524
Renters	29.79	81	27.4	1,112,031

Note: Households by type will not sum to the total because not all household types are shown. Hispanics may be of any race and most are white. Total household spending and market shares may not sum to total due to rounding. For an explanation of terms, see the introduction to this report.
Source: Calculations by New Strategist based on the Bureau of Labor Statistics' 2001 Consumer Expenditure Survey

117. SPENDING ON SAUSAGE, 2001

Total (aggregate) household spending in 2001	$4,360,427,357,940
Total (aggregate) household spending on sausage	$2,815,851,280
Average annual household spending on sausage	$25.52

	AVERAGE ANNUAL SPENDING PER HOUSEHOLD (in dollars)	BEST CUSTOMERS (index)	BIGGEST CUSTOMERS (percent market share)	TOTAL (AGGREGATE) HH SPENDING (in thousands of dollars)
AGE OF HOUSEHOLDER				
Average household	**$25.52**	**100**	**100.0%**	**$2,815,851**
Under age 25	14.63	57	4.5	125,789
Aged 25 to 34	20.06	79	13.2	371,411
Aged 35 to 44	28.88	113	25.1	705,307
Aged 45 to 54	30.40	119	24.1	678,437
Aged 55 to 64	28.89	113	14.9	420,321
Aged 65 to 74	23.16	91	9.3	262,681
Aged 75 or older	23.95	94	9.0	253,774
HOUSEHOLD INCOME				
Average household reporting income	**26.95**	**100**	**100.0**	**2,391,408**
Under $10,000	17.16	64	7.8	187,514
$10,000 to $19,999	23.90	89	15.1	361,194
$20,000 to $29,999	23.62	88	11.9	285,212
$30,000 to $39,999	30.96	115	13.6	325,328
$40,000 to $49,999	32.47	121	11.9	283,690
$50,000 to $69,999	26.26	97	13.7	327,725
$70,000 or more	32.63	121	25.8	616,446
HOUSEHOLD TYPE				
Average household	**25.52**	**100**	**100.0**	**2,815,851**
Married couples	32.85	129	65.1	1,834,344
Married couples, no children	27.55	108	22.6	636,928
Married couples, with children	33.68	132	33.6	944,892
Oldest child under 6	23.45	92	4.2	117,719
Oldest child 6 to 17	36.00	141	19.4	545,220
Oldest child 18 or older	36.24	142	10.2	285,934
Single parent with child under 18	31.48	123	7.4	208,681
Single person	10.71	42	12.5	351,106
RACE				
Average household	**25.52**	**100**	**100.0**	**2,815,851**
Black	36.90	145	17.4	490,143
White and other	23.99	94	82.7	2,328,373
HISPANIC ORIGIN				
Average household	**25.52**	**100**	**100.0**	**2,815,851**
Hispanic	26.61	104	9.1	256,015
Non-Hispanic	25.41	100	90.9	2,559,244
REGION				
Average household	**25.52**	**100**	**100.0**	**2,815,851**
Northeast	27.26	107	20.3	570,824
Midwest	23.53	92	21.6	608,062
South	28.50	112	39.7	1,116,545
West	21.33	84	18.5	520,025

	AVERAGE ANNUAL SPENDING PER HOUSEHOLD (in dollars)	BEST CUSTOMERS (index)	BIGGEST CUSTOMERS (percent market share)	TOTAL (AGGREGATE) HH SPENDING (in thousands of dollars)
EDUCATION				
Average household	**$25.52**	**100**	**100.0%**	**$2,815,851**
Less than high school graduate	28.64	112	17.5	491,949
High school graduate	27.49	108	31.1	875,996
Some college	25.36	99	20.7	583,077
Associate's degree	22.73	89	7.8	220,572
College graduate	22.62	89	23.0	648,289
Bachelor's degree	22.51	88	15.1	424,989
Master's, professional, doctoral degree	22.81	89	7.9	223,082
OCCUPATION				
Average household	**25.52**	**100**	**100.0**	**2,815,851**
Self-employed	26.64	104	4.6	129,843
Wage-and-salary workers, total	24.76	97	65.1	1,832,636
Managers and professionals	24.54	96	23.3	656,838
Technical, sales, and clerical	23.49	92	17.6	496,508
Service workers	25.74	101	9.3	263,243
Construction workers and mechanics	29.76	117	5.3	150,139
Operators, fabricators, laborers	24.37	96	9.4	264,195
Retired	26.07	102	17.9	503,959
HOMEOWNERSHIP STATUS				
Average household	**25.52**	**100**	**100.0**	**2,815,851**
Homeowners	28.31	111	73.4	2,066,913
Renters	20.07	79	26.6	749,193

Note: Households by type will not sum to the total because not all household types are shown. Hispanics may be of any race and most are white. Total household spending and market shares may not sum to total due to rounding. For an explanation of terms, see the introduction to this report.
Source: Calculations by New Strategist based on the Bureau of Labor Statistics' 2001 Consumer Expenditure Survey

118. SPENDING ON SOUP, CANNED AND PACKAGED, 2001

Total (aggregate) household spending in 2001	$4,360,427,357,940
Total (aggregate) household spending on soup, canned and packaged	$4,112,334,530
Average annual household spending on soup, canned and packaged	$37.27

	AVERAGE ANNUAL SPENDING PER HOUSEHOLD (in dollars)	BEST CUSTOMERS (index)	BIGGEST CUSTOMERS (percent market share)	TOTAL (AGGREGATE) HH SPENDING (in thousands of dollars)
AGE OF HOUSEHOLDER				
Average household	**$37.27**	**100**	**100.0%**	**$4,112,335**
Under age 25	18.47	50	3.9	158,805
Aged 25 to 34	34.75	93	15.6	643,396
Aged 35 to 44	40.71	109	24.2	994,220
Aged 45 to 54	43.42	117	23.6	969,004
Aged 55 to 64	39.64	106	14.0	576,722
Aged 65 to 74	32.36	87	8.9	367,027
Aged 75 or older	38.16	102	9.8	404,343
HOUSEHOLD INCOME				
Average household reporting income	**39.14**	**100**	**100.0**	**3,473,088**
Under $10,000	23.08	59	7.3	252,270
$10,000 to $19,999	29.27	75	12.7	442,417
$20,000 to $29,999	36.90	94	12.8	445,568
$30,000 to $39,999	38.33	98	11.6	402,772
$40,000 to $49,999	43.67	112	11.0	381,545
$50,000 to $69,999	43.51	111	15.6	543,005
$70,000 or more	53.53	137	29.1	1,011,289
HOUSEHOLD TYPE				
Average household	**37.27**	**100**	**100.0**	**4,112,335**
Married couples	45.35	122	61.6	2,532,344
Married couples, no children	36.70	99	20.6	848,467
Married couples, with children	51.97	139	35.5	1,458,018
Oldest child under 6	45.85	123	5.6	230,167
Oldest child 6 to 17	49.95	134	18.4	756,493
Oldest child 18 or older	60.90	163	11.7	480,501
Single parent with child under 18	37.96	102	6.1	251,637
Single person	23.53	63	18.8	771,384
RACE				
Average household	**37.27**	**100**	**100.0**	**4,112,335**
Black	23.62	63	7.6	313,745
White and other	39.12	105	92.3	3,796,831
HISPANIC ORIGIN				
Average household	**37.27**	**100**	**100.0**	**4,112,335**
Hispanic	34.85	94	8.2	335,292
Non-Hispanic	37.52	101	91.9	3,778,939
REGION				
Average household	**37.27**	**100**	**100.0**	**4,112,335**
Northeast	42.41	114	21.6	888,065
Midwest	39.23	105	24.7	1,013,782
South	32.63	88	31.1	1,278,346
West	38.23	103	22.7	932,047

	AVERAGE ANNUAL SPENDING PER HOUSEHOLD (in dollars)	BEST CUSTOMERS (index)	BIGGEST CUSTOMERS (percent market share)	TOTAL (AGGREGATE) HH SPENDING (in thousands of dollars)
EDUCATION				
Average household	**$37.27**	**100**	**100.0%**	**$4,112,335**
Less than high school graduate	31.79	85	13.3	546,057
High school graduate	36.70	99	28.4	1,169,482
Some college	36.14	97	20.2	830,931
Associate's degree	38.78	104	9.2	376,321
College graduate	41.43	111	28.9	1,187,384
Bachelor's degree	37.40	100	17.2	706,112
Master's, professional, doctoral degree	48.77	131	11.6	476,971
OCCUPATION				
Average household	**37.27**	**100**	**100.0**	**4,112,335**
Self-employed	38.73	104	4.6	188,770
Wage-and-salary workers, total	37.43	100	67.4	2,770,419
Managers and professionals	42.10	113	27.4	1,126,849
Technical, sales, and clerical	35.03	94	1.8	740,429
Service workers	33.45	90	8.3	342,093
Construction workers and mechanics	36.27	97	4.4	182,982
Operators, fabricators, laborers	35.25	95	9.3	382,145
Retired	37.44	101	17.6	723,753
HOMEOWNERSHIP STATUS				
Average household	**37.27**	**100**	**100.0**	**4,112,335**
Homeowners	41.36	111	73.4	3,019,694
Renters	29.27	79	26.6	1,092,620

Note: Households by type will not sum to the total because not all household types are shown. Hispanics may be of any race and most are white. Total household spending and market shares may not sum to total due to rounding. For an explanation of terms, see the introduction to this report.
Source: Calculations by New Strategist based on the Bureau of Labor Statistics' 2001 Consumer Expenditure Survey

119. SPENDING ON STEAK, 2001

Total (aggregate) household spending in 2001	$4,360,427,357,940
Total (aggregate) household spending on steak	$10,231,735,470
Average annual household spending on steak	$92.73

	AVERAGE ANNUAL SPENDING PER HOUSEHOLD (in dollars)	BEST CUSTOMERS (index)	BIGGEST CUSTOMERS (percent market share)	TOTAL (AGGREGATE) HH SPENDING (in thousands of dollars)
AGE OF HOUSEHOLDER				
Average household	**$92.73**	**100**	**100.0%**	**$10,231,736**
Under age 25	53.83	58	4.5	462,830
Aged 25 to 34	90.89	98	16.4	1,682,828
Aged 35 to 44	102.09	110	24.4	2,493,242
Aged 45 to 54	119.02	128	26.0	2,656,169
Aged 55 to 64	97.43	105	13.9	1,417,509
Aged 65 to 74	81.34	88	9.0	922,558
Aged 75 or older	55.63	60	5.8	589,456
HOUSEHOLD INCOME				
Average household reporting income	**99.78**	**100**	**100.0**	**8,853,978**
Under $10,000	53.33	53	6.6	582,838
$10,000 to $19,999	62.07	62	10.6	938,059
$20,000 to $29,999	98.59	99	13.4	1,190,474
$30,000 to $39,999	97.99	98	11.6	1,029,679
$40,000 to $49,999	106.20	106	10.5	927,869
$50,000 to $69,999	115.44	116	16.3	1,440,691
$70,000 or more	146.78	147	31.3	2,772,968
HOUSEHOLD TYPE				
Average household	**92.73**	**100**	**100.0**	**10,231,736**
Married couples	122.74	132	67.0	6,853,802
Married couples, no children	115.34	124	26.1	2,666,546
Married couples, with children	122.71	132	33.6	3,442,629
Oldest child under 6	109.86	119	5.4	551,497
Oldest child 6 to 17	123.77	134	18.3	1,874,497
Oldest child 18 or older	129.94	140	10.0	1,025,227
Single parent with child under 18	104.56	113	6.8	693,128
Single person	40.22	43	12.9	1,318,532
RACE				
Average household	**92.73**	**100**	**100.0**	**10,231,736**
Black	79.79	86	10.4	1,059,851
White and other	94.47	102	89.6	9,168,880
HISPANIC ORIGIN				
Average household	**92.73**	**100**	**100.0**	**10,231,736**
Hispanic	125.76	136	11.8	1,209,937
Non-Hispanic	89.43	96	88.0	9,007,211
REGION				
Average household	**92.73**	**100**	**100.0**	**10,231,736**
Northeast	96.84	104	19.8	2,027,830
Midwest	79.72	86	20.1	2,060,124
South	95.30	103	36.5	3,733,568
West	98.76	107	23.5	2,407,769

	AVERAGE ANNUAL SPENDING PER HOUSEHOLD (in dollars)	BEST CUSTOMERS (index)	BIGGEST CUSTOMERS (percent market share)	TOTAL (AGGREGATE) HH SPENDING (in thousands of dollars)
EDUCATION				
Average household	**$92.73**	**100**	**100.0%**	**$10,231,736**
Less than high school graduate	84.58	91	14.2	1,452,831
High school graduate	93.37	101	29.1	2,975,328
Some college	95.86	103	21.5	2,204,013
Associate's degree	90.54	98	8.6	878,600
College graduate	95.17	103	26.7	2,727,572
Bachelor's degree	93.26	101	17.2	1,760,749
Master's, professional, doctoral degree	98.65	106	9.4	964,797
OCCUPATION				
Average household	**92.73**	**100**	**100.0**	**10,231,736**
Self-employed	101.46	109	4.8	494,516
Wage-and-salary workers, total	96.40	104	69.7	7,135,142
Managers and professionals	102.19	110	26.7	2,735,218
Technical, sales, and clerical	94.02	101	19.4	1,987,301
Service workers	80.44	87	8.0	822,660
Construction workers and mechanics	117.49	127	5.8	592,737
Operators, fabricators, laborers	93.03	100	9.9	1,008,538
Retired	75.73	82	14.3	1,463,937
HOMEOWNERSHIP STATUS				
Average household	**92.73**	**100**	**100.0**	**10,231,736**
Homeowners	102.29	110	73.0	7,468,193
Renters	73.99	80	27.0	2,761,973

Note: Households by type will not sum to the total because not all household types are shown. Hispanics may be of any race and most are white. Total household spending and market shares may not sum to total due to rounding. For an explanation of terms, see the introduction to this report.
Source: Calculations by New Strategist based on the Bureau of Labor Statistics' 2001 Consumer Expenditure Survey

120. SPENDING ON SUGAR, 2001

Total (aggregate) household spending in 2001	$4,360,427,357,940		
Total (aggregate) household spending on sugar	$1,976,171,490		
Average annual household spending on sugar	$17.91		

	AVERAGE ANNUAL SPENDING PER HOUSEHOLD (in dollars)	BEST CUSTOMERS (index)	BIGGEST CUSTOMERS (percent market share)	TOTAL (AGGREGATE) HH SPENDING (in thousands of dollars)
AGE OF HOUSEHOLDER				
Average household	**$17.91**	**100**	**100.0%**	**$1,976,172**
Under age 25	11.04	62	4.8	94,922
Aged 25 to 34	18.02	101	16.9	333,640
Aged 35 to 44	19.02	106	23.5	464,506
Aged 45 to 54	21.54	120	24.3	480,708
Aged 55 to 64	21.00	117	15.5	305,529
Aged 65 to 74	15.01	84	8.6	170,243
Aged 75 or older	11.84	66	6.3	125,457
HOUSEHOLD INCOME				
Average household reporting income	**18.88**	**100**	**100.0**	**1,675,317**
Under $10,000	16.50	87	10.8	180,381
$10,000 to $19,999	16.41	87	14.8	247,930
$20,000 to $29,999	17.82	94	12.8	215,177
$30,000 to $39,999	20.73	110	1.3	217,831
$40,000 to $49,999	24.13	128	12.6	210,824
$50,000 to $69,999	18.95	100	14.1	236,496
$70,000 or more	19.46	103	21.9	367,638
HOUSEHOLD TYPE				
Average household	**17.91**	**100**	**100.0**	**1,976,172**
Married couples	22.87	128	64.6	1,277,061
Married couples, no children	18.36	103	21.5	424,465
Married couples, with children	24.57	137	34.9	689,311
Oldest child under 6	23.35	130	5.9	117,217
Oldest child 6 to 17	22.30	125	17.1	337,734
Oldest child 18 or older	30.41	170	12.1	239,935
Single parent with child under 18	21.34	119	7.2	141,463
Single person	7.92	44	13.1	259,641
RACE				
Average household	**17.91**	**100**	**100.0**	**1,976,172**
Black	24.81	139	16.7	329,551
White and other	16.98	95	83.4	1,648,011
HISPANIC ORIGIN				
Average household	**17.91**	**100**	**100.0**	**1,976,172**
Hispanic	24.43	136	11.9	235,041
Non-Hispanic	17.26	96	88.0	1,738,393
REGION				
Average household	**17.91**	**100**	**100.0**	**1,976,172**
Northeast	14.93	83	15.8	312,634
Midwest	15.78	88	20.6	407,787
South	20.85	116	41.3	816,840
West	18.00	101	22.2	438,840

	AVERAGE ANNUAL SPENDING PER HOUSEHOLD (in dollars)	BEST CUSTOMERS (index)	BIGGEST CUSTOMERS (percent market share)	TOTAL (AGGREGATE) HH SPENDING (in thousands of dollars)
EDUCATION				
Average household	**$17.91**	**100**	**100.0%**	**$1,976,172**
Less than high school graduate	23.10	129	20.1	396,789
High school graduate	17.72	99	28.6	564,666
Some college	16.20	91	18.8	372,470
Associate's degree	16.08	90	7.9	156,040
College graduate	16.99	95	24.6	486,933
Bachelor's degree	16.98	95	16.2	320,582
Master's, professional, doctoral degree	17.02	95	8.4	166,456
OCCUPATION				
Average household	**17.91**	**100**	**100.0**	**1,976,172**
Self-employed	21.49	120	5.3	104,742
Wage-and-salary workers, total	18.26	102	68.4	1,351,532
Managers and professionals	17.44	97	23.6	466,799
Technical, sales, and clerical	17.36	97	18.6	366,938
Service workers	17.30	97	9.0	176,927
Construction workers and mechanics	18.90	106	4.8	95,351
Operators, fabricators, laborers	22.03	123	12.1	238,827
Retired	12.95	72	12.7	250,337
HOMEOWNERSHIP STATUS				
Average household	**17.91**	**100**	**100.0**	**1,976,172**
Homeowners	19.27	108	71.2	1,406,903
Renters	15.25	85	28.8	569,267

Note: Households by type will not sum to the total because not all household types are shown. Hispanics may be of any race and most are white. Total household spending and market shares may not sum to total due to rounding. For an explanation of terms, see the introduction to this report.
Source: Calculations by New Strategist based on the Bureau of Labor Statistics' 2001 Consumer Expenditure Survey

121. SPENDING ON SWEETROLLS, COFFEE CAKES, DOUGHNUTS, 2001

Total (aggregate) household spending in 2001		$4,360,427,357,940	
Total (aggregate) household spending on sweetrolls, coffe cakes, doughnuts		$2,904,122,480	
Average annual household spending on sweetrolls, coffe cakes, doughnuts		$26.32	

	AVERAGE ANNUAL SPENDING PER HOUSEHOLD (in dollars)	BEST CUSTOMERS (index)	BIGGEST CUSTOMERS (percent market share)	TOTAL (AGGREGATE) HH SPENDING (in thousands of dollars)
AGE OF HOUSEHOLDER				
Average household	**$26.32**	**100**	**100.0%**	**$2,904,123**
Under age 25	13.78	52	4.1	118,480
Aged 25 to 34	20.29	77	12.9	375,669
Aged 35 to 44	33.26	126	28.0	812,276
Aged 45 to 54	32.21	122	24.8	718,831
Aged 55 to 64	25.48	97	12.8	370,709
Aged 65 to 74	22.81	87	8.9	258,711
Aged 75 or older	23.47	89	8.6	248,688
HOUSEHOLD INCOME				
Average household reporting income	**28.09**	**100**	**100.0**	**2,492,566**
Under $10,000	17.34	62	7.6	189,510
$10,000 to $19,999	20.20	72	12.2	305,317
$20,000 to $29,999	26.44	94	12.8	319,263
$30,000 to $39,999	25.68	91	10.8	269,845
$40,000 to $49,999	30.71	109	10.8	268,313
$50,000 to $69,999	31.17	111	15.6	389,002
$70,000 or more	40.02	143	30.3	756,058
HOUSEHOLD TYPE				
Average household	**26.32**	**100**	**100.0**	**2,904,123**
Married couples	33.38	127	64.2	1,863,939
Married couples, no children	23.64	90	18.8	546,533
Married couples, with children	40.18	153	38.8	1,127,250
Oldest child under 6	28.07	107	4.9	140,911
Oldest child 6 to 17	42.39	161	22.1	641,997
Oldest child 18 or older	44.37	169	12.1	350,079
Single parent with child under 18	30.10	114	6.9	199,533
Single person	12.93	49	14.6	423,884
RACE				
Average household	**26.32**	**100**	**100.0**	**2,904,123**
Black	19.63	75	9.0	260,745
White and other	27.22	103	91.0	2,641,864
HISPANIC ORIGIN				
Average household	**26.32**	**100**	**100.0**	**2,904,123**
Hispanic	32.91	125	10.9	316,627
Non-Hispanic	25.66	98	89.0	2,584,424
REGION				
Average household	**26.32**	**100**	**100.0**	**2,904,123**
Northeast	25.91	98	18.7	542,555
Midwest	26.64	101	23.7	688,431
South	24.93	95	33.6	976,683
West	28.58	109	24.0	696,780

	AVERAGE ANNUAL SPENDING PER HOUSEHOLD (in dollars)	BEST CUSTOMERS (index)	BIGGEST CUSTOMERS (percent market share)	TOTAL (AGGREGATE) HH SPENDING (in thousands of dollars)
EDUCATION				
Average household	**$26.32**	**100**	**100.0%**	**$2,904,123**
Less than high school graduate	25.52	97	15.1	438,357
High school graduate	24.92	95	27.3	794,101
Some college	24.76	94	19.6	569,282
Associate's degree	25.31	96	8.5	245,608
College graduate	29.86	113	29.5	855,788
Bachelor's degree	29.67	113	19.3	560,170
Master's, professional, doctoral degree	30.20	115	10.2	295,356
OCCUPATION				
Average household	**26.32**	**100**	**100.0**	**2,904,123**
Self-employed	28.89	110	4.8	140,810
Wage-and-salary workers, total	26.85	102	68.4	1,987,330
Managers and professionals	28.20	107	26.0	754,801
Technical, sales, and clerical	26.64	101	19.4	563,090
Service workers	26.19	100	9.2	267,845
Construction workers and mechanics	26.16	99	4.5	131,977
Operators, fabricators, laborers	25.17	96	9.4	272,868
Retired	24.37	93	16.2	471,097
HOMEOWNERSHIP STATUS				
Average household	**26.32**	**100**	**100.0**	**2,904,123**
Homeowners	29.21	111	73.4	2,132,622
Renters	20.67	79	26.6	771,590

Note: Households by type will not sum to the total because not all household types are shown. Hispanics may be of any race and most are white. Total household spending and market shares may not sum to total due to rounding. For an explanation of terms, see the introduction to this report.
Source: Calculations by New Strategist based on the Bureau of Labor Statistics' 2001 Consumer Expenditure Survey

122. SPENDING ON TEA, 2001

Total (aggregate) household spending in 2001	$4,360,427,357,940
Total (aggregate) household spending on tea	$1,938,656,230
Average annual household spending on tea	$17.57

	AVERAGE ANNUAL SPENDING PER HOUSEHOLD (in dollars)	BEST CUSTOMERS (index)	BIGGEST CUSTOMERS (percent market share)	TOTAL (AGGREGATE) HH SPENDING (in thousands of dollars)
AGE OF HOUSEHOLDER				
Average household	**$17.57**	**100**	**100.0%**	**$1,938,656**
Under age 25	8.41	48	3.7	72,309
Aged 25 to 34	16.28	93	15.5	301,424
Aged 35 to 44	21.23	121	26.7	518,479
Aged 45 to 54	22.13	126	25.5	493,875
Aged 55 to 64	17.43	99	13.1	253,589
Aged 65 to 74	14.28	81	8.4	161,964
Aged 75 or older	12.78	73	7.0	135,417
HOUSEHOLD INCOME				
Average household reporting income	**18.79**	**100**	**100.0**	**1,667,331**
Under $10,000	12.37	66	8.1	135,236
$10,000 to $19,999	13.42	71	12.2	202,774
$20,000 to $29,999	15.49	82	11.2	187,042
$30,000 to $39,999	16.28	87	10.3	171,070
$40,000 to $49,999	16.44	88	8.6	143,636
$50,000 to $69,999	22.13	118	16.6	276,182
$70,000 or more	29.77	158	33.7	562,415
HOUSEHOLD TYPE				
Average household	**17.57**	**100**	**100.0**	**1,938,656**
Married couples	21.47	122	61.8	1,198,885
Married couples, no children	19.95	114	23.8	461,224
Married couples, with children	22.00	125	31.8	617,210
Oldest child under 6	19.19	109	5.0	96,334
Oldest child 6 to 17	21.10	120	16.5	319,560
Oldest child 18 or older	26.02	148	10.6	205,298
Single parent with child under 18	20.48	117	0.7	135,762
Single person	9.19	52	15.5	301,276
RACE				
Average household	**17.57**	**100**	**100.0**	**1,938,656**
Black	14.72	84	10.1	195,526
White and other	17.96	102	89.9	1,743,126
HISPANIC ORIGIN				
Average household	**17.57**	**100**	**100.0**	**1,938,656**
Hispanic	21.20	121	10.5	203,965
Non-Hispanic	17.21	98	89.4	1,733,357
REGION				
Average household	**17.57**	**100**	**100.0**	**1,938,656**
Northeast	24.60	140	26.6	515,124
Midwest	14.56	83	19.4	376,260
South	17.21	98	34.8	674,236
West	15.25	87	19.2	371,795

	AVERAGE ANNUAL SPENDING PER HOUSEHOLD (in dollars)	BEST CUSTOMERS (index)	BIGGEST CUSTOMERS (percent market share)	TOTAL (AGGREGATE) HH SPENDING (in thousands of dollars)
EDUCATION				
Average household	**$17.57**	**100**	**100.0%**	**$1,938,656**
Less than high school graduate	14.03	80	12.4	240,993
High school graduate	17.32	99	28.5	551,919
Some college	16.06	91	19.1	369,252
Associate's degree	17.80	101	8.9	172,731
College graduate	20.97	119	31.0	601,000
Bachelor's degree	19.86	113	19.3	374,957
Master's, professional, doctoral degree	22.99	131	11.6	224,842
OCCUPATION				
Average household	**17.57**	**100**	**100.0**	**1,938,656**
Self-employed	20.76	118	5.2	101,184
Wage-and-salary workers, total	18.53	106	70.7	1,371,517
Managers and professionals	20.97	119	29.0	561,283
Technical, sales, and clerical	16.48	94	18.0	348,338
Service workers	17.02	97	9.0	174,064
Construction workers and mechanics	18.49	105	4.8	93,282
Operators, fabricators, laborers	17.95	102	10.0	194,596
Retired	14.17	81	14.1	273,920
HOMEOWNERSHIP STATUS				
Average household	**17.57**	**100**	**100.0**	**1,938,656**
Homeowners	18.50	105	69.7	1,350,685
Renters	15.76	90	30.3	588,305

Note: Households by type will not sum to the total because not all household types are shown. Hispanics may be of any race and most are white. Total household spending and market shares may not sum to total due to rounding. For an explanation of terms, see the introduction to this report.
Source: Calculations by New Strategist based on the Bureau of Labor Statistics' 2001 Consumer Expenditure Survey

123. SPENDING ON VEGETABLE JUICES, FRESH AND CANNED, 2001

Total (aggregate) household spending in 2001	$4,360,427,357,940
Total (aggregate) household spending on vegetable juices, fresh and canned	$844,093,350
Average annual household spending on vegetable juices, fresh and canned	$7.65

	AVERAGE ANNUAL SPENDING PER HOUSEHOLD (in dollars)	BEST CUSTOMERS (index)	BIGGEST CUSTOMERS (percent market share)	TOTAL (AGGREGATE) HH SPENDING (in thousands of dollars)
AGE OF HOUSEHOLDER				
Average household	**$7.65**	**100**	**100.0%**	**$844,093**
Under age 25	5.22	68	5.3	44,882
Aged 25 to 34	7.54	99	16.5	139,603
Aged 35 to 44	9.37	123	27.1	228,834
Aged 45 to 54	8.85	116	23.4	197,506
Aged 55 to 64	6.84	89	11.8	99,515
Aged 65 to 74	4.94	65	6.6	56,030
Aged 75 or older	7.17	94	9.0	75,973
HOUSEHOLD INCOME				
Average household reporting income	**8.01**	**100**	**100.0**	**710,767**
Under $10,000	5.34	67	8.2	58,357
$10,000 to $19,999	5.79	72	12.3	87,567
$20,000 to $29,999	6.78	85	11.5	81,869
$30,000 to $39,999	6.72	84	9.9	70,614
$40,000 to $49,999	7.64	95	9.4	66,751
$50,000 to $69,999	8.15	102	14.3	101,712
$70,000 or more	13.00	162	34.6	245,596
HOUSEHOLD TYPE				
Average household	**7.65**	**100**	**100.0**	**844,093**
Married couples	9.07	119	6.0	506,469
Married couples, no children	8.01	105	21.9	185,183
Married couples, with children	9.90	129	32.9	277,745
Oldest child under 6	7.11	93	4.2	35,692
Oldest child 6 to 17	10.44	137	18.7	158,114
Oldest child 18 or older	10.80	141	10.1	85,212
Single parent with child under 18	7.36	96	5.8	48,789
Single person	4.40	58	17.1	144,245
RACE				
Average household	**7.65**	**100**	**100.0**	**844,093**
Black	6.47	85	10.2	85,941
White and other	7.81	102	89.8	758,007
HISPANIC ORIGIN				
Average household	**7.65**	**100**	**100.0**	**844,093**
Hispanic	7.54	99	8.6	72,542
Non-Hispanic	7.66	100	91.4	771,500
REGION				
Average household	**7.65**	**100**	**100.0**	**844,093**
Northeast	8.69	114	21.6	181,969
Midwest	6.61	86	20.2	170,816
South	7.42	97	34.4	290,693
West	8.21	107	23.7	200,160

	AVERAGE ANNUAL SPENDING PER HOUSEHOLD (in dollars)	BEST CUSTOMERS (index)	BIGGEST CUSTOMERS (percent market share)	TOTAL (AGGREGATE) HH SPENDING (in thousands of dollars)
EDUCATION				
Average household	**$7.65**	**100**	**100.0%**	**$844,093**
Less than high school graduate	7.13	93	14.5	122,472
High school graduate	6.96	91	26.3	221,787
Some college	7.53	98	20.5	173,130
Associate's degree	8.00	105	9.2	77,632
College graduate	8.68	114	29.5	248,769
Bachelor's degree	9.41	123	21.1	177,661
Master's, professional, doctoral degree	7.34	96	8.5	71,785
OCCUPATION				
Average household	**7.65**	**100**	**100.0**	**844,093**
Self-employed	6.10	80	3.5	29,731
Wage-and-salary workers, total	8.26	108	72.4	611,372
Managers and professionals	10.12	132	32.1	270,872
Technical, sales, and clerical	8.11	106	20.3	171,421
Service workers	6.77	89	8.2	69,237
Construction workers and mechanics	8.10	106	4.8	40,865
Operators, fabricators, laborers	5.90	77	7.6	63,962
Retired	5.95	78	13.6	115,019
HOMEOWNERSHIP STATUS				
Average household	**7.65**	**100**	**100.0**	**844,093**
Homeowners	7.73	101	66.9	564,367
Renters	7.48	98	33.1	279,221

Note: Households by type will not sum to the total because not all household types are shown. Hispanics may be of any race and most are white. Total household spending and market shares may not sum to total due to rounding. For an explanation of terms, see the introduction to this report.
Source: Calculations by New Strategist based on the Bureau of Labor Statistics' 2001 Consumer Expenditure Survey

Spending by Product and Service, 2001

(average annual spending of consumer units on products and services, ranked by amount spent, 2001)

Mortgage interest	$2,695.21
Social Security	2,449.69
Federal income taxes	2,236.81
Rent	2,070.43
Gasoline and motor oil	1,279.36
Property taxes	1,233.20
Health insurance	1,060.65
Electricity	1,008.54
Used cars	993.17
New cars	855.61
Used trucks	854.92
New trucks	829.57
Vehicle insurance	819.23
Telephone service, residential	685.61
Vehicle maintenance and repairs	662.38
Apparel, women's	562.21
State and local income taxes	554.56
Cash contributions to church, religious organizations	519.50
Dinner at full-service restaurants	512.06
Maintenance and repair services, owned homes	478.64
Pensions, deductions for private	411.32
Natural gas	410.62
Life, endowment, annuity, other personal insurance	400.09
Retirement accounts, nonpayroll deposits	393.60
College tuition	369.85
Lunch at fast food restaurants and take-outs	369.11
Finance charges, vehicle	359.45
Cable service and community antenna	353.57
Drugs, prescription	340.51
Vehicle leasing	339.66
Apparel, men's	335.15
Apparel, children's	284.02
Cigarettes	282.79
Lodging on trips	261.59
Airline fares	254.70
Food on trips	252.43
Homeowner's insurance	248.77
BEEF	**248.06**
Water and sewerage maintenance	232.45
Lunch at full-service restaurants	230.57
Personal care services	226.92
Finance charges, except mortgage and vehicles	224.63
Dental services	220.65
Dinner at fast food restaurants and take-outs	219.51
Cellular phone service	210.20
Day care centers, nurseries, and preschools	191.28

Child support expenditures	$189.42
PORK	**177.31**
Snacks at fast food restaurants and take-outs	173.57
Medicare payments	173.47
Home equity loan, line of credit interest	165.99
Vacation homes, owned	163.94
FRESH VEGETABLES	**161.62**
FRESH FRUITS	**160.41**
POULTRY	**151.87**
Household decorative items	147.23
Computers and computer hardware, nonbusiness use	146.06
Shoes, women's	141.69
Recreation expenses on trips	141.40
Cash contributions to charities and other organizations	135.31
CARBONATED DRINKS	**133.55**
Physician's services	132.14
Laundry and cleaning supplies	131.37
MILK, FRESH	**123.50**
Toys, games, hobbies, and tricycles	119.83
Cosmetics, perfume, and bath products	116.03
FISH AND SEAFOOD	**113.67**
Beer and ale at home	111.75
Legal fees	109.61
Social, recreation, civic club membership	107.94
Jewelry	107.07
Elementary and high school tuition	106.76
Maintenance and repair materials, owned homes	101.14
Shoes, men's	100.17
Gardening, lawn care service	96.69
CHEESE	**93.39**
Movie, theater, opera, ballet tickets	91.26
Computer information services	90.33
Breakfast at fast food restaurants and take-outs	88.18
Pet food	87.96
Trash and garbage collection	86.25
CEREALS, READY-TO-EAT AND COOKED	**86.04**
BREAD	**85.37**
Housekeeping services	84.97
Breakfast at full-service restaurants	81.38
State and local registration	79.79
Lunch at employer and school cafeterias	79.22
Sofas	78.43
Television sets	77.13
Fees for recreational lessons	76.64
POTATO CHIPS AND OTHER SNACKS	**75.56**
Cleansing and toilet tissue, paper towels, and napkins	75.47
Cash support for college students	74.85
Fees for participant sports	73.53
CANDY AND CHEWING GUM	**73.49**
Laundry and dry cleaning of apparel, professional	73.18
Lunch meats (cold cuts)	70.88
Deductions for government retirement	69.67
Lawn and garden supplies	69.49
Motorized camper	69.12
Whiskey and other alcoholic beverages at restaurants, bars	67.83
Veterinarian services	64.49
School lunches	63.89

Housing while attending school	$63.40
Fuel oil	63.31
Stationery, stationery supplies, giftwrap	62.52
Beer and ale at restaurants, bars	61.41
Funeral expenses	61.11
Drugs, nonprescription	60.84
Shoes, children's	60.40
Bedroom furniture, except mattress and springs	58.95
Postage	57.70
Wine at home	56.89
ICE CREAM AND RELATED PRODUCTS	**56.79**
Accounting fees	55.81
Athletic gear, game tables, exercise equipment	55.68
Wall units, cabinets, and other furniture	55.67
FRUIT JUICE, CANNED AND BOTTLED	**55.50**
Hair care products	54.80
Hospital services other than room	53.10
Plants and fresh flowers, indoor	52.36
Kitchen and dining room furniture	51.68
Eyeglasses and contact lenses	51.52
Mass transit fares, intracity	50.64
Books, supplies for college	50.13
Refrigerators and freezers	49.79
Mattresses and springs	49.40
Books, except book clubs	49.38
VEGETABLES, CANNED AND DRIED	**48.17**
Bedroom linens	48.17
Vitamins, nonprescription	47.41
Lottery and gambling losses	46.78
Board (including at school)	46.54
COOKIES	**46.13**
Motorboats	45.94
Newspaper subscriptions	45.36
Lawn and garden equipment	42.06
Pet purchase, supplies, and medicines	41.42
Bottled/tank gas	41.07
Occupational expenses	39.76
Babysitting and child care, own home	39.47
Trailer and other attachable campers	39.45
Rental of video cassettes, tapes, discs, films	39.38
Living room chairs	39.37
BISCUITS AND ROLLS	**39.34**
Vehicle rental	39.01
Coffee	38.35
Records, CDs, audio tapes, needles	38.23
Catered affairs	38.08
Eye care services	37.70
SOUPS, CANNED AND PACKAGED	**37.27**
Snacks at vending machines, mobile vendors	37.15
Telephones and accessories	36.86
SAUCES AND GRAVIES	**36.84**
Laundry and dry cleaning of apparel, coin-operated	36.06
Admission to sports events	35.56
EGGS	**34.99**
Hospital room	34.76
Ground rent	34.28
Gifts to non-CU members of stocks, bonds, and mutual funds	34.24

CAKES AND CUPCAKES	**$33.80**
Medical services by professionals other than physician	33.33
Care for elderly, invalids, handicapped, etc.	33.20
Alcoholic beverages on trips	32.94
Power tools	32.84
Convalescent or nursing home care	32.37
Moving, storage, and freight express	31.84
Snacks at full-service restaurants	30.85
Cooking stoves, ovens	30.22
PASTA, CORNMEAL, AND OTHER CEREAL PRODUCTS	**29.57**
Deodorants, feminine hygiene, misc. products	29.09
Alimony expenditures	28.65
FROZEN MEALS	**28.65**
Film processing	28.23
SALAD DRESSINGS	**28.02**
Cash contributions to educational institutions	27.90
Parking fees	27.80
VEGETABLES, FROZEN	**27.50**
Oral hygiene products	27.03
SWEETROLLS, COFFEE CAKES, DOUGHNUTS	**26.32**
Topicals and dressings	26.22
BAKERY PRODUCTS, FROZEN AND REFRIGERATED	**26.06**
Musical instruments and accessories	25.33
Babysitting and child care, other home	25.29
VCRs and video disc players	25.18
FRUIT JUICE, FRESH	**24.86**
FATS AND OILS	**24.53**
Video cassettes, tapes, and discs	24.46
Ship fares	24.19
CRACKERS	**24.05**
Meals as pay	23.83
Checking accounts, other bank service charges	23.69
Used motorcycles	23.63
BABY FOOD	**23.62**
Tobacco products, except cigarettes	23.32
Train fares, intercity	23.06
Floor coverings, wall-to-wall	22.82
Video game hardware and software	22.70
Hunting and fishing equipment	22.27
New motorcycles	22.02
FRANKFURTERS	**22.01**
Washing machines	21.99
Bathroom linens	21.89
NUTS	**21.81**
Photographic equipment	21.56
Butter	21.55
Pet services	21.16
Computer software and accessories, nonbusiness use	21.06
Lab tests, X-rays	21.05
Electric floor-cleaning equipment	20.63
Sound components and component systems	20.58
FRUIT-FLAVORED DRINKS, NONCARBONATED	**20.36**
RICE	**19.95**
SALT, SPICES, AND OTHER SEASONINGS	**19.83**
PREPARED SALADS	**19.55**
JAMS, PRESERVES, OTHER SWEETS	**19.52**
Film	19.43

Photographer fees	$19.39
Cemetery lots, vaults, and maintenance fees	19.09
China and other dinnerware	18.83
Floor coverings, nonpermanent	18.23
Magazine subscriptions	18.18
Outdoor equipment	18.12
Living room tables	18.00
SUGAR	**17.91**
TEA	**17.57**
Small electric kitchen appliances	17.48
BAKING NEEDS	**17.41**
Phone cards	17.15
Watches	16.98
Curtains and draperies	16.43
Home security system service fee	16.31
FRUIT, CANNED	**16.27**
Tableware, nonelectric kitchenware	16.27
Taxi fares and limousine service	15.94
Tolls	15.81
Maintenance and repair services, rented homes	15.55
Window coverings	15.51
Property management, owned home	15.38
Dishwashers (built-in), garbage disposals, range hoods	15.21
Nonelectric cookware	15.05
Books, supplies for elementary, high school	14.99
Wine at restaurants, bars	14.55
Boat without motor and boat trailers	14.50
Shaving products	14.19
Clothes dryers	13.99
Whiskey at home	13.62
Office furniture for home use	13.44
FLOUR MIXES, PREPARED	**12.89**
PEANUT BUTTER	**12.69**
CREAM	**12.35**
Camping equipment	11.54
Local transportation on trips	11.54
Snacks at employer and school cafeterias	11.48
Newspaper, nonsubscription	11.45
MARGARINE	**11.43**
Laundry and cleaning equipment	11.37
FRUIT JUICE, FROZEN	**11.33**
Outdoor furniture	11.22
Bus fares, intercity	11.20
Hearing aids	11.08
Closet and storage items	10.94
Automobile service clubs	10.68
Lamps and lighting fixtures	10.63
PIES, TARTS, TURNOVERS	**10.60**
Bicycles	10.58
Appliance repair, including service center	10.44
Maintenance and repair materials, rented homes	10.41
PREPARED DESSERTS	**10.15**
NONDAIRY CREAM AND IMITATION MILK	**10.09**
Termite/pest control services	10.06
Tenant's insurance	10.01
OLIVES, PICKLES, RELISHES	**9.97**
Microwave ovens	9.77

Sewing materials for household items	$9.62
Infants' furniture	9.51
Magazines, nonsubscription	9.38
Infants' equipment	9.28
Vehicle inspection	9.28
LAMB AND ORGAN MEATS	**9.17**
Electric personal care appliances	8.69
Kitchen and dining room linens	8.41
Medical equipment	8.29
FLOUR	**8.01**
VEGETABLE JUICES	**8.01**
Reupholstering and furniture repair	7.82
Slipcovers and decorative pillows	7.80
Docking and landing fees	7.68
Winter sports equipment	7.59
Radios	7.55
Pinball, electronic video games	7.53
Wood and other fuels	7.50
Compact disc, tape, record, video mail order clubs	7.29
Hand tools	7.26
Books purchased through book clubs	6.97
Taxi fares and limousine service on trips	6.78
Cash contributions to political organizations	6.77
Air conditioners, window	6.62
Sewing patterns and notions	6.48
Hair accessories	6.46
Sound equipment accessories	6.41
Driver's license	6.34
Rental of furniture	6.15
Lunch at vending machines, mobile vendors	6.14
Glassware	6.07
Luggage	6.06
Apparel repair and tailoring	6.02
Towing charges	5.92
Shopping club membership fees	5.58
FRUIT DRIED	**5.54**
Water sports equipment	5.38
ARTIFICIAL SWEETENERS	**5.04**
Management and upkeep services for security, owned home	5.01
Watch and jewelry repair	4.83
Portable heating and cooling equipment	4.79
Safe deposit box rental	4.52
Breakfast at employer and school cafeterias	4.17
Laundry and dry cleaning, nonapparel, coin-operated	4.17
Books, supplies for day care, nursery school	4.11
BREAD AND CRACKER PRODUCTS	**4.05**
Sewing machines	4.02
Repairs/rentals of lawn/garden equipment, hand/power tools,	3.81
Flatware	3.72
Credit card memberships	3.57
Clocks	3.57
Material for making clothes	3.51
Repair of TV, radio, and sound equipment	3.23
Water softening service	3.18
Clothing rental	2.92
Rental of medical equipment	2.61
Tape recorders and players	2.55

FRUIT, FROZEN	**$2.53**
Dinner at employer and school cafeterias	2.53
Playground equipment	2.44
Repair of computer systems for nonbusiness use	2.44
Rental and repair of miscellaneous sports equipment	2.38
Delivery services	2.27
Fireworks	2.15
Deductions for railroad retirement	2.03
Appliance rental	2.03
Septic tank cleaning	1.95
Smoking accessories	1.95
Rental of recreational vehicles	1.92
Satellite dishes	1.91
Visual goods	1.82
School bus	1.70
Adult day care centers	1.68
Silver serving pieces	1.56
Shoe repair and other shoe services	1.53
Laundry and dry cleaning, nonapparel, sent out	1.53
Dinner at vending machines, mobile vendors	1.52
Wigs and hairpieces	1.51
Rental and repair of musical instruments	1.49
Breakfast at vending machines, mobile vendors	1.49
Telephone answering devices	1.48
Business equipment for home use	1.48
Pager service	1.46
Plastic dinnerware	1.45
Calculators	1.43
Souvenirs	1.32
Dishwashers, portable	1.31
Outboard motors	1.21
Smoke alarms	0.71
NONALCOHOLIC BEER	**0.66**
Termite/pest control products	0.65
Clothing storage	0.60
Rental of VCR, radio, sound equipment	0.56
Rental of television sets	0.49
Coal	0.48
Rental of office equipment for nonbusiness use	0.43
Parking, owned home	0.37
Vitamin supplements	0.29
Encyclopedia and other reference book sets	0.23
Repair and rental of photographic equipment	0.20
Newsletters	0.05

*Note: Ranking does not show miscellaneous categories or gift spending, which is
included in each product and service category.*
Source: Calculations by New Strategist based on the 2001 Consumer Expenditure Survey

age The age of the reference person, also called the householder or head of household.

average spending The average amount spent per household. The Bureau of Labor Statistics calculates the average for all households in a segment, not just for those who purchased an item. For items purchased by most households, such as bread, average spending figures are an accurate account of actual spending. For products and services purchased by few households during a year's time, such as cars, the average amount spent is much less than what purchasers spend. See Appendix C for the percentage of consumer units reporting an expenditure and the average amount spent by purchasers.

baby boom People born from 1946 through 1964, aged 37 to 55 in 2001.

baby bust People born from 1965 through 1976, aged 25 to 36 in 2001. Also known as Generation X.

complete income reporters Respondents who provided values for major sources of income, such as wages and salaries, self-employment income, and Social Security income. Even complete income reporters may not have given a full accounting of all income from all sources.

consumer unit Defined as follows:

• All members of a household who are related by blood, marriage, adoption, or other legal arrangements.

• A person living alone or sharing a household with others or living as a roomer in a private home or lodging house or in permanent living quarters in a hotel or motel, but who is financially independent.

• Two persons or more living together who pool their income to make joint expenditure decisions. Financial independence is determined by the three major expense categories: housing, food, and other living expenses. To be considered financially independent, at least two of the three major expense categories have to be provided by the respondent. For convenience, called households in the text of this book.

consumer unit, composition of The classification of interview households by type according to: (1) relationship of other household members to the reference person; (2) age of the children to the reference person; and (3) combination of relationship to the reference person and age of the children. Stepchildren and adopted children are included with the reference person's own children.

earner A consumer unit member aged 14 or older who worked at least one week during the 12 months prior to the interview date.

education of reference person The number of years of formal education of the reference person based on the highest grade completed. If the respondent was enrolled at the time of interview, the grade being attended is the one recorded. Those not reporting their education are classified under no school or not reported.

expenditure The transaction cost including excise and sales taxes of goods and services acquired during the survey period. The full cost of each purchase is recorded even though full payment may not have been made at the date of purchase. Expenditure estimates include gifts. Excluded from expenditures are purchases or portions of purchases directly assignable to business purposes and periodic credit or installment payments on goods and services already acquired.

food Includes the following:

• *food at home* Refers to the total expenditures for food at grocery stores or other food stores during the interview period. It is calculated by multiplying the number of visits to a grocery or other food store by the average amount spent per visit. It excludes the purchase of nonfood items.

• *food away from home* Includes all meals (breakfast, lunch, brunch, and dinner) at restaurants, carryouts, and vending machines, including tips, plus meals as pay, special catered affairs such as weddings, bar mitzvahs, and confirmations, and meals away from home on trips.

generation X People born from 1965 through 1976, aged 25 to 36 in 2001. Also known as the baby bust.

Hispanic origin The self-identified Hispanic origin of the consumer unit reference person. All consumer units are included in one of two Hispanic origin groups based on the reference person's Hispanic origin: Hispanic or non-Hispanic. Hispanics may be of any race.

household According to the Census Bureau, all the people who occupy a household. A group of unrelated people who share a housing unit as roommates or unmarried partners is also counted as a household. Households do not include group quarters such as college dormitories, prisons, or nursing homes. A household may contain more than one consumer unit. The terms "household" and "consumer unit" are used interchangeably in this book.

housing tenure "Owner" includes households living in their own homes, cooperatives, condominiums, or townhouses. "Renter" includes households paying rent as well as families living rent free in lieu of wages.

income before taxes The total money earnings and selected money receipts accruing to a consumer unit during the 12 months prior to the interview date. Income includes the following components:

• *wages and salaries* Includes total money earnings for all members of the consumer unit aged 14 or older from all jobs, including civilian wages and salaries, Armed Forces pay and allowances, piece-rate payments, commis

sions, tips, National Guard or Reserve pay (received for training periods), and cash bonuses before deductions for taxes, pensions, union dues, etc.

• *self-employment income* Includes net business and farm income, which consists of net income (gross receipts minus operating expenses) from a profession or unincorporated business or from the operation of a farm by an owner, tenant, or sharecropper. If the business or farm is a partnership, only an appropriate share of net income is recorded. Losses are also recorded.

• *Social Security, private and government retirement* Includes the following: payments by the federal government made under retirement, survivor, and disability insurance programs to retired persons, dependents of deceased insured workers, or to disabled workers; and private pensions or retirement benefits received by retired persons or their survivors, either directly or through an insurance company.

• *interest, dividends, rental income, and other property income* Includes interest income on savings or bonds; payments made by a corporation to its stockholders, periodic receipts from estates or trust funds; net income or loss from the rental of property, real estate, or farms, and net income or loss from roomers or boarders.

• *unemployment and workers' compensation and veterans' benefits* Includes income from unemployment compensation and workers' compensation, and veterans' payments including educational benefits, but excluding military retirement.

• *public assistance, supplemental security income, and food stamps* Includes public assistance or welfare, including money received from job training grants; supplemental security income paid by federal, state, and local welfare agencies to low-income persons who are aged 65 or older, blind, or disabled; and the value of food stamps obtained.

• *regular contributions for support* Includes alimony and child support as well as any regular contributions from persons outside the consumer unit.

• *other income* Includes money income from care of foster children, cash scholarships, fellowships, or stipends not based on working; and meals and rent as pay.

indexed spending The indexed spending figures compare the spending of each demographic segment with that of the average household. To compute an index, the amount spent on an item by a demographic segment is divided by the amount spent on the item by the average household. That figure is then multiplied by 100. An index of 100 is the average for all households. An index of 132 means average spending by households in a segment is 32 percent above average (100 plus 32). An index of 75 means average spending by households in a segment is 25 percent below average (100 minus 25). Indexed spending figures identify the consumer units that spend the most on a product or service.

market share The market share is the percentage of total household spending on an item that is accounted for by a demographic segment. Market shares are calculated by dividing a demographic segment's total spending on an item by the total spend-

ing of all households on the item. Total spending on an item for all households is calculated by multiplying average spending by the total number of households (110,339,000 in 2001). Total spending on an item for each demographic segment is calculated by multiplying the segment's average spending by the number of households in the segment. Market shares reveal the demographic segments that account for the largest share of spending on a product or service.

metropolitan statistical area (MSA) As defined by the Office of Management and Budget, a large population nucleus, together with adjacent communities which have a high degree of economic and social integration with the nucleus.

millennial generation People born from 1977 though 1994, and aged 7 through 24 in 2001.

occupation The occupation in which the reference person received the most earnings during the survey period. The occupational categories follow those of the Census of Population. Categories shown in the tables include the following:

• *self-employed* Includes all occupational categories; the reference person is self-employed in own business, professional practice, or farm.

• *wage and salary earners, managers and professionals* Includes executives, administrators, managers, and professional specialties such as architects, engineers, natural and social scientists, lawyers, teachers, writers, health diagnosis and treatment workers, entertainers, and athletes.

• *wage and salary earners, technical, sales, and clerical workers* Includes technicians and related support workers; sales representatives, sales workers, cashiers, and sales-related occupations; and administrative support, including clerical.

• *retired* People who did not work either full- or part-time during the survey period.

race The self-identified race of the consumer unit reference person. All consumer units are included in one of two racial groups based on the reference person's race: black or "white and other." The "other" group includes American Indians, Alaskan natives, Asians, and Pacific Islanders. Hispanics may be of any race.

reference person The first member mentioned by the respondent when asked to "Start with the name of the person or one of the persons who owns or rents the home." It is with respect to this person that the relationship of other consumer unit members is determined. Also called the householder or head of household.

region Consumer units are classified according to their address at the time of their participation in the survey. The four major census regions of the United States are the following state groupings:

• *Northeast* Connecticut, Maine, Massachusetts, New Hampshire, New Jersey, New York, Pennsylvania, Rhode Island, and Vermont.

• *Midwest* Illinois, Indiana, Iowa, Kansas, Michigan, Minnesota, Missouri, Nebraska, North Dakota, Ohio, South Dakota, and Wisconsin.

• *South* Alabama, Arkansas, Delaware, District of Columbia, Florida, Georgia, Kentucky, Louisiana, Maryland, Mississippi,

North Carolina, Oklahoma, South Carolina, Tennessee, Texas, Virginia, and West Virginia.

• *West* Alaska, Arizona, California, Colorado, Hawaii, Idaho, Montana, Nevada, New Mexico, Oregon, Utah, Washington, and Wyoming.

size of consumer unit The number of people whose usual place of residence at the time of the interview is in the consumer unit.